W9-BHK-278

Social Psychology
and
Human Values

Social Psychology and Human Values

Selected Essays

by
M. Brewster Smith
The University of Chicago

ALDINE PUBLISHING COMPANY / Chicago

First published 1969 by Aldine Publishing Company,
529 South Wabash Avenue, Chicago, Illinois 60605
Library of Congress Catalog Card Number 69–11229
Printed in the United States of America

To the memory of
Gordon W. Allport

Acknowledgment

My indebtedness to the several publishers of the books and journals in which the reprinted items of this volume originally appeared is acknowledged in notes at the beginning of each chapter.

Here I wish to record my special debt to Mrs. Vivien March, my former secretary at the Institute of Human Development, University of California, Berkeley. She performed with characteristic care the various tedious tasks of readying these materials for publication, including the collation of references (in the course of which she rectified an embarrassing number of previously published inaccuracies on my part). My gratitude for her indispensable role in preparing this volume merges with general gratitude for her intelligent and loyal support in many matters.

Contents

Introduction

1

Social Psychology and Human Values

Of course social psychology must grapple with human experience in society; of course it is inextricably concerned with human values—or so I have always thought. That is why I was originally attracted to the field and began to think of myself as a would-be social psychologist when, still an undergraduate, I had only the dimmest idea of what social psychology was really about. Before I could at all understand it, I had read with mixed fascination and disbelief J. F. Brown's unorthodox text (1936), which combined extremely orthodox commitments to the doctrines of Marx, Freud, and Kurt Lewin—the last just then becoming visible on the American psychological scene. To a young psychologist who was also exploring a tentative identity as a young radical, this was heady stuff that proposed big answers to big questions, even if these theoretical lions seemed most unlikely to lie peacefully with one another. Social psychology, I decided, was psychology that was committed, in the jargon of the 1930's, to "social significance." That was what I wanted, and I settled into a social-psychologist identity without, for a long time, much command of the content to back it up.

As I began to get acquainted with this odd field that on the flimsiest basis I had decided was mine, I could not be entirely happy with the identity that I had acquired. I soon discovered that social psychology was then really two disciplines, not one: an important branch of sociology, on the one hand, and a somewhat marginal application of psychology, on the other. (Matters stayed that way through most of the first half of the century.) Sociologist-social psychologists, beginning with G. H. Mead (1934) and C. H. Cooley (1902), had created an important body of theory concerning the processes of "symbolic interaction" through which the biological raw materials of human potentiality are transmuted into human nature to provide the psychological basis for organized society. But they were slow to refine and test these ideas in empirical research. Generally innocent of theory, their psychologist contemporaries concerned themselves with quantitative studies: measuring attitudes and experimenting on how individual performance is affected by the presence of others.

It was this rather unpromising subfield of psychology in which I found myself: first of all, I was a psychologist. After Floyd Allport's ambitious early attempt (1924) at theoretical synthesis in the framework of Watsonian behaviorism, psychological social psychologists lost their theoretical bearings. They mainly based their shaky claim to the prestigious status of scientist on increasing elegance of measurement (though it was crude enough). It was L. L. Thurstone (1928) who started a long line of research in this vein with his article, "Attitudes Can Be Measured." And indeed, attitudes were measured, but mostly on samples of ever available college sophomores, to no great theoretical or practical end. The appearance of social significance was simulated by measuring such attitudes as radicalism-conservatism and the like and correlating them with other indices. But the psychologist's social psychology of the 1930's had really very little to offer the understanding of man's social experience or to the clarification of his social problems.

Neither did it welcome intellectual contact with speculative social psychology of the sociological variety. The popular view was F. H. Allport's doctrinaire individualism (1933), which sought to debunk the "group fallacy" of attributing reality to groups and social institutions, the stock-in-trade of sociologists. Only the individual and his behavior were "real."

To be sure, there were glimmerings of a new day. Muzafer Sherif's minor classic, *The Psychology of Social Norms* (1936), sought to legitimize the concept of social norms by demonstrating that behavioral norms can be created in the psychological laboratory. The fact that Sherif worked with the perceptual autokinetic phenomenon, a favorite of experimental psychologists, made his case the more appealing, but it was long before his contribution was really assimilated into the thinking of psychological social psychologists.

Most important, there was the emigré Kurt Lewin (see Lewin, 1951), who impressed American psychologists and sociologists alike with his ingenious experiments that brought social reality into the laboratory ("What is 'real' is what has effects") and set a notable example of research on group structure and processes that was at once empirical, theoretical, and practical ("there is nothing so practical as a good theory"). As it turned out, Lewin was a brisk, fructifying wind that began the transformation of social psychology into an intellectually challenging endeavor in vital touch with human experience and social action.

The full impact of Lewin's influence in social psychology was not felt until nearly the time of his death in 1947. I had meanwhile gone to Harvard as a graduate student just before World War II; there I encountered two great psychologists, Henry Murray and Gordon Allport, both mavericks out of sympathy with the mechanistic-behavioristic tradition in American psychology, both theorists in the older grand style, both "personologists," in Murray's term (see Murray, 1938; Allport, 1937). Murray had the appeal of the explorer of human depths, Allport that of the exemplar of a Puritan ego ideal. I vacillated in my attachments to each. Like Lewin, Allport was interested in both personality and social psychology, and he saw no sharp boundary between these interests. Like Murray but unlike Lewin, Allport had strong roots in the humanistic tradition. In personal style as in psychological predilections, he was a man of letters as much as—perhaps more than—he was a scientist. His first commitment was fidelity to the unique individuality of human personality; cleanliness of method for its study was a secondary consideration. In social psychology, he was primarily a scholar and teacher rather than a systematist or empirical investigator. But, again like Lewin, his interests in social psychology showed a deep concern with human injustice, especially the evil of ethnic prejudice (Allport, 1954).

I barely had time to be "imprinted" by Allport and, to a lesser extent, by Murray before the draft and the war intervened—for four diverse years. My final army assignment was to the Research Branch of the Morale Services Division (later, Information and Education Division), where I was fortunate to get to know at first hand two new strands of research that, together with Lewin's legacy and the major tradition of interactionist sociology, underlie the social psychology that we know today. Under Samuel Stouffer, I learned and applied survey research and analysis (see Stouffer, Lumsdaine, Lumsdaine, Williams, Smith, Janis, Star, and Cottrell, 1949), the source of much of the substantive content of a social psychology that has since become increasingly preoccupied with abstracted process. And under Carl Hovland, who directed the Experimental Section of the Research Branch, I became acquainted with the experimental study of persuasive communication. The army studies in which I served a brief apprenticeship (Hovland, Lumsdaine, and Sheffield, 1949) were the springboard for the postwar Yale program in communication and attitude change under Hovland's deft and imaginative leadership, some of the best work in the modern process-oriented vein.

Wartime comradeship on assignment from the Research Branch to North Africa and Italy also served to correct the bias in my hitherto one-sidedly psychological orientation to social psychology. I was teamed with the sociologist Arnold Rose, who was infused with the Chicago symbolic interactionist tradition stemming from G. H. Mead and who had only recently emerged from exciting collaboration on Myrdal's classic study of American race relations (1944). By incongruous chance, typical of army experience, I was the officer and Rose the enlisted man; but in our running private seminar, it was I who was at the junior end of the log. I learned about sociological social psychology and I learned about race and racism.

I was also learning some less bookish realities of social life. In field artillery basic training my eyes had been opened to appreciate the obscene virtuosity of Texan working-class culture; exposure to the disorderly warmth of South Italy gave me a taste of—and a taste for—larger cultural differences. And in Palermo, Rome, Florence, and Ravenna I was enchanted by the visible relics of gloriously elaborated views of man and the world, part of our cultural history, that differed just as widely from our own.

The war over, I returned to Harvard for my degree; I entered the Department of Social Relations, just organized, and shared in its interdisciplinary enthusiasm. By then, Allport's psychologism seemed to me the voice of the past—I did not know how deeply I had been influenced by him in more fundamental ways. There were also new sources of influence, especially Jerome Bruner, whose thoroughgoing functionalism was still directed to the study of public opinion, and Robert White, who was already developing his sane brand of ego psychology in the context of broadly psychoanalytic thought: a man like Allport working in Murray's territory. Fruits of our collaboration are reflected in several essays in this volume. Clyde Kluckhohn in cultural anthropology and Talcott Parsons in sociology, on their part, committed the theoretical resources of their disciplines to a brave if abortive attempt at integration of the human sciences.

But by now a new synthesis of the psychological and sociological versions of social psychology was beginning to emerge; I became firmly identified with it as I came to perceive it with growing clarity. (I had taught social psychology at Harvard and Vassar for at least three years before I felt I had any grasp of my own on the shape of the field: teaching is the best avenue to learning!) According to the synthesis that still prevails, with variations and defections, social psychology is defined, not by boundaries that clearly divide it from other specialties, but by its focal problems, which can be located on two axes, according to whether social behavior is viewed synchronously or across time. From the latter perspective the problems are those of socialization: how by participating in communicative interaction the human animal acquires dispositions that equip him as a member of society and as a carrier of culture. Its synchronic problems, on the other hand, have to do with the interrelations of already socialized persons in social contexts. Here concern centers, at the individual pole, on the learned dispositions (attitudes) that enter into determining a person's social behavior, and, at the sociocultural pole, on the patterning of group structure, process, and symbolic culture that emerges as persons interact. The heated controversies of former years about the priority of individual versus group seem beside the point when viewed from the newer perspective: after early infancy, the isolated individual as social atom is pure fiction. Persons as we know them embody much of society in microcosm, and these socialized persons in their interrelationships are what is meant by the social order.

Social psychology at midcentury was indeed exciting. Suddenly it had made contact with important nodes of theory in general psychology and in sociology; no longer did it illustrate that frequent anomaly in psychology, an "applied" field out of contact with the basic science that it pretends to be applying. Learning theory, cognitive theory, psychoanalysis, social interactionist theory, structural role theory, all emerged as suggesting relevant questions and concepts for social psychological research. And social psychology no longer depended entirely on theories imported from without: in Festinger's dissonance theory (1957), for example, it staked out theoretical claims of its own that led to a flurry of experimentation with forays even into the home territory of general experimental psychology. Traffic with the less theoretically inclined field of anthropology waned, however: the "culture and personality" movement receded from its apogee of the 1930's and 1940's.

In the beginning of this fertile period the spirit of Lewin as carried on by his students also held social psychology to a strong commitment to human relevance. Laboratory studies were paralleled by field studies, and much was written about the benefits to be derived from the complementarity of these strategies. Great promise was seen in "action research," conducted in close collaboration with social programs so as both to provide empirical guidance for social policy and to increase basic knowledge through controlled access to kinds and levels of variables that would elude study in the laboratory. Social psychologists were still predominantly men of social conscience, and the new Society for the Psychological Study of Social Issues, founded in 1936, reflected their conscientiousness and their optimism.

Over the past decade matters have changed. True, a large amount of applied social-psychological research goes on under governmental and commercial auspices, and SPSSI grows in membership. And one off-shoot of the Lewinian tradition—the "laboratory" approach to sensitivity and leadership training, as exemplified by the National Training Laboratory in Group Development at Bethel, Maine—has continued to flourish, now joining forces in a veritable social movement with other practical efforts to break through the impersonality of bureaucratized modern life. But the "training laboratory" with its "T-groups" has lost contact with the main thrust of experimentally based theoretical advance. And experimentalists working in the conventional social psychological laboratory, now transformed by electronic gadgets, have to a surprising extent lost interest in problems of the real social world. This trend, which I deplore, is doubtless a price paid for the successes of theoretically oriented laboratory experimentation. The way of the experimentalist has been intrinsically rewarding, and in a period of increasingly generous government support for basic research—extrinsic rewards, too!—there has been little reason for the most creative investigators to resist reaping these rewards.

New norms, new values have thus largely replaced the Lewinian synthesis. To overstate the case, virtuosity rather than substance seems to have carried the day: manipulative virtuosity in the laboratory, and theoretical virtuosity in experimentally armed controversy about interpretative minutiae that are mainly relevant to the laboratory, not to social life. To be sure, the gains have been real: growth in methodological sophistication and impressive clarification of a number of important social processes and relationships. But the losses have been substantial too. As I write, it is a fair bet that countervailing trends may be afoot to redress the balance (see Ring, 1967; McGuire, 1967). The preciousness of some laboratory experimentation has come under criticism; from various quarters comes the call to invest equal ingenuity in field research, to conduct research that bears more directly on the appallingly urgent social problems of the time. (But the most difficult barriers to the solution of these problems are probably matters of political intransigence and expediency, not of lack of knowledge.)

During this period I have been an outsider to the dominant tradition of experimental social psychology, though many of my best friends—and best students—have been experimentalists; and as teacher, editor, and occasional critic I have followed the progress of experimental work, often with admiration or envy. But as I have discovered, my real investments, values, commitments in social psychology lie elsewhere. I persist, with diminishing defensiveness, in being interested in problems of human values. While I cherish the cumulativeness of the scientific enterprise and thus look askance at some versions of "humanistic psychology" that ignore the basic differences between art and science, increasingly I favor an open pluralism of strategy. One may entertain different grades of evidence without being misled—so long as one remains critically aware of its limitations. One may glean insights and hypotheses from many sources, including common human experience and its refinement in the arts, later to be tested by firmer criteria. I am convinced that there is no royal road to Truth, not even that of the experimentalist. Truth is elusive, and we do best to converge upon it from multiple perspectives.

I persist in seeing value in heuristic conceptual maps when our methods and our knowledge cannot support more adequate theory. Some of my mapping operations have led me to cross disciplinary boundaries: social psychology remains a potential crossroads of the social sciences. Within the central territory of the discipline, I have been most concerned with the common ground that it shares with the psychology of personality. There I have favored natural history over analytical experimentation, not so much in principle (though it does seem to me that social psychology has rushed into experimentation before the tasks of naturalistic observation and description had been carried far enough) as because I find them more congenial. And repeatedly I have been drawn to look at contemporary social problems in the light of conceptual equipment borrowed from the theoretically oriented disciplines. I see merit in substantive social psychology that merges with older traditions of social interpretation, as a complement to the process-oriented social psychology that has recently dominated the scientific stage. Given the aridity of much of our research literature, I think there is a legitimate place for armchair speculation.

In most of these idiosyncrasies I have only recently come to recognize the extent of Gordon Allport's pervasive influence. In my bumptious adolescence as a neophyte psychologist, I sometimes joined fellow graduate students or junior faculty in making fun of his idiosyncrasies; now I find that ever so many of them are my own. It is therefore only appropriate for me to dedicate this volume to his memory in filial gratitude.

The essays that I have selected for inclusion fall into five clusters. The initial group concern some of the interdisciplinary relations of social psychology: with political science, anthropology, and sociology. The first of these essays, touching political science, is my most ambitious attempt at conceptual mapping and draws upon a psychological perspective that is more fully developed in the section that follows. The second, concerning relations with anthropology, is seriously dated, since it takes no account of the "new ethnography" of componential analysis that makes provocative contact with modern cognitive psychology. But in general I would stand by my comments on the earlier and largely still persisting relationships between the disciplines. The biographical essay on Stouffer represents ties with sociology and partly repays a personal intellectual debt.

Attitudes and values as products of socialization that predispose the person to behave distinctively in social situations are the focus of the next group of papers. I have been recurrently preoccupied with this topic ever since my army apprenticeship, most substantially in collaboration with Bruner and White (Smith, Bruner, and White, 1956), as summarized in the initial essay of the section. The final paper, an empirical study of authoritarianism, provides a bridge from the study of attitudes to that of broader constellations of personality, treated in the ensuing section.

The third group of papers, on issues of personality theory, deal with three subsidiary themes. A view of the self—a favorite personality concept among social psychologists—is developed in the first two and elaborated upon in another connection in the final paper of the section. Three papers represent successive stages in my struggle with the concept of "mental health" as an evaluative perspective on personality, initially stimulated by Marie Jahoda's provocative suggestions toward a social psychology of mental health (1950). Like many of my colleagues in psychology, but perhaps without as much personal basis in interprofessional rivalry (as a social psychologist, I am a "mental-health professional" only by courtesy and avocation), I have become progressively disenchanted with the concept—not with the "mental" component of the term, but certainly with the medical connotations of "health." The last two papers are my attempt at an alternative view of psychological effectiveness, drawing upon Robert White's valuable concept of competence (1959). The final essay, the recent outgrowth of long productive interchange with fellow members of the Social Science Research Council Committee on Socialization and Social Structure, is my only serious venture into the terrain of socialization research.

Next come essays that deal with an assortment of social problems. The first is a contemporary polemic that brings the perspective previously developed about competence and "mental health" to bear on issues of social policy toward the psychologically disturbed. The argument is still timely as this book goes to press; hopefully it will quickly become dated. Two essays concerning problems of foreign students and foreign study reflect my association as staff to the SSRC Committee on Cross-Cultural Education in the early 1950's. They are widely spaced in time, and the different problems to which they are addressed mirror shifting national priorities from early in the

Cold War to the recent past, when the salient problem became one of aiding the newly independent developing countries to attain educational and technical competence. The single paper on family planning gives token recognition to an issue of immense importance to which social psychologists, myself included, have paid shockingly little attention. The one on prejudice deals with a topic in which (thanks to Gordon Allport, Arnold Rose, and important people in my personal life) I have had an abiding interest but with which I have only recently come to grips in empirical research. The two recent essays that conclude the section are by-products of collaborative research on student activism, a matter of anxious concern and hope as this book is assembled. Because they focus particularly on the values and moral orientations of protesting students, they form a natural bridge to the papers of the final group, which leave the realm of basic and applied social science for a more direct consideration of humanistic values.

This last group of essays is a mixed bag lacking any hint of organizing theme. Retrospectively, though, I detect signs of a consistent point of view in the miscellaneous papers. Several of them reflect a rather old-fashioned liberalism, a conviction that if there is hope for man in a time of peril, instability, and headlong change, it lies in the further development of his capacities and resources for knowing and responsible choice. These include such cultural aids as social science and democratic institutions. But increasingly I have come to sense that feeling and human communion demand a bigger place in the scheme of human values if people are to sustain the burdens of rational choice—or if such choice is to be worth the candle. Here Murray now takes precedence over Allport among my mentors. Among the essays in this group, the piece on Proust is token payment to the life of feeling; so is my account in the previous section of what I have learned from protesting students.

Choice, however, implies a voluntaristic view of man, one that is out of tune with the mechanistic determinism of traditional American psychology that still persists, but that is much in the spirit of Gordon Allport and of William James before him. How to fit voluntaristic choice into a deterministic science is a truly basic psychological problem, not "merely" philosophical, one that has perplexed me since my days of college bull sessions. The point of view I have come to had best be laid on the table at the risk of exposure to the philosophically more sophisticated, since it seems to me to produce a kind of underlying consistency among a number of my scattered interests and concerns: commitment to deterministic science, involvement in social action, and hope for greater human competence and fulfillment. It seems to help make sense of a version of social psychology as a crossroads of scientific, political, and humanistic interests.

Like Isidor Chein (1962), whose views about these matters fit very well with mine and probably had more influence on them than I can presently recognize, I am unwilling to buy free will at the price of calling upon the

Heisenberg principle of indeterminacy. This particular genie belongs in the bottle of subatomic processes. So far as the physical sciences are concerned, he remains there: macroprocesses are quite adequately determinate. If we let him out into the psychological world in a misguided attempt to preserve free will, we find to our dismay that we have put in jeopardy just what we were trying to save: ethical responsibility and human efficacy. Free will as indeterminacy and chance is no freedom at all. What we mean by freedom is personal causation. This, I have come to see, is an empirical variable, not a philosophical assumption. Some people have more freedom than others, and these differences are subject to causal analysis and to causal intervention.

As we scan the evolutionary scale of organic life from the simple to the more complexly organized, we find that organisms—complex open *systems* of causal processes—show increasing independence of the conditions in their proximal environments. They enjoy increasing degrees of freedom. Metazoa do better at this than protozoa; warm-blooded animals better than cold-blooded. Man, with his self-produced cultural envelope, does best of all. For him causes and effects can be legitimately restated as means and ends. Yet as we compare men, they are far from free and equal. They are manifestly unequal in their freedom. Those who live in poverty or under despotism suffer from major external constraints. They are likely to have been socialized to suffer from major internal constraints as well: inadequate knowledge and skills, stunted motives, paralyzing beliefs such as the self-fulfilling fatalism that is a necessary buffer against hopeless circumstances but itself helps to perpetuate them. Human freedom is not a postulate; it is a fact, which is present or absent in degree. In the course of human history most people have had precious little of it. In the affluent societies of the contemporary world they have more of it than ever before, but they enjoy it insecurely. It can be frightening. Too few of them have been raised so as to be endowed with inner capacities for freedom—responsiveness as a person to the wishes of the self—that match their widened range of outer opportunity. Free will is itself caused; it is an achievement, not a paradoxical assumption.
light on the circumstances that enhance or hamper man's attainment of

Value-oriented research on socialization, from this perspective, can throw freedom. (My chapter on competence is an early attempt in this direction.) By the same token, research toward the solution of social problems no longer appears as an anomaly in deterministic social science. It is a causally relevant strategy, itself caused, for adding to people's resources for doing their will.

Like all knowledge, social psychological understanding is, of course, two-edged. My commitment is to its use in ways that augment human freedom, but knowledge can also be used manipulatively in ways that diminish it. Again we encounter the self-fulfilling prophecy. Social psychologists who believe in the potentiality, if not the full actuality, of human freedom are likely to treat people, in and out of research, with the respect that causally enhances their actual freedom. In this social psychologists do not differ from anybody else. Those who do not hold this belief are likely to treat people in ways that tend to reduce them to the quasi-machines that fit the mechanistic theory. Here lies the danger of a social psychology that is artificially divorced from human values. My hope in these essays is to advance the development of a science of social man that begins to do justice to his humanity—a science *of* man that is *for* man, too.

Some Interdisciplinary Relationships of Social Psychology

2

Personality in Politics

A Conceptual Map, with Application to the Problem of Political Rationality

Progress in the social and behavioral sciences has in general not been marked by major theoretical "breakthroughs." As those of us who profess one or another of these disciplines look upon the succession of research and theoretical interests that capture the center of the stage, we may sometimes wonder if indeed there has been any progress at all. Particularly if we are fixated on the physical sciences[1] as models of what a good science should be, we can easily become discouraged. As therapy for this depressive mood, however, one has only to scan the textbooks of former generations and some of the earlier landmark contributions to our fields: the fact of progress, of the cumulativeness of understanding that is the hallmark of science, is immediately apparent.

The progress that we see, however, is not on the pattern according to which Einstein included and supplanted Newton, or even on that by which the modern theory of the chemical valence bond makes sense of Mendeleyev's descriptive table of elements. In addition to the development and refinement of research methods and the accretion of facts, our kind of progress has involved developing some more or less satisfactory "theories of the middle range" (Merton, 1957), and, especially, a steady increase in the sophistica-

Reprinted by permission of the publishers from Oliver Garceau, editor, *Political Research and Political Theory.* Cambridge, Mass., Harvard University Press, Copyright, 1968, by the President and Fellows of Harvard College. The first half of the essay has been adapted, with minor changes, from Smith (1968c). I am grateful to the editor of the *Journal of Social Issues* and to the Society for the Psychological Study of Social Issues for permission to draw upon it.

1. Other than meteorology, which in some respects offers such an appropriate model that I am puzzled that social scientists have not picked it up. The natural history of cloud formations, the precise physics of atmospheric microprocesses, the statistical treatment of macroprocesses, all have their homologies in the social sciences. The parallel even extends to the continued prominence of folk wisdom in both fields. Yet meteorologists seem to have been spared the self-doubts and soul-searchings to which social scientists are prone.

tion of the questions that we ask and in our sensitivity to the variables that are likely to be relevant to them.

To codify this kind of progress, and to make our gains readily accessible as we face new problems of research and application, we need something other than grand theory in the old literary style. We are not ready for genuinely theoretical integration, and to pretend that we are is to hamper rather than to aid ourselves in attacking new problems with an open mind. Conceptual mapping operations that have only modest pretentions better fit the state of our theoretical resources and can often be helpful in organizing these resources to bear upon particular problems. The sort of conceptual map that I have in mind starts from a particular intellectual or practical problem and attempts to link the pertinent islands of knowledge discovered in the pursuit of middle-range theories and to disentangle relationships among the kinds of variables that current knowledge points to as relevant. When the variables are drawn from the home territory of different academic disciplines (and the concepts of a context-defined field like political science inevitably have such a heterogeneous provenience), ventures in mapping become particularly important. They are the best we can do toward interdisciplinary integration, which in these instances is required of us by the nature of the task.

This essay sketches such a map for the analysis of personality and politics, an outgrowth of my attempts to apply the approach developed in *Opinions and Personality* (Smith, Bruner, and White, 1956; Smith, 1958) to the analysis of various problems involving social attitudes and behavior, particularly McCarthyism, civil liberties, and anti-Semitism.[2] While it obviously bears the marks of its origins, I have had to go considerably beyond the range of variables, mainly psychological ones, that Bruner, White, and I were dealing with.

A map like this is *not* a theory that can be confirmed or falsified by testing deductions against evidence; it is rather a heuristic device, a declaration of intellectual strategy, that is to be judged as profitable or sterile rather than as true or false. On my own part, I have found it useful in coming to grips with topics that were new to me and in organizing what I think we know for my students in teaching. Placing particular variables and relationships as it does in larger context, it may have the further virtue of counteracting one's natural tendency to stress the exclusive importance of the variables or theories that one happens momentarily to be interested in. Many persisting disputes in the social sciences are like the story of the Blind Men and the Elephant. A good map helps us to keep the whole Elephant in view.

In offering this essay in homage to the memory of V. O. Key, I am keenly aware of Key's rare talent for grasping the Elephant whole without

2. In the area of McCarthyism and civil liberties, I prepared an unpublished memorandum for Samuel A. Stouffer in connection with planning for the studies leading to his book, *Communism, Conformity, and Civil Liberties* (1955). The application to anti-Semitism is embodied in my pamphlet (Smith, 1965b), on which I draw heavily here. I am grateful to the Anti-Defamation League for support of the project of which it was a by-product.

recourse to such arid conceptual baggage. It was part of Key's artistry to keep much of his conceptual sophistication implicit, as he brought empirical analysis shrewdly to bear on theoretical and normative problems. The rest of us may need more explicit aids if we are to emulate his openness to the contributions of adjacent disciplines, his distrustfulness of the simplistic explanation.

In the final section of the essay, I seek to illustrate the utility of the map by applying it in an attempt to clarify some of the meanings of political rationality—a theme with which Key was preoccupied up to his death. If the map turns out to help reduce some of the confusions prevalent at this crossroads of normative and empirical concern, I would regard it as an appropriate if partial repayment of debt to Key.

The Map

Schematic as it is, the map is too complicated to take in at a glance. Figure 2.1 presents the gross outlines—the continents in their asserted relationships. In Figures 2.2 and 2.3 we will look in more detail at particular segments of the terrain. The full map, given in Figure 2.4, should then become intelligible. Certain intentional omissions and simplifications must finally be noted by way of qualification. Illustrative examples will be provided casually en route, for the most part without documentation from the literature.

Figure 2.1 diagrams the major components of a framework for the analysis of personality and politics in terms of five major panels. In keeping with

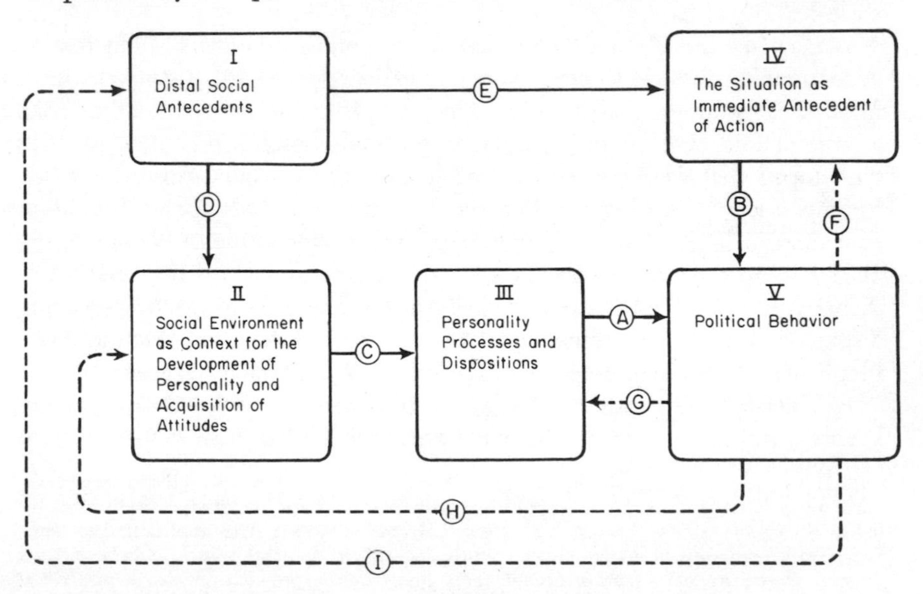

FIGURE 2.1

the psychological focus of the map, Panel III (personality processes and dispositions) occupies the center of the stage. Casual relationships are indicated by arrows. Because we are used to reading from left to right, I have put the payoff in actual behavior (Panel V) at the extreme right. This panel is concerned with personal political decisions as carried into action: voting, information-seeking, policy formation or implementation, influence attempts, or—the source of much of our psychological data—question-answering. The data that come from our observations of people, what they say as well as what they do, belong here; only by reconstruction and inference do we arrive at the contents of the central personality panel.

Panel IV represents the person's behavioral situation as an immediate antecedent of action; Panel II includes features of the person's more enduring social environment to which we turn to explain how he has happened to become the sort of political actor that we find him to be; and Panel I represents the more remote, or distal, facts of politics, economics, culture, social structure, and history that contribute to the distinctive features of the environment in which he was socialized and of the immediate situations in which he acts. From the standpoint of the behaving individual, the contents of Panel I are conceptually distal but may be temporally contemporaneous: an historically given political system (Panel I), for example, affects (Arrow D) the political norms—such as those concerning democracy, authority, and legitimacy—to which a person is socialized (Panel II); it also affects (Arrow E) the structure of the immediate situations of action that he is likely to encounter (Panel IV)—the alternatives offered on a ballot, the procedural rules in a legislative body, and so on. Temporally distal determinants are also assigned to Panel I: thus the history of slavery, the plantation economy, the Civil War and Reconstruction, as determinants of the politically relevant environments in which participants in Southern politics have been socialized, and of the immediate situations that comprise the stage on which they perform as political actors (Key, 1949).

If we start with behavioral outcomes in Panel V, the arrows (marked A and B) that link them with Panels III and IV represent the methodological premise emphasized by the great psychologist Kurt Lewin (1951, pp. 130–154): All social behavior is to be analyzed as a joint resultant of characteristics of the *person,* on the one hand, and of his psychological *situation,* on the other. The behavior of the same political actor may differ substantially as he faces differently structured situations; conversely, different persons who face the same situation will respond differently. Both the contribution of the person and that of his situation, in interaction, must be included in any adequate analysis. To specify the contribution of either requires taking that of the other into account.

For a long time there was a disciplinary quarrel between psychologists and sociologists about the relevance and importance of personal dispositions (primarily *attitudes*) versus that of situations in determining social behavior. To take this feature of our map seriously is to regard the argument as silly and outmoded: both classes of determinants are jointly indispensable. The study of "personality and politics" cannot afford to neglect situational factors, which must in principle be taken into account if only by holding them constant, if we are to isolate the distinctive contributions of personality. In concrete cases in which analysis along these lines is undertaken for the guidance of social action, one may ask, of course, whether the personal or the situational component is more *strategic* in terms of the variance it controls and its accessibility to major influence. It may be more feasible, for example, to influence the normative structure that pertains to interracial relations by authoritative legal action than to carry through a program of mass psychoanalysis to reverse authoritarian personality trends that predispose people toward prejudice and discriminatory behavior. The practical questions of strategic importance and accessibility do not seem to be as charged with disciplinary *amour-propre* as are the theoretical issues that still tend to divide the proponents of personality-oriented and of situational approaches.

The dotted arrows of relationship that leave the behavioral panel require special mention. Political behavior has consequences as well as causes, and for the sake of formal completeness some of these are suggested by the dotted "feedback loops" in the map. As Leon Festinger (1957; Brehm and Cohen, 1962) has argued on the basis of considerable evidence, self-committing behavior may have effects in turn upon a person's attitudes (Arrow G). A political actor who adopts a position for expedient reasons may be convinced by his own rhetoric, or—similar in result though different in the process that is assumed—he may shift his attitudes to accord with his actions in order to reduce feelings of "dissonance." The dotted Arrows F, H, and I merely recognize that individual behavior also has effects in the social world. What the person does in a situation may immediately change it (Arrow F); as we integrate across the behavior of many individuals, the joint consequences of the behavior of the many eventually alter the social environments that shape and support the attitudes of each (Arrow H). In the longer run (Arrow I), the behaviors of individuals constitute a society and its history.

To be sure, this is a psychologist's map that focuses on the attitudes and behavior of individual persons. A political sociologist would have to give explicit attention to matters that remain implicit in the feedback arrows—to the social structures according to which individual behaviors are integrated to have political effects. His map would necessarily be differently centered and elaborated than the present one. V. O. Key (1963, pp. 411 ff.) has given particular attention to the problems of "linkage" between aggregated individual political orientations as a social psychologist studies them and governmental action as the political scientist's ultimate concern.

With the broad framework laid out, we can now look at the details of Panels III and IV, still working from the proximal to the distal determinants of behavior (see Figure 2.2). The contents of Panel IV (the situation as immediate antecedent of action) remind us that an important component

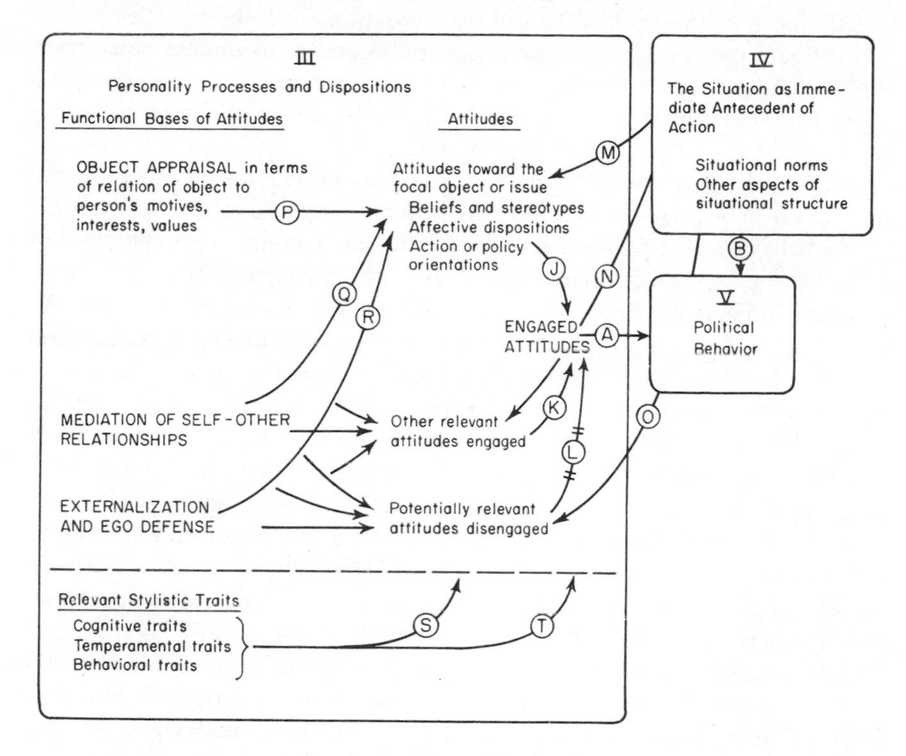

FIGURE 2.2

of any behavioral situation is the set of norms or prescriptions for behavior that are consensually held to apply in it. Students of political behavior at the various levels of governmental organization are concerned with recurring types of situations that confront the citizen, whether as constituent, voter, or petitioner; or as legislator, executive, administrative functionary, or party leader. Much of the variation in personal behavior, not only across types of situations but within the same type in different political structures and at different historical periods, will be attributable to differences and changes in the norms that prevail. Apart from the norms, there are of course many other situational features that are also important as codeterminants of action—among them, the competitive or cooperative relations that hold with other actors who participate in the situation, the degree of urgency with which decision or action is required, the contingencies of cost and benefit that obtain (Thibaut and Kelley, 1959). Lore about the relevant features of political situations is a principal currency of political science.

Turn now to Panel III, personality processes and dispositions. We are concerned here with inferred dispositions of the person that he brings to any situation he encounters, and with their basis in his experience and motivational processes. Social psychologists have come to use the term *attitudes* to refer to such dispositions, when they represent integrations of cognitive, emotional, and conative tendencies around a psychological object such as a political figure or issue. Our problem is a dual one: to formulate how a person's attitudes come to bear on his political behavior,[3] and how these attitudes arise and are sustained in relation to their part in the ongoing operations of the person's psychological economy.

A first point suggested in Figure 2.2 is that we cannot take for granted just which of a person's attitudes will become engaged as a codeterminant of his behavior in a political situation. Political scientists are probably less naive than psychologists about this. A citizen's presidential vote for one or another candidate depends, as we know (Campbell, A., Converse, Miller, W. and Stokes, 1960), not only on his focal attitude toward that candidate, but also on attitudes toward the alternative candidates, toward party, and toward issues. As for situational factors, the privacy of the voting booth is expressly designed to neutralize them insofar as possible, but the weather may keep the voter from the polls, and the form of the ballot also has its effects. For another example, a legislator's vote on a bill will depend not only on situational factors (including whether or not a roll call is involved) and on his attitudes toward the focal issue, but also on other relevant attitudes that become engaged—toward tangential issues, toward the party leadership, toward political survival, or whatever. The situation plays a dual role here: both as a co-determinant, together with his engaged attitudes, of what he does (B) —for example, the legislator may want to vote for a bill but not dare to— and as differentially activating certain of the actor's attitudes (M and N) while allowing or encouraging other potentially relevant attitudes to remain in abeyance (O). In recent years, issues concerning Negro civil rights have come to be posed in the Congress and elsewhere in such pointed terms that political actors probably find it less feasible than formerly to isolate their attitudes of democratic fair play from engagement—attitudes embodied in the American creed to which most citizens have been socialized to some degree (Myrdal, 1944).

Social psychological research may elect to measure and manipulate one attitude at a time for good analytic reasons, but people rarely behave in such a piecemeal fashion. What gets into the mix of a person's engaged attitudes, and with what weighting, makes a big difference. Given the complexity of these relationships, there is no reason to suppose that people's political behavior should uniformly correspond to their attitudes on a single focal issue. It is surprising that some psychologists and sociologists have been surprised at the lack of one-to-one correspondence between single attitudes and behavior, and have questioned the validity of attitude measurement on these irrelevant grounds.

Moving toward the left of Panel III, we turn from the problem of how

3. Key remarks (1963, p. 233) on the unsatisfactory state of basic knowledge concerning the broad problem of the bearing of attitude on behavior. To formulate the problem correctly, I think, is half the battle. The aspects of the map under discussion here are my attempt to do so.

attitudes are differentially aroused to that of how they are formed and sustained. The approach taken here is the *functional* one which posits that a person acquires and maintains attitudes and other learned psychological structures to the extent that they are in some way useful to him in his inner economy of adjustment and his outer economy of adaptation. The scheme for classifying the functional basis of attitudes is one that I have discussed in greater detail elsewhere (Smith, Bruner, White, 1956; Smith, 1968a). It answers the question "Of what use to a man are his opinions?" under three rubrics: *object appraisal, mediation of self—other relationships,* and *externalization and ego defense.*

Under object appraisal, we recognize the ways in which a person's attitudes serve him by "sizing up" significant aspects of the world in terms of their relevance to his motives, interests, and values. As Walter Lippmann (1922) long ago made clear, all attitudes, not just "prejudice," involve an element of "prejudgment": they are useful to the person in part because they prepare him for his encounters with reality, enabling him to avoid the confusion and inefficiency of appraising each new situation afresh in all its complexity. In the most general way, holding *any* attitude brings a bit of order into the flux of a person's psychological world; the specific content of a person's attitudes reflects to varying degrees his appraisal of how the attitudinal object bears upon his interests and enterprises. This function involves reality testing, and is likely to be involved to some minimal degree in even the least rational of attitudes.

A person's attitudes not only embody a provisional appraisal of what for him is significant reality; they also serve to mediate the kind of relationships with others and the kind of conception of self that he is motivated to maintain. Is it important to the decision-maker to think of himself as a liberal Democrat? Then his adopting a liberal stand on any of a variety of issues may contribute to his self-regard. Does he rather set much stock in being right in the light of history? Such motivation, by orienting him toward an ideal reference group, may make him relatively independent of immediate social pressures. To the extent that, by self-selective recruitment, politicians are disproportionately likely to be "other-directed" in Riesman's (1950) sense, however, they may be predisposed by personality to be especially vulnerable to such pressures.

Finally comes the class of functions to which psychoanalytic depth psychology has given the closest attention, here labeled externalization and ego defense. This is the functional basis to which Lasswell (1930) gave exclusive emphasis in his classic formula for the political man: private motives displaced onto public objects, rationalized in terms of the public interest. It also underlies the conception of the "authoritarian personality" (Adorno, Frenkel-Brunswik, Levinson, and Sanford, 1950; Kirscht and Dillehay, 1967)—a posture in which an essentially weak ego puts up a façade of strength that requires bolstering through identification with the strong, the conventional, the in-group, and rejection of the weak, the immoral, the out-group. Given the appeal of depth interpretation in the study of personality and politics, there is little need to expand on these themes; it is more necessary to insist that externalization and ego defense are only part of the story.

The arrows P, Q, and R raise the functional question about the motivational sources of any attitude that a person holds. Arrows S and T, near the bottom of the panel, reflect on their part a different kind of relationship. A person's attitudes and the way they engage with particular political situations bear the mark of his stylistic traits of personality as well as of the purposes that they serve for him. Intelligence or stupidity, incisiveness or vagueness, zest or apathy, optimism or pessimism, decisiveness or hesitation —cognitive, temperamental, and behavioral traits like these have their own history and may perhaps partly be attributed to residues of the person's previous motivational conflicts, but their immediate relevance for his political attitudes and behavior is hardly motivational. His attitudes and actions in the sphere of politics, as in other realms, inevitably reflect such pervasive personal qualities, which can have momentous behavioral consequences. A purely functional account is likely to neglect them.

The foregoing analysis provides us with leverage for identifying aspects of the person's social environment that are relevant to the development,

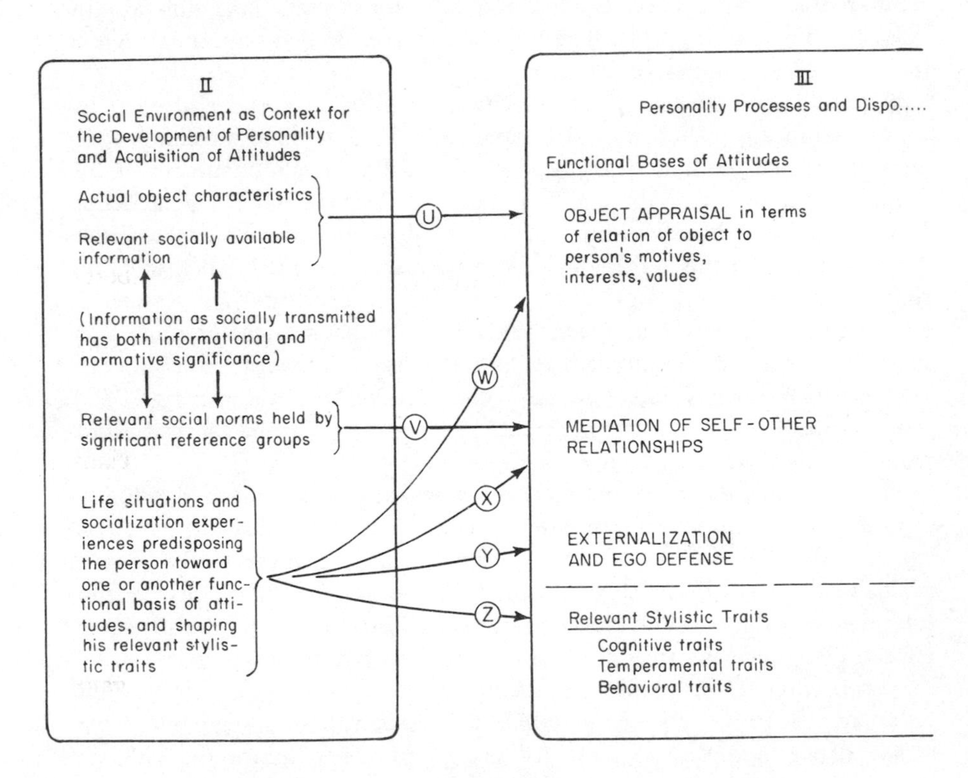

FIGURE 2.3

maintenance, and change of his political attitudes and his stylistic personality traits, as we turn to Panel II at the left of Figure 2.3. To the extent that a person's attitudes in a particular political context reflect processes of object appraisal, he should be responsive to the information that his environment provides about the attitudinal object or issue (Arrow U). The actual facts about it will be important in this connection only as they affect the information that is socially available to him, and, as we know, the quality and quantity of this information vary widely from issue to issue and across the various niches that people occupy in society.

The information on a topic that reaches a person through the channels of communication has a dual relevance, as the internal arrows in Panel II are intended to suggest: not only does it feed into his processes of object appraisal, but it carries further information—a second-order message, so to speak—about the social norms that prevail. When discussion of birth control begin to percolate through Catholic channels, or debates about the pros and cons of China policy through American ones—to take two examples in which, in the mid 1960's, controversy is superseding a previous state of affairs in which one policy position had monopolistic advantages—not only is new grist provided for object appraisal; the important news is conveyed that these previously taboo topics have become moot and discussable. As Arrow V indicates, the second motivational basis of attitudes—the mediation of self-other relations—then may lead to attitudinal consequences that point to a different resultant in behavior. It becomes safe to think in new ways.

Besides providing the environmental data that the first two attitudinal functions can work with to generate new attitudes or to sustain or change esablished ones,[4] the person's life situation and socialization experiences may predispose him—in general, or in a particular topical domain—toward one or another of the functional bases of attitudes (Arrows W, X and Y). What makes the rational man, in whom the first function predominates? The Utopia has not yet arrived in which we know the answer, but recent studies of socialization are beginning to become relevant to the question, and it is a good guess that part of the story is rearing by loving and confident parents who give reasons for their discipline. In the shorter run, environments that augment one's self-esteem and allay one's anxiety should also favor object appraisal. Research in the wake of Riesman (1950), including the Witkin group's studies of field dependence-independence (Witkin, Dyk, Faterson, Goodenough, and Karp, 1962), and Miller and Swanson's work (1958; 1960) on child rearing and personality in entrepreneurial and bureaucratic families, contains suggestions about the sources of primary orientation to the second function, mediation of self-other relationships. As for externalization and ego defense, again the pic-

4. Environmental data play a much more incidental and erratic role in relation to the function of externalization and ego defense.

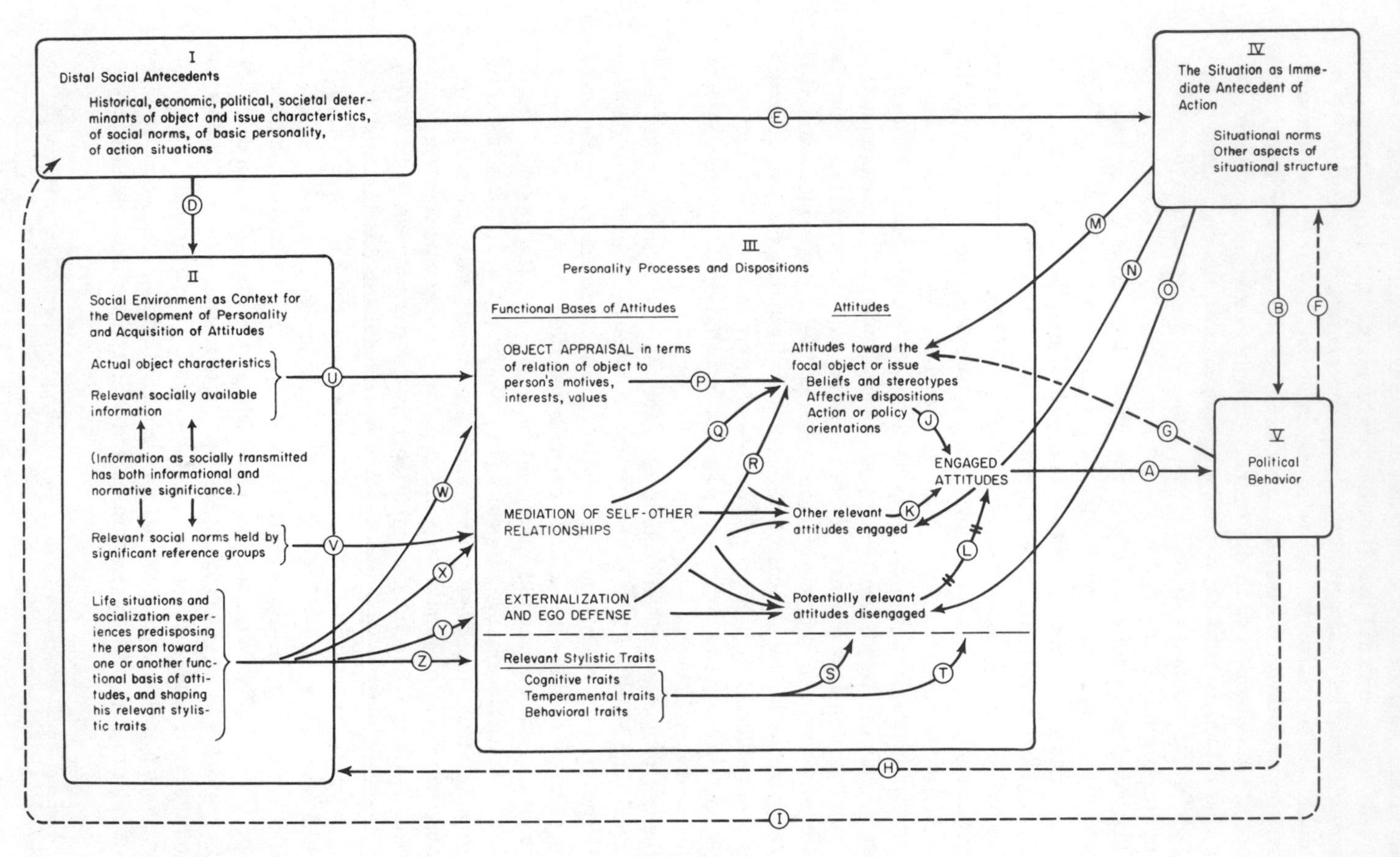
I
Distal Social Antecedents
Historical, economic, political, societal determinants of object and issue characteristics, of social norms, of basic personality, of action situations
II
Social Environment as Context for the Development of Personality and Acquisition of Attitudes
Actual object characteristics
Relevant socially available information
(Information as socially transmitted has both informational and normative significance.)
Relevant social norms held by significant reference groups
Life situations and socialization experiences predisposing the person toward one or another functional basis of attitudes, and shaping his relevant stylistic traits
III
Personality Processes and Dispositions
Functional Bases of Attitudes
OBJECT APPRAISAL in terms of relation of object to person's motives, interests, values
MEDIATION OF SELF-OTHER RELATIONSHIPS
EXTERNALIZATION AND EGO DEFENSE
Attitudes
Attitudes toward the focal object or issue
Beliefs and stereotypes
Affective dispositions
Action or policy orientations
ENGAGED ATTITUDES
Other relevant attitudes engaged
Potentially relevant attitudes disengaged
Relevant Stylistic Traits
Cognitive traits
Temperamental traits
Behavioral traits
IV
The Situation as Immediate Antecedent of Action
Situational norms
Other aspects of situational structure
V
Political Behavior
A
B
D
E
F
G
H
I
J
K
L
M
N
O
P
Q
R
S
T
U
V
W
X
Y
Z

FIGURE 2.4

ture is not clear, but conditions that subject the developing person to arbitrary authority, that deflate self-esteem, that arouse vague anxiety, that provoke hostility but block its relatively direct expression toward the source of the frustration, seem likely sources.

The final arrow Z is drawn not to complete the alphabet but to make place for the findings of personality research, as they emerge, concerning the determinants in socialization of personal stylistic traits.

The entire map can now be reassembled in Figure 2.4. Arrows U to Z, taken together, replace Arrow C in Figure 2.1.

The usefulness of a map and its inherent limitation are two sides of the same coin: its status as a simplification and schematization of reality. There are many complexities that the present map does not attempt to handle. Some of the major omissions, which I note briefly here, arise from the fact that the roles of the basic psychological apparatuses and processes of motivation, perception, and learning are assumed implicitly rather than explicitly delineated.

The triadic functional classification attempts to sort out the ways in which a person's attitudes are rooted in his underlying motives and their fusions and transformations, whatever they may be. It assumes but does not spell out a conception of human motivation.

As for perception, it would elaborate the map to an incomprehensible tangle to give due recognition to what we know about perceptual selectivity—the ways in which a person's existing expectations, motives, and attitudes affect what he will attend to and how he will register and categorize it. A perceptual screening process intervenes between the environmental facts (Panel II) and what the person makes of them (Panel III); likewise between the immediate behavioral situation as it might appear to an objective observer (Panel IV) and how the person defines it for himself, which in the last analysis is the guise in which it affects his behavior.

In regard to learning, the present formulation makes the broad functionalist assumption that people in general acquire attitudes that are useful, that is, rewarding, to them. But it ignores the details of the learning process, and such consequences of learning as the persistence of learned structures beyond their original point of usefulness. A person may acquire much of the content of his political attitudes quite incidentally, moreover, in his unfocused, only mildly attentive effort to make sense of his world. The culture says, in effect, "This is how things are with (Russia) (China) (Republicans) (Southerners) (Negroes) (socialized medicine)," and in the absence of better information, he takes note. Such incidentally learned, psychologically marginal "information," may at the time have little real payoff in object appraisal or social adjustment (the person may have no occasion for dealing with the object or issue, and it may not matter enough to his significant reference groups to become part of the currency of his self-other relationships); yet, should the occasion arise, the basis for resonance to certain political positions rather than others has been laid.

The Problem of Political Rationality

In illustrative comments along the way, I have tried to indicate how the map draws distinctions that help to clarify thinking about personality and politics. But these have been hit-and-run examples. A clearer view of its usefulness—or sterility—should come from applying the map to the elucidation of some major problem of political theory and research. A good one for the purpose should be the problem of political rationality, in which V. O. Key was persistently interested and to which he made substantive contribution in his posthumous book (1966).

In setting the scene for his study of rationality in American presidential voting, Key depicted the current antirational climate of political analysis thus:

> By and large, the picture of the voter that emerges from a combination of the folklore of practical politics and the findings of the new electoral studies is not a pretty one. It is not a portrait of citizens moving to considered decision as they play their solemn role of making and unmaking governments. The older tradition from practical politics may regard the voter as an erratic and irrational fellow susceptible to manipulation by skilled humbugs . . . Nor does a heroic conception of the voter emerge from the new analyses of electoral behavior. They can be added up to a conception of voting not as a civic decision but as an almost purely deterministic act. [pp. 4–6]

As Key sees it, such an irrationalist view itself has political consequences:

> In short, theories of how voters behave acquire importance not because of their effects on voters, who may proceed blithely unaware of them. They gain significance because of their effects, both potentially and in reality, on candidates and other political leaders. If leaders believe the route to victory is by projection of images and cultivation of styles rather than by advocacy of policies to cope with the problems of the country, they will project images and cultivate styles to the neglect of the substance of politics. They will abdicate their prime function in a democratic system, which amounts, in essence, to the assumption of the risk of trying to persuade us to lift ourselves by our bootstraps. [p. 6]

Psychological theory has also contributed its bit to the antirationalist trend that has had the upper hand since the emergence of modern social science. The realization brought by Darwin that man is a member of the animal kingdom has often carried with it a degraded conception of human nature, instead of focusing scientific curiosity on how man is sometimes capable of qualities and achievements that surpass those he once ascribed to the angels.

In psychoanalysis Freud, who himself was ironically devoted to rational values and their promulgation, greatly advanced our understanding of irrational aspects of human behavior, but also showed the way for lesser followers to engage in facile debunking of all human pretensions to rationality. The behaviorists, who for more than a generation dominated academic theorizing in American psychology, held dogmatically to a mechanistic view of man that left no place for rational action. Until recently, only psychologists in the minority Gestalt tradition (for instance, Asch, 1952) and humanistically inclined mavericks like Gordon Allport (1955) held to a model of man as a rational actor that would be recognizable to the liberal proponents of democratic political institutions.[5]

But what do we mean by rationality in such contexts? Our answer will depend on the weight we give to evaluating the *products* of individual and social decision processes, as compared with our interest in evaluating the decision *processes* themselves. Rational decisions viewed as products are ones that select appropriate means to attain specified goals at acceptable costs, within a self-consistent framework of positive and negative goal values and in terms of an accurate appraisal of the situation of action. The complexities and competing models of modern decision theory (Becker and McClintock, 1967) testify to the ambiguities that are latent in common-sense notions of rationality as an objective property of decisions themselves. Yet if we are ultimately concerned with evaluating the political consequences of decisions, we cannot avoid a perspective that looks on the rationality of decisions, as it were, from the outside.

An alternative emphasis, on criteria that pertain to the decision processes as such viewed from the "inside," makes readier contact with the process-oriented predilections of contemporary political scientists and psychologists. In the case of important classes of social decisions, conceptions of "due process" specify minimal norms for properly considered—thus rational—decision-making, setting deliberately aside the correctness of the decision reached. Are there analogous conceptions that apply in the sphere of individual decisions?

In terms of the distinctions in my map, the crux of a processual conception of individual political rationality, it seems to me, lies in the relative preponderance of object appraisal in the person's attitudes that enter into his political decisions and actions. As products, his decisions may be defective and irrational if they are based on the appraisal of erroneous or deficient information. But to the extent that they are grounded in processes of object appraisal, they are rational in the sense that they represent a weighing of

5. The conception that *determinism* is incompatible with a model of man as a responsible actor is wrong and seriously misleading. The best discussion I know of this problem at the border between philosophy and psychological theory—and, incidentally, a trenchant criticism of mechanistic theory and a cogent defense of a view of man as a rational animal—is offered by Isidor Chein (1962). For a social psychological interpretation of rationality as an outcome of symbolic interaction, see my paper (Smith, 1960).

means-end relationships that is corrigible in principle given the availability of better information.

From the same processual point of view, externalization and ego defense are definitely irrational. To the extent that this function prevails as a basis for a person's attitudes, he is distracted from relevant considerations of ends and means. He is likely to cling rigidly to his political postures in disregard of available information, and if he changes at all, the change is likely to be saltatory and "unreasonable." Rather than yielding gradually to the pressure of new facts, he may leap unpredictably from a no longer tenable position to another position that is its symbolic or dynamic equivalent for him, different as its realistic political implications may be. The ardent Communist becomes the equally ardent anti-communist Catholic convert.

The remaining functional basis of attitudes, mediation of self—other relationships, is neutral in rationality from this processual perspective. The motivational agenda that it implies has nothing intrinsically to do with how the person appraises the bearing of a focal object or issue on his interests and values, but neither does it necessarily operate at cross-purposes with rational object appraisal, as is the case with externalization and ego defense. And we shall see that there are conditions under which it may lead to decisions which, as products, must be judged as rational.

The functional analysis of attitudes that is embodied in the map of Figure 2.4 thus makes room for rational processes—and for nonrational and irrational ones as well. It does not settle the problem of rationality by assumption, but leaves it open to empirical inquiry. It avoids treating either the rational or the irrational propensities of man—both consequences of his unique symbolic attainments—as residual. It does not rule out the plausible view that at the individual level most political acts and decisions have both rational and irrational ingredients.

Intermediate between conceptions of individual rationality as process and as product is a characteristic that would commonly be ascribed to rational decisions and judgments: they are reached in a context of relevant considerations that is broad, not narrow, and includes a time perspective in which consequences are viewed in the longer run. Thus personality traits (also placed in Panel III of the map) that characterize the contextual breadth with which a person customarily views new problems become relevant to his level of political rationality. Practically, the narrowness, concreteness, and low sophistication that *The American Voter* (Campbell, A., et al., 1960, pp. 216–265) found in the political thinking of average Americans set stringent limits on the rationality of their political decisions viewed as products, however reasonable these may appear from a person's own limited perspective. A theory of the democratic polity must therefore give special place to the role of opinion elites and attentive publics whose attitudes are freer from such limitations, and to their interplay with the less sophisticated mass (Key, 1963, pp. 536 ff.).

To make a place on the map for process rationality, according to which people's decisions and judgments are reasonable within the limits of their grasp of relevant considerations, may restore a view of the human condition in which democracy is conceivable. But as the foregoing discussion suggests, the practical functioning of democracy depends as well on the factors apart from process rationality that affect the extent to which individual judgments meet the criteria of rationality as products. The map finds a place for several such factors.

In regard to Panel IV (the situation as immediate antecedent of action), for example, we may ask: Does the situation pose a meaningful and intelligible political choice? Is information relevant to the choice readily available? How is the citizen to distinguish information from misinformation? All of these considerations should affect whether, in my jargon, process rationality leads to product rationality. And does the situation present the issue in a context of threat and stress, or in a way more conducive to thoughtful deliberation?

If we turn to Panel II (the social environment as context of socialization) again the question of adequacy and accuracy of political information arises. Most people's political attitudes, even when they are predominantly grounded in object appraisal, surely rest on a scanty and haphazard informational base. If such be the nature of most people's attitudes, what kinds of decisions can they be asked to make, then, with the greatest likelihood of rational outcomes? V. O. Key suggests that the basic electoral decision—in or out with the incumbent—is most likely to be within people's range.

In Panel II we also encounter the social norms held by the person's significant reference groups. If these norms are congruent with the person's own real interests (and of course this is a notoriously treacherous matter to judge), rational political outcomes may result even when his attitudes are grounded in the mediation of self-other relationships rather than in object appraisal. I can follow my crowd to good advantage *if* my crowd happens to be right from my standpoint. If, however, the person is linked through his reference groups to norms that conflict with his real interests, this functional basis of attitudes becomes a source of irrational outcomes for him. The extent to which a person's reference groups correspond to his membership groups is a related matter. A Smith who is keeping up with the Joneses may form attitudes and make decisions that would be rational enough for a Jones, but not for a Smith.

Finally, Panel II calls attention to the role of life situations and socialization experiences in preferentially orienting the person toward one or another functional basis for his political attitudes, and in forming his politically relevant traits. The paranoid style of the radical right—surely a mark of irrational externalization—has been described as a defensive posture of the dispossessed, the sidetracked and downwardly mobile (Bell, 1963). What is the effect on the characterological basis of political rationality of living in lifelong practiced denial of the threat of atomic catastrophe? Of living in economic insecurity or affluence in a marginal, or in an affluent society?

Of being one of the powerless in a time of rising aspirations? And what, for that matter, are the long-term political consequences of trends toward less authoritarian child-rearing? Though it may be impossible in the nature of the case to disentangle such strands of recent history, the idea of ebbs and flows in the bases of political rationality seems entirely plausible.

Just as my map deals with the antecedents of political behavior at the individual level, leaving the problems of articulation in a political system to the political sociologist, so my discussion of political rationality thus far stops short of the questions that would most concern a student of the functioning of democratic governmental institutions. But the map may be suggestive even in regard to matters that fall outside its explicit range.

Beyond the level of the single individual, one may approach relevance to governmental institutions by dealing with persons in the aggregate, or by dealing with them as they articulate in social structures. As I have already remarked, the latter type of analysis requires a different sort of map, and V. O. Key's treatise on public opinion (1963) is cogently addressed to considerations of articulation that would be involved in drawing it. But for some problems the mere aggregation of individual data is appropriate, and because that is indeed how votes are counted, it is especially appropriate to the study of voting behavior. This is the strategy followed by Key in his posthumously published study of presidential voting that I quoted at the outset of this section.

In intent and conclusion, *The Responsible Electorate* asserts and adduces evidence for a considerable degree of rationality in American presidential voting. Key summarizes the book prospectively as follows:

> The perverse and unorthodox argument of this little book is that voters are not fools . . . In the large the electorate behaves about as rationally and responsibly as we should expect, given the clarity of the alternatives presented to it and the character of the information available to it. In American presidential campaigns of recent decades the portrait that develops from the data is not one of an electorate strait-jacketed by social determinants or moved by subconscious urges triggered by devilishly skillful propagandists. It is rather one of an electorate moved by concern about central and relevant questions of public policy, of governmental performance, and of executive personality. [Key, 1966, pp.7–8]

Later, he summarizes his principal evidence, concerning the correlates of voting turnover between elections, thus:

> It can scarcely be said that party switchers constitute a sector of the electorate significantly lower in political interest than the standpatters. . . . Instead, the switchers, who (in company with "new" voters) call the turn, are persons whose peculiarity is not lack of interest but agreement on broad political issues with the standpatters toward whom they shift . . .

> This should be regarded as at least a modicum of evidence for the view that those who switch do so to support governmental policies or outlooks with which they agree, not because of subtle psychological or sociological peculiarities. [Key, 1966, p. 104]

What does the map contribute to the interpretation of these data and conclusions?

For one thing, the suggestion immediately arises that voters in the aggregate may look more rational than they do singly—if true, a fortunate outcome for the democratic system. Such would be the case if two conditions turn out to hold: first, that group norms with respect to the vote reflect genuine group interests, and, second, that the roots of voting choice in externalization and ego defense are personally idiosyncratic and distributed unsystematically through the population.

Consider the second of these specifications. If there are irrational private components in everyone's vote, *but* these vary unsystematically across persons and candidates, their effect should cancel out in the aggregate, leaving a residue that reflects rational choice. And perhaps this is indeed the normal, fortunate state of affairs. The abnormal may be exemplified by episodes of "hysteria" like McCarthyism—mass externalization running parallel?—from which the electorate subsequently emerges with a collective hangover. From this point of view, it is fortunate that political choices seem not to have the standardized unconscious meanings that lay Freudians were wont to look for. Not to everybody was Eisenhower a father-figure.

As for the first condition, concerning the degree to which group voting patterns represent genuine group interests, Key argues from his data that they correspond fairly closely by and large. To the extent that they do, of course, the first two functional bases of attitudes pull together. When group norms reflect individual interests, mediation of self-other relations yields the same result as object appraisal.

Key's vivid rhetoric in dramatizing his point, of course, plays up a needless conflict in interpretation. "Sociological peculiarities" or "social determinants" do not have their influence by any mysterious process of "strait-jacketing" the electorate, and nobody ever claimed that they do. Their influence, indeed a determining one, lies primarily in the fact that common experience and common social position yield similar perceptions of interest, and over time lead to the emergence of norms that reflect these perceptions. Social determination is by no means incompatible with political rationality.

Similarly with psychological determination. Aggregate rationality is entirely compatible with "subconscious urges," so long as they are divergent. Note also that psychological determination cannot fairly be equated with the subconscious—with externalization and ego defense. Orientation toward norms and orientation toward consequences for one's interests and values are psychological too!

We must remember, finally, that presidential elections with their simplified choice, their high salience, may not be typical of other political behavior that the citizen is called upon to perform. Presidential voting may indeed be a rational performance as compared, for example, with voting on the many initiative and referendum measures on a long California ballot.

The tentative principle of aggregation suggested in our consideration of Key's analyses has interesting consequences with respect to other features of the map. One major feature that we have seen as limiting political rationality —people's informational deficiencies—will clearly *not* be distributed randomly in the electorate. Obvious correlations of informational adequacy with educational and socioeconomic level will have consequences for the degree and manner of political participation. Systematic differences in available public media and in subcultural informational habits should give rise to regional variation and persisting rural-urban differences. There should be substantial differences by topical content as well, placing a particular handicap on the rational public consideration of foreign policy issues. If we agree with Key that in the long run and on the major policy alternatives, the electorate is basically rational, it does not follow that it is homogeneously rational across social strata, regions, and issues. The heterogeneities pose challenging problems of articulation for political theory, and of organization and leadership for political practice.

By this point we perhaps have a sufficient sampling of what the map can and cannot do. As a heuristic scanning device, it summarizes the wisdom born of long traditions of research and theory by calling attention to variables and classes of relationships that are relevant to a psychologically focused perspective on political behavior. It further draws explicit attention to the boundary problems involved in articulating such a perspective with the sociologically centered perspective that is equally indispensable in the study of politics. To the extent that the map draws distinctions familiar to political scientists, it codifies what they know. If it also draws some novel ones, it may help to throw new light on old problems. At best, it can be an aid to the attainment of better research and better theory. It is, of course, a substitute for neither.

3

Anthropology and Psychology

To treat the interrelations of anthropology and psychology from the point of view of psychology, as falls to my part in this joint undertaking, should presuppose agreement on the meaning and scope of the terms being related. Yet the state of affairs that makes this venture desirable includes, I think, the fact that the boundaries dividing these disciplines from one another and from sociology are by no means sharp, stable, or justified on obviously rational grounds. A source of fruitless jurisdictional disputes and no little confusion, it also gives rise to the hope of attaining a more comprehensive science of social man.

For a starting point, it is probably best to accept psychology, anthropology, and sociology for the cultural and historical facts that they are: academic specializations that emerged late in the nineteenth century, each blessed today with a distinctive body of literature and shared informal lore—a tradition transmitted mainly in college and university departments through relatively standardized training experiences. Joint departments, to be sure, are a frequent occurrence, and an occasional individual changes his affiliation. But at a time when it would be hard indeed to give satisfactory conceptual definitions that would unmistakably distinguish the three disciplines for the uninitiated, practically no one who is professionally involved in them has any doubt about whether he is a psychologist, an anthropologist, or a sociologist. The only adequate way to define each discipline is to point to its history, and to the current activities of the people who agree on identifying one another as members.

Each discipline has, of course, its subdivisions or areas of specialization. Some of these are most loosely interrelated. Consider, for example, the loose bonds among archaeology, linguistics, cultural anthropology, and physical anthropology on the one hand, and constitutional psychology, personality study, physiological psychology, and psychometrics on the other. All of these specialties and many more have their essential contribution to make to the integral study of man. To make my present task feasible, however, I will

Reprinted by permission from John Gillin, editor, *For a Science of Social Man. Convergences in Anthropology, Psychology, and Sociology*. New York: The Macmillan Company, 1954.

focus on what has come to be known as cultural or social anthropology, with respect to its contribution to general psychology, and, particularly, to social psychology and the study of personality. I am thus concerned with anthropology and psychology as they bear on the social nature of man, rather than on its biological basis.

While it may be adequate to define a discipline by a pointing operation, it is quite unsatisfying. One looks rather, if not for boundaries, at least for a distinctive theoretical perspective, for a conceptual center of gravity. In the case of psychology, what runs through an otherwise heterogeneous history is a prevading focus on the individual. From beginnings in which interest centered on his experience or consciousness, through a brash adolescence in which only his most objectively observable activities were deemed suitable for scientific study, to the present more catholic outlook in which psychologists resort more readily to unobservable constructs and inferential concepts in their interpretation of behavior, the individual has been the primary reference point.

This has not meant that psychologists have always thought of themselves as studying individuals. Often enough, the person has been lost to sight, whether in the early concern with the description of the "generalized human mind," or in the later pursuit of general principles of behavior in studies of the lowly rat. Modern social psychology, moreover, is struggling to attain ways of dealing more directly with the *interactions* of persons, finding too rigid a focus on the individual as an isolated entity a stumbling block in the way of attaining adequate theory. Nevertheless, descriptions of the organization of consciousness and the principles of behavior, whether they dealt with learning or motivation or social interaction, have with few exceptions been conceived as applying at the level of the individual.

The aspects of anthropology with which we are presently concerned, on the other hand, have had a different focus. From the outmoded phases of evolutionism and diffusionism to the current interest in a theoretical account of culture and social structure, and through the persisting strain of descriptive ethnology, anthropology has come to direct its attention on the organized relations of the members of a society, and on the cultural tradition in which these are imbedded.

The role of the individual in this pattern of interest has been controversial. Except when the anthropologist is working with artifacts of "material culture," to be sure, he secures his data from individuals, either as informants or as actors in the drama of society. After serving as a means in the generation of data, however, the individual traditionally dropped out the picture, in favor of cultural or social patterns described so as to be relatively independent of the particular persons who happen to carry or enact them.

At the extreme, this tendency has been given theoretical status in the position, taken for example by Leslie White (1949), that culture exists at a level utterly independent of the individuals who carry it, with special laws of its own. More characteristic of the current temper, however, is the opposing trend, given its initial impetus by Sapir (1934), to look to the individual for a more differentiated version of the cultural process and for a leverage point at which the theorist can come to grips with cultural continuity and change. Once the individual comes within the range of attention, a host of fascinating problems arise that may carry the anthropologist far into the territory traditionally staked out by the psychologist. But the center of gravity of the anthropologist's concern with the individual, if such can be distinguished, is certainly the interpretation of cultural and social processes supra- or interindividual in scope. No longer disembodied, culture is still the primary focus.

My task of examining the contribution of anthropology to psychology is complicated, however, by the fact that it is difficult to distinguish anthropology from sociology with respect to theoretical focus or principal reference point. It would be convenient if anthropology could be identified as the science of culture[1] and sociology as the science of social structure or social systems—of the patterned interrelations of members of a society. But as we all know and Murdock has reminded us[2], anthropologists have paid major attention to social structure with considerable substantive results. The sociologist, on his part, has implicitly studied culture, even when he has held to a general focus on social structure, which, after all, has major cultural components. The distinctions between sociology and social and cultural anthropology, foremost among them the traditional anthropological emphasis on the comparative study of non-literate societies, are historical accidents. Any survey of the contributions of anthropology must therefore treat certain concepts which are also the common property of sociologists.

How Psychology Has Drawn on Anthropology: An Overview

A detailed historical account of the interplay between anthropology and psychology should go back at least as far as Wundt, whose program to study the higher mental processes through their objectified cultural products culminated in a *Völkerpsychologie* that drew heavily on ethnographic materials. But this proved to be somewhat of a by-path in the development of both disciplines. We can more profitably begin by inquiring about some general features of the processes of diffusion and acculturation by which the influence of anthropology has been felt in psychology during the more recent period that includes the present situation and its immediate antecedents.

In cases of culture contact, the anthropologists tell us, items of culture content are more likely to be transferred than the broader configurations

1. I find Linton's definition (1945, p. 32) as useful as any and will try to abide by it: "A culture is the configuration of learned behavior and results of behavior whose component elements are shared and transmitted by the members of a particular society."

2. In his contribution on "Sociology and anthropology" to the symposium volume in which the present essay appeared, pp. 14–31.

that give them meaning in their original setting. So it has been in the contact of psychology with anthropology. With the exception of the broad concept of culture, the bizarre data brought back by the anthropologist from afield have had more impact on psychology than the theories with which anthropologists approached their data. It is the rare psychologist who lacks passing acquaintance with the Arapesh, the Trobrianders, the Kwakiutl, the Zuni, or the Navaho, though a few stock tribes perhaps suffice to establish for him and his students the point that the condition of man is exceedingly various. Much less frequent is the psychologist who has exposed himself to sophisticated analysis of the culture concept, or who has resorted to anthropological descriptions for help in specifying the social environments in which behavior takes place.

This tendency of the psychologist to borrow data rather than theory from the anthropologist is doubtless in no small part the result of the traditional stress in anthropology on sheer descriptive ethnography. The anthropologist had access to the natural laboratory provided by the wide range of variation among the vanishing non-Western societies; he was preoccupied with capturing a record of these societies while they were still accessible. Until anthropological theorizing in recent years itself took a psychological direction, the psychologist found the ethnographic data much more interesting than the anthropologist's speculations about his still meager conceptual framework. And if the psychologist made only superficial use of the riches of anthropological data, he was abetted by the stress on a somewhat monolithic concept of culture in the anthropological writings that diffused to him. One does not have to look very closely at the facts of very many societies to appreciate the importance of culture; it takes a closer look, to be sure, to see that announcing this concept only poses a host of problems that it does not solve.

With the development within anthropology of a strong psychological current in the study of "culture and personality," showing closer affinities to psychoanalytic theory than to the prevalent academic psychology, another line of influence was established. The popular works in this vein—those by Margaret Mead (e.g. 1928) are the most salient example—are probably still the most frequent avenue of psychological acquaintance with anthropology, as witness the names of stock tribes that immediately come to mind to a psychologist. Although the psychological approach to anthropology met with initial unfavorable criticism in the psychological camp as it did in the anthropological, it may well be that this feedback of modified psychoanalytic ideas to psychologists has something to do with the more important role of psychodynamic conceptions in contemporary psychology. As McDougall (1908) foresaw, the social sciences need from psychology an adequate theory of motivation. The borrowings of anthropologists from psychoanalytic motivational theory have at least dramatized to the psychologist the need to get his own house in order in this conceptual area. Paradoxically, the seriousness with which psychological attention is now focused on a re-examination of Freudian psychodynamics may in part represent an anthropological influence on psychology.

In this recent interplay of anthropology and psychology, habits of research and thinking established in the characteristic training patterns of each discipline have influenced the developing channels of communication and borrowing. Anthropological field training has tended to emphasize keen observation, the shrewd use of informants, and naturalistic qualitative description. So long as practical exigencies confront one or two field workers with the task of describing an entire culture on the basis of a year of residence more or less, the field worker is forced into bold extrapolations if he aspires to any synthetic characterization of the culture as a whole. Anthropological methods of collecting and digesting data have therefore had more in common with the procedures of clinical psychiatry than with the methodological nicety of experimental psychology. While the anthropologist, like the psychiatrist, is moved by urgencies in the real situation to glean as much insight as possible from methods that are open to challenge from the purist, the psychologist from the beginning has been ready to risk triviality for the sake of the scientific rigor that is his badge of distinction from philosophy and anecdotal or armchair speculation.

Anthropology, therefore, has had stronger affinity with psychiatry and psychoanalysis than with the hard core of academic psychology. And to a considerable extent, the more tenderminded in both anthropology and psychology have been the agents of contact. During the historical and descriptive phase of American anthropology, concern with theory was itself a mark of tendermindednes. In psychology, students of personality and social psychology, who comprised most of those who paid any attention to anthropological developments, were perforce bucking the current of methodological rigor in concerning themselves with these treacherous areas. In sum, when anthropologists looked to psychology, it was likely to be of the psychoanalytic variety, while the psychologists who were drawn into closest contact with anthropology tended themselves to be of the more clinical persuasion.[3]

Happily, this characterization, never entirely accurate, seems to be becoming outmoded by recent developments. Theory having become respectable in anthropology, toughminded anthropologists are investigating problems that bring them into closer rapprochement with psychology. Psychodynamics having become respectable in psychology, toughminded psychologists are addressing themselves to motivational problems, and the gap between "academic" psychology and the more comprehensive but speculative theories of psychoanalysis is at least diminishing. As the attack on problems

3. Margaret Mead's contribution (1952) to a textbook of psychoanalytic psychiatry at once discusses and itself exemplifies some of the affinities I have described. But Mead has also been concerned with underpinning her approach to personality-as-a-whole in culture-as-a-totality with appropriately rigorous field methods. See, for example, M. Mead (1946), which also contains a valuable discussion of anthropological contributions to the psychology of socialization.

of motivation and personality development advances, moreover, the crucial relevance of the comparative data accessible through the anthropologist is becoming increasingly apparent.

Lest I be too quickly misunderstood, let me say at once that I have no wish to disparage the contribution of the tenderminded. But it is unhealthy for either the toughminded or the tenderminded to have a monopoly on particular problem areas or on the channels between two disciplines in the present stage of development of the human sciences. The present situation seems to me promising not because the rigor claimed by the experimental psychologist is prevailing, but because minds of both persuasions are more nearly meeting in the systematic attack on common problems.

While a genuine interpenetration of perspectives and collaborative marshalling of the joint resources of the two disciplines appears closer to realization in recent years, a less admirable sort of borrowing is perhaps still the rule at the plebeian level of the elementary textbook, where the most frequent if not the most significant occasions occur for the budding psychologist to form his impressions of related disciplines. The social psychologist who takes seriously the mission of his specialty to build a bridge between interpretations of individual behavior rooted in the organism, on the one hand, and phenomena at the social and cultural levels, on the other, must after all do more than merely borrow data and concepts. He has to re-examine the conceptual foundations of psychology to assure himself that they can anchor the individually-oriented end of this bridge effectively. To do this, he has to develop for himself a tentative conception of the structure of the bridge, including its anchoring at the socio-cultural end. More commonly, however, he has in fact tended to take for granted the existing conceptual structure oriented toward the biological individual, and without assuring himself that there is a bridge, to add on to it fragments and snatches casually drawn from the social sciences, particularly anthropology.

Solomon Asch (1952), taking a critical view of the theoretical resources of social psychology, has recently made a similar point:

> It has to be admitted that social psychology lives today in the shadow of great doctrines of man that were formulated long before it appeared and that it has borrowed its leading ideas from neighboring regions of scientific thought and from the social philosophies of the modern period. It is paradoxical but true that social psychology has thus far made the least contribution to the questions that are its special concern and that it has as yet not significantly affected the conceptions it has borrowed. [p. viii]

Intellectual beachcombing of this sort is of course no substitute for serious attempts at synthesis in the social sciences. The presence in a psychological textbook of interesting anthropological case material or of genuflections to "culture" gives no guarantee that the contribution of anthropology has been assimilated. It may, on the other hand, contribute to the misimpression that a fully elaborated psychology would incorporate the entire domain of social science. As a sign of gropings toward a more comprehensive science of social man, it may temporarily be a healthy state of affairs, but it is a stage that needs to be superseded if we are to get ahead with the real collaborative task.

The Concept of Culture

Turning now to some of the specific contributions of anthropology to psychology, we can hardly start elsewhere than with the concept of culture, surely the most influential and perhaps the most important outcome of modern anthropology, particularly as it has developed in America. If the word "anthropology" were presented to a sample of psychologists in a word association test, I would venture, "culture" would probably be the most popular response, with "Indians" a runner-up. As a technical term, the word has filtered into the popular culture of educated people to an extent matched only by some of the language of psychoanalysis; the cautious explanation that anthropologists mean by culture something other than the hoped-for product of a liberal education has become superfluous.

Anthropologists have the privilege of engaging in technical controversy about the definition of their most central concept (Kroeber, A. L., and Kluckhohn, 1952)—controversy that leads to refinement and clarification when it is directed at an examination of common usage or of the logical requirements of the theoretical contexts in which the term is to be put to use, but which is apt to be sterile if it involves conflicting claims about the essence of a supposed real entity. But to a psychologist, there seems to be considerable agreement in the present use of the term. "Culture" in the abstract is a generalization from "cultures," while *a* culture is itself an abstract concept ascribed to some identified social group. The important components of current usage would seem to include (a) a conception of shared ways of behaving, predispositions to behavior, and (perhaps) products of behavior, and (b) the restriction that if something is a part of culture, it is learned—transmitted socially rather than biologically. Trouble enters primarily with the identification of what is shared. If culture is regarded as an abstraction from social behavior, however, the balance between patterned uniformities and individual variation becomes a matter for empirical determination rather than definitional controversy. In practice, the extent of uniformity or of patterning appears to be broad enough to make it convenient to talk about cultures, without dismissing the probable need for more differentiated concepts.

It is important to note that culture is a concept, not a theory. The term itself embodies no articulated propositions from which consequences can be drawn and put to test. It asserts nothing about reality. The psychologist who turns to anthropology after studying his lessons in the logic of science may therefore show some surprise when he encounters statements about the importance of the concept as an anthropological contribution.

It would be grossly unfair, of course, to view the concept of culture in splendid isolation. If it contains no assertions, its definition nevertheless calls attention to phenomena that had previously been neglected. With the *concept* of culture goes an *orientation,* if not a theory, that a very wide range of human phenomena is cultural in nature. The importance of the concept rests, then, on the host of assertions in which it occurs, to the effect that phenomena x, y, z, etc. are cultural in origin, or are influenced in specific ways by culture. It is through facts of this latter order, together with the broader cultural orientation, that the concept of culture has been influential on psychology.

Some Parallels between the Concepts of Culture and Personality

In psychology, personality has much the same status as culture in anthropology, though it may lack the latter's eye-opening properties. As with culture, there is an entire literature of definitional controversy. To by-pass extensive discussion, we can take from Newcomb the modal definition that an individual's personality is the organization of his predispositions to behavior. Strictly speaking, *a* personality is to be distinguished from personality in general, just as *a* culture is from *culture.* Like culture, personality is an abstraction from behavior, mainly in social contexts. It is abstracted, however, from consistencies in the behavior of the single individual. Since personality has been linked with culture in one of the lines of development that has brought anthropology and psychology into close association, we can well afford a detour to examine jointly some of the controversies that have centered on these concepts. As it turns out, there is a striking parallelism in the methodological problems to which they have given rise. The same battles have been fought, apparently quite independently, in anthropology and psychology.

There is in the first place the question of how personality and culture are related to simpler or more microscopic concepts. The polarity of *elementarism* vs. *holism* that has run through the scientific controversies of the twentieth century has taken very similar form in the two disciplines, and in each the holistic emphasis on organization, hierarchy, and "patterning" has tended to gain the upper hand, after an initial period of predominant elementarism.

Anthropology of the diffusionist period concerned itself with the distribution of independent culture "traits" and "items," of which a particular culture was seen as an aggregate or congeries. While trait distributions continue to be studied, recent emphasis has fallen on the integrity of cultures. If the context in which particular traits occur determines their significance, to speak of the "same" trait in two different cultures is likely to require much qualification. A whole vocabulary has sprung up to deal with the hierarchical organization of cultural components, from "patterns" and "configurations" to "ethos"—even the more elementary terms having the flavor familiar to the psychologist from Gestalt doctrine. A similar trend is apparent in the psychology of personality. The "sum-total" conception of personality as a cluster of habits, S-R connections, traits or tendencies externally bound to one another has given way to emphasis on the personality "as a whole," with preoccupation with structure or organization.

In each case, however, the ascendancy of holism has raised a new set of problems that neither science has gone far toward solving. While it is the virute of the holistic approach to recognize phenomena of structure and organization, either culture or personality "as a whole" is a more fitting subject for poetry than for science. Wholeness can be—and has often been —evoked, but it cannot be described in ways that can be checked independently without the use of more elementary terms. Yet if the sterility of crude elementarism is to be avoided, ways must be found of framing subsidiary concepts that are appropriate to dynamically organized phenomena, and techniques must be devised for constituting the appropriate data.

In this respect, the task of psychology may well be simpler than that of anthropology. The wholeness of the functioning organism, it has seemed reasonable to postulate, can readily be involved in complex responses, if, indeed, its involvement is not inevitable. In the development of projective tests, one attack on this problem, the psychologist has sought to obtain strategic samples of behavior from which the dispositional structure of the behaving individual can be inferred. Merest beginnings have been made in the process of grounding these tests more firmly in a rationale of psychological theory and standardizing the canons of inference from the data that they yield. But the persistence of knotty problems leaves reasonably clear the general direction from which a more adequate description of personality organization is to be sought.

The program of holism in cultural anthropology, on the other hand, must face the difficulty that since cultures are abstractions from the behavior of many people, they do not themselves "behave" in ways that can be sampled with a test, projective or otherwise. Analogous data have nevertheless been sought, from at least three directions. One may turn to the individuals who are vehicles of the culture, and borrowing techniques from the psychologist, investigate the organization of culture as it is internalized by its carriers. But the problem then remains of how to reconstitute "the" culture from these data. Or one may systematically analyze such cultural products as mythology and folklore to emerge with "themes" analogous to those that the clinical psychologist identifies in his projective material. Aside from the difficulty shared with the psychologist in arriving at objective canons of inference, the anthropologist faces here a major problem of attaining a definable and adequate sample of the culture for his analysis. Or, finally, one may look for the covariation, relative persistence, and modifiability of cultural components under conditions of culture contact, change, and dissolution. The latter method, attractive since it identifies structure in what is functionally coherent, is applicable only when it is possible to capture adequate data on culture change. Each of these approaches has its instructive parallel in the psychology of personality. As either discipline approaches more closely the solution of its problems of structural description, the other may find leads from it toward the solution of its own problems.

A second realm of controversy has to do with the sort of theoretical context in which culture or personality concepts are to be placed—or, to put it differently, with the explanation of cultures or personalities once they have been described. The polarity, as it became defined in anthropology, is that of *historicism* vs. *functionalism.*

In both disciplines, there has been affinity between historical interpretation and the preference for working with simple and unchanging conceptual elements. The association is a natural one, since if personality or culture is regarded as a chance assembly of elements that preserve their identity and are not significantly influenced by their interaction with one another, the presence of a culture trait or a habit or S-R bond can only be accounted for historically. The presumed rigid identity of the element draws the theorist's attention to the historical line of continuity in its past vicissitudes, and underplays the lines of relationship to features of the contemporary situation.

If the culture trait is independent of the organized cultural matrix in which it is embedded, one can only refer its presence to persistence from an earlier state of the culture, or to accession from processes of invention or diffusion. Conversely, the independent trait as a starting point gives little anchorage for investigating the functioning of socio-cultural systems or studying the relation of cultural components to the presently existing needs of the members of a society. So functionalism of the varieties associated with both Radcliffe-Brown and Malinowski has developed within a descriptive orientation that weights heavily the phenomena of organization and structure.

In psychology, too, elementaristic description has involved predominantly historical explanation: witness the historical phrasing of classical associationism and of its more modern variants in conditioning and reinforcement theory. But the existence of strong functional and structural orientations in psychoanalysis, which has been notably historical in its preoccupation with origins, suggests that the antihistorical bent of functionalism in anthropology may have been accidental rather than the outcome of intrinsic features of a functional approach. Modern psychology, historical or otherwise, is in fact overwhelmingly functional. The dominant strain is oriented toward a model of the organism as a self-regulating system and falls naturally into the use of terms like homeostasis, equilibrium, and adjustment; while the marginal influence of Gestalt theory leads to parallel emphasis on the field determination of phenomenal properties or behavioral tendencies. Rather than putting history and function in opposition, recent psychological discussion has centered on the more clearly articulated dichotomy of *historical* vs. *contemporaneous* explanation, posed most forcefully in the writings of Kurt Lewin (1935).

And the history of even this dichotomy, if I read it rightly, has indicated that once certain tenacious misunderstandings are cleared aside, there is little cause for battle. If psychology were equipped with an adequate set of laws and an adequate description of the situation faced by an individual, as most psychologists would be ready to agree in principle, his behavior could be predicted either from a complete record of his psychological history or from a full analysis of his immediate predispositions—the present state of his personality as a system. In this hypothetical case, which for practical purposes is trivial because it is non-existent, knowledge of the individual's history would be translatable into knowledge about his contemporaneous personality structure. Whether or not one would then elect to work in historical terms would be a matter of arbitrary preference.

The fact of the matter, however, is that psychologists do not and will not in the foreseeable future possess complete data on either the history or the present personality of an individual, to say nothing of adequate laws or procedures for situational analysis. Lacking the equivalent of X-ray techniques to diagnose present personality, the psychologist perforce has recourse to personal history in his reconstruction of the individual as he is at present. Correspondingly, reconstructions of personal history must usually take as their starting point the individual's present dispositions, including most notably his memories.

There is thus no inherent conflict between historical and ahistorical approaches to the study of personality. They are complementary, not antagonistic. Once the air is cleared of the murk of partisanship, investigators can get about their business, some approaching the problem from a focus on antecedent—consequent relations in individual history, others seeking to analyze functional interdependencies within the immediate present, and still others working toward a closer articulation of the two approaches. The lessons of this controversy, which has perhaps been worked through in greater detail in psychology than in anthropology, should be partially transferable to research on culture. Indeed, Murdock (1949) has already demonstrated that analysis of functional dependence among elements of social structure furnishes a powerful tool for historical reconstruction.

The third methodological difficulty running alike through discussion of personality and of culture has also been phrased as a polarity, that between *idiographic* and *nomothetic* approaches. The terms were given currency in psychology by G. W. Allport (1937), who derived them from Windelband. The contrast is that between fidelity to the unique occurrence and the search for general laws that encompass reality by successive approximation without pretending to capture the unique. An idiographic psychology, as proclaimed by Allport, would seek to describe the personality of each individual in terms of its own unique organization. Its quest for laws would be directed at the discovery of principles of development and organization to account for individual uniqueness. The corresponding position in anthropology reiterates the uniqueness of cultures, and shows an aversion to systematic comparative analysis as somehow involving the violation of a culture's integrity. There is, indeed, a strong current of temperamental preference running through the statements of faith from both sides of this controversy: the more tenderminded and intuitive aligned on one side with a nurturant, appreciative attitude toward their data, as against the toughminded and conceptual who have no hesitation in rending apart the presenting phenomena in order to abstract regularities that can be fitted into a causal though approximate interpretation of nature.[4]

In fairness to Allport, it should be noted that he regards the idiographic and nomothetic approaches as complementary. Those who embrace the extreme idiographic position, which I believe is more deeply entrenched in anthropology than in psychology, are vulnerable to a telling argument. If they maintain that cultures or personalities are each unique and incommeasurable, one has only to counter with instances of success in the demonstration of lawful relationships in cross-cultural studies or in experimental psychodynamics to make the position untenable. Meager as our substantive findings are today, they more than suffice to establish this point.

The dichotomy collapses, it seems to me, when it is recognized that all concrete phenomena, whether sticks or stones or behaving individuals in their interrelations, are unique. One may quite legitimately appreciate their uniqueness and even haltingly aspire to describe or recreate it, though researchers of this bent seem to be drawn toward poetry and metaphor. But one may also legitimately seek to abstract from phenomena common analytical elements that can then be lawfully related. The lesson of the history of science is that this detour away from the compelling force of concrete reality greatly increases our powers of understanding it and coping with it in the longer run. Quite apart from the general question of what is profitable science, however, it is clear that the psychologists, sociologists, and anthropologists who are groping toward a more comprehensive behavioral science are committed to pushing the latter sort of program as far as it can be extended.

But the idiographic position deserves serious consideration in the present connection to the extent that its arguments merge with the admonitions of holism. If context matters, as it presumably does, serious difficulty lies in the way of comparative, nomothetic, research that neglects contextual effects in

4. Like most typologies, the present one—introduced by William James—does some violence to the facts. Among ethnologists what is certainly an idiographic approach is often pursued with the most ascetic toughmindedness. Where fact reigns supreme, any attempt at theory may appear tenderminded. The present distinction holds, rather, among different persuasions of the theoretically inclined, dividing those who look for an abstract formulation of particular cultures from those who are more interested in cross-cultural regularities. In psychology the concrete, factual sort of toughmindedness is little represented. Good or bad, psychologists all seem to be theorists.

the definition of its variables. In both personality research and research on cultures, and especially in the research area that deals with the interrelations of culture and personality, one of the most urgent methodological tasks is the identification of variables that are truly homologous in different contextual settings. Such dimensions of personality and variables of culture patterns, as they are progressively refined, should bring increasing areas of untamed natural uniqueness under scientific cultivation. Good beginnings are already being made in this direction. While proponents of the idiographic position will not contribute directly to this essential task, they remain valuable critics who may be relied on to remind us of how little and how tenuously the jungle has been tamed, and, equally important, to give us preliminary accounts of some of the strange forms that lurk there.[5]

Lastly, the very task of defining culture and personality has been beset in each case with uncertainty about the logical status of the terms. Is culture, and is personality, something real in nature whose lineaments we have only to discern truly? Or are these merely terms of convenience, that we use as we like with no implied counterpart in the structure of reality? The foregoing discussion has assumed the now prevailing view which differs from both of these respective realist and nominalist positions. Personality and culture as terms in scientific discourse are both constructs, figments of the scientific imagination. But if they are to play a useful part in the scientific enterprise, the scientist must be highly restricted in his freedom to have his will with them. He must frame and elaborate them with due regard to the requirements of the theoretical context in which they are to be put to use, and this context of theory, in turn, must stand the test of empirical verification. So, in an indirect way, constructs are grounded on reality to the extent that they are embedded in a maturing theory in constant interplay with data. The crucial fit is between theoretical structure and the data that confirm or refute it, not between the several constructs and presumptive entities taken as things-in-themselves.

This perspective, a conceptualist one if you like, is becoming increasingly

5. An additional methodological parallel might be drawn in regard to the role of typological formulations about personality and culture. Typologies have appeal as a compromise between holistic and idiographic concern with fidelity to the particular case in its structured uniqueness and the attempt to attain a degree of generality. A half-way station on the road to science that has usually had more heuristic convenience than empirical validity, the typological approach represented in psychology by Kretschmer (constitutional types), Jung (introversion-extraversion), and Spranger (economic, theoretical, political, social, and religious value types) has given way to the use of interrelated variables. Unlike sociologists, anthropologists have not made very much use of typological concepts. Examples, perhaps, are Redfield's adaptation of Toennies' concepts of Gemeinschaft and Gesellschaft in his treatment of folk versus urban societies, and Ruth Benedict's distinction between Apollonian and Dionysian cultures. Typologies based on kinship terminology are a different case, since the social and biological distinctions around which kinship nomenclature and practice are elaborated are discontinuous. The limited range of possibilities therefore makes the data fall naturally into clear types. But if anthropologists have not been given to typologizing, neither have they done much with explicitly interrelated variables. Until culture theory is more highly developed, the half-way station of typologies may perhaps continue to have its usefulness.

explicit and prevalent in psychology and the social sciences. It has a number of important implications for theory-building and research. As constructs, personality and culture are abstractions. To recognize this is to undercut the greater part of the nomothetic-idiographic controversy. It is things-in-themselves whose uniqueness is defended by the idiographically inclined; the worth of a construct is measured, as we have observed, solely by the extent to which it takes its place in significant propositions that can later be verified. Whether it corresponds or not to unique reality has nothing to do with the matter. But note again that the value of the construct cannot be ascertained in isolation. Only as part of a theory can it be assessed. Much of the "theoretical" discussion of both personality and culture has remained at the level of elaborating concepts, without making explicit the propositions from which they can alone derive significance.

More differentiated concepts at the level of motive, value, custom, or culture pattern may well turn out to be more fruitful than culture in the generation of hypotheses and laws. The global concepts of culture and personality may then end up after all as terms of convenience like mechanics and thermodynamics to identify major research areas, rather than as serious constructs of scientific theory.

In the present state of anthropology and personality theory, however, explicit recognition of the status of personality and culture as constructs is most salutary for the clarification that it brings into discussion in the fashionable culture-and-personality area. Rather than being concerned with the relations between two mythical interacting entities, one is led to look afresh at the different angle of abstraction by which each construct is derived from the data of social behavior. The substantively empirical findings can be assimilated more effectively into the theoretical frameworks of the respective disciplines when one is equipped with a translation formula. Some of the relations between the two concepts, as we will note later, turn out to follow from logical necessity.

The Influence of the Concept of Culture on Trends in Psychology

Our excursion to look at some problematic features of thinking about culture and about personality has laid before us some of the methodological complexities involved in a sophisticated treatment of culture. The gross impact of the concept of culture on psychology, however, has occurred at a less sophisticated level. It is as a general orientation to the determinants of human behavior rather than as a carefully elaborated concept or a developed theory that the cultural approach has been most influential.

Culture and the Influence of the Environment

Recognition of the extent to which the activities of the members of a society are culturally patterned and of the extraordinary range of variation in modal patterns as one moves from society to society led to a veritable revolution in psychological thinking that is still working itself out today. Darwinian biology had brought the importance of environment to attention quite early in the development of modern psychology. But so long as all psychological investigation was carried out in the relatively standard environmental range of Western civilization, it was easy to mistake the consistent results of exposure to this setting for features of a "generalized human mind" or general principles of behavior—a natural fallacy that persistently recurs, as when a Kinsey entitles the report on his researches in American sexual behavior "Sexual Behavior in the *Human* Male." Anthropology raised serious questions as to whether the entire structure of the psychologist's supposedly universal-human doctrine might not be in important respects "culture-bound." The latter term, in fact, compresses to a word the major burden of anthropological criticism.

So well entrenched was the narrowly based attempt at a generalized human psychology in the early twentieth century, new and fragmentary as were its facts, that one early reaction to the beginning influx of accounts of behavior in non-literate societies was to read in them evidence for a child-like primitive mentality. If "natives" did not think like Western adults, obviously they were to be equated to Western children. Western man still furnished the unquestioned standard, and the result did not disturb the prevalent complacency that placed the modern Englishman or German (it varied with the nationality of the author) at the peak of the evolutionary scale. As the last remark suggests, legacies of the initial uncritical response to the Darwinian revolution made this blind alley attractive. The anthropologists of the day were assuming that societies could be placed along a unilinear scale of cultural evolution, while psychologists like G. Stanley Hall had made popular the view that the development of the child recapitulates in microcosm the evolution of the race. Although the doctrine of the primitive mind was promulgated principally by non-psychologists like Levy-Bruhl, it was in keeping with the culture-bound psychology of the day.

Subsequent criticism, of course, has questioned both the description of non-literate thinking (it may often be rational) and that of the thought processes of the Western adult (which seldom follow the rules of logic), as well as discrediting the framework of evolutionary assumptions that made it plausible to equate the child and the primitive. Revulsion against this tangle of error, unfortunately, has diverted attention from genuine problems that the doctrine of primitive mentality approached but wrongly phrased. As Werner (1948) has suggested in an unfortunately neglected work that partakes to some extent in the earlier fallacies, there may well be intrinsic sequences in the mental development of the child, involving progressive differentiation, conceptualization, and articulated integration as the child is exposed to environments of the sort represented in the extreme in Western urban society. If there are indeed psychological grounds for expecting a developmental sequence, the ordering though not the pacing and terminal level of which is relatively independent of culture, critics of primitive mentality may have been too hasty in rejecting concern with developmental levels. In point of fact, there are scarcely any existing data on the development of cognitive processes in differing cultural contexts. Serious comparative research using modern psychological techniques is badly needed to test out the possibility of a truly general though culturally relevant psychology of cognitive development.

It was in the attack on instinct doctrines that the cultural approach made its most important contribution to a revised appreciation of environmental influence, both in academic psychology and, more recently, in psychoanalytic theory. The lists of purportedly universal-human instincts elaborated by James, McDougall, Thorndike, and others were not long in crumbling when confronted with the surprising differences in activities and motives reported from the majority of societies that fall outside the purview of Western history. Once the structure was breeched, it became apparent that even highly "dependable" motives like parental love and gregariousness could as well be attributed to universal features of the human environment (first learnings always occurring in the bosom of the family) as to universal constants of biology.

Self-isolated from these scientific controversies and combining sectarian dogmatism with pragmatic disregard for the niceties of scientific confirmation, Freudian psychoanalysis was still resisting the impact of anthropology after academic psychology had capitulated in principle. It clung tenaciously to a biological libido that unfolded in ways biologically foreordained, including the complicated configuration of the Oedipus complex. While Freud and, later, Roheim drew on ethnology to support a suggestive interpretation of culture in orthodox psychoanalytic terms, one that erred seriously as it pretended to historical reconstruction or to unilateral derivation of cultural from psychological facts, the more advanced thinking in all psychoanalytic camps is at present coming to realize the importance of disentangling what is general in psychoanalytic doctrine from what was actually peculiar to *fin-de-siecle* Vienna or to the broader range of Western culture. The line of criticism initiated by Malinowski, for example, has given the Oedipus complex a less culture-bound interpretation: the patterned residue of the person's early affectional relations with the people who nurtured, disciplined, and socialized him in the family. As the family is universal, so is the Oedipus complex in this broadened sense, which sets the stage, however, for the search for differences in its patterned content corresponding to the wide variety of family relationships that are somewhere culturally prescribed. Recent research on "culture and personality" is only beginning to explore systematic relationships in this area.

We can pass over the extreme environmentalist phase into which the behavioristic psychology of the 1920's swung in reaction against the errors of instinct theory, observing only that psychologists seem to agree today in regarding personality and behavior as complex resultants of a chain of organism-environment interactions, of which genetic and environmental determinants are both inescapably necessary. Anthropological data and insights have also highlighted the importance of environment in a somewhat different sense. While the investigator may attempt to specify a person's environment in objective terms independent of the special perspective of the behaving individual, human beings after early infancy have commerce with such a "real" world only through mediating processes of selection, elaboration, and interpretation made possible by the highly developed symbolic equipment that is at once the badge of humanity and the core of the cultural heritage. The process of mediation is so complex and so little understood that for most purposes a more intelligible account of human behavior can be gained by referring it to the "psychological environment," the "private world" in which the individual is oriented, than by attempting to start with the objective environment of the physical scientist and biologist.

The concept of the psychological environment grew current in psychology through the writings of Koffka and Lewin. Hallowell (1949, esp. pp. 308 ff; 1953b) has reminded us that the data of modern anthropology demand a similar conception of reality as it is defined for the individual by the premises of the culture in which he participates. For "private worlds" are not so private after all; much of their distinctive structure is shared among all people who grow up to speak the same language, believe in the same gods, and, through inheriting a common culture, come to see as through lenses ground to a common formula. These are facts with which the psychologist has to come to terms, difficult as he may find it to discover the transformation formulae relating such inferred subjective structures to "stimuli" within the objective frame of reference. As out-and-out objectivism and interpretation in terms of the psychological environment—sometimes rather unhappily termed the "phenomenological frame of reference" (Smith, 1950b)—compete in contemporary psychology, the weight of cultural anthropology tends to fall on the side of the latter. While the phenomenological psychologist may too readily take the psychological environment as given, the objectivist risks sterility and irrelevance if he evades accepting it as a problem.

Looking back at the revolution touched off in psychology by the cultural approach, the surprising thing is the still limited extent to which it has come to fruition. Psychologists continue to aspire to a general science of behavior —no one responded to the cultural revolution by happy resignation to the explicit study of, say, the special psychology of Americans. Yet overwhelmingly their experimental studies are confined to subjects from modern Western culture or from a trifling number of sub-human species. Of late there has been a resurgence of neo-comparative psychologists who have decried the founding of "general" principles of behavior on the white rat and the chimpanzee. All the more should it be essential, not only for social psychology and personality study but for the development of general psychology as well, that fundamental psychological experimentation be extended comparatively to subjects from a wide variety of cultures. Though dramatic, the impact of the cultural approach on psychology has occurred principally in regard to instinct theory, the interpretation of abilities,[6] and personality study. Surely such important areas as perception and the thought processes, learning, and "group dynamics" need re-examination from a comparative, cross-cultural perspective. The existing anthropological literature suggests that substantial revision of current doctrine might result.

Cultural Relativism

To recognize that each culture defines its own version of reality, its own standards and ethical system, and imposes its own distinctive patterns as "normal" is to take the position of cultural relativism, once modern civilization is accepted as one culture among others rather than taken as in some sense peculiarly human. In terms of lip-service, cultural relativism is almost as widely embraced in psychology as in anthropology. Already avoidant of value judgments, psychologists have found in the relativistic point of view additional armor for safeguarding scientific objectivity and ethical neutrality.

A decade or so ago it would have been easier than it is today to assess the significance of cultural relativism for psychology. One would then have pointed with some assurance to a resulting revision of concepts of psychological normality then in progress. The revision, which we now see left some important problems unresolved, was nevertheless a real and needed one: it turned out that two important meanings of this elusive term were implicitly cultural and had better be made explicitly so. On the one hand are the statistically frequent behavior patterns of a group; on the other, the group's ideals of approved behavior. It certainly cleared the air to recognize that both conceptions of normality—and only confusion results unless they are kept distinct—pose as alternatives either a relativism that makes the cultural reference explicit, or a dogmatic absolutism that is in fact culture-bound. In psychopathology, it became pertinent to re-examine the culturally-given standards of our own society before applying them ethnocentrically to the analysis of bizarre behavior patterns of other cultures.

But psychologists could not be entirely satisfied with the starkly relativist solution that seemed at first to cut through so many problems. In the extreme version, cultural relativism involves an idiographic approach to cultures that excludes the possibility not only of trans-cultural norms and standards, but of general laws and principles arising from cross-cultural comparison. Mixed in with the admittedly cultural meanings of normality as it occurred in psychological parlance were gropings toward more intrinsically psychological criteria of adequate functioning. These gropings have continued unabated, and recently anthropologists as well as psychologists and psychiatrists have given increasing attention to ways of transcending the culturally relative, without denying the importance of the relativistic critique of traditional absolutes. The flavor of the current search for transcultural standards of psychological functioning, inconclusive as it has thus far been, can best

6. Not treated here because of its lesser relevance to existing systematic theory.

be evoked by listing some of the terms under the aegis of which the quest is in progress: maturity, autonomy, competence, productive orientation, mental health. "Adjustment," unless very specially defined, should perhaps be conspicuously absent from this list, since one has only to ask what the person is adjusted *to* for the cultural reference to become obvious and the old alternatives of relativism vs. culture-bound absolutism to be reintroduced.

Volumes have been written on each of these concepts and others like them. Here I can only indicate the direction along which I think progress can be made toward a solution. First, under whatever term psychological adequacy is assessed it seems likely that no single criterion can be sufficient for its evaluation. A set of imperfectly correlated criteria employed jointly seems essential. Value judgment, moreover, is unavoidable in their selection. Under the impact of increasing communication among different value perspectives and in the light of growing psychological and cultural knowledge, there is nevertheless hope for an emerging informed consensus about the marks of psychological adequacy. Say that such criteria turn out to include indices of attributes like creativity, flexibility, self-acceptance, effective intelligence, etc. Then, secondly, characteristic average values of each of these variables can be found for persons growing up in distinctive cultural milieus.

More important, in most actual cultures, an individual can be expected to attain optimal values on certain criteria only at the cost of less than optimal realization of others. In a culture that is characterized by conflicting values as ours is said to be, for instance, adaptation may be attainable only at the cost of personal integration, and vice versa. One can thus look toward the assessment of cultures in regard to the extent to which they permit the joint realization of a plurality of criteria, as well as the assessment of individuals in regard to their standing on the criterion variables.

Since the approach rests fundamentally on evaluative criteria established by consensus, competing patterns of analysis are appropriate as long as value frameworks diverge. But we must abide by this pluralistic state of affairs if we are to avoid traditional or theological absolutism. It differs from the older extreme relativism, however, in its intended movement toward standards of evaluation that are progressively free from restriction to single cultures. Transcultural standards can be approached only with difficulty and through slow successive approximation; there are no lurking rabbits ready to be pulled from the hat by an ingenious maneuver. Whether we like it or not, social science is no *deus ex machina* to replace the God of our fathers in generating full-blown a new set of absolutes. But neither is it irrelevant to the clarification of values (see Smith, 1950a).

Culture "and" Personality

The "culture and personality" movement, which has progressively gained momentum since its launching in the thirties, merits special consideration as the interstitial development that has brought anthropology and psychology into closest contact. The very existence of a movement so designated points up the excessively narrow framework within which investigations of culture and of personality had been respectively pursued in the two disciplines. Except as a disembodied abstraction, culture can hardly be reckoned with apart from persons; from the other side of the fence, personality cannot be viewed in perspective apart from the cultural tradition that furnishes so much of its form and content. The movement was thus an attempt to join together what should never have been held asunder in the first place. While the literature identified with it has tended toward preoccupation with a narrower selection of problems, the broadest interpretation of its objectives would be almost as inclusive as the scope of the present symposium.[7]

By and large the initiative was taken by anthropologists with collaboration from psychoanalysts (notably Abram Kardiner and Erich Fromm), and rather less participation by psychologists. But the problems dealt with are as relevant to psychology as they are to anthropology. While the anthropologist following his traditional interests might look for psychological clues to the processes of cultural continuity and change and to the cohesiveness and range of variability of cultural patterns—the dynamics and microstructure of culture—the psychologist's principal concern centers on how cultural factors enter into the determination of personality structure and into the definition of situations in which the developed personality functions. The former of the psychologist's potential interests, it should be added, has almost eclipsed the latter, which in principle should be equally pertinent.

There is no space here to review the literature on cultural factors in personality formation, which has been rich both in suggestive but fragmentary data and in attempts at theoretical synthesis. I will rather address myself briefly first to an intentionally sweeping characterization of the research situation in relation to present needs, and secondly, to an attempt to clarify some of the conceptual problems that bother a psychologist as he seeks in this area a bridge between his home territory and the social sciences.

It is probably fair to say that anthropological research in culture and personality to date has provided us with highly provocative case material and leads, without, for the most part, the systematic evidence essential for confirmation. There is ample evidence that there are bear in these woods, enough to justify major concerted efforts to track them down. But the tracking operation has been only begun. The reason for this state of affairs is not hard to find: it lies not so much in the deficiencies of research efforts thus far as in difficulties inherent in cross-cultural methodology.

Consider for a moment the case approach in personality study. A skilled

7. Bibliographies of this literature can be found in the contributions by A. Irving Hallowell and Margaret Mead to the Wenner-Gren symposium of 1952. (Hallowell, 1953a; Mead, M., 1953). Notable collections of papers are Haring (1949), Kluckhohn, C.K.M., Murray, and Schneider (1952), the former also containing an extensive bibliography. A symposium discussion of the field may be found in Sargent and Smith (1949). Klineberg (1950) surveys the literature on national character, with particular attention to methodological problems.

clinician, working intensively with a single individual, can build up a highly plausible construction of the causal interplay that has given rise to his present personality. Such a construction can carry great conviction, particularly if there is internal consistency among converging lines of evidence. But it stands up rather poorly against obdurate criticism that insists on the exclusion of alternative and equally plausible interpretations. And, more important, the single case does not yield general principles (here the idiographic-nomothetic controversy comes in). These must be drawn from the study of systematic covariation in series of cases, ideally under experimentally controlled situations. It is from cumulative experience with series of cases that the major psychodynamic insights have come, and it is from more controlled studies approaching the experimental ideal that they are being validated and refined to take their place in developed theory.

But a field report on "culture and personality" in a single society contributes the equivalent of a single case, even if studies of a number of individuals form part of the research. With the best techniques, it can establish beyond question that certain cultural practices and norms—in regard to child rearing, life crises, or whatever—are associated in this instance with certain distributions or modal tendencies in the personality patterns found in the group. The causal interpretation of such obtained associations, however, cannot be substantiated by internal evidence. For this, systematic series of cases—of field studies in different cultures—are essential. Yet the cases accumulate very slowly, even when field work is conducted much more hastily and casually than the complexities of the data would warrant. Small wonder, then, that culture-and-personality theory remains controversial.

Most of the field work with which we are concerned has of course been undertaken from a different point of view toward the task. Working hypotheses and principles have been borrowed from psychodynamics and learning theory and applied to the interpretation of cultural data. There is nothing exceptionable in this procedure, which as we know has redounded to the benefit of personality theory and insight into cultural processes alike. But so long as the doctrines being applied are controversial, their application to the explanation of personality development in a single culture must remain even more so; not only are the principles themselves still in doubt, but there is added uncertainty as to the correctness of their application to the facts at hand. Good fit in the particular case contributes, to be sure, toward the validation of the interpretative principles that are employed, but it does not go very far toward establishing them beyond cavil. And cavil there has been.

The way out of the hardly defensible bootstraps dilemma of seeking simultaneously to validate interpretative principles and interpretations against each other is to move from the single case to the case series. With a statistically adequate sample of cultures, hypotheses drawn from psychological theory can be checked against correlations obtained between cultural variables and variables of modal personality. Since the cross-cultural range of variation in conditions of socialization is much more extensive than that in Western society in which theories of personality development originated, extension as well as revision of existing theory can be anticipated.

Impressionistic comparison of the accumulating body of cultural cases, while superior to reliance on internal consistency within single studies, is still inadequate to the task. For the most part the studies were never conducted with an eye to comparability, and far too many degrees of freedom are left to the insightful scholar who seeks to distill their cumulative message. A half-way station is represented by the attempt to extract quantitative relationships from existing materials by applying objective rating methods or typologies, and statistical tests of significant association. The resources of the Human Relations Area Files (Murdock, Ford, Hudson, Kennedy, Simmons, and Whiting, 1950), which organize in accessible form the major descriptive literature on some 200 cultures, make it possible to go some distance in applying to problems of socialization and personality development this approach, the power of which was demonstrated in another area by Murdock (1949). The recent work by John W. M. Whiting and Irvin Child (1953), who studied the relation of infant training in spheres suggested by psychoanalytic and learning theory to the projective reflection of adult anxieties in magical explanations of disease, carries us considerably ahead of the prevailing impressionism. No doubt they have far from exhausted the potentialities of the Human Relations Area Files for culture and personality research.

The stage nevertheless seems set for a frontal attack through original field work in an adequate sample of cultures to collect systematically the directly relevant data for testing the relationship between different patterned modes of child rearing and selected personality variables. Only by ingenious indirection were Whiting and Child able to explore such hypotheses in a preliminary way in the existing literature. Their work gives promise of even more substantial advance from research planned so as to yield indices that are based on the most direct evidence obtainable through comparable methods. Technical difficulties remain to be worked through in regard to both the isolation of transcultural variables and the construction of practicable indices, but progress is being made on both scores.

When it comes to causal interpretation, however, even the most ideal design we can conceive for cross-cultural research on personality formation runs into the circular chicken-and-egg relationship that we must assume to hold between cultural and personality variables. One of the current insights that is hardly to be controverted has it that in stable societies parents raise their children in ways that lead them to become in turn the kind of parents who naturally want to raise *their* children likewise. Mere correlations between rearing practices and adult personality do not disentangle a primary causal direction within this presumptively circular system. The matter is further complicated by the influence on personality of cultural pressures encountered throughout the life cycle. Important as we have grounds for believing infancy to be, we can be sure that socialization does not stop there. These later influences, if themselves correlated with parental practices, could underlie outcomes mistakenly attributed to infantile experience. Even systematic cross-cultural comparison can therefore offer no royal road to uncomplicated truth. Sometimes we may have sound theoretical grounds for assigning a single direction of causation. And intensive studies of changing cultures may loosen the strands of the causal nexus sufficiently for them to be partially disentangled. For the most part, however, the causal interpretation of the associations turned up by research is inherently ambiguous.

Actual research on culture and personality has focused on process relationships among cultural and personality variables, not on culture "and" personality as presumptively separable entities. Hence the purist's need to put the "and" in quotation marks. Yet some of the theoretical discussion of culture and personality has been seemingly beguiled by the conventional label into neglecting the fact that both abstractions rest ultimately on the same data of social behavior. Once definitions of culture and personality such as those offered earlier are accepted and it is stipulated that phenomena exist to which the definitions can be appropriately applied, some of the matters about which there has been no little controversy turn out to follow tautologically.

So it has been with conceptions of modal personality, basic personality, and their ilk. If in fact the members of a definable social group share a set of traditional behavior patterns that warrant designation as a culture or sub-culture, by the same token these patterns (having no existence apart from behaving persons) cannot fail to be integrated into the personalities of the members. Cultural universals, to employ Linton's term, must turn up in the personality dispositions of virtually all the group members, else they would not be universals; these are ingredients of basic or modal personality. Cultural specialties, such as those that make it relevant to distinguish particular positions or statuses in the society, may be referred accordingly to dispositions shared by the occupants of the respective statuses; Linton has given us the term "status personality" to call attention to this culturally relevant aspect of personality patterning (Linton, 1945). The "existence" of modal personality and status personality is no more controversial than the existence of cultures and statuses. At root these are merely alternative ways of organizing the same data.

If this were all there were to it, however, the concepts would never have aroused the degree of interest that they rightly attract. The interesting features of modal or basic personality, which are far from tautological, are secondary repercussions arising through intrinsic psychological processes in response to the impact and internalization of culture patterns in personality development. Tendencies for parents to respond harshly to their children's aggressive behavior, for instance, if common to the members of a society, are to be referred equally to the culture and to the modal personality of the parents. But the result in the developing child is not a foregone conclusion: present knowledge suggests that under specifiable conditions outcomes as different as rigid politeness or touchy latent hostility may follow. These consequences in turn may lead to cultural elaborations that seem superficially remote from the cultural starting point, yet are dynamically linked with it: a preoccupation with sorcery and witchcraft, for example, arising as an avenue for the discharge of pent-up hostilities. The situation is further complicated by the likelihood that these secondary cultural repercussions, while reinforced by the psychodynamic consequences of other cultural practices, may themselves be learned directly by the participants in the culture. And so we are thrown back into the intricate causal interplay that we noted as complicating the interpretation of cross-cultural research. It is nevertheless well to remember that while the elaboration of modal personality and its ramified implications for the coherence of cultural organization can only be discovered through empirical research, the logical status of the concept is such that whenever sufficient regularities exist to identify a culture, we may be sure it is applicable.

The tendency to reify concepts, to give them "misplaced concreteness," which is a persistent source of confusion in this area, has potentially unfortunate results on personality theory as it digests the implications of culture-and-personality research. It is legitimate and helpful to classify the determinants of personality according to their source in facts of biology, culture, or social role, and to abstract a conception of modal or status personality. But it is misplaced concreteness to assume uncritically that these analytic distinctions are relevant to the functioning of the integral person. Yet one often gets the impression from current writing that personality can somehow be partitioned into concentric segments identified by their source of determination—a biological core, a region of modal personality, and so on. This sort of construction, which is implicit in the frequently encountered definition of personality as the source of residual variation once culturally determined regularities have been extracted, makes no sense psychologically. Psychological accounts of personality functioning need to draw their own relevant distinctions, mindful, of course, that to understand the personal significance of any item of behavior one must know the cultural norms toward which it is oriented.

Some Directions of Convergence

I have already hazarded a number of suggestions about ways in which the collaboration of anthropology and psychology might become more fruitful. There is no need to rehearse them here. Some concluding remarks are nevertheless in order to make some additional observations and point up directions of convergence that are implicit in my treatment.

Broadening the Base of Collaboration: Language and Psychology

Research on culture and personality has tended to concentrate, we observed, on a restricted range of problems. A broadened base of collaboration between anthropology and psychology would bring additional areas into joint focus. So far as psychology is concerned, there is no area in which the gain from collaboration should be greater than that of language research. For the psychologist it is still almost virgin territory.

This is the case in spite of universal agreement among psychologists about the distinctive and fundamental importance of language in human behavior. Aside from an impressive body of research on language development in European and American children—which did not have to await the construction of adequate theory—psychological treatment of language and symbolic behavior has been speculative and relatively barren. Themselves immersed in language, psychologists have seemed unable to discover leverage points at which research could clarify the nature of talking and listening and verbal thinking as psychological processes. And their theoretical speculations and halting attempts to experiment have proceeded in unfortunate isolation from the impressive developments in descriptive linguistics, which anthropologists either claim as their own or respect with more than a nodding acquaintance.

The interest of psychologists has recently been aroused by provocative analyses, such as those by Benjamin Whorf and Dorothy Lee, which purport to show an intimate relation between the structure of a language and the implicit categories of perception and thought shared among its speakers. Psychologists are properly wary of the conclusions of these studies, based as they are on internal analysis of language structure. The linguist's analysis needs to be matched against direct and adequate data on perceptual and cognitive processes, collected by methods as independent of the structure of the particular language as possible. Psychologists are peculiarly qualified to work on this end of the problem, but to do so they need much more sophistication in linguistics than they are likely to have at present. This so-called "Weltanschauung" problem is one of many on which the psychologist and linguist could profitably collaborate. Happily there are indications that promising lines of collaboration are developing (Carroll, 1951; Hoijer, 1953).

Emphasis on More Differentiated Concepts

While our discussion has centered around the broad concepts of personality and culture, psychologists and anthropologists are less likely to talk at cross purposes and more likely to contribute to a common theoretical framework when both employ more differentiated concepts that are better suited to the analysis of process. The psychologist concerned with the discrepancy between what people say and what they do, or with the contrast between unconscious and symbolically formulated behavior, can relate his problems to the anthropologist's distinctions between ideal vs. real, overt vs. covert, implicit vs. explicit patterns. Differentiated concepts of social structure, particularly those of position and role, have been left for treatment in the chapter on "Sociology and Psychology."[8] But these concepts are rooted as deeply in anthropological as in sociological writings, and as Newcomb (1950) and Parsons (Parsons and Shils, 1951) have argued most cogently, their significance for social psychology and personality theory can hardly be overestimated. The related concepts of values and norms, about which much terminological confusion still exists, have as yet been very inadequately assimilated into psychology.

The Emergence of Appropriate Models

If psychologists and anthropologists are not merely to cooperate on problems where their interests overlap but are also to contribute to a coherent and more inclusive body of knowledge about social behavior, they must approach their respective data in terms of mutually compatible conceptual models. Historically, incompatibility—or mutual irrelevance—between psychological and socio-cultural models has been a major obstacle precluding effective interdisciplinary collaboration.

The opposing models most hampering in their consequences were psychological individualism on the one hand and social or cultural realism on the other, the latter expressed in such metaphors as the superorganic or the group mind. Theory in social psychology was long torn between stress on the isolated individual, who somehow had to be related to others to form a society, and on a reified society or group, the basis of which in individual psychological processes then became most mysterious. Since social psychology was committed by its self-imposed charter to concern itself with the bridge between individual and group concepts, the gyrations taken by its developing theory reflect tensions generated by an impossible task. Anthropology was more happily situated, free as it was from commitment to any such bridge-building operation. But similar models offered themselves, and those who adopted the attractive superorganic model of culture as an entity *sui generis* had little occasion to concern themselves with psychological matters.

One of the most hopeful features in the current situation, therefore, is the emergence from diverse quarters of incipient consensus on a model that rejects the sterile dichotomy of isolated individual vs. disembodied group. The model is by no means new; Cooley (1902) and G. H. Mead (1934) had the essential insights early in the century. But the tradition springing from Mead and Cooley tended to remain the private property of sociologists, in whose hands it retained a speculative flavor. What is new today is that the insights are being rediscovered on all sides, and—more important—they are

8. Contributed to the volume in which the essay appeared by Theodore M. Newcomb, pp. 227–256.

being employed, refined, and tested as never before in empirical and experimental research.

This new-old model has many variants in the hands of different theorists. But its minimal features can be quickly delineated. It takes its start not from individuals or socio-cultural entities but from the interactions of persons; hence it is sometimes called "interactionism." In any functioning social group, according to this view, the isolated individual is a msleading artifact. Persons achieve communication and avoid randomness in their relationships because each already embodies much of the socio-cultural system in microcosm. That is, the symbol-systems, beliefs, and expectations of one another shared by members of a social group, the modified or emergent motives, aspirations, and standards of evaluation learned in group experience, so transform man as a biological entity that he exists always in implicit relation to others. The notion of men as social atoms somehow to be brought into significant relation to one another is simply a myth, except when applied to collections of infants where, indeed, it is not inaccurate.

With the demise of the isolated individual, the case for social realism—the "group mind"—loses its pertinence. More, to be sure, than the sum of its *individual* members, a group is comprised of interacting persons in their relationships without the necessity for any *tertium quid.*

So much for the synchronic aspect of the model—its pattern for describing social behavior at a given point of time. Diachronically, the model suggests that in the process of social interaction, the actor learns through time to become the sort of person who is capable of the orderly social relationships in which we later encounter him. Within the framework of the model, therefore, the conditions and consequences of the socialization process in its detail become a central problem for research. Through socialization, culture, which at the outset of the life-cycle is exterior to the person and constraining upon him as Durkheim would have it, becomes internalized—inextricably incorporated in his very make-up.

The implications of this model have as yet to be worked out satisfactorily in psychology, particularly in relation to the theory of motivation, where an unquestionable biological bias has resisted conceptual incorporation in the interactionist framework. Developments in this sphere should be particularly important for their bearing on anthropological problems. They must come, however, from theoretically oriented research, not from armchair speculation and model-building.

If these indeed bear some resemblance to the lines along which a comprehensive theoretical framework for the sciences of social man is to be erected—to hazard a most speculative guess—the need will persists for specialized inquiry from perspectives not very different from those of psychology and anthropology today. Process and patterning at both the personal and cultural levels will continue to require special study, anthropology offering to psychology a detailed account of the social context of behavior, and psychology reciprocating with a corresponding account of the interpersonal processes underlying culture. If the comparative method ceases to be the monopoly of cultural anthropologists and modern society the privileged territory of sociologists, the boundaries between these two disciplines should become progressively indistinct. Workers within all three disciplines can perhaps best contribute to the emergence of a comprehensive structure by giving explicit attention to problems of articulation in framing their working concepts and hypotheses.

4

Samuel A. Stouffer

Samuel A. Stouffer (1900–1960), American sociologist, was a founder of large-scale quantitative social research. His contribution to the analysis of survey data represents a distinctively American approach to sociology. The four volumes of the collaborative magnum opus, Studies in Social Psychology in World War II, of which the two volumes of *The American Soldier* (Stouffer, Lumsdaine, Lumsdaine, Williams, Smith, Janis, Star, and Cottrell, 1949) are best known, remain a landmark and a model in the new tradition of mass production in research, emphasis upon quantitative evidence, avoidance of theoretical speculation except in close contact with the data, and close connection with applied problems. The work has also been a prime target of criticism for those who deplore this trend (e.g., the book reviews quoted by Lerner in Merton and Lazarsfeld, 1950, pp. 212–251). Stouffer's career, as his collaborator Paul F. Lazarsfeld has noted (Stouffer, 1962, p. xv), coincides with the development of empirical social research in the United States, and his writings reflect its strengths and limitations.

Stouffer was born and brought up in the little town of Sac City in western Iowa, where his father was publisher of the local newspaper. He attended the small local Methodist college, Morningside, and after a year's graduate work in English at Harvard, he returned to work for a time on the family newspaper. His career as a sociologist began with graduate work at the University of Chicago, where he received his PH.D. in 1930. There he came under the formative influence of L. L. Thurstone and William F. Ogburn, both pioneers in the development and application of quantitative methods in the study of human behavior. Stouffer's quantitative bent was strengthened by his work with Karl Pearson and R. A. Fisher during a postdoctoral year at the University of London. On his return from England he proceeded to take up successive academic positions at the universities of Wisconsin and Chicago. During World War II he served as director of the professional staff in the Research Branch, Information and Education Division, of the War Department, where he mobilized a large staff of research personnel and planned and supervised the extensive studies that culminated in the four volumes including *The American Soldier.* After the war he established the Laboratory of Social Relations at Harvard University, where he remained until his death.

At the outset of Stouffer's career, demography and social statistics were the only aspects of sociology in which a quantitative approach was well developed. These were the areas on which Stouffer's early contributions were focused, and his interest in them continued. He was, for example. consultant to the U.S. Bureau of the Census; furthermore, during the year immediately preceding his death he was embarking upon a study for the Population Council in New York. His early studies—for example, his analysis of differential trends in fertility in Catholics and non-Catholics (Stouffer, 1962, pp. 165–184) and his study, with Lazarsfeld, of the effects of the depression on the family (Stouffer, 1962, pp. 134–153)—are, like his later ones, marked by his strong talent for getting social data to speak with minimal ambiguity. The data for these early studies were obtained from public records, and much ingenuity was required to develop relevant indices and to control for obscuring factors. In his analysis, he always considered plausible alternative interpretations and tried to find ways to reduce interpretative ambiguity.

Whether he worked with available social statistics or, later, with survey data created by the investigator, Stouffer's forte lay in this ingenious interplay, close to the data, of interpretative hypothesis and empirical check. Theoretical questions tended to arise directly from the data before him and to return him quickly to the data for further analysis. His personal style of research fitted the stage of precomputer technology, when the investigator, running his sets of data cards through the counter-sorter himself, could quickly adapt his tactics of analysis to the emerging results. Stouffer's career ended just as the requirements of modern electronic computers were tending to impose a greater separation between the investigator and his data.

Research in Stouffer's style is not mere fact-grubbing, but neither does it often result directly in broader integrations of theory. One of his early contributions to demographic research, however, provided a precedent-setting example of the kind of mathematically formalized small-scale theory that was later to attract much attention in American social research: his theory of internal migration in terms of *intervening opportunities* (1962, pp. 68–91), which he subsequently elaborated and tested against additional data (1962, pp. 91–112). Stouffer's model seeks to account for the movement of population between cities, and it asserts, in effect, that the number of people moving between two places will be larger the more opportunities there are in the target area and the fewer the opportunities that are interposed between the target area and the place of origin. According to his initial formation, all locations within the circular area centering on the city of origin (with the target city falling on the circumference) potentially present intervening opportunities; direction is ignored. His later elaboration takes direction into account in the estimation of intervening opportunities and introduces such further refinements as adjustment for the general accessibility of the target city to migration from sources other than the origin under consideration. The ingenuity of Stouffer's treatment of migration lies less in the mathematical formulation than in the ways in which he was able to coordinate the formal model with data available in census statistics.

During the 1930s the methods of survey research had been developed in the United States under auspices that were largely journalistic or commercial. Stouffer's use of survey methods in the wartime studies under his direction and the later secondary analysis of the data reported in *The American Soldier* had a substantial impact on the improvement of survey design and analysis as a research approach that generates data convenient for quantitative treatment. His approach to survey research had several distinguishing features. One was largely a matter of historical accident: reliance upon self-administered questionnaires rather than on field interviews. More important were his consistent practice of controlling statistically for the effects of many variables on the relationships under examination and his analytic preference for basing interpretative conclusions upon replicated analyses rather than on strong statistical tests of single sets of observations. Also characteristic was his attention to the need for mathematically sophisticated indices of attitudes, as reflected in his sponsorship of work by Guttman and by Lazarsfeld in developing "scalogram" and "latent structure" analysis (Stouffer, Guttman, Suchman, Lazarsfeld, Star, and Clausen, 1950) and in his own later contribution of the H-technique of scale analysis as a practical improvement upon Guttman's method (Stouffer, 1962, pp. 274–289).

The theoretical concept given the most emphasis in *The American Soldier* is characteristic not only of Stouffer's analytic ingenuity but also of his somewhat data-bound empiricism: the concept of *relative deprivation.* This notion, not formally developed, was invoked to account for such otherwise puzzling findings as that when rank, educational level, and length of Army service are held constant, the *less* the opportunity for promotion afforded by a branch of the Army, the *more* favorably will members of that branch assess their chances of promotion. The explanation is offered that each individual evaluates his chances of promotion in comparison with others who share his situation. The Air Force private, in a service (objectively) characterized by rapid promotion, feels more deprived than the private in Military Police, where promotions are much less frequent. Similar interpretative principles appear to account for a variety of seemingly paradoxical observations. It remained for Robert K. Merton and Alice S. Kitt (in Merton and Lazarsfeld, 1950, pp. 40–105) to explicate and generalize the theoretical notions that are involved and to relate them to the concept of *reference groups;* in this way they developed a conceptually powerful approach to the analysis of social influences on individual persons. Stouffer asserted, as does Merton, that modest small-scale theories are more useful than theoretical systems in the older, grand style that rarely generated predictions accessible to empirical test. Stouffer's theorizing was more modest, more closely tied to the data than is Merton's, but at a cost.

If Stouffer's practically-oriented yet intellectually curious empiricism at once reflected and tended to reinforce a characteristically American orientation in the social sciences, so also did his emphasis on prediction as a touchstone of scientific merit. The wartime studies provide several examples of moderately effective prediction of behavior from attitudinal data (Stouffer et al., 1950). What is missing, however, is concern with the theoretical articulation of the steps that intervene between antecedent and consequent. Prediction thus comes to be valued in its own right, as a matter of practical achievement, rather than as a criterion of the correctness or utility of theoretical formulations.

For Stouffer, the ideal research method was the controlled experiment, in which outcomes are predicted by prior hypothesis and in which variations in the independent variables are manipulated by the experimenter. Ironically, Stouffer never conducted experimental studies himself, although in his wartime role he sponsored the important experimental work on mass communications by Hovland, Lumsdaine, and Sheffield (1949), and later actively encouraged experimental research in the Harvard Laboratory of Social Relations. Always sophisticated and critical in his appraisal of the essentially descriptive and correlational methods of analysis of which he was master, Stouffer's admiration for the magic of experimentation was somewhat naïve. In his methodological writings (e.g., 1962, pp. 290–299), he came close to viewing the experimental method as a royal road to truth, neglecting the ambiguities that bedevil the experimenter in his attempts to translate theoretical variables into empirical operations. Yet progress in the sophisticated application of the experimental method in social research has surely resulted from Stouffer's enthusiastic sponsorship.

As the merger of research and theory that both he and Merton had called for became increasingly the order of the day, Stouffer proceeded, in two of his later studies, published in 1949 and 1951, to test a small-scale theory concerning social roles and role conflict (1962, pp. 39–67). Characteristically, the distinctive contribution of these two studies is in the development of empirical indices of such theoretical concepts as universalism and particularism and in revising the view of role expectations as well-defined social norms, thus yielding more complicated conceptions in closer accord with the facts.

Stouffer's work reflected a meliorist concern with the social problems of the day. He hoped that social research would be socially useful; he held that in the long run the social justification of investment in basic research is in its applications (1962, p. 4). Yet he was deeply concerned lest the exaggerated claims of enthusiasts should jeopardize the long-run prospects for the development and application of the social sciences. About these long-run prospects, he was firmly optimistic. In the shorter run, he saw the danger of dissipated effort and conspicuous failure if social scientists were too eager to solve those social problems for which their tools were still inadequate. Stouffer was ever confident about the prospects of social science, but modest about its present resources.

Nevertheless, on three occasions, Stouffer did direct his skills in social research to matters of urgent social import. He played a major role in carrying out the studies undertaken as part of Myrdal's monumental analysis of the American Negro problem (1944) and continued to take an interest in problems of race relations throughout his career. His deployment of social research to meet wartime needs has already been noted. During the postwar episode in which civil liberties in the United States suffered serious erosion under the attack of Senator Joseph R. McCarthy, he planned and analyzed an important survey of American attitudes toward communism and civil liberties (1955).

Stouffer's influence, in sum, accentuated certain distinctively American trends in social research: toward quantification and small-scale theoretical formalization, toward large-scale collaborative research organization, toward fusion of pure and applied research interests, away from speculative theoretical synthesis. His writings provided models upon which contemporary practice in survey analysis is built. While he valued empirically based theory, his own preference was for a style of inquiry rather closer to the data than is optimal for the development of theoretical conceptions with powerful generality. Stouffer was a master of such empirical analysis, making social data answer to his questioning as they would never "speak for themselves."

Attitudes and Values

5

Opinions, Personality, and Political Behavior

It is gratifying to be able to present to students of political behavior the approach that my colleagues and I worked out for the study of *Opinions and Personality* (Smith, Bruner, and White, 1956), since throughout our explorations political scientists had been what the current jargon would call a "salient reference group" for us. As a psychologist and "outsider," however, I offer these remarks with some trepidation, since the framework that we arrived at in the detailed study of ten men's outlook on Russia was, after all, distinctly psychological; therefore a limited view that embraces but one segment of the processes with which political scientists are properly concerned. Our investigations were long on the description and analysis of *opinions,* but short on the observation of consequential *behavior,* political or otherwise. And our study did not even focus on *public* opinion, in any sense that attempts a close conceptual distinction between the public and the private.

Yet these very limitations of scope and perspective may be instructive if they are explicitly faced. The domain of political behavior is too large, too complex, to be readily comprehended in terms of any single or simple conceptual scheme, any at least that presents itself to the psychological onlooker as immediately available. It may be more profitable to chart a portion of the larger terrain, taking note of its bearings with respect to maps plotted from other bench marks. If the experience of our mapping expedition can be said to point to a single moral, it is that a useful map of the small region comprising men's opinions in their personal context turns out to be complicated enough—considerably more so than many proposed formulations have been wont to recognize.

Historical Perspective

The need for a map of opinions and personality that takes into account a considerable degree of complexity can be appreciated in any attempt such as

Revised from a paper presented to the panel on "Personality and Political Behavior" at the New York meetings of the American Political Science Association, September 6, 1957, and reprinted with permission from the *American Political Science Review,* 1958, *52,* 1–17.

ours to make sense of the opinions of a series of persons with whom the investigator has established a close, quasi-clinical acquaintance. But hindsight supports the same conclusion—the need for a comprehensive framework—when one examines the earlier research on opinion determinants. Since it will be my principal point that it is fruitful to study the interrelations of opinions and personality in terms of a more comprehensive set of assumptions than hitherto, a brief critical look at a few of the earlier efforts is in order.

The first major foray by psychologists into the personal determinants of opinion was anything but promising. To the empirically minded American psychologists of the late 'twenties and 'thirties, newly equipped with pencil-and-paper questionnaires for the measurement of personality traits and of attitudes, what could be more natural than to correlate these scales with one another? So there was a spate of correlational studies in this vein, mostly employing the ever-available college sophomore, a good many of them focused on the personal correlates of radicalism and conservatism (See Murphy, G., Murphy, and Newcomb, 1937). The yield was small, and no wonder. Both on the side of attitudes and of personality, conceptualization was meager and inadequate. Personality as caught in the questionnaires of the day was a congeries of traits. More adequate formulation of motivational dynamics and of personality organization had to await the impact of psychoanalysis and of holistic influences from Europe. Attitudes, on the other hand, were measured by crude scales that compressed the many-faceted nature of opinion to the single dimension of pro-con *direction* usually mingled with *intensity*. Correspondences that such a conceptual armory could establish between attitudes and personality can be regarded as almost coincidental.

Now the correlation of trait and attitude variables makes sense when one's concern is with the *expressive* aspects of opinion—opinion as a manifestation of personal style, whether temperamental (for instance, optimism, pessimism, or apathy) or intellectual (for instance, tendency to focus on discrete detail or on the broad picture). For the study of such correlations to yield returns, however, one must ask the right questions about personality and about opinions; one must discover the aspects of each that are most susceptible to congruent stylistic variation. The approach, in a word, falls into place as a legitimate partial one, when it is guided by more adequate theory. But even in the more sophisticated if not always responsible hands of a modern factor analyst like Eysenck (1954; 1956; also Christie, 1956a and 1956b), the correlational approach yields a limited perspective on personality and a very incomplete view of its contribution to opinion.

The next landmark that demands our attention, Harold Lasswell's *Psychopathology and Politics* (1930), suffered from no such dearth of scientific imagination, bringing to bear as it did on political opinion the rich treasure of hypothesis to be mined from classical psychoanalysis, and illustrating the fruitfulness of case studies for the elucidation of political thinking. Displacement and rationalization were for Lasswell the major devices whereby private motives come to be transformed into political opinions. According to his formula for the "political man," private motives are displaced onto a public object and rationalized in terms of the public interest. The formula and the case material introduced by way of illustration served the important positive function of bringing a dynamic view of human motivation into the ken of American political science at a time when most American psychologists eschewed the psychoanalytic jungle with fear or disdain. Negatively, Lasswell's contribution dealt one more blow to the rationalistic view of man as embodied in the political philosophy of the Enlightenment and of the Founding Fathers. Of course, his formula necessarily oversimplified, even in terms of the earlier Freud on whose writings Lasswell drew. From the perspective of modern Freudian psychoanalysis with its emphasis on "ego psychology,"[1] the distortion appears somewhat greater. "Rationalization" in the formula swallows up rational processes without residue while the constructive role of opinion in the functioning of personality goes unregarded. Again we have a partial truth, more provocative and more penetrating, to be sure, than one pursued by the trait-attitude correlators. But the partial insight comes close to error unless it is placed in perspective as comprising only one of a variety of relationships that can be observed between opinions and personality.

No account of opinion research, however selective, can afford to ignore the impact of the opinion polls, even though the sampling survey did not come to a natural focus on the personal setting of opinion. It is not easy to gather useful data on personality in doorstep interviews, though we have recently seen that it is by no means impossible (Sanford, F. H., 1950). Rather, the line of least resistance was to relate opinions to the demographic facts of age, sex, education, socio-economic status—"face-sheet" data that were normally collected as a check on the representativeness of sampling. Under the leadership of Paul Lazarsfeld (Lazarsfeld, Berelson, and Gaudet, 1944; Berelson, Lazarsfeld, and McFee, 1954), this opinion demography was given a sociological rationale. The demographic uniformities of opinion turned up by the pollsters were attributed to homogenizing pressures of primary group membership. It remained to identify the "cross-pressures" exerted on a person by divergence among the norms prevailing in the various groups with which he was affiliated, and a manifestly powerful tool was in hand for coping with interindividual variation as well as with uniformity. An Index of Political Predisposition such as Lazarsfeld and his collaborators (Lazarsfeld, Berelson, and Gaudet, 1944, pp. 25–27) constructed from the Erie County data left but little for personal idiosyncrasy.

To this sociological account a social-psychological refinement was added, primarily by Herbert Hyman (1942) and Robert Merton (Merton and Lazarsfeld, 1950, pp. 40–105), in the concept of *reference groups*. The groups to which a person looks for norms and standards, they pointed out, need not be identical with those to which he actually belongs. The implica-

1. A good account of these developments from a sympathetic standpoint may be found in Munroe (1955).

tions of this distinction between membership groups and reference groups are still being worked out in research, but the conception is patently a fruitful one.

While an account of political opinion solely in terms of membership groups and their cross-pressures, matters of apparently objective social fact, presents itself as a competitor to psychological interpretation, the complications of reference group theory bring the person's selective orientation to the social world once more into the picture. What enduring personal dispositions underlie an individual's choice of reference groups? What characterizes the conformist, Reisman's (1950) "other-directed" man who finds his reference group in the salient membership group of the moment or in the just-more-prestigeful "Joneses"? What distinguishes him from the maverick whose attachment to an ideal reference group provides him, in Reisman's metaphor, with a gyroscope that frees his judgments from the influence of his immediate associates and social betters? These are legitimate questions for personality theory.

From this perspective, the account of opinion in terms of "group determinants" can be seen to have thrown into focus still another facet of the relational complex linking opinions and personality. The whole story of group influences cannot, of course, be encompassed by the psychology of personality, for opinions and behavior, as Kurt Lewin (1948, 1951) was fond of emphasizing, are a function of personality and situation taken jointly. One can come to grips with this field of interaction from the standpoint of social groups and the constraints that these important constituents of human situations impose on behavior. Or, and this is the tack taken here, one can take personality as the point of departure. In the latter case, the person's orientation to his social world must be seen as one more partial source of his opinions. It too needs to be put in perspective by viewing it together with strands of relationship that other approaches have chosen to emphasize.

An additional line of development remains to be noted. Rensis Likert, Angus Campbell, and the group associated with them, now the Michigan Survey Research Center, gave currency in the study of opinion to an emphasis, adapted from clinical interviewing, on how the respondent himself formulates or "structures" the topic being investigated (Cannell and Kahn, 1953). Their emphasis on the texture of a person's assumptions, beliefs, and opinions in terms of which his particular decisions and actions are to be understood—on "cognitive structure"—provided a much needed corrective, on the one hand to the pollsters' undue reliance on categorical statements of preference about preformulated issues, and on the other, to the oversimplifying tendency of academic attitude research to reduce attitudes to the scalable dimensions of direction and intensity. The task of systematizing the analysis of cognitive structure, to be sure, is formidable, and the "open-ended" questioning of the Michigan group may not have progressed very far on it. But they performed the important task of recapturing for research scrutiny a view of attitudes that opens for exploration a rich array of possible relationships to personality. Just as Lasswell's Freudian view of the motivational dynamics of opinion represents a conceptual enrichment on the side of personality in advance of the earlier trait-psychology, so the approach to attitudes as cognitive structures sensitizes the investigator to relevant aspects of attitude that the tradition of attitude scaling had neglected and still neglects. Some of the old questions concerning attitude-personality relationships could now profitably be reopened.

Perhaps this all-too-casual review has sufficiently established that when Bruner, White and I embarked on our case studies a decade ago, the ingredients were available for attempting to encompass the relations of opinions to personality in a comprehensive framework. The prevalent formulations tended to emphasize single strands of relationship, and thus to be offered as competitive rather than as supplementary lines of explanation. We thought that close attention to the thinking of a few people on a controversial topic, coupled with the study of their personalities along clinical lines, would help us in this task of synthesis. As a venture in the natural history of holding opinions, our study could not prove the correctness of specific hypotheses or the general validity of the framework we arrived at. But the richness of clinical detail that our interviews and tests evoked should, it seemed to us, allow us to scotch simplistic formulations in somewhat more definitive vein.

The Authoritarian Personality

Before turning to what seems to me distinctive in our explorations, I must at least mention *The Authoritarian Personality* (Adorno, Frenkel-Brunswik, Levinson, and Sanford, 1950) not because this monumental study was a source we could draw on—our cases were closed and our thinking about them essentially crystallized before its publication—but because its well-deserved renown among social scientists makes it an essential benchmark in regard to which any subsequent attempt to map the relations of opinions to personality has to be located.

The California investigators, it is important to remember, set out on the trail of the psychological sources of *antisemitism,* and the elucidation of this very archetype of social irrationality remained the focus of their inquiry throughout. As we know, they found—and the finding seems to have stood up in the flood of subsequent research though with some qualification (Christie and Jahoda, 1954; Titus and Hollander, 1957)—that people who fall at the antisemitic extreme not only are likely to give evidence of a cluster of related attitudes (general rejection of "out-groups," super-patriotism, and the like), but are also distinguished by a set of character traits that cohere in a meaningful pattern from the authors' psychoanalytic perspective. The so-called F (Fascism) Scale developed to measure this authoritarian syndrome of superstition, cynicism, punitive moralism and the like has turned out, for all its technical deficiencies, to do a fairly good job of separating sheep from goats with respect to a wide assortment of socially relevant attitudes and behaviors.

As a monographic study of the sources in personality of a socially important set of attitudes, *The Authoritarian Personality* is unparalleled. And the personality syndrome delineated by the California authors has much interest for political scientists, whether for the light it sheds on endemic McCarthyism or for the dimensions it suggests for the analysis of political leadership and followership. What it does *not* provide (it was not intended to) is a generally useful framework for the analysis of relationships between personality and opinions—or a dependable example of the kind of relationships likely to be found in other politically relevant realms. If you start out with a bit of institutionalized irrationality like antisemitism, you are bound to come out with a psychological formula for irrationality, nothing more. In other words, the kinds of phenomena with which Frenkel-Brunswik, Sanford, and their collaborators were dealing were the sort that fit the early Lasswellian formula. One must cast a wider net, or fish in different waters, to bring more representative kinds of political thinking and behavior into view.

A Functional Account of Opinions

I would not argue that our fishing grounds—attitudes toward Russia and Communism during the promulgation of the Truman doctrine—were especially representative. Very likely the topic carried a higher charge of unreasoned emotionality fanned by distorted information than many that we might have chosen. Had we followed the strategy of the California group and singled out the most virulent Russophobes for investigation—or the extreme Communists—we might have come to a formulation more similar to theirs than in fact emerged. But the series of men we studied held positions on Russia covering a wide range of favorableness, involvement, and information and when we sought to trace in each case sources of opinions in personality that the evidence made clinically plausible, no single syndrome dominated the picture but a variety of linkages came to light. Such variety, we suspect, *is* characteristic of opinions on most political issues.

Central to our inquiry was the question, what kinds of *functions* do opinions serve in the economy of personality? A word is, therefore, in order about the legitimate role of a functional approach, as we see it, in such a psychological investigation. When we ask, of what use to a man are his opinions, what good do they do him, we are posing the functional question in the sense we have in mind—a sense that has a venerable lineage in Darwinian biology and in most post-Darwinian psychology. Clearly the question is *not* one of cause or mechanism; one has not given a causal or genetic explanation to a person's opinions when one discovers their contribution to his personal economy. To confuse function with cause is the error of teleology, and we do not mean to be teleologists.

We recognize that in a maturing science, systematic causal explanation replaces functional analysis: witness physiology since Bernard, Cannon and Henderson, where concern with the detailed operation of homeostatic mechanisms has supplanted the earlier emphasis on the functions of organ systems. Yet in the earlier stages of a biological or human science—and surely the psychology of personality must be placed here together with most social science—a functional approach provides a very useful, perhaps an indispensable strategy for coming to grips with ongoing processes. Wherever one has to do with an entity that behaves as a self-maintaining system, a going concern, it is safe enough to assume that functions are being taken care of that keep the system going. Personality has profitably been regarded as such a system, and the Parsonians find it helpful to take a similar view of societies (see Miller, J. G., 1955; Parsons and Shils, 1951; Parsons, 1951; Levy, 1952). And if, as current theories of learning and of personality development lead us to believe, people tend to learn those ways of thinking and behaving that, broadly speaking, *work* for them, the functional approach is not so remote from causal explanation after all. If we can discern the functions served by an item of opinion or behavior, that is, we may be well on the road toward an understanding of—an ability to predict—the circumstances under which the item will be manifested, and those under which it will be modified. The distinctions drawn by a functional analysis, in other words, are likely to be causally relevant. Knowledge of the functions that a particular opinion or belief are serving a man can be put to use without waiting for a full understanding of the underlying causal mechanisms.

The opinions about Russia and Communism held or expressed by our subjects appeared to us to be used by them in ways that we could sort into three broad categories, which we called *object appraisal, social adjustment,* and *externalization.* A person's opinions on a topic are likely to serve all three functions to some extent; the extent to which one or another of the functions predominates varies from person to person and from one topic to another. What, in brief, are these functions?

It should go without saying—but our look at the earlier literature shows that the saying is necessary—that a person's initial orientation to events is not to be thought of as serving purely autistic needs. *Object appraisal* we understand as the process of testing reality in order to assess its relevance to one's ongoing enterprises. It comprises those activities whereby the events and issues in the person's world are appraised for their relationship to his motives, goals, values, and interests. The "input" of information—from personal experience, from the mass media, from hearsay—has to be scanned for its possible bearing on things that he wants, fears, or otherwise cares about. The process of "opinioning" reflects to a considerable extent such scanning for relevance.

A person's stock of *existing* beliefs and opinions, to carry the argument one step further, simplifies his task of scanning, as Lippmann (1922) long ago suggested, by providing him with already evaluated categories to which incoming information can be fitted. To serve this function, his opinions must be closely enough anchored in the reality presented to him to minimize the likelihood of surprise.

People differ greatly from one another in the extent to which a topic like Russia engages their values and interests, in the extent to which their attitudes toward Russia serve the function of object appraisal. Some are sufficiently isolated by social position and habits of attention that the barest minimum of borrowed cliches suffices to satisfy their "placing need" to put in order the modicum of information that filters through. For others, a strong personal commitment to religion, to liberal democracy, or to national interests may organize their view of Russia and the orientation that they take toward it, perhaps leading them even to seek out information that is relevant to their concerns. Even when the interests and values of a person are minimally engaged, however, and his concern with Russia is perfunctory, one can usually see the influence of his central concerns in the aspects of Russia that he singles out for notice.

Under *social adjustment* we consider another major role that opinions play: that of facilitating, disrupting, or simply maintaining an individual's relations with others. Here what matters is not so much the object itself—what Russia is like—but rather the opinions about it that a person thinks are held by other people who are significant to him. In contrast with object appraisal, in which the informational input *about the object* engages with a person's going concerns insofar as he sees the object to be relevant to them, the social adjustment function involves a process in which information about *how other people regard the object* engages with his motives to affiliate or identify himself with them or to distinguish himself from or oppose them. In view of the variety of social motives—needs for autonomy and for recognition, etc., as well as for acceptance and status—the significance of social adjustment for opinions is not just a matter of conformity. The rebel and the autonomous person as well as the conformist give evidence of having come to hold opinions that contribute to attaining or maintaining their distinctive pattern of social relationships.

It is not merely through the *expression* of opinions in the give and take of social intercourse that opinions contribute to an individual's social adjustment. The mere *holding* of an opinion whether or not the person expresses it may symbolize for him his solidarity with some remote reference group; it may be for him a way of saying, "I am like them." Or, for that matter, that "I am *unlike* them": so-called "negative reference groups" must also be recognized. During the period of our study, for example, the views of Russia, and of sundry other topics, held by a good many would-be respectable people undoubtedly served the function of confirming in their minds how different they were from the despised Communists. The possibilities of playing upon such a widely shared negative reference group were not, of course, neglected by the masters of political rhetoric.

The third and final class of functions in our list is *externalization,* which involves response to an external event in a way that is colored by a person's unresolved inner problems. Outside events are treated as if they were analogous to inner ones, and the attitude taken toward them corresponds to attitudes taken in the inner struggle. Himself greedy for a share of the world's goods and prestige to a greater degree than he could afford to recognize, one of our subjects, for example, conceived of the Soviet leadership with imagery of "pigs at the trough." In attempting to appraise the object, the person thus unwittingly carries on some of the work that is necessary in dealing with his inner problems. Insofar as he can cope with them more readily as externally symbolized, and thus better contain his conflicts, his burden of anxiety may be somewhat reduced.

Private dilemmas take Protean shapes, so the evidences of externalization that we found in our subjects' opinions about Russia fell into no single pattern. Certainly any expectation of one-to-one correspondence between "standard" conflicts, Freudian or otherwise, and particular opinion content is doomed to disappointment. As if to underline this observation, our Communist subject, an inveterate externalizer if ever there was one, gave no evidence of the latent father-hatred that some popular versions of the Freudian account would have had us look for; it was his paranoid mother that forced the Sullivan siblings to band together in defensive revolt (Smith, Bruner, and White, 1956, pp. 154–188). But the significant way in which his ideology helped him to cope with almost insupportable dilemmas lay in another highly individual direction.

The relationships we conceptualize as externalization are, of course, essentially those with which Lasswell and the authors of *The Authoritarian Personality* were concerned. Those we treat under the heading of social adjustment include points emphasized by the theorists of group influence, as these appear from a perspective focused on personality. In this day of anti-intellectualism in social and psychological theory, however, one must turn to an earlier page of political thought to encounter emphasis on the reality-oriented processes we discuss as object appraisal.

Not that we would reinstate that admirable fiction, the Rational Man. Human interests are more diverse and less reducible than the rationalists supposed, and the information on which men have to judge and act is more often faulty and misleading. And I suppose that today anyone who came close to displaying the classical rational calculus in his political opinions would be checked off as a sick man, an obsessional-compulsive. But there is an undeniably rational component in men's opinions, rooted in the reality-testing function, which current thinking is prone to underplay. Only a social psychologist like Solomon Asch (1952), writing in the Gestalt tradition, can be accused of giving it too much weight.

The kind of pluralistic scheme we have proposed has advantages, we think, over simpler views of the functions of opinion. It would still be an academic exercise in classification, however, if the primary functional grounding of opinion in object appraisal, in social adjustment, or in externalization did not have divergent consequences. We think there is such a pay-off. When a person's opinions on a topic function largely for object appraisal, it seems reasonable to suppose that he should be relatively flexible in assimilating new facts and in changing his mind when these facts point to different implications for his interests: Information campaigns, as a political strategy, assume that object appraisal is importantly involved in the opinions of the relevant publics. Sometimes this is the case; sometimes not: it should be possible to devise ways of assessing the extent to which prevalent attitudes are responsive to new information.

Opinions that are founded largely on social adjustment should be more readily influenced by what others think than by information about their object. Political as well as advertising campaigns employ the strategies of "prestige suggestion" on the assumption, often apparently justified, that the dynamics of the opinions they would alter are of this kind. The case is different with externalization, which lends to opinions a defensive rigidity not amenable to rational persuasion or to simple social manipulation. We would not expect opinions primarily in the service of such a function to undergo gradual change under the pressure of changing fact or group opinion; more characteristic would be "conversion," the saltatory change from one equilibrium to its dynamic near-equivalent, as from Communism to another True Church. The politics of scare and innuendo thus appeals to externalizing tendencies in people, and tries to focus and channel these tendencies in line with the propagandist's objectives. The good democrat who wants his politics along more rational lines, on the other hand, can perhaps foster the flexibility of object appraisal by striving to create an atmosphere of reassurance minimizing the anxiety that sets defensive dynamisms to work. His motto might well be, "There is nothing to fear but fear itself." In a world that presents so much to warrant real anxiety and to tap neurotic fears of the monstrous and uncanny, this may not be an easy course to follow.

Our excursion into the natural history of opinion was not designed to put such hypotheses to test. Fortunately, Daniel Katz and Helen Peak have recently been directing at the University of Michigan a series of studies, conceived independently of our work, that are providing more systematic evidence along these lines (Sarnoff and Katz, 1954; Peak, 1955; Carlson, 1956; Rosenberg, 1956; Katz, D., Sarnoff, and McClintock, 1956; Katz, D., McClintock, and Sarnoff, 1957).

The Expressive Aspect of Opinion

There is a tempting error to which functional theories are prone: to overinterpret, to seek functions where none exist. If a function can be found for every aspect of a person's dispositions and behavior, or for every institutional arrangement of a society, one comes close to the position of a Pangloss for whom "whatever is, is right." There are *dys*functions, too, as the good functional sociologist Robert Merton (1957, p. 51) reminds us. Not every feature of a person's opinions is currently useful to him, and just as certainly, not all the linkages between opinions and personality are brought to light by inquiry along functional lines. Although much of what was at one point functional for a person gets embedded somehow in his personality structure as it emerges in the transactions that compose his life history, there is no guarantee that the functional basis persists to the present. Yet personality coheres, and students of personality like Gordon Allport have provided us with ample evidence that different samples of a person's behavior bear that person's distinctive stamp (see Allport, G. W., 1937, 1950; Allport, G. W., and Vernon, 1933).

A man's opinions, too, carry his signature. So a comprehensive account of the relations between personality and opinions must go beyond the functional question to examine the *expressive* aspect of opinions, the ways in which an individual's opinions are shaped by the kind of person who has them. Both a person's intellectual and his temperamental qualities are revealed in the nature of his attitudes, as we found in our case studies. But the correspondences seldom determined his stand on gross issues such as, for example, whether he supported or opposed the Truman Doctrine—the kind of datum likely to be provided by an attitude test or opinion poll. Support or opposition for the publicly formulated alternatives on current issues appeared to us in the guise of "final common paths" (to borrow a metaphor from neurophysiology) that people could arrive at from a diversity of private routes. The impress of intellectual and temperamental traits of personality was to be discerned rather in the style than in the gross outcome of political thinking and action.

Stylistic features rooted in personality traits remain practically important, even though they are not predictive of a person's particular policy stand. Take, for example, the effects of differences between people in the abstractness or concreteness characteristic of their thinking. In spite of the fact that without our intending it the men we studied were well above average in intelligence as a group, we were forcibly impressed by the narrow limits within which most of them could cope with political issues in abstract terms—a general feature of their thinking. This common attribute of Nonacademic Man has, of course, a lot to do with the prevalence of stereotypy in political attitudes and of the *non-sequitur* in popular political thinking. As a formal condition of political thought and behavior, to look at the matter from another perspective, such incapacity for abstraction puts the functioning of opinion in object appraisal under major constraint. It goes far to explain why opinions that primarily serve this essentially rational function can fall so short of the standards of logical rationality.

Reservations and Conclusions

Let me return to features of our approach that I noted at the outset, by way of introducing some comments on its possible relevance for political scientists.

Our study, I observed, was long on the description and analysis of opinions, but short on the observation of political *behavior,* a result that followed perhaps from our selection of Russia as a focal topic, perhaps from our method that leaned heavily on interview and discussion. From a political scientist's standpoint as from a psychologist's, this is certainly a deficiency in our case materials. But the theoretical position that we worked out from opinion data may nevertheless have implications that extend beyond "mere" opinions. *Expressed* opinions are, after all, a form of behavior, and opinions *held* are but one type of behavioral disposition. To the extent that we learned about things that our subjects did in the service of their opinions—other than talking to us—this behavior seemed to be intelligible in much the same terms as their attitudes. The Communist who avoided subjecting himself to Party discipline but avidly sought out information to feed his internalized version of the Marxist "line"; the affable real estate agent who rarely discussed Russia but accepted a wide range of favorable or unfavorable information about Russia without being much affected at the core of his beliefs; the cautious accountant who avoided controversy at all costs in spite of a view of Russia as a villainous regime: all of these behaved in ways that were congruent with the functions their opinions about Russia were serving, if not always logically consistent with the letter of their beliefs. Discrepancies between attitudes and behavior pose a logical or moral problem, hardly a psychological one.

That our studies barely touched on *public* opinion in any strict sense is a more serious reservation. There are general implications here, I think, for the political scientist who is interested in psychological approaches. If I understand the uses of the term in political and social theory, "*public* opinion" implies not so much the contrast between public vs. private circumstances of expression, as the existence of *consensually defined issues* in the social group whose opinions are under consideration.[2] Our scheme for describing opinions (which I have not summarized in this paper) did take cognizance of the person's position on public issues, under the rubric of *policy stand.* But the interesting correspondences that we found between opinions and personality primarily involved the richer aspects of attitude content and structure as uniquely patterned by the particular individual. Indeed, we came to see the necessity of arriving at a simple policy stand—"Are you for or against the Truman Doctrine?"—as imposing a kind of

2. See D. Katz, Cartwright, Eldersveld, and Lee (1954, pp. 50–84) for representative approaches to the definition of public opinion.

Procrustean frame on the much subtler distinctions often drawn in the attitudinal object as privately construed, and in the person's orientation toward it. It is in the nature of public opinion, we came to see, that a wide range of personal opinions are brought into focus on a highly limited set of alternative proposals for collective action.

If knowledge of personality does not, in general, permit the prediction of policy stands, need the political scientist who is interested in public opinion concern himself with personal opinions and with personality? This crucial question is not easy to answer. There is undoubtedly a Sirens' lure to personality studies that political scientists who are tempted would do well to view with sturdy suspicion. How easy it is to be enticed into the pursuit of humanly fascinating facts that, in last analysis, have rather little to do with the broader issues that purportedly motivate one's inquiry! For many purposes, the student of political behavior is clearly justified in ignoring personality; he can take people's policy stands as *data* without close inquiry into the private ingredients of which they are resultants.

Yet the burden of this paper is, obviously, that the personal setting of public opinion does matter, and that political scientists will surely have recurrent needs to come to grips with it. Not, usually, through the intensive study of individual cases on our model: this procedure is too inefficient for purposes other than the exploratory search for illustrative specimens. More extensive appraisals can be envisaged, however, as for example of the personal values and interests with which a particular topic engages, in a defined public, or of the degree to which the attitudes prevalent on a topic in a defined population serve one or another of our three functions. Such partial but extensive inquiries into opinion dynamics look particularly promising as avenues to the understanding and perhaps prediction of *shifts* in public opinion in response to events and to different styles of leadership or manipulation.

The final limiting feature of our work that I mentioned at the outset—a matter related to the point just discussed—arises from the fact that our approach maintains a distinctly psychological perspective focused on the individual personality as a functioning system. How is such an approach to be integrated with others that are appropriate to the broad domain of political behavior, particularly that of sociology with its emphasis on roles, groups and institutions? I shall not attempt an easy solution to this chronic source of difficulty, which presents resistant obstacles to empirical research on social behavior as much as it troubles the theorist who ventures across disciplinary boundaries. Aspects of our discussion may nevertheless have suggested, perhaps, some lines along which a *modus vivendi* may be approached among differently focused conceptual approaches. Group-related concepts, we have seen, enter the psychological account among the variety of considerations relevant to the functional analysis of opinion. Had this essay attempted a genetic formulation of how opinion develops, I would also have had to call upon them in identifying the sources of information from which opinions are constituted. Not everything that a group theorist would have to say about public opinion finds its way into this personality-oriented schema, but no matter. The sociologist, on his part, extends his conceptual linkages from the group to the personality level, without any obligation to include in his formulation everything that the psychologist of personality can contribute to the study of opinion. For the political scientist, it seems to me, the profitable question is not, "Which account is more valid, the psychological or the sociological?" but rather, "For what problems of political behavior is the vantage point of personality theory more useful, and for what problems that of groups and institutions?"

My very tentative suggestion with respect to this question runs along lines already hinted at. So long as concern is focused on whether people accept or reject the various positions on an issue as they are publicly formulated at a particular time, a sociological emphasis on group affiliations may well be the more promising. A "cross-pressures" analysis, for example, may account for differences in policy stand where the detailed study of personality does not carry us very far. To look at the matter from a slightly different angle, *public* opinion as a phenomenon of social consensus may best be described in categories of sociological theory. In order to anticipate *changes* in people's policy stands under the impact of attempts to influence them or of events, however, one has to look behind the facade of relatively stereotyped public opinion to the private, individual level. Here a psychological approach may well be the method of choice. The present paper has attempted to illustrate one such psychological approach from the vantage point of personality theory, and to suggest an orderly framework for the study of the complex relations between opinions and personality.

6

Attitude Change

Interpreted broadly, the topic of attitude change is not only a focal preoccupation of theory and research in social psychology; it embraces phenomena and problems that equally concern students of personality, of culture, of political affairs, and of consumer preferences. The molding of public opinion by propaganda and through processes of persuasion is a matter of attitude change, but so also are the development or reduction of prejudice and the socialization of the child to adhere to the sentiments and values of his culture. Even the modification of interpersonal feelings and expectations during the course of personal acquaintance or in psychotherapy is a matter of attitude change.

Scope and Brief History

The concept of attitude, although variously defined, is most commonly employed to designate inferred *dispositions,* attributed to an individual, according to which his thoughts, feelings, and perhaps action tendencies are organized with respect to a psychological object. The topic of attitude change thus embraces the conditions under which such dispositions are initially formed and subsequently modified in the course of a person's transactions with his physical, social, and informational environment. It includes changes both in relatively superficial and specific matters of "opinion" and in deep-seated sentiments or "cathexes" that are properly regarded as constitutive of personality, changes that occur in the natural course of maturation and experience as well as those that result from exposure to deliberate persuasion or propaganda.

Although the scope of the topic is thus embarrassingly broad, substantial research has been brought to bear upon it only along a much narrower front. When attitudes became the central focus of social psychology in the 1920's and 1930's (Allport, G. W., 1935; Murphy, G., Murphy, and Newcomb, 1937) and techniques had been worked out for their measurement by pencil-

"Attitude Change" by M. Brewster Smith. Reprinted with permission of the Publisher from the *International Encyclopedia of the Social Sciences*, David L. Sills, ed. Volume 1, pages 458–467.

and-paper tests, social psychologists came to investigate under this rubric favorable or unfavorable orientations toward consensually defined social objects and issues (war, the church, ethnic groups, etc.), leaving to specialists in personality research the conceptualization and study of man's deeper and more idiosyncratic attachments. The approach characteristic of this early period was mainly descriptive and correlational, with little sustained attention to the conditions under which attitudes are formed and modified and little effort toward linking the psychology of attitudes with more general explanatory principles.

Four developments in the 1930's and 1940's radically changed the complexion of the field, making problems of attitude change salient and for the first time justifying the claim that in attitudes—previously a matter of academic but quite untheoretical preoccupation—social psychology finds one of its most important and fertile topics.

Sample surveys and polling. A major influence on social psychology has been the development of the technology of sample surveys and survey analysis—public opinion polling. The new survey research institutes, equipped to conduct and analyze door-to-door interviews with the general public, escaped the restricted world of the earlier questionnaire studies carried out with readily accessible college student respondents. When repeated surveys asked the same questions, trend data on opinion change brought to the fore the problem of how events and exposure to mass communications influence opinions. With the invention of the "panel" technique of survey design and analysis, involving repeated interviews with the same respondents, the persuasive impact of mass communications on ordinary publics became the subject of fruitful research. The study of voting behavior, in particular, by these methods produced findings relevant to attitude change.

Small group research. A second important trend brought social realities under experimental scrutiny, in the tradition of research on small-group dynamics begun by Kurt Lewin and his students (Lewin, 1951; Festinger, 1950). Conceptual equipment and experimental techniques became available for treating systematically the social influences on attitudes and behavior to which people are exposed by virtue of their memberships and participation in groups. The interrelations between these first two trends—survey research and small-group research—are examined by E. Katz and Lazarsfeld (1955).

Psychoanalytic formulations. Meanwhile psychoanalytic conceptions were gaining favor among American psychologists, revolutionizing their approach to personality research. Following pathways suggested earlier by Harold Lasswell, the authors of *The Authoritarian Personality* (Adorno, Frenkel-Brunswik, Levinson, and Sanford, 1950) illustrated in depth, for the special case of anti-Semitism as well as general ethnic prejudice, how attitudes may be an integral part of the defensive postures that people assume against the consequences of deep-seated inner conflict. From this perspective, the psychology of attitude formation and change became an integral part of the study of personality dynamics.

Experimental studies of communication. The fourth formative development was the concerted deployment of experimental method in the study of conditions governing the effects of persuasive communication begun during World War II and continued in the postwar years by Carl Hovland and his associates (Hovland, Lumsdaine, and Sheffield, 1949; Hovland, Janis, and Kelley, 1953). Planning their experiments within a broadly mapped conception of the process of communication, which accommodated hypotheses arising from a variety of theoretical contexts, these investigators demonstrated the power of carefully designed experimentation to identify the main and interactive effects on attitudes of numerous characteristics of the source and content of communications and of audiences.

By mid-century, the effect of these developments was to make attitude change not only a field of active investigation, via both controlled experimentation and the correlational methods of the sampling survey and panel, but also an arena in which theoretical approaches of general and social psychology were being elaborated and applied. The focus on predictive hypotheses concerning change now made such theories relevant, as they had not been in the earlier, descriptive phase of attitude research.

Before we turn to examine the major theoretical treatments of attitude change, the ensuing section reviews current conceptualization of the origin and development of attitudes.

Formation and Development of Attitudes

In an influential early formulation, G. W. Allport (1935, pp. 810–812) listed four conditions for the formation of attitudes: the *integration* of numerous specific responses within an organized structure; the *differentiation* of more specific action patterns and conceptual systems from primordial, nonspecific attitudes of approach and withdrawal; *trauma,* involving "a compulsive organization of the mental field following a single intense emotional experience"; and the adoption of attitudes by imitation of parents, teachers, or peers. These categories can readily be applied to describing the development of particular attitudes, but it is clear that they are descriptive rather than explanatory and are neither logically coordinate nor mutually exclusive. They variously emphasize different aspects of attitudinal learning, such as its gradualness or suddenness, the emotional intensity of the learning experience, and the informational basis on which attitudes are acquired.

Regarding attitudes as a special case of the more general category *acquired behavioral dispositions,* D. T. Campbell (1963, pp. 107–111) focuses on the problem of informational basis and proposes six different ways of acquiring the information upon which such dispositions are based: blind trial-and-error, general perception, perception of others' responses, perception of the outcomes of others' explorations, verbal instructions relevant to behavior, and verbal instructions about objects' characteristics. Although these represent varying degrees of efficiency, Campbell argues that dispositions acquired by these different modes are psychologically equivalent and that the several modes combine additively to result in stronger dispositions. However, solid evidence for the equivalence of the several modes is lacking.

Theorizing about the modes and processes by which attitudes are acquired should rest upon an extensive "natural history" of the development of attitudes, based on longitudinal and cross-sectional research that would sample a variety of content domains. The research needed for such a natural history largely remains to be done. There have been no long-term longitudinal investigations tracing the development and change of attitudes in the same individuals over substantial segments of the life cycle. Newcomb has contributed two classic short-term longitudinal studies: one (1943) following changes in students' liberalism—conservatism over their college years and another (1961) investigating the development and change of interpersonal attitudes among members of a specially assembled college living group. Cross-sectional research comparing the attitudes of different age groups has focused heavily on the single domain of ethnic prejudice (see Allport, G. W., 1954; Harding, Kutner, Proshansky, and Chein, 1954), with some attention also to the development of political attitudes (Hyman, 1959).

In both these domains, there is evidence supporting Allport's conception of differentiation as characterizing the early stages of attitude development in childhood. The evident manifestations of prejudice in childhood involve diffuse rejection of the out-group and its symbols; only later is the culturally prescribed content of prejudice elaborated. Similarly, American children learn early to identify with their family's political affiliation; more specific attitudes on political issues come only later. Scattered evidence suggests that with increasing maturity, attitudes may become more highly integrated in the sense of showing more internal consistency. But age trends in the organization of attitudes urgently require study, across different topics and different social and cultural groups.

Theoretical Approaches to Attitude Change

Although the natural history of attitude development remains largely to be written, the processes underlying attitude change have nonetheless become the subject of active experimental inquiry. In part, inquiry has been directed toward formulating and refining empirical generalizations about factors that influence attitudes. (Representative findings are reviewed by Janis and Smith, 1965). To a major extent, however, inquiry has been guided by theoretical orientations imported from other areas of psychology.

Although the possibility that attitudes have innate components cannot be excluded (see, for instance, Hebb and Thompson, 1954, p. 549, on innate fear of the strange), the primary contribution of learning to the formation and development of attitudes is beyond question. Theories of learning are thus exploited for their bearing on the conditions of attitude change. Attitudes also embody the results of information processing and in turn affect the way that a person conceives and judges aspects of his world. Theories of the cognitive processes are therefore a second source of hypotheses about attitude change. As organized dispositions toward psychological objects, moreover, attitudes are important components of personality. To the extent that the personality has properties of a dynamic system, a person's attitudes should develop and change under the influence of the roles that they play in personality adjustments and transactions. A third group of theoretical orientations to attitude change thus have their roots in personality theory.

Since the major types of theoretical orientation to the study of attitude change are addressed to different questions and concerned with different variables, they cannot be regarded as mutually exclusive or even as seriously competitive. A comprehensive view of attitude change might require an integration drawn from all of them. Such an integration has not been forthcoming, however, and the *Zeitgeist* of recent theoretically oriented research has tended to seek progress in increasingly precise and formalized models of component processes.

Learning Theories

Although the study of attitude change has not been a major proving ground for the learning theories that flourished in recent American psychology, each of the major variants of learning theory has been applied to it. Thus for Skinner (1957) and his followers, who dissolve the dispositional concept of attitude into overt verbal behaviors, attitude change becomes a matter of the shaping of verbal behavior under the control of schedules of reinforcement. Clark Hull's learning theory has been applied to the psychology of attitudes by Doob (1947). Empirical evidence is available (e.g., Scott, W. A., 1957) supporting the prediction from reinforcement theory that people tend to adopt, as their own, attitudinal positions that they have been asked to espouse publicly in experiments, when their performance has been accompanied by reward. Establishment of attitudes by the procedures of classical Pavlovian conditioning has also been demonstrated (Staats and Staats, 1958).

But the mere demonstration that attitudes *can* be established and modified according to learning principles does not lead very far in research. The more important contribution of learning theory to the understanding of attitude change has come from investigators who have taken its relevance for granted and applied its categories of stimulus—response analysis, reinforcement, generalization, and conflict to empirically derived problems of persuasive communication and attitude change. Such an approach was characteristic of the Yale studies under the leadership of Carl Hovland, which also drew with catholicity on other theoretical traditions. Thus, in one study of the effects of fear-arousing appeals in persuasive communication, the lesser effectiveness of strongly threatening appeals is interpreted in terms of the learning of interfering responses (incompatible with acceptance of the communicator's recommendations) to reduce the induced state of anxiety (Hovland, Janis, and Kelley, 1953, pp. 77–89). No test of a specific deduction from learning theory is involved; rather, the categories of learning theory serve heuristically to set the terms of the empirical problem and to suggest lines of interpretation that give direction to subsequent investigation.

Cognitive Approaches

The theoretical controversies of the generation of American psychology between 1930 and 1950 pitted the cognitive orientation derived from Gestalt psychology against the predominant stimulus—response learning theories of American behaviorism. These controversies carried over into the social psychology of attitude change, particularly with respect to interpretation of the processes of social influence involved in the traditional topic of prestige suggestion. People tend to evaluate objects, such as slogans or literary passages, more highly when they are attributed to a highly valued, prestigious source than when they are attributed to a source toward which their existing attitudes are less favorable. Is this influence of the source to be interpreted in essentially associative terms, in which the positive or negative affect aroused by the source adheres to the message on the model of classical conditioning? Or, as Asch (1952, pp. 387–417) argued eloquently from a Gestalt orientation, does attribution serve rather to provide a new context of meaning that induces changes in the cognitive object, about which changed evaluative judgments and accompanying affect are then appropriate?

At least two issues appear to have been confounded in the controversy. One has to do with the priority of cognitive as compared with affective factors in attitude change. Do people change their feelings about an object because they have come to see it differently, or do they change their beliefs about it to fit prior alterations in their feelings? The evidence now seems clear that both sorts of processes occur; what may be primary is a tendency to bring beliefs and feelings into congruence (Rosenberg, Hovland, McGuire, Abelson, and Brehm, 1960, pp. 15–64). The second issue also seems rather dated from present perspectives. Are the processes of influence to be interpreted in associative or meaningful terms? Recent elaborations of associative theory, in their emphasis on central mediational processes intervening between stimulus and response, tend to converge with the older cognitive theories. Heat has dissipated from controversy as theorists socialized to feel at home with stimulus-response or with cognitive terminologies come to see their differences as more a matter of linguistic preference and conceptual strategy and less a question of truth versus falsity (see Campbell, D. T., 1963, pp. 112–135).

Contemporary cognitive approaches to attitude change have therefore lost the polemical cast that used to characterize cognitive theory when it was a minority systematic position in opposition to behavioristic psychology. Concern has shifted from system building to the clarification of particular aspects of attitude change. Here a minor theme draws upon the psychology of judgment; a major one postulates trends toward cognitive consistency or balance as underlying attitude change.

Judgmental Processes and Attitude Change

As inferred dispositions, attitudes are customarily measured by eliciting acts of judgment: agreement or disagreement with standard statements of opinion. Much of the behavior to which attitudes give rise is mediated by further acts of judgment that involve the placement of the issue or object in an evaluative framework and its assignment to a category. Concepts and principles drawn from the general psychology of judgment should therefore throw light on the processes of attitude change. M. Sherif and Hovland (1961) and Sherif, C. W., Sherif, M., and Nebergall (1965) have made promising beginnings toward bringing about this rapprochement.

As applied to the context of persuasive communication, their thinking may be simplified as follows: A person's attitude on a controversial issue may be coordinated to the range of discriminable opinion positions that he finds acceptable. The person's *latitude of acceptance* will typically be narrower than the accompanying *latitude of rejection* when he is highly ego-involved with the issue or when his position is extreme. In responding to a persuasive communication that advocates some position on the issue, he places it on a subjective pro-con scale of favorability with respect to the issue. The effects of the communication on the recipient will depend heavily on the distance between the recipient's stand and the position advocated by the communication as he locates it in his scale of judgment. The same objective differences in the positions of two communications may be perceived very differently by different individuals, depending on the nature of their judgment scales, which in turn are determined by such factors as their familiarity with the issue and the extremity of their own positions. Maximal persuasive effects are to be expected when the position advocated in the communication falls near the boundary of the recipient's latitude of acceptance; under these conditions the recipient is likely to minimize its judged distance from his own position (*assimilation effect*) and to be open to its influence. When the position of the communication falls within his latitude of rejection, he is likely to exaggerate its judged distance from his own stand (*contrast effect*) and to resist influence. On issues characterized by low ego-involvement, where latitudes of acceptance are correspondingly great, the persuasive effect may be a positive function of the distance between the recipient's stand and the position advocated, within relatively broad limits.

This schematic summary may suggest the promise of reconceptualizing attitudinal processes in terms of the psychology of judgment. At present, the promise has yet to be realized. Major areas of theoretical ambiguity remain to be clarified, and the data that have thus far been brought to bear are not fully consistent.

Helson's theory of adaptation level—a zone of neutrality on the stimulus continuum that is established as a weighted mean of focal and background stimuli and of the residues of previous stimulation—represents an alternative conceptualization of judgment processes that is founded in extensive psychophysical research. In principle, it should be applicable to the analysis of attitude change. In the hands of Helson and his co-workers (Helson, 1964, pp. 609–630), however, its application has thus far been so broadly analogical that it has contributed little to bringing attitude change in conceptual contact with fundamental processes of judgment. What emerges is the assertion that expressions of attitude are a joint function of the presenting stimulus, of the social context and its pressures ("background factors"), and of personality ("residual factors")—hardly a novel formulation.

Consistency or Balance Theories

Since the mid-1950's, the most active front in the study of attitude change has centered on a group of related theories that seek to come to grips with the dynamics of attitude change via formulations of the interplay between the person's postulated tendency toward consistency in specified aspects of his beliefs and attitudes and the incoming information with which he is confronted. The idea of a trend toward psychological consistency is an old one. What is new in the recent attention that it has received is the combination of theoretical formalization and experimental ingenuity to test inferences that go beyond the earlier common sense. The theories to be considered vary greatly in scope and ambition, but none of them purports to offer a general account of attitude change.

Heider's theory of balance. The phenomenologically oriented theorist Heider (1946; 1958, pp. 200–209) initiated the recent emphasis on trends toward consistency with a treatment of the seemingly very narrow problem involved in identifying states of balance and "imbalance" in the cognitive field of an experiencing person *p*, as he entertains specified relationships with another person *o*, and with some attitudinal object *x*. Relations of two kinds are considered: the *sentiment* (or attitude) relation of liking or disliking and the *unit* relation involved in perceiving persons or objects as belonging together in a specially close way. Both types of relations when they exist may be positive or negative (degrees of relationship are not considered). The relations in a *p-o-x* triad are balanced when all three relations are positive or when two of the relations are negative and one is positive. Imbalance occurs when two of the relations are positive and one is negative.

Heider gives as an example of imbalance the following triad: *p* worships *o* (liking, positive); *o* tells a lie (positive unit relation between *o* and *x*);

p disapproves of lying (negative relation of dislike between *p* and *x*). Were *p* to come to dislike *o*, the triad would come into balance. Other routes by which *p* could re-establish balance would be to sever the unit relation between *p* and *x* ("it isn't typical of *o* to lie") or to dissolve the experienced unity of *o* by introducing a cognitive differentiation that segregates the aspect of *o* as liar (disliked) from the rest of *o* (liked)—both differentiated aspects now entering into balanced triads. According to the theory, balanced states are stable; imbalanced states are unstable. Heider postulates a general trend to re-establish balance when it is disturbed by the registration of new information; but his formulation is intuitive and qualitative, containing no basis for predicting the route by which balance will be attained.

Newcomb's theory. The relations with which Heider is concerned obtain within the cognitive field of an experiencing subject *p*. Newcomb (1961), who like Heider has been interested in the relationships between attitudes and interpersonal attraction, offers a slightly modified version of the conditions under which *p-o-x* relations are *subjectively* balanced or imbalanced. (He also uses a different notation.) On the additional assumptions that reciprocated attractions between persons are more rewarding than nonreciprocated ones and that accurate perceptions of the attitudes of *o*'s toward *x*'s will in the long run be more rewarding to each *p* than inaccurate ones, Newcomb goes on to derive the prediction that as interpersonal relations stabilize in established social groups they will approximate conditions of *objective* balance in which, for example, people who share agreement on important issues and feel the same way about other people also come to like each other. His study of *The Acquaintance Process* (1961) in specially convened student living groups provides evidence of strong trends toward subjective balance from the beginning, with increasing trends toward objective balance developing over time. Newcomb thus extends Heider's principle of balance from the private worlds of phenomenology to the objective world of interpersonal relations.

Theory of cognitive consistency. In a provocative recent venture, Rosenberg and Abelson (Rosenberg, Hovland, McGuire, Abelson, and Brehm, 1960, pp. 112–163) introduced a degree of formalization and extended the principle of balance from the restricted scope of *p-o-x* relations to encompass more general conditions of consistency within and between cognitions about an emotionally significant issue.

Rosenberg and Abelson posit a hierarchy of responses to imbalance in a cognitive structure, such that imbalance is resolved by that route that involves the minimal number of changes in the relations and signs of cognitive elements. But the tendency to reduce imbalance is not the only factor that determines how persons go about the resolution of cognitive discrepancies: there is also a tendency, independent of the striving for consistency, for the individual to prefer solutions that maximize his potential hedonic gain.

This model has yet to undergo much testing in research and will undoubtedly have only a short life in its present form. It is nevertheless worth consideration as exemplifying one of the directions in which trends toward consistency are currently being explored in accounting for attitude change. Its virtues of flexibility and generality are in contrast to those of specificity and quantification presented by Osgood and Tannenbaum's congruity model (1955), which generates precise predictions of shifts in the evaluation of both subject (e.g., "Eisenhower") and object (e.g., "communism") when assertions join them in positive (e.g., "praises") or negative (e.g., "condemns") associative linkage.

Festinger's cognitive dissonance theory. Of all the versions in which the consistency principle has appeared, Festinger's theory of cognitive dissonance has attracted the most active investigation in the late 1950's and early 1960's (Festinger, 1957; Brehm and Cohen, 1962). Any two cognitive elements—beliefs or bits of knowledge—may be *consonant, dissonant,* or *irrelevant* to one another. Dissonance occurs when one element follows psychologically from the contrary of the other. The total amount of dissonance that a person experiences is a function of the importance of the elements in a dissonant relationship and of the proportion of relevant relations that are dissonant. There is a tendency for the person to attempt to reduce dissonance when it arises: states of dissonance have motivational properties. Dissonance may be reduced in three major ways: by changing one or more of the elements involved in dissonant relations, by adding new cognitive elements that are consonant with already existing cognitions, and by decreasing the importance of the dissonant elements. A general tendency for cognitions to be brought into correspondence with impinging reality is assumed.

Although this capsule statement sounds like a very general consistency theory, the ingenious program of experimentation that Festinger and his followers have carried out has been primarily concerned with a much more restricted sphere of consistency or inconsistency—that between a person's cognitions of what he has done and his awareness of grounds for not having done it. Typical cases arise after a person makes a decision or when he has been induced to comply with a distasteful request. In the first instance, decisions are supposed to be followed by residual dissonance between awareness of the decision and awareness of the reasons supporting the alternative course of action that was rejected. The attempt to reduce such dissonance may lead the person to seek out informational or social support for the decision that he has taken.

The second case, that of "forced compliance," involves dissonance between the person's awareness of the compliant act to which he has irrevocably committed himself and his cognition of the grounds for not having wanted to do it. One way of reducing the dissonance is to change his private attitude or preference in the direction of consonance with the compliant behavior. Here is the basis for some of the "nonobvious" predictions from the confirmation of which Festinger claims strong support for this theory. Thus, when a person is induced by bribe or threat to voice opinions contrary to those that he privately holds, the weaker the inducement, the *more* likely he is to change his private views in a direction that brings them into accord with the ones that he has been induced to express. So long as the positive or negative inducement is sufficient to bring about compliance, the greater the inducement, the more disproportional the grounds for compliance, and therefore the less the dissonance and the less the motivation for attitude change to reduce it.

Clearly there is a wide discrepancy between the apparent generality of the theory and the rather special character of the experiments that have tested it. Brehm and Cohen (1962, pp. 299–300), in their comprehensive review of the evidence bearing on dissonance theory, seek to plug the gap in part by pointing out that where the antecedents of behavior have been a major concern of other theories, dissonance theory is concerned, at least in part, with the *consequences* of behavior. They go on to suggest that *commitment* may be necessary before the psychologically consonant or dissonant status of particular cognitive elements can be determined. They reformulate the core assertion of the theory to state that "a person will try to justify a commitment to the extent that there is information discrepant with that commitment" (Brehm and Cohen, 1962, p. 300)—a significant and important statement, but one much narrower in scope than Festinger's original propositions.

In spite of the large amount of research recently stimulated by Festinger's theory, most of which purports to confirm it, the status of the theory is still far from clear. The experiments tend to be open to alternative interpretations. The experimental manipulations by which commitment is brought about as a precondition for the arousal of dissonance have not been critically scrutinized and may be important. To a considerable extent, experimental ingenuity has substituted for theoretical explicitness: experimentally, for example, alternative routes for the reduction of dissonance have been eliminated to leave attitude change as the predicted outcome, but the theory has little to say about which of the possible ways of reducing dissonance a person will employ. Where predictions from learning theories of reinforcement and conflict are pitted against predictions based on dissonance theory, as in some recent studies, the outcomes do not consistently support dissonance theory. The conjecture may be ventured that, in the long run, dissonance theory will turn out to have made sense of certain paradoxical feed-back effects of a person's behavior upon his attitudes but to have said little that is important about the main themes governing the formation of attitudes and the direction of behavior. Or it may become incorporated in a more comprehensive theory that deals with these themes. The lure of the paradoxical "non-obvious prediction" can deflect attention from the main story, which may be "obvious" but needs to be formulated and specified.

Approaches Based on Theories of Personality

Learning theories have their sources in rigorous experimentation with lower species and college sophomores; judgmental theories still bear the marks of the psychophysical laboratory; other cognitive theories find their models in rigorous research on perceptual processes; but personality theories trace their origin to the clinic and consulting room. The atmosphere is entirely different. Rigor and precision are likely to be sacrificed in favor of relevance to human experience and problems. Whether the gain justifies the loss is a major issue that divides modern psychology.

Psychoanalysis. Among personality theories, psychoanalysis shows most strongly the characteristic virtues and vices of clinical origins. A generally psychoanalytic, but not doctrinaire, perspective was brought to bear upon the sources of prejudiced attitudes in *The Authoritarian Personality* (Adorno et al., 1950). This suggestively rich, influential, but technically vulnerable study portrayed the prejudiced person as using his attitudes to maintain a rigid and precarious defensive posture, bolstering his self-esteem by identifying with the strong and rejecting the weak, resolving his own uncertainties and keeping his unacceptable impulses in check (while giving them covert expression) by cleaving moralistically to a world of clear-cut alternatives, a world in which the safe areas of conventional respectability seem bounded by unknown dangers and conspiracies. This study did not deal directly with attitude change, but the implications were clear: to the extent that prejudiced attitudes are so grounded, there is little to be hoped from rational persuasion. The expression of prejudice can be controlled by firm authority; its dynamic roots perhaps excised by psychotherapy; and its occasion avoided by wiser child rearing. In present perspective this is a one-sided picture, even for this least rational of attitudes.

Like learning theory, psychoanalytic theory has suggested concepts, categories, and hypotheses to investigators of attitude change whose principal research directives have arisen from the phenomena being studied. Such influence is particularly apparent in the work of Janis (e.g., 1959), whose treatment of decisional conflicts represents an important alternative to Festinger's.

Self theories. Approaches to personality that emphasize self, self-image, and identity have not given rise to formal theories of attitude change. That such theories might well be developed is suggested by the widespread and loose evocation of the term "ego-involvement" (Sherif, M., and Cantril, 1947) as a determinant of resistance to change in attitudes. Also suggestive is Rokeach's (1960) treatment of belief systems, in which he contrasts a central region of primitive beliefs about self and world with a peripheral region comprising the variety of beliefs that a person receives on authority. More directly relevant are the accounts of attitude change under the conditions of extreme coercive persuasion that characterized the so-called brainwashing or thought reform conducted by the Chinese Communists (Lifton, 1961; Schein with Schneirer and Barker, 1961). In cases where deep-seated convictions were substantially shaken and relatively profound changes of attitude brought about, we hear of references to "death and rebirth" being employed. To unfreeze attitudes that have become central constituents of the self, the sense of identity itself is attacked; guilt is evoked, confessed, and expiated. Somewhat similar processes have been described for the transformation of a young layman into a monk (Erikson, 1958) or of a recruit into an officer (Smith, 1949b). The seemingly significance and human cogency of the phenomena touched upon in these descriptions raise doubts about the extent to which the theory of attitude change may have been impoverished by too close confinement to the pallid topics and mild pressures of the laboratory. There are striking similarities between the processes of attitude change in self-involving life settings and in psychotherapy (Frank, 1961).

Functional Approaches to Attitude Change

Not tied to any single theory of personality, a group of recent approaches to the development and change of attitudes is nevertheless oriented to the personality as an empirical system. These functional approaches attempt a relatively comprehensive account of the functions that a person's opinions and attitudes serve in the ongoing economy of personality, on the assumption that knowledge of the motivational basis of attitudes should point to the conditions under which change can be expected. From the functional standpoint, the vigorous resistance with which persuasive efforts are commonly met suggests that people have a strong interest in maintaining their attitudes with as little change as possible.

Smith, Bruner, and White (1956), on the basis of an intensive clinical study, offer a classification in terms of three broad functions served by opinions and attitudes: (1) *object appraisal,* (2) *social adjustment,* and (3) *externalization.* Any persistent attitude is likely to serve all three functions to some extent, but there is considerable variation from issue to issue and from person to person with respect to the function that predominates.

Object appraisal. The first function involves scanning and appraising the input of information from the external world for its relevance to the person's motives, goals, values, and interests, thus giving rise to selective self-exposure and attention to information. A person's stock of *existing* beliefs and opinions simplifies his task of scanning by providing him with already evaluated categories to which incoming information can be fitted. When object appraisal predominates, attitudes should be malleable, in response to rational presentations of information that lead the person to reappraise the bearing of reality factors on his interests and enterprises. Even in this case some resistance may be expected, since relatively stable categories are an advantage to a person in coordinating an effective way of coping with the too unstable world.

Social adjustment. The part played by a person's opinions in facilitating, disrupting, or simply maintaining his relations with significant others is termed social adjustment. Since attitudes may be organized in response to motivated nonconformity, as well as to conformist motives, a better term for this function might be the *mediation of self-other relations.* In contrast with object appraisal, in which informational input about the object of the attitude is the crucial formant and source of change, here the strategic information pertains to how other people regard the object. This information engages his motives to affiliate and identify himself with them or to detach himself and oppose them. The influence of reference groups on a person's attitudes is classified here.

Externalization. The final class of functions, more broadly phrased as externalization and ego defense, involves response to an external object or event in a way that is colored by a person's unresolved inner problems. The attitude taken toward external facts is an overt symbolic substitute for covert attitudes taken in the inner struggle. This function has been emphasized by psychoanalysis to the exclusion of the others, and, of course, it is the function that is one-sidedly stressed in *The Authoritarian Personality* (Adorno et al., 1950). Attitudes so motivated are unlikely to be influenced by rationally presented information, but they may respond to authoritative reassurances that allay anxiety, to changes brought about in self-insight, or to the uncovering processes that go on in psychoanalytic therapy.

A closely related classification of four functions is provided by D. Katz (1960; see also Katz, D., and Stotland, 1959), who develops the implications of each for conditions of attitude change.

Such functional classifications must be regarded as devices of heuristic convenience, not as theories that are true or false. But the hypotheses about attitude change for which they provide a framework are being tested in empirical research. Here difficulties in assessing motivation combine with those inherent in the study of attitudes to make clear-cut results difficult to obtain.

Some Concluding Remarks

This essay has focused on theoretical approaches to the study of attitude change; but the research on which this spate of theories, models, and approaches is grounded is not entirely in good order, and a few cautionary remarks are appropriate in conclusion.

The recent rapid flow of research has not represented, in a way that is adequate for the healthy development of theory, the full range of phenomena implied by the customary definitions of attitude. We have noted the relative dearth of naturalistic descriptive studies. When the relevant variables and relationships are yet to be discerned, premature leaping into rigidly designed experimentation may be costly. The too frequent failure of apparently well-designed studies to stand up to replication should be a warning. Reasons of efficiency have also led to the restriction of experimental studies of change to relatively superficial attitudes and beliefs in regard to which exposure to brief communications might be expected to have measurable effects. Similar reasons have led to a concentration on short-term effects instead of the more important long-term ones.

The integration of attitude research with the study of personality structure and processes is largely still incomplete. By and large, the investigators who study personality change, as in psychotherapy, are different from those who are interested in attitude change; they conceive of their problems within different frameworks and theorize about them in different terms.

More strictly technical aspects of research on attitude change should also cause concern. The care expended by psychometricians on the refinement of sophisticated scaling models for the measurement of attitudes has largely been lost to the experimentalist, who is fastidious about experimental design but slipshod in his techniques of measurement. Although perhaps more serious from the perspective of fostering the specification and development of theory, investigators and theorists alike have been entirely too cavalier in referring to attitude change without specifying the *aspect* of attitude—belief, feeling, or action tendency—in which change is predicted and measured. It often seems as though any stray feature of opinion in which change can readily be produced will do for experimentation. Moreover, researchers would do well to return to the safeguards employed by Hovland, Lumsdaine, and Sheffield (1949) against the contamination of results by the expectations of guinea pig subjects who know that they are under study.

For all these strictures, research on attitude change has made immense strides in recent decades. Knowledge in this field should be advanced and consolidated if current trends in research toward theoretical and experimental virtuosity are balanced by equal concern with representativeness and fidelity to the phenomena.

7

Personal Values in the Study of Lives

This essay is a much-delayed response to a personal challenge from Henry A. Murray, a challenge of at least ten years' standing, to develop some incipient ideas about the formulation of personal values as a topic for personological and social-psychological inquiry. Characteristically, Harry gave enthusiastic support when I first broached the subject; a larval idea can only bask in the glow of his warm receptiveness and is even tempted to fancy itself a butterfly. In the cold awakening that so often follows such a self-indulgent episode, however, the larval state of the ideas was all too apparent; they have been in indefinite pupation ever since.

I still have no butterfly to present. But a number of considerations now lead me to accept the challenge all the same. The topic of values has certainly attracted much more attention in the intervening years than it previously enjoyed; among major efforts, there are the recent book-length bibliography by Albert and Kluckhohn (1960), the comparative cultural studies by F. R. Kluckhohn and Strodtbeck (1961), and by von Mering (1961), and the factor analytic research stemming from Charles Morris' scheme (1956). If anthropologists and sociologists concerned with cultural values as foci of personal and cultural integration have been the largest contributors to this literature, psychologists have also found themselves talking more frequently about values—as features of the philosophical boundary that sets the terms of professional decisions (Lowe, 1959) or as ingredients of accounts that propose to describe the functioning person (McClelland, 1951).

But the increased currency of explicit value concepts among psychologists and social scientists has unfortunately not been accompanied by corresponding gains in conceptual clarity or consensus. We talk about altogether too many

Reprinted from *The Study of Lives*, R. W. White, editor, by permission of the Publishers, Atherton Press, Inc.

probably different things under one rubric when we stretch the same terminology to include the utilities of mathematical decision theory (Edwards, 1954), fundamental assumptions about the nature of the world and man's place in it (Kluckhohn, F. R., and Strodtbeck, 1961), ultimate preferences among life styles (Morris, C. W., 1956), and core attitudes or sentiments that set priorities among one's preferences and thus give structure to a life (Allport, G. W., 1937). And, at the same time, we are embarrassed with a proliferation of concepts akin to values: attitudes and sentiments, but also interests, preferences, motives, cathexes, valences. The handful of major attempts to study values empirically have started from different preconceptions and have altogether failed to link together to yield a domain of cumulative knowledge.

These observations would be grounds for avoiding the topic entirely, except for the fact that each new topic to which I turn seems to transmute itself into one in which questions of values are inescapable. In our study *Opinions and Personality* (Smith, Bruner, and White, 1956), carried out at the Harvard Psychological Clinic with the inspiration of Murray's example and tradition, Jerome S. Bruner, Robert W. White, and I found in the personal values of our subjects a level of analysis that seemed peculiarly advantageous for discerning inner coherence among their political opinions. Subsequent concern with the concept of mental health convinced me that this embarrassingly unsatisfactory term barely conceals an almost pure value problem (Smith, 1961). And in my current explorations of patterns of coping and adjustment in the intercultural situation of Peace Corps service, questions of value commitment arise centrally once more. My fate, apparently, is to be haunted by the problem of the psychological status of personal values, which keeps bobbing up like King Charles' head. This may be an auspicious occasion to face the problem more frontally.

At present, one may hope that a tentative armchair analysis will be fruitful. Thanks in part to the naturalistic study of lives that Murray pioneered, we have the advantage of considerable familiarity with values in relation to personality. Contemporary systematic thinking about "personality in nature, society, and culture" (to echo the title of a book in which Murray was centrally involved) also gives us the beginnings of a framework with which a developed conception of personal values must eventually articulate. This essay attempts to develop a few distinctions and to point to a few of the relationships of values to the framework of thinking about man in society which may make one direction of conceptualization more profitable than another. In keeping with the preliminary character of what I am attempting, I will not try to cover systematically the substantial literature of discussion and the smaller literature of research on values. Any headway we can make toward greater conceptual clarity should have implications for methods and directions of research, in an area in which choice of method has seemed haphazard and direction often lacking.

Selecting a Conception of Value

The first and crucial step in picking a way through the confusion that has enveloped discussions of values is to identify an unequivocal core meaning. Of course, semantic decisions of this sort are in a sense arbitrary. Like Humpty-Dumpty, one may use words as one pleases, so long as one uses them consistently. Yet, unless one is content to live in a Humpty-Dumpty world—an unfavorable environment both for efficient communication and for the cumulative advance of articulated knowledge—one had best take pains about the decision. The conception of values that I am approaching pays due regard to contemporary usage but also is selected with other essential criteria in mind.

To be useful in the study of lives, a conception of values should include in its reference at least some of the important human phenomena that one encounters when one sees people valuing, caring, committing themselves, judging as better or worse. A meaning should be found, if the term is to be at all serviceable, that falls within the vaguely bounded area of discourse evoked by such situations. And further, the use of a special term, rather than others more firmly grounded in general psychological theories not specifically human in reference, will be most clearly justified if it refers to distinctively human phenomena within this broader area—phenomena, that is, that are not exhausted by more general terms like motive, incentive, and valence, which apply equally at human and infrahuman levels.

A further strategic consideration stems from the fact that value terminology has become prevalent in a wide range of social or behavioral sciences besides psychology: sociology, cultural anthropology, economics, political science. There is at least the basis for hoping that value can become one of the important concepts that potentially link different levels of organization and analysis and can therefore play a central part in a developing general science of social man. The hope may be illusory, for the seeming convergence on terminology may merely hide basically divergent meanings: loose efforts at integrating the social sciences too often hinge on the slippery use of terms. In searching for a core meaning of value, however, I will be seeking one that is primarily relevant for personology but also engages with issues and concepts of anthropology and sociology—one that meets the needs of the social psychologist concerned with the development and functioning of the person in his social and cultural context.

Some Alternatives

Before these criteria can be brought to bear, we need to map out, in a preliminary way, some of the major alternatives that are available in recent usage. Because of the prevalent confusion, my final preference will be for a well-bounded, specific meaning that does not pretend to include many of the referents to which the term has been applied. But the preliminary task of mapping requires starting with a highly general conception that embraces most of the meanings in which "value" has been employed. Such a conception, it seems to me, is that of selective behavior—in which a person chooses, rejects, takes interest in, approves, disapproves—with respect to a physical, social, or ideal object.

Whenever we talk about values and valuing, we are confronted—in actuality, in principle, or in retrospect—with persons engaged in processes of selection or choice with respect to objects. We employ the terminology of values as a conceptual handle for discerning and dealing with regularities in this behavior. The selective behavior may be instrumental to attaining some further object or state of affairs beyond that to which it is immediately oriented, or it may be consummatory, an end-term in the behavioral sequence. Or the behavior under inspection may rather be talk about such encounters.

The search for underlying constancies in the flux of behavior turns the theorist, like the Everyman of Heider's (1958) "commonsense psychology," to attend to properties that he attributes to the polar components of the behavioral situation: person and object. So the major cleavage in the use of the term value divides those who focus on the person and his dispositions, on the one hand, and those who apply the term to properties of the object of choice, on the other. For the first group, values are subsumed in one way or another under attitudes, the most general term for personal dispositions toward a psychological object or class of objects. For the second, value is or results from properties of the object that evoke selective behavior—either intrinsic properties of the object or, more commonly, functional properties that emerge in relation to the motivation of the person who is in commerce with it.

In the early years of empirical social research, W. I. Thomas in his methodological introduction to *The Polish Peasant* (Thomas and Znaniecki, 1918) introduced just this distinction with the complementary terms, attitude and value. For Thomas, attitude refers to any disposition of a person toward an object, while any object becomes a value by virtue of being the target of a person's attitude. Here the term value is used very generally and is located explicitly at the object pole. Similarly employing the term for concepts anchored in the object of choice are the economists, when they deal with the value of an object, either in the marketplace or in its utility for particular persons.

Theorists concerned with personological problems have sometimes applied the term to classifications of the objects or goals of behavior. Thus, Lasswell (1946) and Murray (1951, p. 463) offer classifications of sought-for goals under this rubric; and Ralph K. White's *Value Analysis* (1951) is also a catalogue of goals or end-states toward which motivated behavior may be directed. Still others employ terms other than value for related concepts having to do with choice-evoking properties of the object: thus Lewin's (1935) valence, Sigmund Freud's (1957) cathexis, and the concepts of reward or incentive value which are current in the psychology of learning.

More characteristically, however, students of personality have understandably been preoccupied with dispositions of the person, and when they have used the term value, they have had some class of evaluative attitudes in mind. Here the influence of Gordon Allport and, through him, of Spranger's now-familiar typology of aesthetic, theoretical, economic, political, social, and religious values has been substantial (Spranger, 1928). *A Study of Values* in the Allport-Vernon (Vernon and Allport, 1931) and in the Allport-Vernon-Lindzey (1951) versions was for years the only standardized instrument that purported to measure personal values. Its considerable predictive power, as shown for example in studies of creativity and of vocational choice, attests to the fact that it measures something that is humanly important. In the test-oriented field of personality research, its sheer availability, as well as its real merits, led to its widespread use; and its general use, in turn, has tended to center the meaning of personal values, for the student of personality, on essentially the sort of thing that the Allport-Vernon-Lindzey version measures. Spranger's original formulation, in the Germanic spirit of *Verstehen*, has generally been lost to view, and the concept of personal values has come to mean, in common usage, highly general orienting preferences, which are usually assigned a relatively central and hierarchically superior status in the organization of personality.

The view of personal values as general and hierarchically important attitudes, as components of a personal philosophy of life, has also been promulgated in recent research on the psychology of opinons and attitudes. I adopted this usage in an early paper (Smith, 1949a), and it was followed by Bruner, White, and myself in our collaborative work (Smith, Bruner, and White, 1956). In a parallel line of development, Daniel Katz and his students at the University of Michigan employed a closely similar conception in their functional theory of attitude structure and change (Katz, D., and Stotland, 1959). Assuming that values are more general and central than other attitudes, they show that a person's attitude on a specific issue can be predicted from a joint knowledge of his hierarchy of values and of the instrumental relationship that he perceives between his values and the issue in question (Rosenberg, 1956); moreover, changes in perceived instrumentality induced by persuasive communication result, in turn, in corresponding changes in attitude (Carlson, 1956). In this framework of analysis, values are inherently supraordinate to the attitudes under study, but a more precise definition of values, that would distinguish them from other general attitudes, is not required. Some people may well ask whether an additional term is really necessary in this context; the same relationships could very likely be expressed in a terminology of attitudes varying in generality-specificity and related hierarchically to one another.

To round out this sketch, we must finally take notice of a kind of usage that fits the scheme more awkwardly: the phenomenological approach that uses the object language to refer to properties of the phenomenal world of the experiencing subject. For the psychologist not reared to this intellectual tradition, the "objective" givenness of values emphasized by Köhler (1938) may seem confusingly subjective. He is essentially concerned with the descriptive fact that within the psychological world of the experiencing person, values like beauty or repulsiveness are immediately given properties of the psychological object and are not perceived as arising from his own subjective tastes. Depending on one's preferred theoretical strategies, one may elect to emphasize or to ignore such a phenomenological observation; in any event, Köhler's descriptive point is compatible with an explanatory account that treats values as functional properties that objects acquire, in part, by virtue of their relationships to dispositions of the behaving person.

Personal Values as Standards of the Desirable

The foregoing excursion among some of the options offered by recent usage establishes, if nothing else, the need for explicit decision concerning terminology on the part of anyone who would contribute to this area; a variety of distinguishable and worthy concepts have become attached to the single term. It is time to declare my choice.

My starting point will be the definition given by Clyde Kluckhohn (1951), which has had considerable currency:

> A value is a conception, explicit or implicit, distinctive of an individual or characteristic of a group, of the desirable which influences the selection from available modes, means, and ends of action. [p. 395]

Let us put aside for the time being some of the particulars in this definition. Our main interest will be in personal values, so we can set aside the question of the various ways in which values may be "characteristic of a group." We might also do well to postpone facing the difficulties hidden in the phrase, "which *influences* the selection . . ."; the nature of the influence is a matter to be explored. The possibility should also be left open that a person's "conceptions of the desirable" may sometimes play a merely retrospective role in criticizing or justifying his previous selective behavior. The core of Kluckhohn's definition that I would presently stress, then, is its focus on a particular class of personal dispositions: *conceptions of the desirable that are relevant to selective behavior.*

Personal values in the present sense are attitudes, in the sense of object-directed personal dispositions. But they are a special kind of attitude, functioning as standards by which choices are evaluated. Personal values pertain to the desirable, the preferable, rather than to the merely desired or preferred; to the realm of "ought" rather than that of "is" or "want." As standards against which specific choices are tested they have at least to some degree the hierarchically superior status customarily ascribed to personal values. As I will point out later, they are also often central in the organization of personality, to the extent that they are constitutive of the self. But not all central and hierarchically superior attitudes are personal values in the sense of this definition. One may have highly general preferences, consistencies that underlie many occasions of choice, yet these preferences need not necessarily carry the cachet of preferability. An aspect of the commonly noted erosion of values that has accompanied the shift from absolutism to relativism in our modern culture is surely a shift from the "objective" requiredness of the desirable (ought) to the merely desired (want). It is a significant difference.

I want therefore to highlight rather than to slip past the lack of exact fit between the present conception and that underlying the Allport-Vernon-Lindzey *A Study of Values*. According to the operations of item-checking that go into determining a set of scores on this instrument, it gets at consistent patterns of verbally expressed preferences, just as do the Kuder Preference Record and the Strong Vocational Interest Blank. Very likely, these preferences are often sustained by convictions about the preferable, but the content of the items does not guarantee that such is the case, and there are no external checks to give us this assurance. Similarly with respect to Charles Morris' "Paths of Life" (1956). Again the respondent is asked to rank his preferences among complex and widely varying life styles, without any guarantee that the preferences reflect adherence to standards of preferability.

Here I had best pause. The Allport-Vernon-Lindzey is a justly respected test, with which personologists are closely acquainted through long use; and Morris' "Paths" has likewise attracted a good deal of recent interest. It is well enough to establish that the operations involved in these instruments do not correspond precisely to the definition I derive from Clyde Kluckhohn; but why should one prefer the definition to the instruments? It begins to look like a case of everyone out of step but Johnny.

I don't at all intend to disparage the importance of measuring patterns of fundamental preference, as part of the descriptive task of mapping variations in personal philosophy. My objection is simply that these instruments do not come to grips with the distinction that I am presently insisting on. It remains to support my contention that the distinction is worth making.

One ground for the distinction is phenomenological: simply pointing to the vivid qualitative difference commonly evoked by the words "desired" and "desirable." The ensuing section will look more closely at this phenomenal contrast and some possible bases for it. Another reason reverts to one of the criteria touched upon at the outset: reference to distinctively human phenomena within the broader area of selective dispositions. The peculiarly human aspect of selective behavior would seem to be precisely the universal occurrence of standards of the desirable, of "oughts" and "thou shalt nots." Preference and desire and cathexis—motivation and attitude—can be found in a wide range of animal behavior, though of course only one species is capable of completing *A Study of Values*; it is personal values in the sense of Clyde Kluckhohn's definition that pose the challenging theoretical problem at the human level. A final line of justification, to be developed subsequently, is that the conception favored here is fruitful of relationships linking personality to society and culture—relationships of a sort that tantalize the social psychologist.

To fuse preferability with preference for purposes of the descriptive measurement of personality is natural enough, since the distinction is an analytical rather than an empirical one; if we give credence to the sort of strain toward consistency in cognition emphasized by Heider (1958) and Festinger (1957), there is reason to expect people more often than not to prefer what they think preferable, and vice versa. So the student of the architecture of personality may often safely neglect the distinction, unless he is concerned with the genesis and functional correlates of the peculiarly human aspect of human valuing.

Similarly, the anthropologist concerned with the analysis of culture patterns can make other fusions. Thus Clyde Kluckhohn (1951) moves quickly from his definition of values to the consideration of "value orientations," which he defines as

> . . . generalized and organized conception[s], influencing behavior, of nature, of man's place in it, of man's relation to man, and of the desirable and nondesirable as they may relate to man-environment and interhuman relations. [p. 411]

Values—as one concretely encounters them, that is—are embedded in a context of fundamental assumptions, "existential," or "is," rather than "ought" propositions. If one is interested in the comparative study of cultural ethos, one has to deal with this fusion of the existential and the normative, just as would be the case in the study of personal philosophies of life. Florence Kluckhohn and her collaborators (Kluckhohn, F. R., and Strodtbeck, 1961) have pursued the systematic study of value orientations so conceived with much empirical ingenuity. For other theoretical purposes, however, it seems essential to cleave here to the narrower conception of values isolated from the core beliefs with which they are likely to be closely linked (Rokeach, 1960).

The Phenomenal Objectivity of Values

The crux of the present conception of values, then, is the word desirable. As Kluckhohn (1951, p. 398) elaborates, "The desirable . . . is not restricted to what is commonly designated as the 'moral.' It includes the aesthetic and those elements of the cognitive which reflect appraisal. The cue words are 'right' or 'wrong,' 'better' or 'worse.' " All of these words carry for us the connotation that standards apart from personal whim are being applied; in Köhler's sense, "objective" considerations are brought to bear on matters of choice. As with Köhler, the objectivity involved is that of the phenomenal world of the experiencing person. For further clarification of distinctions in this taken-for-granted but elusive realm, it will be profitable to turn to Heider's perceptive analysis of "commonsense psychology"—in this case, his treatment of the concept of "ought" (Heider, 1958, pp. 218–222).

Heider (1958, p. 219) starts with the Wertheimer-Köhler-Asch conception of requiredness, introduced to describe a situation in which we feel that "something ought to happen." "Requiredness, according to this view, is rooted in the gap or incompleteness of the situation. Acting in accordance with this implicit injunction, acting in a manner that brings about the necessary closure, then becomes identified with the right." But he immediately points to the insufficiency of this interpretation:

> Yet, it is not strictly correct to equate gap-induced requiredness with ought requiredness, for clearly there may be many occasions in which the person may experience the tension of an incompleteness in the situation, without at the same time experiencing the tension of an ought. For instance, the person may realize that he wants *x*, the situation being incomplete in the sense that his desire is unfulfilled, and yet that he ought not to have it. Or, in interpersonal relations, the person may recognize that someone else wants *x*, but unlike the case in which *o* needs help, filling the gap by satisfying his wants does not necessarily coincide with what ought to be done. [p. 219]

As a first approximation, Heider notes a degree of parallelism between the content of "I ought to do such-and-such" and that of "somebody wants or commands that I do such-and-such."

> In the case of ought, however, it is not a particular somebody that is felt to want or command people to do *x*, but some suprapersonal objective order. It may also be experienced as a supernatural being who personifies this objective order. In any case, when *p* [the experiencing person in Heider's convention] has the conviction that he ought to do *x* he recognizes a vector in the environment, a vector which is like a wish or a demand or a requirement on the part of some suprapersonal order and which has the validity of objective existence. [p. 219]

From this starting point, Heider goes on to identify the functional properties of "oughts," as they occur in the person's phenomenal world.

> First of all, oughts are impersonal. They refer to standards of what ought to be done or experienced, standards independent of the individual's wishes. That is not to say that personal wishes do not influence the

perception of ought forces; it is rather that they "should not," that in principle the ought is established by objective requirements. [p. 219]

Moreover, oughts are dispositional in character. They refer to invariant standards, to "laws of conduct" which hold in spite of many variations in incidental or momentary factors . . . as long as differences among situations do not alter what are perceived to be impersonal objective requirements. [pp. 220–221]

The objectivization of ought as an impersonal, dispositional concept also implies that ought has interpersonal validity. Not only should ought disregard personal desires, not only does ought in principle appear unchanged in spite of incidental situational factors, but it is also universal and should look alike to everybody . . . If *p* accepts the vector which is given by the objective order and acts accordingly, he feels that he is a "good" person. He may even expect praise. But if he violates the directives of this vector, he may expect punishment.

Thus we see [Heider concludes] that even in this first approximation, the meaning of ought . . . is not a mystical quality somehow attached to the word. It can be defined by investigating the functional role it plays in our thinking and our reactions. We have suggested that it can be represented as a cognized wish or requirement of a suprapersonal objective order which has an invariant reality, and whose validity therefore transcends the point of view of any one person. [p. 222]

The suggestiveness of this phenomenological analysis for a social-psychological and developmental approach is immediately apparent. Before exploring some of the directions that it opens for inquiry, however, we need to place Heider's "ought" in firmer relation to our present treatment of personal values.

The experience of "ought," as Heider has dissected it, would seem to be a prototype of the actual, momentary occurrences of valuing in human behavior; the explicit or implicit standards according to which "ought" is experienced are values in our present sense (Heider employs the term in another way which need not concern us here). "Ought" may not exhaust the occurrences to which values pertain (for example, it seems to fit less aptly experiences of preferability in the realm of the aesthetic), but the phenomenally given objectivity and interpersonal validity that Heider finds characteristic of "ought" would seem to be true of value standards generally.

Some Types of Phenomenally Objective Requiredness

The phenomenologist may be privileged to rest content with discovering the objectivity with which values are given in naive experience. For most psychologists, however, phenomenology is a starting point rather than a goal; one asks immediately (perhaps prematurely, the phenomenologist might say) whence the experience of objectivity arises and what difference it makes. To start in this direction of inquiry, it may be helpful to shift from Heider's concern with the features that experiences of "ought" have in common, to ask if there may not be discernible *types* of value requiredness, all experienced as in some sense objective, but perhaps with different sources and functional correlates. Several such types can be distinguished in a preliminary way.

Social Requiredness

One type that is directly suggested by Heider's discussion may be labeled social requiredness: he or they or, projectively, the gods or God require something of me. Heider began by observing the partial similarity between "ought" and someone else's wish or command; one experiences in both cases an expectation from without as to how one should act. For his purposes, Heider went on to contrast the impersonality of "ought," its phenomenal anchorage in the objective order, as compared with the personal quality of commands and wishes. But we must now note once more the similarity; demands from the other are in any event "objective" for *p*, and, in important special cases, personal demands become phenomenally indistinguishable from requirements of the objective scheme of things.

Thus for the infant and young child, his parents as "others" comprise an enormous segment of his relevant world. Until the child attains a fairly sophisticated level of reciprocity, from which he can discount the "humanness" of his parents' perspective, their wishes and demands are not merely part of the objective order as it emerges for him; they are likely to be among the most important parts to which he has to accommodate. At the beginning of personality, then, we can safely assume that social requiredness provides a basis for the experience of objective requiredness in its full force.

Another special case is that of the traditional culture in which there is a high degree of social consensus on the proper ways of acting in each of the large but finite number of situations that life offers. "They" expect such-and-such of me—but *they* are everyone (probably including the ghosts of my ancestors); they comprise my whole social world, and their wishes for me in effect constitute the requirements of the objective order. As in the case of the young child in relation to his parents, here, too, the person has no choice but to accept the requirements of the "others" as given.

To seek in social requiredness a principal basis for the felt objectivity characteristic of adult values is only to rephrase customary thinking about the birth of conscience in the process of socialization. But as long as we remain on the level of social requiredness as such, the value standards involved in the rules set by others—parents or tradition or the Joneses—can be spoken of as personal values only in a very limited sense if at all. The person is in the last analysis oriented toward whatever "they" require; if he goes on to embrace the rules as his own, a new ingredient has entered the picture. In Kelman's

(1961) terms, pure social requiredness is the sphere of compliance and identification, but not of internalization.

In such an imaginary pure case of social requiredness, there is no difficulty in speaking of cultural values. Thus, the observing anthropologist looks for meaningful patterns that enable him to formulate principles and priorities underlying the many situation-bound rules of a traditional society. These are cultural values at a higher level of generality than the particular rules that specify good and proper behavior in each culturally recognized kind of situation. In learning the cultural maze while growing up, each individual also learns these rules, which have objective requiredness for him; but if he is primarily oriented to the demands of the others who carry the tradition, it could be misleading to conceive that the more general cultural values (as formulated by the anthropologist) are also his personal values. The rules that define what is situationally proper function as values for him, but they may well be learned as so many particulars. At this level, their significance for him depends on the actual or imagined sanctions of approval or disapproval that back them up. They are extrinsically related to his personality rather than constituents of it.

Something approximating the pure case of social requiredness doubtless occurs in the early stages of individual development, but it seems unlikely that entire societies can be fitted exactly to the type without violence to the facts. The proposed dichotomy of shame versus guilt cultures has not fared well in recent discussions (Whiting, 1959). Whether the pure case exists in any concrete society is immaterial, however, to the analytical utility of the distinction.

Personal Requiredness

Out of social requiredness emerges what may be called personal requiredness, under circumstances that have recently been the subject of intensive inquiry by students of socialization and personality development. The process by which the person moves from one to the other level is conventionally referred to as the "internalization" of values, a term that of course explains nothing. Currently prevalent theory can be related to my scheme if we introduce two subtypes of personal requiredness: superego requiredness and self-requiredness.

Superego requiredness may be said to characterize those standards (values) that the person holds in the fashion portrayed in the classical Freudian superego. The values are "internalized" in that their application to a person's behavior does not depend on the presence of others. But they are inflexibly held, irrationally applied, and are typically implicit, or unconscious, rather than explicitly formulated by the person who holds them. A person may feel ridden by these requirements as something alien to his self. He applies the standards in ways that involve only the most primitive cognitive discriminations. When he violates them, he is burdened with guilt. All told, standards adhered to in this fashion have the earmarks of having been laid down early in life, prior to the firm development of a reflective self. If, as Freud would have it, they are acquired primarily by a process of defensive identification, this could account for the heavy predominance of negative over positive content: "thou shalt not" over "thou shalt," guilt over positive affect.

But superego values are only one kind that involve personal requiredness, and in persons who approach more closely the commonly formulated ideals of maturity and good functioning, they fall into the background as compared with values characterized by what I am calling self-requiredness. These are standards that may be implicit but, in any case, are accessible to conscious formulation. They are actively embraced by the person and thus become constituents of the self, part of what the person feels himself to be and to stand for. Characteristically their application involves more finely differentiated cognitive discrimination than is the case with superego values, and they can therefore be applied with more flexibility, appropriateness, and rationality. As one measures oneself and one's behavior against these standards, his self-esteem rises or falls; at low ebb there is a sense of shame or worthlessness to correspond to the superego affect of guilt, but the negative end of the affective spectrum does not seem to be so inherently dominant as in the case of an active superego. Since they are integrated in the self rather than sealed off in an infantile form, they are open to progressive modification and elaboration. They retain the phenomenal character of objective requiredness emphasized by Heider but are sustained by the individual's active commitment to them as the values that he chooses to live by.

Objective Appropriateness

It would best suit the biases of a social psychologist to stop taking inventory of types of requiredness and values at this point, as the stage is well set for an account that would trace all personal values to sources in social experience, along lines parallel to the theories of the self that view it as a mere looking glass of reflected appraisals, a purely social formation. But just as self theory in the Mead-Cooley tradition ignores the presocial ingredients of organic sensation and body imagery, so I fear it would be in error to claim that the objective requiredness of values can be traced exhaustively to social origins. A place has to be reserved for the role of objective appropriateness as a source of standards having the experienced quality of requiredness. Here we return to the home ground of Köhler's Gestalt account.

The "goodness" or correctness of a solution to a mathematical problem, to pick an extreme example, is objectively required in a way that depends, to be sure, on elements of convention or rules of the game, but at the same time follows ineluctably from the inherent structure of the problem. And a good performance is distinguished from a poor one, whether in the accomplishment of a skilled task, the play of a competitive sport, or the re-creation of a piece of music, according to standards somehow intrinsic to the nature of the activity, the potentialities of form that it entails. These examples have the quality of "ought" that Heider found lacking in some instances of Köhler's "gap-induced requiredness": if one sets out to solve a mathematical problem at all, one "ought" to do it correctly; if one undertakes to perform a task, one "ought" to do it as well as one can. Artists may work within the framework of a cultural style or of a set of classical rules that is fixed by convention, but the critic's judgment of artistic quality is not simply a matter of estimating the degree of fidelity with which the rules have been applied, the style exemplified. He is almost sure to be convinced that within the framework of convention, standards are nonetheless intrinsic and objective, hard as they may be to make fully explicit. What seems common to these cases is that although convention or cultural tradition sets the terms of the problem or defines the materials, modes, and ends of the activity, standards of evaluation arise that have some necessary relation to the structure of the activity and are not themselves merely conventional.

These matters are outside my competence and involve perennial questions about which controversy will not soon be exhausted. It is enough for my present purposes to leave my scheme open to the possibility that elements of objective appropriateness may combine in varying degrees with more clearly social ingredients in the actual genesis of values.

Interrelations

The distinctions I have been drawing are analytical abstractions; the requiredness that attaches to the values actually held by real people can be expected to come from mixed sources. But one may speculate, without altogether losing contact with potential facts, on the interrelations among social and personal requiredness and objective appropriateness.

Where social requiredness has the support of virtually complete consensus on the proper behavior for a stable and exhaustive inventory of culturally defined situations—or an inclusive set of rules—there is little occasion for personal requiredness to become salient, if it develops at all. Here we have the ideal type of the tradition-directed character described by Riesman (1950). As I noted earlier, one can appropriately discern a system of cultural values in such a society, underlying the interlocking set of social rules that has shaken down into coherence through long usage; but these cultural values are hardly constitutive of the individual selves of the society's members. Here perhaps lies a reason for the anomic disorganization often observed when the value system of a traditional society is broken by the radically changed circumstances and cultural intrusions occasioned by exposure to the modern world.

In changing societies where traditional social requiredness can no longer specify what is fitting and proper for a definitive inventory of situations, personal requiredness, if there is the basis for it at all, is likely to become more salient. It becomes more salient partly by default, because traditional patterns defined by specified social expectations no longer provide adequately for the predicaments of choice that life brings. And it is reinforced by success; the "gyroscope" of inner directedness, in Riesman's metaphor, has cash value in such circumstances. Of the varieties of personal requiredness, superego requiredness would seem to be the more socially dependable and foolproof when the psychological conditions for its development can be maintained—but at the cost of much personal neurotic suffering and an element of social rigidity. Self-requiredness, a subtler formation, has its special vulnerability.

It is vulnerable because the degree of explicit commitment involved in consciously embracing values as part of the self casts potential doubt upon the objectivity that distinguishes values from tastes or preferences. Remember Heider's analysis of "ought" as impersonal, relatively invariant, and interpersonally valid. For our values to carry the full force of "ought," we need to believe that they have validity beyond our individual fiat, that they are as valid for others as for ourselves. Self-values have this quality of phenomenal objectivity, but it is endangered by the very failure of consensus, the prevalent relativism and pluralistic tolerance, that makes them salient. In other words, they appear to be especially susceptible to change—I was about to say deterioration—into mere tastes and preferences which, since they lack the force of "ought," can hardly play the same central role as values in personal and social integration.

In principle, one can conceive of the person who embraces his values with full commitment in the absence of consensus among his fellows or of belief in a cosmic cheering section rooting behind the scenes for the right. But few of us are like Nietzsche's Superman; all too human, we need the support of cobelievers to remain convinced that our standards are interpersonally valid.[1]

The possible ingredient of objective appropriateness continues to puzzle me. If we think of it as somehow generated by the requirements of historically conditioned human nature, as they mesh or fail to mesh with the situations that people encounter, perhaps we begin to get at intrinsic sources of values in the discovery of value "universals" that recur in most cultures (Kluckhohn, C. K. M., 1954) or by the study of directional, "progressive" trends in history in the development of value standards. Or perhaps Asch (1952) points to a more promising path when, in his intended refutation of cultural relativism, he seeks to maximize the invariance of value standards transculturally by attributing as much as possible of the intercultural variability in value judgments to cultural differences in the real or culturally defined situation. If we give the principle of invariance of values the benefit of every doubt, as Asch does, what "invariant" values do we in fact come out with from a close study of world cultures?

Granted the possible relevance of objective appropriateness, it is at least conceivable that perceived relationships of appropriateness are an important source of values in personality development, together with the influence of parental demands and expectations which we are now better able to formu-

1. Cf. Festinger's emphasis on "social reality," as in Festinger, Riecken, and Schachter (1956).

late. The suggestive evidence for a core of value universals points, albeit weakly, to continued pressure from this source that partly shapes what is socially or personally required.

The Reflexiveness of Self-Values

In the study of lives, it is the self-values that call most insistently for closer investigation, both because of the central part they would appear to play in the organization and integration of the self and because of the instability to which they seem particularly vulnerable under present cultural conditions. Reverting to my previous comments about the most widely used instruments in personological research on values, both *A Study of Values* (Allport, G. W., Vernon, and Lindzey, 1951) and "Paths of Life" (Morris, C. W., 1956) aim primarily at this value sphere, although, as I noted in criticism, they do not permit a clear distinction between value standards and preferences that lack the force of "ought." New approaches are needed if we are to bring data to bear effectively on such psychologically and socially relevant questions as the conditions and consequences associated with the predominance of values or of tastes. Toward this end, the remainder of the essay is devoted to exploratory discussion of some features of self-values that we may expect on theoretical grounds. The theory I draw on is the convergent body of speculation and research concerning the self, to which sociologists,[2] psychiatrists (Sullivan, 1945), and psychologists (Sarbin, 1954; Wylie, 1961) have contributed.

As an institution of personality, the self has the peculiarity of being a subsystem (a functional construct inferred by the observer-theorist) organized around a phenomenal entity existing only for the experiencing person—the self-percept or concept in the sense of the person's organized awareness of his being (Smith, 1950b). The inherent reflexiveness or self-reference of this subsystem (it is hard to talk of these matters without getting into verbal tangles) has been the focus of much theoretical interest.

On the one hand, there is plausible speculation concerning how it comes about, how the direct and naive awareness of the human infant achieves the sophistication for him to view himself as an object in his phenomenal world. G. H. Mead (1934), following earlier suggestions by James (1890, pp. 291–401), Baldwin (1913) and Cooley (1902), developed the most influential formulation of this problem in his proposal that we progessively attain selfhood and a kind of objectivity through covertly or imaginatively adopting the perspective on our actions of the others with whom we interact. We eventually integrate these partial perspectives into a more stable capacity for self-objectification as we become able to take what Mead referred to as the role of the "generalized other." As noted earlier, this account neglects the

2. G. H. Mead (1934) was, of course, a philosopher, not a sociologist; but his formulations are central to the sociological analysis of the self.

contribution of direct body-awareness to the developing self-percept, but its emphasis on social intercourse as an important ingredient of reflective selfhood seems hard to contravene.

And on the other hand, theorists have devoted attention to the special role in the functioning of personality that such a reflexive self can play. For McDougall (1908), the "sentiment of self-regard," just such a reflexive entity, did duty as replacement for the "will" of classical psychology. Sociologists and social psychologists in the tradition of Mead also emphasize the adaptive and integrating value of the self, as the person comes to be able to respond symbolically to his own behavior and attributes in terms that are potentially communicable. The concept of a reflexive self is intimately linked to possibilities of self-control. And, in the personality theory of Carl Rogers (1961), the self is explicitly at the heart of the personality system and, indeed, the source and focus of the most important human motivation.

So much is essential background for approaching the reflexiveness of values that become incorporated in the self. We may begin by considering how values are probably acquired in the course of the processes of socialization that give rise to selfhood. The child before selfhood has no direct contact with values; what he encounters as he emits behavior that his significant others evaluate is sanctions: tokens, more or less explicit, more or less directly rewarding or punishing, of the approval or disapproval that he has evoked. By the time language comes into the picture (an acquisition that Mead believed to be intrinsically linked to developing selfhood), he also encounters requests and demands, and usually reasons—both for the requests made and for the sanctions administered. And he has the example of the behavior of his parents and significant others and of their accounts of themselves. These are the raw materials from the ongoing social world, out of which the child must construct his own values.

If we leave aside the part played by example and modeling, which may well become important only as the child acquires a relatively well-defined sense of self and other, the foregoing amounts to saying that the child's first acquaintance with values is mediated by the consequences of having his own behavior evaluated, usually by his parents. Just as the primitive "ought," to extrapolate from Heider's analysis, has its source in the parental request, so the initial step in the use of value standards is taken when the child covertly adopts the role of the parent and evaluates his own actions, thoughts, and characteristics as his parent has done: when he administers sanctions of approval or disapproval to himself. Like the self, then, values are essentially reflexive from the start. And in this respect they differ intrinsically from preferences or cathexes, direct orientations toward an object that do not require mediation by taking a role.

Whether or not sanctions or requests are accompanied by more or less explicit reasons understandable to the child may be decisive, determining whether the personal values he acquires in this fashion are assimilated to an increasingly autonomous self-system or embedded in the superego. The self-system is flexible, expanding, relatively integrated, and increasingly autonomous of its origins because the growing person is in continual reflexive discourse with himself through linguistic and imaginal symbols. The reasons that accompany parental sanctions or demands provide the child with symbolic handles that tie the perceived parental standard into this system and permit its continual symbolic reworking, so that the ultimate result is firmly interwoven with his developed self-concept. They also enable the child to formulate the standard for himself in a much more differentiated way than would be possible through unverbalized processes of generalization. If, on the other hand, parental evaluations come arbitrarily without intelligible reasons, the child is likely to adopt them just as arbitrarily, with little differentiation and no basis for subsequent reworking and incorporation into an autonomous self.

These are, of course, characteristics of what we call the superego. Superegolike values are to some extent inevitable from the fact that the infant receives many parental evaluations before he has become symbolically equipped to assimilate them into the self. And this isolated, persistently infantile system of child-perceived parental evaluation is also presumably stocked with evaluations that would provoke too much anxiety for verbal symbolization to be tolerable.

Conceptual Implications

If this account of the genesis of personal values in the self, elliptical as it is, comes near the truth, some consequences follow for the conceptual status of self-values and for directions in which they may fruitfully be approached in empirical research. One implication returns us to a feature of Clyde Kluckhohn's definition (1951, p. 395) that we postponed considering. A value, Kluckhohn asserted, is a conception of the desirable which influences selective behavior; what is the nature of the influence? Seeking a definition that would hold for both personal and cultural spheres, Kluckhohn was necessarily vague on this point. With our present attention focused on self-values, we need to be more specific. Taking self-values as inferred, symbolically formulated standards, we can be sure, a priori, only that they will influence evaluation: judging, praising, or condemning as better or worse, true or false, worthy of admiration or of contempt; evaluating the behavior of others or one's own actions and qualities. It is nearly as safe to assume that one's self-values influence his responses when he is exposed to unfavorable evaluation by others or finds his actions somehow called into question. This should follow from the context of socialization in which self-values are acquired. The child soon learns to call selectively on value standards to defend his actions when they have become suspect. "I wasn't either lying!" assumes a shared value of honesty; "I didn't mean to!" carries the implicit value that intentions count more than acts. In the long pull of maintaining "face" before others and self-esteem within, we all become thoroughly practiced in evoking values to justify ourselves. Justification (or rationalization), like evaluation, is a "self-conscious," reflective operation, which is brought to bear on behavior in retrospect.

But these influences may seem rather trivial; what counts, we may protest, is the prospective, not the retrospective. How are we to formulate the bearing of self-values on one's active choices? One alternative, that taken by French and Kahn (1962), whose treatment of the role of values in personality I find congenial in many respects, is to say that a value may also be a motive; that when one's values influence one's choices they do so by virtue of motivational force. The issues here are definitional or analytic rather than substantive, I think, but they are nonetheless real. If we are to avoid unnecessary confusion, we need to use our concepts with as rigorous consistency as we can. The concept of self-value at which we have arrived is that of a symbolically formulated standard of the desirable. A standard is not itself a motive, but in relation to other facts, it may generate motivation. For example, the discrepancy between an evaluated state of affairs and what is optimal for the person may give rise to motivation. To insist on this distinction is more than verbal quibbling. It directs us not to look for motivational and nonmotivational classes of values but to try to identify the value standards that the person has adopted, whatever they may be, and only then to inquire how their application or engagement, or its lack, is motivationally relevant.

Implications for Research

Let us finally turn briefly to some implications of this approach to personal values for research in the study of lives. A person's superego values are primitive and obscure, by definition not accessible to his reflective awareness without distortion. To infer them is a matter of subtle indirection and behavioral detection. But self-values, to the extent that they fit our definition, are ideally approached by verbal means. As ingredients of inner discourse, we can tap them through the interview and its derivatives if we enjoy good rapport with our subjects. To be sure, all verbal communication is indirect, and we can never afford to neglect the possibility of deliberate falsification or unintentional distortion as the subject's verbal behavior is shaped in part by the demands of the interview situation. But in the case of the value constituents of the self, the occasion for concealment is less than we may expect to encounter in many other private areas.

That we are tapping something "merely verbal" is no occasion for dismay: the verbal symbolism by which values are knit into the fabric of the self is a source of their importance, not a limitation. Indeed, the notion that "behavioral values" would somehow be firmer stuff than the verbal values, could we only get at them, seems to me quite mistaken. Overt behavior is never a direct index of any personological variable, being a result of components attributable to personality and the behavioral situation; for the contribution of personality in this case is further resolvable into motivation and ability, and the motivation, in turn, arises only in part from the engagement of value standards. Talk is of course behavior, too, but it is behavior from which we can infer what is revelant to know about a person's values more surely and economically than in any other way.

The more serious problem, which has yet to be solved in systematic research, is to distinguish dependably between values and preferences, between the desirable and the merely desired. Had I solved it, I should probably have been contributing substantive results rather than this essay. Progress toward a solution, however, seems promising in at least three possible directions. One is the complex, informal, recorded interview patterned somewhat after the approach that seemed fruitful in *Opinions and Personality* (Smith, Bruner, and White, 1956), before the present distinction became critically important. Working from transcripts of such interviews, trained raters could be instructed to maintain the distinction with ascertainable and perhaps satisfactory reliability. A second approach would adapt currently available instruments, revising them to employ a consistent language of "ought," "should," and desirability rather than of wish and preference. And the third would depart from the idea that personal values are especially exposed in the context of justification. It would seek some more or less systematic way to trace a person's grounds for choice back as far as possible.

I have been struggling here with a few of the conceptual problems that have hampered progress in the investigations of personal values, in spite of considerable interest in the general topic. If we can only get a firm grasp on concepts and methods, the study of values should become a promising focus of psychological and humanistic concerns.

8

An Analysis of Two Measures of "Authoritarianism" among Peace Corps Teachers

As the flood of research that followed the appearance of *The Authoritarian Personality* (Adorno, Frenkel-Brunswik, Levinson, and Sanford, 1950) abates, one can take little satisfaction in the accretion that remains to substantive social psychology. Beginning with the classical critique by Hyman and Sheatsley (1952), research on "authoritarianism" as measured by the F scale has been heavily preoccupied with technical issues; with some notable exceptions (e.g., Rokeach, 1960) the substantive issues that gave interest and importance to the monograph have been lost to sight in the beguiling pursuit of methodologically oriented research. Now that the necessary technical clean-up job is largely done, however, the original substantive questions are hardly settled: what is the status of "authoritarianism" as a personological syndrome, and what is its significance for important social orientations and behavior?

Keenly aware of such unfinished business, I seized the opportunity to include measures of authoritarianism in a battery of procedures administered to a group of 58 Peace Corps volunteers in training on the Berkeley campus in the summer of 1961, 50 of whom were to teach in secondary schools in Ghana as the first Peace Corps contingent to go overseas. The rationale seemed clear-cut: the qualities of flexibility, interpersonal sensitivity, humanistic orientation, and the like, commonly ascribed to persons who are low in authoritarianism, would seem to be ingredients of an effective performance in the Peace Corps, while alleged authoritarian traits such as rigidity, ethnocentrism, and conventionality should interfere with effective performance. In these predictions, the consideration weighed heavily that the unfamiliar

Reprinted from *Journal of Personality,* 1965, *33,* 513–535, by permission of the publishers, Duke University Press. Written during tenure as Special Research Fellow of the National Institute of Mental Health and Fellow of the Center for Advanced Study in the Behavioral Sciences. The research was supported by Contract No. PC–(W)–55 with the Peace Corps, which, of course, is not to be held responsible for my conclusions. I am indebted to Dr. Raphael S. Ezekiel, Dr. Susan R. Sherman, Dr. James T. Fawcett, and Dr. Cigdem Cizakca Kagitcibasi for assistance in the study, which in the case of the first two mentioned approached full collaboration. See 14, "Explorations in Competence" for an overall account of the study.

intercultural setting of Peace Corps duty would require novel adjustments on the part of all the volunteers, as would the teaching job itself for the majority of them who had had no substantial experience in teaching.

By hindsight, the expectation of a simple, direct relationship between authoritarianism and performance in the Peace Corps shows a certain naïveté, which it is one of the purposes of this paper to dispel. Obviously, many factors besides authoritarianism might be expected to contribute to the effectiveness of Peace Corps teachers—factors of intelligence, technical competence, commitment, and personal stability, among others. More generally, the broad theoretical and methodological question of how to conceive the relationship between core personality and overt social behavior is involved. As Couch (1962) has pointed out in an incisive discussion of this issue, not only a person's deeper motives but also his characteristic defenses and the press of his perceived environment need to be taken into account.

It might be argued that an "ego" variable like authoritarianism, concerned with a person's ways of relating both to his impulse life and to the social world, should be less subject to Couch's (1962) strictures than, say, a motivational variable such as need for aggression. As compared with inferred states of inner need, its theoretical status lies closer to overt behavior. Even so, the likelihood remains that the person's manifest behavior may deviate from that which would best fit his authoritarian dispositions, as a result either of his inner reasons to censor and guide his behavior or of environmental pressures to which he is exposed.

Empirically, the limited available evidence confirms the complexity of relationships between authoritarianism and social behavior. Thus, Haythorn, Couch, Haefner, Langham, and Carter (1956), in their study of discussion groups composed of persons high or low in authoritarianism, found the variable to be related to differences in leader and member behavior that accorded well with the theory of authoritarianism (though a number of differences that might have been expected failed to emerge). On the other hand, the paradoxical results found by I. Katz and Benjamin (1960) for biracial work groups—e.g., among white subjects, high authoritarians were more favorable than lows to their Negro partners—seem to call for explanation in terms of defensive processes of "leaning over backwards" or of differential responsiveness to the norms perceived to apply in the experimental setting. Additional empirical study is badly needed before the considerations that govern the relationship between authoritarian dispositions and overt social behavior can be disentangled. The follow-up study of the Peace Corps teachers provides relevant data.

For the volunteers tested in training, ratings of their subsequent performance overseas were obtained, and their experience as teachers in Ghana was explored in detail in long tape-recorded interviews conducted with them at their schools near the end of their first and second years of service.[1] Tran-

1. The interviews were done by Dr. Raphael S. Ezekiel and the author. First-year interviews averaged about four hours; second-year interviews, two and one-half to three hours.

scriptions of the interviews were subsequently rated in a complex *Q*-sort procedure by graduate students in psychology who were otherwise unacquainted with the volunteers or with the hypotheses under investigation.

These voluminous materials can thus be brought to bear on two major questions: At the time of training, how were the volunteers who scored high in authoritarianism distinguished personologically from those who scored low? And in what respects was authoritarianism, as measured during training, related to performance overseas? The first issue pertains to the construct validity of the measures. The second bears on their predictive validity, though not decisively in view of the many other factors on which success in the Peace Corps must also depend. After describing briefly the measures of authoritarianism, the remainder of this paper is organized around these two themes.

Measures of Authoritarianism

Derived F

The principal measure of authoritarianism was derived from the SSRC S-A schedule.[2] This inventory, developed for the study of "stereopathy" (Stern, Stein, & Bloom, 1956)—a concept essentially synonymous with "authoritarianism"—is comprised of two forms of 100 items each in which the direction and style of item wording are systematically varied. Form P860 is composed of "personality" items similar to those in the MMPI and CPI; form I860 of "ideology" items is similar to those in the original F scale. Each form in turn is made up of 10 scales of 10 items apiece. Items for four of the scales in each form are worded in the stereopathic direction. In two of these, items are worded as categorical generalizations; in two, they are given qualified, probabilistic phrasing. In each of these pairs, one scale is comprised of items that are expressed in relatively "violent" terms, one of items expressed in more "moderate" terms. Four corresponding scales in each form are composed of items worded in the non-stereopathic direction. Each form contains two additional nonstereopathic scales comprised of "antiviolent" items, as distinct from both violence and moderation: one scale of "categorical" items, one of "qualified" ones. In each form, items from the ten scales are interspersed with one another according to a standard pattern. *S*s responded to each

2. This unpublished inventory was developed by Richard Christie, Hugh Lane, Nevitt Sanford, George Stern, and Harold Webster. I am indebted to Drs. Webster and Stern for making copies available for use in this study. A copy of the items of Form I860, together with a scoring key, has been deposited as Document Number 8332 with the ADI Auxiliary Publications Project, Photoduplication Service, Library of Congress, Washington 25, D. C. A copy may be secured by citing the document number and by remitting $1.25 in advance for protoprints or for 35 mm. microfilm. Make checks or money orders payable to: Chief, Photoduplication Service, Library of Congress.

item on a six-point continuum, ranging from strongly disagree to strongly agree. A neutral response was not allowed, and the rare cases in which *S*s failed to respond to an item were arbitrarily given a score of 3.5.

Preliminary correlational and cluster analysis of scores on the twenty scales called the validity of the "personality" scales into question: three of the stereopathy scales in this form turned out to have high loadings on the cluster defined by the first four nonstereopathy personality scales.[3] We therefore confined all further analysis to the "ideology" scales of form 1860, which manifestly belonged to the domain sampled by the F scale and were indeed based on an item pool drawn from the research literature on the measurement of authoritarianism.

Cluster analysis of these scale scores could not effectively disentangle stereopathy from acquiescence. Since we sought a measure of authoritarianism that was independent of acquiescence and had no special interest in the other stylistic variables of item phrasing, we took advantage of the balanced construction of the schedule. Discarding the pair of nonstereopathic antiviolence scales (for which there was no corresponding stereopathic version), we followed the example of Christie, Havel, and Seidenberg (1958) to obtain rational derived measures of authoritarianism and acquiescence from appropriate sums and differences of the eight scale scores for which there were formally matched stereopathic and nonstereopathic versions. Specifically, a Derived Acquiescence score was computed as the sum of *S*'s raw scores on all eight of the ten-item scales. For 57 Peace Corps volunteers in training, the mean was 244.4 (*SD,* 24.7), compared with a theoretical neutral point of 280. The average response tendency thus fell somewhat on the nonacquiescent side for this sample of item content. A score for authoritarianism, here labeled Derived F, was similarly obtained by subtracting the sum of *S*'s raw scores on the four nonstereopathy scales from the sum of his scores on the four corresponding scales that were worded in the stereopathic direction, arbitrarily adding 400 to avoid negative numbers. The group mean was 336.8 (*SD*, 29.0), on the nonauthoritarian side of the theoretical neutral point of 400.

Levinson F

A related instrument then being administered to several Peace Corps training groups provides a second but generally inferior measure of authoritarianism. This was a 24-item version of the F scale, composed of 12 items from the original F scale and 12 items relating to "traditional family ideology" (Levinson and Huffman, 1955).[4] Conventional scoring

3. The details of this analysis are given in Appendix A to Progress Report, April, 1963, "Summary of analysis of data collected during training, Summer, 1961," by Susan Roth, on file with the Peace Corps.

4. A copy of the 24-item scale, as used, has been filed with the American Documentation Institute. See note 2 above.

of items from one to seven was employed, four representing the theoretical neutral point. For the 58 volunteers in training, the mean score on this "Levinson F scale" was 66.7 (*SD*, 18.9), substantially on the non-authoritarian side of the theoretical neutral point, 96.

The Levinson F scale shares with the scales employed in *The Authoritarian Personality* the technical defect that all items are worded in the authoritarian direction. It is thus of interest that while our measures of Derived F and Derived Acquiescence are constructed to be independent of one another ($r = -.02$), Levinson F correlates .66 with Derived F and .41 with Derived Acquiescence. (In each case, $N = 57$.) These results correspond generally with estimates in the literature concerning the contribution of acquiescent response set to F-scale scores based on unidirectional items.

Construct Validity

The Personological Criterion

Experimental procedures in the psychiatric assessment of Peace Corps volunteers that were employed with the Ghana group are the basis for our personological criterion. Early in the training period, each volunteer was seen in two 50-minute appraisal interviews by psychiatrists from the Langley-Porter Neuropsychiatric Institute. Seven psychiatrists participated in the interviewing, each seeing 16 or 17 volunteers on a schedule that as far as possible varied the pairing of psychiatrists who interviewed the same volunteer and also the psychiatrists' participation in first and second interviews. Upon completion of each interview, the psychiatrist made various ratings with which we are not presently concerned. He also wrote a narrative summary of the interview. When typed, the summaries ranged from one to three pages of single-spaced narrative description.[5] Inspection of these summaries indicated that the psychiatrists' skills had been used more fully and appropriately here than in the case of the ratings, and that the summaries would thus provide rich material on the volunteers as they appeared to psychiatric interviewers before overseas service. Where the two summaries on a given volunteer diverged from one another, the reader often experienced a stereoscopic-like effect in which the person interviewed seemed to emerge three-dimensionally from the discrepant perspectives. Our problem was to convert the qualitative narratives into a form amenable to quantitative treatment.

The *Q*-sort method, employing the California *Q* set (Form III) (abbreviated CQ) as developed by Jack Block (1961), seemed ideally suited to the purpose. The CQ deck consists of 100 items printed on separate cards, to be sorted by judges in a fixed distribution according to the extent to which each item is saliently descriptive of a given person or saliently uncharacteristic of

5. I am indebted to Dr. M. Robert Harris for making these summaries available.

him. The items, developed by Block in the course of extensive research with diverse groups, in effect provide a theoretically neutral common language for the dynamic characterization of personality.

Three graduate students in psychology,[6] working independently of one another, read the pair of summaries for each trainee and then sorted the CQ set to characterize him. The correlations between the *Q* sorts of the three judges for a given volunteer provide an estimate of the reliability of these judgments. Across the three pairs of judges, the mean interjudge correlation (via Fisher's *z* transformation) was .61. The composite *Q* descriptions across the three judges provide our criterion data; by the Spearman-Brown formula, an average reliability coefficient of .82 corresponds to this level of interjudge correlation.

Derived F

From the group of 57 trainees, subgroups respectively high and low in authoritarianism were selected, in terms of the 19 highest (350–419) and 20 lowest (279–324) in the Derived F score. Mean composite ratings for the two subgroups on each of the 100 CQ items were then compared by *t* test. The results are summarized in Table 8.1. Correspondence with the formulations of *The Authoritarian Personality* is remarkable. In view of the fact that the psychiatrists' appraisal interviews were in no way focused on authoritarianism nor was the CQ set specially devised for its portrayal, such close correspondence speaks forcefully for the construct validity of Derived F as a measure of authoritarianism.

Levinson F

The same analytic approach was applied to high and low subgroups of 19 trainees each in terms of scores on the Levinson F test. Scores for the "highs" ranged from 75 to 114, for the "lows" from 30 to 55. Based on 24 rather than 80 items, its scores should be less reliable. We have also seen reason to believe that they are confounded by acquiescent response set. Table 8.2 shows the results of the analysis.

In view of the positive correlation between Levinson F and Derived F, one would expect a somewhat similar set of items to emerge as differentiating the subgroups. Inspection of Table 8.2 indicates that such is indeed the case: moralism, hypersensitiveness to criticism, and conservatism remain characteristic of the highs, and conventionality is added; the lows continue to be described as intelligent, unconventional, non-conforming, esthetically oriented, and as having a wide range of interests. But substantially fewer items differentiate significantly, and the portrait of the "authoritarian personality" is somewhat blurred in comparison with the one that arises from

6. I am indebted to Dan and Jeanne Peterman and to Naomi Litt Quenk for conscientious service as judges. They were otherwise unacquainted with the volunteers or with the hypotheses of the study.

Table 8.1. Comparison of Peace Corps volunteers who are high and low in Derived F, in terms of Q sort of summaries of psychiatric appraisal interviews.

Items for which the more authoritarian group had significantly higher means

Significant at .01 level:

9. Is uncomfortable with uncertainty and complexities.
25. Tends toward overcontrol of needs and impulses; binds tensions excessively; delays gratification unnecessarily.
41. Is moralistic. (N.B. Regardless of the particular nature of the moral code.)
76. Tends to project his own feelings and motivations onto others.

Significant at .05 level:

7. Favors conservative values in a variety of areas.
13. Is thin-skinned; sensitive to anything that can be construed as criticism or any interpersonal slight.
49. Is basically distrustful of people in general; questions their motivations.
86. Handles anxiety and conflicts by, in effect, refusing to recognize their presence; repressive or dissociative tendencies.

Significant at .10 level:

12. Tends to be self-defensive.
87. Interprets basically simple and clear-cut situations in complicated and particularizing ways.

Items for which the less authoritarian group had significantly higher means

Significant at .01 level:

62. Tends to be rebellious and nonconforming.
98. Is verbally fluent; can express ideas well.

Significant at .05 level:

3. Has a wide range of interests. (N.B. Superficiality or depth of interest is irrelevant here.)
53. Various needs tend toward relatively direct and uncontrolled expression; unable to delay gratification.
60. Has insight into own motives and behavior.
66. Enjoys esthetic impressions; is esthetically reactive.
83. Able to see to the heart of important problems.
96. Values own independence and autonomy.

Significant at .10 level:

8. Appears to have high degree of intellectual capacity. (N.B. Whether actualized or not. Originality is not necessarily assumed.)
16. Is introspective and concerned with self as an object. (N.B. Introspectiveness per se does not imply insight.)
28. Tends to arouse liking and acceptance in people.
51. Genuinely values intellectual and cognitive matters. (N.B. Ability or achievement are not implied here.)

the comparisons based on Derived F. Derived F is clearly the better measure in terms of construct validity.

Derived Acquiescence

It will be remembered that the Derived Acquiescence score was a byproduct of the method by which a purified measure of authoritarianism was extracted from the SSRC S-A schedule. Delineation of the characteristic features of extreme subgroups in terms of this variable has interest in its own right; it also helps to clarify the consequences of confounding authoritarianism and

Table 8.2. Comparison of Peace Corps volunteers who are high and low in Levinson F, in terms of Q sort of summaries of psychiatric appraisal interviews.

Items for which the more authoritarian group had significantly higher means

Significant at .05 level:

13. Is thin-skinned; sensitive to anything that can be construed as criticism or any interpersonal slight.
41. Is moralistic. (N.B. Regardless of the particular nature of the moral code.)
63. Judges self and others in conventional terms like "popularity," "the correct thing to do," social pressures, etc.

Significant at .10 level:

7. Favors conservative values in a variety of areas.
89. Compares self to others. Is alert to real or fancied differences between self and other people.

Items for which the less authoritarian group had significantly higher means

Significant at .01 level:

3. Has a wide range of interests. (N.B. Superficiality or depth of interest is irrelevant here.)
39. Thinks and associates to ideas in unusual ways; has unconventional thought processes.
66. Enjoys esthetic impressions; is esthetically reactive.

Significant at .05 level:

8. Appears to have high degree of intellectual capacity. (N.B. Whether actualized or not. Originality is not necessarily assumed.)
51. Genuinely values intellectual and cognitive matters. (N.B. Ability or achievement are not implied here.)
57. Is an interesting, arresting person.

Significant at .10 level:

20. Has a rapid personal tempo; behaves and acts quickly.
62. Tends to be rebellious and nonconforming.

acquiescence, as in Levinson F. Table 8.3 presents the items that discriminate between high and low subgroups of 19 trainees each. (Ranges of scores for high and low subgroups were 256–293 and 161–233, respectively.)

The items that distinguish the more acquiescent volunteers seem in general to be congruent with Couch and Keniston's (1960) picture of the "yeasayer" as tending toward impulsiveness and undercontrol; the three items that differentiate the less acquiescent subgroups at the .05 level correspond to characteristics of Couch and Keniston's "naysayers," although the suggestion of manipulativeness and distrust in this group seems new. Since overcontrol is at once part of the picture of high authoritarianism and of low acquiescence, the partial confounding of authoritarianism and acquiescence in measures based on unidirectionally worded instruments like the Levinson F scale can only obscure the view that such instruments afford of the personality correlates of authoritarianism.

Relationship to Overseas Criteria

We now turn to the question of predictive validity: was authoritarianism as measured in training related to the volunteers' performance as Peace Corps

Table 8.3. Comparison of Peace Corps volunteers who are high and low in derived acquiescence, in terms of Q sort of summaries of psychiatric appraisal interviews.

Items for which the more acquiescent group had significantly higher means

Significant at .01 level:

58. Enjoys sensuous experiences (including touch, taste, smell, physical contact).
67. Is self-indulgent.

Significant at .05 level:

18. Initiates humor.
53. Various needs tend toward relatively direct and uncontrolled expression; unable to delay gratification.
73. Tends to perceive many different contexts in sexual terms; eroticizes situations.
80. Interested in members of the opposite sex. (N.B. At opposite end, item implies absence of such interest.)

Significant at .10 level:

15. Is skilled in social techniques of imaginative play, pretending, and humor.
56. Responds to humor.

Items for which the less acquiescent group had significantly higher means

Significant at .05 level:

25. Tends toward overcontrol of needs and impulses; binds tensions excessively; delays gratification unnecessarily.
36. Is subtly negativistic; tends to undermine and obstruct or sabotage.
48. Keeps people at a distance; avoids close interpersonal relationships.

Significant at .10 level:

37. Is guileful and deceitful, manipulative, opportunistic.
49. Is basically distrustful of people in general; questions their motivations.
65. Characteristically pushes and tries to stretch limits; sees what he can get away with.

teachers in Ghana? The follow-up study provides a variety of criterion measures available for 49 volunteers (28 men and 21 women) for the first year of service, and for 44 volunteers (27 men and 17 women) for the second year. These somewhat smaller groups included the full range of scores on both measures of authoritarianism found in the larger group who were tested during training.

Overseas Criteria

The criterion measures fall into three categories: overall evaluative ratings, peer nominations, and scores factorially derived from the analysis of the transcribed interviews.

Overall evaluations. At the end of the volunteers' first year of duty, the Peace Corps representative in Ghana and his deputy representative completed a routine administrative rating form on each volunteer, which included a five-point scale of "overall evaluation." The first-year evaluation scores to be employed here combine the ratings by these two administrators with ratings made on the same scale by the two field interviewers, working jointly after the completion of their field work, but before examining the transcribed interview records. (See Smith, Fawcett, Ezekiel, and Roth, 1963, pp. 22–23.) These composite ratings are thus not fully independent of the interview data. With a possible "best" score of 15, the mean was 10.2 (*SD,* 2.6). At the end of the second and final year, only ratings by the Peace Corps representative on a similar five-point scale are available. On this version, one represented the most favorable rating, five the least favorable. For the entire group, the mean rating was 2.6 (*SD,* 0.9). These scores, appropriately reflected, correlated .79 with the combined first-year evaluations just described, and .71 with the first-year ratings made by the same judge.

Peer nominations. In the field interviews conducted near the end of the first year of service, each volunteer was asked to name several volunteers "who are doing a particularly good job." A simple tally of the number of mentions received by each volunteer provided an additional crude criterion (mean, 4.5; *SD,* 5.1). This index correlated .61 with first-year evaluation and .58 with second-year evaluation (when the sign of the latter is appropriately reversed). No peer nominations are available for the second year.

Interview Q-sort factor loadings. The primary source of data in the larger follow-up study was derived from *Q* sorts of the transcripts of the field interviews—amounting to some 200 double-spaced pages of typescript for each volunteer—made by 12 advanced graduate students in psychology who were otherwise unfamiliar with the volunteers and with the preconceptions of the investigator.[7] We are here concerned with *Q* sorts made on the basis of reading both years' interviews (giving precedence to status as of the final year in cases of evident change). These sorts were done with two specially prepared sets of items that had passed through several revisions: a deck of 65 items pertaining to the volunteer's role perceptions, personal agenda, and role performance; and a deck of 64 items characterizing the volunteer's personality structure and processes while overseas, as displayed through the job-focussed interview.[8] Depending on the degree of interjudge agreement achieved by the first pair of raters to *Q* sort a case, from two to six judges contributed to each of the composite *Q*-sort ratings that underlie the criterion measures with which we are presently concerned. On the basis of the average interjudge correlations for each case (computed via Fisher's z transformation and corrected by the Spearman-Brown formula according to the number of judges contributing to a given composite), the role performance *Q* set was judged with a mean reliability of .76, the personality set with a mean reliability of .68.

We were interested in employing the composite ratings on the two *Q* sets

7. The details of this procedure are described in Ezekiel (1968). A summary of the analytic procedures employed and of the Q-oriented factors obtained from the factor analysis of the interperson correlations is also given by Ezekiel. A full exposition will be provided in the volume being prepared on the larger study.

8. A third Q set was also employed to characterize the volunteer's view of his situation, its challenges and limitations, frustrations and satisfactions. Ratings obtained on it were not technically suitable for the kind of factor analysis that was done with the other Q sets and are not relevant to the present problem.

to identify distinguishable major patterns of personal orientation and performance in Peace Corps service. To this end, we computed the matrix of interperson correlations for each of the two sets and carried out a *Q*-oriented principal components factor analysis on each matrix. Inspection of the items receiving high and low factor scores on the first principal components in the two analyses indicated the highly evaluative character of each. On the basis of the distinctive item content, we labelled the first component in the analysis based on the personality *Q* set "Self-confident maturity," and the first component in the role performance analysis "Competent teaching in Africa." The loadings received by individual volunteers on these factors provide additional evaluative criteria, which are essentially uncorrelated with peer nominations and only modestly related to the overall evaluations. Loadings on the first personality factor correlate .31 with the first-year evaluation, .35 with second-year evaluation (both significant at $p < .05$); whereas loadings on the first role performance factor correlate .17 and .26, respectively, with first- and second-year evaluations. Individual loadings on the two P-1 factors are closely correlated with one another ($r = .89$).

The role performance factors V-1 to V-3 and personality factors V-1 to V-6 in Table 8.5 were obtained through varimax rotation. As defined by the content of the *Q*-sort items with high and low factor scores on each, these represent coherent patterns in terms of which volunteers resembled or differed from one another in their approach to the Peace Corps role and in their personal functioning as inferred from the field interviews. By way of illustration, Table 8.4 presents for inspection the items that have distinctively high and low factor scores on role performance factor V-1, "Constructive involvement with Africa." Similar illustrations of factors derived from the personality *Q* set may be found in Tables 8.6 and 8.7.

Again, each volunteer's loading on a given factor was used as a score to index his resemblance to that particular factor pattern. These factor loading scores could then be employed in R-oriented analyses correlating the patterns with other variables, among them our scores on authoritarianism.

The Relationship Between Authoritarianism and Overseas Criteria

The data bearing on the predictive validity of the two measures of authoritarianism are given in Table 8.5. Correlations with first- and second-year evaluations, with peer nominations, and with the evaluative P-1 factors derived from the field interviews all approximate zero. The initial exepectation that low authoritarianism, however measured, should be predictive of good performance in the Peace Corps is clearly refuted for this group of teachers in Ghana.

The argument might be advanced, however—and the data of the larger study give it strong support—that global indices of effective performance merge psychologically divergent ways of doing a better or poorer job in the Peace Corps into a single resultant score. Perhaps if these disparate routes

Table 8.4. Interview Q-sort items defining performance factor V-1, "Constructive Involvement With Africa."

Item No.	*Items With High Factor Scores*	Score
56.	His African experiences have increased his concern with race relations in the U.S.	67.6
10.	Generally likes his students, treats them with warmth and understanding.	64.7
38.	Has established intimate, continuing relationships with adult Africans.	63.7
34.	Enjoys or admires Ghanaian style of living.	63.5
24.	In his appraisal of Ghanaian life and institutions, is sympathetically critical; forms his own judgments with due regard to historical and cultural differences.	63.2
45.	Is on friendly terms with many Ghanaians (apart from students). (N.B. Disregard depth of the relationship.)	63.0
19.	Has developed close, personal relationships with some of his students.	61.4
22.	Committed to carrying out his job as Peace Corps teacher to the best of his ability.	61.3
32.	In anticipating his return he is concerned with interpreting Ghana and/or West Africa to Americans.	61.1
9.	Judges Ghanaian governmental policies and actions in terms of the needs of Ghana. (Regardless of approval or disapproval.)	60.9
63.	Views his teaching in terms of its contribution to the personal welfare or development of his students.	60.5
16.	Views his teaching in terms of its contribution to the development of Ghana.	60.4
25.	As a result of his experience in Ghana his thoughts and feelings about America show increased depth and perspective.	60.1
	Items With Low Factor Scores	
15.	Has little real interest in Ghana.	25.0
54.	Feels mostly negative about Ghanaians he has met, really doesn't like them very much.	28.0
51.	Reacts to his students as a category or as types, rather than as individuals. (N.B. Regardless of degree of warmth or liking.)	31.0
6.	Shows lack of tact in relations with students.	32.4
13.	Tends to be condescending toward his students.	34.0
21.	His whole life has centered on the school compound.	34.2
18.	His personal problems of finding himself take priority for him over the tasks of the Peace Corps assignment.	35.0
43.	Tends to identify with the authoritarian and punitive aspects of the Ghanaian educational system.	35.3
37.	Gets exasperated by [some Ghanaian characteristics].	37.4
11.	Incompetent in his understanding of the major subject matter that he has to teach.	39.1

to favorably or unfavorably evaluated performance might be disentangled, relationships to predictor variables might emerge that are obscured in the case of overall evaluations. The varimax factor patterns derived from the interview *Q* sorts allow us to examine this possibility.

Consider first, in Table 8.5, the correlations of authoritarianism with the varimax factor loadings based on the *Q* set for role performance. Factor V-1 identifies a pattern that mainly concerns the quality of the volunteer's intercultural and interpersonal relations with his students and with other Ghanaians. The distinguishing items are given in Table 8.4. It is particularly in this aspect of the Peace Corps role that theory might lead one to expect differences between volunteers who differ in their scores on authoritarianism. Though the correlation with Derived F is in the right direction whereas that

Table 8.5. Correlations of measures of authoritarianism with indices of performance and personality functioning overseas, among Peace Corps teachers in Ghana. (N = *44 except for first-year evaluation and peer nominations, for which* N = *49.)*

Index	*Derived F*	*Levinson F*
First-year evaluation	.01	—.08
Second-year evaluation[a]	—.08	—.18
Peer nominations (first year only)	—.03	—.23
Factor-loading scores derived from Q sorts of field interviews:		
Role performance:		
P–1 "Competent teaching in Africa"	—.10	.13
V–1 "Constructive involvement with Africa"	—.16	.14
V–2 "Exclusive teaching commitment"	.20	.03
V–3 "Limited commitment"	.06	.08
Personality:		
P–1 "Self-confident maturity"	—.07	.08
V–1 "Interpersonally sensitive maturity"	.06	.14
V–2 "Intellectualizing future orientation"	—.38**	—.15
V–3 "Self-reliant conventionality"	.23	.22
V–4 "Dependent anxiety"	.14	.05
V–5 "Controlling responsibility"	.03	.05
V–6 "Self-actualizing search for identity"	—.26*	—.33**

[a]The sign of the correlation has been reversed so that a positive correlation would mean that high scores on authoritarianism are accompanied by favorable ratings.

*$p < .10$

**$p < .05$

with Levinson F is not, the relationship remains negligible. The content of the two remaining role performance factors has no obvious relationship to authoritarianism, so the insignificant correlations into which they enter are less surprising.

Correlations with the factor patterns that emerged from the *Q* set descriptive of personality functioning overseas present a somewhat different picture. Again we find that the measures of authoritarianism are quite unrelated to the pattern (V-1) that highlights interpersonal openness, tolerance, and sensitivity (loadings on this factor correlate .74 with loadings on factor V-1 from the role-performance set). There is a suggestion of a relationship, though at a level short of statistical significance, with factor V-3, "Self-reliant conventionality." The prominence of conventionality among the items characterizing this pattern might lead one to expect such a relationship, but equally prominent ingredients of matter-of-fact, self-confident, solid dependability are not parts of the theoretical portrait of the authoritarian. Negative correlations that reach statistically acceptable levels for at least one of the measures appear, however, for factors V-2, "Intellectualizing future-orientation," and V-6, "Self-actualizing search for identity." The items that define these factors are given in Tables 8.6 and 8.7.

In terms of their distinctive item content, both of these patterns involve a

Table 8.6. Interview Q-sort items defining personality factor V-2, "Intellectualizing Future Orientation."

Item No.	*Items With High Factor Scores*	Score
39.	Characteristically maintains a highly articulate intellectual formulation of his situation and problems.	73.9
58.	Can communicate freely about self.	70.8
22.	Has long-term goals.	69.0
12.	The two-year limit on his commitment has been salient for him in helping him accept and adapt to his situation.	67.1
6.	Has a complex, well-differentiated picture of his own future.	66.5
24.	Envisions a challenging and demanding personal future.	66.3
10.	Is actively striving toward a clearer, more complex or mature sense of identity.	65.7
50.	Feels his own life is important, that it matters what he does with his life.	64.6
4.	Can assert himself in a forceful manner when he feels he should.	64.6
57.	Generally self-confident.	62.8
45.	Is emotionally labile, given to highs and lows.	61.4
	Items With Low Factor Scores	
42.	Intense, tends to involve self deeply.	25.5
54.	Tends to expect little of life, pessimistic.	27.9
32.	Feels a lack of worth; has low self-esteem.	33.0
38.	Nurturant; enjoys helping the younger or less adequate.	33.1
43.	Unsure just who he is or who he ought to be or how he fits into the world.	35.8
30.	Characterized by zeal and enthusiasm.	37.1
16.	Would be unable to accept help from others when in need.	39.1

somewhat self-preoccupied, future-oriented outlook; they appear to characterize a person who is in good communication with himself and finds the topic interesting, one for whom the search for identity is still a prominent part of the agenda of young adulthood. All of this agrees nicely with theoretical expectations about persons low in F. Otherwise the patterns are divergent. Volunteers with high loadings on V-2 seem in general to have the upper hand in the identity struggle: they are forceful and self-confident and know very well where they are going. The articulately intellectualized stance that is particularly characteristic of this pattern is accompanied by a lack of intensity or enthusiasm. In contrast, the volunteers who correspond most closely to the V-6 pattern seem to be in the midst of a post-adolescent turmoil that is centered on problems of identity. They are intense, unconventional and impulsive, a bit confused and chaotic, not at all sure of themselves or of what the future may offer. But they are working on the problem hard and constructively, if somewhat erratically: self-cultivation and improvement stand high on their personal agenda.

As the data in Table 8.5 indicate, our measures of authoritarianism correlate only modestly even with these patterns. In spite of reasons to prefer Derived F to Levinson F, the former measure does not enter into strikingly higher correlations. To round out the picture, we may ask what is the bearing of the patterns described by factors V-2 and V-6 on evaluated performance

Table 8.7. Interview Q-sort items defining personality factor V-6, "Self-Actualizing Search for Identity."

Item No.	*Items With High Factor Scores*	Score
50.	Feels his own life is important, that it matters what he does with his life.	72.8
3.	Devotes much of his energy to a deliberate program of self-improvement (creative activity, study, etc.)	72.5
42.	Intense, tends to involve self deeply.	72.3
9.	Is aware of his own feelings and motives.	67.5
23.	The values and principles which he holds directly affect what he does.	65.5
11.	Copes with the novelty of the Ghanaian experience by seeking relationships, activities, and settings that let him continue important personal interests.	63.8
43.	Unsure just who he is or what he ought to be or how he fits into the world.	63.1
25.	Impulsive; undercontrolled. (N.B. Opposite implies overcontrolled.)	60.5
10.	Is actively striving toward a clearer, more complex or mature sense of identity.	60.1
	Items With Low Factor Scores	
8.	Basically a dependent person; characteristically leans upon others for support.	28.7
40.	In times of stress, would characteristically tell himself that the troubles will soon blow over.	28.7
59.	Accepts difficulties as inherent in the situation, is not bothered by them.	28.8
61.	Conventional in thought and actions.	29.7
51.	When the going is rough, would tend to take a long-run view.	33.5
53.	When things go badly, would tend to stand back and look at the situation objectively.	35.1
6.	Has a complex, well-differentiated picture of his own future.	35.3
18.	A major component of his stance has been his assumption that one meets one's daily obligations as a matter of course.	37.6
31.	When discouraged, would tend to talk over his problems with somebody else.	39.4
64.	Tends to be preoccupied with matters of physical health.	39.6

in the Peace Corps. The answer is clear: very little. As compared with V-1, which accounts for 26.5 per cent of the common factor variance, V-2 accounts for only 12.7 per cent, V-6 for 6.5 per cent. And loadings on the factors have little to do with evaluations of performance.

	First-year evaluation	*Second-year evaluation*	*Peer nominations*	*P–1 (Role perf.)*	*P–1 (Personality)*
Correlations with V–2	.01	.09	–.04	.48	.57
Correlations with V–6	–.10	.08	.04	–.15	–.11

V-2 does correlate significantly ($p < .01$) with the evaluative first principal component factors from both *Q* sets, but this relationship, rather suspect because it is rooted in the same interview data as rated by the same judges, is not supported by results for the other criteria. Otherwise, the results are null.

Results of analyses of the interview *Q* sorts at the item level may be noted briefly for the sake of completeness. When the *Q*-sort ratings received by subgroups of volunteers who scored high or low in Derived F ($N = 16$ and

15, respectively) are compared by t test, only a chance proportion of items emerges as differentiating significantly at the .05 level or better. In general, such differences as do appear fall in the expected direction:

Items for which the more authoritarian group had significantly higher higher means:

Role Performance Deck

(none)

Personality Deck

31. When discouraged, would tend to talk over his problems with someone else. ($p < .05$)
61. Conventional in thought and actions. ($p < .01$)

Items for which the less authoritarian group had significantly higher means:

Role Performance Deck

64. Has an intelligent grasp of the problems of political and economic development in Ghana. ($p < .05$)

Personality Deck

3. Devotes much of his energy to a deliberate program of self-improvement (creative activity, study, etc.) ($p < .05$)
39. Characteristically maintains a highly articulate intellectual formulation of his situation and problems. ($p < .01$)

What, then, are we to say about the predictive validity of our measures of F in this Peace Corps setting? Do the modest correlations with the V-2 and V-6 personality patterns require us to qualify the negative answer given by all other criteria? Hardly. In the first place, the relationship was not *predicted,* even though it seems reasonable enough after the fact. More important, although scores on these patterns were obtained at a later time, in a different setting, by a very different method from those characterizing our measures of authoritarianism, the correlations seem to be interpretable more legitimately as extensions of our data on the *construct* validity of the measures than as evidence for their predictive validity. Like the pencil-and-paper instruments for measuring F and the congruent evidence from the psychiatrists' appraisal interviews, the content of the V-2 and V-6 patterns pertains especially to how the volunteers conceive and feel about their selves and worlds. It tells us much less about what they characteristically *do,* about the kinds of relationships that they establish. In this connection, the failure of the F measures to predict standing on the V-1 personality and performance patterns involving open, nurturant, tolerant, and empathic relationships and low ethnocentrism must be taken seriously. The evidence before us would seem to support the view of Derived F, and to a lesser degree Levinson F, as good measures of a coherent mode of presentation of self *to* self and others, the bearing of which on consequential interpersonal relations and behavior remains to be shown.

Discussion

With the data in hand that refute our initial expectation about the bearing of authoritarianism on the performance of Peace Corps teachers, we must ask if our predictions put the claims for authoritarianism to a fair test. By hindsight, there are several considerations that require us to qualify our conclusions. On the one hand, these pertain to possible effects of self-selection, and on the other, to unanticipated features of the situation of secondary school teachers in Ghana.

One possibility that comes immediately to mind is that the Peace Corps sample, after all, is a very special group, self-selected in ways that might well reduce the correlations obtained between measures of authoritarianism and other variables. There are two issues here. The narrower one concerns the effects of a restricted range in authoritarianism scores, as such. Although the central tendency of the group was toward low F scores, substantial variability remained, enough to permit the clear relationship that we have seen to emerge with the *Q*-sort judgments of the psychiatrists' summaries. Sheer restriction of range seems inadequate to account for the consistently negative predictive results.[9] But other consequences of self-selection for Peace Corps duty in Africa cannot be discounted so readily.

If one assumes, for the moment, that the conception of F developed in *The Authoritarian Personality* is entirely valid, the high-scoring young people who volunteered to spend two years in a foreign land teaching young Africans under the auspices of an as yet unknown Peace Corps must have been quite atypical of young people in the population at large who would earn similar scores. The prominent special features of the prospective Peace Corps assignment may well have led to self-selection that reduced the normally to be expected correlation between authoritarianism scores and ethnocentrism or prejudice, while leaving intact some of the other personological ingredients of the syndrome. That something of the sort may indeed have happened can be given at least anecdotal support. One of the higher-scoring women in the group, whose outlook on self and world impressed the field interviewer as a close replica of the authoritarian personality, was notable for her genuine friendship with an American Negro and an East Indian. The residue of authoritarians who volunteered for Ghana may largely exclude those who would have manifested the expected interpersonal and intercultural handicap.

Acquaintance with the actual situation of secondary school teachers in Ghana, acquired in the course of the field work of the study, also throws light on a degree of naïveté in the initial expectation of a direct relationship

9. However, the central tendency toward low authoritarianism has the result that our t-tests compared very low scorers with medium scorers. The tendencies of the extreme "lows" toward impulsiveness or undercontrol may have counterbalanced the advantages that accrued from their low-authoritarian virtues.

between authoritarianism and Peace Corps performance. In the lives of volunteers overseas, the teaching job loomed much larger and intercultural relations rather less prominently than the investigator had anticipated. Most of the volunteers lived on the compounds of modern residential schools. Often the school compound became a small, engrossing world, one heavily committed to modern Western ways, from which the teacher might make forays into the surrounding environment of traditional and modern Africa, but at his own pace and only when he could get free from demanding job commitments that were likely to tie him closely to the compound. Under these circumstances, and contrary to expectation, the phenomena of "culture shock" as described by anthropologists were not prominent among the volunteers. In this respect, the qualities supposedly measured by tests of authoritarianism were clearly less relevant to successful adjustment than they had seemed initially.

As for the teaching job itself, here too the criterion situation presented some surprises. The Ghanaian secondary school is patterned on British models, with differences arising from the cultural novelty and high status of formal education. The authority of the headmaster approaches the absolute; the status distance between master and pupil is great and is marked by many symbols of formal respect. The expectations of students are heavily geared toward didactic presentations, toward "notes" that are dictated and memorized. Classroom discipline is rarely a problem; other infractions are customarily dealt with through an elaborate system of penalties that may include corporal punishment. All told, the Ghanaian school atmosphere is probably much more authoritarian than any experienced by the volunteers in the course of an American education. How such a setting affects the relevance of the teacher's own authoritarian dispositions is not clear, but the problem of prediction is obviously more complex than the investigator had assumed.

A final word is in order lest these findings for Peace Corps teachers be generalized unduly. More than half the volunteers in the Peace Corps are assigned to teaching jobs, like *S*s in the present study. Even for these, there is a question of generalization. For 41 volunteers teaching in Nigeria, Mischel (1965) reports a correlation of $-.45$ ($p < .01$) between scores on the identical 24-item Levinson F scale and criterion ratings. There is reason to believe that the situation of volunteers in Nigeria closely resembled that of volunteers in Ghana. Other kinds of projects, particularly those concerned with community development, surely make substantially different psychological demands. Traits such as flexibility and tolerance of ambiguity, part of the portrait of persons who score low in authoritarianism, would seem to be essential for a volunteer who is left to define and discover a job for himself and must put up with long periods of apparent uselessness. The definiteness and predictability of a teacher's core obligations in the classroom may have served to blur the relevance of our measures to performance in Ghana.

The study of Peace Corps teachers in Ghana leaves us, then, with encouraging evidence for the construct validity of Derived F as a measure of authoritarianism. As for predictive validity in this particular setting, our evidence is negative. But the closer look at the criterion situation to which these results have led us questions the fairness of our predictive test. Pending the availability of appropriate comparative evidence from other performance settings, we must ourselves tolerate ambiguity for a while longer.

Summary

Two measures of "authoritarianism" were given to 58 Peace Corps volunteers in training. High scorers differed from low scorers essentially as theory would predict on ratings based on psychiatric appraisal interviews. For 44 volunteers completing two years' teaching in Ghana, scores on authoritarianism were correlated with overall evaluative ratings, peer nominations, and scores on factor patterns derived from *Q* sorts of long transcribed interviews conducted near the end of the first and second years of duty. Authoritarianism was unrelated to evaluations, to peer nominations, and to factorial patterns describing role performance. It was modestly correlated in a negative direction with scores on two personality factor patterns: "Intellectualizing future orientation" and "Self-actualizing search for identity." The lack of relation to performance criteria is discussed.

The Self, "Mental Health," and Competence

9

The Phenomenological Approach in Personality Theory

Some Critical Remarks

The "phenomenological approach" has recently come to be something of a rallying cry to a number of psychologists who share the "tender-minded" bias that psychology must, after all, come to terms with human experience, and who go so far as to believe that careful attention to this experience will leave the science of psychology not merely more satisfying to like-minded people, but also better science. Sharing this point of view and agreeing heartily with the program recommended by MacLeod (1947) in his article on "The Phenomenological Approach in Social Psychology," the present writer has been dismayed by some recent publications which, it seems to him, misconstrue the appropriate role of a phenomenological approach in a way that invites the critical to reject a humanized psychology lock, stock, and barrel. Sine the writer would regard such an outcome as highly unfortunate, he feels that a clarification of the issues is badly needed, and herewith makes an attempt in this direction.

The position with which he would take particular issue is that of Snygg and Combs (1949; also Combs, 1949) whose point of view has also been espoused by Rogers (1947). These authors contrast the objective or external frame of reference in psychology with the phenomenological, or internal frame of reference, and, declaring their stand firmly with phenomenology, proceed to muster on their side the names of Lewin, Lecky, Allport, Murphy, and Angyal, among others, even including the seemingly less tractable father-figure of Freud. In essence, their contention is that the locus of psychological causation lies entirely within the phenomenal field of conscious experience, and that it therefore behooves the psychological theorist—and therapist—to formulate his problems and concepts accordingly. Snygg and Combs give much attention to the individual's perceptual-cognitive field,

Reprinted by permission from *Journal of Abnormal and Social Psychology,* 1950, *45,* 516–522.

particularly to the *self,* as its most salient feature. Written from this standpoint, psychology comes close to a rapprochement with common sense.

While applauding their emphasis on perception and the self, the present writer proposes that they are confusing phenomenology with what may be termed the subjective frame of reference. Sharply maintained, this distinction further helps to clarify certain persistent ambiguities in the theory of ego and self.

Phenomenology and Common Sense

One of the genuine merits of the phenomenological approach is that it brings psychology somewhat closer to the world of common sense. There is always the danger that psychology, in its concern for rigor and neatness, may divorce itself too completely from this source of problems and partial insights. Focussing scientific attention on the phenomenal world as it is presented to us, the world from which common sense also takes its start, the phenomenological approach can bring into the ken of the psychologist data and problems too often left to common sense by default. Like common sense, and unlike some current varieties of psychological theory, it does deal with experience, and thus presents itself as an attractive alternative to those who find a behavioristic psychology uncongenial.

But phenomenology is not common sense, nor can it rightly be called upon to justify a common sense psychology. In MacLeod's phrase, the phenomenological approach "involves the adoption of what might be called an attitude of disciplined naïveté" (1947, p. 194). In many respects, its result may run exactly counter to common sense conclusions. Common sense, with its preconceived categories and stock explanations, neither disciplined nor naïve, is full of pseudo-scientific theory, while phenomenology limits its concern to the unprejudiced *description* of the world of phenomena. To take the phenomenal world presented in conscious experience as completely explanatory of behavior is closer to common sense than to phenomenology or adequate science.

Yet this is essentially what Snygg and Combs have done in their attempt to rewrite psychology in a "phenomenological frame of reference." "*All behavior, without exception,*" they say, "*is completely determined by and pertinent to the phenomenal field of the behaving organism*" (1949, p. 15, italics theirs). And they go on to explain that

> by the phenomenal field, we mean the entire universe, including himself, as it is experienced by the individual at the instant of action . . . Unlike the "objective" physical field, the phenomenal field is not an abstraction or an artificial construction. It is simply the universe of naïve experience in which each individual lives, the everyday situation of self and surroundings which each person takes to be reality. [p. 15]

While they bow unnecessarily to current prejudice in avoiding the word *consciousness*, their meaning is clear, and their index spells it out: "Consciousness, *see* Phenomenal field."

It is one variant of common sense that consciousness completely explains behavior, but at this juncture, it is hard to see how such a view can be regarded as an acceptable scientific postulate. Quite apart from the metaphysical controversy about the status of consciousness as "real" or respectable, we have behind us Würzburg and we have behind us Freud, to mention but two major sources of evidence that a psychology of experience or consciousness has distinct explanatory limits. Where is the determining tendency represented in the phenomenal field? What of the inacceptable strivings that warp our behavior, what of our defensive techniques of adjustment that so often prove most effective precisely when we are least aware of them? It is no satisfactory solution to speak, as Snygg and Combs do, of a "unified field of figure-ground phenomena of which the individual is more or less conscious . . . [in which] the vague and fuzzy aspects of behavior correspond to and are parts of the vague and incompletely differentiated aspects of the field" (p. 17). The clinical literature abounds with instances of unconsciously determined behavior which, far from being "vague and fuzzy," is on the contrary highly differentiated.

One suspects that such a psychology of consciousness has an element of common-sense appeal not unlike the attraction of allied forms of psychotherapy. It does make sense to the layman: it accords with what he is ready and able to recognize in himself. And it has distinct value within limits that it refuses to recognize. Because it over-states its claims, however, it may tend to promote the state of affairs away from which we have been striving—every man his own psychologist.

But MacLeod (1947, p. 207) has already made the relevant point succinctly: "The phenomenological method, in social psychology as in the psychology of perception [and we would add, psychology generally] can never be more than an approach to a scientific inquiry." It provides certain kinds of data, not *all* the data. It furnishes the basis for certain valuable theoretical constructs; it does not give birth to them in full concreteness. It sets some problems and provides some clues; the psychologist, theorist or clinician, must *infer* the answers.

Subjective Constructs and the Observer's Frame of Reference

Here we reach the crux of the matter. If a psychology of consciousness is necessarily incomplete yet we do not abandon our hope for a psychology that comes to terms with human experience, what is the solution? A discussion of two lesser questions may indicate the nature of the answer. In the first place, does the decision to frame our psychological concepts and theories in terms appropriate to the "private world" of the behaving person commit us to the exclusive use of phenomenal concepts? Secondly, what is the appropriate role of the phenomenological approach in the service of this kind of theory-building?

Lewin, whose psychological life space Snygg and Combs (1949, p. 15) equate to their phenomenal field, was entirely clear in maintaining a sharp distinction between the two concepts. He said:

> It is likewise doubtful whether one can use consciousness as the sole criterion of what belongs to the psychological life space at a given moment in regard to social facts and relationships. The mother, the father, the brothers and sisters are not to be included as real facts in the psychological situation of the child only when they are immediately present. For example, the little child playing in the garden behaves differently when he knows his mother is at home than when he knows she is out. One cannot assume that this fact is continually in the child's consciousness. Also a prohibition or a goal can play an essential role in the psychological situation without being clearly present in consciousness. . . . Here, as in many other cases it is clear that one must distinguish between "appearance" and the "underlying reality" in a dynamic sense. In other words, the phenomenal properties are to be distinguished from the conditional-genetic characteristics of objects and events, that is, from the properties which determine their causal relationships. . . . As far as the conceptual derivation is concerned, one may use effectiveness as the criterion for existence: "*What is real is what has effects.*" [Lewin, 1936, p. 19]

Lewin's life space, then, is *not* merely the phenomenal field. And he adds to our previous considerations cogent reasons for thinking that a psychology of the phenomenal field cannot be adequately explanatory. His life space is not immediately given in the concreteness of experience; it is an abstract, hypothetical construct, inferred by the psychologist-observer to account for the individual's behavior.

It is, however, a construct of a type that differs from constructs of behavioristic psychology. It is formulated in terms of what is behaviorally real to the acting individual, not primarily in terms of what is physically observable to the scientist. Hence it is legitimate to speak of theories like Lewin's as anchored in a *subjective* (not phenomenological) *frame of reference.* Lewin's concepts and many of Freud's are in this sense *subjective constructs*, not because they are built of the stuff of conscious experience, but because they attempt to deal with what is effectively real to the individual, even when it is real to the scientific observer only in this secondary, indirect way.

The subjective frame of reference in theory construction is to be contrasted with the *objective frame of reference*, wherein concepts are chosen so as to be rooted as closely as possible in effective realities shared by any qualified observer. This is the distinction that Snygg and Combs seek, which makes them see both Freud and Lewin as precursors. There is no absolute difference between the two frames of reference; it is rather a question of which criteria are weighted most strongly in the selection of constructs.

Both the subjective and objective frames of reference pertain to the choice of constructs and the theoretical context in which they are embedded. They in no sense conflict with what has been called the *observer's frame of reference*, which, indeed, lies at the foundation of all science. The problem of establishing a bridge between the point of view of the observer and *either* subjective or objective inferential constructs is the familiar one of operational definition. It cannot, in the last analysis, be avoided unless one chooses the alternative of claiming *direct* access to the point of view of the observed. This is the position of intuitionism, which asserts that the observer's and subject's points of view can be merged. But is this science? Not in the sense of a systematic search for understanding that can withstand the equally systematic doubt of the man from Missouri.

Subjective constructs framed in terms of the "private world" of the behaving individual remain constructs, and as such must ultimately be rooted in data accessible to the observer's frame of reference. There is no reason at all why their source should be restricted to the data of communicated conscious experience, in answer to our first question. But the phenomenological approach, or, more generally, any means of access to the experience of the subject, is of course crucial to the formulation of subjective constructs and the investigation of their relationships. Perhaps the point has been labored, but it is an essential one: the phenomenological approach, the clinical interview, the projective protocol, the behavioral observation—none of these yield direct knowledge of psychological constructs, subjective or objective, while all of them can provide the basis for inferring explanatory constructs and their relationships. If the canons of inference can be made sufficiently explicit, they provide the operational definitions that secure the constructs in the scientific home base of the observer's frame of reference.

Methods that get the subject to reveal his private world as he sees it need to be supplemented by others which permit the observer to infer effective factors that are distorted or disguised in the subject's awareness. But the broadly phenomenological methods remain a signally important source of data. Certain important subjective constructs such as the *self*, moreover, are anchored fairly directly in the data of phenomenological report.

Ego, Self, and Phenomenology

Although there is still considerable confusion in usage, a degree of consensus seems to be emerging to employ the term *self* for the phenomenal content of the experience of personal identity. A salient feature of the phenomenal field that has figured largely in personality theory, the self in this sense has the conceptual properties of a phenomenal object. G. Murphy (1947) and Chein

(1944) use it with this meaning. Snygg and Combs agree, writing with somewhat franker circularity:

> Of particular importance in the motivation of behavior will be those parts of the phenomenal field perceived by him to be part or characteristic of himself. To refer to this important aspect of the total field we have used the term *phenomenal self*. [1949, p. 111]

Within the phenomenal self, they distinguish as a stable core the *self-concept*: "Those parts of the phenomenal field which the individual had differentiated as definite and fairly stable characteristics of himself" (p. 112).

Sharing with Murphy a strong emphasis on responses to the self as fundamental to motivational theory, Snygg and Combs go so far as to state that the basic human need is "the preservation and enhancement of the phenomenal self" (p. 58). Changes in the perception of the self play a major role in the theory of the therapeutic process that they share with Rogers (1947).

Let us look more closely, however, at how these writers actually use the term. Passages like the following can readily be found:

> . . . when the self is free from any threat of attack or likelihood of attack, then it is possible for the self to consider these hitherto rejected perceptions, to make new differentiations, and to reintegrate the self in such a way as to include them. [Rogers, 1947, p. 365]

> A self threatened by its perceptions, may deny the perception by simply refusing to enter the situation where such a perception is forced upon him. [Snygg and Combs, 1949, p. 148]

Can a phenomenal self consider perceptions and reintegrate itself; can a threatened phenomenal self deny perceptions; or is this rather double-talk resulting from the attempt to make one good concept do the work of two? If, as this writer suspects, the latter is the case, what is the nature of the hidden second concept, which evidently is not merely a percept or phenomenal entity? To give it a name he would suggest the conventional term *ego*, realizing that usage in this respect is even more ambiguous than with the term *self*. The important point is that the concept, implicit in the writings of Rogers and of Snygg and Combs, is a subjective construct but does not refer to a phenomenal entity, whereas the self, on the other hand, is a coordinate subjective construct that does. The relation between the two will bear closer examination.

It is not necessary, at this juncture, to propose a definitive theory of the ego, nor to enter into an involved discussion of alternative views about its nature. What is relevant is that starting from an attempt to write a psychology in phenomenal terms, our authors in spite of themselves give implicit recognition to organizing, selective processes in the personality which are somehow guided by the nature and status of the self (among other things) and somehow, in turn, have an influence in its nature and status. So conceived, the relation of ego and self is highly interdependent[1] but by no means an identity. The distinction is that between a dynamic configuration of on-going processes, inferred from many facts of biography and behavior, and a phenomenal entity resulting from these processes and affecting them in turn, inferred primarily (but not exclusively) from phenomenological report.

Approaching the problem on a slightly different tack, we may find it rewarding to consider three of the eight conceptions of the ego listed by G. W. Allport (1943, p. 459) in the light of the distinction just made: the ego "as one segregated behavioral system among others," "as knower," and "as object of knowledge." The fundamental conception advanced here is not unlike the first of these senses, if one reads into it a dynamic quality not expressed in Allport's formulation. As an on-going system of organizing and selective processes mediating the individual's intercourse with reality, it includes a variety of processes without being coterminous with the total personality.[2] Among these processes or functions is that of the ego as "knower," which the writer would take in a less metaphysical sense than Allport's to embrace the cognitive-perceptual functions of personality. These have been described with reason in psychoanalytic theory (Freud, S., 1933, pp. 105–106) as an integral aspect of the ego system. Among the phenomena that the ego "knows" is the *self*, Allport's "ego as object of knowledge." Like any cognitive-perceptual object, the self only imperfectly mirrors the physical, psychological, and social facts that underlie the perception. And also like similar phenomenal objects it serves as a guide to appropriate behavior. But the relation of self to ego-processes is no more and no less obscure than the relation of cognitive structures to behavior generally.

"Ego-Involvements" and "Ego-Defense"

We have sought to reinstate the ego as a subjective but non-phenomenal construct mainly through an examination of the pitfalls encountered by the attempt to avoid such a concept. If the ego-self distinction as outlined above is worth making, however, it should make a difference in the formulation of other knotty problems. Does it? Two such problems—the nature of "ego-involvements" and of the "mechanisms of defense" will be examined briefly as test cases.

As it emerges in the work of M. Sherif and Cantril (1947), the concept of ego-involvement lacks clarity and focus. Widely divergent sorts of psy-

1. The writer doubts that it is advisable to construct the ego as narrowly around the self as do Chein (1944) and G. Murphy (1947).

2. How to distinguish within the personality between *ego* and *non-ego* is, of course, an important problem, though it will not be attempted here. The distinction, however, is not the same as the phenomenal one between the *self* and *not-self* (often described, confusingly, as *ego-alien*).

chological facts turn out to be embraced by the term, which like so many in popular psychological currency rather identifies a disparate group of problems than clarifies them. More often than not, ego-involvement means the involvement of a person's pride and self-esteem in a task; he feels put to the test and ready to be ashamed of a poor performance. In other instances, the term is invoked to cover immersion in a cause, or falling in love—cases in which the person, to be sure, cares as deeply about outcomes as in the first type, but may be engrossed to the point of losing self-awareness.

Now the present self-ego distinction makes excellent sense when applied here. Since the distinctive character of the first sort of examples lies in the fact that the individual's conception of his self and its worth is at stake, these can aptly be described as *self-involvement*. The second type of case can often still be called ego-involvement without inconsistency. The situation in the latter instances touches on the person's central system of on-going psychological processes so closely that he may lose himself in it. Similar engrossment can, to be sure, result from the involvement of equally imperative non-ego processes: who is to say, without intimate acquaintance with the principals, whether being in love should be called ego-involvement or "id-involvement"! However that may be, note that self-involvement and ego-involvement thus conceived may vary independently. A person may care about a task both because of its intrinsic meaning for him and with afterthought for its bearing on his prestige and self-esteem. Or either or neither may be the case. The behavioral conditions and consequences of ego- and self-involvement should furthermore be quite distinct.

The situation is somewhat different in regard to the theoretical status of the mechanisms of defense. Here the classical formulation by Anna Freud (1946) regards the defense mechanisms as employed by the ego (the term is used essentially in our sense) to protect itself, primarily from disruption by strong unassimilated urges, but also from threats from the external world. As a more or less precariously balanced system mediating between inner strivings and outer reality, the ego, in this view, has recourse to these sometimes drastic techniques in order to preserve its balance, and maintain the course of behavior at a lower level of adjustment if need be rather than run the risk of its catastrophic disruption. G. Murphy (1947), and later Snygg and Combs (1949), on the other hand, say in effect that it is rather the self that is defended. Under conditions of threat, enhancement and preservation of the self may be achieved by the classical defense mechanisms. Is it necessary to choose between these divergent formulations, or can the conflict be resolved?

The present writer would maintain that the mechanisms of defense can ultimately all be conceived as defenses of the ego, since they serve to bolster up the ego's adjustive compromise. As contributors to this compromise, they can also best be regarded as a part of the activity included in the ego system. But in a more immediate sense, any particular one of an individual's defenses may or may *not* be a *self*-defense mechanism. Since the maintenance of a favorable self-image is important to sound ego functioning, though not its only requisite, the end of ego defense can often be served most efficiently by self-defense mechanisms. Certain mechanisms, like identification, may, indeed, always take effect through the defense of the self. There are, however, instances of ego-defense mechanisms which involve the self only indirectly if at all. In regression, for example, one can hardly suppose that the self is enhanced in any way. What is more likely is that by retreating to an earlier, more deeply established, or simpler level of ego organization, the person seeks, perhaps ineptly, to cope with disturbing experiences that, by reason of circumstance, constitution, or previous learning, he has not the strength to meet maturely. In most cases, the relative significance of the self in the defensive process probably cannot be assessed in any simple way, since changes in the self for better or worse may be the *consequence* of the fortunes of the ego and its defenses, as well as the focus of defensive techniques.

A formulation of this sort, which seems to agree with present clinical experience, again suggests the usefulness of a distinction between phenomenal and non-phenomenal (shall we say *functional*?) subjective constructs, with both employed in proper coordination. A purely phenomenological psychology, on the other hand, cannot adequately describe *all* the defensive processes, since neither all the effective threats to the ego nor all the defenses against them are registered accurately in conscious awareness. Indeed, it is largely the consequence of "silent" defensive processes that phenomenological reports must be viewed with so much circumspection in personality research.

Conclusions

Starting from a discussion of Snygg and Combs' (1949) proposal of a phenomenological frame of reference for psychology, the writer has sought to establish the following major points:

1. While common sense may favor an explanatory psychology framed entirely in terms of conscious experience, such a psychological system does violence to currently available knowledge.

2. Phenomenology, as distinct from common sense, is descriptive, not explanatory. It is an approach or method ancillary to the formulation of problems and derivation of constructs, and does not give birth to these constructs full blown.

3. The subjective and objective frames of reference, which denote relatively different alternative contexts within which constructs may be selected, are both entirely compatible with the observer's frame of reference. Subjective constructs to be scientifically admissible must ultimately be anchored in the data of observation.

4. The phenomenological approach provides one method of deriving subjective constructs. But not all subjective constructs need represent phenomenal entities. They may, thus, denote functional entities that are either absent from the phenomenal field or inaccurately presented in it.

5. The coordinate use of phenomenal and non-phenomenal subjective constructs, maintained in clear distinction from one another, serves to clarify the theory of the ego and the self. It is proposed that an adequate theory of personality must distinguish, among other constructs,

a. the *ego*, a *non-phenomenal* subjective construct representing a configuration of on-going processes, among which is the cognitive-perceptual function. Through exercise of this function, the ego "knows," among other things,
b. the *self*, a *phenomenal* subjective construct.

6. When carried into current problems concerning the nature of "ego-involvement" and of the "mechanisms of defense," the above distinction seems productive.

10

The Self and Cognitive Consistency

The seemingly straightforward notion of a psychological trend toward consistency comprises a host of problems that require explication, as shown by the entire volume in which this essay first appeared. If we ask how such trends are conditioned by relations to the self or self concept as a cognitive structure, we immediately face similar complications. In spite of the apparent solidity of the term self concept, even a mildly critical look at the literature of research and theory bearing on the topic should suffice to indicate that the solidity is illusory. Concerning neither conceptualization nor measurement is there satisfactory agreement, and what traditions of measurement have emerged—particularly the self-report methods—are not very well grounded in theory. Wylie's (1961) review volume displays this unsatisfactory situation, which remains essentially unchanged since 1961, without doing much to improve it.

Given this state of affairs, a necessary preliminary to the present chapter is to sketch in the bare bones of a working conception of the self. Here I will be brief and dogmatic, so as to get on with the main task, even though the state of self theory would call for tentativeness, qualification, and prolixity. The minimal distinctions that I introduce are conceived within a general frame of reference I outlined some years ago (Smith, 1950b).

Phenomenological inspection yields references to the self as actor in relation to other actors, as ground against which experience of an external world is figural, as maintaining identity in time, as reflexive object. Some tender-minded theorists, playing by rules that I do not accept, try to put such a phenomenal self to immediate theoretical work. However, I have always thought that proper scientific discourse requires us to use what insights we can glean from what is given phenomenally so as to frame subjective constructs—ones conceptualized from the actor's point of view—that are as

Reprinted from *Theories of Cognitive Consistency*, R. P. Abelson, E. Aronson, W. J. McGuire, T. M. Newcomb, M. J. Rosenberg, and P. H. Tannenbaum, Editors, by permission of the publisher, Rand McNally & Company.

firmly grounded in the observer's frame of reference as we can make them. We cannot expect to find good theoretical concepts given directly in experience. The question is, rather, what inferential conceptual distinctions do we need in the domain vaguely identified by phenomenal experiences of self?

One distinction seems to me clearly useful in the present context; a couple of others will be noted as likely to be useful, though I am less clear about how. The one I would stress is between the person's more or less stable *self concept,* and the transitory *self percepts* that are evoked in the course of his transactions with the environment. Self percepts will depend not only upon the individual's persisting beliefs about himself (self concept), but also upon his ongoing behavior and the informational feedback that it brings, as well as upon the treatment he is accorded by others as it varies from one situation to another. The responses evoked by self-report procedures are highly fallible means for developing inferences about either level of construct, and the sloppy habit of *identifying* self-reports with constructs is sure to lead to confusion.

Within the sphere of the self concept, a further minimal distinction will probably turn out to be necessary, though I will not put it to use here. One can probably distinguish a *core of identity beliefs* that have persisting trans-situational relevance for a person's view of himself (these varying in centrality or importance and saliency—thus sex vs. eye color) from the set of subidentities that correspond to William James' notion (1890, pp. 293–296) of the person's multiple social selves, systems of beliefs that are bound to the major distinguishable contexts of role relations in which the person participates. One may expect pronounced individual and societal variation in the extent to which such subidentities are differentiated from one another and from core identity.[1]

The psychoanalytic tradition suggests the relevance of additional distinctions, which are introduced here not because I intend to use them directly, but to suggest the absurdity of treating *the* self concept as a concrete entity. We may infer that a person entertains views of himself that he fears or disavows, "negative identities" that may not be accessible to self-report; he also has conceptions of himself as he would like to be (research has picked up the latter theme for emphasis). In the sphere of percepts, he may reject self-regarding experiences as 'ego'-alien, as not pertaining to the acknowledged self.

With this sketchy foundation, we can return to the task at hand. In order to consider what the self has to do with trends toward consistency, we can begin by noting, with Lecky (1945), the importance of such trends in the very constitution of the self. As consistency theories become more mature, we can expect that one important direction in which social psychology may seek integration with personality theory is in further specifying the role of consistency-directed processes in the formation and development of the self. Pend-

1. See D. R. Miller (1963) and French and Sherwood (1965) for more formal treatments of self theory that are generally congruent with the approach taken here.

ing such an elaboration and application of formal theory, several things can be said.

First of all, the formation of a person's core identity, the differentiation of his subidentities, and the extrusion of his negative identities would seem to be heavily influenced by trends toward consistency of two kinds: toward internal consistency with as simple a structure as possible, and toward external consistency, such that surprise and disconfirmation by new percepts are kept within tolerable bounds. Heider (1958) emphasized how differentiation can be one outcome of strains toward cognitive balance; the theories derivative from Heider would seem to hold more promise than dissonance theory as aids toward the understanding of differentiated structure in the self.

But secondly, consistency-seeking processes operate in conjunction with an essentially unrelated trend, a bias toward thinking as well of oneself as one can get away with. Just as Festinger's version of consistency theory weights the discrepancy between cognitions by their importance, so the self-esteem-maximizing trend would seem also to involve a weighting by importance or centrality to one's self concept (see French and Sherwood, 1965). Among social psychological consistency theories. McGuire's formulation (Rosenberg, M. J., Hovland, McGuire, Abelson, and Brehm, 1960, pp. 65–111), which pits logical consistency against wishful thinking, runs somewhat parallel here.

The joint operation of these trends over the course of a life in progress, moreover, will likely give rise to affectively charged cognitive structures that have great stability, exceeding that of all but a very few "primitive beliefs" (Rokeach, 1960) about the external world that also operate like Kantian categories as ground for the whole succession of perceptual experience. The self concept as comprised of such structures is not likely to be much disturbed by single bits of incoming information, or by brief communications. We know how resistant it is to change in psychotherapy, and we know the heroic (or diabolical) efforts that seem to be required for 'brainwashing' to have substantial impact. When experiment manipulations and communications purport to produce measurable changes in the self concept, we may rightly be suspicious and look rather for momentary changes in self percepts—or for temporary yielding to the demand characteristics of the experimental situation (see Orne, 1962).

Finally, if the inferred self concept of a normal person is bound to be a strong and stable structure, the same cannot be said about momentary self-perceptions. These are also subject to pressures toward internal and external consistency and toward high self-evaluation. They should be under particularly strong pressure toward consistency with the person's enduring self concept, given the greater stability and importance of the latter. Their relation to the self concept should be asymmetrical: in the single encounter, the percept should give way, not the self concept. If there is not enough stimulus ambiguity for the self-perception to be brought into line, other maneuvers of isolation, rationalization, and so on, will be drawn upon, including the ones explored in dissonance theory.

So much (and little it is) for consistency phenomena in the self. What of the bearing of self on consistency phenomena as currently under view in social psychological research and theory? Let us first sample some of the ways in which the recent literature reflects explicit or implicit reference to the self.

Perhaps the most interesting of these involves implicit reference. As I read the focused reformulation of dissonance theory in Brehm and Cohen (1962) and in Festinger (1964), the claims for dissonance theory are now restricted to a sphere in which one of the terms in the cognitive relationship involves a self-perception. Although Festinger's original (1957) formulation was extremely general, purporting to deal with the relations between any two cognitions, research as it developed was preponderantly concerned with the important but very special class of situations in which one of the cognitive elements is the subject's knowledge of how he has in fact behaved. Brehm and Cohen's contribution, in their own research and in their thorough review of the work of others, was to stress the role of commitment and voluntary choice as requisite for the generation of dissonance. But knowledge of how one has behaved is an instance of self-perception, and the requirement of choice and commitment insures that the percept will be in relatively close communication with the self concept. Festinger's own recent (1964) reaffirmation of dissonance theory as a theory of postdecisional processes is congruent: the act of decision binds the self to a particular alternative or course of behavior.

The suggestion that the phenomena of dissonance depend upon involvement of the self has been made by others outside the directly Festingerian research tradition (see Deutsch, Krauss, and Rosenau, 1962). Intuitively, it makes good sense that the trend toward consistency should be particularly noticeable in matters that touch on the self. But are consistency effects limited to such matters? Evidently not: witness the success of Osgood and Tannenbaum's (1955) congruity model in its even more restricted sphere that in effect excludes the self; witness also the success of Rosenberg and Abelson's potentially very general balance model (Rosenberg, M. J., et al., 1960, pp. 112–163) and of McGuire's narrow syllogisic one (Rosenberg, M. J., et al., 1960, pp. 65–111), neither of which involves self-reference. For each of these cases the research data are limited, but there is no reason to doubt the existence of consistency effects that fall outside the sphere of self. Is the restriction of dissonance theory to self-related cognitions a matter of historical accident? Or can reasons be found for this restriction?

Three considerations occur to me as pertinent. For one, there is the formal defect of dissonance theory that, unlike balance and congruity theories, it does not deal explicitly with the unit relation. To limit its scope to relations that involve self precepts resting on voluntary commitment may, as Brehm and Cohen imply, make it more likely that the cognitions in question will be taken as relevant to one another.[2]

2. McGuire's special case may assure the mutual relevance of cognition through its restriction to highly artificial materials drawn from the formally defined domain of propositional fragments of syllogisms.

Perhaps also germane is the iceberg-like quality of dissonance theory as it is revealed in practice, in which experimental ingenuity tends to substitute for theoretical explicitness. Buried in experimental manipulations that are arrived at intuitively and refined through pilot work is a lot of implicit theory about how to 'con' subjects into voluntary engaging in dissonance-producing behavior, as well as additional implicit theory about how alternative channels of dissonance reduction may be blocked. The high valuation that Festingerians set on experimental ingeniousness may have helped to disguise the extent to which the generality of the theory had in effect become limited until Brehm and Cohen did their stock-taking.

Finally, there is the effect of the competition between dissonance theory and conflict theory cast in terms of incentives and reinforcement (Janis, 1959). The pressure to make dissonance theory distinctive pushed it to make its special claim for postdecisional processes, leaving predecisional ones to conventional conflict formulations. But, as we have seen, postdecisional phenomena are intrinsically self-referential. To get outside the bounds of self, dissonance theory would have to leave the postdecisional domain where its claim for exclusiveness rests.

So far, we have been considering ways in which dissonance theory has been implicitly concerned with the self. In regard to *explicit* self-reference, at least two lines of research may be noted. One suggests that high momentary self-esteem (presumably a composite dimension of self-perceptions rather than of the enduring self concept, since it is manipulated experimentally) may be an essential condition for the generation of dissonance under certain circumstances. Thus, Bramel (1962) predicted and found that subjects in whom high self-esteem had been induced engaged in more dissonance-reducing behavior than subjects whose self-esteem had been lowered, when all subjects were given credible information implying that they had strong homosexual tendencies. Similarly, in an experiment in which subjects who were opposed to the research use of electric shock on human beings were induced to administer apparently painful shocks to a seeming fellow student, Buss (1961) found that only the subgroup among whom high momentary self-esteem had been experimentally induced showed the predicted indications of dissonance-reducing behavior (increased unfriendliness toward the target of their aggressions). In both these cases, it is implied that negatively valued information about the self should produce more dissonance for subjects whose self-esteem is momentarily high than for subjects who for the nonce have been made to think less well of themselves. The employment here of concepts relating to the self seems to be well within the bounds of conventional dissonance interpretations.

The other line of research, exemplified by Aronson and Carlsmith (1962), pits the predictions of dissonance or consistency theory against those that would follow from people's general tendencies to maximize their self-esteem. They found that subjects in whom an expectation of failure on an experimental task had previously been established and who were then led to experience strong success used an opportunity with which they were provided to revise their performance in a downward direction, just as those in whom an expectation of success had been established and who then were made to fail used the opportunity to improve their performance. Put in general terms, subjects who were given information about their performance that was inconsistent with their expectancies changed a significantly greater number of their responses than those who were given consistent information. The results are startling, because common sense, which knows about self-esteem and the desire for success, has not yet been educated in dissonance theory. Theoretically, these results only begin to open the problem of what conditions govern the relative weight of consistency-producing and esteem-enhancing processes when these compete with each other. Certainly the existence of neither sort of process is in doubt.

As for the versions of cognitive consistency doctrine other than dissonance theory, we have already noted that neither Osgood and Tannenbaum (1955), McGuire (Rosenberg, M. J., et al., 1960, pp. 65–111), nor Rosenberg and Abelson's (Rosenberg, M. J., et al., 1960, pp. 112–163) version of balance theory has anything distinctive to say about the self. But Heider's own formulation of balance theory in his chosen domain of cognized interpersonal relations requires reference to sentiments toward the self. Thus, Heider (1958, p. 180) introduces his discussion of balance and imbalance with the following intuitive examples of imbalance:

> *p* hates *o* because he is similar to *o*.
> He always imitates people he dislikes.
> He avoids people he likes.

For these examples to represent imbalance, according both to common sense and to Heider's noncommonsense version of commonsense psychology, one must assume—as will usually be the case but not always—that *p* likes *p;* in other words that *p* has relatively high self-esteem. For a person whose self-esteem is pathologically low, it is plausible enough to regard the examples as balanced.

Evidence that self-esteem can indeed be a predictive variable in a version of Heider's theory that is modified to treat relations between elements as continua rather than as dichotomies is provided by Wiest (1965), who finds with sociometric data from schoolchildren that the extent to which a person believes that his evaluations of others are reciprocated by them is a positive function of his self-esteem.

Involvement of the self presumably also bears upon stability and change in attitudes in ways other than those mediated by consistency-seeking processes. (For the conventional term ego-involvement read self-involvement in the present context.) For example, consider the so-called discrepancy-involvement controversy as recently summarized by McGuire (1966, pp. 485–487). M. Sherif and Hovland (1961) and, most recently, C. Sherif,

M. Sherif, and Nebergall (1965) have claimed in the context of assimilation-contrast-judgmental theory that with stronger involvement, larger discrepancies between a person's own prior attitudinal position and the position advocated by a persuasive communication should result in decreased attitude change, because of the narrower latitude of acceptance that accompanies high involvement. Zimbardo (1960) arrived at contrary predictions from dissonance theory, and found evidence to support them. The confusing array of results from the series of studies that have ensued suggests the importance of differentiating types of 'involvement,' and the relevance of other features of the experimental situation. The bearing of this entire controversy on consistency theory is ambiguous, however, in that dissonance theory must be stretched a good deal beyond what its formal properties can strictly support if it is to deal with quantitative phenomena such as degree of discrepancy. Dissonance-consonance, after all, is presented as a dichotomous relationship, with quantification entering only through the manipulation (not rating) of importance and the fictive counting of consonant vs. dissonant elements.

Outside the laboratory, the work on "brainwashing" (Lifton, 1961; Schein with Schneier and Barker, 1961; Biderman, 1963) contains suggestions that processes involving the self may set some limits to predictions that follow from consistency principles in other settings. Thus, dissonance theory predicts that the more coercive the sanctions that are applied to a person to secure his compliance, the less he will change his private opinions in the direction advocated. On the whole, this prediction seems to have been well enough sustained in the experience of Korean POW's (see Biderman, 1963), among whom conversions were few in spite of some token compliance. The more intensive and efficient procedures that the Chinese Communists applied to American and other civilian prisoners seem to have led to a somewhat different outcome, if we are to believe Schein et al. (1961) and Lifton (1961), who report instances of pronounced attitude change. Here the crux of the matter would seem to have been a prolonged and efficiently contrived assault upon the self, in which coercion was an essential ingredient. The central use of self-produced confessions, of course, can be interpreted in terms of dissonance theory as a technique that undermines the prisoner's previous self-structure and helps to reformulate it along desired lines. Attitudes deeply anchored in the self could thus be susceptible to coercive persuasion by this painful indirect route.

This sampling of ways in which conceptualizations of the self have come in contact with consistency theories can be summed up in a few declarative sentences to which the reader can add his own qualifications:

1. The formation, structure, and dynamics of self concepts and percepts is a field of personality study to which the present crop of consistency theories and their successors can profitably be applied.

2. Those consistency theories to which the topic is directly relevant seem to have no difficulty in bringing the self into their formulations. As a class

of cognitive structures, the self concept has properties of stability, differentiation, and importance that should weight it heavily when it is out of balance with other types of cognitions. These features do not seem to require the special modification of consistency theories, however.

3. The tendency to think well of oneself may complicate predictions from consistency theories, since it appears to be independent of trends toward consistency.

4. The variable(s) of self-involvement should be played against less ambiguous questions of consistency theory than the issue concerning the effects of communication discrepancy.

5. Dissonance theory seems to have limited itself in practice to cases in which one of the terms in the cognitive relationship involves a self-perception. Whether this is a necessary restriction warrants closer examination.

6. To be useful in the development of consistency theory, more precise and better specified conceptions in the sphere of self are obviously called for.

11

Optima of Mental Health

A General Frame of Reference

Much effort has been expended in the attempt to arrive at a positive conception of mental health. Difficult as it has been for the investigator and the therapist to formulate the problems of mental disease and abnormality, they have found these problems far less elusive than the criteria of psychological adequacy implied in discussions of mental health, so-called normality, and therapeutic goals. The catalytic impact of cultural anthropology on psychiatric thinking has added its share of confusion as well as enlightenment. Impressed by the fact that the symptoms of one culture appear as the norms of another, and as disregarded trivia in yet a third, students of the developing area of culture and personality tended initially toward a relativism that equated mental health with conformity to the values and practices of one's particular cultural milieu (Benedict, 1934). On the other hand, the cultural application of a dynamic psychology (Kardiner, 1939, 1945; DuBois, 1944), with its assumption of universal modes of reaction to recurring human situations, reopened the possibility of transcultural standards. To the promise shown by these attempts to establish dynamic correlation between formative institutions and the basic personality structure characterizing members of a society should probably be added another influence favoring the reaction against cultural relativism—our natural war-time reluctance to accept the equivalent worth of enemy value-patterns.

The tentative outcome of studies of personality formation in different cultures does suggest that cultures can be analyzed according to their pro-

Reprinted by permission from *Psychiatry,* 1950, *13,* 503–510. The frame of reference elaborated in this article is largely based on a conception of mental health presented by Dr. Marie Jahoda in her paper "Toward a Social Psychology of Mental Health" prepared for the Midcentury White House Conference on Children and Young People (Jahoda, 1950). The ideas I develop here first took form in a discussion with Dr. Jahoda and Dr. Stuart W. Cook during the latter stages of preparation of her paper. I am glad to acknowledge my indebtedness to Dr. Jahoda and to Dr. Cook for the impetus to work through these problems and for many of the views expressed in this article.

motive or disruptive influence on the mental health of the individual. But existing studies go only part of the way toward articulating with the analysis of differences in mental health *within* a culture. What is more, there has been insufficient explicit attention to the development of criteria of mental health that can be applied inter- or intra-culturally.

It is not my primary aim in this paper, however, to submit from the armchair my own proposal for this elusive philosopher's touchstone. Until "normal," happy people, people engrossed in their human relationships and work, in our own culture as well as in others, have been studied with some of the perspicacity and thoroughness that have been expended on the troubled and deviant, such speculation must remain highly tentative and is likely to be wasted. Rather, my purpose is to suggest a frame of reference for the analysis of mental health both within and between cultures, that may pose significant problems for research and help to separate empirical questions from value judgments in this difficult area. Necessarily, I must present this discussion in terms of a specific set of criteria. I hope, however, that the frame of reference developed may prove useful even if these particular criteria turn out to require radical reformulation.

First, let us consider the tentative criteria of mental health. The essential feature of this approach is the employment of *multiple* criteria which though related are assumed to have at least some degree of independence of one another. For present purposes, three may be considered: adjustment, integration, and cognitive adequacy, each of which has been advanced with good reason as the essential feature of psychological well-being. Yet each by itself seems insufficient to comprehend all that good mental health connotes.

Adjustment as a criterion stems from the functional biological approach underlying the great advances in psychology and psychiatry during the present century. The well-being of the organism in interaction with its environmental field is seen as depending on the satisfaction of the needs that arise on varying levels of complexity during the conduct of its life-processes. The vocabulary of need, tension-reduction, frustration, and adjustive mechanisms—a major component of psychoanalytic thinking—has also served as almost the entire conceptual armory of academic experimental psychology in its analysis of mental health problems. Mental health from this point of view becomes synonymous with *homeostasis*—a dynamic equilibrium in which the needs and capacities of the organism are so attuned to its environmental matrix that it can maintain a steady state with minimal disruptive tensions.

The concept of adjustment is neutral in respect to the degree that the organism contributes actively to this state of affairs: homeostatic equilibrium may be approximated either from passive compliance to environmental pressures, or from active mastery of environmental conditions. Undoubtedly one of the limitations of the concept as it is found in current usage is the ease with which this ambiguity permits one to equate mental health with adjustment, and adjustment with acquiescent acceptance of a social environment that may be fundamentally unsatisfactory on other grounds. It is this chain of assumptions that lays open much psychiatric practice to the charge of implicit conservatism.

Yet even if this pitfall is avoided, adjustment by itself is an insufficient criterion of mental health. Today it is all too easy to think of situations in which effective adjustment is impossible. Granted that full mental health is equally impossible in such situations, other standards are still needed to evaluate the *relative* adequacy of one or another mode of orientation to these situations. Besides, a consideration of the humanistic tradition and of the variety of cultures man has developed calls into serious question the appropriateness of minimal tension level as the sole index of optimal functioning of the human animal. Were one to accept this view with full consistency, death would indeed appear to stand as the goal of life rather than its antithesis.

Some concept allied to *integration* has usually been put forward to meet this dilemma. Within the biological orientation, it is the integrity of the organism as a complexly coordinated system that is emphasized rather than its interaction with the environment. Here, too, psychoanalysis has made important contributions, in its theories of intrapsychic conflict and its conception of normality as a state of affairs in which the full energies of the person are free to be mobilized in the service of his central purposes rather than being bound in the containment of unintegrated strivings. Particularly with the cultivation of ego psychology, integration became a central concern of psychoanalytic theory. Related facets of the problem have been stressed by writers such as Angyal (1941), Lecky (1945), Goldstein (1948), and Fromm (1947) with their emphasis on self-realization and self-consistency that echoes a theme traditional among ethical philosophers. In a sense, those who choose the criterion of integration would set a relative independence of environmental vicissitudes as their therapeutic goal.

In itself, however, the concept of integration is also neutral in a crucial respect: the degree of complexity or differentiation of the integrated system. Integration refers to the degree of coordination of needs, means, and goals, and to the resiliency of this organization under the pressures it encounters. It says nothing about complexity. Unless one imports a concept of *levels* of integration, one can hardly speak of the richly cultivated person as reflecting a higher degree of integration than the simple mountaineer. And to do this confounds disparate concepts, as well as implying what is hard to justify: namely, that complexity of organization is in itself a useful measure of psychological adequacy.

Intrapersonal integration as a sole criterion neglects the embeddedness of the individual in a social and physical reality. There is a sense in which the paranoid psychotic, for example, has attained a high degree of integration at the expense of his relations to the real world. To conceive of mental health narrowly in terms of psychological integration runs the risk of confusing encapsulation with health. Part of the difficulty is resolved if integration and adjustment are taken as dual criteria. Further clarification of what seem to be productive lines of thought in this area, however, may be gained by introducing yet a third standard.

The final tentative criterion, then, is the *adequacy of the individual's cognition of reality*, both of self and of his behavioral world. Insight has long been regarded as at least an index of successful psychotherapy, if not a primary condition of its attainment. Experimental as well as clinical evidence points to the readiness with which perceptions may be distorted in the pseudo-solution of psychological conflicts (Bruner and Postman, 1948). Equally compelling data (Adorno, Frenkel-Brunswik, Levinson, and Sanford, 1950) lead to the conclusion that adequate perception of self and of one's social environment go hand in hand: distortions in the one are likely to imply complementary distortions in the other. While to erect cognitive adequacy as the primary criterion of mental health, as Rogers (1947) appears to be inclined to do, makes for an unduly intellectualistic and undynamic approach, it seems likely that in the long run, accuracy of perception is an essential accompaniment of maximal adjustment and integration.

In long-run and ideal terms, indeed, all three of these criteria must probably be maximized if any one of them is to attain its maximum value. The person who achieves a smooth adjustment at the expense of personal integrity lacks the resources of strength and resiliency to maintain his adjustment against environmental stresses that a more highly integrated person could withstand. If it is accuracy of perception and belief that is sacrificed for the sake of short-run adjustment, one's behavior lacks reliable direction, and he risks compounding further difficulties for himself. Since personality structure arises out of social experience and remains functionally interdependent with one's pattern of interpersonal relations, the attempt to maintain integration at the expense of adjustment, say in a splendid nonconformity, is precarious at best and likely to involve dysfunctional features that stand in the way of the free utilization of the person's full energies. As in the case of adjustment, integration based on warped perceptions is potentially vulnerable. Brute experience may penetrate the perceptual defenses, undermining the shaky premises on which such a personality structure is grounded. Finally, present knowledge of the dynamics of perception and belief makes it quite unlikely that human beings are capable of sustained cognitive adequacy unless they are satisfactorily adjusted and integrated in personality.

Thus, if we maintain a long-run orientation and are concerned with ideal conditions in which maximal mental health is possible, any one of these criteria may well do service for all three. But in empirical investigations one is almost necessarily confined to the short run in the collection of data. For this reason, if the conception of mental health is to retain long-run validity, some approximation of these suggested triple criteria seems called for in evaluating the short-run data. If one could weigh the relationship among indices of a person's present adjustment, integration, and perceptual adequacy, he would be in a better position to estimate the subject's long-run prospects for satisfactory psychological functioning than if any single criterion is relied upon. The joint employment of the criteria also gives some promise of making it unnecessary to place primary emphasis on such qualitative distinctions as those between active and passive adjustment, and higher and lower levels of integration. Verifiable hypotheses could be formulated with respect to a specified milieu: for example, that adjustment to be compatible with a given degree of integration and perceptual adequacy must involve active mastery; or that integration, to be compatible with a given degree of perceptual adequacy must be attained at a definite level of complexity and differentiation.

It is one thing to speculate that *maximum* adjustment or integration or cognitive adequacy requires that each of the other two criteria be at a maximum; in other words, that ideal mental health is indivisible. To say that a similar relationship holds for the *optimal* degree of mental health that is *possible in a particular socio-cultural milieu* is a quite different assertion, and, it seems to me, a false one. In fact, the imperfections in known human societies have been such that it might be a fairer statement to maintain that for most people, most of the time, these three criteria have been at least to some extent mutually incompatible. While this is a matter for research rather than speculation, the trend of contemporary thinking points in this direction.

Consider, for example, the value conflicts such as those between "Christian" altruism and competitive individualism that Lynd (1939), Horney (1937), and other writers have found in present American culture. Adjustment to this cultural environment may often be achieved only at the cost of defective integration—through internalizing conflicting values—or of distorted perception of self or of the society to which one is adjusting. The point is certainly not a new one. Or take the lot of people cast in a nearly unsupportable situation, such as the inmates of the concentration camp described by Bettelheim (1943). Here some of the open alternatives were passive adjustment with regressive disintegration, active resistance and consequent annihilation, or the pursuit of a tenuous encapsulated integration, made possible by translating the threatening experience to a level of unreality. What seems clear is that one or more features of ideal mental health had to be sacrificed for the sake of mere psychological existence, and that even in this extreme situation more than one pattern of adjustment, integration, and cognitive adequacy was possible.

A case with broader implications is that of members of oppressed or underprivileged classes in which the frustrations of life weigh heavily against the gratifications. The Marxian expectation that the proletariat would act in behalf of its objective economic interests may have run afoul of this restriction of the psychologically possible alternatives. Perhaps those who suffer most from the economic system can appraise their situation accurately only at the cost of the integration or "ego strength" essential for the effective organization of a revolutionary movement. The more popular alternative seems to have been to maintain a measure of integrity and adjustment by grace of the opiates of cognitive distortion—perhaps less through religion than through myths of social mobility or sheer restriction of the psychological field. The frequently cited observation that revolutions are likely to break out at a time when social conditions are improving, rather than at their nadir, supports this interpretation, as does the fact that revolutionary leaders have tended to arise from social strata other than the most oppressed classes.

Perhaps, on the other hand, the golden ages of history can be looked to as periods when, at least for some substantial segment of the population, these three criteria of mental health approached compatibility to an extraordinary extent. For the free citizen of Periclean Athens, or for the courtier and burgher of the Renaissance, untrammelled cognitive clarity, psychological integration permitting a focusing of productive energies, and zestful adjustment to one's milieu seem to have been fostered by the spirit of the age. If the records and traditions of these high ages paint a true picture, one may well ask under what socio-cultural conditions these three criteria are interrelated in a way that makes maximal mental health possible on such a scale.

This analysis, therefore, indicates the possibility both of absolute standards of mental health and of contingent criteria adaptable to the pragmatic requirements of particular situations, all within a common framework and applicable at both individual and societal levels. Consider first the absolute standards, which, like most absolutes, are likely to have rather limited practical and theoretical significance. The absolute measure of a person's mental health is the extent to which he approaches maximal values on all three criteria. Many factors beyond the reach of practical intervention, of course, set a ceiling on his possible attainment. A mentally deficient person, for example, can reach neither the adjustment, the integration, nor the cognitive adequacy of a normally endowed person in the same situation. Here the primary impairment of the cognitive factor imposes severe limits on the alternatives open for adjustment and integration. Analogous limits on cognitive adequacy are set by the level of dependable or scientific knowledge accumulated by the culture in which a person participates. Where belief in witchcraft and magic is the norm, a person is in this respect less adequately equipped for commerce with his environment than in a more sophisticated culture. Value conflicts in a malintegrated culture, as it has been suggested, may also restrict the possibilities for the attainment of mental health. The very pursuit of certain values, such as asceticism or aggressive individualism, may directly or indirectly set restrictions on mental health as I have defined it. And finally, unintended psychological consequences of the culturally prescribed process by which the person is inducted into his social roles may prove to be limiting factors.

A full statement of the extent that a person falls short of maximal mental health appears to require a separate evaluation on each of the three criteria, for a combined index would necessarily involve a value judgment as to their relative importance, on which consensus would be difficult to attain. Depending on one's value premises, different weighting schemes and different conclusions could legitimately be arrived at in particular cases. Which should be rated more highly, for instance, adjustment at the cost of integration, or the converse? This is clearly a question of ethics rather than science, although scientific findings might help to clarify the ethical problem.

Cultures as well as individuals can be evaluated in these absolute terms. Here two avenues are open. One may inquire as to the distribution of individuals in a particular socio-cultural milieu according to these criteria. Or, perhaps more incisively, one may look for the extent to which optimal values on the several criteria are psychologically compatible for individuals in that milieu. The degree to which the culture necessitates sacrifices along one dimension for the sake of optimal values on the others suggests itself as a possible approach.

The real importance of absolute standards ends, however, with the demonstration of their possibility. For clarity of thinking it is helpful to dispose once more of the relativism that would make each culture a norm to itself. But little theoretical and less practical purpose is likely to be served by attempts to classify cultures or individuals according to absolute criteria of mental health. People cannot choose their culture any more than they can select their parents, and utopias cannot be cut to order out of whole cloth. Absolute standards lack practical relevance. In both research and practice, one is usually concerned with the relation among certain strategic variables in a definite setting in which certain features must be taken as given, and these givens, although not subject to manipulation, determine as parameters the nature of the relationship among the variables. Where these tentative criteria show real promise is in their contingent application within the limits set by specific cultures and situations.

My assumption has been that the simultaneous maximizing of all three criteria—adjustment, integration, and cognitive adequacy—is possible only in the limiting case of the well-endowed individual in an ideal environment. In all other cases—which, for practical purposes, means in all cases—*optima* rather than maxima are possible on the several criteria. If, furthermore, adjustment, integration, and cognitive adequacy are not fully compatible with one another in cases short of the ideal, it follows that for each situation defined by a set of individual and socio-cultural characteristics, not just one optimal set of criterion values but a family of such sets can be determined. Each set specifies the value of the three criteria under the given conditions when one of them is at its optimum. Perhaps in some cases a unique solution might be found in which the three together reach their greatest value. The variety of psychological alternatives available in this family of sets would seem to depend on which factors are taken as fixed parameters—givens not subject to manipulation or control—and which as strategic variables. The more factors that must be regarded as fixed, of course, the more narrowly are the psychological alternatives determined.

Thus, in the concentration camp described by Bettelheim, given the extraordinary stresses of the situation as fixed, several optimal patterns of mental health emerged, each of which, however, met no criterion very satisfactorily and required the almost total sacrifice of at least some other criterion. If factors of individual endowment and previous personality as parameters are introduced, the range of alternative optimal patterns should be progressively narrowed. A thorough exploration along these lines of mental health in a variety of situations should add considerably to the understanding of the relation between mental health and the factors on which it depends.

A conception of the patterns of optima possible under specified conditions is well suited as an orienting framework to guide remedial measures. It has the particular merit of organizing the relevant empirical facts in a conditional, "if-then" form free of implicit value judgments, leaving explicit the points at which value decisions and practical exigencies enter into determining one's course.

Suppose, for example, one is concerned with mental health in the urban working class. It is up to the investigator to decide which factors in the situation he will take as given. If the study is under the auspices of an agency which has the power to introduce changes in certain aspects of the situation but not in others, these facts may dictate what is regarded as fixed. A general exploratory study is likely to be guided in its selection by estimates of the likelihood that particular factors may become subject to social manipulation, or by value judgments that the *status quo* should be preserved in certain areas. It is better that the basis of these decisions be made explicit.

If one assumes that no major institutional changes are considered feasible or desirable, then the major features of the existing working-class situation then become the parameters. What is the joint distribution on the three criteria of a sample of the population living under these conditions? This is an empirical problem and, of course, no easy one. An inspection of the distribution should yield an initial assessment of mental-health assets and liabilities in terms of the criteria. The data may then be analyzed to determine the standing on each of the other two criteria of those people who reached the optimum on any particular one. This analysis would isolate the patterns of optima in which I am particularly interested, since they exist for the given setting with its defining parameters. It would throw light on the psychological cost of given therapeutic goals, the extent to which they might be achieved, and the possible combinations of psychological desiderata within the limits of the situation. Misguided attempts to make palliative measures accomplish the impossible might be forestalled by this analysis, and the outcome of particular strategies predicted. A more intensive analysis of the uncontrolled variables in the situation associated with optima on particular criteria should suggest measures for promoting those aspects of mental health within the situation. Experimental tests might follow appropriately.

There is, of course, no need to take the institutional features of the situation as fixed. By broadening the base of study and introducing relevant comparison groups, the range of optima can be found when more and more factors are regarded as strategic variables rather than parameters. The limit of this process, starting with the analysis of particular situations and subcultures, lies in cross-cultural comparisons in which the fewest factors will remain as defined parameters. This scheme provides a frame of reference for ordering the large amount of data needed for an adequate theory of mental health and a sound strategy of social change. It incidentally indicates the need for some caution in generalizing from broad cross-cultural studies, where the variables are so many and the parameters so few.

At whatever level one sets one's parameters, however, one would expect to find not just one optimal pattern of mental health, but alternative patterns, depending on which criterion happens to be optimized. Empirical knowledge of the criterion values of each optimal pattern, and of the independent variables with which each is associated, should permit more enlightened value judgments in the choice of therapeutic goals, and more effective strategy in their pursuit.

The point at which this scheme is most vulnerable, of course, is in the selection of the triple criterion of mental health. A value judgment rather than a verifiable hypothesis, it may be argued, underlies the entire discussion. In a limited sense, this is true. The hypothesis and the value judgment are, nonetheless, separable. It is a matter of hypothesis, unfortunately very difficult to verify, that a *maximal* degree of adjustment, integration, or cognitive adequacy, when the situation permits its attainment, depends in each case on the maximizing of the other two variables. If such should indeed turn out to be the case, a high degree of social consensus could probably be reached in favor of the value judgment that selects these variables as criteria of mental health. Such a working consensus grounded on a correct appraisal of empirical relationships is the only nontheological source of standards possible.

It is undoubtedly true, of course, that the criteria as presented here have gross inadequacies. As more operational definitions are attempted in actual research, they are sure to be refined and clarified, and may well be superseded. Granted the provisional character of the present statement, the frame of reference in which patterns of optima on multiple and partially incompatible criteria are conceived to be specific to definite values of situational parameters may still retain its usefulness. For whatever standards of mental health may eventually be elected by social consensus, it seems quite probable that such multiple criteria will prove necessary.

12

Research Strategies Toward a Conception of Positive Mental Health

I think it is fair to say that the recent shift in interest in the mental health movement away from exclusive concern with mental illness and its treatment toward greater concern with positive mental health has not been accompanied by proportionate gains in research and scientific understanding. The phrase remains more of a slogan, a rallying cry, than a scientific concept. If this is an accurate impression[1] and we have actually met something of an impasse in our attempts to give conceptual content to mental *health,* we ought first to try to locate some of the difficulties that the term presents to those who would work with it in a scientific framework. The initial job for this paper is thus a diagnostic and a critical one. If we can gain some perspective on what the difficulties have been, we should be in a more favorable position to examine how research may be brought to bear to advance our understanding of optimal human functioning.

Some Conceptual Difficulties With "Mental Health"

What of the difficulties? One real if superficial obstacle may be noted and dismissed at the outset: that presented by the rather inappropriate connotations of "mental" and "health," which for historical reasons we are undoubtedly stuck with whether we like the terms or not. Neither of them would be just the choice of a scrupulous psychologist: "mental" with its echoes of an outworn dualism, or "health" with its gratuitous invocation of a medical

Reprinted by permission from *American Psychologist,* 1959, *14,* 673–681. Revised from a paper presented to the Second Institute on Preventive Psychiatry, State University of Iowa, April 10, 1959. The author is indebted to Barbara Dohrenwend and to Lillian Robbins for a critical reading of the earlier version.

1. It is certainly supported by W. A. Scott's reviews (1958a, 1958b) of the research literature bearing on mental health, in which there is little evidence of research attention to positive aspects.

context. But the serious trouble is not merely semantic, and revision or clarification of terminology will not suffice to resolve it.

The crux of the matter, it seem to me, is that mental health is inherently an *evaluative* concept and that science has not yet learned how to deal surefootedly with values. To say as much is no counsel of despair; it is rather to specify the nature of the problem. Mental health is personality evaluated, measured against certain criteria that either have the status of values or are derivatives of implicit values. If we are to use the results of research on personality to clarify our conceptions of mental health, we come face to face with the more general problem of how scientific knowledge of empirical facts and relationships can be made to contribute to the clarification of values. It is just here that scientists, humanists, and theologians have traditionally parted ways in a cloud of controversy.

Values are involved, whether mental illness or positive mental health is at issue. But so long as the mental health movement was preoccupied with pathology and malfunction, it was easy for the value issues to remain implicit, since values are taken for granted when everybody agrees about them. Everyone could agree that the grosser forms of mental disease are evils to be eliminated as much as possible. A scientific psychopathology could therefore get about its difficult task of seeking a causal account of the varieties of "mental illness." (Note that once our cultural horizons are broadened beyond the reach of this value consensus, even pathology becomes problematic as value differences become explicit: how are *we* to decide whether or not a shaman's trances—or a saint's—are a sign of poor mental health? cf. Devereux, 1956.)

Habitual ways of thinking about "normality" and "adjustment," as long as they seemed to work for us, shielded us from facing the value problems that lurk in notions of positive mental health. But they no longer work. Jahoda (1958) is only the most recent of many critics of these once fashionable concepts to note that neither is at all satisfactory as a criterion of mental health. Of the various meanings of "normality" that we learned to distinguish some time ago, the one that seems closest to being value-free—the statistical average—turns out on examination to be irrelevant for our purposes. Averageness is surely a far cry from optimal functioning, however we are to define it; and it is easy to conceive of whole populations that are sick, to a degree, mentally as well as physically. Nor, on closer examination, is the concept as value-free as it appears at first glance: a value judgment is involved in selecting the dimensions for "averaging." Any other meaning of psychological normality than the statistical either shifts the question "What is health?" to a new terminology without getting us any closer to an answer or uncritically substitutes the cultural *norms* of a given time and place for more universal criteria. We have somehow to transcend cultural perspectives if there is to be much point in talking about positive mental health.

Adjustment as a criterion of mental health runs afoul of just this pitfall of culture-boundedness. Adjustment to *what?* And why *adjustment* rather than, say, autonomy and creativity? Of course, adjustment is still a perfectly good concept, in spite of the eclipse it has suffered among intellectuals in a post-McCarthy era as a result of its linkage with conformity. We will continue to need to talk about the degree to which a person has come to terms with the demands of the situations in which he finds himself. The point is, rather, that to take adjustment as our single standard for evaluating personality is to give entirely too much weight to essentially arbitrary characteristics of the person's situation, and to adopt implicitly the value position that persons *ought* to come to terms with situations as they encounter them. Inherently relative to culture and to situation, the concept of adjustment fails to give us the leverage that we need in order to transcend situational and cultural boundaries. And in the context of mental health, adjustment *is* a value, one that conflicts with other values to which we would give priority. Once we see it as a value—not as a value-free importation from biological, hence scientific, thinking—we perceive its insufficiency for guiding our thought and action.

Let us agree that neither normality nor adjustment—nor, I will flatly state, any other conceptual panacea—excuses us from facing a choice of values if we are to concern ourselves with mental health. How, then, are mental health values to be distinguished from other values? And how can research be brought to bear in making the distinction? These complex issues lie at the heart of our problem, and there is little sign of consensus on either of them.

There seems to be an increasing tendency to treat positive mental health as a kind of *summum bonum,* a synonym for the "good life." When richness of life, self-actualization, and creativity as well as the more homespun virtues of honesty, faith, hope, and charity are embraced as aspects of mental health—and sometimes even *justified* by this classification—we may wonder just what is happening. Does it add to our appreciation of older values, or give us a concept that is at all workable, to regard mental health as a kind of latter-day substitute for salvation? Provisionally, it seems clear that, if mental health is to be a useful term for other than propagandistic purposes, it will have to be confined to some more restricted sense.

For the institutional psychiatrist still baffled by the treatment of gross mental disease (cf. Barton in Jahoda, 1958, pp. 111–119), there is no problem here: mental health, for his practical purposes, is the absence of flagrant mental illness. More than his colleagues treating character disorders and neuroses in clinic or private practice, he can and perhaps should leave to others the whole array of positive values beyond merely adequate functioning. But the parent, the teacher, the psychological counselor can hardly avoid concern with the positive end of the spectrum. We need guidelines to distinguish the values we would promote in the name of mental health from ones we embrace simply as citizens and people of good will. Because we are scientists, or professionals who seek their nourishment from science, we look to research for guidance. Can we find it?

Of one thing we can be sure at the outset: research is not going to solve our value problems for us, to absolve us from having to make responsible decisions. It is a commonplace that no amount of empirical knowledge about what *is* can settle the issue of what *ought* to be. Who is to convince the mystic that he ought not to mortify the flesh, because it "isn't healthy"? The choice of values involves an irreducible element of individual option; and consensus on values, to the extent that it is attainable, is catalyzed by social intercourse out of communalities in the response of human potentiality to human situations. Granted all this, psychological evidence can still be very relevant.

To the extent that there is already consensus on human values, empirical evidence, when there is some, can tell us how to maximize the values we have selected. Research can also provide the occasion for revising existing consensus or for approaching consensus where none presently exists. Indirectly, and always in conjunction with personal choice, it furnishes grounds for re-evaluation. As research displays the causal nexus in which values are embedded, that is, we see the *cost* in terms of other values of attaining the particular goals we have set our sights upon. With increasing knowledge we should be in a better position to make choices among values in the light of the consequences that these choices entail. And, as Gardner Murphy (1958) has recently emphasized, new choices become possible as knowledge extends our conception of what is attainable.

Ideally, research can thus contribute to the identification of values, and to the clarification of choices among them. Can it help us decide which values may usefully be included in the boundaries of "mental health"? Here we are handicapped by the relatively primitive state of our science of personality. If we are to understand mental health as "personality evaluated," a well developed theory of personality might be expected to suggest boundaries of relevance. As it is, we are faced with competing perspectives among which the degree of congruence is a matter for debate, and scattered areas of reasonably well established fact following up broader reaches of clinically informed opinion.

Under these circumstances, a modest inductive approach is in order. An overview of recent research in this spirit suggests that there have been three principal strategies for gaining a research toe hold on positive mental health. These range from what amounts to frontal assault to an indirect approach that may not be regarded as dealing with mental health at all. Let us sample these presently available strategies to see what kinds of contributions we may expect of each.

The Frontal Assault

First, the frontal assault. If you want to isolate the features of a disease syndrome, you single out a series of cases that share what you believe to be the diagnostic symptoms and note what other features of history and of present status these cases have in common that distinguish them from the population at large. Pursuit of this strategy tells you whether or not your initial diagnostic hunches are fruitful; and, if they turn out to have some validity, it provides the basis both for elaborating your conception of the syndrome and for drawing inferences about its etiology. Why not apply the same strategy to problems of mental *health?* The idea has considerable appeal, but I know of few examples of its actual use.

A. H. Maslow (1950), who for some time has been asking psychologists to pay more attention to health, love, and creativity and less to deficit phenomena, tried such a direct approach in his exploratory study of self-actualizing people. To get a relatively pure criterion group of people who had realized their potentialities to the fullest, he spread his net to include historical figures as well as acquaintances and notable contemporaries; his specimens included Beethoven, Lincoln, Jefferson, and Thoreau as well as Einstein and Eleanor Roosevelt. Inspection of what distinguished this remarkable group from the run of the mill suggested a number of characteristics, including: a more efficient perception of reality; acceptance of self, others, and nature for what they are; spontaneity; problem-centeredness rather than ego-centeredness; the quality of detachment, with a need for privacy; autonomy in relation to culture and environment; freshness rather than stereotypy of appreciation; openness to mystical experiences though not necessarily religious ones; identification with mankind; capacity for deep intimacy in relations with others; democratic attitudes and values; strong ethical orientation that does not confuse means with ends; philosophical rather than hostile sense of humor; creativeness.

This list of traits is certainly suggestive, and the study well serves Maslow's purpose of calling our attention dramatically to the interesting and important problems that optimal functioning poses for research. But apart from deficiencies of data and method that Maslow recognizes, we cannot be satisfied with this study as *evidence* for a self-actualizing syndrome of positive mental health. So much depends on the kind of people Maslow liked and admired enough to select for his self-actualizing group. Actualization of potentialities is a slippery concept; for, unless one assumes built-in goals of human nature on the model of Aristotle's entelechy (which in this context is to beg the question), human potentiality is manifold: to be a Napoleon or a Khrushchev as well as a Cellini or a Dostoevski. One may actualize oneself in many ways, and tastes as to which are preferable differ. Maslow's list, like his selection of people, tells us more about his own values and preferences than it does about positive mental health as such.

A second illustration of the frontal assault may be found in the more rigorous program of research into excellence of human functioning that has been in progress for some time at the California Institute for Personality Assessment and Research. Barron (1954, 1963) has reported one aspect of this program in a study of the *personal soundness* of some 80 advanced male graduate students, mostly doctoral candidates in the sciences. Judgments by professors in the student's major department provided the main criterion. By way of guidance the raters were told that "all-round soundness as a person" refers to "the soundness, balance, and degree of maturity which the individual shows in his relations with other people." After a three-day assessment at the institute using a variety of procedures, the staff rated the subjects on a number of personality variables. They also made their own global ratings of the subjects' inner psychological soundness.

Barron (1963) summarizes the traits that were found to be most consistently related to personal soundness as conceived by both major professors and institute staff. They are effectiveness and organization in working toward goals, correct perception of reality, character and integrity in the ethical sense, and interpersonal and intrapersonal adjustment. Scrutiny of the subjects' personal histories led the assessment staff to the conclusion that

> . . . psychopathology is always with us, and that soundness is *a way of reacting to problems, not an absence of them*. . . . High Soundness subjects are beset, like all other persons, by fears, unrealizable desires, self-condemned hates, and tensions difficult to resolve; they are *sound* largely because they bear with their anxieties, hew to a stable course, and maintain some sense of the ultimate worthwhileness of their lives.... [pp. 64–65]

While there was a substantial core of agreement between the conceptions of soundness as reflected in the departmental ratings and in those of the assessment staff, there were also differences. According to the pattern endorsed by the departments, high stability tended to the combined with low responsiveness. Soundness as they conceived it was apparently to be achieved at some cost of spontaneity and personal warmth. The psychologists, on their part, placed a premium on some other traits besides the goal oriented ones: friendliness, lack of affectation, tolerance, etc. Indeed, the study provides interesting insights into the values of psychologists and of science professors! Does it do more?

Barron's study at least has the advantage over Maslow's of recognizing explicitly that its central criterion variable is socially defined. From a practical standpoint, the judgments of a graduate student's major professors have a lot to do with the opportunity he will have to realize his potentialities; it is useful to make the basis of their judgments explicit, as this study does, and to uncover the psychological correlates and antecedents of earning their favorable or unfavorable regard.[2] The use of two sets of criterion judgments —the professors' and the psychological staff's—has the further advantage of partly escaping the limitations of reliance on the judgments of a single group. Where there is agreement between the two sets of judges, there *may* be an area of general value consensus on which a conception of mental

2. This rationale for personality assessment is essentially the one elaborated by Stern, Stein, and Bloom (1956).

health can begin to build. And the divergences between the sets are mutually illuminating; they foster critical reconsideration of the assumptions implicit in each, with the possibility of subsequent movement toward closer consensus.

There remain obdurate sources of ambiguity that limit the usefulness of this study for our purposes. How much did the definition of personal soundness that was offered for the judges' guidance influence them? If the definition had little influence, the judgments may be saturated with "halo effects" of general favorableness, and the analysis of their correlates amounts essentially to dissection of the halo. In this case, mental health has not been distinguished from other human values after all. If, on the other hand, the judgments turn out to be highly specific to the definition provided, then we face anew the problem of how to choose among alternative definitions. Clearly a complex program of research, not a single study, is required to throw light on these questions; yet even such a program would offer no guarantee of a conception of positive mental health that is dictated by the evidence.

What of the frontal assault as a strategy? Certainly, there is much to be learned by pursuing it, especially about the tacit ingredients of our conceptions of mental health. When one is in the position to start with a well specified defining criterion, as will be true for some practical purposes, such an approach can give useful information about antecedents and correlates. We get less help here on the central problem of what criterion to employ.

A further limitation, and a major one, remains to be mentioned. There are ample grounds, some of them to be reviewed shortly, for questioning whether optimal mental health can appropriately be regarded as a unitary syndrome. The frontal assault prejudges this issue in its commitment to seek what is common to persons who function well. Perhaps it would be more fruitful to start, not with global judgments of soundness or health, but with more specific criterion measures. How these criteria are related to one another could then be explored empirically. This is a second major strategy through which research can contribute to a concept of positive mental health, and to it I turn next.

The Multiple Criterion Approach

Among students of mental health, Marie Jahoda (1950) has developed one of the more articulate conceptions in terms of multiple criteria, and her recent survey (1958) of current mental health concepts is also conceived along these lines. In her later work, she has identified six major themes or categories of criteria in the recent theoretical literature—a literature that for the most part reflects clinical wisdom rather than systematic evidence. To list them concisely is to pass over what is probably the most valuable contribution of her monograph: her insightful commentary on distinctions and convergences in the writings of significant recent theorists of different schools. But here they are in brief: (a) attitudes toward the self, including its accessibility to consciousness, correctness of the self-concept, self-acceptance, and sense of identity; (b) growth, development, and self-actualization; (c) integration, including the balance of psychic forces, a unifying outlook on life, and resistance to stress; (d) autonomy; (e) perception of reality, including freedom from need-distortion, and empathy or social sensitivity; and (f) environmental mastery, under which she groups a number of proposed criteria in order of decreasing specificity: ability to love and to experience orgasm; adequacy in love, work, and play; adequacy in interpersonal relations; efficiency in meeting situational requirements; capacity for adaptation and adjustment; and efficiency in problem solving.

Such a list of recurrent, related, yet diverse themes reflects a degree of convergence in contemporary discussion that is heartening or disappointing according to one's expectations. Jahoda proposes in effect that we give serious consideration to each of these proposed criteria and give up the idea of settling for any single candidate, at least until much more evidence is in. After all, they have each been proposed by competent authority, and few of us would rule out any one of them as *un*desirable. How much redundancy there is in the list remains to be seen.

Jahoda would have us move from speculation to research on positive mental health by first translating the theoretical criteria into empirical indicators—test scores, *Q* sorts, rating variables, behavior in test situations, and the like. One could then study in different populations the interrelations among the several criteria and perhaps reduce the list by attention to the way they cluster empirically. And one could seek, with respect to each criterion in turn, the conditions under which mental health is acquired and maintained. If mental health as measured by different criteria turns out to share the same conditions of development and maintenance, there would be further grounds for combining or collapsing the list into a simpler one. But if different criteria yield distinctive patterns of correlates, we need to know it and to treat them separately.

Any apparent modesty in this proposal is of course grossly deceptive. True, one takes as a starting point the views of informed authorities, not abstract principles, and is prepared to be satisfied at the end with a set of partly correlated criteria, rather than a single overarching definition that generates a single dimension. But there is a wide and treacherous gap between abstractly formulated criteria and empirical indicators. The crux of the research problem lies in the finding of a finite number of satisfactory indices to represent the proposed criteria, and our experience with indices in other research situations hardly warrants optimism here. Each facet of a complex category like integration—say, unity of personal philosophy, or resistance to stress—seems all too likely to dissolve into a host of slightly correlated measures, and the attainment of a single score that validly represents a person's over-all degree of integration seems a distant goal at best. The problem may be one for factor analysis, but in comparable domains the factor analysts have achieved only moderate success.

Evidence for the complexity of indexing mental health variables, but also for the promise of a multiple criterion approach, may be found in the survey of mental health in a representative national sample, done for the Joint Commission on Mental Illness and Health by Gurin, Veroff, and Feld (1960). In this ground-breaking study, randomly selected respondents throughout the country were interviewed at length concerning the satisfactions and problems they found in life. Their self-perceptions were explored, and their adjustments in marriage, in parenthood, and in the world of work. Crude indices of symptomatology were also obtained. The foregoing could then be related to the extent to which respondents were ready to seek professional help should they find themselves in difficulty, and to their actual employment of such resources.

One of the many possible illustrations of the index problem in their work concerns perception of the self, an area that corresponds to one of Jahoda's categories. The Michigan investigators had available for their analysis responses to three open-ended questions:

1. People are the same in many ways, but no two people are exactly alike. What are some of the ways in which you are different from other people?
2. If you had a son [daughter for women], how would you like him to be different from you?
3. How about your good points? What would you say were your strongest points?

It was possible to use the coded answers to these questions to derive a number of indices, among them these: perception of difference from others, admission to shortcomings, and denial of strong points. The authors sought to explore the meaning of these indices and to get at more fundamental distinctions by examining their interrelationships and their associations with other variables, following much the strategy that Jahoda would recommend. I can summarize only one small aspect of their analysis here.

Each of the three indices just named may be viewed as reflecting the acceptance or rejection of one of the three self-percept questions. As it turned out: perception of difference from others is quite unrelated to admission of shortcomings in the self, admission of shortcomings is likewise unrelated to denial of strong points, but there is a strong relationship between perception of difference from others and denial of strong points (persons who saw themselves as different from others in some respect were much more likely to mention strong points about themselves in their initial response to the third question). A fine kettle of fish!

Actually, this pattern of relationships was predicted by the authors on the basis of the rationale that led them to include the questions in the interview. Running through all three questions is a focus on the person's ability or willingness to introspect, to look inward at the self. Introspective tendency might be expected to go with perception of differences from others and with the awareness both of strong points and of shortcomings, while the less introspective people should tend to fall on the "rejection" end of all three indices. But each question also taps certain affective or attitudinal aspects of the self-percept. As the authors point out:

> To reject the idea that one is in any way different from other people not only implies a lack of introspection but may also imply a negative evaluation of the self, reflecting an impoverished identity. To reject the idea that one has strong points also reflects a negative self-image. Rejection of the idea that one has shortcomings, on the other hand, has obvious implications for a *positive* view of the self. [1960, p. 59]

For two of the relationships between the indices, the direction of correlation that one would expect on the basis of introspective tendency runs counter to that which self-attitude by itself should produce. One might expect these contrary trends to "wash out" the relationship, and in fact just these instances yielded null correlations. The strong positive relation found between indices of perception of difference and denial of strong points, on the other hand, corresponds to parallel predictions from both supposedly underlying variables.

I have gone into this much detail because I think the foregoing analysis fairly illustrates the complexity of working with empirical indices, which seldom tap without contamination the single conceptual variable in which one is interested. Disentangling the underlying variables in their relationships is at best a complicated business, and the program laid out in principle by Jahoda is probably to be regarded as an ideal rather than as a working plan.

The Michigan survey also provides a demonstration—convincing to me—of the advantages of working with multiple criteria of mental health. For in relation to other variables the different indices enter into distinctive relationships that would be lost to sight with a less differentiated approach. Let me illustrate by quoting in part from the mental health profile of education, one of several important demographic variables employed in the study.

> Two important themes run through the differential responses of persons at varying educational levels. First, people with more education seem to be more introspective about themselves, more concerned about the personal and interpersonal aspects of their lives. Secondly, more educated people seem to have, coupled with this introspectiveness, a greater sense of well-being and satisfaction. Their introspection is reflected in the greater prevalance among the more educated respondents of

> (1) feelings of inadequacy both as a parent and as a husband or wife, (2) reports of *both* shortcomings and strong points in the self, and (3) more of the psychological immobilization symptoms. . . . They are happier—in their over-all evaluations of their current happiness, in their marriages, and in their jobs—and are more optimistic about the future than the less educated respondents. These two themes which appear so clearly in our data seem to point to education as broadening one's perspective and raising one's aspiration level—which leads to both an increased realization of problems and unfulfilled expectations, and a greater awareness of life satisfactions. [1960, pp. 210–211]

These differences were maintained even when income level was held constant, and therefore cannot be discounted as a mere reflection of greater material advantages. Advantages—and disadvantages—that education entails for psychological functioning became apparent as they would not had a single yardstick of mental health been applied. Features of mental health that go together in distinguishing the more educated from the less, moreover, pull apart in other demographic comparisons.

The parallelism with Jahoda's approach is closer than might superficially appear. Several of Jahoda's suggested aspects of mental health figure prominently in the Michigan study, but as rubrics or categories around which questioning was directed rather than as unified criteria. In the translation to indices, things suddenly get more complex. Fascinated by the empirical relationships revealed, the authors hardly bother with a conception of mental health. Yet they surely contribute to our understanding of the multifaceted functioning of people.

Perhaps this may be the fate of the multiple criterion strategy: to provide a map for research in the course of which the initial criteria get lost in the complexity of the relationships discovered. Yet, from the point of view of the practitioner and professional who needs standards of human functioning and wants them to be grounded in empirical fact, the data reported by Gurin et al. can be quite relevant to the reformulation of mental health criteria. To mention one conclusion that I draw from several interrelated findings in their material: an awareness of personal problems is more properly to be regarded as an aspect of good rather than of poor mental health—an extension of Barron's observations as previously quoted.

Generally, an approach to mental health via multiple criteria has a major advantage that I have explored in more detail elsewhere (Smith, 1950a): it recognizes the possibility that, in the life situations most people face, optimal functioning in terms of one criterion is likely to be attained only at the cost of some limitation in other respects. Put differently, reality enforces a choice of values. At the unfavorable extreme (one thinks of the concentration camp), it seems clear that people cannot at once be adjusted *and* integrated *and* accurate in their grasp of the presenting reality. I have suggested (1950a) that human environments can perhaps themselves be evaluated by the extent to which they are compatible with jointly optimal values on several criteria.

But for all these advantages, multiple criteria offer no philosopher's stone for distinguishing mental health from other human values. Given a provisional list of criteria, research can clarify their interrelations. Decision on what to include in the list to begin with—which will partially determine the end result—would seem, however, to rest on a priori or consensual grounds external to the research logic of the multiple criterion approach.

FUNDAMENTAL RESEARCH IN PERSONALITY

The readiness with which multiple criteria dissolve into a multitude of empirical indices to be studied in their relationships, once the evaluative perspective becomes secondary in actual research, leads directly to the third major strategy through which research contributes to a concept of positive mental health. From one standpoint it is not a mental health strategy at all. I have in mind, of course, the main stream of research in personality, its functioning and development, pursued for the sake of understanding structure and causal relationships without any immediate concern for evaluation. Personality research becomes a source of insight into positive mental health when its results can be interpreted secondarily in an evaluative framework. Since the apparently more direct research approaches, with their inherent pitfalls and ambiguities, turn out not to be so direct after all, I have little doubt that this roundabout strategy will prove the most fruitful in the long run. It has the merit of being governed by the intrinsic patternings of phenomena as they become progressively accessible to the tools of investigation. Sometimes these patternings may be relevant to the evaluative interests of mental health; often they may not. But research is likely to be more creative if it follows its own bent with a healthy opportunism, rather than being forced prematurely into an evaluative frame.

It would exceed the scope of a single paper to try to identify the strands in this central research tradition or to illustrate their contribution, actual and potential, to our thinking about positive mental health. There are nauralistic studies of individual personalities (Smith, Bruner, and White, 1956; White, R. W., 1952), with their demonstration that personal assets take many forms and are quite compatible with elements of pathology; these strongly favor a complex view of mental health in which multiple criteria stand in some sort of alternative relationship to one another. There is the long line of studies centering on the authoritarian personality (Adorno, Frenkel-Brunswik, Levinson, and Sanford, 1950), which in spite of some methodological detours have unquestionably added greatly to our thinking about the goals of personality development. There are developmental studies, and factor analytic studies, and studies of personality dynamics deriving, at long last, from some sophistication in psychoanalytic theory, with the result that this previously isolated source of insights itself stands to be refined and enriched. Just how personality research contributes to an emerging concept of positive mental health is as hard to state formally as its substance is difficult to itemize; yet its contribution has surely been substantial.

Systems Theory as a Frame of Reference

During the course of this paper, we have looked at several paths by which research contributes to the elucidation of positive mental health: the direct assault, the multiple criterion approach, and the evaluation of fundamental research on personality. We have found merit in each, though greatest promise in the last, to which I devoted the least attention. But I have left dangling the question posed near the outset of our inquiry: how, in the light of research, are the ingredients of mental health to be distinguished from other values?

Neither the strategy of direct assault nor that of multiple criteria turns out to give us much assistance on this problem, although the empirical relationships brought to light by research that follows either strategy may aid us in the volitional decision as to where to draw the boundaries. Both seem likely to come out with distinctions already built into the procedure of investigation, either explicitly or surreptitiously. Both are compatible with either narrower or more expanded conceptions of mental health.

At an earlier point I suggested that, if mental health is personality somehow evaluated, we are handicapped by the relatively primitive state of the science of personality. So long as personality theory must be represented by *theories* of personality (cf. Hall and Lindzey, 1957), we are in a poor position to set our boundaries according to guidelines suggested by any one of the several competitors. Here lies still another reason for the support of fundamental research in personality in the interests of mental health.

In the meantime, we do well to note some formal convergences among the various conceptualizations of personality. Most views of personality conceive it as some sort of open system with tendencies toward self-maintenance and growth in commerce with the environment. A closer look at the functional interdependencies that warrant the term *system* identifies two distinguishable though interrelated *loci* of organization, which for convenience I can label the external and the internal subsystems. The external subsystem lies in what Angyal (1941) called the biosphere and concerns the dispositions and processes underlying adaptation, as newly emphasized in the psychoanalytic "ego psychology" of Hartmann and others (cf. Gill, 1959). The internal system, on the other hand, stressed in the theories of G. W. Allport (1937) and of Murray (1938) and in the orthodox psychoanalysis of Freud, has to do with stable interrelations among the institutions and processes of personality, including the management of anxiety and tension. If we take the notion of system seriously, mental health can be identified with the stability, resiliance, and viability—in a word the system properties—of these external and internal subsystems of personality.

I do not propose to elaborate a "systems theory" of personality in more detail, as the effort would surely be premature. For present purposes, it is sufficient merely to suggest in principle that system properties can provide a referent for mental health concepts on which students of personality may eventually agree. Of course such a framework answers no empirical questions, including the crucial one for students of positive mental health as to the relationship between positive mental health values (e.g., growth, differentiation, and autonomy as system properties) and resistance to mental illness under stress (viability and resiliance). As Clausen (1956) remarks, we must eventually face this question.

The systems framework as a way of thinking ties mental health to our most general conceptions of personality in a schema that permits or, better, requires elaboration by research. It calls for the development of multiple criteria of mental health and provides a framework for sorting out many of the ones that have been proposed, in terms of internal system properties (e.g., self-attitudes and integration) and properties of the external system (e.g., perception of reality, environmental mastery). And it finds in these directional properties of personality *qua* system a natural basis for evaluation. This evaluative standpoint, which transcends culture and situation, is distinguishable, moreover, from other ethical values and is by no means all-inclusive. We may regard a Khrushchev as mentally healthy at the same time we judge him to be socially destructive; a Dostoevski may be mentally ill yet artistically creative. Mental health, thus viewed, is complex and not easily schematized. It is a cluster of values that compete with other values in the arena of personal and social choice. We will not always want to give it priority. That, I think, is as it should be.

13

"Mental Health" Reconsidered

A Special Case of the Problem of Values in Psychology

The signs are increasingly clear that "mental health" and its complement, "mental illness," are terms that embarrass psychologists. Many of us do not like them (cf. American Psychological Association, 1959). Unable to define or to conceptualize them to our satisfaction, we use the terms in spite of ourselves, since they label the goals, however nebulous, of many of our service activities and the auspices of much of our research support. Even when we try to avoid them, we are swept along in the social movement of which they are shibboleths, and our scruples make little difference. Little wonder, then, that we and our colleagues in the other "mental health professions" seek to clear our consciences by continuing to engage in sporadic attempts to give them more precise and explicit meaning.

Having contributed from time to time to this discussion, I feel entitled to some skepticism about where it has got us. True, we have made some gains in disposing of several unprofitable ways of thinking about mental health that used to be prevalent. We have come to see that statistical notions of "normality" are no real help in giving psychological meaning to mental health and illness: they beg the question or fail to come to grips with it. We have become suspicious of the once regnant concept of adjustment, as it has fallen into disrepute at the hands of social critics and moralists (e.g., Riesman, 1950) who see it as a pseudo-scientific rationalization for conformist values, and of psychological theorists (e.g., White, R. W., 1959) who are challenging the sufficiency of the equilibrium model in which it is rooted. And from many quarters we encounter the call for a more positive view of mental health than is involved in the mere absence of manifest mental disorder. Since the appearance of Jahoda's useful book (1958) that reviewed the

Reprinted by permission from *American Psychologist,* 1961, *16,* 299–306. Adapted from a paper prepared for the Work Conference on Mental Health–Teacher Education Research Projects, Madison, Wisconsin, November 10–18, 1960. I am indebted to Barbara Biber, Robert Peck, Fred Wilhelms, John Withall, Nicholas Hobbs, Erich Lindemann, Ronald Lippitt, Ralph Ojemann, Hildegard Peplau, Carl Rogers, and the other participants in the conference for their reactions to the earlier version of the paper.

considerable array of proposals toward such a conception of optimal human functioning, the flow of suggestions has not abated. The discussion goes on in articles, conferences, and symposia, with little evidence of consensus in the offing.

The various lists of criteria that have been proposed for positive mental health reshuffle overlapping conceptions of desirable functioning without attaining agreement—or giving much promise that agreement can be reached. The inventories repeat themselves, and indeed it is inevitable that they should, since each successor list is proposed by a wise psychologist who scrutinizes previous proposals and introduces variations and emphases to fit his own values and preferences. Some give greater weight to the cognitive values of accurate perception and self-knowledge (e.g., Jahoda, 1950); some to moral values, to meaningful commitment, to social responsibility (e.g., Allport, G. W., 1960; Shoben, 1957); some to working effectiveness (e.g., Ginsburg, 1955); some to the blander social virtues (e.g., aspects of Foote and Cottrell, 1955); some to zest, exuberance, and creativity (e.g., Maslow, 1954). The terms recur, but in different combinations and with connotations that slant in divergent directions. By way of illustration, Table 13.1 gives the six headings

Table 13.1. Two Illustrative Conceptions of Positive Mental Health in Terms of Multiple Criteria.

Jahoda (1958)	*Allport (1960)*
attitudes toward the self	self-objectification
growth and self-actualization	ego-extension
integration	unifying philosophy of life
autonomy	
perception of reality environmental mastery }	realistic coping skills, abilities, and perceptions
	warm and deep relation of self to others
	compassionate regard for all living creatures

Note.—Rubrics rearranged to bring out parallels.

under which Jahoda (1958) organized the proposals for mental health criteria that she encountered in her review of the literature, and Allport's most recent proposal (1960), rearranged to bring out correspondences and discrepancies in the two lists. While it is an advance that psychologists are now looking for multiple criteria of good functioning rather than seeking the single touchstone of a unitary definition of mental health, we may well ask: How are psychologists to decide what items belong in such a list? By what warrant may we assign priorities to alternative criteria? Surely we need something closer to *terra firma* on which to build our research, from which to guide our practice.

There is little to be gained, I think, from adding to these competing lists. Conceptual clarification, on the other hand, may be more profitable, and my attempt in the present essay lies in that direction. Starting from the now prevalent recognition that mental health is an evaluative term, that personal and social values as standards of the preferable are somehow crucially involved in any discourse about mental health, I try first to show that this intrusion of values into psychology, lamented by some, applauded by others, is entirely legitimate. But I question, secondly, whether there is any profit in the argument about which evaluative criteria for appraising human personality and behavior are to be included in a concept of mental health. Rather, I suggest that, at least in the present stage of personality theory, "mental health" should not be regarded as a theoretical concept at all, but as a rubric or chapter heading under which fall a variety of evaluative concerns. I try to show that such a view of the term may help to clear the ground for both practical and theoretical purposes.

In an earlier effort (Smith, 1959) at clarification in this area, I observed that at the crux of the difficulty of assimilating "mental health" to psychology is the fact that "science has not yet learned how to deal surefootedly with values" (p. 673). Any progress toward clarity in psychological thinking about mental health, I am increasingly convinced, depends on our becoming clearer, as psychologists, about how we are to think about values. Whatever advances we make on the problem of values in this setting should also stand us in good stead in other contexts where issues of value confront psychology. The value problem is worth a close and sustained look.

Why the Search for a Value-Laden Conception of Positive Mental Health?

While evaluative criteria and judgments are involved in the notion of mental disorder, our consensus about what is *un*desirable is close enough for practical purposes that the role of values tends to remain implicit. It is when we want to talk about positive criteria of psychological functioning that we encounter the value problem head on. A good starting point for the present discussion, then, is to ask why we ever got ourselves into this difficult, intellectually treacherous business of positive mental health. Are not the problems of mental disorder enough? Why should the mental health movement be impelled, as it had been since the days of Clifford Beers (cf. Joint Commission on Mental Illness and Health, 1961), to extend itself to concern with the "mental hygiene" of promoting positive mental health—in the absence of firm knowledge or clear guidelines?

The answer to such a question cannot be simple. But I think a generally critical onlooker from England, R. S. Peters (1960), has hit the essential point when he addressed the BBC audience thus:

> We have a highly specialized society and we are often warned that we are developing not merely two nations but a league of nations without a

common culture and shared ideals. This should not surprise us; for where are such unifying ideals to be fostered? The study of literature, history, and the classics has had to be cut down to make room for the vast expansion in scientific education without which our society cannot survive, and the Church is rapidly losing the authority it once had as a source of unifying ideals. We tend to treat the doctor who looks after our bodies and the psychiatrist who advises us about our minds with more respect than we treat the priest who advises us about our souls—if we still think we have one. For they are scientists; and it is scientists who are now coming to be thought of as the repositories of wisdom about the mysteries of life.

This general trend explains why the educationist sometimes inclines his ear towards a new expert, the psychologist, when he is at a loss to find new unifying educational ideals to replace the old religious ones. There is thus much talk in educational circles of "the mental health of the child," "wholeness," "integration," "adjustment," and all that sort of thing. We no longer talk of turning out Christian gentlemen; we talk of letting people develop mental health or mature personalities. Indeed in America Freud's priestly role is much more explicitly acknowledged. . . . Nevertheless the general trend is [also] with us, as is shown in the frequent references to psychological notions such as "mental health" in discussion about educational ideals. [p. 46]

Discount the bias of perspective arising from Peters' assured stance in the tradition of British class education, and hold in abeyance reaction to his critical undertones: his point remains that a good many thoughtful people have turned, appropriately or otherwise, to notions of mental health in order to fill a void left by the attrition of traditionally or religiously sanctioned values. There is consumer demand for psychologists to enter the discussion of goals and aspirations for human behavior; but we had better be clear about our warrant for doing so.

The demand for a psychologically informed phrasing of objectives—for conceptions of positive mental health—comes most compellingly from those concerned with the rearing and education of children. The psychologist or psychiatrist who mainly deals with hospitalized psychotics has enough to do in trying to treat severe mental disorder and get his patients to function at some minimally adequate level; since consensus on these objectives is immediately given, the value problem hardly rises to the surface. But responsibility for the raising of children calls for positive criteria against which the success of one's efforts on their behalf can be measured. Perhaps a counselor may appropriately leave it to his adult client to set the goals for his therapy; the case can hardly be extended to the child as ward of teacher and parent—who in turn look to the psychologist for guidance.

Of course there are intellectual positions from which the responsibility appears to be minimized. If you take a Rousseau-like view that regards optimal development as the unfolding of a benign inner potential, you can at least pretend to leave goal setting entirely to the child's own nature. This doctrine of benign potentiality, which is still very much alive in educational and psychological theory (witness Maslow, 1954), strikes me as involving psychological half-truths and philosophical error. It is we ourselves, in terms of our tacit values, who single out, as optimal, one of an infinite set of possible environments for the developing child, and distinguish the way he develops in such an auspicious setting as the actualization of a naturally given potential. We ignore the infinite variety of other developmental trends that he simultaneously has the potential to actualize, many of which we would not think highly of—and ignore the silent and therefore not fully responsible intrusion of our own values involved in distinguishing one class of possible trends as self-actualizing.

Another way of minimizing responsibility for educational goal setting in terms of mental health is to accept as ultimate the values of the culture, to define the function of education as cultural transmission and, in effect, leave matters of value-choice to parents and school board. The trouble is that this option is no longer really available, even if we prefer it. The state of affairs evoked by Peters is with us: there is no longer such a solid traditional consensus for us to fall back on. Parents and school boards too are confused and involved in the fray. Under these circumstances education can hardly avoid a complex role that combines and balances cultural transmission, on the one hand, and social criticism and reconstruction on the other. This characteristic American philosophy of education has thus become virtually a policy of necessity. It calls for clear-headedness about goals, and has tended to draw on psychology for their formulation.

Insofar as we take the requirements of education seriously, then, we cannot help trying to grapple with conceptions of optimal human functioning. We also need them in planning and assessing programs of counseling and of environmental change. In the face of a waning consensus on traditional values, we join our lay clientele in hoping that psychology can help in this endeavor. But hope does not guarantee success. The strength of our needs may head us the more rigidly down blind alleys, unless we have our wits about us.

The Value Problem

The skeptical reader imbued with the distinction between scientific objectivity, on the one hand, and the humanistic cultivation of values on the other will have balked at an earlier point, and stayed with the question: By what warrant do psychologists assume the right to posit any set of human values, as we do when we propose criteria of positive mental health? The psychologist has no more right to do so, he will say, than anyone else. Let him stick to his last, and recognize the limits of his competence. My serious rejoinder, which requires somewhat of a detour to develop, reverses this conventional view: the psychologist has *as much* right to posit values as anyone else, in some important respects more. It is time to dispel the shopworn bromide that the humanist (or moralist or philosopher) has a corner on pronouncements about values, while the psychologist (or sociologist or scientist generally) must restrict himself to facts. Things are just not that simple.

For most of us, the two sources to which everyone once looked for what were then regarded as "absolute" values—Tradition and Theology—speak only equivocally if at all. We are still suffering from the crisis of personal and social readjustment occasioned by this loss. As we regain our bearings, our nostalgia for the old illusion of Absoluteness, of givenness in the eternal scheme of things, begins to fade. But in spite of the pessimism of those who hunger after Absoluteness, we still have values, in the sense of personal standards of desirability and obligation. We see them, now, as commiting choices that people make (often unwittingly) in the interplay of cultural tradition and individual experience. We see them as "relative," yes, but relative not only to culture (an exclusive focus on *cultural* relativism was the mistake of the last generation of anthropologists). They are relative also to human nature —in the diverse varieties of this nature that have emerged in human history with a degree of continuity and cumulativeness—and relative to the opportunities and limitations of human situations. Thus the warrior virtues held validity for the traditional Sioux; for the reservation Sioux they no longer make any sense (Macgregor, 1946). And one can fairly doubt whether the petty competitive values of the Alorese studied by Cora DuBois (1944) ever made much sense: she showed them to be part and parcel of a wretched and demeaning way of life that I doubt whether any Alorese would choose were some magic to give him a wider range of opportunity.

If values are social products, they rest, ultimately, on a personal commitment. Everybody, scientist or humanist or man in the street, has the right to posit values. And, since people in society are interdependent, everyone has a right to try to persuade others to his ways of valuing: *de gustibus non disputandum est* may apply to tastes and preferences, but it has never prevented controversy about values, as the course of human history well reveals. We *all* have the right to dispute values, and most of us do it. The humanist and the humane scientist nevertheless have potentially different specialized roles in the argument.

Their roles arise from the peculiar nature of argument about values that follows from the basis of values in an optional personal commitment. If you want to persuade someone to value something as you do, you can follow one of at least two strategies (assuming that physical or social coercion is ruled out, which historically has unfortunately not been the case): You can, first, try to open his eyes to new ways of seeing things—increase the range of possibilities of which he is aware, create the conditions for differentiations and restructurings in his experience from which it is possible (not necessary) that, seeing things like yourself, he may come to value them likewise. Or, second, you can give him evidence that the position he takes on a particular value has consequences for other values to which he is also committed. For the fact that values rest on a personal option does not make them arbitrary in the sense of being detached from cause or consequence. If you show a person that his chosen value of racial purity conflicts with the values of the American Creed that he also embraces, he *may* reconsider it (Myrdal, 1944). Or if you show him that his prejudiced value rests causally on evasive covert tactics of defense against inner weakness, you again have a chance to win out (Adorno, Frenkel-Brunswik, Levinson, and Sanford, 1950). The *ad hominem* argument, in ill favor as it is, is fair play in this peculiar and important realm, so long as it is not taken as conclusive. Since values rest on personal option, *no* argument is conclusive, though many can be persuasive, and appropriately so.

I am thus suggesting that the humanist and the moral philosopher are especially equipped to employ the first of these strategies: drawing on the fund of human history and culture, with its stock of transmitted discriminations, they can sensitize us to differentiations and potentialities of human experience which, unaided, we could never attain individually. Our value choices are enriched and modified by this exposure. The second strategy, that of displaying the causal network in which value choice is embedded, is one for which the humane or behavioral scientist is uniquely qualified.

The old myth had it that man lost his precultural innocence when, biting the fruit of the Tree of Knowledge, he became aware of Good and Evil. In becoming modern, Man has taken a second portentous bite of the same fruit. There are alternative versions of Good and Evil, he discovers to his discomfiture, and it is up to him to choose the commitments he is to live by. From this emerging view that can no longer turn to authoritative interpretations of tradition or divine revelation to resolve questions of value, it makes no sense at all for us to encyst ourselves behind a pass-the-buck notion that we can leave value judgments to some other discipline that specializes in them. There is no discipline that has this mythical competence: the humanist and the theologian speak with no greater authority than we. We are all in it together.

The List Problem

I think I have shown the legitimacy, the clear warrant, for psychologists to concern themselves with values, as we do when we involve ourselves with mental health. But my argument gives no help at all on the other problem: what value dimensions are to get on our lists of mental health criteria, and why? If anything, it makes things more difficult. For if values are matters of a committing personal option, how are psychologists—let alone people at large—to come to agree on any particular list any more closely than the limited extent to which they already do? Even with a richer exposure to the humanistic tradition than is customary for psychologists, even with a far more adequate fund of causal knowledge than is presently available, psychological "experts" are not going to agree on the proper goals for human nature, and these are what we are talking about.

The actual situation is well typified by the experience of the Cornell Conference (National Assembly on Mental Health Education, 1960). To quote the conference report:

> Everyone at Cornell seemed to agree that the good life for all was to be desired. They split, however, on what that good life was—as they had split on the definition of mental health, and they split on who, if anyone, should have the right to try to "impose" it on others. [p. 20]

The definition of mental health, of course, *involves* a conception of the good life, which nobody *can* impose on anyone else (barring "brainwashing" and physical coercion), though, at least among colleagues and equals, it is fair enough for each of us to try to persuade the rest.

But the time has come to cut the Gordian knot, to restructure the problem along more profitable lines. The place to cut, I think, is the notion that the lists we have been considering itemize criteria of some entity called "positive mental health," and are equivalent to a definition of it. Even though we may have forsaken the view of mental health as a unitary phenomenon, and may have no intention of adding up a single score across our multiple criteria, we remain beguiled by the assumption that an articulate theoretical concept or construct of mental health lurks somewhere ready to be discovered. It is the pursuit of this will-o'-the-wisp that has made the procession of lists of mental health criteria so fruitless.

As we actually study effective functioning—or commit ourselves to social or educational programs that seek in various ways to promote it—our focus then becomes, not "mental health" variously indexed, but any or all of a number of much more specific evaluative dimensions of human functioning: any that we are ready to commit ourselves to take seriously as relevant and valued potential psychological outcomes of the programs that we are working with, any that we can begin to pin down in operational terms, as many of them as seem important to us and as we can feasibly cope with. Here I find myself in essential agreement with the position recently taken by Levine and Kantor (1962).

From the standpoint of research, the problem of attaining consensus on criteria is thus scaled down to the workaday dimensions we are used to: the practical difficulty of trying to convince at least some of our colleagues to study some of the same things we are studying by similar methods, so that our results can dovetail or add up. There is no reason at all why study of the causes, consequences, and interrelations of status on various mental health dimensions has to await consensus on a common list that may never be attained—and by my personal value commitments would not even be desirable!

In the long run, it is possible that our understanding of interrelated system properties of personality may advance to a point that warrants a more theoretical conception of mental health—one related, say, to empirically based estimates of such properties as self-maintenance, growth, and resilience (cf.

Smith, 1959). We are certainly still far from being able to envision such a conception except in the most schematic terms. But if it is to be attained at all, the road to it should lie through nonevaluative research on personality development and functioning, on the one hand, and, on the other, through the strategy I have just been advocating: modestly exploring the empirical correlates of valued attributes of personality.

But what of the public demands for mental health "expertise" with which we started? What implications does our analysis have for the role of the psychologist in school, clinic, or consulting room? The very fact that no simple rule book of prescribed conduct seems to follow from it gives me greater confidence in the appropriateness of the approach we have taken.

Knowing that he lacks a scientifically sanctioned single set of mental health criteria, the psychologist in his consulting or service or educational relationships will hesitate to prescribe the nature of the good life to others in the name of psychology. Since values rest on a personal option, he will find it easiest to keep a clear scientific and professional conscience when he can use his knowledge and skill to help others identify, clarify, and realize their value commitments—provided that he can reconcile them with the values that he himself is commited to. Yet his own psychologically informed personal commitments about the nature of good human functioning cannot exist in a vacuum. They may lead him to avoid or to terminate service relationships that appear to violate them, to seek relationships that promote them. When his role as teacher or therapist vests him with more direct and personal responsibility for goal setting, he will not hesitate to act in terms of his convictions about what is desirable in the relationship and of the best knowledge and wisdom he can muster. But he will seek to move such relationships in the direction of increasing the responsibility of the other party for choosing his own goals. To his colleagues in and out of psychology and to various publics, he may often appear as an advocate of particular values. But his advocacy will consist in displaying the nature of his personal commitment and of using his psychological knowledge and insight to explore the linkage between holding or attaining a value and its conditions and consequences. In a word, explicitness about values goes with responsible scientific and professional behavior, and when we are explicit about such values as truthfulness, competence, care, responsibility, creativity, we add nothing consequential by labeling them as dimensions or criteria of positive mental health.

MENTAL HEALTH AS A RUBRIC

If "mental health" is to lose its presumptive conceptual standing, what does its status become? I see it rather as a rubric, a chapter title, a label for the common concern of various disciplines involved in evaluating human functioning from the perspective of the psychology of personality. Its usefulness in this respect does not depend on its dubious status as a theoretical concept. As chapter title, "mental health" is analogous to "mechanics" in classical physics: a rubric under which we treat a number of theoretical constructs (e.g., mass, force, velocity) and the laws relating them. You do not argue very violently about where chapter boundaries should be drawn.

There remain many meaningful problems concerning the contents and organization of such a chapter, even about its name. Personally, I agree with Levine and Kantor (1962) and with Szasz (1960) that the term "mental health" is unfortunate for our present purposes, biasing the issues as it does toward a model of physical health and illness that seems quite inappropriate to the analysis of effective and disordered conduct. But with the focus shifted to specific evaluative dimensions, I do not find myself caring very much about this argument, any more than I worry about the chapter titles in a book of applied science. This is an editorial problem, not a substantive one.

As for the contents of the mental health chapter, a variety of pragmatic considerations come to mind to assist in culling, augmenting, and refining the items in the available lists. Candidates for treatment as dimensions of mental health or of goodness of psychological functioning might be expected to meet most of the following criteria, none of which seems to require elaborate justification:

1. They should be serious contenders in the arena of human values (though an impossible consensus is of course not required). The posited value should be explicit.
2. They should be capable of measurement or of inference from identifiable aspects of behavior.
3. They should articulate with personality theory (a weak requirement, since the proviso must be added immediately that personality theories will probably need to be extended and modified to make contact with value dimensions chosen on other grounds).
4. They should be relevant to the social context for which the chapter is being written. In the context of education, for instance, this is to ask: What kinds of psychological assets would we like to see the schools develop in our children? Quite different considerations would come to the fore in the context of a correctional agency.

Considerations such as these make it unlikely that the entire range of moral, esthetic, and cognitive values will vie for inclusion in the mental health chapter. But no harm is done if a venturesome soul decides to study the natural history of some utterly "unpsychological" value under mental health auspices.

A more fundamental choice concerns short vs. long versions of the chapter: in other words, minimal vs. extended conceptions of mental health. I can illustrate this choice best if I introduce at the same time a possible principle for organizing the chapter. Jahoda (1958) observed that "one has the option of defining mental health in at least two ways: as a relatively constant and enduring function of the personality . . . ; or as a momentary function of personality and situation" (pp. 7–8). Klein (1960) makes a similar point in his distinction between soundness or general stability, and well-being. We want, that is, to distinguish, on the one hand, the person's present state and behavior as an interactive resultant of his personality and features of the momentary situation that he confronts, and, on the other, the corresponding dispositions of his present personality, with situational effects discounted. Add a time dimension—here in terms of an assessment of mental health in childhood with prognosis to adulthood, since a primary ingredient of our interest in the mental health of children is the foundation it is assumed to provide for adult functioning—and minimal vs. extended views of mental health may be illustrated as in Table 13.2.

Table 13.2. Illustration of Narrow and Broad Conceptions of Mental Health.

Scope	MENTAL HEALTH OF CHILD		*Adult Prognosis*
	Present Behavior	*Present Disposition*	
Minimal Conception	Freedom from incapacitating symptoms	Good resistance to stress	Absence of mental disorder in adulthood
Extended Conception	Momentary well-being (in specified respects)	Capacities for competent, happy, zestful, etc. child life	Capacities for competent, happy, zestful, etc. adult life

To me, this way of mapping the contents of the chapter seems clarifying. As I look at the top row, the narrow conception of the scope of mental health seems thoroughly viable. I am led to think that Jahoda (1958) may have dismissed this version too quickly, that the psychiatrist Walter Barton in his postscript to her volume was certainly right about its relevance and adequacy for the context of institutional psychiatry. But as I compare the top and bottom lines, I agree with her that the narrow version of the chapter is not in itself adequate to the evaluative concerns of education—to pick one relevant context with which psychologists are involved. And it is of course the bottom line, the extended version, that potentially expands greatly as various dimensions of good functioning are specified. Comparison of the two lines reminds me to agree with Clausen (1956) that we know very little about their relationship to one another: no longer regarding mental health as a theoretical concept, we have no particular reason to expect resistance to mental disorder to correlate with various aspects of positive functioning, but the problem calls for research. And finally, the presence of the right-hand column calls to mind how little we know about the continuities of behavior seen in evaluative terms.

So long as we grope futilely toward a *concept* of "mental health," minimal or maximal, the advantages of specificity and researchability appear to be on the side of the minimal conception. Viewing these versions as different locations of chapter boundary lines, however, we can be as specific as we want about our positively valued criteria. It may well turn out to be the case, then, that the extended version includes the valued dimensions of behavior and personality that are most responsive to our interventions. "Mental health promotion" in this sense may not be as impractical as some of us have come to assume.

CONCLUSION

Where has this analysis of "mental health" as a problem of values led us? It may free us, I hope, from some of the embarrassment that has motivated psychologists' attempts to treat it as a theoretical concept—attemps that have not been additive and have not made the term theoretically respectable. If we understand "mental health" not as an unsatisfactory and vague theoretical concept but as a reasonably adequate rubric or label for an evaluative psychological perspective on personality—even though the term is not of our own choosing—we can get about our business without wasting our efforts on the search for consensus on a unique set of mental health criteria when consensus is not to be had.

Under this rubric, our business, be it research or service, is properly concerned with specific valued dimensions or attributes of behavior and personality. In our focus on these dimensions we are not at all handicapped by the lack of a satisfactory conceptual definition of mental health.

Nor need we be embarrassed by the intrusion of values in our focus on various specified aspects of desirable or undesirable psychological functioning. What is to be avoided is the *surreptitious* advocacy of values disguised under presumptive scientific auspices. The lists of psychological desiderata that psychologists have continued to propose, each reflecting the value commitments of its proponent, have this drawback insofar as they are offered as "criteria of positive mental health." But there is nothing surreptitious, nothing illegitimate, in using evaluative dimensions such as those that appear on these lists to appraise behavior and personality, so long as the value position one takes is explicit. And there is much to be gained from psychological study of the empirical antecedents, consequences, and interrelations of realizing different values in the sphere of personality.

In the study of optimal human functioning, I have argued, behavioral and social scientists can put their special qualifications to work toward the clarification of values among which people must choose and of the causal relations that are relevant to value choice. From it we should not only increase our knowledge about ways and means of attaining the values we agree on; we should also bring to light factual relationships that have a bearing on our choice of what values to pursue, individually and socially. To the extent that the behavioral sciences develop in this direction, they contribute to providing a badly needed bridge between what C. P. Snow (1959) has called "the two cultures" of the scientists and the humanistic intellectuals.

14

Explorations in Competence

A Study of Peace Corps Teachers in Ghana

One of the hopeful aspects of our affluent society—and I persist in believing that there are many—is our increasing concern with psychological effectiveness and fulfillment. Like the hierarchy of needs that Abraham Maslow (1954) has proposed, there seems to be a hierarchy of human goals that underlie fashions of value-oriented research. When people are undernourished and die young, as they still do in much of the world, research and action on public health is the first order of business. Achievements in this initial sphere have brought us to realize belatedly that successful attack on the "underdeveloped syndrome" requires knowledge and action on two additional fronts: economic development, to provide a better livelihood for the growing and now impatient numbers who survive; and population control, lest economic gains dissolve into net losses. Psychologists are beginning to find a challenge for research in the former topic (McClelland, 1965); they have still to rise to the need and the opportunity in regard to the second.

The basic problems of human survival and maintenance are never permanently solved, but social priorities do shift. Over the last generation American psychologists have found a good deal of social support in their preoccupation with derangements of conduct and social relations among physically healthy people—a concern that would have seemed an unwarranted luxury in a society where the more exigent problems of health and hunger had not been substantially tamed. These problems are still with

Reprinted by permission from *American Psychologist,* 1966, *21,* 555–566. Invited address, Division 8, American Psychological Association, Chicago, September 1965; written during tenure as Fellow of the Center for Advanced Study in the Behavioral Sciences and Special Research Fellow of the National Institute of Mental Health. The data reported are based on a study at the Institute of Human Development, University of California, Berkeley, under contract No. PC–(W)–55 with the Peace Corps, which of course is not responsible for the opinions and judgments that I have ventured to express. I am especially indebted to my closest associates in this research, Raphael S. Ezekiel and Susan Roth Sherman; to George Carter, the initial Peace Corps Representative in Ghana; and to the volunteers themselves whose tolerance and hospitality made my research both possible and gratifying.

us, and as we extend our attention to the submerged and essentially underdeveloped sectors of our own society, they will rank high in our scheme of priorities for a good while longer.

All the same, psychologists are beginning to bring psychological research to bear upon the forms and conditions of more positive aspects of human functioning, under such rubrics as "positive mental health," psychological effectiveness, creativity, and competence. These may still be middle-class luxuries, but it is now politically astute, not merely visionary, to conceive of a "great society" in which such phrasings of the good life become relevant for everybody.

When we turn from the bottom of the hierarchy of social goals, where consensus on values is easily had in regard to the minimal essentials of life in society, to the unimagined variety of paths along which people may seek fulfillment, it is easy to lose our bearings, to confuse tendentious pleading for our own versions of the good life with the exploration of empirical fact. I have done my own share of floundering in these waters, fishing from the armchair in discussions of "positive mental health" (Smith, 1959; 1961). From the armchair, the critical need seemed to me to be for more adequate mapping of facts and relationships concerning widely valued modes of behavior.

I therefore grasped the opportunity to make an intensive study of a group of promising young people who were faced with a challenging assignment: the first group of Peace Corps volunteers to go overseas, who trained in Berkeley in the summer of 1961 and served for two years as secondary school teachers in Ghana. The combined idealistic-practical asupices of the Peace Corps seemed right, and Nicholas Hobbs (then Director of Selection and Research for the Peace Corps) was encouraging. I saw the study as an investigation of psychological effectiveness (let us put aside the awkward terminology of "mental health"). More recently, the cogency of Robert White's (1959, 1963) conceptions to my emerging data has become increasingly apparent, so that I now think of myself as having been engaged in "explorations in competence."

There were 58 young people who entered training in Berkeley, 50 of whom completed one year[1] and 45 completed two years of overseas service. Our most intensive data are for 27 men and 17 women who finished the two-year term. I met my obligations to the Peace Corps with a technical report (Smith, 1964), and since then have been working on a volume that intends to illuminate the statistical findings with a series of illustrative case studies.

Here I must be selective. I shall draw on our findings to develop several themes that represent things I think I have learned about competence in this special Peace Corps setting.

1. Their mean age of entry was 24.0 (range, 19–34); subsequent groups averaged about a year younger. As many as 46 per cent had had a year or more of teaching experience; subsequent groups were less experienced.

My major points will be four. First, in regard to the nature of competence in this group, time, and setting: Our data support the view that competence has a coherent core of common psychological attributes. But, second, competent performance takes various forms, which people reach by different psychological routes. Third, in regard to the prediction of competent performance: Two reasonable possibilities, grounded in the respective thought patterns of social psychologists and of psychiatrists and clinical psychologists, turn out not to work at all, while a third predictor, introduced on a hunch, shows promise. Both the failures and the relative success have something to say about the psychological nature of competence. Finally, we have some evidence about the maturing effects of Peace Corps service, which lends itself to speculation about motivational aspects of the Peace Corps experience.

From Field Interviews to *Q* Sort Patterns

Before I can turn to the first of these topics, a word is needed about the kind of data that we will be dealing with. Of course we had a kit of pencil-and-paper tests, some of them administered both before and after overseas experience. We also had various staff ratings from the training period and from the field. Our central information about the experience and performance of the volunteers, however, came from long and detailed interviews that R. S. Ezekiel and I recorded with the volunteers at their schools in the early summer of 1962 and 1963.

Our reliance on informal interviews made a virtue of necessity. Practical considerations excluded the systematic use of classroom observation, or of data from students, fellow teachers, or headmasters. The spirited touchiness of the volunteers themselves in regard to psychological assessment procedures—partly a residue of their experience during selection-in-training at Berkeley—required us to establish an essentially collaborative relationship with them if we were to do the study at all. Fortunately, the volunteers liked to talk about their lives and jobs, and we were able to gain a satisfying degree of rapport with them—which still continues.

We planned the guide for the first-year interviews on the basis of my quick reconnaisance during the volunteers' first Christmas in Ghana. As it turned out, the roughly four hours of interviewing apiece the first year, and two and a half the second, gave a highly informative picture of what the volunteer had made of his job and Peace Corps role and of his qualities as a person as they were brought out in this novel and challenging setting. We were well satisfied with the quality of our interviews. But how to process them to preserve their richness yet assure the maximum degree of objectivity that we could attain?

Our first and crucial decision on behalf of objectivity was made at the onset: to record and transcribe the interviews in full. Following the lead of my colleague Jack Block (1961), we then invested major effort in constructing two decks of *Q* sort items that "judges" could use to extract and quantify the meat of the interview transcripts. One deck, of 65 items in the final version, dealt with the volunteer's role perceptions, personal agenda, and role performance. The second, of 64 items, permitted judges to characterize the volunteer's personality structure and processes.[2] These sets of items were in development over much of a year. Our procedure was to hold "clinical" conferences in the attempt to formulate what the interviews could tell us about the personality and performance of particular volunteers, then to translate our intuitive insights into items. There followed the usual tedious process of trial use by the research staff and by naive judges, and endless editing and revision.

Once the decks had been refined to our satisfaction, we had 12 advanced graduate students in psychology use them to characterize each volunteer after studying the transcript of his interviews. The judges were given a brief orientation to the setting and special terminology of "Peace Corps–Ghana" and discussed their discrepancies in the rating of a practice case—the investigator carefully holding back his own version of "the truth"—but they were otherwise unfamiliar with the volunteers and with the preconceptions of the investigator. Their task in each case was to sort the items of a given deck in a prescribed nine-point distribution, ranging from the three items that appeared to be most saliently characteristic or newsworthy about the volunteer (given a rating of 9) down to the three that seemed most saliently uncharacteristic of him (a rating of 1). Clearly, normative considerations about what might be expected of people in general and of Peace Corps volunteers in particular intrude into these ipsative ratings. The advantage of the ipsative task over normative ratings would seem to lie, rather, in its focus on the *patterning* of personality and performance, thus reducing the potency of general halo effects that might otherwise obscure patterned differences among volunteers.

We will be concerned here with *Q* sorts made on the basis of reading *both* years' interviews with a particular volunteer (giving precedence to status as of the final year in cases of evident change). Depending on the extent of interjudge agreement achieved by the first pair of raters to *Q* sort a case, from two to six judges contributed to each of the composite *Q* sort ratings that constitute our central data. On the basis of the average interjudge correlations for each case, appropriately transformed,[3] the role performance *Q* set was judged with a mean estimated reliability of .76; the personality set with a mean estimated reliability of .68.

2. A third *Q* deck characterizing the volunteer's view of his situation, its challenges and limitations, and aspects of morale and job satisfaction was also developed; results depending on this deck are drawn upon in the larger study but will not be cited here.

3. Average r's were computed via Fisher's z transformation and corrected by the Spearman-Brown formula according to the number of judges contributing to a given composite.

The composite ratings of each volunteer on the two *Q* sets allows us to identify distinguishable major patterns of personal orientation and performance in Peace Corps service. The first step was to compute the matrix of interperson correlations for each of the two sets. We could then carry out a *Q* oriented principal-components factor analysis on each matrix. The first principal component that was produced from each of the two analyses, which accounted for 41 per cent and 44 per cent, respectively, of the communality of the role performance and the personality matrices, defined a highly evaluative dimension, as we could see from the items that received high or low factor scores, and from our acquaintance with the volunteers who received high or low factor loadings. Loadings on these factors thus provided us with measures of general competence as reflected in the interviews, and refracted through the *Q* sorts for role performance and for personality. Volunteers' loadings on these factors correlated .26 and .35, respectively, with administrative ratings of overall performance as of the end of the second year—modest correlations to be sure, but better than 0 at $p < .05$ for the personality factor. Loadings on the first personality and first performance factors were closely intercorrelated: $r = .89$.

The evaluative halo extracted in the first principal component factors was thus of interest to us in its own right, for its item content and for the evaluative criteria that the factor loadings provided against which to test predictor variables. But we were also interested in penetrating and dissecting this halo, insofar as possible, to distinguish recurrent patterns of role performance and of personality functioning overseas: coherent ways in which volunteers resembled or different from one another in their handling of the Peace Corps role and in their traits and coping styles as inferred from the field interviews. To this end we carried out varimax rotations of the factors obtained through the principal-components analysis. Three clearly interpretable patterns of role performance and six of personality emerged from this analysis—much to our surprise after months of delayed gratification while interview tapes were transcribed, *Q* decks built, transcripts judged, and cards punched. But now it is time to look at the data.

Some Patterns of Competence

A Picture of General Competence

Let us first look at the evaluative first principal components, beginning with the one based on *Q* sorts with the personality deck. Table 14.1 lists the items that were especially characteristic of volunteers who received high loadings on this factor: items with factor scores a standard deviation or more above the mean. The items defining what is *un*characteristic of these

Table 14.1. Items with High Factor Scores on Personality Factor P-1: Self-Confident Maturity.

Item	*Factor score*
Generally self-confident.	73
A genuinely dependable and responsible person.	69
The values and principles which he hold directly affect what he does.	65
Feels his own life is important, that it matters what he does with his life.	65
Open to experience, ready to learn.	62
Tolerant and understanding.	61
Characteristically maintains a highly articulate, intellectual formulation of his situation and problems.	60

Table 14.2. Items with Low Factor Scores on Personality Factor P-1: Self-Confident Maturity.

Item	*Factor score*
Feels a lack of worth; has low self-esteem.	24
Basically a dependent person; characteristically leans upon others for support.	33
Has had a characteristically high level of anxiety during the time in Ghana.	33
Tends to expect little of life, pessimistic.	33
Seems generally to lack energy, to operate at a markedly low key.	35
Tends to be suspicious of others.	35
Tends to give up easily when faced with setbacks.	36
Would be unable to accept help from others when in need.	37
When things go badly, would tend to let them drift.	37
Tends to be preoccupied with matters of physical health.	38
Irritable and overresponsive to petty annoyances.	38
Engages in "posturing" to self and others; concerned with maintaining "face."	39
Tends unrealistically to minimize or deny the difficulties that he faces.	40

volunteers—those with distinctively low factor scores, are given in Table 14.2. Inspection of the tables shows a pattern of self-confidence, high self-esteem, energy, principled responsibility, optimistic realism, and persistence with flexibility, among other virtues. We felt justified in labeling this P-1 pattern "Self-Confident Maturity."

The corresponding first factor based on the role performance deck really gives us an alternative perspective on the same facts, since it is based on the same interviews and much the same people obtained high loadings. Table 14.3 shows the items that have high scores on this factor. Commitment to and competence in the teaching role top the list, with liking for one's students a close third. Other items emphasize qualities both of the volunteer's teaching and of his involvement with Africa. In Table 14.4 are given the *un*characteristic items, with low factor scores. These items paint a picture of low competence and commitment, and of a variety of ways in which a volunteer might perform his role less than well. We label this P-1 performance pattern "Competent Teaching in Africa."

Table 14.3. Items with High Factor Scores on Performance Factor P-1: Competent Teaching in Africa.

Item	*Factor score*
Committed to carrying out his job as Peace Corps teacher to the best of his ability.	72
Is, all-in-all, a good competent teacher.	71
Generally likes his students, treats them with warmth and understanding.	66
Values his Peace Corps assignment as relevant to his career plans.	63
Views his teaching in terms of its contribution to the personal welfare or development of his students.	62
In his appraisal of Ghanaian life and institutions, is sympathetically critical; forms his own judgments with due regard to historical and cultural differences.	62
As a teacher emphasizes challenging students to think.	61
His African experiences have increased his concern with race relations in the United States.	61
Judges Ghanaian governmental policies and actions in terms of the needs of Ghana (regardless of approval or disapproval).	61
His approach to teaching integrates the formal curricular and examination requirements with his own sense of proper educational objectives.	60
Has shown consideration in his dealings with adult Ghanaians.	60

Table 14.4. Items with Low Factor Scores on Performance Factor P-1: Competent Teaching in Africa.

Item	*Factor score*
Incompetent in his understanding of the major subject matter that he has to teach.	25
Feels mostly negative about Ghanaians he has met, really doesn't like them very much.	27
Overidentified with Ghana, attempts to "go native."	30
Has little real interest in Ghana.	31
Shows a lack of tact in relations with students.	33
Imposes own educational objectives at expense of preparing student for formal curricular and examination requirements.	34
Sees his school job as one restricted almost entirely to the classroom—the "9 to 5" attitude.	36
Tends to be condescending toward his students.	36
His personal problems of finding himself take priority for him over the tasks of the Peace Corps assignment.	37
Reacts to his students as a category or as types, rather than as individuals (N.B. regardless of degree of warmth or liking).	39

The pictures that emerge from the two *Q* sort decks readily coalesce. We find a pattern defined on its good side by qualities of warranted self-confidence, commitment, energy, responsibility, autonomy, flexibility, and hopeful realism together with other skills and attitudes more specifically appropriate to the role of Peace Corps teacher. The pattern has psychological coherence, in that having some of these virtues should make it easier to have the others. (If you lack most of them, it is very hard to get a start on acquiring any of them—as we are learning from efforts to relaunch culturally deprived youth.) Undoubtedly, raters' halo exaggerates the coherence of our data: To a degree that we cannot ascertain, raters will have attributed miscellaneous virtues to the volunteers of whom they came to think well, on whatever grounds. We will assume, all the same, that this syndrome of general competence rests on underlying psychological fact. Other coherences in our data tend to lend to this assumption at least some support.

Patterns of Role Performance

Turn now to the discriminable patterns of role performance that emerge from varimax rotation. For the sake of economy, we will look only at the items with distinctively high factor scores. Under rotation, the generally evaluative dimension of Competent Teaching in Africa pulls apart into two distinct patterns, one emphasizing involvement with Africa, the other an exclusive commitment to teaching.

Table 14.5 shows the items with high scores on Factor V-1, "Constructive Involvement with Africa."[4] They emphasize good personal relations with students and with other Africans, and a thoughtful integration of the experience of Africa, coupled with commitment to the teaching job.

Table 14.5. Items with High Factor Scores on Performance Factor V-1: Constructive Involvement with Africa.

Item	*Factor score*
His African experiences have increased his concern with race relations in the United States.	68
Generally likes his students, treats them with warmth and understanding.	65
Has established intimate, continuing relationships with adult Africans.	64
Enjoys or admires Ghanaian style of living.	64
In his appraisal of Ghanaian life and institutions, is sympathetically critical; forms his own judgments with due regard to historical and cultural differences.	63
Is on friendly terms with many Ghanaians (apart from his students). (N.B. Disregard depth of the relationship.)	63
Has developed close, personal relationships with some of his students.	61
Committed to carrying out his job as Peace Corps teacher to the best of his ability.	61
In anticipating his return he is concerned with interpreting Ghana and/or West Africa to Americans.	61
Judges Ghanaian governmental policies and actions in terms of the needs of Ghana (Regardless of approval or disapproval.)	61
Views his teaching in terms of its contribution to the personal welfare or development of his students.	60
Views his teaching in terms of its contribution to the development of Ghana.	60
As a result of his experience in Ghana, his thoughts and feelings about America show increased depth and perspective.	60

Note.—Twenty-seven percent of communality; r with P-1 (performance) = .84, r with P-1 (personality) = .68.

4. See Table 8.4, above, for the items with low factor scores.

Quite in contrast is the picture of Factor V-2, "Exclusive Teaching Commitment" (Table 14.6). Volunteers who loaded high on this factor were skillfully devoted to their teaching almost to the exclusion of other involvements with Africa: their contact with Africa was deep but narrow, through their school and students.

Our third varimax performance factor looks the opposite of "gung-ho." From the items with high factor scores in Table 14.7, we see that this pattern

Table 14.6. Items with High Factor Scores on Performance Factor V-2: Exclusive Teaching Commitment.

Item	*Factor score*
His whole life has centered on the school compound.	78
Absorbed in his work.	70
Committed to carrying out his job as Peace Corps teacher to the best of his ability.	69
Is, all-in-all, a good competent teacher.	69
Spends much time preparing lessons, correcting papers, etc.	67
As a teacher emphasizes challenging students to think.	64
Has well defined teaching goals and objectives.	62
Has worked out a balance between informality and closeness to students, on the one hand, and the requirements of discipline and authority on the other.	62
Generally likes his students, treats them with warmth and understanding.	61
His approach to teaching integrates the formal curricular and examination requirements with his own sense of proper educational objectives.	61
Concerned with setting Ghanaians a good personal example.	61

Note.—Nineteen percent of communality; r with P-1 (performance) = .32, r with P-1 (personality) = .31.

Table 14.7. Items with High Factor Scores on Performance Factor V-3: Limited Commitment.

Item	*Factor score*
Most of his time outside of class is spent in reading, recreation, or other activities unrelated to work.	71
Establishing relationships with the opposite sex has been an important aspect of his period of Peace Corps service.	68
Is, all-in-all, a good competent teacher.	67
Sees his school job as one restricted almost entirely to the classroom—the "9 to 5" attitude.	66
His approach to teaching integrates the formal curricular and examination requirements with his own sense of proper educational objectives.	65
Was quick to become aware of difficulties in communicating with students in the classroom and to adapt his teaching accordingly.	65
Has many, or close, contacts with expatriates (off school compound).	63
Interested in traditional Ghanaian life and customs.	61
Meets his teaching obligations day-by-day with little long-term planning.	61
Concerned with introducing American educational approaches and techniques.	60

Note.—Nine percent of communality; r with P-1 (performance) = —.50, r with P-1 (personality) = —.39.

characterizes volunteers who, by and large, were good teachers, but were low in commitment both to modern Africa and to the teaching job. They were "9-to-5ers" who nevertheless often made a substantial contribution to their schools. The negative correlation of —.50 between factor loadings on "Limited Commitment" and on the P-1 competence factor reflects the relatively low evaluation they tended to receive from the *Q* sort judges; they did not fare so badly in administrative evaluation.

The results so far carry a message of some practical importance. They show that although a syndrome of general competence in the Peace Corps role can be identified, two quite different patterns of competent performance emerged, both "good." We will see that different personality patterns accompanied these distinctive performance styles. Selection policies based on a stereotyped conception of the ideal volunteer could readily go astray.

Personality Patterns in the Field Interviews

Since six intelligible patterns appeared in the varimax analysis of the personality *Q* sorts, I must hold myself to a summary treatment. The labels we gave them appear in Table 14.8, together with the correlations between loadings on each of them and loadings on the evaluative first principal components. The table also shows their relationships to the varimax performance factors, again correlating factor loadings taken as scores.

Three of the patterns are associated with competent performance. V-1, Interpersonally Sensitive Maturity, differs little from the P-1 factor based on the same *Q* sort, except that it gives greater emphasis to interpersonal openness, nurturance, empathy, and intensity of self-involvement. Women were more likely than men to fit this pattern. The other two "good" patterns

Table 14.8. Personality Patterns Derived From Interview Q *Sorts and Some of Their Correlates.*

Pattern	% communality	*r* WITH P-1 LOADINGS		Closest correlates among role performance factors	
		Perf.	*Pers.*		
V-1, Interpersonally sensitive maturity	27%	.80	.82	V-1 (Involv. in Afr.):	.74
				V-3 (Limited commit.):	—.43
V-2, Intellectualizing future orientation	13%	.48	.57	V-1 (Involv. in Afr.):	.40
V-3, Self-reliant conventionality	12%	—.07	.08	V-3 (Limited commit.):	.50
V-4, Dependent anxiety	11%	—.76	—.87	V-1 (Involv. in Afr.):	—.58
				V-3 (Limited commit.):	.40
V-5, Controlling responsibility	11%	.46	.50	V-2 (Exclus. teach.):	.62
				V-3 (Limited commit.):	—.51
V-6, Self-actualizing search for identity	7%	—.15	—.11	V-2 (Exclus. teach.):	—.38

were more characteristic of men: V-2, Intellectualizing Future Orientation, and V-5, Controlling Responsibility.

One pattern, when it appeared, strongly tended to be incompatible with good performance: V-4, Dependent Anxiety. Finally, there were two well-defined patterns that showed little correlation with loadings on the evaluative P-1 factors: V-3, Self-Reliant Conventionality, and V-6, Self-Actualizing Search for Identity.

The right-hand column of the table shows the main lines of relationship between these personality patterns and the varimax performance factors. Let us note the major correlates of each of these performance patterns in turn. We see that performance factor V-1, Constructive Involvement with Africa, is positively linked with Interpersonally Sensitive Maturity and with Intellectualizing Future Orientation—alternative routes toward getting involved with Africa—and negatively with Dependent Anxiety. V-2, Exclusive Teaching Commitment, is closely tied with Controlling Responsibility, and negatively linked with Self-Actualizing Search for Identity. Finally, V-3, Limited Commitment, is associated with both Self-Reliant Conventionality and with Dependent Anxiety, as alternative psychological bases, and is negatively related to Interpersonally Sensitive Maturity and to Controlling Responsibility. Diverse personal styles are indeed involved in the patterns of performance that our method has discerned in the interviews.

We can put a little meat on these bones by looking at the items that define patterns V-5 and V-6, to which we will have occasion to refer subsequently. Factor V-5, Controlling Responsibility, is presented in Table 14.9. Volunteers who were high on this factor tended, we remember, also to be high on Exclusive Teaching Commitment. They were steady, somewhat rigid people, self-contained but given to intense involvement. Highly *un*characteristic items (not shown) indicate that self-control was as important to them as control over the situations that they faced. They tended to be low in empathic sensitivity but high in nurturance. They had considerable personal resources.

In contrast to them are the interesting volunteers who showed the pattern to which we have given the perhaps pretentious but nevertheless descriptive label, Self-Actualizing Search for Identity. The defining items with high factor scores appear in Table 14.10.[5] These volunteers, like those who were high on V-2 (Intellectualizing Future Orientation),[6] appear to have been in good communication with themselves and to have found the topic interesting; the search for identity was still a prominent part of their agenda of young adulthood. But whereas the volunteers who were high on Intellectualizing Future Orientation seem in general to have gained the upper hand in the struggle for self-definition, those who were high on V-6 were clearly in the midst of a postadolescent turmoil. The *Q* sort items describe them as

5. See Table 8.7, above, for the items with low factor scores.

6. See Table 8.6, above, for the items with high and low factor scores on this variable.

Table 14.9. Items with High Factor Scores on Personality Factor V-5: Controlling Responsibility.

Item	Factor score
Control of his situation is important to him.	75
A genuinely dependable and responsible person.	69
Engages in "posturing" to self and others; concerned with maintaining "face."	67
Preoccupied with the power aspects of relations.	66
Intense, tends to involve self deeply.	65
Is uneasy when the situation is not clearly defined.	65
The values and principles which he holds directly affect what he does.	65
High in initiative; active rather than reactive.	65
Nurturant; enjoys helping the younger or less adequate.	62
A major component of his stance has been his assumption that one meets one's daily obligations as a matter of course.	61
Generally self-confident.	60

Note.—Eleven percent of communality; *r* with P–1 (personality) = .50, *r* with P–1 (performance) = .46.

Table 14.10. Items with High Factor Scores on Personality Factor V-6: Self-Actualizing Search for Identity.

Item	Factor score
Feels his own life is important, that it matters what he does with his life.	73
Devotes much of his energy to a deliberate program of self-improvement (creative activity, study, etc.).	73
Intense, tends to involve self deeply.	72
Is aware of his own feelings and motives.	68
The values and principles which he holds directly affect what he does.	65
Copes with the novelty of the Ghanaian experience by seeking relationships, activities and settings that let him continue important personal interests.	64
Unsure just who he is or who he ought to be or how he fits into the world.	63
Impulsive; undercontrolled (N.B. opposite implies over-controlled).	60
Is actively striving toward a clearer, more complex or mature sense of identity.	60

Note.—Seven percent of communality; *r* with P–1 (personality) = —.11, *r* with P–1 (performance) = —.15.

intense, unconventional, and impulsive, a bit confused and chaotic, not at all sure of themselves or of what the future might offer. But they were working hard and constructively, if somewhat erratically, on the problem: Self-cultivation and improvement stood high on their personal agenda.

Some Problems of Prediction

It is one thing to explore, as we have been doing, the relationship between patterns of role performance and of personality overseas, both derived from judgments of the same field interviews. This is to extract, as objectively and sensitively as we can, what the interviews have to say. To do so has obviously been informative. But to *predict* performance from independent measures of personality is quite another matter, in regard to which the entire experience of personnel psychology must caution us against optimism. I now turn to three attempts at prediction of competence, two of them failures, one a qualified success. For criterion variables we will use factor loadings on the evaluative first principal component factors, and also second-year evaluative ratings, made on a 5-point scale by the Peace Corps Representative in Ghana. We will also refer to loadings on some of the varimax patterns that we have just examined.

Authoritarianism

Since I will be having some sharp things to say about the predictive value of mental health assessments, it is only tactful to begin with a failure of a prediction made on what I thought were good social psychological grounds. Persons high in authoritarianism, I would have supposed, should be hampered by traits of ethnocentrism and rigidity, among others, from performing well as teachers in Africa. To make a long story short,[7] we employed two measures of authoritarianism: one, a 24-item version identical to that used by Mischel (1965) and closely similar to the versions employed in *The Authoritarian Personality* (Adorno, Frenkel-Brunswik, Levinson, and Sanford, 1950); the other a more sophisticated 100-item instrument carefully balanced to eliminate the effect of response sets. We obtained surprisingly good evidence that these measures, particularly the more sophisticated one, sorted the volunteers out at the time they were in training along a composite dimension, the ingredients of which were essentially as the authors of *The Authoritarian Personality* had claimed, including intolerance of ambiguity, over-control, moralism, projectivity, conservatism, distrustfulness of others, and repressiveness. Yet scores on authoritarianism showed essentially null correlations with loadings on the general competence patterns and with administrative evaluations. The only appreciable correlations involving our better measure of authoritarianism were with V-2, Intellectualizing Future Orientation ($-.38$, $p < .05$) and with V-6, Self-Actualizing Search for Identity ($-.26$, $p < .10$), both patterns that involved good communication with and about the self.

Second thoughts after direct experience in the field suggest that the prediction was naive in giving insufficient weight to a job analysis of the requirements on a teacher in an essentially authoritarian educational setting.[8] In any case, it is apparent that although our measure did relate sensibly

7. A full account of methods and results is given in Smith (1965a), reprinted as, "An Analysis of Two Measures of 'Authoritarianism'," above.

8. It would be particularly interesting to know the predictive value of measures of authoritarianism for performance in community development settings, where higher levels of flexibility and tolerance for ambiguity (as compared to levels required in classroom teaching) would seem to be essential.

to certain personality patterns overseas, it did *not* contribute to the prediction of competent performance.

Psychiatric Ratings

Early in the training period at Berkeley, each volunteer was seen in two 50-minute appraisal interviews by psychiatrists from the Langley-Porter Neuropsychiatric Institute.[9] Each of the seven participating psychiatrists made a variety of predictive ratings. The most reliable of these required the psychiatrist to rate the "predicted psychological effectiveness" of the 16 or 17 trainees that he had seen, on a 7-point scale with a prescribed distribution. The correlation between ratings given by first and second interviewers was .41.

On what did the psychiatrists base their predictive ratings? We were able to find out, since they also wrote 2- or 3-page freehand summaries of each interview. We had these summaries translated into ratings by independent judges on Jack Block's (1961) California *Q* set for the general dynamic description of personality, and performed an item analysis by *t* test looking for *Q* sort items that discriminated between the 20 volunteers whom the psychiatrists rated highest in "psychological effectiveness" and the 20 rated lowest. Not surprisingly in view of the psychiatrists' professional training, their responsibility for weeding out disqualifying pathology, and their essential ignorance of the criterion situation, the discriminating items corresponded closely with the ones listed by Block (1961, pp. 144–145) as defining, positively or negatively, "the optimally adjusted personality" as viewed by clinical psychologists—what amounts to a "mental health stereotype." The mean item *Q* sort ratings for the group regarded more favorably by the psychiatrists correlated (rho) .78 with Block's item data for the mental health stereotype; for the less favorably regarded group, the corresponding rho was .07. The items ordered in much the same way with respect to discriminatory power (*t*) as they did with respect to the degree to which they were seen by clinical psychologists as characterizing the "optimally adjusted personality" (rho = .83).

The psychiatrists' "mental health" ratings had a close to 0 correlation with our criterion measures of competent performance. Within the admittedly restricted range of volunteers actually sent overseas, the degree to which a person's adjustment as appraised by the psychiatrists approximated the "optimal" pattern simply had nothing to do with the adequacy with which he performed in the Peace Corps role.[10]

9. This procedure was tried out by the Peace Corps for experimental purposes and does not represent subsequent practice. I am grateful to M. Robert Harris for making the results of the psychiatric interviews available to me.

10. Apart from self-selection by the volunteers and preselection by the Peace Corps on the basis of letters of reference, 8 of 58 volunteers in training were not sent overseas. Of these, one fled training in panic; for four others, judgments regarding personal adjustment played a substantial role in deselection. My present hunch, for what it is worth, is that two or three of these would have been quite successful had they been sent to Ghana. The really dubious case would have been deselected by nonprofessionals relying on the naked eye.

An intriguing footnote to this convincingly null overall relationship emerges when we divide the volunteers according to whether their schools were located in the major cities, in provincial towns, or in more remote "bush" settings. The groups are small, but striking differences in correlation appear. In relation to second-year administrative evaluations, for example, where the overall correlation with psychiatric ratings is —.02, there is a positive correlation of .54 for the city teachers, a correlation of —.02 for the intermediate ones, and one of —.36 for those with bush assignments! Other data support the view that this is not a chance finding. Clearly the implications of the psychiatrists' ratings were situationally specific, rather than pertaining to general competence. I will forgo speculation about what situational factors were involved, except to suggest that city assignments, which diverged greatly from the volunteers' expectations, seemed to give rise to certain special morale problems among this initial Peace Corps group.

Dimensions of the Personal Future

After this dismal but familiar story of predictive failure, now for a modest success! At the time the Ghana volunteers were in training at Berkeley, Raphael Ezekiel, then a beginning graduate student, was working with me on the psychology of time perspectives. It occurred to him that a subject's view of his own personal future should have a clearer psychological significance than indices derived from Thematic Aperception Test stories and the like. We adapted a procedure that he was currently trying on other groups, and included in the battery for the trainees the assignment of writing three essays: one about their alternative immediate plans if they were not accepted in the Peace Corps, one a brief "mock autobiography" covering the three years after return from Peace Corps service, and the third a similar mock autobiography covering the year in which they would be 40 years old.[11]

These essays were rated with satisfactory reliability by independent judges (Spearman-Brown *r*'s of .70 to .80 for the several dimensions, once the protocols of certain volunteers who were independently judged to have rejected the task had been eliminated) on three 7-point scales: *Differentiation,* the extent to which each essay showed complex and detailed mapping of the future; *Agency*, the extent to which the essays as a whole showed the future self as the prime agent in determining the course of the person's future life; and *Demand,* the extent to which they described a life viewed by the respondent as demanding long-term, continuing effort. Each of these correlated dimensions has its own distinctive pattern of correlates, but we will be concerned here only with correlates of a sum score across all of them.

The sum score correlated .41 ($p < .01$) with the overall administrative evaluation of the volunteers' effectiveness as of the second year. As for our *Q* sort dimensions based on the field interviews, correlations with the generally

11. A fourth essay, an imaginary letter from Ghana to a friend describing the volunteer's life and activities, was dropped from analysis when it appeared to evoke a highly stereotyped regurgitation of official doctrine received in training.

evaluative P-1 factors were insignificant but positive. The stronger correlations were with loadings on two particular personality patterns, both moderately correlated in turn with the measures of overall competence derived from the interviews: V-2, Intellectualizing Future Orientation ($r = .41$, $p < .05$), and V-5, Controlling Responsibility ($r = .43$, $p < .01$). We have already seen the items defining the latter factor. Those that define Intellectualizing Future Orientation include: "Characteristically maintains a highly articulate intellectual formulation of his situation and problems," "Has long term goals," "Has a complex, well-differentiated picture of his own future," "Feels his own life is important, that it matters what he does with his life"—items that correspond strikingly to the dimensions on which the Mock Autobiographies were rated.

We may gain a fuller picture of the psychological meaning of the sum scores by looking at the *Q* sort items from the personality and role performance decks that discriminate high scorers from low scorers significantly by *t* test. The ones that are more characteristic of high scorers are given in Table 14.11. Apart from items that constitute further construct validation of the index, the picture of inventiveness, initiative, job-elaboration, and self-testing or responsiveness to challenge indicates that the procedure has indeed tapped qualities that should contribute to a more than routine performance.

But it is time to introduce a note of qualification that has its own substantive interest. When, on a hunch, Ezekiel looked separately at data for Protestants and Catholics, who performed equally well on the average, he found that the predictive relationship is entirely concentrated in the Protestant group. For them, the correlation with second-year evaluation is .64 ($p < .01$), while it is only .13 for Catholics. Furthermore, the subordinate dimensions of which the sum score is composed do not intercorrelate as highly for the Catholics as they do for the Protestants. We are of course dealing with such small numbers here that in the absence of replication one can have little confidence. Speculatively, however, exposure to the Protestant Ethic may be required to consolidate the variables on which the Mock Autobiographies were rated into a coherent psychological dimension.

With this qualification, Ezekiel interprets his measures as tapping the volunteer's readiness to commit himself to demanding tasks and to take active initiative in bringing about desired futures, the pathways to which he sees with some clarity—dispositions exceedingly relevant to the core content of competence as we are beginning to conceive of it. True, there is a bias toward the intellectualizer; but our small sample of strategically evoked verbal behavior does seem to have caught some of the motivational basis for response to the challenge of the Peace Corps assignment with commitment, initiative, and effort. We seem to be on the right track here.[12] Maybe mental health or adjustment (except at the sick extreme) and authoritarianism really were blind alleys.

12. For a full discussion and analysis of the Mock Autobiography technique as used in this research, see Ezekiel (1968).

Table 14.11. Items that Are Characteristic of Volunteers with High Sum Scores on Mock Autobiographies.

Item	p^a
Personality Q sort	
Envisions a challenging and demanding personal future.	.05
Characteristically maintains a highly articulate intellectual formulation of his situation and problems.	.05
Shows inventiveness, ingenuity.	.05
Has developed a well-balanced, varied, and stable program for self of work, relaxation, relief or escape.	.05
Devotes much of his energy to a deliberate program of self-improvement (creative activity, study, etc.).	.10
High in initiative; active rather than reactive.	.10
Performance Q sort	
Elaborates his performance of teaching duties in non-routine imaginative ways; invests self creatively in teaching job in and out of class.	.01
Values his Peace Corps assignment as relevant to his career plans.	.05
Actively employs self in useful, school-related activities outside of class.	.10
Concerned with using his Peace Corps experience to test himself.	.10

[a] By *t* test comparing extreme thirds of distribution.

The Peace Corps and Personality Change

Since our data concerning personality change over the period of Peace Corps service are complex and untidy, I will summarize them cavalierly. In regard to short-run changes, analysis of the field interviews indicated a degree of shift from initial all-out enthusiasm in the first year to more of a "veteran" mentality in the second, in which the volunteers came to be sustained more by their principles than by sheer enthusiasm. In the second year there seems to have been some decrease in involvement on all fronts, a partial withdrawal from full engagement with the opportunities and challenges of the situation. But there were also indications of greater self-insight and raised aspirations for the future. As for the longer run, comparisons are available on two pencil-and-paper questionnaires taken in training and at termination. Consistent shifts in response would appear to indicate that the volunteer became more tough-minded and realistic, more autonomous and independent of authority, and much more concerned with the plight of the American Negro. This was at the time of Birmingham; in the absence of a control group, we cannot assess the importance of the fact that it was from Africa that the volunteers were indignantly viewing events at home.

Messy data aside, my personal impression from knowing a number of the volunteers rather well was that important personality changes in the direction of maturity were frequent. I think I know why. My reconstructed account is at least consistent with our data, though it goes considerably beyond what I could use them to establish. It will also serve to put in context some of the themes with which we have been concerned.

When they joined the Peace Corps, many of this initial group of volunteers were not very clear as to why they did so: This was one of the reasons why they prickled when psychologists, psychiatrists, journalists, friends, and casual passers-by insistently asked them the question. Toward the end of their service, one could get a better and I think more accurate answer. The most frequent motivational mix, as I interpret it, was composed in varying proportions of two major ingredients and some minor ones. First, they needed a "psychosocial moratorium," in Erikson's (1956) sense. They were more often than not somewhat unclear about where they were heading, perhaps somewhat dissatisfied with their current directions. Two years' time out for reassessment and self-discovery was welcome, not a major sacrifice. (How the volunteers resented talk of the sacrifices they were making!) But second, and this must be stressed in almost the same breath to give a fair picture, the volunteers wanted to earn and justify this moratorium by doing something that seemed to them simply and intrinsically worthwhile, cutting through the complexities and hypocrisies of modern life and international relations. The Peace Corps as an opportunity for direct personal action toward good ends was strongly appealing. And third—less important—the appeal of adventure and foreign exposure was a factor for some, and the possibility of career-relevant experience for others.

But this account of the volunteers' private motives for joining the Peace Corps does not fairly describe the motivation that *sustained* them in their efforts. Once in, most of them saw and were captured by the challenges of the job and role: students and schools that needed everything they could give, a window on Africa that invited exploration. Their effective motivation was emergent: a response to opportunities and difficulties as challenges to be met, not as frustrations to be endured or "adjusted" to. If this reaction was typical of the group as a whole, it was truest of volunteers who were rated high in competence, and least true of those rated low or characterized by the Limited Commitment pattern.

How did the volunteers' particularly engrossing commitment to the job come about? It was not prominent in their motivation for joining, although their attraction to worthwhile activity as such obviously foreshadows it. Partly, to be sure, it must have been induced by the example and precept of the excellent training staff and Peace Corps leadership in the field. Given the volunteers' initial need to find themselves while doing something valuable intrinsically in simple human terms, however, I think the definite two-year limit may have been important, though for most it was not salient. One can afford to make a fuller, less reserved or cautious investment of self in an undertaking if the demand is explicitly time limited.

It was this high degree of committed but disinterested investment in a challenging undertaking, I think, that was so auspicious for psychological change in the direction of maturity. Experiences from which the self is held in reserve do not change the self; profit in growth requires its investment.

Largely by self-selection, the volunteers who came to training fortunately contained a majority who were predisposed to respond to the Peace Corps challenge with high commitment. Our experimental Mock Autobiographies seem to have sampled this predisposition, though only crudely. In contrast, the "mental health" orientation, which received considerable weight during selection-in-training, turned out to be essentially irrelevant to the prediction of competent performance—and even of the volunteers' ability to carry on as teachers given the unforeseen press of stresses and supports that Ghana presented. Psychologists who assume responsibility for Peace Corps selection: please note!

This opportunistic study in the Peace Corps has suggested certain common strands in competence, and also illustrated that in this setting, there were various psychological routes to competent performance. We have not asked, how can young people be raised and educated to cultivate the emergence of competence? What social innovations are needed to capitalize upon existing potentials of competence? How can social and psychological vicious circles be reversed to allow the socially deprived to gain in competence? These questions should stand high on our agenda.[13] Our experience with the Peace Corps as an imaginative social invention carries some suggestions worth pursuing.

13. For a preliminary scouting of these questions, see Smith (1965c), where I report on a conference at which these topics were discussed.

15

Competence and Socialization

What do we know, and what do we need to know, about the conditions under which people come to function as competent members of society? The question arises with urgency as the first generation of crash programs to instill competence in the poor and "culturally deprived" comes under skeptical review, and the path to the millenium remains to be discovered. It was in this context of contemporary social action that, near the end of its tenure, the Committee on Socialization and Social Structure of the Social Science Research Council considered the topics of socialization for competence.

In its preliminary discussions, the Committee identified a number of currently active lines of research that seemed to bear upon positive outcomes of socialization—outcomes viewed from a frankly evaluative perspective. Several of these diverse, but potentially convergent, strands—ranging from the effects of early experience on the neonate to the evocation of competence among the citizens of newly independent developing countries—were brought together for examination and critical discussion at a conference held in San Juan, Puerto Rico, in the spring of 1965. This chapter builds on the conference discussion but departs freely from it in the attempt to see the bearing of socialization on the origins and development of competence from a more coherent perspective than the lively exchange between specialists of disparate interests and backgrounds could attain.[1] As the reader will see, a coherent framework within which questions are posed rather than a substantive synthesis is aimed at: too many pieces of the puzzle are still missing. To the extent that synthesis is attempted, it must remain conjectural.

From *Socialization and Society,* John A. Clausen, ed., pp. 270–320. Copyright © 1968, Little, Brown and Company (Inc.). Reprinted by permission of the editor and publisher. I am indebted to Arlene Skolnick for stimulating discussion, to Dieter Bruehl for extensive bibliographical assistance, and to an informal seminar with Neil Altman, Dieter Bruehl, Diana Solar, Ronald Weisberg, and Arlene Vadum that helped me to explore concepts of self-evaluation.

1. Since an account of the conference has been published elsewhere (Smith, 1965c), and some of the working papers have since been printed in revised versions (Colson, 1967; Inkeles, 1966), I have made free use of the ideas that it stimulated without feeling the obligation to treat them in the form presented at the conference.

Toward a Conception of the Competent Self

In any attempt to look evaluatively at the processes and outcomes of socialization, terminology makes a difference. The terms we use carry with them a freight of implicit assumptions, and the changing fashions in evaluative terms reflect shifts in what goes without saying, what is taken for granted. Thus before World War II sealed the fate of extreme cultural relativism in the social sciences, a favored concept to which a highly productive committee of the Social Science Research Council devoted its attention was *social adjustment* (Young, 1941), which for present-day readers bears an unwelcome connotation of uncritical obeisance to the sociocultural status quo. *Mental health* (see Jahoda, 1958), more recently fashionable and probably more durable because of the institutional recognition it has received in law and government, is currently under attack as connoting a bio-medical frame of evaluation that is out of tune with the contexts in which we want to employ it (Smith, 1961; 1969). The term *competence* (*Webster's* defines *competent* as "answering to all requirements, adequate; fit; capable"), on the other hand, is presently acquiring connotations that commend it for our purposes. This chapter is intended to increase its popularity—but also to clarify some of the issues that arise in conceptualizing the nature and development of competence.

Alternative Conceptions of Competence

In adopting *competence,* we were influenced particularly by Robert W. White, who in a series of important essays (1959, 1960, 1963) urged the relevance to human development of intrinsic motivation toward competence —toward effective interaction with the environment—that, in White's view, man shares with the higher mammals. White marshalled evidence for the separate and major role of such motivation, which he designated *effectance,* in distinction from the "drives," based on tissue needs, of the motivational theory that until recently prevailed in experimental psychology, and from the quiescence-seeking instincts of orthodox psychoanalysis. For White, the important motivational ingredient missed by traditional theories is contributed by the feedback that the developing person gets about the environmental consequences of his own actions. Later, we will compare White's view with alternative possible emphases on *social* feedback from the approval or disapproval of significant others—social reinforcement—or on intrinsically motivating aspects of information processing as such. We will see that important issues are involved here that as yet are far from resolved. At this point, however, we are not ready to pursue them. Rather, what is relevant is to note that we are attracted to competence as an evaluative concept partly because of the connotations that White has given it: rootedness in a view of the organism-person as an *active* (rather than merely *re*active) participant in *inter*action with the environment, and close linkage to motivational processes.

These connotations point to a focus on biological origins and concern with the developmental vicissitudes of individual motivation and capacities. Given the Committee's task and orientation, however, a complementary focus on societally relevant outcomes was required of us. In his paper for the Puerto Rico Conference, Inkeles offered a definition of competence that stresses the societal referent: "the ability to attain and perform in three sets of statuses: those which one's society will normally assign one, those in the repertoire of one's social system that one many reasonably aspire to, and those which one might reasonably invent or elaborate for oneself" (Inkeles, 1966). At the Conference he argued vigorously—as he does in the book where this essay first appeared—that the study of socialization should be approached from the standpoint of societal requirements and socialization outcomes rather than from that of biological origins and the impact of practices of child rearing. His proposed definition of competence is well adapted to this strategy.

It is also congruent with the emerging public interests in finding ways in which *all* citizens may become equipped for effective participation in modern society, with the public distress that a submerged minority have been trained in *in*competence that leaves them unable to benefit from most "opportunities" that are opened to them. This concern was paramount to a group of staff members of the Community Research and Services Branch, National Institute of Mental Health (Rae-Grant, Gladwin, and Bower, 1966), who proposed a concept of social competence quite similar to Inkeles' as the focus of an alternative to the traditional mental health strategy that centered on psychotherapeutic intervention to reduce inner conflict.

In a report on a conference of mental health professionals held at the National Institute of Mental Health shortly after the Puerto Rico Conference, Gladwin (1967) develops the implications of this concept in an important statement.

> Competence . . . develops along three major axes, all closely interrelated. First is the ability to learn or to use a variety of alternative pathways or behavioral responses in order to reach a given goal . . . Second, the competent individual comprehends and is able to use a variety of social systems within the society, moving within these systems and utilizing the resources they offer. Third, competence depends upon effective reality testing. Reality testing involves not merely the lack of psychopathological impairment to perception but also a positive, broad, and sophisticated understanding of the world. [p. 32]

Programs of remedial intervention appropriate to this conception were seen as operating primarily

> through the provision or adaptation of a social environment designed to maximize rewarding and effective social experience within a setting relevant to the real world in which [the] clients lived. The modality through which such an experience must be achieved can be referred to as an ecological unit encompassing within a single interacting system the individual and as much of his social environment as is relevant to the behavior under consideration. [p. 32]

The approach to social systems implied in the concept of the ecological unit is highly congenial, it will be seen, to the point of view developed in the present chapter, and the examples that Gladwin provides of current programs that seek to maximize social competence through deliberate intervention with ecological units of differing scope supplement my treatment very usefully. What I wish to emphasize here, however, is the essential congruence of Gladwin's conception of social competence with Inkeles': the three components of competence that Gladwin offers to define goals for programs of social intervention are, in effect, abilities to use social systems to achieve one's goals—to perform effectively for self and society in one's social roles. In contrast with White's conception and with the view of competence to be developed in this chapter, the motivational aspect of competence remains implicit. Reference is rather to knowledge and ability.

It is instructive to view Inkeles' conception of social competence in relation to an earlier sociological formulation on which Gladwin (1967) draws, which also contributed connotations that predispose us to be attracted to it: *interpersonal competence,* as introduced by Foote and Cottrell (1955) in their programmatic framework for family research. These authors, seeking an evaluative concept for family research from a "planning" orientation (a context similar to the present one), conceive interpersonal competence as skill or ability "in controlling the outcomes of episodes of interaction" (p. 36) and as comprising six components: health, intelligence, empathy, autonomy, judgment, and creativity. They organize their suggestions for research around hypotheses concerning the antecedents and correlates of each of these presumptive aspects.

Viewed in historical perspective, the variant versions of competence offered by Foote and Cottrell and by Inkeles correspond rather neatly to the two major strands in modern sociological role theory. For both, indeed, competence is a matter of capacities for role performance. What differentiates them is the frame within which role performance is conceived. Inkeles writes in the structural tradition of role-status theory, anchored near its origins by Ralph Linton's *The Study of Man* (1936), and more recently summarized and codified by Gross, Mason, and McEachern (1958). In this tradition, adequacy of role performance is to be measured against the role requirements of the various statuses or positions in the social structure that a person may occupy. Foote and Cottrell, on the other had, embody the so-called symbolic-interactionist tradition stemming from George Herbert Mead (1934) and assimilating congenial influences from neo-Freudian psychiatry, especially Harry Stack Sullivan (1945). Emphasis in this tradition is on interactional *process* in role relationships that are conceived primarily in interpersonal rather than social-structural terms. Socialization is viewed more as a process through which personality and selfhood emerge in the course of role-taking in progressively more sharply attuned communicative interaction than as one in which persons become equipped with beliefs, knowledge, skills, motives, and values that fit them to occupy a sequence of niches in the social structure. While Foote and Cottrell do not exclude a constitutional-genetic component from their criteria of interpersonal competence, their conception amounts to a view of successful socialization—successful within the framework set by Mead and Sullivan, just as Inkeles' definition states a conception of successful socialization within the structuralist framework.

Clearly there is no necessary clash here between competing versions of the Truth. Just as modern versions of role theory have sought to weave together the strands deriving from Linton and from Mead (an early attempt was made by Sarbin, 1954), so a role-relevant conception of social competence as successful socialization might well incorporate ingredients from both the Foote-Cottrell and the Inkeles versions. A comprehensive view of social competence should also keep in simultaneous view the two perspectives that are differentially emphasized by Inkeles and by Foote and Cottrell: that of society and its "manpower" needs, and that of the person himself as the locus of humanistic values. To repeat, competence involves effective role performance for self and for society.

Competence as Differentiating Vicious and Benign Circles of Development

As we contemplate these two sociological concepts of competence in relation to White's bio-psychological one, bridging the gap between them with explicit conceptual and empirical links becomes in effect the major agenda of the study of socialization, when it is phrased evaluatively. It is the problem of how to get from beginnings in the infant organism to the person participating competently in communicative interaction within the framework of a social system. Intuitively, it looks as though the gap from White to Foote and Cottrell is narrower than that from White to Inkeles: Inkeles' concern with outcomes for the larger social system introduces a variety of specific requirements beyond the more generalized capacities in which Foote and Cottrell are interested. Be that as it may, the view of competence that emerges in the foregoing discussion creates severe problems for the writer of this chapter. For if the topic of competence is to be identified with the outcome of socialization taken evaluatively, the task of this chapter is hardly distinct from that of the entire volume in which it appeared. What would be its distinctive content? Indeed, the chapter by Inkeles[2] works out the implications of

2. "Society, social structure, and child socialization," in J. A. Clausen (ed.), 1968, pp. 73–129.

his conception of competence for the study of socialization in such rich detail that there would be no gain from reviewing the same considerations here.

Faced with this predicament, I have adopted a strategy of selection based on empirical assumptions that go beyond the bounds of knowledge that can currently be regarded as firmly established. I will assume, in implicit agreement with a good many contemporary theorists, that there is a core of interrelated personal attributes—short of the entire complement of cognitive, motivational, and behavioral variables implied by Inkeles' conception, and even of the more limited list proposed by Foote and Cottrell—which in some way plays a crucial role in the person's effectiveness in interaction with the environment. The cluster of attributes that I am looking for is one that would make a decisive difference in the cumulative direction of the outcome of a person's interactions.

Underlying my search for such a key cluster is a view of causation in personal and social development as inherently circular or spiral, rather than linear in terms of neatly isolable causes and effects. As the very concept of interaction implies, developmental progress or deficit is typically a matter of benign circles or of vicious ones, not of persistent effects of clear-cut single causes (see Myrdal, 1944, Vol. 2, pp. 1065–1070). In social life, there is much bitter truth to the biblical maxim, "To him who hath shall be given; from him who hath not shall be taken away even that which he hath." Launched on the right trajectory, the person is likely to accumulate successes that strengthen the effectiveness of his orientation toward the world while at the same time he acquires the knowledge and skills that make his further success more probable. His environmental involvements generally lead to gratification and to increased competence and favorable development. Off to a bad start, on the other hand, he soon encounters failures that make him hesitant to try. What to others are challenges appear to him as threats; he becomes preoccupied with defense of his small claims on life at the expense of energies to invest in constructive coping. And he falls increasingly behind his fellows in acquiring the knowledge and skills that are needed for success on those occasions when he does try.

The picture is familiar. In instance after instance of contemporary attempts at planned social intervention to remedy human ineffectiveness, whether under the aegis of the schools, of poverty programs, of corrections, or of "mental health," the practical problem is becoming conceptualized as one of how to break into well-entrenched vicious circles of social causation so as to convert them into benign ones, in which Hippocrates' "curative power of Nature" can then be relied upon. The *practical* problem is typically immense because of the way in which a multitude of causal factors interlock, so that remedial efforts applied to any single factor are ineffectual: the inertial properties of the rest of the system suffice to drag the person down again in spite of initial gains. The *conceptual* problem is that of distinguishing the components of the interdependent system and, especially, of identifying those that are central and strategic in regard to causal linkage with other variables in the system and also in regard to accessibility as leverage-points through which the state of the system as a whole can be altered from a "vicious" to a "benign" condition.

Related Concepts and Themes in Recent Research

Provisionally, then, I want to focus in this chapter on attributes of the person that are likely candidates for such a strategic role. For the developed person who has attained selfhood, the place to look for them is in attitudes and motives related to the *self,* as the entity around which a person's enduring orientations to the environing world are organized. The recent literature contains a number of terms and concepts that seem to belong in the domain with which we are concerned. Some of these are common English terms that have acquired enriched meaning from the sensitive commentary of Erik Erikson (1959): trust and confidence, initiative and industry, autonomy, and, especially, hope. On the other side of the coin, there are self-doubt, passivity, dependence, fatalism, and despair. No one will question which of these lists goes with the Haves, which with the Have Nots! Nor is the idea novel that these are important human qualities: humanistic wisdom has always known it. What is new is their recognition within the specialized and deliberately cumulative enterprise of social and behavioral science.

This recognition has also engendered a technical and not very rewarding literature concerning the dimension of self-evaluation usually called self-esteem (Wylie, 1967; Rosenberg, M., 1965; Coopersmith, 1967). While the technical difficulties of measurement, given people's motivation to put on as good a face as they can manage for themselves and others (Goffman, 1959), still elude satisfactory solution, the persistent research that is being invested in the study of self-esteem as an independent or a dependent variable reflects the common acknowledgment of its key status. Perhaps, indeed, part of the difficulty that has hampered empirical research on self-esteem has followed from the assumption that it *can* be treated as an unidimensional variable; we might profitably return to McDougall's conception of the *self-regarding sentiment* (McDougall, 1908) as suggesting a complex, multidimensional structure more in keeping with the part that we expect it to play in human experience and behavior.

Developments in the post-Freudian psychoanalytic tradition of ego psychology make further terms available to us for dealing with these decisive properties of the self. Erikson, of course, writes from within this tradition, as does White, whose contributions to the conceptualization of competence might be seen as an attempt to follow through on the otherwise unrealized invitation extended by Heinz Hartmann (1958) for an integration of psychoanalytic ego psychology with the findings of "academic" psychological research. Lois Murphy's (1962) conception of the child's emerging *coping strategies* for mastering the environment—as distinguished from the defenses against anxiety stressed by earlier psychoanalytic writers—initiated a productive shift of emphasis; the distinction has been further developed by

Haan (1963). The notion of *ego strength* (Barron, 1963) as resiliency in handling stress may be too globally evaluative to be satisfactory in the long run, but it too can be seen as a foray into the present area of concern. Recently, Jane Loevinger (1966) has cast a variety of current ideas about ego functioning into a coherent and sophisticated developmental perspective. Her proposed progression of ego development, from impulse ridden through opportunistic and conformist to conscientious, autonomous, and integrated stages, offers a framework, with diagnostic "milestones," for treating the emergence of qualitative features of the personality system that make for personal integrity and for relative independence from the vicissitudes of biological impulse or environmental contingency.

Essentially out of contact with the foregoing developments, a succession of loosely-linked experimental approaches to the study of goal-setting behavior is just now coming into coherent focus as highly relevant to our concern. These began with the studies of *level of aspiration* by Kurt Lewin and his students (Lewin, Dembo, Festinger, and Sears, 1944), who investigated the effects of success and failure on a person's hopes and expectations for performance on experimental tasks. These studies gave rise to a number of interesting experimental findings and conceptual distinctions, but the line of research that they stimulated seemed until recently to have been played out without major impact on personality or developmental theory. From the standpoint of his social-learning theory of personality, Rotter and his students (Rotter, 1954) carried out a relatively independent program of research on goal setting, in which the value of the goal and the subject's expectancy of success were central variables. This line of work, too, seemed to have found its place, without major impact, in the not very coherent literature of personality research.

Meanwhile, Atkinson and his students (Atkinson, 1964; Atkinson and Feather, 1966) began a series of studies of goal setting in relation to McClelland's conception of achievement motivation (McClelland, Atkinson, Clark, and Lowell, 1953)—a topic to which we return later in the chapter. Sharing with Rotter a value-expectancy approach to conceptualizing goal setting, the Atkinson group found different patterns of goal setting to distinguish persons whose orientations toward achievement stemmed from hope for success from persons who orientations stemmed from fear of failure, the latter characteristically setting their levels of aspiration unrealistically high or very low. Level of aspiration now became relevant to the study of the person's fundamental orientations that affect his engagement with challenge and opportunity.

New research developments, again under the leadership of Rotter, bring us to the present, when research on this interrelated cluster of issues is very active indeed. Rotter's group had observed that success on an experimental task has very different consequences for a person's subsequent goal setting, depending on whether the person believes that the outcome—the "reinforcement" received—results from chance or from his own skill. In a number of studies this belief was manipulated experimentally. Recently Rotter has developed and validated a measure of "generalized expectancies for internal versus external control of reinforcement," and has shown that people differ consistently from one another in their general tendency to attribute the outcomes of their endeavors to external factors, such as chance or fate, or to internal ones, such as their own skill and effort (Rotter, 1966; Lefcourt, 1966). As Rotter summarizes the substantive findings that bear upon the construct validity and hence the theoretical interest of his I-E scale, there is

> strong support for the hypotheses that the individual who has a strong belief that he can control his own destiny is likely to (a) be more alert to those aspects of the environment which provide useful information for his future behavior; (b) take steps to improve his environmental position; (c) place greater value on skill or achievement reinforcements and be generally more concerned with his ability, particularly his failures; and (d) be resistive to subtle attempts to influence him. [1966, p. 25]

Rotter notes the relationship of perceived internal versus external control to research on achievement motivation (high need for achievement implying some belief in one's capacity to determine the outcome of his efforts), to White's conception of competence motivation, and to the sense of *powerlessness* as an aspect of the sociological concept of alienation (Seeman, 1959). He also notes apparent, but less direct, convergences with Riesman's (1950) well-known distinction between inner-directed and other-directed character types, and with the distinction between "field-dependent" versus "body-oriented" tendencies that the Witkin group derived from the study of individual differences in perceptual responses (Witkin, Lewis, Hertzman, Machover, Meissner, and Wapner, 1954).

Still an additional line of investigation that warrants notice in this partial roll call is Mischel's work (1966) on children's preference for small, immediate rewards or larger, deferred ones. Capacity for delayed gratification as an aspect of impulse control has figured prominently in discussions of ego strength. Whether such a capacity for forbearance is at issue or rather an attitude of trust that promised gratifications will actually be delivered, Mischel has provided methods that permit the systematic study of one component of an effective orientation toward the environment. The relevance of voluntary inhibitory control is further indicated in a study by Eleanor Maccoby and her collaborators (Maccoby, Dowley, Hagen, and Degerman, 1965), who found among nursery school children, both boys and girls, that although an index of general activity level in free play was unrelated to measures of intellectual functioning, the children's ability to inhibit movement voluntarily showed moderately strong correlations with these measures.

This hasty overview of concepts and research themes from the recent past serves to define a terrain of relevance: from a variety of intellectual heritages and research traditions, students of personality have been converging on a cluster of interrelated, overlapping ideas that seem to bear upon the extent to which a person is oriented to make the most of his opportunities in the world, upon the likelihood that the interactive circles of causation in which he involves himself will be benign, not vicious. Having spread a sampling of these ideas and themes before us, let us see if we can find in them some provisional order.

A Provisional View of the Competent Self

In a first approximation to a formulation of the competent self, then, we would look for distinctive features in the person's attitudes toward self and world. The self is perceived as causally important, as effective in the world—which is to a major extent a world of other people—as likely to be able to bring about desired effects, and as accepting responsibility when effects do not correspond to desire. In near equivalent, the person has self-respect. With self-respect go at least moderately favorable levels of general self-evaluation—self-esteem or self-acceptance—but favorable self-evaluation in the general terms according to which is has predominantly been studied would seem less important than the sense of efficacy or potency. (In terms of Osgood's semantic differential [Osgood, Suci, and Tannenbaum, 1957], research on the self has overstressed the preemptive evaluative dimension, to the neglect of the coordinate dimensions of activity and potency.)

Distinctive attitudes toward the world are linked with these attitudes toward the self as the opposite side of the same coin. Coordinate with the feeling of efficacy is an attitude of hope—the world is the sort of place in which, given appropriate efforts, I can expect good outcomes. Hope provides the ground against which planning, forbearance, and effort are rational. Corresponding to generalized favorable self-evalution is an attitude of optimistic trust. While as Erikson has asserted, some degree of basic trust is essential to personal adequacy, I would think that given that essential minimum, hope is the more critical attitude. In the lack of hope, attitudes of fatalism and passivity that make a bad world tolerable at the cost of giving up the possibility of constructive action are natural adaptations that have been rediscovered perennially by individuals and cultures the world over.

With these positive attitudes toward self and world goes a characteristic behavioral orientation that throws the person into the kinds of interaction that close the benign circle. Here we find alternative phrasings that amount to much the same thing. The person is attracted to moderate challenges that have an intermediate probability of success. By setting his goals realistically at a level somewhat higher than that of his previous performance, he reaps the maximum cumulative gain in sensed efficacy from his successes. This is, in effect, an active, coping orientation high in initiative, not a passive or defensive one characterized by very low goals (which can yield little sense of efficacy when attained) or unrealistically high ones (the main virtue of which is the readiness with which non-attainment can be explained away and "failure" neutralized).

These attitudes and behavioral orientations, I propose, constitute the generalized core of the competent self. As I will shortly suggest, they seem to be relevant across societies and cultures. Accompanying these dispositions of the self are the array of knowledge, habits, skills, and abilities that are required to translate hopeful expectations and active orientations into effective behavior. This equipment for competence is clearly part of the interlocking system, since its possession gives a person warrant for feelings of efficacy and for hopeful expectations, and his constructive engagement with the environment in turn establishes habits of industry and provides the experiential background from which he can acquire knowledge and skill and make the most of his potential abilities. But these attributes are bound to be more specific to the person's particular roles and station in society than are the ones I have proposed for the generalized core.

Some of these cognitive and behavioral qualifications nevertheless have rather broad applicability, such as Foote and Cottrell's (1955) proposed components of interpersonal competence—intelligence and empathy. Also high in generalized relevance are skills in inquiry and in the use of informational resources—particularly valuable in a fluid world in which pat solutions and right answers answers do not stay valid. But these suggestions already seem to arise with special relevance to contemporary middle-class society; one can think of other cultural situations where their payoff would be small. From another perspective, however, modern technical society is itself increasingly universal (with the middle class embodying its major values). As Inkeles points out, within this modern framework one can go a long way toward specifying the repertory of cognitive and characterological equipment that is necessary for effective participation in terms of modern society's common role requirements: orientation to the clock and attendant habits of temporal regularity and dependability, verbal and numerical facility, accommodation to work relationships of authority and collaboration in complex organizations, and many others.

In keeping with the strategy that I proposed at the outset, I will focus henceforth on the proposed core of the competent self, without intending to minimize the importance of these additional personal dispositions that engage with particular societal role requirements. Before turning to issues pertinent to the relation of this competence syndrome to socialization and social structure, I need first to strengthen somewhat the case for its relevance as a syndrome and to examine more closely the case for its transcultural generality.

Illustrative Evidence for the Competent Self

My own conviction about the relevance and coherence of the syndrome arose in the course of my study of Peace Corps teachers (Smith, 1966), whom a colleague and I interviewed near the end of their first and second years of service in Ghana.[3] From close study of selected tape-recorded interview transcripts in the light of field experience, we developed a set of descriptive items to characterize the personalities of the volunteers as they appeared through the job-focused interviews. These items were then used by judges other than ourselves to characterize each volunteer as his interviews portrayed him, by "Q-sorting" the cards according to a prescribed distribution in nine categories, ranging from items seen as saliently characteristic of the volunteer to ones seen as saliently *un*characteristic of him. We intercorrelated the resulting personal profiles of item ratings and factored the matrix of correlations (by the principal components method) to get at patterns of personality as displayed overseas in the challenging situation of Peace Corps service.

As might be expected, the first principal component turned out to be a highly evaluative factor. Table 14.1 lists the items that were especially characteristic of volunteers who received high loadings on it, in order of declining factor scores; the items that defined what is *un*characteristic of these volunteers are given in Table 14.2 in order of increasing factor scores. Items referring to basic self-attitudes of self-confidence and self-esteem head each list, and the positive list contains the further item, "feels . . . that it matters what he does with his life," reflecting self-respect and efficacy. The negative list contains opposites of autonomy (dependence), hope (pessimism), active orientation (low energy, gives up easily, lets things drift), and trust (suspiciousness). Both lists contain items pertaining to realistic openness to experience. All of these traits are highly congruent with our tentative picture of the competent self.

The lists contain some other items whose presence is instructive. On the list of positively distinguishing characteristics, the qualities of principled responsibility and tolerance are clearly dictated by the requirements of the Peace Corps role. Perhaps they are intrinsically related to general competence, but we cannot be sure. The remaining items on the negatively distinguishing list are accounted for by those psychological states and processes which especially interfere with competent coping: anxiety and the psychological defenses through which anxiety is contained.

The Peace Corps study contains further evidence for the present formulation of the competent self in its sole modest predictive success. My colleague Raphael Ezekiel (1968) had devised a procedure in which the volunteers-in-training wrote three mock autobiographical essays: one on their immediate alternative plans should they not be accepted by the Peace Corps, one covering the three years after their return from Peace Corps service, and a third covering their fortieth year. The essays were rated for *differentiation,* the extent to which the essays showed complex and detailed mapping of the future; *agency,* the extent to which they showed the self as the prime agent

3. This account is adapted with only minor changes from Smith (1969). See 14, "Explorations in Competence" above for a fuller account.

in determining the course of the respondent's future life; and *demand,* the extent to which they described a life viewed by the respondent as demanding long-term, continuing effort. The sum of these ratings correlated moderately (.41) with the overall administrative evaluation as of the second year.

Table 14.11 shows the Q-sort items, again based on the overseas interviews, that were characteristic of the high-scoring volunteers. Apart from items that primarily show personal consistency from the time of essay writing until that of the interviews one and two years later, the picture of inventiveness, initiative, job-elaboration, and self-testing or responsiveness to challenge indicates that the procedure indeed tapped qualities that contribute to a more than routine performance. Ezekiel's interpretation of his measure is highly relevant to the picture of the competent self with which we are concerned here. The volunteer's readiness to engage himself with demanding tasks and to take the initiative in bringing about well-cognized futures that he desires, as crudely indexed by the ratings developed from the essays, provides a basis for his response to the Peace Corps assignment with commitment, initiative, and effort.

Volunteers for the Peace Corps are undoubtedly a self-selected elite in regard to these qualities, and my study of them, though intensive, was small in scale. More convincing evidence of the cogency of one central component of the proposed competence syndrome comes from the massive study, under the auspices of the United States Office of Education, of factors affecting the educational achievement of children of various ethnic groups (Coleman, Campbell, Hobson, McPartland, Mood, Weinfeld, and York, 1966). Data were gathered in the fall of 1965 from 645,000 pupils in grades 3, 6, 9, and 12 in 4000 American public schools. To quote the summary of this unprecedented study:

> A pupil attitude factor, which appears to have a stronger relationship to achievement than do all the "school" factors together, is the extent to which an individual feels that he has some control over his own destiny. . . . The responses of pupils to questions in the survey show that minority pupils, except for Orientals, have far less conviction than whites that they can affect their own environments and futures. When they do, however, their achievement is higher than that of whites who lack that conviction.
>
> Furthermore, while this characteristics shows little relationship to most school factors, it is related, for Negroes, to the proportion of whites in the schools. Those Negroes in schools with a higher proportion of whites have a great sense of control. This finding suggests that the direction such an attitude takes may be associated with the pupil's school experience as well as his experience in the larger community. [p. 23]

The three agree-disagree items on which the score for sense of control was based are:

Good luck is more important than hard work for success.
Every time I try to get ahead, something or somebody stops me.
People like me don't have much of a chance to be successful in life.

The theme is obviously the same as that of Rotter's I-E scale discussed above. As the researchers of the study observe: "There is an objective basis for this difference in feelings of control, since these minority children have less chance to control their environment than do the majority whites." For a slum Negro child, agreement with each of these items is likely to be the "right answer." The relatively powerful correlation of these reality-based attitudes with educational achievement within each ethnic group is impressive, though the findings of course suffer from the inherent causal ambiguity of all correlational data.

The Problem of Transcultural Relevance

If the cogency of our formulation of the competent self be granted, what of its general relevance? Is this only another projection of middle-class values reflecting culture-bound bias? My suggestion is that while different cultures would indeed value the competence syndrome differently, in principle it has transcultural relevance, as the content of specific goals and the knowledge and skill required to achieve them do not.

Surely the competence syndrome has special relevance for modern technical society where particular knowledge and skill is rapidly obsolescent—the more so to the extent that individualistic values prevail. If modern society is to remain viable as an open, free society, its major roles need to be adequately manned by persons sufficiently endowed with the qualities that we have been discussing. Persons who are seriously lacking in these qualities tend to be barred from effective participation. This is the problem of the ghetto minorities. When a conspicuous number of young people from elite groups in the society also show signs of a failure of hope, a loss of sense of efficacy, and withdraw hippie-style into passive noncommitment or explode in symbolic protest, there is indeed occasion for alarm at the dawning crisis of confidence that is implied. The context in which the agenda for this chapter is framed takes for granted that the fostering of competent selves is now an urgent social need.

What of traditional folk societies? Contemporary wisdom tells us to emphasize their variety, not their sameness. Nevertheless, the sharp contrast with our unique modern situation permits some things to be said. The traditional world was a small, parochial one in which the dramatis personae of hamlet and village could be well known to each of the players. The compass of daily life was finite and familiar, though it was surrounded by a great Unknown of fearsome natural forces and dangerous strangers. The ritual life of the community supported the individual in a sense of significance and worth. Given his embeddedness in traditional communal life, the individual was probably less saliently aware of his isolated selfhood than he is in the fluid modern world. Yet in the limited sphere within his purview, in social life and in agriculture and the associated crafts, he could earn honest feelings of efficacy; very likely he could know his effectiveness with less ambiguity than is characteristic in complex modern society, since the feedback was direct and the criteria were intrinsic or traditional. Cultural elaborations in the creative arts attest to the prevalence of motivation toward excellence beyond the requirements of mere conformity or survival.

Within a framework of scarce cognitive and technical resources that in fact imposed narrow limits on people's ability to master their environment and control their own lives, people could nevertheless develop a sense of self-respect and efficacy. The stable round of events in the life cycle gave a basis for hope. Outside the limits within which competence could be real and unambiguous, the fatalistic beliefs and propitiatory or controlling ritual and magic provided by the culture relieved the individual of some of the burden of inventing his own neurotic defenses against the anxieties of living in a world where so much was beyond his understanding and control.

This generalized and no doubt idealized picture ignores dramatic intercultural variation that clearly has a bearing on the prevalence of competent selfhood. One has only to read a perceptive ethnographic and psychological report like DuBois' account of *The People of Alor* (1944) to recognize that traditional societies can sustain themselves in persisting culture patterns that entail a very high cost to individual selves. DuBois' Alorese seem so hag-ridden by anxieties and so preoccupied with cultural and individual defenses against them, at the expense of effective coping, that one is forced to conjecture that the society could endure only in a remarkably protected environment.

It is thus germane to inquire about the extent to which conditions that prevail in traditional societies are compatible with the development of competent selves, even though the questions arise from concerns that are part of our own social predicament. When we turn to instances of disintegrating culture at the margins of modern life, as depicted in Oscar Lewis' accounts of the "culture of poverty" (for example, 1959), the relevance of our conception is unmistakable. What is dramatically evident is the absence of the competence syndrome, the presence of the vicious circle. For life to be at all endurable in the mutually exploitative jungle world at a nearly "animal" level of existence, where trust would be folly and self-respect is unattainable, people *have to* adopt a fatalistic view. They *have to* seize upon such fleeting gratifications as come their way. And the very adaptations that make a bad life minimally supportable trap people in "the life." From within this system there is little chance of escape.

If further grounds are needed for regarding our approach to competence as transculturally relevant, they may be found in the fruitful use of the closely related concept of *civic competence* in Almond and Verba's (1963) comparative study of political culture in five countries. Almond and Verba's concept is a direct equivalent of the one developed here, as focused on the more restricted sphere of political attitudes and action. The authors find striking national differences, to which they give a major role in interpreting the functioning of the formally democratic political systems in these countries, in people's actual political competence—their ability and readiness to take the initiative in influencing political decisions that affect them—and in their *sense* of civic competence—their belief that they can exert such influence. The data of their study do not settle whether civic competence is most usefully regarded as part of a general competence syndrome or may be so much influenced by special features of national political systems as to require separate assessment. As one of the most fertile recent studies of comparative politics, however, this work is testimony to the cross-national relevance of competence as a strategic variable.

Akin to the question of cross-cultural relevance of competence is that of the relevance of competence to the two sexes. As the cross-cultural data reported by Barry, Bacon, and Child (1957) for 110 cultures make clear, there is a widespread pattern, corresponding to what prevails in our own society, according to which there is greater pressure toward self-reliance and striving for achievement in boys, toward nurturance, obedience, and responsibility in girls. Any measure of the competence syndrome is likely not to be "fair" to girls—but neither are the traditional cultures of the world in this respect. Our concept appears relevant to both sexes, though it will be important to examine how the antecedents of competence are structured differently for boys and girls, and how competence strivings may be channeled in girls and women under cultural circumstances that limit their direct expression.

The Early Development of Competence

The competent self, as we have examined the concept in the first section of this chapter, is planted squarely in the midstream of socialization and personality development, after the important achievements underlying selfhood have already occurred but leading, under favorable circumstances, to productive spirals of further growth. What are the precursors of competent selfhood? By what processes and subject to what essential conditions does the baby human animal get set on a trajectory that creates the grounds for its favorable further development? Recent research on infancy and early childhood identifies some of the possibilities and allows us to formulate questions that could not have been posed only a few years ago. But it still does not provide the answers that we need. Wise social policy must still hedge its bets while entertaining alternative views of what is strategic in the course of development. Meanwhile, further research is urgently needed, and profitable directions for it to pursue are reasonably clear. For good reason this is currently a field of very active investigation.

R. W. White's initial article (1959) in which his concept of competence was introduced reviewed a variety of evidence from research on animals and infants that cast serious doubt upon the then still current, though shaken, assumption that the organism's reaching out to the environment in curiosity, exploration, and manipulativeness could be accounted for in terms of learned by-products of biological drives, based on tissue needs, directed toward end-states of quiescence. His negative argument, questioning the inclusive adequacy of motivational theory rooted in tension reduction, was persuasive to many readers. But his positive case, for a special category of biologically given motivation toward the production of effects in the environment, was less satisfying.

As an interim schema that frees the imagination to consider possibilities ruled out by prevailing orthodoxies in motivational theory, it undoubtedly made a major contribution. But it left open the question of what *sort* of effects would lead to intrinsically rewarding feedback, and indeed left the details of effectance or competence motivation and its development essentially unspecified. His subsequent monograph (White, R. W., 1963), an epistle to the gentiles of psychoanalytic persuasion, did not help matters in its gratuitous assumption of "independent ego energies" to account for competence motivation, though it added a rich and provocative discussion of the part played by competence motivation in later ego development. The time for motivational theories based on the energy metaphor that Freud adopted from Helmholtz had already past; too much was being discovered in modern neurophysiology to which the energy metaphor with its associated hydraulics was not at all relevant, and it was beginning to appear equally misleading in regard to the facts of behavior. White leaves us, then, with the assumption that man's active commerce with the environment has a biological basis other than the satisfaction of tissue drives. The job of clarifying what that basis might be essentially remains.

Mammalian Precursors of Competence

A good empirical starting point for us is provided by the results of a major program of research on the behavior of captive white-footed mice, reported by Kavanau (1967) since the appearance of White's papers. Psychologists have a predilection for rats and mice, but unfortunately they have found it convenient to work mostly with domesticated strains that are uninformative about the behavior traits that have emerged as products of mammalian evolution—and hence about the biological endowment of man as a domesticating but still (genetically) undomesticated animal. Not only have they preferred to study creatures that have had much of the native behavior repertory of the wild species bred out of them, but they have also chosen to investigate the animals' behavior in very restricted settings such as Skinner boxes and discrimination apparatuses. The zoologist Kavanau follows a wiser strategy with richly rewarding results. He has placed members of a wild species in an ingeniously constructed artificial environment with many potentialities for variation under the experimenter's or under the animal's control: a special cage with nest box and activity wheels for running under free and motor-driven conditions, provided with switches by which, when the experimenter wishes it, the animal can itself control major features of its environment (illumination, motor-drive for the wheel, and the like). Many aspects of the animal's behavior are automatically recorded.

What do the white-footed mice tell us about one variant of mammalian behavior? Here are some excerpts from Kavanau's summary of his detailed findings from a six-year program of research.

> Confined animals are likely to seize upon and repeatedly exercise virtually any opportunities to modify (and alter their relationships with) their surroundings. In addition they have a strong tendency to counteract non-volitional and "unexpected" deviations from the status quo. As a result, their responses do not bear an immutable relationship to the nature of the stimulus or other variable being modified; stimuli and activities that are rewarding in certain circumstances are avoided in others. These aspects of behavior have been illustrated by studies of nest occupancy, running in motor-driven wheels, and control of intensity of illumination. [p. 1638]

Thus, mice will frequently leave the nest when the experimental enclosure is disturbed during the day. Sometimes they will immediately return to the nest; sometimes not. But if they are put back in the nest by hand, they will dependably leave it immediately, no matter how many times they are put back. So much like men! "In this relatively clear-cut case, an act or situation which is rewarding when carried out volitionally is avoided when initiated by force—the animal responds by doing the opposite."

Similarly with the motor-driven wheel. If the experimenter starts the motor while the mouse is in the wheel and the mouse can turn it off by a lever, it does so promptly, no matter what the speed or how experienced the mouse may be with motor-driven running. But if the mouse itself starts the motor-driven wheel and the experimenter turns it off, the mouse predictably and promptly turns it back on again.

> The results of the control-of-illumination studies suggest the complex interplay of tendencies to modify features of the environment, to avoid conditions imposed compulsorily, and to select preferred levels of illumination. [p. 1638]

By ingenious experimental variations Kavanau has shown independent tendencies in this nocturnal animal to prefer low illumination, but also to initiate change in illumination apparently for its own sake, yet to resist change imposed by the experimenter (though, of course, from the mouse's point of view the imposed change just happens; the experimenter does not figure in the mouse's world).

Still other studies showed that under training regimens that give the mice experience with a variety of running wheels, some requiring split-second timing and quick reflex action (for example, square "wheels" and wheels with hurdles), the mice prefer these more "challenging" tasks to running in plain round wheels.

Kavanau further reports:

> White-footed mice readily master complex regimes in which several different levers and shutters must be pressed or rotated in certain sequences within seconds for different rewards. They quickly learn to traverse mazes containing hundreds of blind alleys and do so frequently without extrinsic reward. It is unlikely that these remarkable learning performances even begin to approach the capacities of the animals. [p. 1638]

One can share Kavanau's enthusiasm for these attractive little creatures, for they provide more cogent evidence in regard to White's thesis than any animal research that was available for him to cite. For the types of captive mouse behavior that we have sampled, the rules appear to be these:

1. If things stay the same for very long, change them if you can.
2. To the extent that you can resist imposed change, do so.
3. All the same, there will be some environmental conditions that suit you better than others. Pick those conditions, unless rules 1 and 2 supervene.
4. When you are out for exercise, use your skills and capacities to the hilt.

"Effectance" describes what these mice are up to, but it is a pallid summary. They also show both autonomy and need for variety (Fiske and Maddi, 1961), as well as relatively stable preferences for certain environmental states over others. The gratifications of self-initiated action and the aversive quality of imposed environmental change are clearly evident.

Psychologists have sometimes written as though a fact about people cannot be regarded as legitimate unless it can also be demonstrated in lower animals. No such odd reasoning is intended here, of course. I have no doubt that children show curiosity and negativism and test their capacities in play. What is at issue is whether they do so as part of their evolutionary heritage as mammals. Even the most careful study of one species cannot settle the matter, but Kavanau's research in conjunction with other recent work, especially on primates, creates a strong presumption that these precursors of the competence syndrome have a biological basis. Certainly the behaviors that he describes should yield an evolutionary advantage.

The Emergence of Intrinsic Motivation

How, then, are we to conceive of the human infant's active involvement with the world? Piaget (1952), whose ingenious and detailed observations of the behavior of his own children as infants undoubtedly provided the most important single stimulus to current research interest in early development, took the motivational aspect of this involvement for granted. We simply find the infant engrossed in the process of actively constructing his world, building "schemata"—cognitive-behavioral structures—to which he *assimilates* the presenting stimulation at the same time that he *accommodates* to its refractoriness. During the sensorimotor period of infancy, these schemata are pre-symbolic action-patterns, the achievement of which involves mastery of the instrumental resources of the body and stabilization of a world of objects as two sides of the same coin. Attainment of the schema of directed grasping, for example, establishes for the infant the primitive reality of the object grasped as implied in the complex pattern of sensorimotor coordination. In his waking hours, the infant is constantly busy practicing and applying his existing repertory of schemata, and with increasing maturity, trying out new ones that when perfected increase his cognitive and behavioral command over an ever widening world. Paradoxically, the infant gains in real power over the world to the extent that his emerging cognitive structures provide a coherent formulation of its existence and structural properties as relatively independent of his own actions. The infant comes to construe the world in polar relation to the self and discovers its properties in an endless program of behavioral "experimentation" as it shapes the consequences of his actions.

Given Piaget's enduring preoccupations with developmental epistemology, it is only natural that he has left the motivational aspect of cognitive development implicit in his formulations. The closest that he comes to its explicit recognition is in his metaphorical reference to schemata as feeding upon (receiving "aliment" from) the experience that is assimilated to them. Yet the motivational relevance of his account is obvious, and R. W. White (1959) found some of his most persuasive illustrations in Piaget's descriptions of infant behavior.

J. McV. Hunt, who had previously (1961) examined in detail the bearing of Piaget's research and theories on the very American question (in which Piaget himself was little interested) of how to promote and accelerate intellectual development, has recently (1963, 1965) turned his attention to explicating their motivational implications, grounding his reinterpretation of Piaget in recent research and theory about arousal, attentional processes, curiosity, and exploratory behavior. With White, Hunt sees in Piaget's descriptions evidence for intrinsic motivation, which he spells out as "motivation inherent in information processing and action." Reflecting his background in positivistic behavior studies, he is critical of formulations that give an illusory appearance of dealing adequately with motives by naming them—a fault that he finds in White's "effectance"—or that bypass the problem by postulating spontaneous activity. The details of how Hunt seeks to avoid these errors by recourse to mechanisms and relationships currently entertained in neurophysiologically oriented accounts of motivation need not concern us. But the essentials of his explication and simplification of Piaget are worth considering, as pointing to an epigenetic sequence which, if firmly established, would provide a framework within which social influences on the development of intrinsic motivation might be studied.

Hunt draws upon the idea, put forth by McClelland, Atkinson, Clark, and Lowell (1953) among others, that the affective value of informational input to the organism—pleasant and reinforcing or unpleasant and aversive—depends on its relation to the organism's then-existing adaptation level. Small discrepancies between a characteristic of input and the adaptation level of the organism for that particular characteristic and modality of input arouse pleasant affect; large discrepancies arouse distressing affect. Affective arousal, according to this view, underlies the development of persisting motives. But the very young infant has yet to establish internal standards of reference. During the first four or five months, in Hunt's first stage which corresponds to Piaget's first two, the infant is reactive, a captive of his field of stimulation. Change in this field evokes from him the "orienting response," which is followed by reduction of tension and arousal.

> In this first stage of intrinsic motivation, the standard of reference against which new receptor inputs become incongruous is the ongoing input of the moment. . . . This responsiveness to change in input, especially through the eyes and ears, indicates that a basis for motivation inherent in the infant's informational interaction with his circumstances exists, ready-made, even at birth. [1965, p. 232]

Since the neonate's only standard that governs affective arousal in informational interaction is that of ongoing input, the absence of change—as in neglectful orphanage environments in which input is relatively homogeneous—means the absence of intrinsic motivation, which in the short run means apathy and in the long run should lead to retardation.

This view of the motivational aspects of informational commerce with the environment puts a different interpretation on the often-cited observations of Spitz (1945), who attributed the depression and retardation of orphanage foundlings to the lack of mothering. The new view is congruent with increasing skepticism among careful students concerning the consequences of maternal deprivation as such (Yarrow, 1964). Also working with institutionalized infants, B. White and Held (1966) have since provided decisive evidence that enriched opportunities in the world of the institutional crib have striking effects on the development of the infant's capacities for attention and prehension. At the Puerto Rico Conference, B. White voiced the conviction that these measurable specific effects were accompanied by a generally more positive engagement with the world, which looked like a precursor of competence.

Hunt's second stage appears when the infant begins acting to regain perceptual contact with various kinds of receptor inputs as "interesting spectacles"—in Piaget's phrasing. No longer merely responsive and also commanding a more efficient motor apparatus, the infant can now be said to show intentional activity, in that the instigation of his actions is based on discrepancy from an internal standard. He acts to reestablish sights and happenings to which he has become emotionally attached during the process of increasing familiarization. (Hunt leaves open the question as to whether familiarization as such leads to the attachment or whether it follows upon changes in input that are contingent on the infant's own actions—a theme we remember from the work with white-footed mice.)

Some time in the first year, the infant's cognitive world becomes sufficiently furnished that the familiar loses some of its appeal, and the infant is attracted more to novelty as such. Much remains to be clarified in this formulation, because as Hunt notes, this third stage is also the time at which really serious attachments to persons and places begin with concomitant fear of the strange. It is at this period that Hunt thinks that R. W. White's conceptions of competence motivation toward original constructive activity become relevant.

Some of the other puzzles not resolved by this provisional formulation may be noted briefly. What *are* the characteristics of the stimulus environment that attract the infant's attention, engage his awakening curiosity, draw him outward in cognitive involvement with the world? Novelty and discrepancy from expectation are a first approximation, but what of complexity, what of innately attractive figural properties, like the simple bull's-eye that predictably draws an infant's attention? To what extent is it critical that the infant produce the changes in stimulation by his own actions? Bower (1966) has shown that three-month-old infants acquire the capacity to perceive visual depth through response to the relative motion within the visual field —"motion parallax"—that results from their gross head movements. That their own self-induced movements are crucial is suggested by the research of Held and Hein (1963) on kittens, who found that self-induced movement was essential for normal visual-motor development, and externally-produced movement in the presence of a dependable surround was insufficient.

Is the relationship between early stimulation and the development of intellective competence and intrinsic motivation a continuous function—the more the better? Or a curvilinear one? We no longer hear warnings about over-stimulation, but that is not because the facts are clear. Amid the current excitement about the potential benefits from early stimulation, a note of caution is in order. The possibility that there may be such a thing as over-stimulation is suggested by the observation of B. White and Held (1966), in their study of institutionalized infants already cited, that the introduction of an enriched visual surround when the infants were about five weeks old did not immediately produce favorable effects. Rather, the group with visual enrichment actually exhibited *less* visual attention during the first five weeks of exposure, and the investigators reported their impression that during this period the infants engaged in much more crying than the control group. Favorable effects began only at about ten weeks of age. Timing would seem to be critical. The possibility that there is some minimal level of stimulus variation needed for normal development, beyond which additional dosage makes less difference, also needs to be explored.

What, for that matter, is the interplay between emergent intrinsic motivation, as emphasized by Hunt, and the sense of well-being that presumably arises from the contact comforts of good mothering? Until about 1960, mothering was evidently made to carry too heavy and exclusive a developmental burden. (In his critical review of professional advice to parents over forty years, Brim [1959] found that virtually no attention was given to cognitive development.) But even though some of the consequences previously ascribed to inadequate mothering can now be interpreted more plausibly in terms of the lack of stimulating interplay with the environment (of which the mother is usually a salient component), it would be foolish to assume that mothering makes no difference. Perhaps contact comfort is necessary from the beginning, and an emotional relationship with a stable, affectionate caretaker becomes important in Hunt's third stage? In our enthusiasm for progress in understanding cognitive development, we might wisely dampen any pendulum swing away from recognition of the probable importance of maternal love.

Unfortunately, different sorts of investigators are likely to care about these two topics, and in general research and theory have not been directed toward knitting them together, as an adequate account of the Anlagen of the competent self in infancy would seem to require. We need to know more about how mothering or its lack affects the infant's readiness for active exploration, as is suggested by Mary Ainsworth's finding (Ainsworth and Wittig, in press) that one-year-old infants (like baby chimpanzees) engage in much more active environmental exploration in the presence of their mothers than when with a stranger. The present stage of research and theory opens up many important questions but does not settle them. I recently heard a prominent child psychiatrist assert with some assurance that whether or not a child will ever attain self-respect is probably decided by the time he is two—and that maternal love versus deprivation makes the difference. Fortunately, our present knowledge radically undercuts that assurance, but it does not yet provide the needed answers.

Hunt's version of Piaget has provocative implications for the impact of social structure on socialization for competence. The extent to which slum children actually do suffer the effects of deprivation in infancy is a matter for debate, as their subsequent deficit is not, but the foregoing account helps to focus our inquiry about likely causes of deficit. For one thing, the untidy confusion of a crowded tenement flat certainly does not deprive the young infant of varied stimulation unless he is parked unattended in a convenient crib. Nor, as the infant construes his world, is the chaos that appalls the middle-class visitor necessarily so chaotic from the perspective of the burgeoning schemata of later infancy. Things are things, whatever their disarray, and the baby on the floor has as good a chance as his middle-class counterpart to explore their properties. If he is left in a crib for the convenience of mother or granny, he *may* indeed be deprived, but such deprivation is hardly specific to the slum. One is led to conjecture that before major handicaps appear as the child enters the symbolic world of language, the main liabilities are to be looked for in instability of temporal scheduling (conceivably relevant throughout infancy) and in such social factors (presumably most relevant in later infancy) as erratic scheduling of social reinforcement and instability of relationships with caretakers—items that do not figure prominently in the cognitively focused account of development we have just reviewed.

Continuity versus Discontinuity between Infancy and Early Childhood

By the time the infant is a year old, the terminology of competence seems to fit very well the coherent ways in which infants differ from one another. This impression is supported by evidence in Wenar's study of "competence at one" (1964). Defining "executive competence" as "the child's ability to initiate and sustain locomotor, manipulative, and visually regarding activities at a given level of complexity and intensity, and with a given degree of self-sufficiency" (p. 336), he found a significant tendency for indices of his proposed components of competence to vary together, with the exception of self-sufficiency. What remains in doubt, and this is an area of uncertainty where research is most badly needed, is the linkage between competence in infancy and in early childhood.

At about two years of age, the preschool child emerges out of babyhood. He begins to talk, not with faltering words, but using language as a major channel of increasingly efficient communication with other human beings, at the beginning principally his parents. With language goes a new level of organization of his mental life.

Once, psychologists were wont to assume that the symbolic tokens of language and of thought as inner speech, acquired from the culture, transformed the young child's capacities for problem-solving, for future orientation, and for self-regard; a single causal direction was assumed from language to thought, fitting the now discredited view of the infant mind as *tabula rasa.* Better contemporary understanding of the constructive aspects of language learning (for example, Lenneberg, 1967) now suggests that only after the child has already grown into capacities for symbolization and for the induction and creative application of sentence-producing rules (a process that cannot be explained by passive imitation)—only after his thought is already in the process of being transformed—can he conceivably display the creative, productive use of language that is characteristic even of beginners. We must now give much more weight to the maturing capacities and cognitive dispositions that underlie the onset of language. But once the child can talk and understand, language becomes the preeminent tool for further cognitive elaboration in development.

Piaget labels the distinction between infancy and the preschool years as that between the sensory-motor and the "pre-operational" periods. Though Piaget is less interested in this aspect of development, reflective selfhood (Mead, G. H., 1934) emerges along with symbolization and language. In spite of the apparent sharp discontinuity between infancy and childhood, does favorable development in infancy predict competence in childhood and later? The evidence is slim. Flavell (1963, p. 150) cites Piaget as noting that the period from two to four years is the least investigated period in the entire developmental span.

The issue of predictive continuity or discontinuity across this little known boundary makes a considerable difference for social policy. It is considered in Hunt's discussion of the development of intellectual capacities, in particular how their further development might best be stimulated (1961, p. 314). Citing Bayley (1940) on the high reliability but absent predictive validity of infant mental tests, Hunt argues that "predictive validity could be expected only by assuming fixed intelligence and predetermined development" (which Hunt denies); low predictive validity in relation to later childhood and adulthood does not discredit the validity of the tests as reflecting the intellectual attainments of infancy. On the same page, however, we find him also arguing that "inasmuch as developmental rates are most rapid, in absolute terms, during the early months and the first couple of years, this is probably the period of most importance for maximizing intellectual potential"—an argument that is currently reaching the popular literature with little more empirical evidence to back it up than was at Hunt's disposal. (We may be at the point of overemphasizing the early years in the cognitive realm before the evidence is in, just as the Freudian revolution led an earlier generation of parent advisors to overemphasize them in the emotional realm.) But note the logical problem in joining the two statements. *If* what happens in the first two years is so important for later intellectual attainment, *why* is measured intellectual status near the end of that period so poor a predictor of later intelligence? If the linkage between infant and childhood intelligence is as feeble as the empirical correlations indicate, what grounds do we have for believing that stimulating infant intelligence can produce gains that will be preserved in childhood and later? Major decisions on the ages at which social investment should be made in remedying incompetence and promoting competence hinge—or ought to hinge—on how this issue is resolved.

Bayley (1966) has recently summarized a variety of evidence from the Berkeley Growth Study, concerning not only the stability and predictive value of intelligence-test scores but also the changing nature of correlations between mental scores and a variety of other behaviors and conditions, which sharpens the case for a substantial realignment of mental functions in the two-year-old. But perhaps there is reason to expect continuities in intrinsic motivation even if there is discontinuity in the organization of intellective functions. Intuitively such continuity makes sense.

There is at least some empirical evidence for motivational continuity across the infancy-childhood barrier, in the longitudinal correlations of the Menninger "coping" study (Murphy, Lois, 1962). For this small, intensively studied sample, infancy ratings on protest, termination, and resistance in the feeding situation—which might be interpreted as precursors of autonomous mastery—were substantially correlated, among the boys, with such preschool variables belonging to the competence cluster as impulse control, reality testing, overall ability, clarity regarding own identity, persistence in the face of failure, ability to restructure the environment, determination, drive for mastery, sense of importance, and problem-solving attitude toward life. Bearing on my earlier plea for the integrated study of the consequences of good or poor mothering together with those of productive interplay with the environment, Lois Murphy further reports substantial positive correlations (also for boys) between "oral gratification" in infancy—which sounds like a reflection of good mothering—and a number of competence-related preschool variables: clarity of perception, sense of self-worth, strength of interest, ability to control the impact of the environment, and reality level. The negative correlations with depreciation of others, loss of perceptual clarity under stress, and tendency to get fatigued are equally pertinent and interesting. Given the limitations of this exploratory study, these relationships have to be regarded as suggestive rather than conclusive. On the side of discontinuity are the Kagan and Moss (1962) findings, in the Fels longitudinal study, that ratings of achievement behavior in the first three years show low negative correlations with comparable ratings in later childhood, in spite of evidence for substantial continuity between later childhood and adulthood in this motivational area. Better evidence in regard to continuity versus discontinuity of both intellective and motivational functions is badly needed, especially in regard to the persistent effects of interventions intended to improve the course of development.

Pending new light on this question, we may nevertheless be sure that the onset of talking creates new opportunities and challenges for some children, and begins or accentuates a cycle of intellectual handicap and failure for others. To the extent that children from the Negro slums learn as their native tongue a "substandard" dialect that makes them foreigners when they come to school, they are handicapped at least in regard to communication with teachers and possibly in social contacts with other children. Beyond this de facto disadvantage, however, patterns of language usage in the lower class may entail intrinsic intellective handicaps to the child who acquires them. In his sociolinguistic studies of the English middle and working classes, Bernstein (1964) proposes that speech is, indeed, "the major means through which the social structure becomes part of individual experience." As compared with the "elaborated code" of middle-class speech, the working class communicate by a "restricted code" in which meaning is organized via selection among a severely limited range of alternatives. Bernstein holds that the two modes of speech "elicit and sustain particular forms of relationships to the environment and so establish different orders of learning and relevance" (p. 258). The restricted code, with its limited structural organization and lexicon, is adapted to solidary communication about a limited stock of culturally shared referents. Within this framework, concrete, global, descriptive relationships are expressed at a low level of conceptualization. Communication of subjective intent is typically not well elaborated. As Bernstein puts it, the restricted code "signals the normative arrangements of a group rather than the individuated experience of its members" (p. 255). While warm solidarity is promoted, so is passivity and projectivity. Bernstein suggests that children reared to the restricted code may not progress in cognitive development from concrete to formal operations in Piaget's terms.

The Chicago studies by Hess and his colleagues (for example, Hess and Shipman, 1965) provide systematic evidence in support of these plausible hypotheses. These investigators observed Negro mothers, drawn from contrasting levels of social status, in interviews and in interaction with their four-year-old children as the children worked at various tasks. Mothers from the lower strata indeed used speech in a restricted way, which tends to foreclose the need for reflective weighing of alternatives and consequences. But Hess, though he follows Bernstein's analysis of speech patterns, is more interested in the entire teaching style that mothers use with their children, and how different styles of teaching shape the children's learning styles and information-processing strategies. As Hess and Shipman summarize the import of their research:

> The picture that is beginning to emerge is that the meaning of deprivation is a deprivation of meaning—a cognitive environment in which behavior is controlled by status rules rather than by attention to the individual characteristics of a specific situation and one in which behavior is not mediated by verbal cues or by teaching that relates events to one another and the present to the future. This environment produces a child who relates to authority rather than to rationale, who, although often compliant, is not reflective in his behavior, and for whom the consequences of an act are largely considered in terms of immediate punishment or reward rather than future effects and long-range goals. [p. 885]

These considerations carry us beyond the impact of class-related speech patterns as such, to issues with which we will be concerned in the next major section of the chapter. Research now in progress in the presently very lively field of sociolinguistics should throw further light on the channel that language provides for the transmission and perpetuation of class-linked aspects of competence. The period from one to three years old, before most children become readily accessible to observation in the nursery school, would seem to be a particularly strategic phase of development to study, crossing as it does the apparent major discontinuity in the development of intelligence and including the major steps in the development of language.

Competence and Emerging Selfhood

With language comes selfhood, and we make contact with our starting point in this chapter: the *person* as possessing attributes of competence or incompetence. From this point on, to speak of the "organism" reflects a deliberately partial perspective. Our earlier discussion has already made a case for assuming that once the child attains the level of communicative social participation as a conscious self, the motives and attitudes in which we are interested are organized around or channeled through the self as reflexive object and enduring structure.

Apart from the diffuse background of bodily awareness, the child's sense of self would appear to have its origins in two distinguishable sorts of input, only one of which has been emphasized in the major line of social-psychological theorizing. One is the feedback that the child gets about the effects of his actions on the world of physical objects and people, as stressed by R. W. White (1959) and throughout this chapter. The other is feedback from the mirror of social response and appraisal, as emphasized by the great names in the symbolic-interactionist tradition. Both sorts of ingredients, I propose, are necessarily involved in the constitution of the self. How they are integrated in the self as it becomes stabilized as an established structure is a matter of decisive importance for the child's orientation toward the world, since the self continues to be the vehicle both for approval-seeking motivation guided by social comparison and for intrinsic competence motivation toward the production of valued effects. The interplay between these motivational aspects of selfhood will be examined in more detail in the next section.

The development of these two aspects of the self requires description in different terms, and different social factors emerge as likely to be influential in the development of each. Consider first the component of reflected social appraisal, as initially suggested by James, Baldwin, and Cooley and brought to its most sophisticated statement by G. H. Mead (1934) in his formulation that reflective self-awareness depends upon adopting toward one's own attributes and actions the perspective of people at large, generalizing across the various particular role relationships in which one is in communicative interaction. From this vantage point, development of the self depends upon the ever-widening and more complexly organized sets of role relationships in which the child is involved, starting with the mother-child pair, extending to the more complicated role system of the immediate family, and, beginning with the school years, broadening to include the peer group, extra-familial adult authorities, and, progressively, the entire complex structure of society at large as the individual is related to it. As the "generalized other" whose perspective the child adopts becomes progressively *more* generalized, his reflected view of himself becomes more "objective"—less dependent upon the contingencies of particular role relationships—at the same time that he becomes equipped with the role repertory to participate effectively in the full range of social life.

Throughout this course of development, the theme of reflected *appraisal* calls our attention to how the child is evaluated by the various "significant others" and to the categories of people that enter his world of relationships, as primary determinants of his emerging self-evaluation. It is through who these others are and how they treat him that the social structure has its impact on his feelings of worth—a theme introduced by neo-Meadians under the influence of Sullivan (1945). Since the generalized other of the preschool child is restricted to the immediate family, it is how the child perceives their feelings about him that makes the most difference to this aspect of the beginnings of selfhood.

This is the familiar social-psychological account of the development of the self, and while it would seem to be correct and useful so far as it goes, it is clearly one-sided. Along with interactionist role theory generally, it looks like the theory that Riesman's "other-directed man" (Riesman, 1950) would naturally invent to give an account of himself. It needs to be balanced by attention to those aspects of the self that continue to channel intrinsic motivation.

It is clear that intrinsic motivation *does* become channeled in the course of development. The infant, like the captive white-footed mouse, may seek his effects from the environment in rather randomly selected directions; not so the older child nor, of course, the adult. Just any effect won't do. The developing person comes to specialize in seeking environmental effects in particular realms, and he acquires values or standards against which he measures the adequacy of the effects that he has produced. Progressive definition of one's sense of identity is in good part a matter of such limitation and specification of one's claims on life.

One aspect of this process of progressive motivational differentiation was given an early formulation by Gardner Murphy (1947) in his concept of *canalization*—the tendency to seek gratification in the particular modes and from the particular activities that previously have been found gratifying; that is, one's areas of success point the direction for focusing one's further efforts. But this idea, which is really a variant of commonplace concepts of reinforcement, does better as an account of the differentiation, say, of the general biological hunger drive into a set of culturally specific food preferences and appetites than it does as a formulation for the development of elaborating, self-feeding, insatiable interests and endeavors that are intrinsically motivating to the mature person. In his discussion of *propriate* (self-related) striving, G. W. Allport (1961) captures descriptively this aspect of motivation as involving the person's self-directed intentions.

With the development of the self, then, the person's initial diffuse orientation toward effective engagement with the environment becomes *differentiated* and specialized. At the same time, however, his self-conceptions and self-attitudes, formed in the light of feedback from effects achieved *and* from social appraisal, provide the basis for *generalized* orientations of competence or incompetence, relatively stable across the vicissitudes of particular transactional encounters or role relationships. It is the dialectic interplay of trends toward generalization *and* differentiation that gives rise to the integrated organization of personality structure.

Social Approval, Social Comparison, and Intrinsic Motivation

Some Interrelations

But the developmental sequences involving the results of reflected appraisals of the child's qualities and performances, on the one hand, and the intrinsic effects of his own self-initiated activities, on the other, do not proceed independently of one another. The distinction is analytic and does not at all correspond to neatly separable aspects of personality development or structure. Thus, the two sorts of motivation can run parallel and fuse, as when parents or teachers bestow their approval on the child for performances that are also intrinsically rewarding. Gratifications from social effectance can supplant and substitute for those of social approval when the latter are not to be had—as when the "bad" child settles on getting a rise out of adults whose approval he has no hope of receiving (at the same time probably reaping social rewards from his peers). Or—one suspects more commonly with the middle-class child—extrinsic rewards of approval, grades, and, later, money may come eventually to replace intrinsic satisfactions, at heavy cost to the person's zest, creativity, and sense of meaningfulness.

I want to avoid giving the impression that intrinsic motivation is uniformly good and social-reinforcement motivation bad in socialization and personality development or that it makes any sense to conceive of the individual as unfolding autonomously under the guidance of pure effectance. Children and people generally need to feel well regarded by the others they care about, and if they do not, they are thrown into all manner of defensive maneuvers. Some sense of goodness coming from benign reflected appraisal is probably essential if the person is to be free to cope. Then, too, the child has to acquire some routine skills—for example, the "times tables"—that depend on rote practice under extrinsic reward, intrinsic rewards during their acquisition being notably lacking.[4] Moreover, often the standards by which a person can recognize an effective performance that is intrinsically rewarding are not themselves given intrinsically. Social convention defines the

4. O. K. Moore's electronically controlled "responsive environment," described in Hunt (1965), manages to enlist intrinsic motivation even in the service of rote learning; hence its appeal and efficiency as a teaching device.

good performance in football and in banking, to a greater extent than in felling a tree or weaving a robe, but that does not eliminate the joys of effectance in playing the game. In large areas of personal and social behavior, as Festinger (1954) has emphasized, one can evaluate one's attributes and performances only through some process of social comparison. People appropriately turn to others to know how they stand when directly informative feedback from the results of their actions is unavailable.

The clear separation of what is extrinsic from what is intrinsic becomes the more difficult because, as G. W. Allport (1961) liked to stress, the motivational basis of particular activities does not stay put. Something that is not initially rewarding for its own sake becomes intrinsically rewarding as one achieves skill—whether playing the piano, dancing, or doing a problem in calculus. Conversely, something that was rewarding may cease to be so once mastered, especially if it is not highly valued by others. Socially derived values assist in defining what tasks are worth working on, what kinds of mastery worth pursuing. Moreover, since different segments of the social structure entail diverse definitions of worthwhile activities and tasks, social factors undoubtedly contribute to the channeling of competence, to the focusing of intrinsic motivation.

Despite the fact that the intrinsic and extrinsic, the personal and the social, strands become inextricably entangled, we must pursue the fate of intrinsic motivation. We must be particularly interested in identifying approaches to socialization that dampen intrinsic motivation and replace it by motivation for social approval and preemptive orientation toward extrinsic rewards. The procedures of our educational institutions invite examination from this perspective. The late president of Vassar, Sarah Blanding, told of a dewy-eyed freshman who approached her at the President's Reception to pronounce solemnly, "Miss Blanding, I think every young student has a spark of genius somewhere within her . . . and it is the duty of the faculty to *water* that spark." What in the educational process is likely to water the spark of intrinsic motivation, producing results that are familiar to saddened teachers and discouraged parents?

One obviously unfavorable factor, which is critically important in the lives of many children, is a consistent history of failure and disapproval attending their independent efforts. Using a Reinforcement History Questionnaire that inquired about characteristic parental reactions in a variety of situations of effort, success, and failure on the part of the child, Irwin Katz (1967) found that among Negro boys (though not among girls) low school achievement, anxiety, and a propensity for self-devaluation, which as we might expect were all interrelated, were each in turn related to the predominance of negative reinforcements from parents—reports of low parental interest and acceptance and high parental punitiveness. When a discouraging start at home is followed by disparagement and ego-assault at school, the damage is only compounded. In *Death at an Early Age,* Kozol (1967) gives a poignant account of such factors as they impinge on Negro children in a segregated Boston school. Intrinsic motivation is bound to be quenched in settings where effort is predictably followed by failure (no intrinsic satisfactions) and accompanied by social indifference or disapproval (no extrinsic ones, either).

But let us assume well-intentioned parents and teachers, and more fortunate children. Good teaching by the agents of socialization, whether parents or teachers, would often seem to require more skill and forbearance than these people possess. It is easier to lecture than to develop a collaborative teaching relationship in which the child is encouraged to take the initiative. It is easier to lay out the facts for rote learning, necessarily sustained by extrinsic reinforcements, than it is to arrange curricular experiences in which knowledge and skills are seen by the child as instrumental to his own problem-solving efforts. It is easier to help the child who is in difficulty by giving him the "right" answer, the "right" method, than it is to point his attention in directions that support him in making the discovery for himself. How to give the right amount of the right kind of help at the right time, and not too much? It is easier to lay down rules by fiat than to go into the reasons for behavioral requests and on occasion to modify a request when the child has good countervailing reasons of his own. Educational theory since the days of Dewey has recognized the importance of building upon the child's active participation in the learning process, but realization of this aim in crowded classes led by teachers who, as the products of traditional educational experiences are themselves far from ideal models of competence, is another matter. The spark gets watered.

Achievement Motivation and Competence

At the Puerto Rico Conference, some of the most provocative talk about intrinsic versus extrinsic motivation in socialization for competence centered on the need for achievement—a concept that at first blush appears to have much in common with White's concept of competence. For McClelland et al. (1953), the concept meant striving to attain standards of excellence. They carried out an exemplary program of research on its antecedents and results based on scoring for achievement motivation imaginative stories told by subjects about a standard set of pictures—an adaptation of the Thematic Apperception Test (TAT) technique. The scoring system was derived empirically by noting the categories of content that distinguished the stories of students whose achievement motive had supposedly been aroused, as compared with stories written in a "neutral" condition. For the condition in which achievement motivation was to be aroused, subjects were given a difficult prior task—just before writing their stories—which was presented to them as a test of intelligence, a trait that most students can be assumed to want to excel in. Subsequent research (summarized most recently in Atkinson and Feather, 1966) has found high need for achievement to be associated with achievement training by both parents and independence training by the father. Warm but dominating mothers who are much concerned with their sons' performance contribute to high need for achievement in sons; dominating fathers, to low achievement motivation. A central influence in the learning of achievement motivation is the parents' conditional approval.

There are a good many difficulties with the concept of achievement motivation as embodied in this fantasy-based measure, most of which are reviewed by Irwin Katz (1967). There are questions about its generality, its applicability to women, its openness to influences that contaminate its value as a measure of motivation. The findings in regard to its relationships to achievement-oriented behavior have been ambiguous, except as a predictor of entrepreneurial striving in business men. Given this less than encouraging record, one suspects that there has been slippage between the theoretical definition of the motive and what has actually been captured in the measurements.

The technique of arousal that was employed in developing the scoring system did not directly arouse "standards of excellence"; rather, subjects were led to be concerned about their competitive standing in a quality that was important to them: intelligence. Perhaps, after all, the motive thus imperfectly tapped has more to do with competitive striving in a context of social comparison than with intrinsic effort toward excellence. Atkinson and Feather entertain this possibility: "Under some conditions thematic apperceptive n Ach scores may reflect *extrinsic* motivation instead of, or in addition to, achievement motivation. The possibility is sufficiently important to make this one of the most significant problems for future study" (1966, p. 350). Evidence in support of this conjecture is provided in Skolnick's finding (1966) that, for men, McClelland-style fantasy scores for achievement correlate more highly with the California Psychological Inventory scale for *Achievement via conformance* than with that for *Achievement via independence* (contrary findings for women perhaps being explicable in terms of the culturally prescribed feminine sex role, according to which competitive achievement striving, as deviant, requires independence of prevailing norms).

If we give weight to these misgivings and to the emphasis on conditional approval in the antecedents of achievement motivation, the apparent similarity between *n Ach* and our competence syndrome is dispelled. Achievement motivation would seem at root to involve performance for the sake of social approval; competence motivation involves being able to risk disapproval in order to master a task on one's own terms. No doubt, effective performance is often for the sake of approval; but at what psychological cost?

A congruence seems apparent between achievement motivation and the approach of the "traditional" school with its competition and grades, its reliance on extrinsic motivation to power the learning of facts and specific skills. More congruent with the development of competent selves is the "modern" orientation according to which the school tries to build on the child's native and intrinsic curiosity, on his active initiative in the learning process. In such schools, intellectual mastery in terms of the child's own organization of knowledge is valued rather than the level of factual attainment. The child is helped to discover the self-relevance of what he learns; interplay between the subjective and objective is encouraged.

But the value question that brings heat to arguments about humanistic child rearing and progressive education remains: Is the development of strong need for achievement an asset or a liability? American society obviously thrived when it was manned by a middle class that was competitively oriented toward achievement—at a toll for the individual. If the school and the home train children so as to maximize their sense of competence and autonomy, they will not want to do all the things that society calls upon them to do; they may not choose to do things that society needs to have done, including things that later on they may themselves wish they had chosen to do. One can imagine supporters of traditional education, competitive achievement motivation, and the associated values of the Protestant ethic putting up a strong argument for the older way. At root, a choice of values is at issue.

These issues are beginning to become clarified in recent research on the child-rearing antecedents of competence-related behavior. Two studies that are interesting to compare in this regard share as a valuable common feature the collection of systematic data on parent-child interaction in a standard situation. In the classic study of the antecedents of achievement motivation, Rosen and D'Andrade (1959) found that mothers of boys who scored high in need for achievement were distinctive in being more intrusive, setting high standards for their boys' performance, and insisting on a superior performance. They did not allow the child much autonomy in decision making. Helen Bee (1967) reports a contrasting pattern of behavior for parents of nine-year-old children of both sexes who had been selected for their ability to resist distraction, a feature of inner control that would seem to belong to our competence syndrome and should certainly contribute to effective performance in many settings. Bee found that in comparison with parents of distractible children, parents of non-distractible children give less specific suggestions about how to accomplish the task, give more positive encouragement, pay more attention to their child's contributions in decision-making interaction, and make relatively more evaluative comments than suggestions. They seem to be concerned that the child's achievement be his own. In congruence with Wenar's (1964) finding that self-sufficiency did not cohere with other indices of infant competence, Bee reports that contrary to expectation, non-distractible children make more bids for help, but they also reject help more often. Perhaps what is relevant to competence is not so much self-sufficiency as the ability and disposition to make use of others' help on one's own terms.

Diana Baumrind has recently contributed evidence that bears more directly on the parental practices associated with competence in nursery school children. In one study (1967), she identified for comparison three groups of children selected on the basis of their behavior in nursery school: a competent group who were assertive, self-reliant, self-controlled, bouyant, and affiliative; another group who were discontented, withdrawn, and distrustful; and a third group who had little self-control or self-reliance and tended to retreat from novel experiences. Parents of the competent group tended to be controlling, demanding, communicative, and loving; parents of the unhappy and disaffiliated group were relatively controlling and detached; and parents of the least self-reliant and self-controlled group of children were noncontrolling, nondemanding, and relatively warm. A second study (Baumrind and Black, 1967) examined the relations among parent behaviors, parent attitudes, and child behavior in an unselected sample. While the results of this research show important sex differences in relationships that are too complex for ready summarizing, the findings again suggest:

> Parental practices which are intellectually stimulating and to some extent tension-producing (socialization and maturity demands, punitiveness, firmness in disciplinary matters) are associated in the young child with various aspects of competence. Techniques which fostered self-reliance, whether by placing demands upon the child for self-control and high level performance or by encouraging independent action and decision-making, facilitated responsible, independent behavior. Firm discipline in the home did not produce conforming or dependent behavior in the nursery school. [p. 325]

For engendering competence, it is clear, love is not enough, though it matters. Challenge, respect for the child, perhaps even some abrasiveness in relations with the child that provokes his assertiveness, good communication with an emphasis on the reasons for directives—these would seem important too, and are supported by convergent evidence. Baumrind's particular stress on high parental demands, firmness, and even punitiveness remains controversial, and no conclusion can be drawn about competence versus need for achievement when the relatively few relevant studies available employ different criteria and measures and draw their observations from different populations.

Our discussion has carried us rather far from the topic of achievement motivation, as treated in the work of the McClelland-Atkinson group. Achievement motivation can of course of studied by methods other than fantasy-based measures; other investigators have sought to save the concept by introducing differentiations that take into account some of the criticisms we have noted. For example, Veroff (1967), in the recent paper that also reviews an impressive program of related research done with his students, contrasts *autonomous* achievement motivation, which brings internalized personal standards into play, with *social* achievement motivation, in which the standards of excellence are based on social comparison. He offers a conjectural developmental sequence with three stages: an early one in which autonomous motivation predominates, a second stage in which social comparison is central (in the early school years), and finally a third one in which these components of achievement motivation are effectively integrated. He interprets various defects in the development of achivement motivation in terms of deficiencies in motive acquisition at the several stages. His data very broadly accord with the scheme, without giving it compelling support. But they do not answer the question of whether we are indeed dealing with an intrinsic sequence or instead with the consequences of dumping curious and autonomous youngsters into conventional, competitive schools. Nor is his concept of the integrated stage well developed. Rather, the question would seem to be: *how* are the autonomous and social components put together?

Irwin Katz (1967), whose paper we have already cited, is concerned with the much more concrete problem of accounting for the motivational aspect of Negro deficit in school achievement and in this context finds the McClelland-Atkinson approach wanting, as focusing exclusively on motive strength while providing no useful information about the inferred self-regulatory behaviors that are supposedly involved. His decision to bring the children's normally covert responses of self-approval and self-disapproval under direct observation in an ingeniously contrived situation nicely complements the studies of Rotter (1966), Coleman et al. (1966), and Crandall, Katkovsky, and Crandall (1965) on children's beliefs in their own control of reinforcements in achievement situations. Rather than focus on their *beliefs* that reinforcing outcomes are under their own control, Katz studied how they actually administer reinforcements of approval or disapproval to themselves, while performing simple standard tasks.

He found that under conditions of supposed privacy, low achieving boys were more likely than relatively high achievers to indicate disapproval of their own performances, actual quality of performance being equivalent for the groups. The relationship does not hold for girls, a finding of sex differences that recurs throughout the complex literature of achievement research and cannot be pursued here, though with clarification of their basis should come much better understanding of the socialization antecedents of achievement motivation and behavior. If we hold in abeyance Katz's interpretation of his data in terms of internalized processes of covert reinforcement or their lack, on the surface his findings portray the low achievers' generalized unfavorable view of their own performance, which carries over even to situations in which the performance is not deficient. This discouraged outlook is entirely compatible with their giving voice to unrealistically high goals. Indeed, as Katz plausibly suggests, verbal subscription to high goals can substitute for constructive action toward achieving them.

This foray into recent research and theory about achievement motivation cannot produce tidy solutions from a field that is not yet ready for them. Hopefully, it may have sensitized the reader, as it has the author, to the complexity and difficulties of conceptualization and measurement that hamper attempts to disentangle intrinsic and extrinsic motivation in regard to a person's tendencies to engage constructively with the world.

Anxiety and Need for Approval

We may close this section by brief attention to some motivational dispositions that are clearly incompatible with intrinsically motivated competence. The first to be considered, need for approval as studied by Marlowe and Crowne (1964), sounds like the concern with social appraisal that we have been discussing. However, their method of assessing individual differences singles out as high scorers persons whose need to be well regarded by others is in defense of a very vulnerable self-regarding sentiment. The social desirability scale that Marlowe and Crowne use in their research allows people to endorse statements—outside the realm of psychopathology—that are commonly regarded as desirable attributes but are usually false. It thus identifies, at the high end, people who will go to considerable lengths to make a favorable impression. If the straightforward desire to be liked and receive social reinforcement can sometimes interfere with competence motivation, its defensive equivalent is unquestionably disadvantageous. Marlowe and Crowne present evidence that is generally consistent with this view, showing that while high scorers learn well under conditions of social reinforcement, they are dependent and compliant, and show themselves as defensive and avoidant in psychotherapy. But it is not clear whether it is their underlying low self-esteem that is incompatible with the competence syndrome, or, on the other hand, the defensive posture that they have adopted in order to bolster it.

In common psychodynamic theory, defensiveness is linked to anxiety. Anxiety as a momentary state may energize the person toward emergency action, but as an enduring trait the evidence shows according to expectation that it generally goes with low competence. This is not the place to consider the technicalities of pencil-and-paper anxiety scales and their use in research, which have been reviewed by I. G. Sarason (1960) and by Ruebush (1963). The most thorough work relating anxiety to achievement and competence in children has been that of S. B. Sarason and his colleagues (for example, Sarason, Davidson, Lighthall, Waite, and Ruebush, 1960; Hill, K. T., and Sarason, 1966), who focused on a measure of test anxiety. Test anxiety tends to lead to poor school achievement, and in its antecedents and correlates is clearly part of the incompetence cluster. The Mandler-Sarason Test Anxiety Questionnaire has been used as an index of "fear of failure" by the Atkinson group (Atkinson and Feather, 1966).

Social Structure and Competence

At scattered points throughout the chapter, we have noted ways in which factors of social structure—especially social class and ghetto status[5]—impinge on the development of competence. Having looked at its sources in infancy and tried with only partial success to disentangle some of the motivational factors that affect competent functioning in childhood and later, it is time for us to return to our provisional model of the competent self, established in benign circles of productive engagement with the environment, and its incompetent counterpart, mired in vicious circles of self-defeat. To expand our view of the self-sustaining system we can now look for strategic factors of social structure that gear into these vicious or benign circles. In the personal system centering on the self, I suggested that attitudes of hope and of self-respect are at the crux of competence. Are there corresponding features of a person's location in the social system that play an equally strategic role?

Power, Respect, and Opportunity

I think there are such strategic aspects of location in the social structure: *opportunity, respect,* and *power*. Opportunity corresponds to hope and provides its warrant. Respect by others—more important in this regard than love or approval—provides the social ground for respect of self. And power is the kingpin of the system. Power receives respect and guarantees access to opportunity.

Restriction of opportunity not only blights hope; it excludes the person from the chance to acquire the knowledge and skill that would in turn enable him to surmount the barriers to effectiveness. Contempt and withheld respect may lead to "self-hatred" (Lewin, 1948, pp. 186–200) and may necessitate debilitating postures of self-defense. Absence of power entails general vulnerability and creates dependence. When opportunities are offered without a sharing of power, we have paternalism, which undercuts respect, accentuates dependence, and breeds a lurking resentment that the powerful are likely to condemn in righteousness as ingratitude.

The current world has fully displayed the inadequacy of paternalism and resounds with the claims of the powerless. Former colonial peoples, American Negroes, college students and other youth—all are engaged in strident power claims. And the prophets, the apologists, the critics of Black Power have almost succeeded, among them, in washing out all stable meaning from the term. Yet fundamentally the prophets and apologists are right, since power is objective control over what affects one's destiny.

5. An excellent integration of research findings concerning child rearing and family-life patterns associated with poverty, with implications for action programs, has been recently provided by Chilman (1966).

As many commentators have noted, the currently escalating power claims by the disadvantaged are not to be explained by their extreme deprivation; rather, the contrary. The fact that these claims can be made at all is a sign of growing competence among people who before were fatalistically adapted to their powerless positions as apathetic students, colonials, or Uncle Toms. Loosened bonds of paternalistic authority, expanding opportunities, and instant mass communication across classes and countries and from campus to campus lead to rising expectations in an affluent society and modernizing world—the glimmerings of hope—and as the movement gathers momentum, models that the still powerless and incompetent can identify with to gain vicarious strength become available. The unreasonableness and unrealism of the claims to power, the frequently self-defeating tactics are understandable as stigmata of the persisting incompetence produced by powerlessness. Given unrealistic and insecure hopes that are bound to be frustrated, given competition among the leadership elite in the outrageousness of their claims, and given the predictable "backlash" from whoever constitute the relevant Establishment, the potentialities for continued explosive violence are very great indeed.

If social chaos can somehow be avoided, even spurious compensatory claims to respect and power have their value in what we must hope will be a transition to more fully shared power and greater competence for the presently deprived. The problem here is not the powerlessness and incompetence of individuals but that of massive social groups with shared, mutually reinforcing sentiments about self and world. Even flagrant reversals of white racist values, even transparent fabrications of a glorious history can help people who have little basis for realistic hope to develop the beginnings of a sense of worth and a feeling that they can have important effects in this world. The models furnished by conspicuous leaders provide a vicarious basis for the feeling of competence. In this regard, sinners like Adam Clayton Powell and Kwame Nkrumah may make more difference than saints like Martin Luther King. They are closer to their followers and more understandable.

Of course, extreme power claims by all social groups can never be simultaneously satisfied. The logical end point of pressing these claims would be a war of all against all—the Hobbesian "state of nature" that still exists in principle among nations. We may hope that as the powerless gain in real power and in both the feeling and the fact of competence, they may abate their more extreme claims, while the holders of power relax their resistance. The resulting state of shared power and accompanying responsibility, as and if it is approximated, could create a community fit for competent selves.

In this excursion about power and competence, I have neglected the asymmetrical power relationship that is most germane to socialization—that between parent and child, socialization agent and socializee (let us regard college students as quasi-adults). Age grading is itself a fact of social structure.

Do the same considerations apply here? Yes, I think, with a difference. The difference is that the asymmetry in real power and competence is inherent, and hence some variant of paternalism—call it parentalism?—can hardly be avoided. And the attempt to disguise it can amount to an abdiction of responsibility or can undermine the honesty of the relationship.

But with this important qualification, I think the fundamental relationships between power and competence hold. The authoritarian parent who uses his age-status for the naked assertion of power over his children gets dependence and passive resistance; maybe, if he is lucky, revolt. The wise nurture of competence in the young would seem to call for a deliberate progressive sharing of power and responsibility as the growing competence of the child enables him to use it. A little faster, perhaps, than is securely warranted by what the child can do: good "parentalism," unlike conventional paternalism, sees to it that the child has real problems and challenges to face, and that his solutions are his own.

Deviant Forms of Competence

Throughout this discussion I have knowingly overdrawn the picture of incompetence that goes with powerlessness and hopelessness, especially in the urban ghetto, so as to lay forth as clearly as possible an interpretative perspective which, though conjectural, seems to me to make a variety of salient current developments intelligible. True, the incompetence is there (along with remarkable instances of competence in spite of great handicap), and much deviant and problematic behavior can be interpreted as an attempt to seek escape from self and world, or to gain a short circuited, illusory sense of efficacy—thus drug use and the search for kicks. Much, but not all. Some antisocial behavior, deviant from the point of view of the environing and superordinate society, may in part be directed toward alternative modes of competence that remain available and indeed become normative in the ghetto subculture when legitimate channels of effectance are closed off. The combative prowess of the gang leader and member, virtuosity in aggressive "mother talk," audacity in sexual exploits, and competence in the risky skills of the hustler belong under this heading, though these directions of activity obviously also yield extrinsic rewards. The larger society will regard these directions of activity as bad, but those who plan and direct rehabilitation programs will do well to remember that for many slum youth, all of their resources of competence motivation get channeled in these deviant directions. A lot of self is invested in them.

Small wonder that when youths from the slums are asked to give up these known avenues for intrinsic motivation for the sake of the uncertain benefits of a square world to which they have no commitment, they often "blot out" in some disastrous act that rescues them, at the very brink of successful rehabilitation, from the dangers of this fate. (This pattern was described in the conference paper by Nathan Caplan.) Such unsuccessful outcomes are the more likely to represent "healthy" strivings toward competence and autonomy when rehabilitation programs can still appear to the clients to be aimed mainly at satisfying the social workers' needs for achievement, not the clients' autonomous desires.

Even the "floating" that characterizes many slum boys, a manifestly incompetent pattern of behavior, testifies to residual effectance motivation under conditions that exclude true effectiveness. Observations that Caplan reported in connection with street club work identified two distinct recurrent patterns of daily activity. On the one hand were boys who did not get into trouble, whose sequence of activities seemed highly organized along culturally approved lines. Interviews suggested that for many of these boys achievement was primarily a matter of cultural conformity. The "floaters," on the other hand, spent much of their time trying to find something to do by exploring their environment. They spoke of "hanging around," "messing around," or "roaming." When asked for a more definite description of their behavior, they were at a loss to give a more precise account except in terms of looking or waiting for something to do or happen.

Very likely some of the most promising talent in the slums is channeled in socially deviant directions. If the planners of rehabilitation programs hope to be effective, they will have to find ways of building on this competence and redirecting it, not quelling it.

There should be no summary to this chapter, which, as we end with the social concerns that stimulated the Committee's initial interest in the socialization of competence, closes in a neater pattern than the state of research-based knowledge really justifies. We have encountered many issues that call for better theory and further investigation. Characteristically, it has been easier to write coherently and "wisely" about those subjects, near the head and tail of the chapter, for which the facts are thinnest—and most malleable. The somewhat more rigorously worked areas of early development and achievement motivation are also the hardest to bring into focus.[6]

6. After the completion of this chapter, the valuable contribution of Richard de Charms in his volume *Personal causation* (New York and London, Academic Press, 1968) came to my attention. The perspective from which he covers much of the ground examined here seems congruent with mine.

Some Social Problems

16

The Revolution in Mental Health Care—A "Bold New Approach"?

American society is now well launched into a third mental-health revolution—a revolution that promises to end the isolation of the mentally disturbed and bring them back into the community as fully accredited human beings. And yet this revolution is in great danger of faltering, of being prevented from ever realizing its magnificent potential.

The first mental-health revolution unshackled the insane. By calling them sick, it managed to treat them as human. Its monuments and symbols are the great, usually isolated, state mental hospitals. The second revolution came from the spread of dynamic psychiatry (mainly Freud's) and was characterized by individual, one-to-one psychotherapy. Now the third revolution throws off the constraints of the doctor-patient medical model—the idea that mental disorder is a *private* misery—and relates the trouble, and the cure, to the entire web of social and personal relationships in which the individual is caught.

Perhaps the depth and significance of this new revolution are not so obvious as they should be. The first two revolutions were great steps forward, but they could not come to grips with the problems that afflict most of the disturbed, and they brought in a number of unintended evils. The new revolution offers new solutions to old and unsolved problems, and seeks also to cope with urgent new problems of our seething urban society.

The first revolution goes back to the birth of institutional psychiatry in the nineteenth century. It was a progressive movement then, under medical auspices. What it offered to insane people was *asylum*—a humane alternative to almshouses and jails. This revolution respected their humanity, accepted some responsibility for their care, and offered at least some hope for cure. The state hospitals that came into being gave psychotic people at least a modicum of care. At the beginning, there was a hopeful—and surprisingly modern—emphasis on moral treatment.

This system, we now know, became by and large a bad one. It served mainly to ease the public conscience by putting crazy people out of sight and mind—in hospitals, typically built out of the country, in the district of some powerful legislator. There a large number of chronic patients were trained, in effect, to be nothing but patients for life.

The second mental-health revolution occurred in the wake of Freud's insights and discoveries. The forefront of innovation was the consulting room of the private practitioner; the method, treatment by talk. And the patients were limited almost entirely to those who could afford this expensive new treatment.

Furthermore, the medical language of illness and health, disease and cure, had to be stretched beyond comfortable limits. In the beginning the patients Freud saw were mainly hysterics—troubled people whose difficulties mimicked organic disease, and who therefore tended to turn up in the offices of physicians. But in recent years the problems that middle-class patients bring to therapy are increasingly those of the sick soul—malaise, meaninglessness, a vague sense of missing out on the satisfactions of life. The language of health and illness doesn't really fit such complaints.

This second revolution brought mostly sorrow to the big state mental hospitals. It could not give them much help. There was simply no real possibility of extending individual psychotherapy to the great mass of inmates—though some attempt was made. Hospital psychiatry had to rely on the organic therapies (like lobotomy and electric shock) and fell into even lower repute. Private practice, with its well-heeled and sophisticated patients, is what attracted the bright young psychiatrists and clinical psychologists—even if, now, they were trained largely at public expense.

Yet the doctor-patient medical model, as embodied in the first two revolutions, got attached to mental disorder more for historical reasons than for intrinsic reasons. Why should medicine, more than religion or education, provide the framework for helping disturbed people cope with their problems? "Mental illness" *is* very different from physical illness, even if some physical illnesses produce disturbed behavior. It is not just somebody's private misery. Mental illness usually grows out of—and contributes to—the breakdown of a person's normal sources of support and understanding, especially in his family. It is part of a vicious circle. Not only has he himself faltered, but the social systems on which he depends have failed to sustain him—family, school, job, church, friendship, and the like. The task is not to cure an ailment inside his skin, but to strengthen him to the point where he can once again participate in the interactions that make up the warp and woof of life. It is also one of helping those subsystems function in ways that promote the well-being and effectiveness of all people who take part in them. Of course, genetic and other organic factors may contribute to a troubled person's difficulties. But primarily, as the new community approach sees it, his troubles amount to malfunctions of ordinary social participation.

Creating A Therapeutic Community

In the great mental hospitals, the hours of therapy—whether individual or group—are few and far apart, if the patient is lucky enough to get *any*. It is therefore obvious, according to the new approach, that the day-in and day-out routine of ward life has more effect on a patient's progress—or lack of it—than all formal therapy. Moreover, the discovery of tranquilizing drugs has ushered in a whole new revolution of its own, making possible an entirely new role for the hospital as well as new concepts of therapy. Thus was born the idea of remaking the mental hospital into a *therapeutic community*, rather than a mere treatment center.

Next, the enormous gap between the state mental hospital and the patient's home and community had to be bridged. As this idea gained general acceptance (aided considerably by the report of the Joint Commission on Mental Illness and Health, 1961), the third mental-health revolution was under way.

The first big step in the third mental-health revolution has been to bring the treatment of the seriously disturbed back from the remote state hospital into the community. That means, among other things, taking patients away from the dehumanizing damage done by the old state hospitals with their isolation, their locked doors and back wards. We must keep patients in their home communities even if they go to hospitals there—this first of all.

It follows that we must:

—Leave the hospital doors unlocked—if people are *expected* to act crazy, most of them will.

—Make it easy to enter the hospital voluntarily, and depart voluntarily; make it easy for the individual to return and feel free to return in times of stress and extra need. The "open door" and the "revolving door" help to lower the barriers that stand between mental hospital and community life.

—Integrate in-patient and out-patient services so that there is continuity of care within the mental-health system. Provide intermediate way-stations between complete hospitalization and out-patient status—night hospitals for those able to work during the day, day hospitals for those who can more profitably spend nights and weekends at home.

—Cut down the waiting, so help is provided when it is needed. To those in crisis, make emergency help immediately and conspicuously available.

All this constitutes the essential, giant first step. But it is still not enough, and I predict that this new revolution will peter out in disillusionment unless we quickly go beyond it.

This first stage is inadequate for several reasons:

—Present models of "treatment" generally do not reach or help those with the most serious problems.

—If we use only the mental-health professionals we use now, the expanded programs will be impossible to staff.

—The importance of the community for bad or for good—for sustaining vicious circles of human misery and ineffectiveness, or for helping people achieve satisfying lives—is not yet grasped in the hospital-clinic-centered program.

Let me elaborate on these points:

Present methods don't reach those who need help most. The second, Freudian, mental-health revolution set the standard for the most prestigious technique of treatment: intensive individual therapy, the more like psychoanalysis, and the longer, the better. This is what most psychiatrists and clinical psychologists are trained to do, and get most satisfaction from. They are themselves middle-class; and they work best with relatively sophisticated patients, who can appreciate both them and what they are doing.

But it is the poor, the dispossessed, the uneducated—the "poor treatment risks"—who have the really serious mental-health problems. And these people—less verbal, less subjective—tend not to understand dynamic psychotherapy, or want it, or benefit from it. They don't see their troubles in psychological terms, and don't believe that talk can be a treatment. The modern professional, with his fixation on psychotherapy, is a little like the drunk who kept looking for his keys under the streetlight, not because he had lost them there but because it was easier to look there.

Radical departures are needed. And there are promising new models. Some draw on the behavior therapies. They try, unabashedly, to use learning principles to remove troublesome symptoms directly rather than concentrating on remote, "underlying causes." A variety of promising therapies emphasize action—such as role-playing—rather than talk, and explore the real problems of people in their real lives, rather than in their subjective fantasies.

Expanded programs cannot conceivably be staffed on present patterns. The federal program for community mental-health centers began with a appropriation for bricks and mortar. This was a big mistake. Buildings are *not* the strategic ingredient of a community mental-health center. The key ingredient is *services*—and services mean professional people. There are not enough of them to go around, and there won't be in the foreseeable future. The lack of mental-health manpower is on the verge of becoming a national disaster.

Clearly, to cling to the model of one-to-one individual psychotherapy, even if there were no doubt about its effectiveness, is downright irresponsible. We need to employ scarce professional resources in ways that *multiply* their effectiveness. Community mental-health programs need to make more use of very carefully selected and briefly trained nonprofessionals. In working with unsophisticated, poor people, carefully selected "indigenous" nonprofessionals may achieve better communication than the scarce middle-class professional ever can (Hallowitz and Riessman, 1967). It would be better to employ his scarce talents in selection, training, and supervision of nonprofessionals.

The potential of the community for bad or good isn't recognized in the hospital-clinic-centered program. We are not dealing with isolated disease processes, but with vicious circles of human misery and ineffectiveness, with patterns of self-defeating behavior that are hard to break because they are embedded in the very texture of people's lives. We need to invest more in working on the social contexts in which troubled people are involved, and to count less upon the effectiveness of the isolated therapeutic hour.

PROJECT RE-ED

In this connection, I think of my colleague Nick Hobbs' very important Project Re-Ed, centered at Peabody College in Tennessee (see Hobbs, 1966). This was a boldly innovative demonstration project that is now ready for export. Project Re-Ed is a residential-school program. It seeks not to "cure" the "sick" child but to give him sufficient strength and resources so that—when he is reintroduced into family and school—constructive, benign circles of causation replace the earlier, vicious ones. When you think about it, investment in working with the child's normal environment is just as essential as investment in re-education itself. The child is not released as "cured," but reintroduced into his everyday life in such a way that he is more likely to gain progressively in competence and satisfaction.

The teacher-counselors—the frontline staff of these residential schools—are recruited from the large pool of would-be teachers, rather than from the highly restricted one of identified mental-health professionals. The job attracts the same sort of dedicated people as those who join the Peace Corps.

The Re-Ed program recognizes that learning takes place 24 hours a day. For continuity, night-teacher-counselors plan programs and activities together with day-teacher-counselors. The teacher-counselors are backed up by expert psychiatric and psychological help; they accept and support the children without setting themselves up as junior psychotherapists. Hobbs has found that the *liaison teacher* is the crucial link between the residential school and the child's real school in the community he will return to.

The Re-Ed programs have had gratifying success. They have now been accepted as regular parts of the North Carolina and Tennessee state systems of Mental Hygiene. Tennessee is using the model as its basic approach in treating emotionally-disturbed children.

PROGRAMMING FOR HUMAN EFFECTIVENESS

Still, the Re-Ed program is only one model. The general picture is a good deal less gratifying. Why have we not made better use of what we know? Obviously, we have not been bold or radical enough; we have not asked the hard questions.

For instance, why don't we have better coordination between the agencies that are supposted to serve people—especially those people who need it most? Why do we so arbitrarily parcel out human problems among diverse agencies, departments, and professions? The new mental-health revolution is not an isolated phenomenon—it is part of the whole urban revolution, a revolution that poses the question of how we can make urban life more tolerable, satisfying, and effective. And most of us are now urbanites. At present the schools, the great proliferation of public and private welfare agencies, the mental-health system, and the legal-correctional system all nibble at the edges of these problems. We must integrate efforts.

Consider, for example, what happens to an alcoholic. Who handles his case? Whether it is the police, courts and jails, mental-health institutions, or some special welfare agency depends pretty much on circumstances—most of them accidental.

Or what of the unruly, disturbed, truant child who commits an act of vandalism? Will he be handled by the schools and their psychological services or by the police and the courts? (Whether he is rich or poor, black or white, will help decide.)

The absurdity and injustice of all this are obvious. As a result, there is ferment in every field that must deal with the hard-core problems of malfunctioning in a modern, urban society. The basic wrong-headedness of present public-welfare policies is just short of a national scandal, and the search for alternatives has brought on a national debate. The field of justice and corrections is going through its own revolution, modeled largely on the new mental-health revolution—the emphasis has shifted from a punitive-custodial orientation in the prisons to therapy and a greater use of community treatment, especially for juveniles. In the Negro ghettos, at long last—even if we still move with tragic slowness—we have begun to do something about the appalling problems instead of trying to sweep them under a rug. In sum, there are signs of an impending rational attack on urban problems. But the needed coordination is still a hope, not a reality.

In mental-health programming itself, a key impediment to effectiveness has been its separation from such services as schools, courts, and welfare. Agencies often work at cross-purposes, or in ignorance of one another's programs. This is partly because we are still defining mental disturbance as an illness, establishing hospitals and clinics as the appropriate places of treatment, and insisting on semi-medical qualifications for its treatment specialists.

Current recommendations that a person in trouble be admitted to the total mental-health system, and not just to one component of it, fall short of coming to grips with the problem—though the aim is laudable. In treating distressed people, we must not artificially isolate a "mental-health sector." Mental-health professionals should take the lead in ensuring that mental-health activities are no longer isolated from the schools, from urban planning, from the poverty program, and from police recruitment and training.

Let there be no misunderstanding: I do not claim all human welfare is covered by "mental health." But professionals can no longer find smug comfort in some supposedly well-defined area of "mental-health problems." There is no such well-defined area. "Mental health"—a better description is "human effectiveness versus ineffectiveness"—is one aspect of concrete problems that are also likely to be educational, medical, moral, and maybe religious. No single family of professions or institutions can grasp and manage all the mental-health concerns to which we are committed—from serious neurological disorders through the whole fabric of human experience. Mental health is everyone's business. None of us has sufficient competence to deal with all of it. No mental-health center can be comprehensive enough.

Mental-health professionals must therefore ask how their scarce skills can be used best in conjunction with the skills of others. The staff of a community mental-health center must set up joint programs with the other systems—school, industry, welfare, and the rest. As staff members do this, they will need to develop new skills—ways of helping based on action rather than talk, as well as indirect forms of help and consultation.

Consultation is essential. People interact with their social environment; to change aspects of that environment can make great differences in the mental health of whole groups. The people and institutions that in large part influence or determine that environment—government agencies, churches, schools, business, industry—are amateurs when it comes to the psychological effects of their policies and decisions, and they are preoccupied with other matters. This does not mean that the mental-health professionals know best how the community should operate—such a claim is presumptuous and foolish. Rather, they contribute a special perspective that can help the agencies and institutions perform their functions better. Through consultation, at all levels, mental-health people can improve the quality of community and family life for all citizens.

New Approaches to Therapy

What existing programs embody the new approaches? I have already mentioned Nick Hobbs and his Project Re-Ed. I must also hasten to add, in all fairness, that though I have been arguing for a community mental-health progam that breaks free of the old medical model, some of the most imaginative programs—and those least medical in the traditional sense—have been launched by physicians.

I have been much impressed by the program led by two psychiatrists, Sheppard Kellam and Sheldon Schiff (Kellam and Schiff, 1967; Schiff and Kellam, 1967). They have been working primarily with children in the Chicago Negro community of Woodlawn. In developing this community mental-health program, they had the great advantage of building upon an already active community organization with identified leadership, whom they could work with closely. Consultations, therefore, could go into motion quickly—without the usual faltering.

Woodlawn wanted the program to focus on the problems of first-grade children in their encounter with school. School represents the initial occasion when all children are touched by organized society. The approach taken by Kellam, Schiff, and their associates made the teachers themselves collaborators and principals in the enterprise, drawing heavily on their skills and experience. The program included screening for existing psychological problems, and consultation with teachers and classroom groups of children. The psychiatrists also keep a running assessment of the impact of their program. The scarce skills of the mental-health professionals were used strategically—they even trained the teachers, in effect, to be valuable assistant diagnosticians and treatment specialists.

A couple of other examples might be introduced. Frank Riessman's application of the technique of *role-playing* is especially helpful with the nonverbal poor (Riessman and Goldfarb, 1964). In role-playing, the participants act out parts in selected, simulated situations. Working with slum-dwellers in the Mobilization for Youth program, Riessman found this approach more congenial to them than just talking. The poor prefer doing to talking, presenting their real problems rather than their fantasies. He found that this approach also reduced the gap between practitioner and client—a real barrier when middle-class professionals try to work with the poor, especially in the usual bureaucratic settings. It also tends to develop the articulateness of people who usually lack verbal skill and self-confidence.

Another example of imaginative innovation: In Cambridge, Mass., Charles Slack and R. R. Schwitzgebel, working with delinquents, in effect tried using tape recorders as therapists (see Schwitzgebel, 1964). They hired the youths to talk at length into the recorders about their lives and problems, carefully using rewards and bonuses to bring them into increasingly responsible relationships, and to give them, and the professionals, insight. Although Slack and Schwitzgebel describe this approach in terms of B. F. Skinner's reinforcement theories, I think that its scrupulous honesty and complete reciprocity were the most important reasons for its success. Help and knowledge were sought from the young people as well as given (at first, in fact, *more* sought than given).

All these new approaches have broken the mold of the doctor-patient relationship, and achieved some success; we can expect many more.

But success is not inevitable. In fact, in a fundamental sense the work has hardly begun, and many snares lie ahead. It was President John F. Kennedy who sponsored this revolution, and the "bold new approaches" he called for are still, for the most part, gleams in the eyes of pioneers, or pilot ventures not yet part of standard practice. Moreover, we are finding to our dismay that we must fight a two-front war: While we try to push ahead, we must also fight vigorously merely to preserve yesterday's gains from short-sighted budget-mindedness. The situation in California[1] provides a good example. In

1. In 1967-68, the state mental health budget was under attack from Republican Governor Ronald Reagan.

self-defense, mental health has now entered politics, and if we are serious about "bold new approaches," we will have to stay in politics, and fight.

The greatest danger perhaps is that the third mental-health revolution will be (in Harold Lasswell's phrase) "resisted by incorporation"—that is, confined to existing models while lip-service is given to "new" ideas. Already the plans for "comprehensive community mental-health centers," stimulated and supported by federal legislation, are following discouragingly tame and conventional paths. Most are hospital-centered—on the old medical model, under medical control. Do they help orchestrate and coordinate existing services? Generally, no. Usually they appear as just one more package among all the other proliferating, ill-coordinated packages.

What seems to be happening is that the revolution is being frozen in its first phase. This early ossification around the mental-health center idea reflects the thinking of leaders in the National Institute of Mental Health—and it is deplorable. Effective "community mental health" cannot be fitted inside existing professional biases, habits, and territorial rights.

We must have explicit and built-in evaluations of new programs, with continuous feedback of adequate information about results. These we must use, with great flexibility and innovation, to meet *community*—not professional—needs.

We must set forth in new directions. We must be radical. It will be a national shame and scandal if the "third national mental-health revolution" finally peters out into little more than the substitution of shiny, sterile, glass-and-aluminum institutions in the city for the old dismal red brick ones out in the sticks.

17

Some Features of Foreign-Student Adjustment

In the fall of 1953, nearly thirty-four thousand students from abroad—about ten thousand of them at the graduate level—were enrolled in American colleges and universities. Nearly fifteen hundred institutions of higher education reported that they had foreign students enrolled (Institute of International Education, 1954). These impressive figures represent a postwar phenomenon, an influx across our borders that shows no signs of abating. It is the counterpart in the world of education of America's powerful political, economic, and technological position.

As in the economic and political realms, so in the educational: power brings responsibilities. Not so long ago, foreign students appeared to most college administrators as a marginal luxury. They brought to the campus a touch of exotic color; they enriched the educational milieu of American students; they often, to be sure, presented bizarre and troublesome problems. But there was no "foreign student problem" then, and little concern with what American education meant or could mean to these scattered visitors from abroad. It was the day of the Y secretary and the Cosmopolitan Club; the era of the foreign-student adviser had yet to come.

Since the war we have become much more self-conscious about our relations with foreign students. The participation of government in the support of student exchange has made explicit the statement of objectives of national policy. No longer are we content to maintain the campus as a free market place of skills and ideas, under the rule of *caveat emptor*. We not only ask whether the foreign student is getting the education and training that he came for, but inquire whether his training will contribute to his country's social and economic development. Will his experience unfit him for a constructive role in his less-advantaged homeland? And perhaps most insistently, will his voice be heard as a friend of America in the forum of world ideological conflict? Sometimes, indeed, the question reduces to a plaintive, will he love us?

It is by no means clear that this heightened concern with objectives beyond

Reprinted by permission from *Journal of Higher Education,* 1955, *26,* 231–241.

the traditional goals of education has been all to the good. Issues are involved that have their counterpart in the broader debate between educational *laissez faire* and paternalism. There can be little doubt, however, that the old assumption that educational exchange under all conditions is inherently a good thing needed to be re-examined. We are no longer taking it for granted that cross-cultural contact automatically breeds understanding and good will, nor do we assume without question that the best American technical training is necessarily the most useful for a student from an underdeveloped country. Under a variety of auspices, research has recently been launched to throw light on what in fact happens to foreign students here and on their return, and what circumstances lead to different outcomes of this experience. In this paper I shall draw mainly on preliminary findings from a research program with which I am familiar, sponsored by the Committee on Cross-Cultural Education of the Social Science Research Council.[1]

To begin with, a too convenient stereotype must be dispelled: it is even more misleading to speak of "the foreign student" than it is of "the American student." "Foreign-student problems" are to a large extent simply student problems. The pressure of work, the testing of personal goals, the need to know how one stands with one's teachers, the search for social roots in the lonely crowd of a major university—these problems and many others bear no tag of nationality. We need hardly be reminded of the wide variation of individual student ways of coping with them, and there is doubtless as much variation among foreign students as among Americans. However, there are ways in which nationalities seem to differ from one another. While it does less violence to the facts to speak of "the Indian student" or "the Scandinavian student" than it does to talk about "the foreign student," it is important to bear in mind the range of variation that such abstractions deliberately ignore.

The Foreign Student's Tasks

All the same, there are some problems inherent in being a foreign student, and we may well take these problems for a starting point. Simply to list them directs our attention to major factors that affect a foreign student's adjustment and the outcome of his American educational experience. What can we say of the tasks that he faces when he is temporarily transplanted to an American campus? In very general terms, these may be grouped under

1. The program of the Committee was supported by grants to the Council from the Carnegie Corporation of New York, the Ford Foundation, and the Rockefeller Foundation. (See Smith, 1954b). The Committee consisted of the following persons: Ralph L. Beals, University of California at Los Angeles, chairman; Cora DuBois, Harvard University; Herbert H. Hyman, Columbia University; Ronald Lippitt, University of Michigan; Charles P. Loomis, Michigan State College. I should also like to express my indebtedness to my colleagues on the Committee's staff, Joseph B. Casagrande and Bryce Wood of the Social Science Research Council.

such topics as communicating, learning the cultural maze, gaining acceptance, balancing loyalties, maintaining personal integrity and self-esteem, and achieving academic goals.

It is hardly an exaggeration to say that during the foreign student's sojourn, everything hinges on his ability to communicate adequately—with his teachers, his books, his fellow students, and his associates in daily life. Most of what he learns must be filtered through a communication process. Good communication provides the setting in which other problems of adjustment are most easily solved, while blocked or distorted communication can give rise to a vicious spiral of other personal difficulties. The problem of communication is not peculiar to foreign students, but they have difficulties in this area beyond those of most other student groups.

Little need be said about the language problem as such; it has properly received central attention from teachers and administrators. Procedures are now available for screening applicants by their working command of English, though such tests could profitably be used more widely than at present. Methods have also been developed for the rapid teaching of English as a foreign language, so that, when time and resources permit, initial command of English need not be an overriding criterion of selection. While I do not question the importance of language competence, I would rather draw attention to some subtler barriers to communication.

Among these, contrasting or conflicting values are probably the most important and the least tractable. Anthropologists and other experienced observers tell us that each culture is organized around widely shared assumptions, fundamental preferences, and standards of judgment. Behind the bustle and efficiency of American life, for example, lies the belief that time is money, an orientation by no means shared in many other quarters of the world. Psychologists, on their part, have contributed the principle that a person's values serve as a filter or lens, through which he selects and organizes a coherent view of his situation, out of the much richer range of possibilities with which life confronts him. Foreign students and Americans, approaching facts from different value perspectives, may define them differently, and talk—or act—at cross-purposes.

An American may extend a casual invitation to a Japanese student in the spirit of open friendliness. But the Japanese, bringing with him a way of life involving the etiquette of a hierarchical society organized around delicately balanced obligations, may see at first not the opportunity for informal friendship, but rather the danger of incurring social debts that he may not be in a position to repay. An American points with pride to the labor-saving conveniences of American homes as part of a complex that includes the active participation of women in community activities and the virtual absence of a servant class. The same gadgets may be perceived in a different context as evidence of American materialism, especially by students from many less advantaged parts of the world that nevertheless enjoy a rich cultural heritage. Different values lead to different perceptions, in this case partly because of a defensive readiness to find Americans blind to the higher things in life.

A person's basic values are slow to change. Insight across cultural boundaries into one another's values—the foundation for mutual understanding if not admiration—is achieved only with difficulty and over time. The wider the gap between cultures, the harder is this task.

When an American student comes to college, he is likely to "know his way around". In myriad ways that he could never formulate, he knows what is expected of him in the situations that he is likely to face, and how to comport himself to get what he wants; he is an unwitting expert on American culture. All this the foreign student may have to learn, particularly if he has not been reared to some other variant of western civilization. Until he learns the cultural equivalent of Basic English, he is handicapped indeed.

For students whose previous education has followed European models—and this includes a large proportion of students from abroad—the folkways of the American campus present a common hurdle. Not the least mysterious is that formidable document, the college catalogue. In contrast with the European standard, required courses, compulsory attendance, frequent examinations, and a fragmented curriculum are likely to appear novel and unwelcome. The informality of classroom relations between student and professor, on the other hand, is a novelty that may initially disturb and perplex, but in time is almost universally appreciated. While the graduate school, with its assumption of greater maturity, is less likely to clash with the student's expectations than the undergraduate, there are even at this level special difficulties to be encountered in the transition from European-style to American universities. In regard to the balance of emphasis on permissive self-direction or prescribed discipline, American practice exactly reverses the European sequence of lycée or Gymnasium and university. High school for us is not a very serious business, and with college the student encounters tightening requirements and fairly close adult supervision. In contrast, traditional secondary education in Europe bears down hard on the student, leaving him little leeway. For those who go on to a university—it is important to note that these constitute a much more highly selected, élite group than their American counterparts—a new vista of freedom opens out, in which, still enjoying the privileges of youth, they are treated as adults. Even the relative freedom of the American graduate school, impressive enough to the product of our undergraduate curriculums, is likely to seem restrictive in comparison with the European university.

In the long run, an individual's personal well-being and effective functioning depend to a large extent on his feeling accepted by persons who are significant to him. Foreign students especially need this sense of social support because the stresses of adjustment to a radically new setting leave them with a feeling of inner depletion. Home is far away, and social ties tenuously sustained at a distance still leave a need for warm companionship.

Precisely in this regard peculiarities of American culture are likely to tantalize the foreign visitor only to disappoint him. In comparison with what is customary the world over, Americans seem to be notably friendly, easily accessible to relative strangers on an informal basis. Indications of *friendliness* in this characteristically American version are often mistaken by the visitor as tokens of *friendship,* and interpreted as implying a degree of personal commitment that is far from intended. Friendship in this deeper and necessarily more restricted sense may be no less frequent in the United States than it is elsewhere, although some cultures certainly give it more explicit recognition and formal standing. It is the "come-on" of American openness and good will that is potentially misleading, giving rise to false expectations and subsequent disillusionment. Here is one of the reasons that Americans are often dismissed as superficial.

The foreign student who has passed the first flush of pleasure at his initial acceptance may seek his social support in cliques of fellow internationals with perhaps a sprinkling of the self-selected fringe of American students that gravitate toward such groups. International Houses serve a valuable function in providing a haven to which the foreign student can turn when he feels barred from other meaningful relationships. The student who permanently secludes himself in a foreign clique, however, effectively shields himself from some of the more important incidental values of an American education.

Balancing memberships and loyalties is the fourth task imposed on the foreign student by the fact he has two homes—the country to which he is committed to return, and the American setting in which he finds himself. Unlike the emigrant, who is breaking old ties as he forms new ones, and also unlike the casual tourist, who does not seriously involve himself in the life of the country that he visits, the foreign student must at the same time maintain significant orientation to two cultures. He lives at once in two situations—the world of "back home" which he inescapably carries with him, and that of "here and now."[2] How he balances these simultaneous memberships is a matter of considerable moment, especially when they impose upon him conflicting prescriptions about how he ought to act.

Suppose he avoids inner conflict by emphasizing the back-home orientation at the expense of the here and now. He finds a congenial clique of fellow nationals, carefully preserves home-country ways and, in effect, insulates himself as much as possible from being significantly touched by his American experience. Clearly the advantages of foreign study are largely thrown away in such a case.

The opposite reaction is equally sterile. The person who in Rome does with facility what the Romans do, keeping in mental isolation those aspects of his home ways that conflict with his new practices, is likely to be the very person who on return reverts to the old, quite untouched by his intervening experience. In their study of German leader teams here and after

2. I am indebted to Ronald Lippitt for this formulation.

return to Germany, Jeanne Watson and Ronald Lippitt (1955) found that members who were most uncritically accepting of things American during their sojourn were likely to shed their new ways of thinking, once on home soil. Which Germans were touched most deeply by their American experience? According to Watson and Lippitt, those who had managed to keep both home and American considerations in some sort of precarious balance throughout their sojourn, without losing sight of either. These members were by no means the most popular with their American group leaders. They were the ones who would ask embarrassing questions; who would object that this or that vaunted American practice might work here but would never do in Germany; who had to be shown. What they learned was more likely to find application, because they learned it with the home situation in mind.

Still another possibility, exemplified in the German study and in experience with foreign students, is the seduction of the visitor from his home culture. When the student is alienated from the ways of his homeland, personal tragedy and social waste are likely. He becomes an emigrant in spirit if not in fact. If he manages actually to emigrate, or to have his cake and eat it too through a career in foreign service or international trade, he may work out a satisfactory personal adjustment, but from the standpoint of most programs of international exchange, such instances can hardly be scored as successes.

The fundamental task of adjustment, to which all others are subsidiary, is the maintenance of personal integrity and self-esteem. Psychiatry has made us familiar with the devious ways in which persons who feel threatened in this regard go about protecting themselves—the standard defense mechanisms of withdrawal, rationalization, displaced hostility, and the like.

In the nature of the case, foreign students are likely to face major problems in this area. Largely cut off from the support of home ties, faced with difficult adjustive tasks, they are all too likely to feel beleagered and diminished. Defensive reactions may then come to the fore that complicate rather than simplify their problems of coming to terms with life in America. Defensiveness easily becomes a self-perpetuating vicious circle.

Students from certain countries, however, seem especially vulnerable. These are the representatives of underdeveloped countries embued with the spirit of emergent nationalism. Strongly identified with their country's fate and good name—the more so because of the role of "unofficial ambassador" into which they are frequently thrust willy-nilly—they are bound to be antagonized by the low regard in which they find their country held in America. Richard Lambert and Marvin Bressler (1954) have described this pattern in detail for students from India, and common observation indicates that it is by no means peculiar to visitors from this subcontinent. Equally affronted by American ignorance of their homeland and by what passes for informed discussion of it in the public media, these students are likely to develop a view of America that is more a reflex of their defensive needs than a reflection of personal experience. These are the students who cite American race relations as a counter to criticisms of caste, American materialism to balance home-country poverty, and so on through a long list of standard reactions to the probing of standard "sensitive areas." In any case, the image of America developed by such students is apt to be emotionally charged, deeply involved as it is with their own sense of personal and national worth. As such, it is likely to be both one-sided and unstable—all black or all white depending on whether their defensive nationalism is momentarily aroused, or, on the other hand, they see a chance of throwing their lot with the superior host country.

Scandinavian students, as studied by Franklin Scott (1954) and by Sewell, Morris, and Davidsen (1954), exemplify the other extreme. Coming to America with few doubts about their national worth, they characteristically take a much more realistic, matter-of-fact view of their American experience. For them it is not a question of either-or. Rather than reacting globally to America, they are likely to pick and choose what is interesting, relevant, or applicable back home from the experience available to them. Far from uncritical, their attitudes are too highly differentiated to be neatly characterized as pro or con. We came to refer to their Smörgasbord approach—an orientation that facilitates effective learning.

The task with which the college teacher and administrator is most directly concerned is that of specific learning within the formal curriculum. I have no intention of minimizing its prime importance; I treat it last because my main point here will be that what a foreign student learns, and how he later puts it to use, depends on the manner and adequacy with which he meets each of the tasks that we have previously considered.

Let us look at the list again from this point of view. Communication is fundamental. Until the foreign student is able to communicate, he cannot be reached. Imperfect communication means learning that is wrongly focused, off-key. The cultural maze that the student has to learn extends even into the classroom. Until he has "learned the ropes," he can hardly pursue academic goals efficiently, and is likely to be distracted by frustrations encountered in the pursuit of nonacademic ones. The task of gaining acceptane has probably a more complex relationship to the student's academic accomplishment. We all know of students, not necessarily foreign, who throw themselves effectively into their studies simply to compensate for a lack of social acceptance. Yet we like to believe that work engaged in for its own sake or as a direct step toward valued goals is more satisfactory than work motivated by threat and defense. The balance that a student strikes between his memberships and loyalties to back home *versus* the here-and-now, on the other hand, is directly related both to his learning while here, and, more important, to what he does with this learning upon return. Too exclusive an orientation toward back-home, we have seen, leaves him unreceptive to new facts and perspectives. A stance that involves both orientations in interplay seems most conducive to creative application of his sojourn gains. Finally, in regard to the problem of self-esteem, our research has focused on effects in the realm of attitudes. We are far from sure that parallel effects could be shown on academic learning, but we believe that an attitude of objective realism, founded on inner security, is most suitable for the academic task. Measures that strengthen the student's sense of inner worth and relieve him from the burden of defensive maneuvers, we believe, also further the narrower goals of education.

Stages in Adjustment

Such, then are the tasks of adjustment that foreign students face. How they cope with these tasks is subject to the widest individual and national variation; this cannot be overemphasized. Certain very general stages in the process of adjustment seem nevertheless to be distinguishable, each involving its characteristic orientations and problems. It need hardly be added that the rate at which students progress through these stages is a highly individual matter, depending on a variety of personal and situational factors, and that the boundaries between one stage and another are not clear-cut.

On first arrival, the visitor is likely to find himself in the role of *spectator*. Things are new, exciting, perhaps somewhat overwhelming, but both the pleasures and frustrations of the new experience lack reality, since he has yet to commit himself to the pursuit of real goals in his new environment. While the tourist or visitor on a brief junket may never pass beyond this phase, most foreign students, by virtue of their purposes, leave it rather shortly. Those who do not, persist in the spectator role as a protective maneuver, fearing that were they to become involved, they would be too vulnerable to being hurt. We suspect that little learning of importance occurs in the spectator phase. Things may be interesting, but they are hardly significant.

Some time during the first weeks or months of their sojourn, most foreign students begin to struggle seriously with the tasks of cross-cultural adjustment that have previously been outlined. Having taken the plunge, they become more vulnerable to the inevitable frustrations that are entailed by the trial-and-error process of acquiring new ways of thinking and acting not previously available in their repertories. It is during this *adjustive phase* that fundamental learning, involving reorientation of attitudes, is likely to occur if it occurs at all.

If the student's sojourn is long enough, he eventually works out some sort of a stable *modus vivendi* in American culture. He settles on the tentative patterns of adjustment that worked most satisfactorily for him in his previous period of trial and error. These may take any of a variety of forms, Americanization or encystment, manipulativeness or compliance, approval or disapproval. While some of these patterns may be more favorable than others to professional and academic learning, it seems plausible that the student who continues his sojourn to the point of coming to terms with America is freer to devote his attention to specifically educational goals. Fundamental attitudes are learned in the adjustive phase; specific skills and knowledge may be acquired most efficiently in the third of our stages.

As the time of return looms near, a final phase may be distinguished in which *preoccupation with problems of readjustment* is likely to come to the fore. Even if he has thus far kept considerations of back home in a relatively isolated compartment, the student is likely at this point to wonder what it will be like when he gets back, and what he will be able to do with his new training and experience. The longer the sojourn, and the more fundamental the changes it has wrought in his ways of thinking and acting, the more uneasy he may be in anticipating his problems of readjustment. The student's natural concerns during this phase provide a strategic opportunity for counseling and group discussion to help him transfer his learning constructively.[3]

While the timing of these phases varies with the individual and the situations that he encounters, gross differences between national groups may nevertheless be expected. The wider the cultural gap to be bridged—the more difficult the task of cross-cultural adjustment—the longer the student may have to flounder in the adjustive phase before he manages to come to terms with the requirements of life and study in America. Scandinavian students, for whom the task is relatively easy, appear to come to terms in a matter of months. For Japanese, the evidence suggests that considerably more time may be needed (Passin and Bennett, 1954). A fixed one-year term of study may send the student home just as he is beginning to work through his initial severe problems of adjustment. Even though the administrator must properly fend off the efforts of some foreign students to prolong their stay indefinitely, it can reasonably be argued that where sharp cultural contrasts are involved, the sojourn should either be long enough to allow for coming to terms, or so brief that the student remains a spectator.

Another approach to the course of the foreign student's adjustment is to consider the trend of his morale or satisfaction through time. Converging evidence from several quarters suggests that the typical finding may be represented as a U-shaped curve, running from relatively favorable morale at the outset through a trough associated with the frustrations of the adjustive phase, to a subsequently higher level in the favorable cases in which the student has had opportunity to come to terms. This formulation necessarily leaves unspecified the amount of time involved and the absolute level of morale or satisfaction at various points in the curve. Awareness of the general trend may nevertheless furnish a relevant perspective for the appraisal of foreign-student problems.

One widely cited questionnaire study of Indian students, for example, gave evidence of appalling shifts of attitude in a direction critical of the United States (Kiell, 1951). But the plan and analysis of this study did not allow for the effects of varying lengths of sojourn; it is entirely possible that quite

3. This formulation was arrived at in a conference of participants in the first phase of the Council's research program. See Smith and Casagrande (1953).

different conclusions would have been reached if students longer in residence had been examined separately. The problems and the criticisms that are characteristic of the trough give little indication of the sojourn's outcome as the student may later come to appraise it.

Simply to recognize the trough as a trough, not a failure, can be reassuring, and it can also support the teacher and administrator in bearing with the foreign student at times when he seems excessively difficult. It is just at the trough of the adjustive phase, when the student's frustrations are at a maximum and his self-esteem is at low ebb, that he is most likely to indulge in his own brand of self-defensive maneuvers, to the exasperation of those responsible for providing him with educational facilities.

There may well be some characteristic national differences in the way foreign students react in this trying period. Japanese seem especially prone to withdraw to themselves, cutting themselves off from potentially corrective processes of communication and swallowing their resentment. The Indian students whom Lambert and Bressler studied, on the other hand, were more likely to direct their hostilities outward, wearing a noticeable chip on the shoulder. Knowing that both these reactions are likely to be temporary, and that each is a reflection of a potentially constructive struggle for adjustment, the wise administrator is less likely to reject the latter group as troublemakers or to give reluctant thanks for the former as presenting few major administrative problems.

The Role of the Foreign-Student Adviser

The foreign-student adviser is clearly here to stay. The current directory of foreign-student advisers issued by their national association lists twelve hundred names, each at a different institution of higher education. This is an impressive figure when compared with the fifteen hundred institutions that report the presence of foreign students. Of course, not all of these persons bear the adviser title, or have any of their time officially released for advisory purposes. Some of them are foreign-language teachers, some are registrars, and some are even deans. Nevertheless, each is officially designated as the person at his institution who is supposed to cope with the problems of foreign students. Evidently, the need for specialized concern with foreign students is widely recognized.

A large part of the foreign-student adviser's job is necessarily concerned with petty but highly important routine. On the one hand, foreign students have to be led through the maze of requirements, prerequisites, and procedures that is recorded for the ages in the college catalogue. This part of his job is like that of any adviser, only more so, but he must also be master of a strange and different maze contrived by the immigration regulations and the Bureau of Internal Revenue. The importance to foreign students of accurate and adequate advice on these matters can hardly be overstressed. Maintaining a current understanding of these complex and shifting requirements, let alone interpreting them to foreign students, is a job to tax the capacities of the best of us. Only one who understands the workings of the bureaucratic mind is likely to master it.

These duties, pertaining as I say to administrative routine, form the solid core of the foreign-student adviser's job. He is also likely to be confronted, however, with all sorts of other problems that foreign students can bring him, problems of the less tangible sort to which this paper has been primarily devoted. The foreign student needs some identifiable person to turn to for understanding counsel as he struggles with the special problems of cross-cultural adjustment. What sort of person can fill this place?

Clearly he should have the tact and sensitivity of the counseling psychologist. He must be able to see behind hostility or general obnoxiousness to its defensive motivation, and thus avoid reacting in kind or feeling personally hurt. He must be a good listener. He should know through experience that in the realm of personal problems, the best advice is rarely effective. How not to advise and yet to assist the student in solving his problems, is one of his crucial skills. He cannot rightly be expected to be a universal expert on world cultures and national character, but he needs to be culturally sophisticated to the extent of realizing that there are different valid ways of doing things. Especially, he should be unusually aware of his own American culture, and alert to the distinctive ways in which it is likely to contrast with what is customary in the rest of the world. This sort of awareness is not easily acquired; the fish, as an anthropologist has pointed out, would be the last creature to discover the water. Some anthropologists go so far as to insist that adequate perspectives on one's own culture can only be gained from intensive experience of other cultures. The more sensitive the adviser is to the characteristically American, the more helpful he can be to the foreign student whose troubles spring in part from a misunderstanding of Americans. And he should be correspondingly less likely to contribute unwittingly to further misunderstanding.

But this paragon, granted that he can be found, does not sound at all like the kind of adviser we were just talking about, the guide to the maze of academic and governmental bureaucracy. I should like at least to suggest that it may be a mistake to expect to find the two sorts of skill in one person; to me they sound antithetical. When the foreign-student adviser is a specialist in administrative regulations, I suspect that the foreign student with a personal problem is likely to seek out someone else—perhaps a sympathetic teacher of his own language. If the adviser is a culturally sophisticated counseling psychologist at heart, whatever his academic credentials, I wonder where the student is to turn for authoritative advice on regulations. Perhaps he is most likely to find help in the registrar's office.

I doubt if there is any pat solution to the issue raised by this analysis.

Different administrative arrangements will fit different campus situations. The only suggestion that I would offer is that somehow, both of the two advisory roles be explicitly provided for. It may be misleading to think of the good all-around foreign-student adviser. He may be an imaginary creature.

18

Foreign vs. Indigenous Education

The question at issue in this essay—the advantages and disadvantages of foreign vs. indigenous higher education from the standpoint of economic and political development—carries for an American social scientist involved in the surge of research interest a decade ago in foreign students and their problems a sharp reminder of the parochialism of much of our research attention to cross-cultural education.

We were startled by the rapid rise in the numbers of foreign students on American campuses, which grew from 6,000 or 8,000 in the pre-World War II years to 15,000 in 1946–1947, 30,000 in 1950–1951, and reached 58,000 a decade later.[1] Faced with this influx, largely unplanned but with the increasing participation of a congeries of private organizations and governmental programs, we began to scrutinize more closely our optimistic assumptions that (as John Gardner [1951–1952, p. 637] put it in an influential article in *Foreign Affairs*) "all concerned will benefit if foreign peoples get to know us . . . [that] knowing us, they will like and respect us . . . that, if people can be placed face-to-face, they will find a common human basis for understanding. . . . So great is our belief," he added, "that we have tended to assume that the process will inevitably be successful, no matter how haphazardly planned and carried out. This is almost certainly untrue."

The stock-taking that ensued in research and program evaluation focused primarily on the attitudes and the problems and processes of adjustment of the foreign students during sojourn and on return. The implicit evaluative

Reprinted by permission from *Post-Primary Education and Political and Economic Development,* D. C. Piper and T. Cole, editors, by permission of the publishers, Duke University Press. This essay benefits from perspectives attained when I served as staff to the Committee on Cross-Cultural Education of the Social Science Research Council (1952–1956), which, with the support of the Carnegie Corporation of New York, the Ford Foundation, and the Rockefeller Foundation, planned and supervised a program of research on the effects of sojourn in the United States upon foreign students. It also reflects my more recent experience with post-primary education in West Africa in connection with research for the United States Peace Corps concerning its operations in Ghana.

1. The Institute of International Education publishes an annual census of foreign students in institutions of higher education in the United States under the titles *Education for One World* (1948–1954) and *Open Doors* (1955–1963).

criteria underlying these emphases arose from the context of American national interests in the Cold War arena of world opinion and from the objectives of many private sponsoring organizations concerned with educational exchange as an avenue toward international understanding. Research was therefore more concerned with the impact of the educational sojourn on the foreign student, his attitudes and prospects, than with the contribution of foreign education to national development (Scott, F. D., 1956; Sewell and Davidsen, 1961; Lambert and Bressler, 1956; Beals and Humphrey, 1957; Bennett, Passin and McKnight, 1958; Morris, R. T., 1960; Selltiz, Christ, Havel, and Cook, 1963; DuBois, 1956).

The present topic reflects a shift in perspective, centering attention not on our "foreign student problem," but on the alternatives open to developing countries as they struggle to meet their needs for higher education as a facet of elite recruitment and socialization to man the responsible and specialized positions of a modernizing state and economy. One suspects that this shift can be understood in the context of a revised conception of American national interest, in a world in which an Afro-Asian bloc, newly arrived on the international stage, plays an increasingly important role, and in which "international understanding" appears to depend not so much on good will and enlightenment as on security and prosperity in nationhood, in a setting where aspirations have become high and prospects are precarious. At all events, the priorities and terms of relevance are discernibly different today from what they were when much of the American research on foreign students was undertaken. In consequence, one must pick and choose and extrapolate from this research if it is to bear on present issues; large lacunae remain to be filled, and we can at present aspire only to a suggestive analysis of problems and prospects linked respectively with foreign and indigenous education.

The Expansion of Foreign and Indigenous Higher Education

A salient fact to be noted at the outset is the way in which the rapid expansion of both foreign and indigenous higher education has affected the developing countries in recent years. Consider first the flow of foreign students to the United States. If for purposes of crude comparison, we group the students from Europe, Oceania, Japan, and North America (apart from the United States) as coming from relatively advanced areas in contrast with other areas in varying stages of development, we find that, in 1952–1953, 58 per cent of the 33,675 foreign students on American campuses came from the less-developed regions (Institute of International Education, 1953, Table 2). By 1961–1962, the corresponding percentage was 71 (Institute of International Education, 1962, pp. 21–23), a proportion that holds for both undergraduate and graduate levels of instruction. In that year, 37 per cent of the students were from the Far East (including Japan), 17 per cent from Latin America, 14 per cent from the Near and Middle East, 12 per cent from Europe, 11 per cent from North America, and 7 per cent from Africa. The 3,930 African students represented a 39 per cent increase over the previous year (which in turn showed an increase of 44 per cent over the year before) and included some 2,500 students from south of the Sahara. Europe and the Far East sent more graduate students than undergraduates (Europe: 47 per cent graduates, 42 per cent undergraduates; Far East: 56 per cent graduates, 37 per cent undergraduates). The balance for Latin America and for the Near and Middle East fell in the reverse direction (Latin America: 24 per cent graduates, 68 per cent undergraduates; Near and Middle East: 32 per cent graduates, 62 per cent undergraduates). African students were more closely divided between graduate and undergraduate study, 40 per cent being graduates and 52 per cent undergraduates.

In absolute number of foreign students, though not in the proportion of its total student body at the collegiate level, the United States far exceeds any other nation, playing host to about one-fourth of the world total of more than 200,000 foreign students (UNESCO, 1961a, pp. 674–676). This figure represents about 2 per cent of the world student body of 11.5 million in institutions of higher education. (At the time of the first UNESCO survey in 1951–1952, approximately 85,000 foreign students were reported.) The other major countries with more than 10,000 foreign students (in 1959–1960 when the United States reported 48,500) were the Federal Republic of Germany (19,200), France (14,400), the United Kingdom (11,300), and the Soviet Union (11,000).

Factors of educational, linguistic, religious and cultural tradition, proximity, financial support, political ideology, and intangible prestige appear to govern the flow of foreign students from developing countries. Except for the former French colonial area where educational ties to the Métropole remain particularly strong, it is rare for a single host country to enjoy a virtual monopoly of foreign students from one particular developing nation. The United States is heavily favored as a goal of foreign students from Latin America, but appreciable numbers also go to European universities. Sampling UNESCO (1961a, pp. 678–683) data for 1959–1960 (which do not include the national sources of the 11,000 reported foreign students in the Soviet Union), we find that from Burma, 74 students went to the United Kingdom, 102 to India, 196 to the United States; from India, 843 to West Germany, 1,513 to the United Kingdom, 4,835 to the United States; from Ceylon, 36 to Australia, 248 to the United Kingdom, 79 to the United States; from Indonesia, 282 to Australia, 417 to the Netherlands, 54 to the United Arab Republic, and 526 to the United States; from Iran, 622 to Austria, 549 to France, 2,507 to West Germany, 276 to Switzerland, 261 to the United Kingdom, and 2,880 to the United States; from Ethiopia, 35 to France, 23 to the United Arab Republic, 11 to the United Kingdom, and 171 to the United States; from Sierra Leone, 174 to the United Kingdom and 60 to the United States; from Ghana, 353 to the United Kingdom and 160 to the United States; from Sudan, 406 to the United Arab Republic, 109 to the United Kingdom, and 109 to the United

Table 18.1. World Statistics on Enrollments in Educational Institutions[a]

	ESTIMATED TOTAL POPULATION IN 1,000'S		PERCENTAGE OF POPULATION IN SCHOOL ALL LEVELS		PERCENTAGE OF SCHOOL ENROLMENT IN SECONDARY LEVEL		PERCENTAGE OF SCHOOL ENROLMENT IN HIGHER EDUCATION		ESTIMATED ENROLMENT IN INSTITUTIONS OF HIGHER EDUCATION IN 1,000'S	
Continent and region[b]	*1953*	*1957*	*1953–54*	*1957–58*	*1953–54*	*1957–58*	*1953–54*	*1957–58*	*1953–54*	*1957–58*
Africa	214,048	232,569	5.3	7.2	10.1	8.5	0.8	0.8	91	128
Northern Africa	45,588	49,310	6.7	8.7	21.2	15.5	2.2	2.1	66	92
Middle and Southern Africa	168,460	183,259	4.9	6.8	6.0	6.1	0.3	0.3	25	36
America	348,781	379,634	16.3	18.3	17.0	18.0	4.7	5.2	2,675	3,590
North America	175,278	188,682	21.0	23.5	20.8	22.0	6.2	6.9	2,287	3,085
Middle America	54,959	61,150	12.3	13.8	6.5	7.2	1.8	1.8	121	156
South America	118,544	129,802	11.2	12.7	11.8	13.1	2.0	2.1	267	349
Asia (except U.S.S.R.)	1,405,417	1,511,608	9.6	10.3	15.6	16.8	1.3	1.6	1,724	2,460
South West Asia	63,880	68,056	6.9	8.8	11.0	13.1	1.1	1.4	51	83
South Central Asia	473,593	499,702	7.3	8.4	21.9	22.5	1.8	2.1	630	871
South East Asia	165,794	177,508	10.6	11.8	8.4	10.4	1.3	1.5	229	321
East Asia	702,150	766,342	11.2	11.3	14.7	15.9	1.0	1.4	814	1,185
Europe (except U.S.S.R.)	400,928	413,985	14.8	15.5	23.6	25.9	2.3	2.5	1,341	1,642
Oceania	13,330	14,661	17.4	19.4	20.2	21.5	2.3	2.4	54	69
U.S.S.R.	192,700	203,600	17.3	16.0	58.9	41.5	4.7	6.4	1,562	2,099
World Total	2,575,204	2,756,057	11.6	12.4	22.1	20.8	2.5	2.9	7,447	9,988

[a] From UNESCO (1961b), pp. 18–19.

[b] The world regions given in this table, where not self-explanatory, are constituted as follows:

Northern Africa: Spanish West Africa, Spanish possessions in North Africa, Morocco, Algeria, Tunisia, Libya, United Arab Republic (Region of Egypt).

Middle and Southern Africa: The remainder of Africa.

Northern America: Alaska, Canada, Greenland, St. Pierre and Miquelon, Bermuda, United States of America.

South West Asia: Turkey, Iran, Iraq, United Arab Republic (Region of Syria), Lebanon, Israel, Jordan, Cyprus, the Arabian Peninsula.

South Central Asia: Afghanistan, Pakistan, India, Nepal, Bhutan, Ceylon, Maldive Islands.

South East Asia: Burma, Thailand, Malayan Peninsula, Philippines, Indonesia and other islands south-east of the mainland.

East Asia: China, Japan, and the remainder of Asia, except the Asian parts of the U.S.S.R.

States. This list includes only the countries receiving an appreciable proportion of the foreign students of given nationality. The United States, it is evident, draws substantially from Commonwealth countries even where the United Kingdom predominates.

Now consider how the countries of the world themselves provide for higher education. Table 18.1 selects UNESCO data for 1953–1954 and 1957–1958 to place enrolments in higher education in the various major regions in the context of the scope of the entire educational endeavor in these regions. Granted the uneven quality of these data and the fact that reported enrolments need not reflect the standards that prevail in educational facilities, curricula, and instructional staff, several obvious comments are supported by the table. The world trend over the brief period spanned by the data is toward expansion of higher education, not merely in absolute numbers of students but also in terms of the proportion of all students enrolled in institutions at the post-secondary level. Among world regions, Africa is notably deficient in enrolments. Although the absolute numbers in higher education did increase, there was such rapid expansion at the primary level that the proportion of all students enrolled in universities did not show a gain.

Within Africa, it is the tropical region where higher education is most novel and its bearing on political and economic development most problematic. The UNESCO data permit a closer look at the development of higher education in tropical Africa—the region identified in Table 18.1 as Middle and Southern Africa, minus French Somaliland, the Portuguese colonies, the Republic of South Africa, and the High Commission territories. The thirty-two countries in this area grew in estimated population from 119,778,000 in mid-1950 to 154,454,000 in mid-1959, of which 4.3 per cent were enrolled in educational institutions in 1953–1954 and 6.4 per cent in 1957–1958. Of the population group from age five to nineteen, the enrolment ratio for primary schools was estimated at 24.9 per cent in 1957–1958; the corresponding ratio for secondary schools was 3.5 per cent. But this mean figure hides a range from 0.2 per cent for Niger to 7.2 per cent for Southern Rhodesia.[2]

There were facilities available for higher education in only thirteen of the thirty-two African countries. Table 18.2 shows the 1958–1959 enrolments in different fields of study for the ten countries for which these data are available. The approximately 8,000 students accounted for in this table were probably more than matched in numbers by students from tropical Africa enrolled in institutions outside the region.[3] At this recent date, just prior to the "year of independence" for many of the states, indigenous and

2. The value of 29.7 per cent tabulated for Ghana is surely in error by an order of magnitude.

3. "No satisfactory figures are available on the number of students from tropical African countries studying in France, the United States, and the Union of Soviet Socialist Republics. Excluding these important host countries it appears that in 1958/59 there were some 7,000 students from the countries under review who were studying abroad, principally in the Federal Republic of Germany, India, Lebanon, Senegal, the United Arab Republic, and the United Kingdom" (UNESCO, 1961b, p. 42).

Table 18.2. Enrollment in Higher Education in 1958–1959 by Field of Study[a]

Country	*Total Enrolment*[b]	*Humanities*	*Education*	*Fine Arts*	*Law*	*Social Science*	*Natural Science*	*Engineering*	*Medicine*	*Agriculture*
Belgian Congo	398	41	58	—	41	91	54	37	61	15
Ghana	1255	215	66[c]	75	93	323	116	226	56	85
Kenya	797	30	442[d]	43	—	65	37	78	40	62
Malagasy Republic	424	30	—	—	282	—	112	—	—	—
Federation of Nigeria	1984	529	117	91	—	272	631	146	176	22
Federation of Rhodesia and Nyasaland	125	—	28	53	—	—	37	—	—	7
Senegal	1458	317	5	—	576	21	312	14	178	35
Sierra Leone	371	108	1	—	—	105	57	10	—	—
Somaliland (It.)	245	—	—	—	—	245	—	—	—	—
Uganda	837	282	78	22	—	7	246	14	101	87
Total	7894	1552	885	284	992	1129	1602	525	612	313
Percentage by field	(100)	(20)	(11)	(4)	(12)	(14)	(20)	(7)	(8)	(4)

[a] From UNESCO (1961b, p. 42).
[b] Includes enrolments from other African countries, most of which had no facilities for higher education.
[c] Includes only students enrolled in education at the university; excludes teacher training colleges.
[d] Includes higher teacher training courses.

foreign education were in close balance numerically, with expansion in progress on both fronts.

Indigenous Education and Social Development

But the numbers that we have been examining only begin to set the terms of our problem. They suggest how deep is the commitment both to foreign study and to the growth of indigenous educational institutions throughout the world; the trends in progress derive support from so many sources that it is most unlikely that expansion on either front will be brought to a halt in the near future, whatever the rational case for doing so might be. Among the new nations where the relative costs of this expansion are such that it is dearly bought, the data attest to the high value set upon educational advance at all levels by nations and by individuals. But they tell us nothing about the actual contribution of the alternative educational channels to political and economic development. Recent discussion as exemplified elsewhere in this volume has taken a much more critical, even skeptical, view of this contribution than has hitherto prevailed among donor nations or among eager would-be recipients.

Holding this skepticism momentarily in abeyance and granting that expansion in the number of highly educated persons on whatever terms will be regarded as a necessity by the new nations, we suggest that there are certain obvious advantages that favor throwing the main emphasis toward the creation and expansion of indigenous institutions rather than toward the support of expanded foreign study that should be noted at the outset. Other things being equal (and except for some highly specialized kinds of training), it will cost less to establish and man an educational institution at home than to ship the same number of students to universities abroad and maintain them there. In principle, the curricular emphases in such an institution can be directed more closely to national and regional needs than is possible in the case of foreign institutions, which must be primarily responsive to the needs of other clienteles. Also it should be possible in principle to integrate the indigenous institution with the local society so that patterns of student recruitment and placement direct the flow of newly trained talent to the positions in the emerging social order where it is most needed, and thus avoid the cultural uprooting, social dislocation, and the always potential alienation inherent in prolonged foreign sojourn. In the new nations, moreover, the indigenous institution offers an attractive potential agency for welding and solidifying national identity and a focus of pride and prestige in the competition for national status. Given the association of reliance on foreign study with dependent colonial status and the symbolic value of the indigenous university as a badge of national autonomy and parity, the strong appeal of investing heavily in the development of indigenous higher education is evident.

But other things are obviously not equal. The ways in which institutions are embedded in their societies diverge from the rational ideal. What may be possible in principle for the indigenous institution may be difficult or highly improbable to realize in fact. Comparison of indigenous and foreign education, if it is to be useful in the present context, must start from a review of existing patterns of indigenous higher education. When we turn to the assets and liabilities of foreign study, our consideration is likely to be profitable to the extent that we aim not so much at a balance sheet of indigenous vs. foreign, but at a clarification of strategic ways in which the judiciously planned use of foreign study can supplement indigenous education, correct some of its liabilities, and hopefully serve as a source of ferment to catalyze modifications in directions that have greater promise for fostering desirable consequences in political and economic development.

The ground to be covered in this review already has been treated expertly by Mr. Eisenstadt (1964) from a theoretically sophisticated perspective, so the kind of schematic and cursory overview that is compatible with my lack of specialized competence in this area may suffice for present purposes. The field of consideration is higher education in developing countries generally, but special attention will be given to the situation of the new nations of tropical Africa.

For an instructive starting point, we cannot find a better case than that of Japan, a uniquely successful instance of controlled modernization in which higher education played a central role. The outlines of the story are familiar. Upon the opening of Japan in the mid-nineteenth century, a segment of the feudal elite sought to promote the rapid modernization of the society while maintaining firm controls to preserve the traditional hierarchical social order with its values of honor, respect, duty, and fealty to the emperor. Soon after the Meiji Restoration in 1868, the Education Law of 1872 made formal provision for the support of overseas study, and the trickle of Japanese who had found their way into Western schools during the later years of the Shogunate was augmented by a substantial flow of officially sponsored government scholars, going under the close supervision of the Ministry of Education and committed to work for the government upon their return. Initially directed especially toward America, the flow of officially sponsored students turned more to Europe, especially Germany, by as early as 1880.

Meanwhile, the government took rapid steps to convert or replace the traditional academies of classical learning to meet the urgent need for institutions devoted to the study of the sciences, technology, and social institutions of the West and staffed them heavily with expatriates. By 1877, when Tokyo Imperial University was established, Americans on the faculty were gradually being replaced by Germans in the preponderant role.

The authors of *In Search of Identity* (Bennett, et al., 1958), on whose account I have been drawing, make in this connection a comment with suggestive overtones for the appeal that Eastern European models may currently have for some of the new nations:

> It is important to remember that it was not by accident that Germany provided the model for the principal government university. In seeking models for various modern institutions, the Japanese often found other countries more suitable than the United States, where conditions were too different to be extensively imitated. The fact that European conditions more closely approximated those of Japan—the feudal background, the importance of hierarchy, the relative scarcity of resources—suggested that although American technological development was worthy of respect, it was Europe, especially Germany, to which Japan should look for the models for such important institutions as the Diet, the constitution, and the university [pp. 32–33].

The centralized system of higher education that rapidly emerged, culminating in the highly prestigious Tokyo Imperial University, was from the beginning closely integrated with the elite structure of the society. The provision for highly competitive standards for entry to the university, however, introduced a major emphasis on achievement criteria to balance the continuing importance of the traditional ascriptive criteria of class and connections. The academic system culminating in the university was thus not primarily an institution for legitimizing the prerogatives of an existing elite and for socializing them with respect to the traditions and qualities required for generalized elite roles. For youths predominantly of "good" family, it provided a setting for the stringent competitive selection of those who were to attain the high positions of leadership in modern Japan, a setting in which they were also to form the networks of close personal association upon which their subsequent influence and advancement were to depend heavily. It was purposefully geared toward specialized mastery of Western knowledge and technology. And surely, given its heavy competitive emphasis on standards of excellent, it could hardly have been better designed to instil and augment achievement motivation in the future leadership of the nation, which, if we follow David McClelland (1961), is a most important step in providing the conditions for economic growth.[4]

Once this system became firmly established

> the elite universities, particularly those supported by the government, became the privileged training ground and provided the connections needed for acquiring desirable positions in bureaucracy and management; the lesser universities provided channels to lesser businesses and bureaucracies. The student who went abroad in the early years of Meiji was virtually guaranteed success, so urgently needed were foreign skills. But after about 1900 the young Japanese who wished to make a success of his career found it necessary to chart his course very skillfully, to establish

4. The point of greatest competitive pressure was prior to admission to the university. See Passin (1965).

his connections as early as possible, and to maintain them carefully [Bennett, et al., 1958, pp. 34–35].

Through the strategic placement of their graduates, the various faculties of Tokyo Imperial University came to enjoy a virtual monopoly on channels to top positions in many spheres of business, industry, and government.

Under these circumstances, foreign study took on changed significance. The growing prestige of the national system led the government to restrict its sponsorship to finished products of Japanese education, who went abroad to acquire further specialized training, secure in their linkage to the elite channels. Tightly competitive as the system was, unsponsored students continued in substantial numbers to find ways to go to the West for higher education, but on their return many of them found themselves cut off from the preferred avenues for using their training. Until the special circumstances of the American Occupation, they tended to gravitate to marginal social and occupational roles.

The Japanese experience will not be duplicated elsewhere, but it exposes to view in virtually ideal type one institutional pattern that marshaled educational resources very effectively in selecting, motivating, training, and deploying an elite well equipped to carry out spectacularly rapid modernization, if not to lay a firm basis for political democracy. It also illustrates the complex relationship between indigenous and foreign higher education: it would be folly to ask which contributed more, or what were the general advantages and disadvantages of each. Over the seventy years prior to World War II, the weight and role of these two indispensable ingredients repeatedly shifted and were to shift once more in postwar reconstruction.

The more typical case outside the industrialized West is one in which indigenous higher education is only ambiguously linked to the prospects of modernization. The established universities in Latin America and the Middle East have tended to maintain their traditional role in the service of an entrenched elite with little interest in modernization. Emphasizing the traditional liberal arts and professions, they have typically contributed to development in none of the ways—selective, motivational, scientific, or talent-channeling—that we noted in the case of Japan. Indirectly, they may contribute to change as a by-product of social instability; volatile student bodies, hardly engrossed in their studies or tied by a sense of social purpose or personal consequence to their pursuit, become a fertile field for the politics of violence and radical protest. Political stability is further endangered when grossly excessive numbers of students enter training for prestigious, genteel professions such as law, with many having little prospect of putting their skills to constructive use (Lewis, W. A., 1961; Curle, 1962).

The problems of these established, often honored, universities are augmented by, if not rooted in, genteel impoverishment. With the lecture system, part-time faculties, deficient libraries and laboratories, and minimal contact between students and staff, the opportunity for favorable educational impact would seem to be small. These problems are also to a considerable extent shared by the universities of the Indian subcontinent, originally founded along English patterns as a recruiting and training ground for the lower ranks of the colonial civil service.

In countries where such conditions prevail in the major institutions of higher education, the urgent priority should logically be to reform and upgrade indigenous education, not its expansion or foreign study. Educational facilities are needed to support serious encounter with modern knowledge and technology; instructional methods should be modified to place less emphasis on verbalism and rote knowledge (smacking of an initiation test en route to gentility) and more on thought and performance. The structure of reward and opportunity for students should be manipulated so as to channel enrollments into fields of social and economic needs, and better provision is essential for the placement and utilization of graduates whose skills are actually needed but are presently little used. Major changes of this order are of course not readily accomplished. Members of American faculties teaching in such a setting on Fulbright exchange programs have frequently found the limitations on what they could individually accomplish quite frustrating (Macgregor, 1962).

It would seem to be a mistake, where these educational conditions are involved, to look to massive programs of foreign study as a replacement for or *general* supplement to deficiencies in the indigenous institutions. Unlike the case of new countries where each highly educated person from abroad makes a highly discernible difference, the students returning to older countries are all too likely to get lost in the shuffle. By sheer numbers, they are less likely to influence the prevailing educational pattern, which is well established, than is the case in a new nation still in the process of forming its educational policies. On the other hand, strategically planned programs of foreign study can play a part in institutional reform. They can also supplement indigenous institutions in training for critically needed specialized skills. In a later section we return to consider ways in which programs of foreign study might be more appropriately focused toward this end.

A different case is represented by indigenous higher education as a historical novelty in the developing nations of tropical Africa. In some, the founding of a first institution of higher education is an early item on the agenda of new nationhood. For others, firm patterns of educational policy had been set near the end of the period of colonial tutelage, but these are likely to be under continued scrutiny in the early years of independence and subject to the conflicting pressures of admission, costs, and shifting conceptions of national interest. In spite of obvious differences in the social and historical setting, the situation parallels in some ways that of early Meiji Japan, in that all specialized Western education at a high level is at a premium, expatriates necessarily play a major role in staffing faculties, and foreign study remains an indispensable massive supplement to the products of indigenous institutions.

To understand the significance of higher education in tropical Africa, one must remember that it occupies a nearly stratospheric position atop a steep pyramid of status in which an immense gulf separates the still illiterate from those with primary schooling, and another gap perhaps as large divides the latter from successful graduates of academically oriented secondary schools—in the formerly British areas, the holders of the coveted General Certificate of Education (G.C.E.), which is commonly seen as the open sesame to a white collar career. By American standards, the G.C.E. carries more status than a routine college degree. The secondary school graduate is already an accredited participant in the modern world; the university graduate, a fortiori, occupies a pinnacle of status that may be so highly valued in its own right as to overshadow the instrumental competences and capacities that higher education inculcates. It is the legacy of colonial rule that this status, and to a lesser degree that of the secondary school graduate, is that of an assimilated European.

Indeed, the often-cited contrast between the French policy of assimilation and the British one of fostering indigenous institutions and indirect rule breaks down in the secondary and higher educational institutions that eventually were established in the French- and English-dominated territories: the institutions in both cases are frankly assimilationist with language, institutional forms, curricular content, and academic standards adopted from or closely modeled after those of the Métropole.

Both the classical European model and its African version were geared to produce scholars and gentlemen—members of an elite held together by shared familiarity with a classical cultural tradition, one that in the African case might still be only superficially grafted on a radically alien background. As Francis Sutton (1965) remarks:

> The traditional structure of European secondary education fits the assimilationist doctrine very well. It provides a screen through which aspirants to power and high position must pass and which assures their possessing diffuse cultural attainments.

The correspondence in institutional outcome in this respect between the British and the French areas in spite of divergence in colonial policies reflects the charismatic power of Europeans as a super-elite in colonial African eyes, and the consequent immense prestige of things European. To quote Sutton again:

> The English and French are now criticized by Africans (and by Americans too!) for the excessively "literary" character of the education they offered to Africans. In rebuttal they can and do point to African demands that the distinctions between metropolitan and African education be eliminated. This became a matter of principle.

It was a matter of principle at the university level too. Melville Herskovits (1962) writes:

> The problem of adapting subject matter to African requirements, which we encountered in discussing the curricula of the lower schools, was also present in the universities. Aside from the fact that for the Europeans who founded these institutions, the validity of the home curricula seemed self-evident, there was also the point of view of the African to be taken into account. Almost everywhere the value of a university degree was recognized to the extent it was like that of the Métropole, and deviations introduced by European teachers were resented as attempts to dilute the purity of the degree, and hence its worth. . . . At times the insistence on equivalence was so strong that it would go beyond curriculum to traditions which had only symbolic value, such as that attached to wearing the academic gown to lectures and other university exercises by undergraduates in certain university colleges established under British auspices [p. 256].

One is reminded of the vehement and principled insistence of the older-generation female faculty at an American woman's college that the curriculum be in all respects equivalent to that currently fashionable in the Ivy League—any difference surely would mean inferiority!

As a result, one contrast between indigenous and foreign education that is often important hardly holds in the African case: *both* are likely to involve alienation from cultural roots and from major segments of the current society. In essential respects, this indigenous education *is* a foreign education. The African university exists apart from the immediately surrounding society and culture, as does the residential secondary school in its compound.[5] With its confluence of students from different tribal origins, different vernacular languages, different nationalities, it is a melting pot where national or pan-African identity as well as quasi-European status may be established.

These features of academic education in tropical Africa raise a number of problems with respect to its role in political and economic development. While the university may fan national or pan-African sentiments, the salience of status considerations in higher education accentuates new lines of social cleavage to supplant the old tribal ones. The high emotional charge attached to the university life and the academic degree is likely to hamper the rational and utilitarian consideration of educational policy. And the European model of a gentleman's education, for all its solid ingredients of modern knowledge, may still serve more to validate elite, quasi-European status than to equip and motivate the student in ways consonant with national development. It seems

5. Marvick's recent questionnaire study (1965) of Fourah Bay College, Sierra Leone, vividly portrays an institution with European faculty and curriculum, nationally and tribally diverse students, and, in effect, no hosts. The students whom he describes are more uprooted and culturally homeless in their college years than the sojourner at a foreign university, where there is at least an integral culture shared by host nationals at the staff and student levels.

to exert a pull even on institutions marginal to the main stream of academic life: the technical schools at the secondary level, which may strive to be as academic as the traffic will bear, or the higher institutes or universities of science and technology, which may find more prestige in basic science along the lines of a would-be Massachusetts Institute of Technology than in the down-to-earth practicality of a California Polytechnic.

Furthermore, if national development fails to keep pace with unrealistically high aspirations and if opportunities for prestigious employment of the university-trained should dwindle, the heterogeneous assembly of uprooted students on African campuses may become fertile soil for the development of volatile extremist movements along Latin American lines.

This catalogue of existing and potential problems should not obscure the important positive function that the new universities are performing in creating new national elites well educated in modern knowledge and well acquainted with exacting standards of excellence. Indigenous higher education of this type will surely expand, although its exclusiveness, its standards, and the European flavor of its curricula may not be immune to political controversy.

In the case of tropical Africa, foreign study for the present must be relied on as a massive supplement and, for some countries, as a substitute for indigenous undergraduate education. At the post-graduate level, the training of African senior staff to replace expatriates on the faculties of African institutions of higher education has high priority. Given the status-oriented aspect of the present African university (which I may have overemphasized but which surely has a factual basis to be reckoned with), the channeling of well-selected, highly qualified Africans into relevant instrumentally oriented, specialized programs of foreign study might prove a strategic contribution. The aim should be not merely to add to the class of prestigious "been-tos," but to return exemplars of well-motivated technical competence to key positions in the new national life.

While relatively few students from the French-speaking areas will come to America, the United States stands in a special position with respect to the former British colonial areas. Data sampled earlier in this chapter indicate that in spite of the divergence between British and American educational systems, substantial numbers of Africans from the Commonwealth countries study in the United States, and the flow will undoubtedly increase. Given the entrenchment of British educational patterns at the outset of nationhood, we must consider whether these students will be sidetracked on their return. In view of the thinness of the stratum of highly educated persons in African society, this seems quite unlikely. Rather, the growth on the African scene of an appreciable segment of intellectuals trained in the more pragmatic and instrumental tradition of American higher education might serve as a catalyst to induce change in the status-oriented features of indigenous higher education, which we have suggested has disadvantages for political and economic development. To encourage such trends, sponsored programs of American study for Africans should maintain strict selective standards, the fields in which foreign study is supported should be carefully chosen, and the students should be directed to American institutions of high quality.[6]

This is not to suggest that American institutions of higher education—say, the land-grant colleges—can or should be transported whole to African soil to replace British ones. It is rather to suggest that providing British-oriented Africa with alternative educational models may widen their range of effective choice and increase the likelihood that indigenous educational institutions may develop along lines more closely adapted to national needs than is possible for any post-colonial echo of overvalued metropolitan practice.

Foreign Study As Related to Social Development

In our consideration of indigenous higher education, we have noted that the contribution of foreign study to modernization depends upon the situation in the recipient country and that the circumstances that prevail in its indigenous educational institutions are an important consideration. It remains to draw upon evidence and conjecture to examine in greater detail the impact or lack of impact of foreign education from this perspective.

In order for study abroad to advance national development, a chain of many links has to be completed. Sufficiently able persons have to be enrolled in training institutions overseas, they have to learn something that is potentially transferable to use in their home country, they must return, and after return they must be motivated to put their training to use in opportunities where its use makes a difference to the national society. There are many opportunities for this chain to be broken to nullify the contribution of foreign education to national development, whatever other values it may entail.

Concerning several of these steps, there is little if any systematic evidence available. We know virtually nothing about the effect of an American study sojourn, for example, on arousing in foreign students higher levels of the achievement motivation that David McClelland (1961) holds to be the central ingredient of the entrepreneurial spirit and an important precondition of economic growth. Joseph Veroff (1963) provides a shred of suggestive evidence (from data obtained by administering a crude measure of need for achievement to a subsample from the Institute of International Education African student survey) in his conclusion that when newcomer and long-sojourn groups of African foreign students (matched for nationality) are compared a substantially higher proportion of the "oldtimers" receive high achievement scores.

Sufficient evidence is at hand, however, to make it clear that obstacles to the utilization of knowledge and skill after return are the strategic factor that limits the effectiveness of much foreign study.

6. Preferably, however, they should be encouraged to attend institutions which have not been wholly captured by the ethos of pure research for its own sake.

On this point, the earliest and still one of the best intensive studies of returned foreign students is that carried out in 1953–1954 by John and Ruth Useem among a sample of American- and British-trained men in Bombay State. Their findings suffice to dispel any notion that educational exchange offers a panacea to underdeveloped countries: of men who had studied abroad before and after independence and had been back in India from one to eighteen years, they report that "less than 10 per cent ever have jobs in which they work full time in the field for which they have taken specialized training" (Useem and Useem, 1955, p. 81). Even among those whose foreign sojourn had been sponsored by the state or central government, 55 per cent were not employed in work for which they had been trained. The picture, over-all, is one of underutilization and ineffectiveness. In the absence of a comparison group of Indian-trained men of similar background, we do not know that the returnees were at a relative disadvantage. The Useems think not and regard foreign education still as marginally advantageous in the highly competitive job market of the Indian middle classes. Even if the secondary skills of the foreign-trained could be brought to bear in their own work, it is clear that in this case specific foreign training would have only very limited effect on national development.

The less systematic study by Ralph Beals and Norman Humphrey (1957) of Mexican students who returned after being trained in the United States tends also to be discouraging. Although they trace in their interviews ways in which the returnees believed they had transmitted techniques, skills, and knowledge acquired during their sojourn—more often by those employed in business and industry than by those employed in government, and by those trained in science than by those trained in the humanities—their respondents tended to give neutral or negative judgments of the value of their sojourn for their careers. Often American training was seen as a source of handicap, failing to produce degrees or credentials that corresponded to those locally honored, and involving, as it did for many, the loss or restriction of potentially influential contacts. Given the anti-*Yanqui* climate of opinion, they had in any case to avoid the appearance of Americanization.

What is common to the two instances is a society in which the foreign-returned is not perceived as having in his training any scarce commodity to offer: not only is he one of many, but he also finds himself in competition with the products of an established indigenous system. He enters an inefficient job market where he is likely to be entrapped in the particularistic morass of nepotism, traditionally expected bribery, and red tape, which are themselves the symptoms of a widespread syndrome of underdevelopment.

In terms of sheer numbers, it seems likely that a substantial part of the stream of educational exchange flows under these relatively unpromising conditions, particularly at the undergraduate level, and often without sponsorship. The locally available facilities for higher education are not very attractive; for many members of the middle class, chances at home are not very promising and hopes readily develop that foreign training is a way out.

When, near the end of their planned sojourn, such students look ahead with increasing realism to the dismal prospects awaiting them on return, they are all too likely to employ every available stratagem to prolong their stay, presenting a recurring problem that is familiar to American foreign student advisers, immigration authorities, and sponsors of educational exchange programs. These dignitaries are likely to tell themselves that to the extent that such a student eludes attempts to send him home, exchange has failed. His country needs his skills, so there is a moral obligation to get him back. Too often this seemingly hardheaded position is insufficiently cynical. His country *needs* his skills, yes, but it is precisely because it is very unlikely to *use* them that the student bends every effort to postpone his return.

Among the means available for fostering political and economic development in countries that present this kind of picture, we have already assigned relatively low priority to programs of foreign study. But the flow of foreign students from these countries will continue because of private motives and public policies pursued on other grounds. To the extent that the resources for support of foreign study can be deployed strategically, they obviously should be concentrated on the problem of utilization. Thus, the Useems (1955) recommend that much more administrative and financial attention be given to supporting the returned student, such as placement services, subscriptions to professional journals, and preferential use in lieu of "foreign experts" in programs of technical assistance to his country. Noting that older persons who are established before studying abroad in definite jobs to which they are committed to return are a better bet for short-run gains in utilized training, they suggest that focusing support on particular organizations or departments which send a number of individuals for training, either as individuals or as a team, has the advantage that on return they are more likely to give one another support in modifying traditional practices. Younger persons embarking on foreign study might appropriately be counseled to stress basic methods and principles and practical experience, on the expectation that they will probably not have the opportunity to use any more narrowly specialized training. Higher standards of selection and in the dispensing of degrees and recommendations, moreover, would help protect the negotiable value of foreign training from further depreciation. Concern with utilization thus calls for a redistribution of emphasis in educational exchange, a challenge that still largely remains to be met.

The social and historical circumstances in which foreign study has contributed in conspicuous and important ways to social development are not well documented, but one suspects that these most favorable circumstances have applied to only a relatively small proportion of the total flow of persons in educational exchange. The historical case of Japanese modernization supports the intrinsically plausible view that returned students have the greatest impact when they fill a virtual vacuum of Western training and such training is in high demand. This pair of conditions would seem to arise when a previously isolated and backward area is suddenly opened to the modern world under auspices promoting high national aspirations: it is the common ground we noted between Meiji Japan and contemporary sub-Saharan Africa. In other less isolated areas of underdevelopment, persons seeking to trade on their Western knowledge and skills cannot count to such a degree on their novelty, scarcity, and prestige. Less isolated national and colonial systems more often have accommodated gradually to Westernizing influences in ways that protect the position of traditional elites. To use a gross metaphor, these social systems tend to develop a kind of immunity reaction against influence by such foreign bodies as returnees from abroad.

In the newly opened country, the small numbers of returned students in the early years will surely have an impact. They cannot be absorbed unnoticed in the traditional scheme of things. Just what this impact may be, however, cannot be taken for granted. Whether or not it points in the direction of solid economic growth and stable political development will depend on a multitude of factors other than the infusion of foreign educational experience as such.

At the outset, selection for foreign study is likely to be haphazard, as is choice of the kind and quality of training that the students actually obtain. As early cohorts of these casually selected and trained students return, they have the first-comers' advantage in manning the key social positions that require Western higher education. It therefore becomes an important consideration whether or not a fluid opportunity structure is developed that meets the aspirations for advancement of subsequent waves of returnees (and, for that matter, of graduates of the new indigenous institutions), and opens channels for putting their probably superior abilities and preparation to effective use.

A related consideration is whether and how soon haphazardness in selection and training is supplanted by deliberate policy. The inception in 1960 of the American Universities Program for Africa (Committee on Educational Interchange Policy, 1960), administered for a large number of participating universities by the African-American Institute, is a most important step in improved selection as well as in the extension of financial support for training at leading American campuses. The early and understandable major role of southern Negro colleges and universities in training Africans—their very existence as segregated institutions being a questionable anomaly in the American social and educational scene—was not entirely fortunate.

In this initial period when foreign study must be relied upon to substitute for or to supplement heavily the limited openings in indigenous institutions, undergraduate training abroad is proportionally more important than it should be later. Apart from the sheer unavailability of the indigenous alternative, the one consideration favoring foreign over indigenous undergraduate education is the greater malleability of the younger student in personality and basic attitudes. But this very feature raises as serious potential problems as it presents opportunities: at the undergraduate level there is greater danger of alienation of the student from his home society, greater likelihood that his morale may become dependent on facilities and consumer benefits that will not remain available to him at home.[7] Given the intrinsically lower costs of indigenous undergraduate education, planning should aim at shunting the sponsored segment of the undergraduate flow to indigenous institutions as soon as feasible.

The urgencies of educational development in tropical Africa, the shortage of private funds that permit the undirected choice of foreign study at the student's whim, the scarcity of public funds which imposes selectivity—all converge to favor the early development of the sort of intensive rather than extensive, programmed rather than haphazard employment of foreign study in the interest of national development for which the Useems argue in the case of India. By way of prophylaxis, many of the measures that they recommended to correct deficiencies in the Indian use of educational exchange can be instituted before the problems become so serious. Their recommendations on following through with the foreign student after his return—maintaining contact, supporting some of his needs for professional or scientific communication, seeking his advice, perhaps providing refresher training after a period—seem particularly appropriate. To the extent that resources for foreign study are focused on the particularly important sector of staffing new and expanding indigenous universities and technical institutes, this kind of follow-through can be integrated with technical assistance to the indigenous institutions, an equally important topic outside the scope of this essay.

The new nations of tropical Africa thus present a situation in which higher education is strategically needed for social development at an early stage when both indigenous and foreign education have important potential contributions to make.[8] The opportunity is available, through planning, to avoid in this instance mistakes that have severely limited the social contribution of foreign study in other countries outside the industrialized West.

7. In the case of African students in the United States, however, immigration does not seem to present the lure it has for other foreign student groups: "An estimated 10 per cent of all foreign students either remain permanently in the U. S. or eventually return to the U. S. In contrast to this, 97 per cent of the Africans stated they were *certain* to return to their home countries. An additional 2 per cent indicated they would *probably* return." (Davis, Hanson, and Burnov, 1961, p. 32).

8. Since this chapter was written, the report of the Tananarive Conference makes available a valuable source of data and of African perspectives on achievements and needs in regard to indigenous institutions of higher education. See UNESCO (1963).

19

Motivation, Communications Research, and Family Planning

The fertility of a population can be viewed as the resultant of many individual acts and decisions, made within a framework of biological and environmental constraints. Questions of human motivation and motivational change thus have an important bearing on the viability of efforts to attain social control over population growth. Such questions enter the picture in two logically separable respects. On the one hand, the number of children desired by fecund couples varies from society to society, and, over time, within the same society. What factors lead parents to aspire to a particular size of family, and how may their desires be influenced in the direction of the small families required for slowly growing populations in an era of low mortality? On the other hand, couples differ in the extent to which they are motivated to employ rational and effective means of limiting their families to the size they desire. What motivational factors are involved in the acceptance and effective use of birth control, and how may the more effective use of birth control procedures be promoted?

These two kinds of motivational questions are thus respectively concerned with the private ends and means that affect fertility and population growth. So long as the sizes of families that actually prevail in a population exceed the size that is typically desired—as when effective birth control techniques are not generally employed—the second type of question, concerned with the promotion of birth control, should have the top priority because of its strategic relevance to population growth. But in populations (typical of the economically well-developed countries) in which birth control has gained widespread acceptance, questions concerning the motivation of desired family size become increasingly important from the standpoint of population policy. The main body of this paper is focused on the first problem: What implications can be drawn from social psychological research and theory that can contribute to the acceptance and promulgation of effective birth control prac-

Reprinted from *Public Health and Population Change,* Mindel C. Sheps and Jeanne C. Ridley, editors, by the permission of the publishers, University of Pittsburgh Press. Copyright 1965, University of Pittsburgh Press, Pittsburgh, Pennsylvania. I am indebted to Mr. Richard Gardner for bibliographic assistance.

tices? At the end, I will revert to the problem of desired family size in connection with a discussion of research needs.

Practitioners and scientists in other fields often look to the student of human motivation for near-magical solutions to problems that *they* cannot handle—and are ready with contempt when the magical solution is not forthcoming. If he is mindful of these ambivalent expectations, the social psychologist who ventures into the strange territory of population control and family planning will be wise to assume a posture of extreme modesty. In order to appreciate what research on communications and motivation *can* contribute, we had best begin by examining some of the reasons why such modesty is called for—not by way of apology, but to clear the ground so that relevance can be established.

Types of Communications Research

The years since World War II have seen the burgeoning in the United States of research on persuasive communication, and the emergence of a body of tentative empirical generalizations that Nathan Maccoby (1963) has dignified as "the new scientific rhetoric." In spite of substantial progress in this field, however, communications research has been addressed to much easier problems than those confronted in the motivational aspect of family planning, and its empirical propositions have been worked out in much simpler, more promising settings.

One impressively cumulative research tradition has used controlled experimentation to identify factors that determine the effectiveness of communication once the recipient has been exposed to the message (Hovland, Janis, and Kelley, 1953; Janis and Smith, 1965). This body of work on "captive audiences," primarly the contribution of psychologists, has yielded a considerable array of generalizations. But apart from the simplification involved in starting with the captive audience, research in this tradition has characteristically chosen its ground so as to increase the likelihood of obtaining substantial effects, which facilitate the comparison of various factors in the modification of attitudes and practices. It has dealt more with short-term effects than with long-term ones, more with trivial or superficial issues than with emotionally laden and central ones, and more with changes in beliefs and feelings than with consequential behaviors. It has also been heavily based on conveniently available American student populations. Thus, we cannot be sure that the same variables will remain important or have the same weights when communication with widely differing kinds of audiences on very different topics is at issue, but we can certainly expect that the magnitude of effects achieved will often be substantially smaller than in these experimental studies.

A second tradition, to which sociologists have been the main contributors, has used techniques of interview survey research in field studies of the effects of the mass media (Klapper, 1960; Hovland, 1959). In contrast with the results of experimental studies, the typical finding in these field studies of "free" audiences has been one of rather minimal effects, primarily in the direction of reinforcing or activating existing attitudes, not of conversion. Again, the research has been primarily on American publics, and the range of issues explored has not been great. Voting and purchasing, as identifiable acts, have nevertheless made available a research focus on consequential behavior that goes beyond attitudes and beliefs.

Field research in this tradition becomes most relevant to population planning when it has been directed at the role of communications in the promulgation and diffusion of new techniques and practices. Converging evidence seems to point to a two-step linkage in which the public media have their effect primarily upon a limited subpopulation of "opinion leaders" (it turns out that they are different people depending on the issue), who in turn spread the message in their own spheres of personal influence (Katz, E., 1963; Katz, E. and Lazarsfeld, 1955). But the kinds of decisions involved in buying a new product, adopting a new drug, introducing a new farming practice (all topics of studies in this vein) are a large step from those involved in family planning.

Even the most cursory thought about family planning highlights ways in which its motivational context differs so radically from the setting of most recent communications research as to represent a difference in kind, not in degree. The neutral language in which family planning is discussed scientifically and professionally should not let us forget that we deal here with sex and the marriage bed, around which surely are woven some of the strongest and least rational motives, the most intimate and private relationships, and the firmest institutional norms and taboos known to man. The very idea of introducing planful rationality in this "sacred" area could initially have been conceived only in a society trained to give unprecedented priority to rational-technical considerations by long experience with them in more public, less emotionally charged spheres of urban and industrial life.[1] Yet we are under imperatives to promote birth control in traditional societies that are just beginning to attain a modicum of rationality in their public, economic, and political spheres! Any attempt to extrapolate to the motivation of family planning from research on other topics runs the risk of sheer fatuity.

On this appraisal, the social psychologist who shares concern with the population problem has several options. On the one hand, he may proclaim the irrelevance of existing social psychological research and call for an enormous expansion of basic research on the motivation of change in birth-producing or birth-limiting decisions and behavior. It always seems both easy and virtuous to ask for more research, and more is obviously needed here, but I will nevertheless reject this option with respect to the promotion of family plan-

1. Methods of population control have, of course, been practiced in many traditional societies. But the use of such methods may reflect adaptations gradually developed in the culture, rather than deliberate decisions of rational planning.

ning. For all its limitations, existing research has its relevance in ways I hope to suggest below. And I agree with Berelson (1963) that given the current urgencies and limitations of resources, the highest priorities for investment ought to be assigned in other directions.

A second option that I will follow in part is to draw cautiously on the results of existing research for hypotheses that seem relevant to social intervention in population control. The research will seldom warrant prescriptive advice to the practitioner. It may help to sensitize him, however, to potentially important factors that he has not considered explicitly. Particularly the negative conclusions of communications research—conclusions about circumstances in which persuasive communication is likely to be *ineffective*—may, *a fortiori,* help him to avoid wasted effort in the more difficult case of family planning. To the extent that action programs incorporate features extrapolated from the results of research on other topics and contexts, these action hypotheses need to be checked in program evaluation—but so do all the hunches and insights around which programs are built, whatever their source.

In addition, the present fund of research experience can be drawn upon for aid in the better *theoretical* definition of the practical problem. Often to redefine a problem is to see the contingencies that bear upon its solution in a different light. My impression is that in the present modest state of research in motivation and communication, the greatest probable contribution of social psychology lies in this direction. With these preliminaries behind us, I therefore begin with an attempt to illustrate this third option.

Some Theory with Practical Implications

A little theory can often cast a useful searchlight upon silly practice. My favorite example comes from a wartime venture in venereal disease control, so far as I know unrecorded. The American troop information officers in Manila—high-ranking recruits from Madison Avenue—had the inspiration of modelling their appeals over Armed Forces Radio on a recently notorious and perhaps successful campaign of cigarette advertising, in which the advertisers of Lucky Strikes had filled the media for weeks with the unexplained slogan, LS/MFT, at long last announcing—after suspense had presumably built up to the point of nationwide breathlessness—LS/MFT: Lucky Strikes Mean Fine Tobacco. The Manila version, also repeated sententiously for weeks, went: VD/MT. . . . VD/MT—with the final elucidation to a supposedly breathless audience: VD/MT . . . Venereal Disease . . . Means Trouble! A moment's theoretical consideration of the radically different behavioral objectives involved in raising the saliency for smokers of one among many closely similar alternative brands, and in motivating soldiers to avoid intercourse or employ prophylactic measures, should have stopped this pretentious effort.

The modification of birth-producing practices is a special and difficult case of the more general problem of the induction of another's behavior by an outside agent. One of the most cogent analyses of the psychological processes involved in such "behavior induction" remains that of Dorwin Cartwright (1949), which he presented in the context of selected findings from research on the sale of United States war bonds in World War II. To quote Cartwright:

> What happens psychologically when someone attempts to influence the behavior of another person? The answer, in broad outline, may be described as follows: To influence behavior, a chain of processes must be initiated within the person. These processes are complex and interrelated, but in broad terms they may be characterized as (i) creating a particular cognitive structure, (ii) creating a particular motivational structure, and (iii) creating a particular behavioral (action) structure. In other words, behavior is determined by the beliefs, opinions, and "facts" a person possesses; by the needs, goals, and values he has; and by the momentary control held over his behavior by given features of his cognitive and motivational structure. To influence behavior "from the outside" requires the ability to influence these determinants in a particular way.
>
> It seems to be a characteristic of most campaigns that they start strongly with the first process, do considerably less with the second, and only lightly touch upon the third. To the extent that the campaign is intended to influence behavior and not simply to "educate," the third process is essential. [p. 255]

Cartwright's entire analysis is so pertinent that if space permitted, I would like to summarize it at great length. He points out that to *create the desired cognitive structure*—gain acceptance for the relevant facts and beliefs—the message must first reach the sense organs of the persons to be influenced. Once it is received, whether the message is accepted or rejected will depend on how the person identifies it with more general categories to which it appears to belong. He will tend to fit new messages into his stock of categories in ways that serve to protect him from unwanted changes in his cognitive structure (change is resisted). *Creation of the required motivational structure* in a person involves getting him to see the given action as a step toward some desired goal—the more goals that are seen as attainable by a single path, the more likely the path is to be taken. Finally—and it is the implications of this last step that I want to develop here—*creating the required behavioral structure* so that the given action will in fact occur depends on establishing conditions such that the appropriate cognitive and motivational systems gain control of the person's behavior at a particular point in time. Cartwright suggests and illustrates three subprinciples in this connection:

The more specifically defined the path of action to a goal (in an accepted motivational structure), the more likely it is that the structure will gain control of behavior.

The more specifically a path of action is located in time, the more likely it is that the structure will gain control of behavior.

A given motivational structure may be set in control of behavior by placing the person in a situation requiring a decision to take, or not to take, a step of action that is a part of the structure. [pp. 264–265]

In the case of war bond sales, the advantages of specifying the path of action concretely (the first two of the foregoing principles) were illustrated by the substantially greater effectiveness of campaign appeals that said, in effect, "Buy an extra $100 bond during the drive from the solicitor where you work," than of appeals of an earlier, expensive campaign that in substance merely recommended, "Buy War Bonds." The effective technique of personal solicitation, which required the solicited person to make a decision to buy or not to buy a bond then and there, embodied the third principle. It is easy to think of parallels in communications advocating birth control.

But the search for parallels reveals instructive differences between the two cases. Buying a bond is a single well-defined act, to which the principles just noted can be readily applied; the barrage of wartime appeals and solicitation was designed to make it easy to buy, difficult to refuse. By the technique of payroll deduction, moreover, one decision can be made to commit the person to a whole series of purchases, which become equivalent to a single act rather than a set of independent actions. Once committed, the war bond subscriber has to make a separate decision to terminate his purchases—and the promotional campaign, of course, does nothing to encourage *such* decisions. In the sphere of birth control, however, all of the methods that depend on modifying the conditions of each specific act of sexual intercourse fall outside the scope of ready influence, according to these principles. It is simply not possible to arrange the equivalent of war bond solicitation to guide the decision processes affecting each separate act of intercourse. Neither is it possible, where these methods are at issue, to secure the kind of externally binding commitment to their practice that is represented by payroll deduction. The behavioral objective for their advocates must therefore be *not* the motivation of specific acts, but rather the establishment of consistent habits or the development in people of strong and consistent internalized controls. Both of these objectives are intrinsically much more complex and difficult to achieve. It is dubious whether even the best planned promotional campaigns can often attain them.

The present analysis therefore highlights the probable relevance of a dimension along which techniques of birth limitation may vary, ranging from fully committing single acts (male and female sterilization), through infrequent acts the motivation of which can be separately induced (the insertion of intrauterine rings, long-term medication, perhaps abortion), to the entire range of chemical-mechanical procedures that must be carried out daily or before each occasion of intercourse. Included in this last, least promising category are not only the rhythm method and withdrawal, but also the daily "pill," since each of these techniques requires multiple decisions to act or refrain from acting.

The initial middle-class leadership of the birth control movement has favored techniques that fall in the latter category, perhaps just because they seem to maximize voluntary decision—planfulness—about parenthood and thus appeal to middle-class values. It should be recognized, however, that any procedure that maximizes and multiplies voluntary decisions is *disadvantageous* from the standpoint of permitting coordinated social intervention to limit births. If, as seems likely, promotional methods cannot instill sufficiently consistent contraceptive habits and self-discipline in enough people to achieve acceptable target reductions in birth rates, consideration might well be given to focusing promotion on more attainable goals. Sterilization and chemical or mechanical procedures that require attention only at infrequent occasions would seem to be more feasible subjects for promotional campaigns.

Note in passing that the dimension I have been emphasizing is closely related to one emphasized by Berelson (1963) in his grid of three main factors that he proposes for the orientation of field experiments on the promotion of birth control. Berelson ventures that the practically important variables which in combination define a framework for the planning of program testing are, first, the nature of the *society* (traditional or modern), second, the nature of the *contraceptive method* (hard to use or easy), and, finally, the nature of the *approach* (through whom the informational, educational, or promotional campaign is addressed, saying what, to whom).

For his second variable, he contrasts the traditional methods of withdrawal, condom, foam tablet, rhythm, etc., with the steroid pill and intrauterine device, saying that:

> What makes [the former] methods hard to use is the requirement for sustained motivation, the need in most cases to do something preparatory at the time of intercourse, and in some cases the sheer bother and nuisance value. Beyond such problems is the further difficulty that such methods are not always effective—so that the user or potential user may feel justified in thinking that the result is not going to be worth the effort. [pp. 163–164]

Berelson calls for field studies aimed at providing an adequate basis for such gross administrative decisions as whether the "hard" methods can be effectively promoted in traditional societies, even with maximum effort.

Clearly Berelson is making much the same distinction as mine. But his unduly pessimistic dismissal of motivational theory leads him to couch the distinction in the more commonsense terms of "hard" vs. "easy," which in turn leads him to neglect ways in which male sterilization (easy) and female sterilization (hard) both carry one feature of his "easy" list to an even higher degree.

The kind of motivational theory that I have borrowed from Cartwright differentiates analytically the cognitive, attitudinal, and decisional components of the problem of motivating a change in behavior. One may also look at the process temporally. In their generally perspicacious distillation of the literature of communication research for the guidance of written communication on birth control, Bogue and Heiskanen (1963) offer as their first principle that "The complete adoption of a new idea or a new mode of behavior is not a simple act, but is a PROCESS comprised of several steps or stages." For the adoption of birth control practices, they suggest the following four stages as a useful framework:

> Stage I. *Awareness and Interest.* This stage includes *learning that birth control is possible, respectable, and practical; becoming interested in it; and wanting to learn about it.*
>
> Stage II. *Information-Gathering, Evaluation, and Decision to Try.*
>
> Stage III. *Implementation.* This stage includes *taking action, learning how to use, correcting mistakes, and overcoming wrong ideas.*
>
> Stage IV. *Adoption and Continued Use.* This is the stage of full adoption. Couples who arrive at this stage feel that birth control is right and normal. They would be uncomfortable or fearful to have sex relations without it unless they positively wanted a pregnancy to occur. [pp. 7–9]

While such a scheme of stages certainly does not represent an ambitious level of theorizing, it again illustrates the advantage that even low-level theory can provide; it functions as a scanning device in terms of which judgments are called for that might otherwise be neglected. Thus, we are reminded that individuals and populations will be located at different steps along this continuum: the planning of communication strategy obviously requires information about the target population in this respect. Special surveys may be required. Further, the advantages become apparent of developing materials and approaches geared to the readiness and interests characteristic of a particular stage—and of finding or devising channels of distribution that match the materials to the readiness of the recipient. Once such a scheme is proposed, the consequences are obvious.

Some Implications of Research on Communication

Of all the results of communications research, the central finding that ought to be kept before all would-be communicators is the fact of resistance. In general, people's beliefs, attitudes, and behavior tend to be stable. Demands and arguments for change, uncomfortable new facts that do not fit neatly into accustomed categories, are likely to be resisted. Whenever communications attempt to change pre-existing beliefs, attitudes, and habits that engage important goals and values, strong resistances are likely to arise at each stage of the communication process. Thus, some communications are so strongly resisted that they fail to achieve even the first step of eliciting audience *exposure* to the message. The self-selective tendency by which audiences become restricted to the already informed and converted is a recurring and major source of frustration to organizers of persuasive campaigns (Hyman and Sheatsley, 1947). Other communications that are somewhat more successful at the outset may end up by being just as ineffective because resistances are mobilized in members of the audience while they are exposed to the message, which interfere drastically with *attention, comprehension,* or *acceptance* (Hovland et al., 1953, pp. 287–293). No change or even "boomerang effects" may occur as a consequence of selective inattention to disturbing ideas, misperception of the message, or subsequent selective forgetting (Klapper, 1960, pp. 18–26). And as we have seen, even when a persuasive message is accepted, the recipient may fail to act upon it or lack the skill to act effectively.

Much effort is wasted in futile persuasive efforts because this paramount fact of resistance is neglected or underestimated. Before any major campaign in the difficult area of human reproductive practices is embarked upon, the would-be communicator should consider his chances of overcoming resistance sufficiently to justify his investment. Some pilot testing of materials and approach is normally called for before any substantial outlay of funds and effort is warranted.

One touchstone for distinguishing promising from unpromising situations is suggested by Hovland, Janis, and Kelley (1953, pp. 293–298) in their analysis of an essential difference between instruction and persuasion. They point out that in communication consensually defined as instructional, in which acceptance is more readily elicited, the setting is typically one in which the recipients anticipate that the communicator is trying to help them, that his conclusions are incontrovertible, and that they will be socially rewarded rather than punished for adhering to his conclusions. In situations commonly regarded as persuasive, on the other hand, interfering expectations are likely to be aroused that operate as resistances. These interfering expectations seem to be of three major kinds: (1) expectations of being manipulated or exploited by the communicator (distrust); (2) expectations of being "wrong"—out of tune with reality as they understand it; and (3) expectations of social disapproval (from people important to them whose norms do not accord with the communicator's position).

The situations encountered by communicators in the sphere of population control surely cover the full range between these two ideal types. The more that inculcation of the desired knowledge and practices can be conducted via the established educational, medical, and religious institutions of the community, the more the "instructional" conditions should apply. Conversely, the more the campaign is seen as a foreign body at variance with the natural and established order, the more closely the "persuasive" type is approximated under conditions that maximize the likelihood of resistance. To the extent that the latter conditions prevail, it is always an open question whether the effort is warranted.

Janis and Smith (1965) summarize the research evidence concerning the major sources of resistance to persuasive communication, classifying them under two rubrics: resistance due to the anchorage of a person's attitudes and practices in his group affiliations, and resistance due to anchorage in personality needs. Factors related to the former source of resistance have been extensively studied, documenting the obvious but important point, among others, that the more strongly attached a person is to his group, the more he is likely to resist "counter-norm communications" at variance with the standards and precepts of the group to which he belongs. Techniques of persuasion that emphasize a community orientation, legitimation by established leaders, discussion and group support and the like are intended to take these sources of resistance into account (Lippitt, Watson, and Westley, 1958).

Resistance to change anchored in personality needs arises inevitably from the fact that each person has a major investment in his own pattern of beliefs, attitudes, and behaviors that he has worked out in the give-and-take of living or adopted from his parents and mentors. Attitudes and practices are particularly obdurate to rational persuasion insofar as they form part of the person's armament for dealing with his unrecognized inner problems, containing and allaying his anxiety, and helping him to maintain adequate "face" toward self and world. It is in this respect that strong personality-anchored resistances may especially be anticipated in the intimate and emotionally charged area of sexual beliefs and practices. One implication, to the extent that such defensive sources of resistance are otherwise likely to be evoked, is that those techniques of birth control that dissociate the contraceptive decision from the intimacy of sexual life should meet with less resistance than others: the oral "pill" and, to a lesser extent, the implanted intrauterine device (which is associated with the sexual anatomy but not with specific sexual acts). And here, of course, lies the great obstacle to sterilization, where the motivational advantage that it requires only a single act of decision is counterbalanced by the fantasies of impotence, castration, or defeminization that it may invoke.

We have already noted a special source of personal and perhaps cultural resistance that becomes particularly relevant as efforts at population control are directed toward the rural and urban poor of traditionally oriented societies, or even of modern ones. Rationality, planfulness, capacity for delayed gratification, and broad time perspectives, all middle-class virtues that are called for by some approaches to birth control, become psychological luxuries that the extremely deprived, the hope-foresaken of the "culture of poverty" (Lewis, O., 1959; Blake, 1961; Rainwater, 1960) can ill afford. Culturally supported attitudes of resignation, fatalism, and present—rather than future—orientation are presumably clung to because they permit a measure of equanimity in the face of predicitable frustrations; gratifications are grasped heedlessly when they are available because there is no warrant for confidence that forbearance will pay off. Programs aimed at reducing birth rates in such populations will obviously encounter the passive resistance of apathy and erratic performance, if they make demands on resources of planfulness and committing decision-making that are unavailable.[2]

The emphasis in the foregoing has advisedly been placed on obstacles and resistances to persuasive communication as an avenue toward population control, since an over-valuation of the power of the "persuader" seems to be a contemporary culture trait shared by professionals and laity alike. Yet research does suggest circumstances under which persuasive efforts are likely to meet with more success.

One such type of situation is that to which D. Katz and Schanck (1938, pp. 174–175) called attention a number of years ago, with the label "*pluralistic ignorance.*" "People will stay in line because their fellows do, yet, if they only knew that their comrades wanted to kick over the traces too, the institutional conformity of the group would quickly vanish." Where there are taboos or strong barriers against free communication, as is so likely to be the case in regard to sexual matters, states of pluralistic ignorance are especially likely to develop. Surveys of individual attitudes in the area of family planning will often turn up such instances, which then suggest points of vulnerability in the traditional norms that persuasion can capitalize upon.

Thus in their Puerto Rican survey, Hill, Stycos, and Back unearthed pluralistic ignorance that was giving vulnerable support to the *machismo* tenet that men are expected to want large families, especially of sons, as a proof of their masculinity. In fact, however, the men turned out to be even more oriented than their wives to small families. Their wives were unaware of this fact (Hill, R. Stycos, and Back, 1959). To the extent that such constellations of misinformation prevail, programs that seek to induce freer communication can contribute to the emergence and stabilization of more appropriate norms.

A second class of situations that affords optimal opportunities for influence involves the "captive audience." We noted at the outset, as a limitation on the generalizability of psychologists' experimental studies, that they have tended to focus on captive audiences with which exposure to the intended message is guaranteed. Certainly, results from such studies cannot be generalized to situations in which people are freely exposed to competing messages in the mass media, but there *are* important types of situations in which one can count on people receiving the desired message. In these situations there are many reasons to expect communications to be more effective, especially when the circumstances permit prolonged and repeated exposure

2. As noted in other papers in this symposium, the increasingly uprooted urban concentration may be more amenable to innovation than is a traditional peasantry. Other accompaniments of modernization, such as the reduction of high infant mortality and compulsory education, may make individuals more accessible to new ideas and freer from the restraints of group-anchored resistances.

under favorable institutional auspices. An ideal case is provided when the schools are available for instruction in family planning or for the promulgation of small-family values. Whatever messages can be channelled through the classroom not only have the advantage of a guaranteed audience; they participate in the context of "instruction" which as we have seen is likely to circumvent the resistances to which "persuasion" is vulnerable.

While no other case comes to mind that presents equivalent opportunities, there are others that share some of its advantages. For example, a program that enlists the participation of the specialists who officiate at childbirth—be they physicians, nurses, or midwives—gains access for communicating with women during a period when they may be expected to be especially receptive to information about family planning.

Political and Logistical Considerations as Strategic Factors

This selective and speculative survey points to tentative conclusions that come to me almost as a surprise. Existing knowledge, for all its uncertainty, calls into serious question the effectiveness of current effort and practice to attain population control by persuasive means. Even were the many "pilot" ventures to be regularized and multiplied, it seems to me unlikely that enough people would be reached, enough persuaded, enough confirmed in consistent birth-limiting practices, to achieve the socially desirable degree of reduction in birth rates. These doubts follow from the minor impact of persuasive campaigns under most circumstances, the major fact of resistance, and the motivational complexity of many of the widely recommended techniques of birth control. The most strategic class of factors that govern the effectiveness of persuasive communication in this application seem to me to be essentially *political,* not scientific or technical.

Thus, access to the schools and other respected and central social institutions—particularly medical—for the free and legitimate communication of facts and recommendations about family planning is clearly a political matter. Where the dissemination of birth control information is illegal, common agreement would see the strategic problem as one of how to get the law changed—not as a need for research on how to achieve more effective clandestine dissemination. So with the school: there is good reason to believe that schools could play a much more effective role than presently available channels; the political problem of access thus becomes more strategic than research on how to achieve more effective persuasion outside the legitimate institutional framework.

Political considerations are also involved in social decision about the acceptability of particular techniques of birth control, regardless of their effectiveness. The acceptability of the rhythm method and the inacceptability of all others to the Catholic Church is of course a matter of engrossingly strategic politics outside and within the Church. But quite parallel issues involve non-Catholics in value conflicts and potentially political disputes about such undoubtedly effective means as abortion and voluntary sterilization.

Gains on the political front would permit persuasive efforts to be directed to a larger extent than is presently the case in most countries toward objectives and via channels that have a fair chance of circumventing human resistances and producing substantial differences in people's reproductive habits and attainments. *Logistical* problems would then emerge as a close second to political ones in strategic relevance. Well supplied and staffed clinics must be readily available if favorable motivation is to be converted into the desired action. Health educators in large numbers would be needed to convert existing pilot programs into operational ones. Not least, persuasive efforts toward population control will be immeasurably furthered by the cheap and ready availability of chemical and mechanical means of contraception that are designed to fit the specifications of human motivation as well as of human reproductive physiology. The more effectively the design problem is solved, however, the more strategic will political factors become in determining the logistical availability of the perfected techniques!

The Need for Research

In spite of the uncertain and far from adequate state of psychological knowledge about persuasive communication, therefore, I cannot assign high priority in the grand strategy of population control to basic research in this area. There are too many greater urgencies. But there is great need for the feeding back of dependable knowledge of results to guide the development of more effective persuasive programs, and equal need for dependable knowledge about the relevant beliefs, attitudes, and practices of each population that becomes the target of persuasion. The efforts that are called for fall at various locations on the continuum between informal observation and appraisal, systematic surveys and evaluations, and well-controlled experimentation in the field. A limited number of full-scale field experiments—the Puerto Rico study (Hill et al., 1959) is in many respects a model—should amply repay the investment required, in providing the grist from which fresh insights can be developed into the processes by which limitation in birth rate can be induced. But the larger share of investment should go toward incorporating modest provisions for fact-finding, pre-testing, and evaluation into all major action programs. Were this investment made (at a level of ambitiousness roughly proportional to the scope of the associated action program), wasted efforts could be avoided and cumulative wisdom developed about sound practice.

Applied research and program evaluation, then, fits the short-term urgencies concerning the promulgation of birth control techniques. The other motivational problem noted at the outset—that of individual goals for family size and how they may be modified—acquires its priority in a broader time perspective. There is time for basic research on this problem, and there is need. If, as has been suggested, American couples are converging on preference for families of two to four children, what are the factors that tip the decision (which in the long run has vast consequences for population growth) toward the higher or the lower number? How may these preferences be modified? Surveys on American samples provide some leads (Freedman, Whelpton, and Campbell, 1959; Westoff, Potter, Sagi, and Mishler, 1961; Westoff, Potter, and Sagi, 1963). Other hypotheses have been suggested in speculative essays by psychologists (Hoffman, Lois W., and Wyatt, 1960) and by popular writers (Frieden, 1963). Judith Blake (1965) has advocated an indirect approach via the encouragement of female employment outside the home. Basic research now by psychologists and sociologists could provide knowledge that will be badly needed when effective birth control programs have succeeded in narrowing the gap between desire and achievement in family size.

Apart from the priorities that I see as inherent in the field of population control, I hope that my colleagues in psychology will move the field of population research to a position considerably higher in their own scheme of priorities than the less than marginal position that it presently occupies. Because of the intimacy with which fundamental human passions and relationships are involved, the motivational and decisional processes associated with human fertility should provide a rewarding context in which psychologists may come to grips in research with important aspects of personality and social psychology.

20

The Schools and Prejudice

How shall we approach the large and intricate topic of the schools and prejudice? The family, the church, and the school—these are the major institutions of society for the socialization of the young, for inducting them into their roles as participants in a social order that is also a moral order. In our secular times of accelerating social change, both family and church have suffered attrition in their traditional functions. Families, moreover, are hardly more accessible to concerted influence than the individual citizens of whom they are composed. The churches, on their part, no longer reach all children, and they speak to their participants with less assurance and authority than in times past. The school has thus become the preeminent institution through which the perspectives and social orientations of new generations are accessible to influence. We probably ought to reject the romantic conception of the school as an Archimedean fulcrum through which leverage can be brought to bear on society to reform or reconstitute it; the American school system with its traditions of local autonomy is too deeply and complexly embedded in society for that. Nevertheless we must still turn to the school if we wish to rear children who are better fitted for participation in a pluralistic democracy. We must still look to it if we want to understand and to change the processes that keep producing new generations of American citizens who are only partly equipped for democratic participation—and in some ways are badly disqualified for it.

Prejudice, U.S.A., edited by Charles Y. Glock and Ellen Siegelman, published by Frederick A. Praeger, Inc., Publishers, New York, 1969; prepared in cooperation with The Anti-Defamation League of B'nai B'rith. Reprinted by permission. Prepared for the Symposium on Patterns of American Prejudice, University of California, Berkeley, March 25, 1968. The research drawn upon here was supported by grants from the Anti-Defamation League of B'nai B'rith to the Survey Research Center, University of California, Berkeley, for a program of research of anti Semitism under the general direction of Dr. Charles Glock. I am indebted to Mr. Oscar Cohen of the Anti-Defamation League for his encouragement and patience, and to my colleague in the research, Dr. Jane Allyn Hardyck, to whom major credit should go for the execution of the study.

How, then, are we to approach this central and difficult topic? A number of options are open to us.

The ghetto school with its mare's nest of acute and chronic problems has recently attracted belated public attention. As described by Kenneth Clark (1965), Herbert Kohl (1967), Jonathan Kozol (1967), and now James Herndon (1968), the school in the core city ghetto is all too likely to represent an educational system that is *itself* prejudiced against the slum child—especially the Negro slum child. It *prejudges* the child's life chances and arranges matters so as to confirm its pessimistic prophecies about them. It disparages the child—and by undermining the basis on which he could develop self-respect and a sense of efficacy, it cripples his inborn human potentialities for taking advantage of the meager opportunities that remain open to him. It subjects the child to all manner of indignities. The system is manned by teachers and administrators who themselves have more or less prejudiced attitudes. Given their difficult and thankless task and their scant resources for coping with it, prejudice against their educationally unsuccessful pupils is understandable as a last bitter line of self defense. But discrimination against slum children, prejudgment of the child's fate, is built into the system itself. The individual attitudes of teachers and administrative staff are only components of the system, not prime causes or, probably, even strategic ones. If we are looking for the glaringly acute problems of prejudice and the schools, matters of national shame that cry out for drastic remedy, we should surely start with the system itself.

Or we might consider how prejudice is built into the materials of the school curriculum to which virtually *all* children are exposed—innocently by the purveyors of prettified textbooks designed to appeal to middle-class selection committees, or not so innocently, when publishers edit their offerings to appeal to a national market that includes the South. Self-conscious attention to this problem has doubtless led the writers of recent school texts to pay more attention to America's ethnic diversity, and to give more attention to Negro history and to Negro contributions to American history (but not very much, or very honestly: it is hard to be honest with children about the embarrassing facts). For the most part, though, the new textbooks make only feeble gestures in this direction: color a few of the smiling faces black! The persistently bland middle-class orientation of most school materials subtly purveys prejudice, both to the middle-class child, who is given a censored and misleading picture of the social world in which he is later to play a part, and to the slum child, who cannot find his own experience validly represented—who can only conclude that his experience is a matter for suppression and shame, or that school is something irrelevant to be endured and resisted, an agency of "their" world, not of his own.

Or we might start with the young child as he enters the school system. This is a child who has already acquired some crude social categories for sorting people out into "good guys" and "bad guys," who already has his own notions of group identity, who already has absorbed from his parents and from the ever-intrusive TV some of the adult culture of prejudice, but who is still relatively innocent, open and fluid, inconsistent, ready to be educated. We might follow his career to learn how his school experience works upon his initial beliefs and attitudes. We badly need such a longitudinal perspective on the development of prejudice and of democratic orientations, in which the role of the school could be seen in interplay with that of the family, of peer groups, and of the mass media in the lives of individual children. Nobody has done it yet.

Or we might start at the other end, with the adult products of schooling. We might take heart in the secular trend toward greater acceptance of minority groups, toward less agreement with anti-Negro and anti-Semitic statements, as reported by the national polls over the last generation while the educational level of the population has steadily risen. We might note with Stouffer (1955) that younger and better-educated people are more tolerant generally than their less educated elders, and with Stember (1961) that higher levels of education go with less prejudice. Surely we need just now all the sources of optimism that we can glean, and the secular trend toward decreased prejudice is one of these. But we would only delude ourselves if we were to credit the schools with this trend. The decrease in anti-Semitism accompanied not only the world-wide shock at Nazi horrors, but also the disappearance of the Ghetto Jew as an American social type and the replacement of second-generation by third-generation Americans—increasingly inappropriate targets for prejudice. The decline in anti-Negro prejudice (we can hardly count on its continuing) has paralleled the emergence of a Negro middle class and the articulation of civil-rights goals that have the blessing of the established majority elite as well as of Negro leadership. The inverse relationship between educational level and prejudice may mean only that the better educated are more sophisticated, more in tune with the spirit of the times, more closely in touch with liberal values. Those who go on to the higher levels of education are initially a select group, whose qualities—including lower prejudice—cannot be credited with any assurance to the schools.

In the study that I will draw upon here, Dr. Jane Hardyck and I did not do any of these things. Ambitious as our study was, it tried to come to grips with only a small part of the problem of prejudice and the schools. We decided at the outset that we would focus on the development of patterns of prejudice among teenagers in junior and senior high school—an age, as it seemed to us, when the attitudes that young people will carry into adulthood become stabilized, and also—in American culture—a period of potential youthful idealism when young people should be particularly responsive to democratic influences—if such influences are to be had. In order to secure data that were relevant to our focal concerns, we had to make strategic decisions of study design that limit what we can say about other equally important aspects of the problem.

STUDY DESIGN

Through the Survey Research Center at Berkeley, we had the facilities and skills available for a survey-style study of intergroup relations and attitudes in adolescence. This style of research, as its practitioners well know, lends itself to subtle analyses of interrelationships, but runs the risk of overweighting what people say as compared with the more consequential things that they do. We could hardly expect to catch virulent instances of hostile and discriminatory behavior in our net, which was primarily suited for getting at the beliefs and attitudes that young people are able to report under conditions of confidentiality. So we set particularly high priority on securing valid data in one area close to actual behavior where survey methods can go beyond "mere" expressions of belief and feeling: friendship choice. We wanted especially to know the extent to which students' choices of friends cross ethnic and religious lines or are confined to their own ethnic groups. We could find this out by the simple expedient of asking students to name their best friends (a straightforward approach that has been dignified by the label of "sociometric method") and collating these with the responses of the students named to find the self-identified ethnic and religious membership of each. We could collect the data on friendship before the topic of prejudice and intergroup relations had ever been raised, so as to avoid possible distortion on the part of students who knew the democratic "right answer" and might wish to make a favorable impression. But to map out these friendship patterns requires that all the friends named by all the students questioned also be included in the study, and that each student's ethnic and religious membership be self-identified independently.

To secure such unambiguous data on friendship choice, we decided to include *all* the students in entire grades of entire school systems in the study —thus deliberately giving up the advantages of scope and representativeness that a national sample would have offered. As it was, the data that we wanted stretched the tolerance of school administrators and school boards. Of necessity we had to invade regions of considerable privacy. Students had to name names; they had to shed their anonymity temporarily so that their own ethnic identity could be entered in the sociometric analysis; they were also asked quite personal questions about themselves, their beliefs and feelings, and their family backgrounds. Considerable school time was required for the undertaking—three class hours spaced a week apart. This was a lot to ask for, and many school administrators thought, understandably, that it was too much—or preferred to let sleeping dogs lie.

In our initial attempt, we were thrown out of our own Berkeley school system in the fall of 1962. We ended, fortunately, with the full cooperation of three school systems in the East: one, near metropolitan New York, which we call *Commutertown*; another, also in the urban East but farther from

New York, which we call *Oceanville*; and a third eastern industrial city in the midst of a rural area outside any metropolitan orbit, *Central City*. By good fortune rather than by design, all three systems turned out to have about the same proportions of Negro students—14 or 15 per cent. And they varied dramatically in the proportion of Jewish students: 43 per cent in Commutertown, 27 per cent in Oceanville, and less than 1 per cent in Central City.

Of course, the three communities were far from comparable in other respects—we cannot claim a neat "experimental design." Commutertown was clearly the most sophisticated, and its Negro students included children of middle-class professionals. Central City had larger numbers of blue-collar industrial workers and few Catholics. In each of the three communities we studied the entire tenth and twelfth grades in the central high school, and the eighth grades in the elementary schools or junior highs that fed into it. We collected our data in 1963. We are dealing here with substantial numbers of students—2,300 in Commutertown who identified their own race and religion and were therefore suitable for our analyses, 1,200 in Oceanville, and 1,800 in Central City. But it must be remembered that despite the safeguards provided by variation in community characteristics and by the use of large numbers, our study was not representative of the United States. It did not include the segregated ghetto high schools of major Northern cities, nor did it extend to the South or to rural or small-town America.

Thus our focus on intact grades in the differing school systems of three very different communities obviously does not allow us to generalize safely about levels of prejudice among teen-age students in the nation at large. Indeed, it makes no sense to add up our results across the three school systems: we kept them separate throughout our analysis. But our strategy has other advantages besides the possibility of yielding valid data on intergroup friendship. The causal processes that engender, support, or modify prejudiced attitudes are embedded in school and community; they may differ from one school system to another. Our approach gives us the chance to detect such differences when they exist and not wash them out in national averages. Where relationships hold across communities as diverse as Commutertown, Oceanville, and Central City, we can have a good deal of confidence in their general relevance. Where the relationships differ, we have the opportunity to track the differences down to special features of particular situations, and, hopefully, to move through these particulars to a higher level of generalized understanding of the underlying processes.

Main Findings

Here I can only draw selectively on some of the main findings, using a broad brush, in anticipation of our detailed report. A good starting point is the picture of in-group and inter-group friendship that emerged from our analysis of the sociometric data.

Friendship Choice

We had asked each student to name his or her five closest friends of the same sex and grade. (Responses of boys and girls were analyzed separately.) For each category of student, defined jointly by race (Negro-White), religion (Catholic-Protestant-Jewish), sex, and grade in school, we first examined the extent to which the students' choices of friends were concentrated within their own racial-religious group. This analysis made use of an index that takes into account the proportions of students of each race and religion who are available as possible friends in each sex, grade, and school. A first fact —hardly surprising as it reflects one of the more dependable constants of social human nature—is that in all three communities, students tend to choose their friends from their own racial-religious group. This is particularly true of Jewish students, and even more so of Negroes. (Guess why!) Among the Protestant and Catholic boys and girls of the white "majority," this tendency toward in-group choice is by no means extreme. There is some trend from the eighth to the twelfth grade for an increasing proportion of choices to go to the in-group.[1]

The same data can be looked at to answer the further question, Do students belonging to the two "minority groups," Jewish and Negro, *receive* friendship choices from members of the other ethnic-religious categories in proportion to their representation in each sex and grade? Of course, they do not. The indices of cross-group choice to Jews and to Negroes are overwhelmingly negative, with the exception of white Protestant boys and girls in one of the Oceanville eighth grades and white Protestant girls in one of the Commutertown eighth grades; these name Jewish friends at a level a bit higher than chance.

But the story is clearly different for Jews and for Negroes. In Commutertown and Oceanville (the two communities in which there are enough Jewish students to make this analysis possible), white Catholic and Protestant high-school seniors underchoose Jewish students as friends at a level represented by indices ranging from —.15 to —.87 (where —1.00 represents total exclusion and 0 represents nondiscrimination in friendship); the mode is around —.50. As for choices to Negroes, they are very few in any of our three communities, at any grade level. At the twelfth grade, our indices for the various choosing groups center around —.95. The indices are near the absolute ceiling of under-choice; indeed, there is not enough variability to permit us to explore the factors that are linked to friendship with Negroes, either as causes or as effects.

Thus far, then, we have learned that students in each ethnic-religious group tend to find friends among themselves; Gentile students somewhat under-

1. Our data are cross-sectional, not longitudinal (following the same individuals through time), so caution is in order here and elsewhere in drawing inferences about trends. We have considerable confidence in these inferences, however, since differences between eighth, tenth, and twelfth grades generally hold up for smaller special samples from which transfers into the schools and drop-outs (as of a year later) are eliminated.

choose Jews as friends; and white students hardly choose black ones at all. (Incidentally, Negro students name whites as friends substantially more often than they are named by whites—an indication of where the problem lies.) I would not want to ascribe these findings *entirely* to prejudice. Although it has become customary in the social sciences to use "ethnocentrism" as a fancy synonym for prejudice, one can prefer one's own, and preferentially seek one's friends from among them, without derogating the other. In a pluralistic society that finds value in diversity, we should expect and even welcome some persisting bias toward choice of friends from within one's own ethnic or religious group. But the virtually unpenetrated barrier against even same-sex friendships between Negro and white students clearly reflects prejudice. And at the same time it is itself a major obstacle to the reduction of prejudice. Desegregation that fails to lower this barrier remains in essential respects a token gesture.

Who Chooses Jews?

So far, we have been examining the patterns of friendship choice that prevail among broad ethnic-religious categories of students. Our next step is to inquire about the social characteristics that go with naming a friend from a religious or ethnic group other than one's own. But we have already seen that so few of our white students name Negro friends that we cannot pursue the question in regard to intergroup choices of Negroes. So we are left with the alternative question, echoing the old jingle, who "chooses Jews?"

Our analyses of the social characteristics of non-Jewish white students that go with their naming a Jewish friend emerge with two indices which, taken jointly, go far toward accounting for whether a student in Commutertown or Oceanville, where the possibility exists, will indeed have a Jewish friend. The first combines several aspects of family background: whether the student is Protestant or Catholic, whether his father does white-collar or blue-collar work, and whether his father's educational level is relatively high or low. (In each case, the first term mentioned goes with intergroup friendship). These are student characteristics that the school cannot do anything about; they are aspects of its input. The second index, on the other hand, combines three features of the student's school experience: whether or not his eighth-grade school was attended by a substantial proportion of Jewish students, whether or not he participates in extracurricular school activities, and whether or not he is enrolled in the college preparatory program.

Figure 20.1 shows the degree to which these two indices, taken jointly, can predict whether a "majority" student in Commutertown or Oceanville will name a friend who is Jewish. Up and down in the chart are differences in our index of family background; from left to right is our school index. Note that only 8, or 15 per cent, of the students who are low on both indices have a Jewish friend, while 72, or 86 per cent, of those who are high on both indices name at least one.

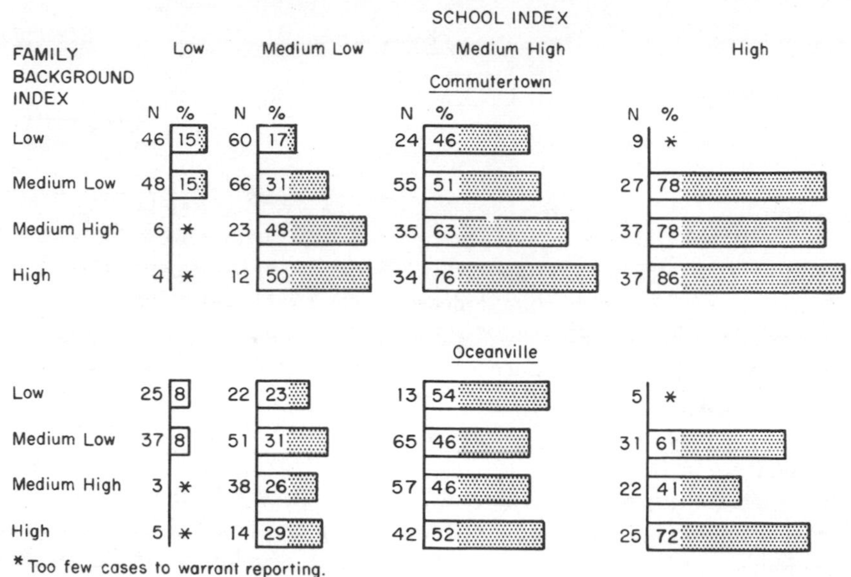

FIGURE 20.1. WHO CHOOSES JEWS?
Percentage of non-Jewish white students who name at least one Jewish friend

We began this analysis with the thought that the two indices represent the familiar factors in friendship of similarity and propinquity: Gentile students who are higher on the index of family background should be more similar to the Jewish students in their schools, and those who are higher on the school index should be thrown into more frequent interaction with them—and friendship should thrive. The only trouble with this interpretation is that two closely similar indices that are usable in all three communities[2] correlated not only with friendly attitudes toward Jews, but with friendly attitudes toward Negroes as well—where the argument from similarity and propinquity cannot hold. The revised school index, based only on participation in activities and in the college prep program, is a particularly strong and consistent predictor of unprejudiced attitudes. It looks as though this index reflects the influence of liberal values and life style as much as that of opportunity for friendly contact.[3]

Opportunity for friendly contact between groups, reflected unambiguously in the ethnic balance of the student's eighth-grade school as a component of

2. Since Central City had very few Jewish and relatively few Catholic students, religious preference had to be omitted from the index of family background, and composition of eighth-grade school from the school index.

3. Note in the figure that in both communities the school index is related to friendship with Jews, but the index of family background—which is substantially a matter of social class—shows a clear relationship only in Commutertown. When we turn from actual friendship to data on attitudes, the relationship of social class to prejudice, which was marked in Commutertown, also failed to appear consistently in the other two communities. This is one of the community-specific findings that our study highlights.

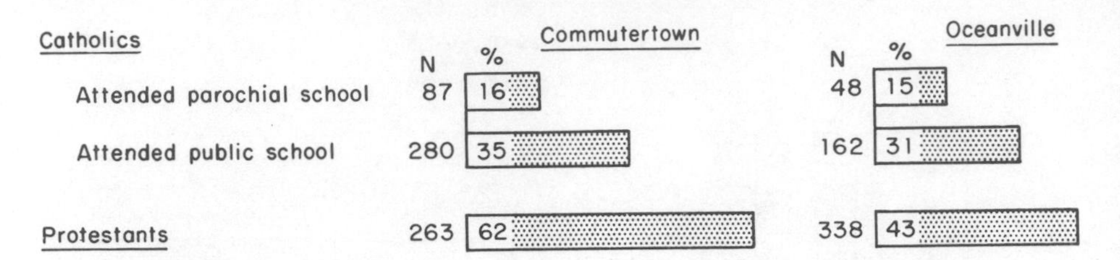

FIGURE 20.2. RELIGION, PAROCHIAL SCHOOL, AND FRIENDSHIP CHOICE
Percentage of non-Jewish white students who name at least one Jewish friend

our school index, clearly influences the development of friendships and, as we shall see later, of unprejudiced attitudes, in its own right. Its influence accounts for part, but not all, of the difference between Catholic and Protestant students in friendships with Jews, as in Figure 20.2. Catholic students who entered the public high school from parochial school were of course barred from school contacts with Jews during their parochial years; their friendships with Jewish students, if they were to develop at all, began after they entered the public high school where we encountered them. This account of the difference they show from Catholics who had attended public school seems the most plausible one, though specific influences of parochial-school teaching or of differential family background cannot be excluded.

Even though the subjects of our study were adolescents, the role of their parents should not be totally ignored. The students reported substantial pressures from their parents against Jewish-Gentile friendships. These pressures, as the students report them, are greater for twelfth-graders than for eighth-graders, are stronger for girls, and increase most over the grades among students who are dating. Our data suggest that parental pressures in Jewish families may actually restrict the friendships of their children. For Gentile students, the picture is inconclusive: parental pressures may be effective in Oceanville, but seem even to backfire in Commutertown where the school leaders are Jewish.

Prejudice Against Negroes and Jews

From patterns of friendship we can now turn to attitudes. We used two principal measures of prejudiced attitudes. One was an index of "social distance," or willingness to accept minority persons in social relationships of varying intimacy; the other was an index of agreement or disagreement with unfavorable beliefs or "stereotypes." We could not safely assume that prejudice when it exists extends to all members of ethnic groups that differ from one's own: perhaps students might feel differently about fellow teenagers from minority groups and minority members of the adult world. With half the students, we therefore inquired about their attitudes toward minority adults; with the other half, about their attitudes toward minority teenagers.

The measure of social distance presented the students with four hypo-

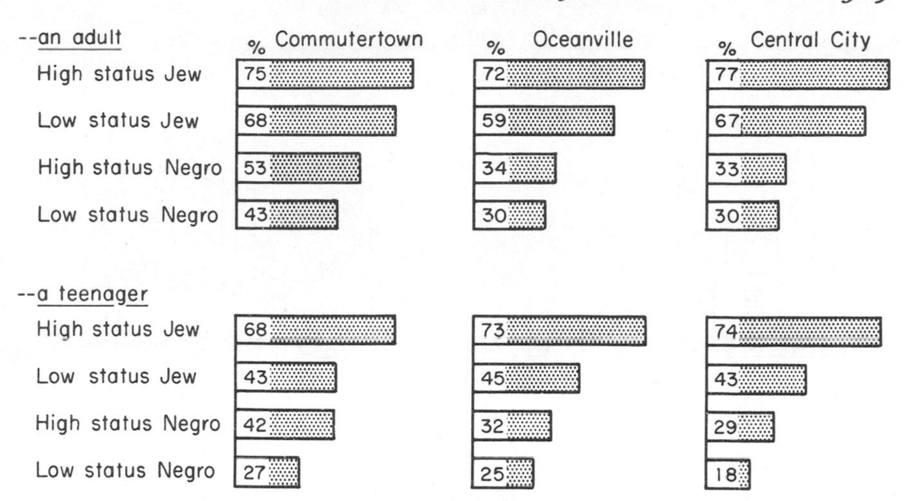

FIGURE 20.3. A COMPONENT OF "SOCIAL DISTANCE"
Percentage of non-Jewish white students who express willingness to have "as a close personal friend" an adult or teenager of a minority group

thetical people in turn (either adults or fellow teenagers of the same sex as themselves); two Jews and two Negroes, whose relative social status was indicated by information about their educational level and job, for the adults, or about their school program (academic or vocational) and average grades, for the teenagers. About each of these "stimulus persons," the student was asked ten items, representing different degrees of intimacy. Results for a representative item in the more intimate half of the scale—willingness to have "as a close personal friend"—are shown in Figure 20.3. About three-quarters of the students say they would be willing to have a high-status Jew as a close personal friend—perhaps a high figure, but remember that one quarter would not. Note also that while one-third to one-half of the students say they would similarly accept a high-status Negro, we have already seen that very few of the students actually named any Negro among their five best friends.

The measure of prejudiced beliefs was based on the student's degree of agreement or disagreement with twenty items suggested by previous research on anti-Semitic and anti-Negro prejudice. Figure 20.4 shows comparative results for seven representative items, including one favorable item concerning intelligence. We have adjusted our net here to catch even the mild prejudice of agreeing "a little" to each item.

Our major analyses employed summary scores based on all ten social distance and all twenty belief items. The salient facts for our present purposes are these:

1. Children come into the eighth grade already furnished with prejudices. They do not change greatly in prejudice, for better or worse, over the high-school years.

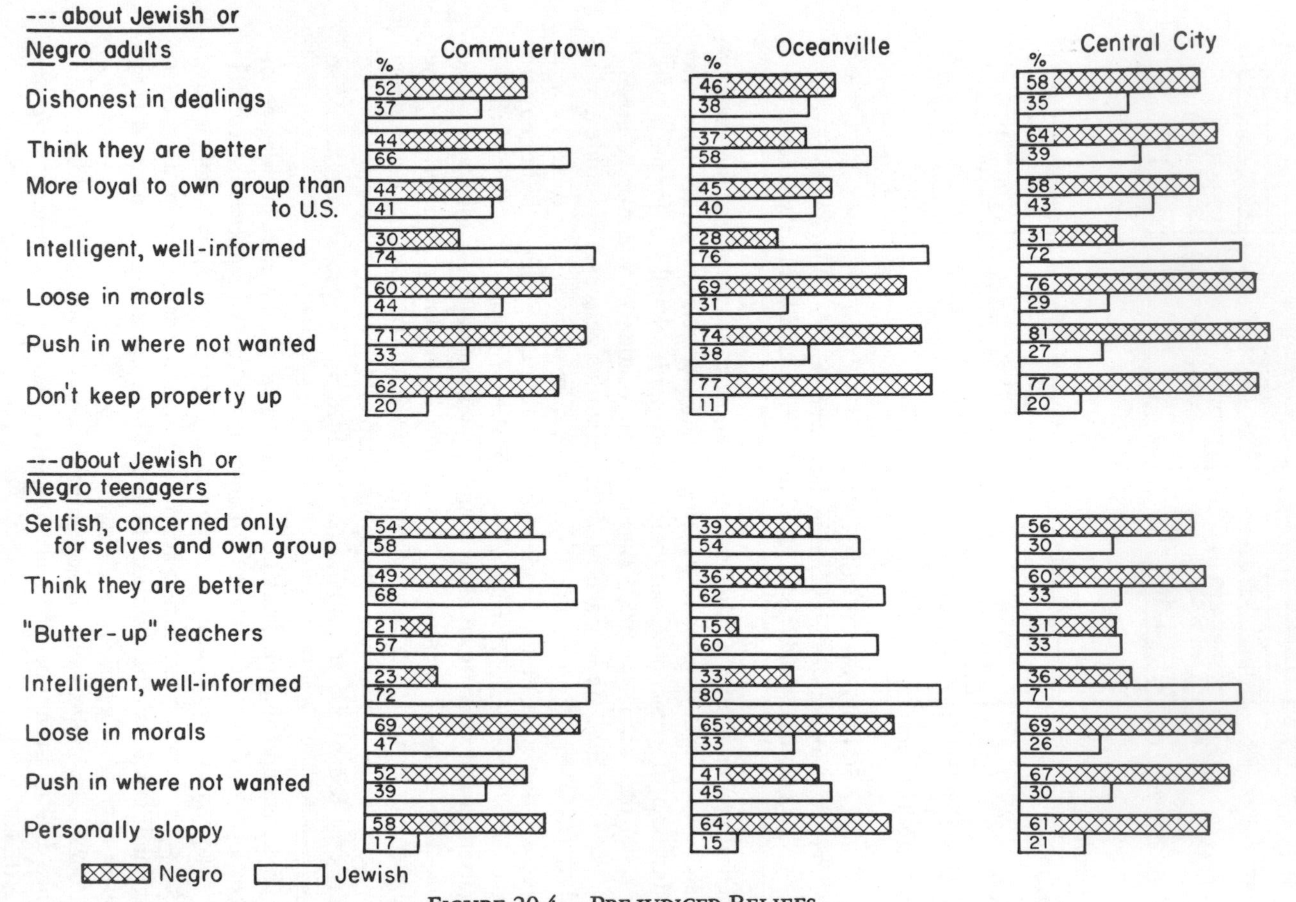

FIGURE 20.4. PREJUDICED BELIEFS

Percentage of non-Jewish white students who agree at least "a little" to the items listed above

2. Over the grades, there is a trend toward some decrease in expressed social distance toward Jews (counter to the trend we observed in *actual* intergroup friendships). In regard to Negroes, what changes appear are in the direction of *increased* social distance. Community differences appear in regard to social distance toward Negroes—most in Central City, least in Commutertown—but not in social distance toward Jews.

3. In regard to acceptance of unfavorable beliefs about Jews, the two communities with appreciable numbers of Jews show an *increase* in stereotyping from eighth grade to twelfth grade. (Central City, with few Jews, shows some decrease). The contrast with the trend for social distance is one of the puzzles in our data. In general, the larger the proportion of Jews in the community, the more the stereotyping by the non-Jewish whites.

4. Prejudice is not all of a piece. While in all communities and samples there are positive relationships between various indices of prejudice—of beliefs, feelings, and preferred social distance—and between prejudice toward Jews and toward Negroes, these relationships are only modest. Prejudice toward minority teenagers appears to be somewhat less firmly structured than prejudice toward adult members of minority groups (most likely because it depends more on the student's own varied experience with the objects of prejudice, and less on the transmission of prejudiced culture), and it enters into a somewhat different pattern of relationships. As for the *content* of prejudice, the profile of anti-Semitism most closely resembles the profile of anti-Negro attitudes in that community (Central City) where there are virtually no Jews; the resemblance is least in heavily Jewish Commutertown. In the absence of Jews, attitudes toward Jews evidently reflect generalized ethnic prejudice, especially when attitudes toward minority adults are concerned.

5. As we would expect, prejudice toward Negroes is very substantially stronger than prejudice toward Jews, on all measures and in all communities.

6. In the two school systems that have appreciable numbers of Jewish students, Jews are much *less* prejudiced than white Gentiles toward Negroes, and slightly less prejudiced toward white Gentiles than the latter are toward Jews. When we examined the attitudes of Jewish students to members of their own group, we found little indication of so-called "Jewish self-hatred" among these young people.

7. Our data produced no evidence for specifically Negro anti-Semitism. On the whole, the Negro students were, if anything, somewhat *less* anti-Semitic in their feelings and beliefs than the non-Jewish white students in the same schools. Their slightly greater social distance (in two of the communities) seems an inevitable reaction to the social realities that in fact exclude them from real friendship with virtually all white students, Gentile or Jewish.

Prejudice, in these schools, is a white Gentile problem!

Value-Similarity and Prejudice

We were particularly interested in identifying factors related to prejudice that might furnish leverage for remedial action in the school. One such appeared dramatically in the results of a restudy by Dr. David Stein of the Commutertown eighth-graders when they reached the ninth grade (Stein, 1966; see also Stein, Hardyck, and Smith, 1965, for confirmatory evidence.) In a complex research design (the sort that earns one a Ph.D.!), he got the ninth-graders to indicate their feelings and preferred social distance toward several fictitious students, part of whose purported questionnaires from the previous year were excerpted as a basis for reaction. Background information about the race and social status of the fictitious students was varied systematically, as was also each fictitious student's supposed responses to a set of questions about his personal values—so as to present fictitious response patterns either very much like the student's own (as determined the year before) or contrasting with his own. For white Gentiles, Jews, and Negroes alike, similarity or dissimilarity of personal values turned out to be a far more powerful determinant of liking and social distance than is social status, race, or religious affiliation—a finding very much in line with the theories of prejudice advanced by Milton Rokeach (1960).

But there is a catch. When information is *not* available about similarity of beliefs and values—and in real life this information remains hidden except in intimate relationships—the students' preferences, by default, are much more strongly influenced by the race and religion of the "stimulus person" and to a lesser extent by his status. Moreover, when "majority" students are asked to give their feelings about an otherwise unspecified "Negro teenager" —embedded in a long list of kinds of people that our main study inquired about—they react to this unspecified teenager much as they do to the *particular* Negro teenager whom Stein presented as having lower status and values unlike the respondent's own! Prejudice reveals itself in the *assumption* of dissimilarity.

Clearly there are implications here for the kind of educational experience that might penetrate and dislodge prejudiced attitudes. If young people can get to know one another well enough to discover essential similarities where they had previously assumed differences, prejudice can crumble. But they must *encounter* one another for that to happen. Cross-racial encounters at this level of intimacy were rare events indeed in our three school systems.

Schools, Teachers, and Prejudice

So far, we have been talking about the patterns of friendship and prejudice among adolescents in three school systems. We have said nothing about the schools and the teachers. We have almost treated the schools as "catchment areas"—mere geographical locations where eighth, tenth, and twelfth graders can be counted upon to be when you look for them. So far as deliberate teaching or programming for intergroup education is concerned, the metaphor is not far amiss. Not much was going on.

Our data, to be sure, contain hints of things going on among the students themselves that affect their attitudes toward other groups. In Commutertown, for example, where school life is dominated by a mainly Jewish leading crowd, the distinctive relationship that appears there between social class and prejudice seems to be the consequence of a class-linked polarization of informal student leadership that is also polarized along religious lines. WASP's and white Catholic students who belong to the in-group of the Jewish dominated system tend to set their followers a pattern of very favorable attitudes toward Jews. But there is a second, lower-class leading crowd of outsiders, the white Gentile participants in which tend to be more anti-Semitic than their followers. It seems likely that their antagonism to the official school leaders as upper-crust Jews has much to do with the relation between social class and prejudice in Commutertown High School.

But what of the teachers? In each of the schools, we asked teachers of the classes included in the study to fill out a questionnaire that focused on their own experiences with intergroup incidents and with educational approaches to promote better intergroup relations. Not all the teachers cooperated, but most did, presumably including the ones who were most constructively involved with the topic. A majority of them indicated that matters concerning minority groups or intergroup relations should be discussed in a matter-of-fact way when they come up, in or out of class. The striking finding, however, is how very little they claimed to have actually discussed these matters. Only one-third said they had ever discussed Negro history and culture in class, and only one-fourth any issue of Negro-white relations. For the corresponding Jewish topics, the proportions were about one-fourth and one-tenth. Very few claimed to have discussed intergroup topics with individual students outside of class. And we may be sure that these very rough figures are substantially inflated.

I would not claim that talk by teachers and classroom discussions are the only ways, or the best ways, that schools can contribute to the education of their students for democratic living in a pluralistic society. Probably they are not: decisions in regard to classroom and activity grouping, for example, are surely more important. But the picture we gain from the teacher questionnaires is one of passivity and unconcern. The results are depressing to inspect.

In summary, the complete barrier that excludes real friendship between black students and white in all three of our school systems is shocking and cannot be accepted for the future.

The big problem for the schools studied was not anti-Semitism but anti-Negro attitudes and behavior. The fact that cross-group friendships were most likely to develop on the part of students who spent the eighth grade in ethnically well-balanced schools is important and encouraging. This is a finding we can do something about. It indicates that desegregation is a minimal condition for the development of good intergroup relations and attitudes. But desegregation per se is not enough. It is also important that similarity of beliefs and values overrides considerations of race and religion—when students know one another well enough to become aware of the similarities that exist. Unless schools take steps to encourage communication and human encounter, students will go their blithe way ignoring members of other groups on the assumption that they are "different."

At root, our story is one of the school's missed opportunities—one of what did *not* happen educationally to these teenagers, not of what happened. Change in prejudice was minor—but then, nobody was trying very hard to do anything about it.

21

The Crisis on the Campus

My subject is the crisis on the campus, and by now it should be clear enough that "the campus" is not just an elliptical reference to Berkeley. The disturbances of the 1964 Free Speech Movement (FSM) and its sequellae were the first to catch public attention in the United States, and for better or worse, Berkeley seems to be stuck with the uncertain honor of symbolizing these developments. But variations on the theme soon burst forth at major institutions throughout the country, and recent events in Eastern and Western Europe suggest a worldwide dimension to the present unrest of college and university youth. (In Latin America and many of the developing countries, such unrest has been endemic.) Confronted with signs of crisis that may indeed have far-reaching implications, a psychologist's first responsibility, I think, is to struggle toward whatever clarity he can attain in understanding what it is about—and to avoid the posture of immediate condemnation that seems so natural to the spokesmen of established adult society. First, facts and interpretations; then we can begin to think responsibly about what ought to be done.

I think there *is* a crisis. I do not at all agree with Robert Nisbet (1968), who pooh-poohs the idea in defense of the university's traditional mission of professional scholarship. According to Nisbet, the universities have always been in crisis anyway, and they are hardly in crisis now, except perhaps for the schools of liberal arts, which he thinks are in danger of responding unwisely to the siren call for a new wave of "life adjustment education." Nevitt Sanford (1962) is his *bête noire.* No, I think there is a crisis, a substantial failure of established patterns that, on medical analogy, offers hope as a potential turning point in the welfare of the patient. The wave of student protest is a surface symptom, a sign that the patient is alive, if you will, rather than an indication of mortal illness.

The campus crisis is interlocked with the other crises under consideration in this symposium. Were there not among many young people a feeling of desperation about the Vietnam war and about the rights and opportunities of Negroes—a loss of faith in normal governmental processes, a con-

Presented at the Symposium on "Ethics and Responsibility in Social Crises," New York State Psychological Association, New York City, May 4, 1968.

viction that the Establishment is both monolithic and evil—the crisis would be much more hopeful than it is. Because of desperation and cynicism among many of the more articulate students about these larger matters, which for the most part lie outside the range of their effective action, they are likely to be more intransigent, less reasonable, in their demands on the institution that *is* within range. And they have learned the tactics of intransigence: in Mississippi and in the early, successful phase of the civil-rights struggle generally, they discovered how the powerless can wield power after all. Student Power and Black Power are both offspring of the early glories of the civil-rights effort.

Iceberglike, the crisis on the campus has massive components that lie beneath the surface, as well as visible crags and peaks. There is the financial crisis that accompanies sky-rocketing costs, the increasing proportions of youth that seek undergraduate and graduate training, the exhaustion of the states' taxing powers and of private philanthropy and endowment funds, and the irrationality and instability of support from the federal government, which has come to bear an ever-increasing part of the load. This is not my area of competence. There the matter of scale and its attendant problems: the "multiversity," the large municipal or state university with its impersonality and bureaucratized procedures—"Do not fold, spindle, or mutilate." There is the rising conflict between traditional educational values and the requirements of rational technology as applied to mass higher education. Closed-circuit TV, automated teaching, and rationally programmed educational planning and cost accounting may be compatible in principle with values of the obsolescent sort of higher education that we idealize in our memories, but in actuality the conflict is real. Too often progress seems to have meant specialization, fragmentation, and dehumanization.

We are also surely experiencing the impact of a massive cultural change in sense of relevance on the part of the young—a change that puts a strain on classroom communication with their elders on the teaching faculty. No one has seen the educational challenge of this change more clearly, I think, than the Berkeley historian Carl Schorske (1967), who puts the crisis of the university squarely in the context of the larger cultural crisis. Faith in Reason, the heritage of the Enlightenment, is faltering, says Schorske, since

> the unity of normative and instrumental reason, so fundamental to the practical idealism of the philosophers and our founding fathers, has broken down. . . . Reason is increasingly perceived by the most sensitive men of our culture . . . to have run amok at the expense of life. . . . The promise of life, liberty, and the pursuit of happiness emerges hideously distorted as death, repression, and the rat-race in the America of the Vietnam Era. What is the consequence of these perceptions of our most sensitive citizens? That the claims of life, liberty, and the pursuit of

happiness are reasserted no longer in the name of Reason, but against it now, in the name of Feeling.

But, according to Schorske's diagnosis of the situation at the best liberal-arts institutions, the faculty remain committed to rear-guard defense of the legacy of eighteenth-century rationalism, while their more thoughtful students are attentive to the new drumbeat. Let me continue to quote him:

> [The major critiques of the shortcomings of the Enlightenment—by Marx, Kierkegaard, Nietzsche, Freud—that cried out against the persistence of suffering within the self-proclaimed rational order, all] point to the great cultural movements of our own day, to the return of the repressed: to social revolution, religious revolution, existential revolution, and sexual revolution. Put all four together and you will know what it is to be young in the America of the 1960's. Realize that all four involve a critique of pure reason and rational values—of pure knowledge, of learning "for its own sake," of scholarly "authority"—and you will know why the University is in crisis. Precisely in the university, those who feel most strongly, the young, espouse the cause of feeling. For the revolt is against the logic of domination with which, for good historical causes, reason has become identified: a revolt on behalf of the suppressed class, suppressed *caritas,* the suppressed person, suppressed *eros.* Those who think most cooly, the old, the faculty, defend the coolest of human activities, reasoning. Geriatrics reinforces the dichotomy of the cultural confrontation. In the struggle of the disciples of Feeling and the champions of Reason at its fruitful best, the sensitive face the reasonable; at its vicious worst, the righteous stand arrayed against the rigid, the men of mindless passion against the men of passionless mind.

In this context, strident protest on the part of a small minority gains a degree of significance that accords more nearly with the extraordinary journalistic attention that it has received than with the relatively small numbers involved. The facts about this protest that have been coming in from recent research lack the drama and evocative brilliance of Professor Schorske's humanistic account, but they are cogent all the same, and in key respects they bear it out. Here I will draw on findings from a number of recent studies, including one at Berkeley and San Francisco State College that Jeanne Block and Norma Haan have collaborated with me on.[1] I will cut through details to some of the central conclusions that they support.

1. Organized student protest has been primarily a phenomenon of the best campuses, not of the marginal ones (Peterson, 1966, 1968). It tends

1. Recent research on American student activism is summarized and discussed in Block, Jeanne H., Haan, and Smith (1968) and in Sampson (1967). A comparative international perspective on students and politics may be found in Lipset (1966) and in the Winter, 1968, issue of *Daedalus*.

to occur, furthermore, on the sorts of campuses on which administrative policy sets the smallest obstacles in the way of freedom of student expression (Williamson and Cowan, 1966). Like most political and social revolutions, student protest is *not* the revolt of the extremely deprived at the nadir of their deprivation.

2. Furthermore, on these campuses the activists tend to be better-than-average students. They are not the marginal students, the dregs or "kooks" of journalistic imagination. They are more oriented than others toward intellectual and humanistic values (see Sampson, 1967). They do tend to come disproportionately from the social sciences and humanities.

3. Like the alienated drop-outs, protesting students are more likely than their classmates to share the new values of feeling that Schorske depicts. They subscribe to the ethic of spontaneity, love, authenticity, curiosity, creativity, and freedom, and (in comparison with students at large) tend to reject the older Protestant ethic of rationality and planfulness, order, control, and wordly ambition (see Smith, Haan, and Block, 1969).

4. When the quality of the thinking by which they resolve classic moral dilemmas is assessed (by Lawrence Kohlberg's Moral Judgment Scale), the protestors are substantially more likely than the common run of students to display a morality of well-internalized principles—and less likely to reason in terms of conventional "good-boy" or "law-and-order" morality (Haan, Smith, and Block, 1968). The activists, that is, include a high concentration of morally sensitive young people. The quality of their moral judgments is, on the average, at a higher developmental level of considered reciprocity and individual conscience as compared with the received conventional morality that predominates among their less involved and committed peers. Their morality, we see, tends to differ both in *content* (the values to which they subscribe) and in *process* (the qualitative features of their moral thinking that we have just noted).

5. The protestors tend to come from family backgrounds that are humanistic rather than authoritarian. For the most part, they are not in revolt against their parents so much as against the failings of society that their upbringing has left them intolerant of (see Smith, Haan, and Block, 1969; also Flacks, in Sampson, 1967).

6. But, of course, they are not all of one stripe. When we sort out the protesting activists in our study into subsamples who are in relatively good rapport with parental values or who are in sharp clash with them, it is the *former* group who distinctively report a humanistic upbringing. (Note that I do *not* say a "permissive" one.) The latter seem, indeed, to be in revolt against an authoritarian personal past, and not surprisingly, they show more signs of personal conflict and disorganization. Their values also come closer to the "hippie" orientation (Block, Jeanne H., 1968).

As we scan research findings such as these, we find evidence here of something more than the perennial generation gap, something more than the accustomed idealism and dissidence of youth. This is not to deny the differential impact of historically contingent factors that instigate student protest at different periods. In the 1930's there were the Depression, the threat of war, fascism, and the prominent appeal of Marxism; today there is the civil-rights movement, Vietnam, and the ever-present threat of nuclear holocaust as the silent background of contemporary life. The earlier set of prominent issues and causes may have tended to propel students who were politically and socially aware in the direction of ideology and pragmatic political organization, the present set more toward moral concerns and direct existential gestures. Without at all discounting such relevant contrasts in the historical scene, I think that the distinctive style and content of today's protest indeed reflect a shifting ethos, a more radical challenge to established values.

This essay gives me little scope to speculate about the historical causes of this deep-seated change, a change of vital human importance if my perception of it is right. My quotation from Schorske suggests one line of interpretation; the latter half of Kenneth Keniston's insightful book (Keniston, 1965) catalogues many others, with particular emphasis on the psychological consequences for youth of the headlong acceleration of sociocultural change. But there is one historical trend to which I should like to call your attention, since I think it especially bears on what ought to be done about our current generation of protestors and their more passive sympathizers. This is the worldwide trend, not so much toward democracy, as against paternalism.

Wherever one turns in recent discussions of the management of human problems, one finds the insight being proclaimed, as if by parallel spontaneous generation, that human problems stay solved only if those affected play the major part in their solution. The idea crops up from all quarters—mental health and psychotherapy, corrections, industrial management, Indian affairs, national and community development, poverty programs, and *even* the school and campus. Looked at more closely, the idea concerns both ends and means. As to means, the increasingly prevalent assumption is that paternalistic intervention is self-defeating, breeding passivity or resentment or both. But underlying the choice of means that involve people in matters that affect their fate are shifting priorities in regard to ends—the spread of the view that social competence and self-determination, not "adjustment" or "mental health" or security, is the proper state of man. There is a good deal of research that bears upon these issues (Smith, 1968b), but I think it is fair to say that the shifting intellectual climate in regard to them is to be viewed as part of a general change in the cultural atmosphere —a change of the same order as the shift in balance from Reason to Feeling that Schorske has emphasized.

Why is this change happening just now? Why are the new insights, proposed as general human truths, being promulgated today instead of thirty or sixty years ago? I suspect it has something to do with the ripening general affluence of Western industrialized society, with the pace of social change, with the erosion of traditional authoritarian religion as a survival of earlier traditional society, with attendant changes in the family and in child-rearing practices. Whatever the complex causes, the phenomenon is surely a major feature of our present historical situation, one that we tend not to see clearly as a whole because we are so much immersed in it. On the campus we ignore it at our peril. It seems to me that the urgent, strident call for student self-determination is an ingredient of the crisis on the campus that is coordinate with the revolt against rationalism.

"Student power," like Black Power, has its substantial compensatory values but can readily turn to viciousness. And the romantic nonideology of "participatory democracy" shared by the student New Left identifies the problem but falls far short of offering institutionally workable solutions to it. If the major challenge to the teacher is to regain relevance to the perspectives and concerns of the present generation of students, the challenge to campus administration is to find institutional ways of enlisting the collaboration of students in a joint educational enterprise in which the student has something to say about his educational fate. In facing the challenge, educators might remember that the objective is one called for (on the campus, largely in vain) by the mainstream of American educational philosophy since Dewey.

The challenge is exceedingly difficult, like the others discussed in this symposium. Part of the difficulty stems from intrinsically asymmetrical features of relations among students, faculty, and administration. Any socialization relationship has its asymmetrical aspects that pose the problem of how to attain essential mutuality when the flow of influence remains stronger in one direction than in the other. Besides that, even the mobile faculties of today have a half-life that considerably exceeds the brief academic generations of the student body. The faculty inevitably and appropriately have a greater investment than the students in the enduring stability of their educational institution. The faculty understandably tire and go sour when, as at Berkeley, each new cohort of students wants to experience the heroic days of the FSM all over again. This may be very educational for the students, but it is hard on professors. Perhaps unattainable levels of inventiveness, and of tolerance and maturity, will be required to devise and establish, with student participation, institutional forms that are consistent with radically increased reciprocity of respect and influence in a situation thus asymmetrical. "Mickey Mouse" pseudo-solutions will not do. When the starting point is a polarized situation of mutual distrust, the difficulty is much compounded.

On the part of the activist students, we know that this distrust often regrettably takes the form of a new absolutism, a tendency to stereotype the Establishment, the opposition, the past-thirty as beyond hope. It is hard for even an enlightened and well-meaning administration to deal sensibly with that "hard core" of activist leadership whose pose combines romantic anarchism, provocative toughness, and the conviction that, in the face of what they see as a hopelessly corrupt or evil opposition, ordinary political processes with their underlying assumption of good faith are obsolete.

And there are the problems that arise from the embeddedness of the campus in the environing society—dramatized by the debacle of police invasion at Stony Brook but present as a constraining and often disruptive influence on all campuses that are taking their educational responsibilities seriously. If the better campuses concentrate the widespread social ferment of youthful dissatisfaction with the established order, their movement toward a desirable state of "educational community" (my analogy to the "therapeutic community" is intentional) is likely to be at the cost of tense and perhaps untenable town-gown relations. Regents and trustees, legislatures and alumni stand ready to intervene. If the campus is to be a channel for cultural and social renewal, capitalizing on the idealism and commitment of the young—if, in other words, it aspires to go beyond the safely restricted roles of trade school or Ivory Tower—it pays the price of vulnerability to outside interference, censure, and retribution. Truly, the role of a conscientious campus administrator is an unenviable one.

Failure to rebuild community on the campus will have sad consequences for the young and for society. It will push increasing numbers of promising young people into the two extremes of social-political irrelevance that George Kennan (1968) decries, in the most sophisticated critique of student protest from a conservative standpoint that I have seen. (But he tends to blame the young more than I think is helpful.) As Kennan sees it, the illusory subjectivism of the hippie and the destructive absolutism of the alienated rebel are opposite sides of the same coin—both drop-outs from the democratic process by which social and educational problems get solved. Only from an apocalyptic view that gives up the prospect of salvation in this world can one admire either posture, except as a stage of growing up.

So much for diagnosis. What about prognosis and prescription? (Since I am not wearing my "mental health" hat, I can play free with medical analogies!) As in the case of the ghetto slums, I see little hope for rational solutions to the campus crisis so long as Vietnam preempts our resources and attention and undermines our moral hopefulness. In the meantime, faculties and administrations should accept the challenge to regain relevance, to share responsibility more widely, to decentralize. Willy-nilly, they will have to keep reasserting the legitimacy of institutional order on the campus against idealistically anarchist challenge. They can hardly expect to reattain "peace in our time." Hopefully, they will put most of their effort into *earning* legitimacy through increased relevance and through sharing and diffusing the power that they wield. Given the cross-pressures on the university from its various public constituencies, enduring solutions will be very hard to accomplish. We may expect many failures, much ill-feeling and conflict. As with the problems of the urban ghetto, there will be much "backlash" pressure for authoritarian repression, from which can come no good whatsoever.

What can psychologists do? Those of us in the academic world have a full agenda before us. As teachers, we need to reexamine our own teaching and the classroom relationships on which it stands. We need to see whether we can make our teaching help, more than it presently does, to channel the moral enthusiasm of youth into deeper understanding and constructive action. As faculty members, we can do our part in the difficult task of rebuilding the academic community. As researchers, more of us might well study the fascinating social processes that are going on right under our noses. Though psychologists have been notoriously dependent on college sophomores for our "Ss," we know surprisingly little about them as people in a college society that is embedded in a larger social order.

But *all* psychologists are deeply connected with academia and share a formative academic past. We are in an advantageous position to be informed about the nature of the educational challenges that the campuses face and to help to communicate to the larger public their difficulty and complexity, their human importance, and their promise. We can all play a part, major or minor, in recruiting the understanding and support that we so badly need—and so little enjoy—for the colleges and universities as sources of renewal in a disoriented and troubled society.

22

Morality and Student Protest

First, Berkeley—still Berkeley, but now also Columbia, and many other fine campuses. Confrontation becomes a way of life. Tempers fray in the Faculty Room and the Board Room, in the legislative chamber. They also fray where students gather. Tolerance dissipates, mutual distrust mounts. And the events at Columbia—in Europe, too, if we include the worldwide picture, as we probably should—give grim new reality to Mario Savio's rhetoric at Sproul Hall in the days of the Berkeley Free Speech Movement of 1964:

> There is a time when the operation of the machine becomes so odious, makes you so sick at heart, that you can't take part; you can't even tacitly take part, and you've got to put your bodies on the gears and upon the wheels, upon the levers, upon all the apparatus and you've got to make it stop. And you've got to indicate to the people who run it, to the people who own it, that unless you're free, the machines will be prevented from working at all. [Lipset and Wolin, 1965, p. 163]

A minority of student "protestants" can indeed stop the machine, bring it to a grinding halt.

The famous Savio quotation was a call to moral action—action for principle rather than expediency. It is also a cry of moral nausea, of disgust with the established order and of despair for its democratic reformation. Student protest, I will try to show, is a manifestation of strong moral concern on the part of intelligent and sensitive young people. But—in historical perspective the paradox should not be surprising—moral protest readily turns to outrageousness, so that the baffled onlooker, particularly when he

The data reported in this paper were collected in a program of "Studies of the Moral Orientations of Student Activists" in which Norma Haan, Jeanne Block, and I were joint collaborators. The opinions expressed in this paper are my own and do not reflect necessarily the interpretations of the other collaborators. The research was supported by generous grants to the Institute of Human Development, University of California, Berkeley, from the Rosenberg Foundation and the Foundations' Fund for Research in Psychiatry. The paper was presented as the Psi Chi Invited Address at the annual meetings of the American Psychological Association, San Francisco, 1968.

is past thirty, finds it hard to see the morality at all. And indeed, protest can disrupt and destroy what ought to be preserved as well as what ought to be changed or done away with: moral motives by no means guarantee moral outcomes. Romantic radicals and pragmatic conservatives have always disagreed as to whether the really mortal sin is hypocritical exploitation or, rather, the fanatical pursuit of good causes. That argument will not soon be resolved, but it seems clear enough that both have contributed their share of evil to the human lot. Recognition that each side of the argument is right in its charges about the other is, I suppose, the hallmark of the liberal!

The turbulence of the current student generation is heightened for us perceptually by its contrast with the complacent passivity of the Eisenhower era. Today we can be nostalgic as we remember our complaints about yesterday's passive student, who now looks like a postwar aberration, not the product of a long-term trend. In modern Western society, adolescence and youth have traditionally been viewed as a period of Sturm und Drang, which often turns against the established order. Margaret Mead (1928) was surely right that storm and stress are not necessary, pan-human features of adolescence. But they are predictably recurrent characteristics of youth in the modern West, whether we attend to the religious crises of late Victorian youth, the flaming youth of the 1920's, the young radicals of the Depression era among whom I once counted myself, or the New Left activists of today. We do not need to search far, I think, for the reasons why adolescents in Western society have recurrently revolted against the cultural status quo. The status quo has not stayed put. The recent era has been one of accelerating social change, creating "generation gaps" and discontinuities, as well as glaring dislocations of human values (see Keniston, 1965). As the discrepancy between biological maturity and social adulthood widens for the young, moreover, and the culturally provided links between youth and adult roles become more tenuous, the Sturm und Drang of adolescence is bound to increase.

And this Sturm und Drang inherently predisposes youth to be preoccupied with moral issues. It is a sociological truism that society is basically a moral order in which commitment to consensual norms and values forms the warp of the social fabric, and it ought to be a psychological truism that moral commitments, positive and negative, lie at the core of personal identity. Rapid sociocultural change therefore both weakens the moral consensus of society and magnifies the problems of the adolescent in finding an identity for himself. The search for identity now increasingly requires a deliberate, perhaps frightening, choice among *alternative* values. Erikson's concept of the identity crisis has given this common modern predicament a phrasing that has become a part of contemporary intellectual folk culture. When young people can no longer take their moral values for granted, receive them from an unquestioned stable culture, but are recurrently faced with momentous issues for existential choice, it is no wonder that morality—and moral outrageousness, the other side of the coin—take the center of the stage.

Student protest today has its novel aspects, but we should not lose sight of this strand of continuity. If we keep it in view, we should be better equipped to grasp what is distinctive in the present turmoil of confrontation.

Shortly after the eruption of FSM, two colleagues of mine at the Institute of Human Development at Berkeley—Jeanne Block and Norma Haan—and I decided that the moral orientations of protesting college youth called for systematic study. We sensed something new in the moral stance of young people in the 1960's, and we expected to find the new themes in high concentration among the students who had riskily committed themselves in social protest. During the spring of 1966 we therefore collected a variety of data from undergraduate FSM arrestees who still remained at Berkeley and from a comparable cross-section of students at large. The following year we extended the study to San Francisco State College and to groups of Peace Corps volunteers in training. Our technical findings are being reported elsewhere in detail.[1] Here I will draw selectively on our data in order to clarify the distinctive moral position of student activists. But I will not hold myself to a report of research. I am more interested in using the research for purposes of social interpretation. If we can see the moral dilemmas posed by protesting youth in a broader sociohistorical context, we may be able to draw some implications for those of us whose roles call upon us to deal with the young.

Any sociopsychological account of the new student protest has to attend both to characteristics of the students that make them protest-prone and to characteristics of society and its institutions that evoke the protest. When my colleagues and I presented an account of our early findings to the American Sociological Association in 1967, the FSM leader Bettina Aptheker took us to task roundly for focusing on the psychology of the students when, from her Marxist perspective, we ought rather to have been studying what is wrong with society and the university. From her standpoint, what we had to say was not so much wrong as irrelevant. So far as priorities for action go, her point is well taken, and later on I hope to make some amends. But we are psychologists, and in the division of labor it is on the side of student characteristics that we have a distinctive contribution to make.

The Morality of Protesting Students

What can we say, then, about the "new morality" of the college youth who have been engaging in social protest that distinguishes them from their fellow students? There are two ways of looking at the moral posture that

1. See Block, Jeanne H., Haan, and Smith (1968), Smith, Haan, and Block (1969), and Haan, Smith, and Block (1968).

characterizes a person or a set of persons. On the one hand, we can specify the *content* of the moral values to which the person subscribes. On the other, we can examine the distinctive *processes* by which he arrives at his moral judgments. Moral content and moral process need not be independent of one another empirically—we find that they are related—but they should be distinguished conceptually.

Obviously, these two aspects of morality might be studied in various ways. Our choice of methods was dictated by availability in the current kit-bag as backed by research tradition, and by suitability for self-administration in the packet of materials mailed to our respondents.

To get at their distinctive values, we employed a Q-sort in which the respondents were asked to describe their "ideal selves" by sorting 63 adjectives into seven equal piles, ranging from those most saliently descriptive of the ideal self to those most saliently contrary to the ideal self. This amounts, of course, to rating the adjectives on a seven-point scale with a forced rectangular distribution. (We also had the subjects describe their actual selves by the same device, but I will not be drawing on the latter data.) It seems reasonable to view people's descriptions of how they would most like to be as expressive of a major aspect of their moral values.

To get at the respondents' processes of moral judgment, we were fortunately able to draw on Lawrence Kohlberg's impressive recent research (1963, 1964) in the cognitive tradition of Jean Piaget (1932). In personal interviews Kohlberg presented his subjects with ten stories in turn, each posing a classical moral dilemma. One situation, for example, describes a husband stealing a drug for his wife who is dying of cancer. The husband is unable to afford the drug, and all other means of securing it are closed. Was the husband right or wrong to steal the drug and why? the respondent is asked. Further probing questions inquire about the rights of the drugstore owner, a husband's duties, one's obligations to his relatives, and the appropriateness of punishment for the husband. Kohlberg scores the protocols so obtained to gain an index of the level of moral judgment that the individual has attained. Just how the person resolves the dilemmas is less important than the kind of rationale that he gives for his solution. According to Kohlberg's scheme, there are three levels of moral development: I. Premoral, II. Morality of Conventional Role-Conformity, and III. Morality of Self-Accepted Moral Principles. Each is subdivided into two types. Kohlberg has presented evidence that the levels do indeed represent an intrinsic developmental sequence, though of course the controversy continues between his position and that of learning theorists who emphasize reinforcement and continuity.

With Kohlberg's advice, we selected five of his ten stories to use in our study and adapted the probing questions for pencil-and-paper self-administration. From our various samples, 957 subjects responded to the moral dilemmas. Kohlberg trained the judges who scored the protocols of our subjects, using his scoring manual, with a gratifying degree of interjudge reliability.

We thus have a rough-and-ready appraisal of our subjects' values and the most sophisticated available assessment of their level of moral judgment—the sensitivity of which is nevertheless somewhat reduced by the fact that we had to give up the interchange of a personal interview. Before I summarize what we learned about the distinctive morality of student activists, I must first describe briefly the two ways in which we classified our subjects' orientations toward political-social action.

For a first approximation, we simply compared, for each campus, the responses of an activist sample with those of a corresponding cross section of students at large. We had to define "activism" differently on the two campuses. At Berkeley it was a matter of having been arrested during the Sproul Hall sit-in—a single criterial act that, of course, would have a variety of personal meanings. At San Francisco State, which at the time of our study had been spared hostile confrontations, we defined activism for our purposes as membership in one of three organizations that were committed to work in the ghetto or to radical educational innovation. Obviously the criteria are entirely different; where the results of our comparisons run parallel on the two campuses, we may have the more confidence in them.

For a more refined analysis that could use all of our data, including the Peace Corps trainees and special U.C. samples from various student political organizations, we constructed a set of five types of orientation to political-social action on the basis of responses to a biographical questionnaire. *Inactives* belonged to and participated in nothing in college, according to their questionnaires. Since the significant thing about this group *might* be their social isolation, we also identified a group of *Conventionalists,* who belonged to fraternities or sororities but were below the median of the total sample in both social service activities (volunteer work) and protest activities (such as picketing, demonstrations, and sit-ins). Differential participation in social service and protest activities was the basis for defining three additional types. Those who were high on social service but low on protest activities we called *Constructivists;* those who were high on both, *Broad-Spectrum Activists;* those who were high only on protest activities (and indeed checked *no* social service activities), *Dissenters.* We can now look at representative data on the moral orientations that distinguish young people when we sort them out in these different ways.

Moral Content

First in regard to content: values as reflected in the ideal Q-sorts. What items differentiated the FSM arrestees from students in the comparable cross section? For the men, there were a large number, and I will list only the ones that differentiated the two groups at the .01 level by t-test. As you read the items that were more characteristic of the FSM participants, it should be helpful if you adopt a mental set somewhat like that of the subjects in Asch's (1946) classic study of forming impressions of personality from lists of traits—only ask, how would you characterize the value systems of young men who described their ideal selves in these terms? Artistic; critical; idealistic; creative, imaginative; impulsive; doubting, uncertain; rebellious; free, unfettered, not hung up; sensitive. In the same comparison, the terms that were more characteristic of men in the cross section were: conventional; ambitious; competitive, likes to be the best; self-controlled; proud; practical, shrewd; foresightful, plans ahead; orderly; self-confident; masculine.

We made all our analyses separately for men and women. Somewhat fewer items proved to differentiate the two corresponding groups of women, so in their case I list items that distinguished FSM women from the cross section at the .05 level. On the FSM side of the comparison were: assertive; critical; creative, imaginative; rebellious; free, unfettered, not hung up; perceptive, aware; effective. On the side of the cross section: ambitious; foresightful, plans ahead; self-denying; conventional; competitive, likes to be the best; practical, shrewd; orderly; responsible. Remember, these are not necessarily the ideal traits that each group rated highest; they are rather the traits that *discriminate* the activists from the cross section.

What about the corresponding comparisons at San Francisco State College, where the institutional setting, the political climate, the student population, and the criteria of activism all differed from Berkeley? For the men, the two lists of items that distinguish activists from others at the .05 level are these (and I will let you guess which list characterizes the ideal selves of the activists): conventional; ambitious; competitive, likes to be the best; proud; orderly; foresightful, plans ahead; amusing; masculine—versus creative, imaginative; doubting, uncertain; rebellious; empathic, feels for others; open, frank; perceptive, aware; free, unfettered, not hung up; sensitive; responsive. Of course it is the second set that is distinctive of the activists. For the women at San Francisco State: ambitious; self-controlled; practical, shrewd; foresightful, plans ahead; conventional; informed; orderly; sociable, gregarious—versus artistic; sensitive; empathic, feels for others; creative, imaginative; open, frank; perceptive, aware; free, uninhibited, not hung up.

Very clearly, on both campuses, and for both men and women, the activists are comparatively low, and the cross section students high, in a pattern of values that can fairly be labeled the Protestant ethic, perhaps best identified by the four items that appear on all four lists: ambitious; foresightful, plans ahead; orderly; and conventional. The positive characterization of activist values comes through less clearly, since the FSM arrest criterion used at Berkeley pulls in the direction of dissent and protest and the organizational criterion at San Francisco State in the direction of altruism and good works. Nevertheless, there are two items that hold up on both campuses as discriminating for both men and women: creative, imaginative; and free, unfettered, not hung up. These are clearly anti-Puritan humanistic values that the activists share with the hippie drop-outs (who unfortunately remain quite inaccessible to our sort of study).

We made similar comparisons of self-values across the five types of political-social orientation, using analysis of variance and pooling the data from all our samples. To avoid surfeiting you with lists, I will give only the items that discriminate between the five groups of *men* at the .05 level. Among these discriminating items, I will list for each type the ones which respondents of that type rated higher, on the average, than any of the other groups rated them. *Inactives:* conventional, orderly, self-controlled, proud, self-denying, needs approval. *Conventionalists:* ambitious, competitive, foresightful, masculine, practical, responsible, self-confident, dominating, considerate. (Both these groups evidently tend to subscribe to variants of the Protestant ethic. Other data show that in general they differ little from each other.) *Constructivists:* empathic, helpful. (This at least validates our definition of the type, though it throws little additional light on the values that are associated with it.) *Broad-Spectrum Activists:* critical, impulsive, sensitive, restless, empathic, perceptive, artistic, creative, curious. (Here clearly we are in a different realm of values. These people, like the final type, had engaged in two or more types of social protest activity.) And finally, the *Dissenters:* rebellious; free, not hung up; idealistic; open and frank. Again we see a contrast between the Protestant ethic of the Inactives and Conventionalists, on the one hand, and the humanistic, anti-Puritan values of the two types of "protesters," the Broad-Spectrum Activists and Dissenters.

Moral Process

We can now turn to our data on moral process, comparing activists and others on the Kohlberg scale according to the same classifications that have guided our inquiry into moral content. With appropriate procedural safeguards, the protocols of responses to each moral dilemma were independently scored by two judges, story by story, and according to explicit rules detailed elsewhere (Haan, Smith, and Block, 1968), each respondent was assigned to a major and, often, a minor modal type according to the pattern of his scores for the several dilemmas. We will be concerned here only with the 53 per cent of the respondents to the Kohlberg instrument who, by our rules, could be regarded as exemplifying relatively pure types in the Kohlberg scheme. (Had we been able to administer the scale in personal interviews, we should probably have found fewer mixed types and unclassifiable protocols.) Five of Kohlberg's six types were well represented in our sample (only one protocol was classified as representing Kohlberg's Type 1, Punishment and Obedience Orientation.) For the sake of simplicity, I will group the types according to Kohlberg's three levels of moral judgment: I. Premoral, II. Morality of Conventional Role-Conformity, and III. Morality of

Self-Accepted Moral Principles. It should be remembered, however, that Level I's in our data are entirely composed of Type 2's—Instrumental Hedonists. Even these were relatively rare.

Figure 22.1 shows the quite dramatic results of our first comparison—between activists and cross section samples on the two campuses. Data are also given for Peace Corps trainees. What is interesting is the percentages at the highest level, that of principled morality, shown to the right of the solid lines in the figure. On both campuses, the activists are very substantially more likely to be classified at the highest developmental level on the basis of their moral reasoning.

Some details in the figure are worth noting. Among the male FSM arrestees, who were predominantly at Level III, there is a substantial minority of Instrumental Hedonists at Level I. Are these really "moral primitives," corresponding to the public image, or are they rather a special worrysome breed of "postmoral" young people, who are unprincipled "on principle"? It is hard to say, but I would venture that these students are quite unlike people in the general population who would be so classified. The Peace Corps trainees are not markedly different from the two cross section samples. And the activists on the Berkeley campus, where civil disobedience was part of the criterion, are considerably more likely to be classified at the highest level than are their counterparts at San Francisco State, where it was not.

When we play the Kohlberg typology against our own typology of orientations toward political-social action, further light is cast on the connection

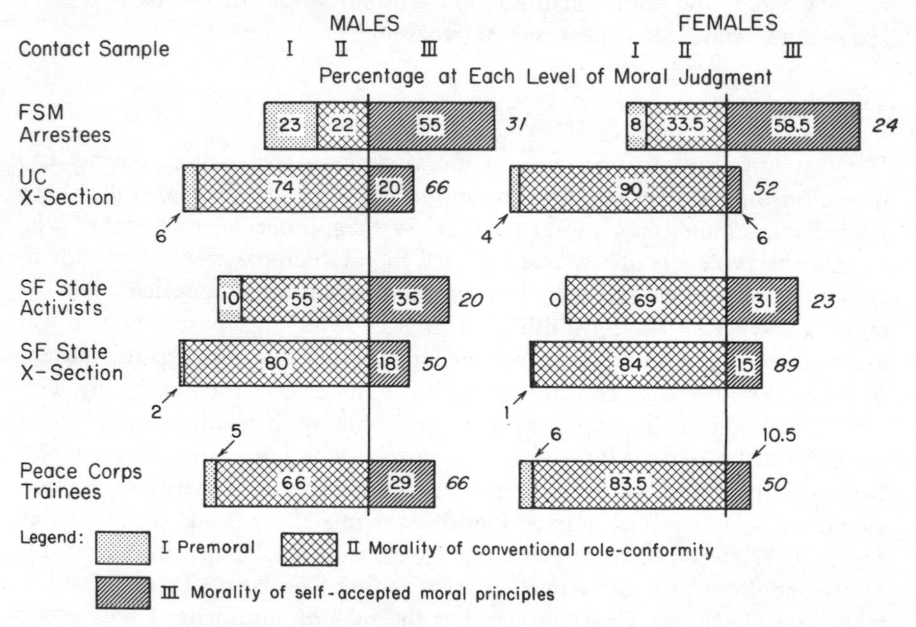

FIGURE 22.1. LEVEL OF MORAL JUDGMENT ACCORDING TO CONTACT SAMPLE

between protest and principled morality. Figure 22.2 shows the data. The Inactives, the Conventionalists, *and* the Constructivists all fall mainly at Level II—Morality of Conventional Role-Conformity. It is the two types who had engaged in substantial protest activity, the Broad-Spectrum Activists and the Dissenters, in which principled morality is especially frequent. When we take into account the nondistinctive pattern of the Constructivists, it seems clear that social protest, not good works, is the hallmark of our principled young people. The data in these two figures, incidentally, are the clearest evidence that I know for a definite relationship between moral thinking and consequential moral behavior.

The Relation Between Moral Process and Moral Content

By now it should be apparent that while our approaches to the study of moral orientations via moral content and via moral process are conceptually and methodologically independent, they are likely to be related to each other empirically. Such is indeed the case. For men and women separately, we used analysis of variance to discover the items in the ideal Q-sort that discriminated significantly (.05 level) among the five Kohlberg types that were represented in our sample. Here are the adjectives that received the highest rating from respondents classified in one of the two types at Level II, for *both* men and women separately: ambitious, competitive, foresightful,

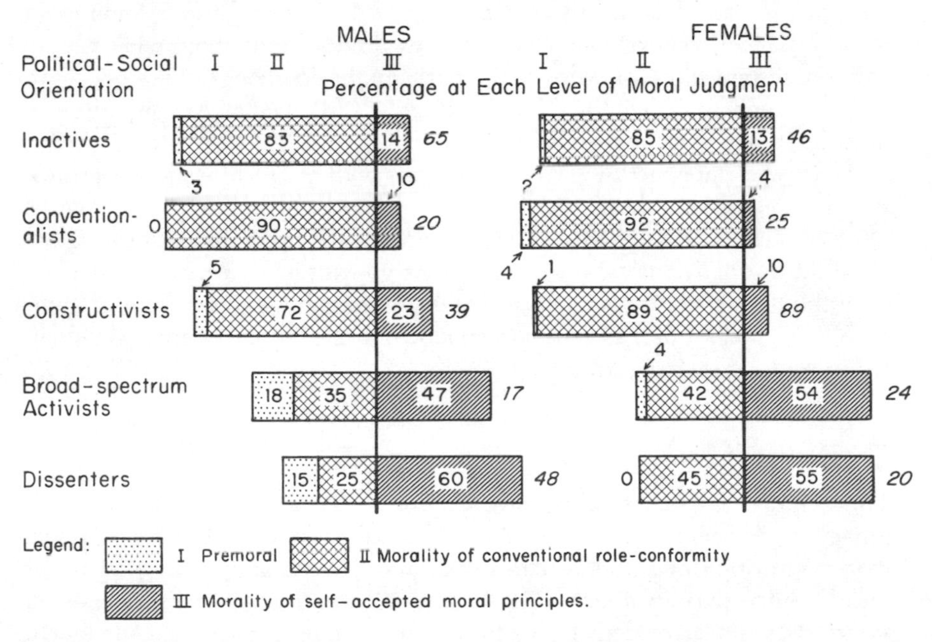

FIGURE 22.2. POLITICAL-SOCIAL ORIENTATION AND LEVEL OF MORAL JUDGMENT

orderly, sociable, and responsible. The familiar values of the Protestant ethic pattern thus are linked, in our data, to Kohlberg's level of the Morality of Conventional Role-Conformity. Our sample at Level I is too small, and probably too special, for attention here. At Level III, the distinctive adjectives are somewhat different from men and women, so I give them separately. The men would distinctively like their ideal selves to be rebellious, idealistic, creative, sensitive, loving, self-controlled, perceptive, empathic, and altruistic.[2] Fewer items emerge as distinctive of the women: again rebellious and sensitive, but also free and individualistic.

At this point in history, then, conventionality in moral judgment goes with a particular, presently conventional pattern of moral values. The Morality of Self-Accepted Principles seems, rather, to be linked with the humanistic values of self-actualization (Maslow, 1954). Spectulatively, one might suggest that the Kohlberg scheme, which is already being used cross-culturally, may be less bounded than the content of moral values by cultural and historical contingency. In other areas and cultures, it seem likely that both conventional morality and self-chosen principled morality might have quite different content.

Morality and Protest in Social-Historical Context

So much for our data. In my remaining time I want to put our findings in social-historical context, so as to draw a few implications about what people who are responsibly concerned with youth might do about the present wave of protest and confrontation. Here I will take full advantage of my hitherto unsullied amateur standing as social critic.

As I try to integrate my own observations with my readings in the professional social critics, I detect four interrelated themes of sociol-cultural change in recent history, each of which seems to me to bear upon student protest and upon the distinctive moral orientations that go with it. These are: the decline of authoritarianism, the waning of the Protestant Ethic, the failure of community in modern life, and the consequent moral exposure of the individual. Let us consider each in turn.

The Decline of Authoritarianism

This century has seen a progressive decline in the claims, power, and legitimacy of arbitrary authority, whether in family, church, or state. I suspect that the attrition of authoritarianism has roots in the accelerating course of social change that we noted at the beginning, which on its part depends on the momentum of modern technology. Technology in turn has contributed

2. Among Level III men, Type 5's would also especially like their ideal selves to be self-controlled, but this anomaly is cancelled by the fact that Type 6's set the *lowest* value on self-control of all five types.

to undermining the religious world view that shored up authority in traditional society, and has produced for most but not all Americans a general affluence that emboldens young people to assert themselves. Be that as it may, one can hardly doubt the trend against arbitrary authority and paternalism.

Convergent data from our own study and that of Flacks (1967) in Chicago suggest that protesting students come from families in the vanguard of this trend. Parents of activist youth are less authoritarian, more humanistic, in relation to their young than is the case with the parents of students at large. Their more rational and more child-respecting, less arbitrary approach to discipline provides the basis for the internalized morality of self-accepted principles that we find especially characteristic of dissident youth.

But the decline of arbitrary authority and the mounting protest against it on the part of the turbulent young proceed falteringly, with friction and mismeshing of gears. Parents who were reared to more paternalistic models are unsure of themselves as they move to newer styles of parenthood; they communicate their lack of assurance to their young. Parental diffidence and vacillation about the assertion of authority, even when it is rationally based, make it especially hard for the children to grasp Erich Fromm's (1941) important distinction between arbitrary or "inhibiting" authority and rational authority, legitimacy based on competence.[3] All too easily they can become the sworn enemies of any authority whatsoever—the posture of the romantic anarchist. Predictably, young people raised in the more humanistic tradition will be triggered into protest and defiance when they encounter —as they do on most campuses—institutional relics of the no longer viable paternalism. As such confrontations escalate, increasing minorities of protesting young people are likely to move toward general and indiscriminate rejection of institutional authority, arbitrary *or* rational.

The Waning of the Protestant Ethic

Accompanying the decline of authoritarianism has been the waning of the Protestant ethic—a relaxation of inner authority, if you will. For young people of the more affluent and culturally sophisticated strata from which our activists are largely drawn, the punitive Freudian superego, the rigidly implanted gyroscope of Riesman's (1950) "inner-directed man," is a museum curiosity. The seeming secular decline in achievement motivation that McClelland (1961) claims to have charted is part of the same picture.

We have already seen evidence that the young activists, like the hippie drop-outs, are also at the forefront of this trend.[4] How we are to view their defection from the values of order, control, rationality, foresight, and success

3. See also Baumrind (1966). David Riesman has emphasized the present relevance of this distinction in personal communication.

4. Note, however, that their academic achievement is high, as Heist (1965) has documented.

depends very much on our own values. If, like McClelland (1961), we take our stand firmly on the ground of the Protestant ethic, we are likely to mistrust the new morality as a sign of the decadence that affluence and pampering brings in its wake. But if we are in more sympathetic touch with the new spirit, we may see it as an adaptive accommodation to a "postindustrial" society that no longer requires of us heroic sacrifice at great psychic cost. We can hope that the trend may bring about a better balance in the human values that people can realize in society, a step toward the goal of "self-actualization" for more people.

But clearly, the new balance has yet to be attained. Young people who are preoccupied with rejecting the rationalism of the Protestant ethic are likely to adopt a romantic style of protest that can be especially vexing to well-meaning adult authorities who would like to negotiate rationally. It also doubtless poses organizational problems for the politics of the "New Left."

Failure of Community

Robert Nisbet, in his scholarly account of *The Sociological Tradition* (1966), has recently pointed to the loosening of the traditional bonds of community as one of the central preoccupations of the great sociological theorists. The quickening pace of sociocultural change has strained some of these bonds to the point of failure, as we all know. Between rich and poor, black and white, the preindustrial and the modernized world are appearing ominous gulfs, reflecting an absence of common experience, common interests, common values, and of the sense of sharing a common human fate. Discussions in a task force of the Joint Commission on the Mental Health of Children and Youth, in which I have been participating, have come to the shared view that a similar failure of community is affecting the relations between young people and the adult world. This is the meaning of the much belabored "generation gap."

Failure of community in all these spheres lays the setting for mutual mistrust, in which inevitable conflicts tend to escalate rather than getting resolved. When, as the saying has it, young people cannot or do not trust anyone over thirty, and we older adults on our part tend to mistrust most adolescents over twelve (the age gets progressively younger!), the scene is set for difficult confrontations, especially when, as we have seen, there are real dissimilarities of values, real grievances, and, in addition, small organized groups of young people who have deepening commitments to stopping the machines of corrupt adult institutions.

Even *among* the young, community is evidently a problem. How else are we to interpret their groping so touchingly for communion (*not* communication: that is too rationalistic) with one another? The mystique of "participatory democracy," as a touchstone of the New Left, perhaps reflects the yearning for community as much as it does the youthful "hang-ups" over authority. The problem is real, the yearning legitimate, but workable institutional mechanisms remain to be devised.

Exposure of the Individual

Failure of community, decline of authority, and attrition of received conventional moral values, all result in the individual's moral exposure. His individuality becomes uncomfortably salient. He is on his own, without the customary supports and guidelines. The predicament is especially severe for the sophisticated young who are in touch with the dissolution of standards and the attendant cultural chaos in contemporary arts and letters, as well as in civility and morals. The most sensitive are most exposed. (And it is true that student protest is most common in the humanities and social sciences, where contact with these cultural currents is closest.)

Our Level III young people are also perilously exposed by virtue of the quality of their moral thinking. It is one thing to make one's moral principles genuinely one's own when they also have the support of a consensual cultural tradition. In this case, the principled Level III's would enjoy much the same benefits as the conventional Level II's, with the added resource that their values are more maturely internalized. But it is quite another matter to choose one's principles all alone, from a field of nonconsensual alternatives. In this predicament, people are likely to cling together. They are also apt to start talking existential philosophy.

The strained individuality of which existentialism is one expression tempts people in dangerous directions. The violent or outrageous act is a notorious way in which the morally exposed individual can reassure himself that he exists. Che Guevara the martyred guerrilla, though he is undoubtedly a hero by traditional criteria, also appeals to such motives in the dissident young. Passionate fellowship in crisis—jointly confronting the police in sit-ins or at the barricades—is another, which at once provides reassurance both through intense experience and through communion. Or one can become a True Believer in some new absolutism, perhaps clung to the more absolutely because it was initially chosen by a kind of existential fiat. (I think Leon Festinger [1957] could give a plausible account of *that.*) Erich Fromm's classic *Escape From Freedom* (1941), which I cited earlier, remains a very cogent analysis. When people's individuality is made to carry more of a load than it can bear, they are likely to flee from it. As Fromm reminds us, fascism could be one outcome—not just from the backlash of reactionary retribution, but from tendencies arising from the activists' own predicament. Again, morally admirable motives can lead to immoral outcomes. I am optimistic enough not to take this possibility very seriously, but one of my oldest friends thought otherwise, when the disturbances at Columbia last spring reminded her of the Nazi street clashes that she saw in the Germany of the early 1930's. German youth of the Wandervogel were idealistic and, in their own new way, also moral.

Some Constructive Implications

After this gloomy note it is time to take stock constructively and look for whatever implications we can find to guide us in the difficult situations that we are facing on the campuses. On the campus, as in the other conspicuous spheres of social disorder, the general tasks are ones of rebuilding community (or building it from scratch where it never existed before) and establishing rational authority. Obviously neither is a simple matter, and success is far from guaranteed. And little headway can be expected as long as principled young people feel moral despair about the Vietnam war and about the plight of black Americans. There will have to be convincing signs that these salient moral provocations are being coped with by the constituted authorities before young people can regain the moral hopefulness that they need if they are themselves to deal in good faith and mutual tolerance with the problems of the campus microcosm. For too long reality has seemed to confirm their stereotyped view of an evil Establishment.

Suppose, however, that the larger scene justifies a new hopefulness. Solution to the campus crisis, if it is to be had, will require the *joint* efforts of the young and their elders—of students, faculty, and administration. No durable or desirable solution can be imposed by a single party to the conflict. In this mutual effort there is obviously a differentiation of roles.

The activists will, of course, remain active, whatever their elders say. They can play a valuable part in desirable social reconstruction by their principled activism. Administrators are required by *their* roles to be pragmatists, balancing the conflicting pressures that impinge upon them. Pressures to retain the status quo are certain; for there to be liberalizing change, radical pressures need to be part of the mix. But I hope, without much optimism, that the more principled activists will exercise restraint in their protest. Vandalism and violence—and vituperation and verbal defilement—only exacerbate the conflict and make its solution less likely. In a more hopeful atmosphere, fewer students should want *that* outcome. Those who do will have to be restrained, either by their fellows or by administrative authority.

Administrators and faculty will necessarily have to assert the legitimacy of their authority when it is challenged; but they, too, need practice in restraint. Especially they need to resist the temptation to rely on punitive coercion, the phenomenon of authoritarian backlash. By a wider sharing of power, and by initiative in developing mechanisms that permit greater mutuality in coping with common tasks, they need to *earn* legitimacy, not just to assert it. Though the tactics of confrontation may have pressed them in the direction of asserting arbitrary authority, their main endeavor should be to move in all possible ways in the direction of exercising rational authority. In seeking to regain community, they need first of all to learn to *listen* to the students. Of course, it might help the listening if the students did not curse and shout.

On the campus as in many other aspects of contemporary life, this is a time both of moral opportunity and of danger. The protesting young people, with their deeply held principles and their humanistic values, are part of the opportunity. In a climate of moral nausea and despair, they are part of the danger, too.

Humanistic Values and Psychology

23

Psychology in a Liberal Education

Psychologists, being relative newcomers on the academic scene, often like to excuse themselves with the claim that, after all, psychology is an infant science. Now this cannot be strictly true, since men calling themselves psychologists have been around for some seventy years. A more accurate observation would be that psychology has shown some of the marks of a delayed adolescence, particularly in its tendency to reject its good parents, philosophy and the humanistic study of man. It is time we psychologists attained enough confidence in our mature powers to feel free to draw on our humanistic forebears—and contemporaries—where they can give us help. Somewhat in that spirit, I should like to cite, by way of preamble, an "Ode on a Distant Prospect of an Absconding Bookmaker":

> Alas! what boots it that my noble steed,
> Chosen so carefully, the field outran?
> I did not reckon, bookie, on *your* speed:
> The proper study of mankind is man.

I think that jingle, and not Alexander Pope's famous verses, provides the text in terms of which the present surge of interest in the study of man should be understood. Since the depression and the war, students throughout the country have been flocking into psychology and the social sciences—why? Not to understand and appreciate the nobility of man and his creations, I think, but for help in predicting and coping with his cussedness. Too often in the past the bookie has absconded when the stakes were high. Toward the end of the last century, the successes of technology and the spread of democracy led people to stake much on perpetual progress. These stakes vanished in the chaos of World War I. During the 1920's, in America, we bravely rebuilt, perhaps somewhat feverishly, a faith in "normalcy," the Republican Party, and the rising stock market. Again the stakes were lost, and with the outbreak of another world war, we came nearer catastrophe

Reprinted by permission from *Journal of Higher Education,* 1951, 22, 181–187.

than ever before. Since then, as we all know, catastrophe lurks just around the corner.

Having lost so much, and standing to lose so much more, we look anxiously for the culprit. Lesser culprits are easy enough to find—Hoover, Roosevelt, Hitler, Stalin, the warmongers, the communists, the capitalists, the Jews, the Negroes—sometimes it turns out that we have set upon scapegoats who are not culprits at all. We begin to suspect that the ultimate culprit is man himself, and the way he has organized his social relations. People turn to the study of man in the hope, perhaps optimistic, perhaps desperate, that it will show them a way out of our present impasse.

But it is more than a concern for the general social plight that has interested so many people in psychology. Living in a troubled world and a changing society produces troubled people. Perhaps fundamentally they are no more troubled than their parents and grandparents were—such comparisons are virtually impossible to make. But they are probably more aware of their troubles, since there is less stability in the social framework for them to lean on. So, again, they look to psychology for help. Here one needs only to follow the plots of the movies and best sellers to see that the call for psychology is a widespread social phenomenon. People want help in understanding and coping with their own problems as well as those of society at large.

All this imposes serious responsibility on the psychologist and his fellow social scientists—a responsibility to do his share in seeking solutions to our pressing problems, to give what help he can where people genuinely need it, but above all, to keep his head—to be sure that his efforts are focused where he has the ability to make a real contribution, to be sure that he has a real contribution to make and is not just wishfully acceding to inappropriate demands. Psychologists who are engaged in clinical practice have their way clear: they only accept patients whom they think they can help. Psychologists who are engaged primarily in research also face a relatively straightforward problem in the choice of their topics for investigation. It is the psychologist who is primarily devoted to undergraduate teaching who must really search his soul about his response to the new demands that are being made on psychology. He knows how little we really know about the matters that most concern us, and he cannot escape knowing how eager his students are to be told things that it is beyond his powers to tell them. It is he, above all, who must keep his head, if he is to deal honestly with the students who turn to him. I think he has a real contribution to make, but let us first see what pitfalls lie in his way.

One is the temptation to substitute jargon for insight, and buy off his students with this counterfeit currency. This is a major failing that few of us avoid completely, however honorable our intentions. Any field striving for exactness needs its technical terms. How much of our elementary instruction, all the same, is wasted on teaching this new vocabulary, without our students' ever really using the concepts that the words label—or worse, without their really grasping them! The danger is not that we are fooling ourselves, but that we may fool our students as well into thinking that giving a thing a name somehow explains it. Another jingle comes to mind:

> When Little Willy's thinking machine
> Was unsupplied with gasoline
> And Angelina's mental dome
> Was mostly filled with vacu-ome
> We used to think their works were busted;
> But now, we know they're—maladjusted.[1]

The magical power of the scientific-sounding label is potent enough in our culture of irium, hydramatic drives, and activated gasolines without the psychologist's contribution. Let us use technical terms when they serve a purpose, yes, but first let us assure ourselves that the net result is to increase the clarity of our students' thinking, not to numb their initial curiosity.

A second pitfall is to put off the demands of our students with righteousness and say, in effect, first learn thoroughly the traditional, well-worked areas of psychology; then, if you are still with us, you will be ready to cope with the more treacherous matters where your interests lie. Learn now about reaction time and the mechanism of space perception; later on there will be time for the study of personality and social relations. If most of our students were going on to graduate school, or even if most of them were going to major in psychology, there might be some reason for this approach; though, even so, it runs the danger of violating the established principle that the most effective teaching builds on existing interests. But the fact is that most of our students come to us for a single course or so, and if this course is limited to what we may think of as time-tested fundamentals, we stand in danger of giving our students nothing of lasting value to them. Somehow we have to face their needs more squarely.

But there a third pitfall lies. So, we may say to ourselves, what our students really want is to be able to understand their own problems and get along better with other people. Well, let us do what we can, and see if we cannot turn out better-adjusted, or happier, or more effective young persons —whichever way we prefer to phrase our goal. There are several things wrong with setting out on this tack. For one thing, it is likely to fail. For all the commercial success of popular psychology books, people rarely make major changes in their personalities through reading books or taking courses. If we are really aiming to produce the results that psychiatrists produce, we must use the psychiatrists' methods. And these do not include teaching courses in psychology.

But it would be a serious mistake to think that what our students really want or need is a watered-down psychotherapy. To be sure, they have their

1. I am indebted for this to my father, M. Ellwood Smith.

problems—as what person young or old does not? To be sure, many of them are groping, and psychology may seem to them a newfangled approach to some of the things they are groping for. But they are growing as well, and need to find for themselves their own ways of living with themselves and others. We should rightly be concerned that they have the fullest possible opportunity to arrive at a mature pattern of living, but this must be their achievement. We do them no favor if we pretend to do it for them. The few in serious difficulty need psychiatric help. For the many who take psychology looking for some orientation toward themselves and society, we can offer courses which, like the other courses that contribute to a liberal education, may introduce them to facts, ideas, and perspectives that enrich their understanding and increase their resources for coping with a problematic world. But just how can psychology contribute to a liberal education?

Perhaps the most valuable thing psychological training can offer is to make real to our students the meaning of a scientific approach to human nature. If they only succeed in grasping this exciting and potent idea, they have engorged a sizable piece of education that is likely to grow in importance for them as they begin to digest and assimilate it. It is surely more important than any single body of facts with which psychologists can acquaint them. Not that we would substitute the scientific point of view for a humanistic one: our task, rather, is to add this to their resources for interpreting and acting on their experience.

When the student first comes to college, his knowledge of human nature is rather narrow and rather shallow. He has not had much time for living, and the chances are that he tends to take himself and his own narrow world of experience for granted: people do, until something makes them probe further. Much of his conception of human nature is made up of common sense, a workable amalgam of truth and error that we have traditionally got along with, but which is antiquated equipment for an age in which people and customs refuse to stay put. All of us, in a liberal-arts college, conspire to encourage him to grow out of this comfortable but insufficient shell. Through literature, and history, and the arts, his eyes—and emotions—are opened gradually to the full range of human experience as lived out and expressed by men who have had far more occasion to know and feel the implications of the human situation than he. The humanities add to his range of receptivity; the sciences go on to invite him to question, and indicate ways of finding dependable answers. A scientific approach to human nature is one that questions what common sense takes for granted, and is guided by the rules of scientific inference in its search for a cumulative understanding of the way people behave—one that can be depended upon to stand up under test and criticism, and can be added to or corrected where it is shown to be inadequate.

For the humanities do not lead to cumulative knowledge. Artists and writers re-create and present human experience. They have done this honestly and skillfully in every age from ancient Greece up to the present. They tell us, this is what life can mean. But altogether, the picture is as rich and contradictory as life itself. If we think we find an established truth in literature, we can surely find its opposite expressed just as convincingly. Once we begin to aspire to a knowledge about human nature that can provide a more dependable guide to action than the intuitive *savoir faire* that comes from a broad acquaintance with it, we have taken the crucial step into the scientific perspective.

A student who has been infected with this healthy virus will not lose his capacity to respond fully to experience and its artistic re-creation. Unless he has an adolescent need to do so, he will not use science to debunk; he misses the point if he thinks that experiences, or works of art, or religious or political beliefs are necessarily any the less valid in themselves because one can look for their causes or explanations. He will, however, prick up his ears when he hears an alleged statement of fact about human nature. People are inherently aggressive, they say, so there will always be wars. How do we know this? Because there have always been wars? Yes, but how much were they the inherent result of human nature, and how much of persistent historical circumstances in which people have grown up and act? What would you need to know in order to prove that people are inhertently aggressive? Even if they are aggressive, our knowledge makes it unlikely, does it not, that there should be a specific instinct for war? Is it not possible that conditions could be discovered in which human nature would not lead to wars? And so on. Notice that this entire train of thought has gone on without the benefit of facts, and there are scientifically established facts that are pertinent to this problem—the anthropologists tell us, for example, of peaceful societies where people are not aggressive. The point is that simply from a habit of questioning factual assertions, asking himself what kinds of evidence are possible and what are necessary for proof, the student is in a position to think intelligently about possibilities to which his mind would otherwise very likely have been closed. This is a valuable habit for people to have today.

Another result of acquiring a scientific approach to psychological problems is a healthier attitude toward the ubiquitous expert, including the scientist, yes, the psychologist himself. Our growing specialization has made us all rely increasingly on experts whether we like it or not, to service our automobiles, teach our children, defend our morals, administer our government, and tell us how to raise our families. Specialization has brought with it an enormous increase in the possibility of a full and satisfying life. But it has also often led to a sense of personal helplessness and inadequacy, and a dangerous tendency to depend on experts even where their judgment cannot possibly be any better than our own. If we have some idea of the basis of the scientist's expertness, we are less at his mercy, and can be more self-respecting when we follow his guidance. The lurking doubt, how does he know this, which every scientist expects from his professional colleagues, is equally important for the dignity and independence of the plain citizen.

So far, I have been considering what the teaching of psychology can contribute simply by communicating a scientific outlook on human nature. This cannot be done in a vacuum, or just by lecturing. Students develop the scientific attitude in connection with concrete factual problems, and learn to think like scientists by behaving like scientists in laboratory experience. And, of course, we hope our students will gain more from the study of psychology than just a feeling for the scientific approach to human behavior. Armed with both a scientific way of thinking and some understanding of what is currently known about human behavior, the student is doubly at an advantage.

The things we know go only a small way toward answering the important questions that the alert student is likely to bring to us. If, however, we succeed in arousing in him the scientific point of view, our knowledge, even though small, can be a considerable help in getting him to ask the right questions—to help him identify some of the blind alleys in thinking about human nature into which much wasted thought and effort are still going, and to raise some of the considerations that any intelligent attempt to deal with our current problems must surely take into account. If we set this as our goal, we can hope to build on the student's practical concern and put him in touch with some of the important facts and perspectives of modern psychology, without stifling his curiosity with pretended answers or letting it die a natural death from long exposure to isolated facts or trivia.

For modern psychology has facts and perspectives to offer that should add to his resources for making sense of himself and his world of human relationships. As both a biological and a social science, psychology is in an especially strategic position. Since we get our start in life as helpless young animals, we need to know as much as we can about the functioning of our biological equipment if we are to understand human behavior. What do we start with? How do we build up our picture of the world through experience? What urges and strivings set us off on the restless lifelong course of activity, and how are they transformed into the complicated design of wishes, desires, strivings, purposes that each of us can discern when we look inward as human adults? How do we learn? What is the nature of this capacity to change, to benefit by experience, in which human beings among all the animals are so richly gifted? Anything we can offer toward an answer to these problems adds its bit to our understanding of man, of what we may expect of him and what can be done about him.

But, as Aristotle noted so long ago, man is also a social animal. Each of us reflects indelibly the society we have grown up in, the cultural tradition that we have made a part of ourselves. At the same time, each of us makes his contribution to the workings of this larger society and culture. It is here that the small but growing body of facts at our disposal can be so important in guiding our thinking about the kinds of social arrangements that will produce the human results that we want, and the ways of attaining our social goals, starting with the human materials we find around us. How should we raise our children to be happy and productive in the kind of society they will face? What social changes might we promote so that people may live fuller, more effective, and more satisfying lives than so many of us are able to live today? Again, I am far from suggesting that psychologists have the answers. We have, however, learned some dependable things that should prove valuable to all who are searching for answers, things ranging from the most general conclusions about the malleability of human nature to the different consequences we have learned to expect from reward and punishment.

But even if we could discover all that we could hope to know, as psychologists, we would still lack the full diagnosis of the social crisis that sends so many students in our direction. Psychologists are most unwise if they forget that human relations are too complex to be accessible from the standpoint of the individual alone. There are facts of human organization and behavior in the mass that have to be studied at their own level—by the sociologist, the political scientist, the economist, the historian. As psychologists, we must turn to the other social sciences to fill in their half of the picture. A tragic fact like war cannot be explained as a reaction to individual frustrations any more than it can be laid to an individual's fighting instinct. The psychological facts are important, but only when they are fitted into their proper places along with facts about governments and their relationships, economic interests, social institutions, and historical events. The student who turns to psychology can find there some of the data that he needs to piece out a mature perspective on modern society. However much we want and try to help, the piecing out is something he must ultimately do for himself. But this, of course, is the way a liberal education works.

The same is true when it comes to the student's desire for self-knowledge. Facts of the sort I have already mentioned go a small part of the way toward the kind of information he would like about the way he works. He is likely to be more keenly interested in the findings and speculations of psychologists about personality in all its complexity. It is unfortunately true that the nearer psychologists come to the matters that people care most about, the shakier are our conclusions and the more we disagree with one another about the most promising leads for future investigation. We cannot hide this from our students and we should not try to. If we take them into our confidence and let them see the difficulties that stand in the way of full understanding, and in addition give them what we have to offer by way of fact and hunch, we have still been of real use.

Again, however, even if we imagine some happy future state of affairs when we can know the things we only speculate about today, we may be sure that we can never offer our students the key to self-knowledge. As scientists, we have only one kind of self-knowledge in our province—the analytical, systematic kind that seeks to put the facts of human existence in neat order of cause and effect. The knowledge that involves appreciation, that involves depth of awareness and sensitivity to moral implications, must for the most part come from other sources, though we may do our bit to turn the students' attention in directions that might otherwise not have occurred to them.

But this is only to say that the old precept, "Know thyself," defines a goal toward which an entire liberal education should point, one that transcends any limited field of knowledge. Perhaps one touchstone of how well we teachers have done our job is whether our students come to realize that we can no more hope to attain complete self-knowledge than we can expect to find the final truth about the nature of the world around us. It is a continuing problem that we carry with us throughout our lives. We hope our students may greet it not with dismay but as a welcome challenge.

24

Toward Scientific and Professional Responsibility

How are responsibility and values related? By *values* I shall mean a person's implicit or explicit standards of choice, insofar as they are invested with obligation or requiredness. Values are closely related to ends or goals, but not all goals are values in this sense; for the American child, the eating of spinach becomes much more value-laden than the eating of ice cream cones. *Responsibility* has to do with the relation of a person's behavior to his values. One could also include the kind of values to which the person subscribes. To simplify my task, however, I will assume that our new code of ethics[1] indicates that we are in fair consensus on a number of generally acceptable values. Our ethical problems, it seems to me, may have more to do with the relation of our values to what we actually do as psychologists than with what our values happen to be.

As I intend to use the term, then, a person acts responsibly to the extent that his behavior meets at least these conditions: First, he is aware of the value context in which he is acting. His goals have been subjected to conscious scrutiny, and his behavior is explicitly related to his values. Second, his choices are made in the light of as adequate an understanding of their probable consequences as he can achieve. The relations that he assumes between means and ends are examined critically, not taken for granted. Third, he is ready to be judged in terms of his choices of both ends and means, and has the flexibility to reconsider both. In a word, he assumes responsibility for his decisions and actions.

If these remarks sound like pious platitudes, perhaps it is an indication that there is indeed consensus on responsibility, so conceived, as itself a value. Yet as we know, personal motives and conflicts between values often stand in the way of responsible action. Some of the other members of the symposium are addressing themselves to sources of irresponsibility in the social situation of psychology. For my part I should like to examine some of its forms. I have eight sins—mortal or venial—for your consideration.

Reprinted by permission from *American Psychologist*, 1954, 9, 513–516.

1. The code of ethics adopted by the American Psychological Association in 1953.

Fixation on means. One can easily find in the activities of psychologists examples of a kind of "functional autonomy of motives," in which too narrow a focus on means leads to behavior that hardly advances the goal values toward which it is still presumably oriented. Consider, for example, fixation on the trappings of science. Are we really pursuing the advancement of understanding, we may from time to time ask ourselves, or are we being sidetracked by our indiscriminate enthusiasm for a particular fashionable gadget, or research technique, or convention of statistical analysis? Fads in research topics and methods may result, to a larger extent than we like to admit, less from the concerted pursuit that follows a significant "breakthrough" than from failure to keep our sights set on goals within the larger context that gives significance to our scientific activities. Fixation upon trivia is the easier for us because of the naiveté with which "common sense" and college sophomores pose problems for psychology. From legitimate insistence on formulating our own questions in ways that permit scientific investigation, it is only a step to smugness that sometimes seems to attribute ritual significance to the forms of science.

Means can become ends in the professional as well as the scientific aspect of psychology. Shall the patient be vertical or horizontal; is the tradition of Rorschach interpretation to be preserved intact at all costs; how sacred is the feeding schedule or the permissive attitude? Heat tends to exclude light when means are taken as ends in themselves. Happily, functional autonomy in this setting is incomplete, and the ends of effective therapy, diagnosis, or upbringing, though sometimes latent, are rarely abandoned. A clear view of means *as* means—that is, in relation to goals—is the best safeguard against fixation on them.

Absolutism of means. The second form of irresponsibility in my list shades into the first without sharp distinction. By "absolutism of means," I mean positing such an invariant, rigid, or fool-proof relation that the need for evaluating the appropriateness of means to end is supposedly by-passed. The examples I have in mind here—controversial ones, to be sure—involve conscious commitment to the means rather than blind fixation. But the results may be much the same. Through the insistence that things are conveniently simpler than they are, the psychologist excuses himself from responsible choice.

Consider first the gospel of democratic group process. Impressive data indicate that when a teacher, leader, or "change-agent" thrusts the members of a group on their own resources, the changes that occur in their knowledge, attitudes, and behavior, coming as they do from within, have stability and personal significance that cannot be attained through more didactic or "authoritarian" procedures. This is an important discovery. It does not follow, however, that *authoritative* intervention may not often be indispensable, nor does it mean that the democratic techniques—or reasonably exact facsimiles thereof—may not be employed in the service of questionable objectives. What is irresponsible, because it rules out discriminating choice where choice is needed, is to set such stock on the technique per se that questions of its suitability to the objective, or the desirability of the objective itself, are overlooked. It is misleading to assume, for instance, that democratic group process as employed by management consultants automatically guarantees a democratic result in keeping with the best interests of worker and supervisor alike. Much manipulation is rationalized in the name of democracy.

When it is elevated to dogma, the parallel non-directive technique in psychotherapy may present similar pitfalls. Only to the extent that the therapist is aware of the degree and nature of his intervention can he direct his *own* role in therapy responsibly.

The foolproof technique, the "simple and sovereign" relationship, has appeal as it promises to let us avoid or delegate responsibility for judgment in the face of complexity. Even if our attempts at simple principles turn out to be valid, however, their application to complex real situations will surely continue to require the best and most explicit judgment we can muster.

Absolutism of ends. Here I turn to another controversial matter. Psychologists and other social scientists have helped to undermine the absolute standing of traditional, theologically supported ends and values. We are perhaps ready enough to detect an abdication of responsibility when persons justify their choices by recourse to a superhuman scheme of things, or to the ways of our own culture writ large as the proper ways of humanity. Yet the search for values to fill the gap left by theology has often remained a quest for other absolutes with some of the old magic. Psychologists have on occasion offered or imposed their own partial values as absolutes blessed in the name of science. I am thinking for example of "adjustment," which as a be-all-and-end-all is already in sufficient disrepute to make my point clear. It is certainly not irresponsible of psychologists to favor adjustment and to seek to promote it; the difficulty comes when we mislead ourselves and others that science lends its authority to an obligation to be adjusted. Science can of course do no such thing, and the pretense that it can closes off prematurely the exploration of alternative standards.

The choice of ends is a personal matter, which can be exercised responsibly or irresponsibly, or abdicated in favor of tradition or mere conformity. As scientists, we have the special competence to consider the bearing of an important realm of facts on the choice of ends—facts about the side consequences, the boomerang effects of our choices. The pitfall for us to avoid, however, is losing sight of the element of personal choice that remains once the facts are in.

Escape into relativism or "value neutrality." Seeing that science yields no absolutes, psychologists may, conversely, try to make peace with themselves by raising the anthropologists' banner of cultural relativism—values are a chance of nurture to be accepted without fuss as one accepts table etiquette. Or they may flatly deny that the realms of scientific fact and value have anything to do with one another. But the psychologist cannot stop making choices, as scientist, teacher, therapist, or human engineer. The choices may be witting or unwitting, responsible or irresponsible, but they are made, and they entail consequences. Acceptance of the values of one's culture as given and beyond reconsideration implies a conservative choice; it can add the psychologist's voice, in fact, to the crescendo urging total conformity, a trend which in the long run may be not at all conservative of our traditional values. And the claim to a value-free science, when it goes beyond insistence on a disciplined regard for fact whether or not it accords with our wishes, only obscures the value elements in the choice of problem, of research setting, of conceptual framework, in the decision as to when to rest with negative findings, when results are reportable, and so on endlessly. Only if we know what we are choosing, only if the values involved in our choices are explicit, do our decisions become responsible ones.

Isolation of conflicting values. Some of the devices we have already listed, as well as still others, may have their appeal because they serve to isolate conflicting values from one another. Insistence on value neutrality may, for instance, serve to contain a conflict between major values for the psychologist who must depend for the support of his work on sources that are not equally disinterested. Isolation—"logic-tight compartments"—may be an essential expedient in the functioning of a less than perfectly integrated society or personality. It excludes, however, the productive interplay in which new means of resolution may be invented and previously held values redefined, and from which can emerge—much as the common law grows from successive judicial decisions—workable consensus on fundamentals and priorities. Conflict, after all, is a serious and difficult matter that is hard to face, harder to tolerate, and hardest to resolve. But the more squarely we are able to confront the alternatives in making our choices, the less frequently we are likely to encounter basic conflicts that exceed our powers.

Token payments to conscience. One response that many of us make to value conflicts in science and profession as in personal life could be tagged as "token payments." We have our cake and eat it too, but only because we take a small, not very nourishing, bite. Caught between our obligations to research and to our teaching, professional, or administrative duties, we appease conscience by writing little research papers—not very good or very significant, to be sure, but neither do they detract *very* much from the performance of our other obligations. In a program of applied research to satisfy a client, we work in somehow a methodological study to present at the altar of science. Vacillating between commitment to science and responsibility as citizens, we act as if doing a little study of, say, prejudice would show that we are on the right side.

Good results obviously come from these compromises. But if we were more fully on to ourselves as scientists and professional and citizens, perhaps we might advance our values more effectively. Much research that is done for the sake of such a token payment to social responsibility might as well not be done. The topic picked as a compromise is often not strategic either for scientific advance or for social action. And the effort that can be committed to the investigation is often insufficient to achieve more than token, "suggestive" results. If the conflict were squarely faced, perhaps one would then be in a position to choose between making a more ambitious effort or none at all; perhaps one would decide to capitalize on the advantages of the ivory tower rather than bemoaning its isolation; or to play scientist and citizen on separate occasions, not in combination. Or one might come back to the same compromise as the most satisfactory resolution. At all events, the decision would be a considered one.

Parochialism. Involved in most of the blind alleys we have explored is, in fact, a kind of blindness—of cognitive inadequacy that precludes explicit and adequate decision. The parochialism of our particular perspectives as psychologists can also limit the range of appropriate choice. The vogue of perception-centered theory in social psychology, for example, may without our intending it leave us preoccupied with social perceptions at the expense of social facts. The facts are outside the competence of our psychological kit bag, while it is easy for us to ascertain what people think the facts are. Important as it is to understand people's perceptions, such a partial description points more obviously to the techniques of the public relations man than to more direct measures for coping with unsatisfactory situations. Psychological warfare and employee relations programs seem, indeed, to be most popular where the juggling of appearances appeals as a painless short cut that does not disturb the *status quo.* Perhaps psychotherapies that center on altering the person's self-perceptions have a similar appeal.

Whenever we seek to apply psychological knowledge to the world of affairs in which the psychological is only one of several relevant aspects, parochialism is a real danger. Psychologists could make a more valid claim to be consulted in councils of high policy if we were less prone to regard the factors that we know most about as the only important ones. Problems of communication and its failure, for example, seem to us inherently psychological; we leave power conflict between organized social structures to the political scientist. But if we then prescribe better communication as a panacea for situations of power conflict, we give poor and irresponsible advice. If "wars are born in the minds of men," individual tensions, frustrations, and misunderstandings take on political significance only as they occur in organized social contexts. Responsible recommendations on policy require of the psychologist an understanding of the place of his distinctive contribution among those of the other social disciplines. Knowledge of our limitations should increase our real power.

Professional vanity. It is still a new thing for psychologists to find their advice on important practical affairs sought and sometimes heeded. Perhaps it would be well for us to remember the limited aspects of our field that have actually paid our way and won for psychology the ear of practical men: aptitude testing, clinical counseling, and a few others, none of which are very close to what we like to think is the theoretical core of the science.

As scientists we are still groping—perhaps as professionals, too. When we are tempted by fantasies of power to try to set the world in order, we need an occasional dose of scientific humility. The hardheaded approach that insists on systematic doubt in the absence of confirmation, and holds even established propositions with tentativeness, remains our special contribution. We can ill afford to neglect our function as scientists in the pursuit of problems that are too big for us to cope with. Our responsibility must be measured against our competence.

My strategy in this paper has been to focus our attention on the implications of responsibility, on the assumption that since it is a value that we already share, explicitness about it should make us more likely to act responsibly as psychologists. Explicitness about the relation of values—including this one—to our behavior would seem to be a necessary if not sufficient condition of rational progress toward valued goals.

25

Conflicting Values Affecting Behavioral Research with Children

What limits, if any, should be set on research into children's behavior? Who should set these limits? These, and other questions related to them, are being asked these days by many people in and out of research—parents and lawmakers included.

Only recently, when research on behavior was a marginal activity of a few college professors and their graduate students, carried out with little financial support and that support received mainly from private donors and foundations, such questions hardly arose. From the professor's standpoint, the responsibility for decisions about the nature of the research was solely his—a matter of academic freedom and privilege within the framework of formal or informal codes of professional ethics. Nobody was likely to challenge him: the whole enterprise of research in the behavioral sciences was unimportant and inconspicuous, and public funds were not involved.

Today, however, the behavioral scientist has to pay the penalty for success. Behavioral research is no longer inconspicuous: even though it is not as affluent as the physical sciences, it is now big business. And since most of its financial support now comes from the federal government, its errors of judgment as well as its successful results now attract political attention. Public concern with the methods that scientists use in studying other people is of course warranted on grounds quite apart from the basis of funding.

For perspective on the special problems of controls on research with children, we had best begin with a brief look at the anxieties and misgivings about the political and ethical aspects of the behavioral sciences that figure prominently in the current climate of discussion.

Many people, including United States congressmen, are worried about many loosely related issues. Do personality questionnaires violate the citizen's right to privacy when used in government personnel procedures or in

Reprinted by permission from *Children*, 1967, 14, 53–58. *Children* is the publication of the Children's Bureau, Welfare Administration, U. S. Department of Health, Education, and Welfare. I am grateful to colleagues at the Institute of Human Development, University of California, Berkeley, for comments on an earlier draft of this paper.

research (Testing and Public Policy, 1965)? Is it ever permissible for experimenters to deceive the subjects of their experiments, as some types of investigation seem to require (Kelman, 1967)? If deception is used, how can the "informed consent" of subjects be obtained (Reubhausen and Brim, 1965)? Do the potentialities for computer retrieval of data collected for administrative purposes (tax returns, census files, and the like) threaten the privacy and perhaps even the liberty of the individual citizen? What of government-sponsored research in foreign countries—how can the sensitivities of the citizens of other countries, the interests of the United States government, and the needs of the social sciences for comparative data all be taken into account (Camelot and Psychological Tests, 1966)? How can the government and the public be assured they are getting their money's worth out of social and behavioral science? Is adequate support available for the study of socially important problems (Carter, 1966)? All these questions and many others have found their way into the legislative hopper. Several congressional committees have held hearings that bear upon them. Suddenly, the social and behavioral sciences are politically visible.

Issues Concerning Children

Each of these issues has its counterpart for research on the behavior of children, though issues concerned with studies of children in foreign countries have not yet received much attention. But the issues look and are different when children are involved.

Personality questionnaires and the right to privacy. When children are questioned for research purposes, the privacy and sensitivity of parents have to be considered in addition to the possible effects of the questioning on the child. Some kinds of questions—those about sexual attitudes, knowledge, and practices, for example—are likely to be regarded as intrinsically inappropriate in questionnaires for use with children; questions about child-rearing practices, on the other hand, may be seen as invading the parents' right to privacy and perhaps even as undermining parent-child relations.

Parents who have little understanding of the methods or objectives or value of behavioral research have objected to their children's being asked about their parents' education and other indicators of socioeconomic status—seemingly incidental information that is often essential in a research project. Very likely only a few parents would be disturbed by the kinds of questions a responsible investigator would find necessary and proper to ask, but their objections have to be taken seriously, not dismissed impatiently as "crackpot." The narrowest interpretation of what is permissible would put many important problems beyond the range of possible research. The most lenient would affront many citizens.

Deception. In this regard, the issues concerning children shape up differently from those concerning deception with college students and adults. In a typical case, the problem under study requires the subjects to undergo a standard sequence of successes and failures on an experimental task. To produce this standard sequence, the subjects are provided with believable false reports about their performances of the task, according to the requirements of the experimental design.

Generally, investigators working with adults or college students attempt to meet the ethical problem in such deception by carefully explaining the reason for the deception to each subject after the experiment is over. When the subjects are students in psychology courses, such a "debriefing" procedure usually makes sense (though it may not balance the harm done to the students by conveying the idea that a manipulative approach to people is acceptable). When "debriefing" is carried out scrupulously, the participant may learn something relevant to his studies, both about psychological research and about his own reactions.

In research with young children, however, no one can argue for "debriefing" as an adequate solution to the ethical problem of deception. A full explanation of procedures to the young child is seldom desirable or possible. In the example that we have been considering, the usual scrupulous practice would be to so contrive matters that by the end of the session every child would leave with a solid experience of success.

Yet such a solution leaves one uneasy. The experimenter who knows that he must subsequently explain to his adult subjects just how he has deceived them may be likely to exercise self-restraint in his procedures. The experimenter with children is under no obligation to explain himself to his subjects, and if he is not required to justify his procedures to others, everything hinges on his private judgment. Can the experimenter's unavoidably self-interested judgment of what is best for the child be trusted?

Consent. The difficult but crucial issue of when the participant in research may be regarded as having given his informed consent appears in a different guise in respect to research with children. Legally, only parents can consent on behalf of children. But when is parental consent "informed"? How much do parents have to know about a particular research project before their consent may be so regarded? When, if at all, may the responsible authorities in schools and other social agencies give consent *in loco parentis?* When, if at all, may implicit consent be assumed? Any call for a rigid enforcement of a requirement for explicit parental consent presents serious obstacles to research studies that hinge on obtaining data from a representative sample of children. This is because, in ways that affect their children, the parents who neglect to return consent forms may differ from those who do return them. A narrow interpretation of the consent issue could very seriously hamper behavioral research with children.

Uses of information. Whether information collected for administrative purposes that can be retrieved and collated by a high-speed computer for other purposes presents risks to the privacy and liberty of adults is still a matter for conjecture, since such data banks are not yet generally available.

However, the cumulative school records of children's psychological tests are already with us and may do real harm.

Useful as ability tests undoubtedly are, they are clearly a mixed blessing (Goslin, 1963; Goslin, 1967). The low test scores of a child who gets off to a poor start may exclude him from opportunities to improve his position. Teachers who rely on the predictive power of a poor score help confirm the prediction. On the other hand, without test results, social stereotyping might play a larger part than it does in deciding a child's educational future. Much careful thought and further research are needed to find ways of using ability tests so as to maximize each child's educational opportunities instead of accentuating existing inequalities of opportunity. Because the testing technology is a product of scientific psychology, problems concerned with the administrative use of tests naturally get entangled with the logically distinct problems of their research uses. It is important to keep the issues separate.

Information collected from children for research should never be used to their disadvantage. When the nature of the research permits data to be collected and stored anonymously, the interests of the individual child can be readily protected. When, on the other hand, identification of individual persons is essential to the research—as in "longitudinal" studies that follow the same persons over a period of time—elaborate precautions are essential to safeguard confidentiality. In such research, protecting the anonymity of the persons studied is an absolute about which there can be no compromise.

Competing Values

As we explore these issues, it is easy to become preoccupied with the dangers of using children as subjects of behavioral research and the safeguards necessary to protect them, at the expense of appreciating the actual and potential contributions of behavioral research to child welfare. The cumulative findings of research on child development are just beginning to break the cyclical fashions in child-rearing advice (Hoffman, M., and Hoffman, 1964, 1966). In this country we are just launching a host of new and expensive programs in the schools based on extrapolations from current knowledge about behavior that urgently require monitoring and rigorous evaluation through research. Now is not the time to stifle behavioral research with severe restrictions.

In its own interest, the public needs to make some accommodations to the requirements of research. Behavioral scientists and the agencies that support their work should be actively involved in educating the public and its representatives in government to the characteristics and value of such research.

The beginning of wisdom in this regard, it seems to me, is to recognize that we must come to terms with competing values. Humanitarian values require that we never harm the individual child and always strive to advance child welfare. Libertarian values require us to respect the integrity and privacy of the child and his parents. Scientific values prescribe the extension of knowledge for its own sake, usually with the faith that in the long run knowledge contributes to humanitarian ends. Legal values require us to respect the status of minors and the rights and obligations of parents, though legal rights in relation to behavioral research are still in the process of clarification (Reubhausen and Brim, 1965). Often these different frames of evaluation point to the same conclusion. The cases in which they do are the simple ones that pose no serious practical or ethical problem. But often they conflict with one another. For example, the child's privacy and perhaps his integrity are violated for the sake of advancing knowledge of a topic that is theoretically and humanly important when, in a study of how moral character develops, he is tempted to cheat and whether he does so or not is surreptitiously observed. In such instances, we need principles and mechanisms for adjudication.

Both principles and mechanisms become indispensable once we grant that decision on these conflicts in values can no longer be left to the unaided conscience of the individual investigator. Now that behavioral science has grown so important that it captures public attention, forces are clearly such that decision will not be left to the individual investigator. Nor should it be. He is likely to be a biased judge, one who will set a higher priority on scientific values than nonscientists are likely to do. He wants so much to conduct research and to advance knowledge that, being human, he may underestimate or rationalize away the costs and risks to his subjects. At any rate, he is open to the legitimate suspicion of being vulnerable to bias. Anyone who has been privy to discussions among tough-minded behavioral scientists about the "trade off" between ethical risks and potential scientific gain will have no doubt that this bias exists.

Codes of Ethics

Further codification of ethical principles by the scientific disciplines concerned to help guide decision in the difficult cases is a much needed first step. Existing codes of ethics provide a good start but they stop short of some of the harder issues before us. Thus, the code adopted in 1959 by the American Psychological Association (1959) provides for the confidentiality of research materials and calls upon the psychologist to show "sensible regard for the social codes and moral expectations of the community in which he works." In what is probably the critical principle, it states:

> Only when a problem is significant and can be investigated in no other way is the psychologist justified in giving misinformation to research

subjects or exposing research subjects to physical or emotional stress.

a. When the possibility of serious aftereffects exists, research is conducted only when the subjects or their responsible agents are fully informed of this possibility and volunteer nevertheless.

b. The psychologist seriously considers the possible harmful aftereffects and removes them as soon as permitted by the design of the experiment. [Principle 16. *Harmful aftereffects*]

Such a code of principles typically contains some absolutes. (Provision *a* above approaches an absolute requirement for voluntary consent, though the decision about when a "possibility of serious aftereffects exists" remains judgmental.) More of the principles will point to strongly desirable or highly undesirable practices that are nevertheless open to some kind of negotiation.

I would like to see some nearly absolute principles added that, I think, are essential to maintaining a relationship of trust between researcher and human subject, a relationship that is a prerequisite to society's continued tolerance of the behavioral scientist. Under very few circumstances is an investigator justified in violating a pledge of confidentiality given to a research subject, even though the interests of the subject are fully protected. The frequency with which hidden devices are used to identify supposedly anonymous questionnaires is deplorable. I would also like assurance that when an investigator *has* employed deception and subsequently explains his action to his subjects in a "debriefing" session, he presents the literal truth—and does not, as sometimes has been the case, use the session for further experimental manipulation.

However, in general, I would prefer to keep the absolutes to a minimum and would open even the few absolutes proposed to debate and to legitimate exceptions, under safeguards of a sort to be discussed shortly. Thus, I can imagine a research situation in which the covert identification of questionnaires might be an essential and justifiable method for checking on the effects of lack of anonymity on questionnaire responses.

The inherent limitation in ethical codes is the leeway they leave for human judgment and for balancing competing values. Without such leeway, any code would be unworkable; with it, the code is open to evasion. Application of ethical principles to real cases is literally a problem in casuistry and is vulnerable to the abuses that gave casuistry a bad name. In the principle I have quoted, what determines "when a problem is significant"? How much unsuccessful search do we require of an investigator before we allow him to decide that the problem "can be investigated in *no* other way"? How big a probability is a "possibility" of serious aftereffect, and how much does the experimeter have to hurt people for it to be "serious"? And who is to decide all this?

I am not criticizing the ambiguous wording of the principle. Insofar as there is no objective, common measure by which competing values can be "traded off," the fallibility of human judgment cannot be eliminated from decisions about the ethics of research. The question is whose judgment should it be and under what safeguards. What we need, therefore, are mechanisms of responsible "due process."

A Due-Process Mechanism

At present, universities throughout the country are having their initial experience with one type of such a due-process mechanism. Through regulations promulgated in February and July 1966, the Surgeon General of the United States Public Health Service requires every institution receiving a USPHS grant to develop principles and procedures governing the use of human subjects in research. A crucial feature of these requirements is a review of the judgment of each principal investigator or program director by a multidisciplinary committee of his institutional associates. Since the procedures became operative only on November 1, 1966, it is too early to report the experience that universities have had in administering these controls. After an era of laissez-faire, an attitude that can no longer be justified, I can safely predict that loud complaints from academic investigators will be heard for some time. Nonetheless, with only slightly less assurance, I also predict that a decentralized system of institutional review on the USPHS model will become the pattern for the social control of federally financed research on human subjects, including children. I think it is a desirable pattern, for all the nuisance it is creating.

What will this decentralized system accomplish?

1. It will assure the public and its representatives that the welfare of human subjects is protected by adequate safeguards. The acceptability of an investigator's procedures will be reviewed by others and will be justified to them. The requirement that the review committee be interdisciplinary promotes the development of common ethical standards across disciplines and professions and is likely to have a corrective influence on disciplines or subdisciplines that have become habituated to dubious practices.

2. Because the investigator's possible bias in regard to the ethical acceptability of research procedures is checked by making the judgment a matter of shared public responsibility, it will for the most part obviate the need for rigid and absolute rules and allow flexible judgment that takes the particulars of a research situation into account. The same considerations by which a jury system is a proper device for administering justice "beyond reasonable doubt" make a system of collegial review appropriate to the inherently judgmental issues research deals with.

3. At the cost of some initial confusion and inequity, it will encourage creative and responsible thinking within institutions as they formulate and revise the ethical codes under which the review committees will operate. Some may wish to keep formal principles to a minimum and evolve a kind

of common law from the precedents that are established in borderline cases. Others may try to spell out more fully elaborated codes. Through their scientific and professional associations, the disciplines concerned would be well advised to watch these developments closely and to take the lead in preparing statements of principles for the institutional committees that reflect the special problems of their own areas of research.

4. It will avert the stultifying rigidity of federal centralized administrative or statutory control over research practices.

I think the special problems of research on the behavior of children can best be dealt with in such a framework of decentralized institutional self-monitoring according to explicit principles and procedures, which can and should be modified as we learn from experience in working with them. Reviewing committees will naturally be slow to approve procedures that they are at all dubious about when the subjects to the research are young children.

A Special Problem

The issue that may demand the closest attention and give the greatest trouble is the one involving explicit parental consent. In regard to this problem, and to many others, behavioral research does not parallel clinical medical research (Ladimer and Newman, 1963) closely enough for the medical research codes to be particularly helpful.

The relationship of physician to patient, involving as it does the highly charged issue of life and death, can when it is diverted to research objectives be perverted to an unspeakable evil (as in the Nazi death camps), unless the strictest controls protect the patient's interests. If patients are to be able to turn confidently to their physicians for help, they must know that they will not be used in medical experimentation without their knowledge and consent. In the case of minors, parental consent is the legally required equivalent of the patient's consent. (Yet matters here are not simple either: advances in pharmacology that none of us would forgo depend on the use of placebos and "double-blind" designs, practices that are hard to reconcile with the principle of voluntary consent.)

In contrast to medical research, much behavioral research, with children or with adults, is concerned with far less sensitive matters. When the requirement of explicit parental consent would defeat the purpose of an otherwise important behavioral study requiring a representative sample of children *and* no reasonable person would expect the study to harm the child or insult the parents' values, an exception to the requirement seems justifiable.

The sort of responsible review of the investigator's justification of his research procedures that the Public Health Service is now requiring makes it possible to consider such exceptions on their merits. Review groups will have to develop their own guidelines for deciding when the explicit consent of a parent or guardian should be obligatory, when parents should be given the opportunity to consent implicitly by failing to object to an announced research plan that involves their child, and when the responsible head of an institution such as a school system or a school might appropriately consent to the research being done without consulting the parents. School authorities will of course base their decisions to give or withhold permission not only on their own judgment about what is ethical but also on the compatibility of the research with the school's educational objectives for the child. The latter judgments are more appropriately made by superintendents and principals than by investigators, review committees, *or* parents.

Respect for the Subject

Lest I give the impression that the due-process mechanism the Public Health Service has decreed for American campuses will of itself fully allay the concern about the proprieties of research with children and other human subjects, which many social and behavioral scientists share with other citizens, I need to draw, by way of conclusion, a distinction between what is ethically permissible and what is ethically desirable. My own view is that the predominant cast of much permissible behavioral research falls short of the desirable in too often adopting a manipulative or condescending attitude toward its human subjects rather than a genuinely respectful, collaborative one.

Much public resentment toward the behavioral sciences arises, I think, from correct perception of this tendency toward manipulation. Review committees and codes of ethics will not directly improve this state of affairs because inevitably they are concerned with ruling out what is not permissible, rather than with making what is desirable prevail. If and as behavioral scientists come more characteristically to grant their subjects the respect they accord to collaborators in an enterprise they understand and accept, they should, by the same token, help create a more favorable atmosphere for behavioral research. The styles of research that prevail may be more important than skill in public relations in creating a favorable "image" of behavioral science.

In research with children, an atmosphere of respect and care is particularly important. Improvement in what is normative practice in research in the behavioral disciplines must be the outgrowth of continued discussion in the professional societies and in the universities and of resultant changes in graduate training.

Such discussions are in process as a by-product of the review procedures the Public Health Service is requiring of the universities. As a result of participating in them, social and behavioral scientists may come increasingly to realize that they have lost their innocence. They can no longer live in a world of simple good and evil in which their research decisions follow unambiguously from academic-scientific values. Like it or not, they are now faced with picking their way among conflicting values and resolving the conflicts as best they can. It comes to many of us as a surprise, though it should not, that the modes of resolving such conflicts are in the broadest sense inherently political.

26

Rationality and Social Process

At a time when rational problem-solving, informed by a scientific approach, is urgently demanded by the larger problems that confront mankind, social rationality with respect to these problems seems to be the exception rather than the rule. This situation, I submit, has been disheartening to psychologists with some commitment to concern about social issues. Our research morale has rested in part on an unexamined assumption of social rationality: that if we as scientists could ascertain the relevant facts, the truth would prevail. Our morale has therefore been vulnerable to experience that has seemed to question this assumption. Perhaps as social psychologists we should inquire more closely into the conceptual status of rationality in our models of human nature. From a modern social psychological point of view, is there a place for rationality? To me, this is not very different from the question recently posed by Robert M. Hutchins[1], "Is Democracy Possible?"

Rationality and the Traditional Psychological Models

The model of man embraced by the traditional political philosophers of democracy, we remember, assumed generous components of rationality. Over the years, the liberals, the friends of democracy have generally espoused the view of man as rational and perfectable, in opposition to the conservative apologists of authority and tradition, who typically have shown little faith in man's rational capacities and propensities. In one guise or another, an assumption of underlying rationality is closely woven into the fabric of democratic ideology.

British empiricism. Yet the psychological status of rationality was already suspect in the philosophical psychology of the British tradition, close as it was to major strands of democratic political philosophy. With the de-

Reprinted by permission from *Journal of Individual Psychology,* 1960, *16,* 25–35. Adapted from the presidential address to the Society for the Psychological Study of Social Issues, American Psychological Association, Cincinnati, Ohio, September 7, 1959.

1. Sidney Hillman Award address, 1959, distributed by the Fund for the Republic, Santa Barbara, California.

mise of faculty psychology, Reason lost its honored place as an active power of the mind (a place reserved for it, to be sure, in Continental thought that was later to influence the doctrines of the Gestalt school). In the writings of British empiricism we encounter rationality as something extrinsic and a little incongruous. Thus *reflection* in Locke, a principle of mental activity out of keeping with his view of the sense-given composition of the mind. By the time that the British school had arrived at the pat amalgam of associationism and hedonism that formed the psychological underpinning of utilitarian doctrine, to speak, as Bentham did, of *enlightened* self-interest was to beg a large psychological question. Whence, psychologically, the grounds for assuming enlightenment? Indeed the machinery of contiguous association seems ill equipped to perform the rational feats of hedonistic calculus, unless guided by some sort of "invisible hand," as in Adam Smith's metaphor for the convergence of individual and general interests. The individual and social rationality so dear to the laissez-faire liberals was a matter of faith and assumption in its own right, hardly congruent with the central aspects of their psychological model.

Evolution. When we turn to currents in the systematic psychology of yesterday and the day before, we find little reason for encouragement. True, the Darwinian revolution that set the scene for contemporary psychologies called attention to the adaptive functions of intelligence. But the emphasis in evolutionary doctrine on continuity between man and beast, on instinct, and on residues of the eternal struggle of tooth and claw, counterbalanced the biological sanction that it gave to concern with man's rational potentialities. If the theory of evolution set Galton and his successors to considering individual differences in intelligence, it also, and in our present context perhaps more significantly, contributed to dethroning man from his erstwhile special position as a uniquely rational being.

Psychoanalysis. Freud and psychoanalysis of course carried the dethronement much farther; ironically, when one considers Frued's personal devotion to rational values, his therapeutic and social goal of extending the boundaries of reality-tested critical awareness at the expense of blind impulse and its derivatives. The Freudian assault on man's pretentions to rationality had at least three prongs. First, it elaborated upon the pleasure-pain doctrine of hedonism by identifying specific instinctual drives. As sources of motivation, these sexual and aggressive strivings are not merely *non-rational,* like the unspecified wants blanketed under the utilitarian formula of self-interest, but distinctly *irrational* in that operating outside the scope of normal awareness, they are repugnant to a person's conscious standards. The devious manifestations of these drives in thought and behavior, as revealed by psychoanalysis, secondly, showed no respect for the canons of logic. The lawfulness seen by Freud in dreams and psychotic delusions as well as in normal behavior has little to do with rationality. The third prong in the psychoanalytic attack is a corollary of the foregoing. All that glitters is not gold, said the psychoanalysts, opening the way for the enthusiastic and indiscriminate debunking of human pretensions by those who caught this much of the psychoanalytic message. Where rationality is claimed, suspect rationalization; where values are asserted, look for sublimated drive derivatives! The significant psychological events, the important determinants of behavior, lie outside the sphere of conscious rationality, which now takes the aspect of a facade, and a misleading one at that. It was this version of psychoanalysis, no doubt a selective caricature, that in popular versions worked as a strong corrosive to disfigure the image of human rationality.

Behaviorism. Under behaviorism and its successors in American psychology, this image has fared little better. Watson preached the doctrine of association by contiguity all over again, together with rejection on metaphysical grounds of intention and awareness, ingredients of most views of rational action. Hull and behaviorists of the later generation set out on their part to account for "knowledge and purpose as habit mechanisms" and to find, in the spirit of Darwin, a mechanistic explanation for adaptive behavior. But the principles of reinforcement on which they relied seem ill-designed to encompass behavior in which immediate tension reduction or reward is forgone for the sake of consequences envisioned in a broader contact or a longer run. Psychologists in this tradition (Mowrer, 1950) have written of the "neurotic paradox," that organisms can pathologically persist in self-defeating responses in spite of reinforcement principles. If one grant that neurotic symptoms evade or palliate immediate anxiety, it is "normal" rational behavior, with its delayed gratifications, its postponement of reinforcement, its orientation to spatially and temporally distal "stimuli," that would seem the more paradoxical from the standpoint of reinforcement theory.

Gestalt psychology. Of the major strands in recent psychological theorizing, only Gestalt psychology and the loosely derivative cognitive and "phenomenological" theories can be regarded as at all hospitable to the notion of human rationality. These views have of course had only a minority voice in American psychology, although it cannot be accidental that social psychologists have more frequently been influenced by them than others.

As we know, the Gestalt tradition recognized, even emphasized the phenomena of intelligent thought and behavior. But as a contending model for depicting the place of rationality in human nature, it presents its substantial difficulties. There is, for one thing, the difficult leap to be made between the phenomenal or brain field with its intrinsic tendencies toward good structure, on the one hand, and events in the non-psychological world, on the other: the problem of relations between psychological and objective environments, or, phrased differently, that of veridicality, a crucial one for the conceptualization and analysis of socially rational behavior. And the indubitably irrational is left, in Gestalt treatments such as Asch's (1952), as a residual category rather than explored for its own kinds of lawfulness; the manifest aspects of blindness and cussedness in human nature rather than its reasonableness now are matters for perplexity. To make much headway in understanding the conditions and limitations under which rational—and irrational—thought and behavior occur, we must proceed, it seems to me, in terms of functionalist principles that have somehow been foreign to the orthodox Gestaltist. Cognitive functional psychologies such as Bruner's (Bruner, Goodnow, and Austin, 1956) may give us more help here.

Recent developments along these lines, and perhaps others such as the formal decision theory that is currently taking shape through related efforts by psychologists, economists, and students of organization (Edwards, 1954), may be changing the picture that I have drawn. But it still seems just to conclude from our scanning of the psychological currents that have brought us to today that these currents have for the most part flowed in directions unsupportive of faith in man's rational potentialities.

A Social Psychology of Rationality

Where do the perspectives of social psychology fit into this picture? Solomon Asch (1952), in introducing his eloquent polemic for a Gestalt-inspired version of social psychology, offers at once a bleak appraisal and a challenge when he writes:

> It has to be admitted that social psychology lives today in the shadow of great doctrines of man that were formulated long before it appeared and that is has borrowed its leading ideas from neighboring regions of scientific thought and from the social philosophies of the modern period. It is paradoxical but true that social psychology has thus far made the least contribution to the questions that are its special concern and that it has as yet not significantly affected the conceptions it has borrowed. [p. viii]

Asch's answer to his own challenge, as we know, was primarily one of importing "the leading ideas" of Gestalt psychology, and the many of us who have been moved and impressed by his book can only agree that they are a leavening influence at his hands.

But need we accept his indictment of social psychology apart from what Gestalt can bring to it? Has it had nothing to add to our perspective on the place of rationality in human nature?

What was once the conceptual core of social psychology, the stock "mechanisms of social interaction"—imitation, suggestion, and sympathy—are surely vulnerable to Asch's critique. Borowed from French psychopathology or heavily influence by it, they give an oddly lunatic portrayal of the basis of social relations if we take them as a literal and sufficient account. Asch is also quite correct, I think, that much of what has passed as social psychological theory has consisted of applying theories and concepts developed in other contexts, and embraced and defended for reasons fundamentally extrinsic to the problems of social psychology.

The interactionist approach. Granted all this, I still think that Asch is selling social psychology short when he omits explicit notice of the tradition that, as I would think, can make the most valid claim to being distinctively social-psychological. His neglect is the more surprising in that much of his own analysis of social interaction so clearly belongs to it. I have in mind, let me say at once, the line of thought initiated primarily by G. H. Mead (1934), and C. H. Cooley (1902), nurtured by social psychologists bearing the credentials of sociology, assimilating relevant contributions from Piaget (1932) and Sullivan (1945), and embraced and developed by a recent generation of social psychologists within psychology—Newcomb (1950) among others—who derive from it a distinctive focus for social psychology among the behavioral sciences. As I observed elsewhere, it seems to me:

> One of the most hopeful features of the current situation . . . is the emergence from diverse quarters of incipient consensus on a model that rejects the sterile dichotomy of isolated individual vs. disembodied group. . . . This new-old model has many variants in the hands of different theorists. But its minimal features can be quickly delineated. It takes its start not from individuals or socio-cultural entities but from the interactions of persons. . . . In any functioning social group, according to this view, the isolated individual is a misleading artifact. Persons achieve communication and avoid randomness in their relationships because each already embodies much of the socio-cultural system in microcosm. That is, the symbol-systems, beliefs, and expectations of one another shared by members of a social group, the modified or emergent motives, aspirations, and standards of evaluation learned in group experience, so transform man as a biological entity that he exists always in implicit relation to others. The notion of men as social atoms somehow to be brought into significant relation to one another is simply a myth. . . .
>
> Diachronically, the model suggests that in the process of social interaction, the actor learns through time to become the sort of person who is capable of the orderly social relationships in which we later encounter him. . . . Through socialization, culture, which at the outset of the life-cycle is exterior to the person and constraining upon him, as Durkheim would have it, becomes internalized—inextricably incorporated in his very make-up. [Smith, 1954a, pp. 64–65]

Within this frame of reference, social psychology has dual foci: *socialization,* when our concern is with the events and processes that build into people the potentiality for orderly social behavior, and *communication,* when we are concerned with social behavior at a particular point of time. Each of these focal processes intrinsically depends on the other.

I submit that this is really the way that most of us have come to frame our thinking about the problems of social psychology, that it is different from the orientations predominant among psychologists a generation or so ago, and—to revert to Asch's challenge—that viewing social psychology from this perspective casts many of the "great doctrines of man" in a usefully different light. It has cut aside venerable pseudo-problems and posed new sets of fundamental issues for research. Attaining it, I would argue, is no mean achievement for social psychology.

A social psychological look at the problem of rationality from this standpoint sees it not as a given, inhering in human nature in fixed amount, but as a primarily social *achievement* and a social *process.* Our principal clues here come from G. H. Mead (1934) and from Piaget (1932); my general approach is also obviously much indebted to John Dewey (1922). Mead had the insight, still insufficiently checked and elaborated by direct investigation, that in psychological development, reflective selfhood and language are jointly acquired in the course of social interaction that becomes increasingly communicative as the process continues. Because a person becomes able to react to or interpret his own words and actions as his partner does—able to "take the role of the other," in Mead's phrase—he can steer his own participation in the interaction to his instrumental advantage. By the same token he anticipates the reaction of the other and acquires perspective on his own activity. Participating in different relationships within socially structured contexts he comes eventually to internalize the role of the "generalized other," as a stabilized source of self-perspective and of community of meaning.

Piaget's familiar early studies enrich and supplement this account. We see the child—and it may very well matter that the child is a participant in modern Western civilization—moving from egocentricity and absolutism in his judgments to reciprocity and the perspectival relativism more characteristic of adult thinking. And we get inklings of the underlying social process.

Social ingredients of rationality. Analysis along these lines suggests that at least four indispensible ingredients of rationality are products of social interaction, acquired by the child during socialization: first, a stock of symbols, counters for rational manipulation, the meanings of which have become more or less dependably stabilized through his participation in a social and linguistic community; second, a set of "rules of the game" for their combination, implicit versions of what the logicians once liked to call the "laws of thought," a syntax of thought as well as of language; third, the ability by shifting perspective to attain a degree of objectivity toward one's own behavior and mental operations; and fourth, by slight extension, the ability to check the results of one's symbolic processes by "consensual validation" or its internalized equivalent. Rational thought becomes understandable as a kind of inner dialogue, an inherently social process.

Rationality versus irrationality in human development. For this schematic and elementary account to become relevant to my theme, however, I must broaden the context to rough in a few other features of what seems to me to be a plausible eclectic view of the way rationality develops. We can probably agree that the baby who is to acquire rationality and selfhood in interaction with those representatives of the socio-cultural *status quo,* his parents, starts out utterly non-rational, a creature of urges, lacks, and unexamined immediacies, much as the psychoanalysts suppose him to be. Let us grant him developing sensory and motor capacities, and satisfactions in putting them to use. Let us further assume that from early in his life, if not from the beginning, he tries to put his experience in some sort of order. Next comes a moot point: What assumptions shall we make about his intellectual curiosity or laziness? If we can count on curiosity, it will provide an intrinsic push to expand his horizons as he gains access to new ranges of information. But laziness, a principle of least mental effort, seems to be part of the picture, too, as Gardner Murphy (1958) has pointed out. Perhaps the best we can do here is to equivocate: The laziness that favors simplicity and sameness over complexity and change in one's cognitive structures, as long as one can get away with it, seems real enough; whether or not curiosity also develops may depend on a variety of factors, probably social ones. We leave unresolved how these opposed but not necessarily contradictory tendencies may interact.

With the achievement of language and the complicated symbolic and social processes that it makes possible, the developing creature is now a person. But symbolic complexity, necessary condition for rationality that it is, also lays the foundation for irrationality. Already he is subject to stresses that disturb the still quite unstable equilibrium that he has been able to achieve, and exceed his powers of problem-solving, uncertainly augumented as they are by his new symbolic equipment. Parental demands to put off the gratifications of being a small animal for the measured satisfactions of civilized restraint; parental disapproval itself internalized and thus a threat to the weak and incipient self; sensed weakness before the assaults of inner and of outer stimulation—all these are sources of the universal phenomena of conflict, anxiety, shame, and guilt. Meanwhile the same, distinctively human symbolic equipment that he has now available for use in problem-solving can be turned to evading problems that threaten to overwhelm him, or to making them more supportable without solving them. Soon he begins to learn the many all-too-human ways of manipulating himself symbolically when threats are too great or too obscure for realistic coping; the loss of innocence that comes with reflective awareness makes possible the insidious comforts of dissimulation to the self as well as to others. The possibilities of neurotic irrationality and of rational problem-solving thus lie on opposite sides of the same symbolic coin.

Factors promoting rationality versus irrationality. We may now ask, what are the factors that may tip the balance toward rationality, what toward evasiveness? The clinical lore on which I am drawing is quite explicit about determinants of irrationality. Among them, it tells us that irrationality proliferates when the challenge to a person's adaptation is too severe, or too obscure, to be met head-on with the resources then at his command, or when it engages residues in his personality structure accrued from previous evasive reactions to equivalent challenges. Irrationality arises by default in the absence of sufficient frustration tolerance and of the requisite knowledge and skill; it may be postively encouraged by example and reward.

As for rationality, the "clinical" lore is less explicit, but suggestions are at hand which go beyond mere negation of the unfavorable determinants that we have just considered. For one, there is the discipline of experience with the world of things, and here I would include factual encounter with the functional properties of other people as well as with those of the inanimate world, as these condition the success of a person's instrumental efforts. As long as experience can be kept a gentle rather than a severe taskmaster by the appropriate scheduling of developmental tasks, instrumental encounter with thing and fact keeps autism in check and may goad even the lazy intellect to revising assumptions and expanding the environmental context within which behavior is oriented. As a determinant of rationality, *thing-encounter* is not specifically social, although it may be socially "programmed" and facilitated.

A second factor promoting rationality, opportunity for the *social validation* of the steps and outcomes of one's symbolic processes, follows directly from our standard account of the interactive genesis of complex symbolic thought. Continual opportunity to test one's assumptions and expectations in social interaction keeps one's "generalized other," as Mead might put it, under constant revision, and like thing-encounter, also serves to control autistic tendencies that unless somehow counteracted would gradually warp one's thinking with respect to his private wishes and fears.

Social or consensual validation has of course been emphasized particularly by Sullivan (1945) and his school of psychiatry, on the one hand, and more recently by Festinger (1950), on the other. One can hardly exaggerate its importance, yet as a determinant of rationality, it is equivocal in some respects. The trouble is that the interactive checking that corrects unwarranted idiosyncrasy (and therefore plays such a major role in psychotherapy) does no good when autisms are common to a social group, or when culturally provided information happens to be wrong. And our studies of culture and personality give us good reason for expecting the shared autism to be a frequent phenomenon, not a rarity. Insufficiently dependable by itself, social validation needs to be checked and supplemented. Direct thing-encounter, when there is opportunity for it, provides one such corrective. But the symbolic world of modern man extends far beyond the rather limited range in which it is sufficiently feasible to be of much help. Still a third factor in rationality thus becomes of crucial importance.

This is the body of socially transmitted "rules of the game" for effective thinking and problem solving, and the values associated with their use, that I will call for convenience *"rational culture"*—"know-how" and "think-how" if you will. At a rudimentary level, this begins with the implicit rules of logic and syntax that, as our model has it, the young child acquires with his first skills in communicative interaction. It goes on to include the full range of skills and aids for coping with reality that his culture makes available without his having to discover or invent them afresh.

Historical cultures have differed enormously in their constructive and critical resources for bolstering rationality. And among them, contemporary industrial civilization is unique in the actual and potential power of its rational culture. The point has been put eloquently in recent essays by Bronowski (1956) and by Gardner Murphy (1958), and I can only rephrase it briefly to fit the present context. The message is an important one for the problem that we started with.

The point, of course, is that the dynamic factor, and the amazing novelty, in our contemporary culture is *science,* as a rational progam for discovery, a cumulative social endeavor, a "habit of truth," a way of life with its own values that have emerged from the inescapable conditions of its practice. As a rational subculture without precedent, it gives new meaning to the concept of rationality, and warrants new aspirations for what man may make of himself.

The trouble is, science is a *sub*culture. The values that go with its technological products have diffused far more widely than its own values and thought-ways. Indeed, it is the former that are undoubtedly responsible for the ineluctable spread throughout the world of the urban industrial complex—as well as for the critical urgency of our current dilemmas. What we most urgently need, implies Bronowski, is more general diffusion of the values and of the spirit of science (which he sees as essentially those of responsible democracy); where as psychologists and behavioral scientists our challenge and our hope lie, says Murphy, is in marshalling our immense powers of discovery and invention to release new dimensions of human potentiality.

In the pursuit of a social psychological perspective on rationality, we began with the liberal's implicit faith in the basic reasonableness of human nature, which, as it seemed, has been rather badly undermined. We then took a look at some of the principal currents in general psychological theory, asking what they had to say about rationality. On the whole, our review yielded little to support a faith in rationality—rather to the contrary—while it also raised some doubts about the adequacy of the theories to deal sensibly with the question that we put to them. We turned then to social psychology, and found that according to the frame of reference that is emerging as predominant, rationality is a social achievement, not a given, and rational thought a social process. Examining the roots of rational problem-solving in the context of the rather jerry-built model of human development that embodies my present convictions, we came to the paradox that if rationality is a social product, so is irrationality; both depend on manipulations of the symbolic equipment, cultural in content and social in genesis, that is distinctive of mankind. Here, I think, we have managed to clear away some of the confusion occasioned by an unwarranted *faith* in human rationality, and set the stage for a more *rational* examination of the conditions under which rational or irrational dispositions are likely to develop and become manifest.

Embarking speculatively on such an examination, we tried to itemize some of these conditions, possible determinants of rationality and irrationality that, once explicitly recognized, can give us reason to hope that higher levels of rationality may be socially attainable. Among these, we singled out for special attention what we called "rational culture," of which the values and thought-ways of modern science are a unique and portentous variant.

Our psychological tour can hardly be said to warrant optimism. Technology may outdistance science, and blow us up; irrationality may get ahead of rationality. No unseen hand has necessarily stacked the cards in our favor. Perhaps, however, the perspective we have attained may embolden us to stick by our values in a spirit of adventure and rational determination. We need not faith, which is vulnerable, but resourcefulness, courage, and determination.

27

On Rereading Proust

"Every psychologist should read Proust." Like many other psychologists, I had long subscribed to this pious maxim without doing much about it. Years ago when I was in basic training in World War II—more or less on a dare to myself—I had read *Swann's Way* and got through much of *Within a Budding Grove* before I bogged down and returned to Dashiell Hammett as more compatible with army life. Since then, the two fat volumes of the Random House edition had sat on my shelves for a quarter century. What returned me to Proust was the definitive two-volume biography by Painter, the second volume of which appeared recently in an American edition. Reading Painter, a biographer who admirably meets the dual criteria of sound scholarship and discriminating love for his subject, naturally sent me back to Proust. And the novel on its part returned me to Painter. Here I report on my involvement in this dialogue between novelist and biographer, in the hope that other psychologists may be enticed to expose themselves to it. Many should find it interesting, and even profitable.

That *A la Recherche du Temps Perdu* is a psychological masterpiece as well as an artistic one is a truism. There are the famous descriptive passages, in which Proust offers a sensitive phenomenology of some of the more fleeting and impalpable aspects of subjective experience. And there is his explicit psychologizing—in such observations as these:[1] "For as the dead exist only in us, it is ourselves that we strike without ceasing when we persist in recalling the blows that we have dealt them" (Vol. 2, p. 115). "That fear of suffering in the immediate present which condemns us to perpetual suffering." (Vol. 2, p. 814); what better capsule formulation of the neurotic character? "Affecting laudable sentiments is not the only way of concealing reprehensible ones, but a newer way is to make a show of the latter in order at least not to appear to shut one's eyes to them" (Vol. 2, p. 903).

Proust's performance as a psychological phenomenologist and theorist

Reprinted by permission from *Contemporary Psychology,* 1967, *12,* 337–340, where it appeared as a review of G. D. Painter, *Proust,* Vol. 1. The *Early Years,* 1959; Vol. 2, *The Later Years,* 1965. Boston and Toronto: Little, Brown & Company.

1. Page references are to the two-volume Random House edition, translated by C. K. Scott Moncrieff and Frederick A. Blossom.

may impress us, but after this second encounter, I now see that it does not constitute his primary value to psychologists. After all, the *aperçus* do not really add to our stock of formulated knowledge; the phenomenological descriptions may on their part contribute to sensitizing our own awareness, but as exhibits for a human museum, they come in a cluttered jumble like the collections of the old Smithsonian. They have potential value, but finding it may not be worth the trouble.

It is rather from Proust the great novelist and *implicit* psychologist that we have the most to learn. In this capacity, Proust does not theorize or describe; he recreates and presents. As readers we can then make the psychology explicit if we wish.

Here we encounter a puzzle. *A la Recherche* is cast as reminiscence. Yet as Painter traces out in fascinating detail, the novel transmutes the materials of Proust's life in an artistic reconstruction. The Narrator speaks with Proust's voice, yet with modifications and rearrangements; the characters of the novel have their sources in Proust's experience, yet are seldom lifted bodily from life: we read in Painter of multiple sources for single characters, of fusions and recombinations. It is clear that some alterations involve a kind of censorship, changes like those a psychologist would make in preparing a case history for publication. But for the most part the transmutation appears to be in the service of artistic rather than pragmatic ends, to extract meaningful patterns from the less orderly events of life. Are we likely, then, to be informed or to be misled as psychologists by the way that Proust the artist has modified biographical fact? Must we read *Remembrance* as a *roman à clef?* Or can we read it as a self-contained work of art, as Proust himself would have us?

Moving back and forth between Proust and Painter, I soon decided that Proust's implicit psychology can be sorted into two categories: a general psychology fully embodied in his novel, to which the facts of his own biography are irrelevant, and a special psychology of people like Proust and his Narrator, where we need the help of the biographer. Here, I can only suggest the contents of these psychologies, and invite other psychologists to read Proust and Painter for themselves.

What of the general psychology? Each psychologist-reader will find contributions that reflect his own concerns as much as Proust's achievement. The ones that most interest me pertain to person perception and the integration of personality. In keeping with Proust's preoccupation with Time, both of these topics are explored developmentally.

Nowhere else is the temporal unfolding of how we see other persons—from first encounter through the full course of a personal relationship—so richly, suggestively, and I think accurately exhibited. Time and again, Proust displays for us what is bound to be elusive in our retrospective views of our own lives. In our own attempts at reconstruction, our later, firmer, more differentiated frames for cognizing another person have preemptive force;

try as we will, we cannot recapture the innocence, the arbitrariness of our initial impressions, or the vicissitudes through which our views have developed. In achieving this miracle, Proust provides indispensable raw materials for theorists of person perception.

Proust's treatment of person perception is part and parcel of his approach to personality, one that suggests the dramaturgical models of Goffman (1959) and Sarbin (1954). In what we know of one another, we are mostly captives of the perspectives entailed by our positions, our interests, and our preemptive assumptions, and also influenced by how each party to the relationship consciously or unconsciously chooses to present himself. In a convincing reconstruction of a living world, Proust's novel vividly illustrates the pervasive importance of such perspectives.

Personality as we see it through Proust is insubstantial, at least at first glance. Public and private faces do not correspond, self-awareness is self-deceptive, roles and selves are only loosely linked, over time there are marked discontinuities. Is this depiction a matter of deliberate strategy, on analogy with the impressionism that Proust so admired in painting, in which shimmering surfaces are deployed so as to evoke in the beholder subtler experiences of three-dimensional solidity? Or is it partly the accidental result of the juggling by which Proust formed earlier and later phases of the same character on different living models? Since we are concerned here with Proust the novelist rather than Proust the explicit psychologist, such questions must remain open. Our thinking about the integration of personality is, all the same, bound to be enriched as we encounter Proust's world of complex and believable people.

On all these matters, the psychologist can read Proust's novel profitably without any key to the underlying facts of personal biography on which he has drawn. Not so when it comes to the special psychology, where our interest is in what we can learn from Proust's formulations about people like himself or his Narrator. The lack of complete identity between the two poses the problem. Proust devotes whole volumes to the nature and course of possessive love and jealousy, to mourning and subsequent oblivion. Clearly not all love has the tortured, self-defeating quality that is portrayed. Just as clearly, a repetitive pattern in Proust's own life is being expressed. But the author holds back things we need to know as psychologists if we are to use his report.

Most serious is the problem presented by Proust's well-documented homosexuality. Any psychologist reading the novel would probably decide on internal evidence alone that Proust's personal entanglements with homosexuality were more direct than those of the Narrator. Sodom and Gomorrah are central to the novel. The "transposition" of the Narrator's heterosexual relationships from their homosexual origins in Proust's life is not wholly convincing psychologically—how could it be?—or, I think, entirely successful artistically. (These are judgments that Painter avoids.) In a characteristic passage near the end of his novel, Proust might be said to put us on guard.

He is talking rather about how the *reader* may introduce such transformations.

> The writer should not be offended to see his heroines given masculine countenances by the invert. . . . In reality, each reader reads only what is already within himself. The book is only a sort of optical instrument which the writer offers to the reader to enable the latter to discover in himself what he would not have found but for the aid of the book. . . . Furthermore, the book may be too learned, too obscure, for the simple-minded reader and therefore provide him with only a cloudy glass, through which he will be unable to read. But other peculiarities, such as inversion, may make it necessary for the reader to read in a certain way in order to understand, and the author should not take offence but should give the reader the maximum liberty, saying to him, See whether you read better with this glass or that, or with some other. [Vol. 2, p. 1024]

For the psychologist, the biographical detail that Painter gives us provides the right "glass." We learn, and it is important, that Proust had several relationships with girls and women before he became confirmed in his homosexuality. We find that love and jealousy as he depicts them represent a fusion of hetero- and homosexual experiences. One can then puzzle over the ready intertranslatability of such experiences for Proust. The Narrator's poignant memories of Mama, moreover, become for us part of a history of homosexuality as well as of dependency and asthma.

Knowing of Proust's adult homosexuality, knowing also of the equation between the "captive" Albertine and Proust's former chauffeur Agostinelli, puts many perplexities in order and allows us to read as psychologists, leaving the detective work to others. New puzzles, psychologically more interesting ones, come into view. Thus we learn from Painter that earlier apprentice versions of Proust's life-novel, completed before Proust had lived out the Agostinelli episode, also came to a climax with such a great, jealous, and unhappy love. As Painter writes,

> It is as though Proust imposed upon his love for Agostinelli the pre-existing pattern not only of his total previous experience of love in his own life, but of the climax of his novel. Agostinelli was conducted along the road to his tragic end by the ineluctable mechanism of a work of art; he was killed by *A la Recherche;* and when he seemed a free agent, like Albertine in her flight to Touraine, he journeyed to his death. *A la Recherche* is a work consecrated by two human sacrifices, the deaths of Mme Proust and Agostinelli, for which Proust himself, in his own mind and in fact, was partly responsible. [Vol. 2, p. 209]

The interplay here between life and art becomes accessible to us only through Painter's biography.

Once we possess the essential biographical facts, new questions about the novel arise. Why is Proust's brother absent from the novel? Why is his bereavement for his mother shifted in the novel to his grandmother? And whence the fusion that produces the magnificent tragic figure of Charlus?—the tragedy now uncovered as Proust's own creation, not drawn from the living models. Some major biographical questions remain open despite Painter's efforts. What are we to make of the Narrator's horrified fascination with Lesbianism? Just what sort of potential or actual misbehavior on Agostinelli's part was Proust actually jealous of?

Proust's prominently displayed theory of "unconscious memory" is best considered as another topic of his special psychology, though Proust would have us regard it as a general theoretical contribution. Beyond any doubt, Proust is presenting his own seriously held views when he portrays the writer as a translator and evoker of symbols, who uses the avenue of "unconscious" (read involuntary) redintegrative memory to escape from the ephemeral to a realm of timeless essences. Painter also takes this doctrine at face value as a serious contribution to aesthetics, abandoning for once the dialogue between man and novel.

Yet the theory can hardly stand on its own. Proust never makes it clear *why* the redintegration of early-experienced scenes and moods is so deeply satisfying. Is the magic of the madeleine a general truth that Proust has had the fortune to discover (as Proust and Painter seem to believe), or is it something special to Proust and people like him? If we agree with Painter that the *Recherche* as a whole is a mythical reconstruction of Proust's life as a writer, we must treat his theory of writing as a part of this reconstruction, and ask whether the independently established facts of his life throw light on its special meaning for him. They clearly do.

A la Recherche as an account of its own gestation and birth is indeed a myth. Near the end of the immense novel, we see the Narrator about to begin his masterwork, an aging man whose life thus far has been indolent and ineffectual. But we learn from Painter about Proust's life-long apprenticeship as a writer—the hard work, the writing and rewriting, the false starts, the incorporation of new material in reconstructed frames. We see him struggling for years with the techniques of writing and with the materials of his life experience. Proust's theory of memory deals retrospectively with the inspiration of his writing, not with its craftsmanship.

One may well doubt whether he actually relied much on "unconscious memory" as he wrote. My guess—Painter is too respectful of his subject to help us directly here—is that it played rather little part. We know from Painter that the climax of the novel in the Narrator's tragic relationship with Albertine was written not in calm recollection but in the immediacy of contemporaneous grief and mourning: no unconscious memory here. Nor is there any question of it in his expertly contrived story of Swann. On the other hand, there is no reason to doubt that Proust derived a sense of the timeless that stirred him deeply from early memories that were evoked by association with present sensory fragments. As readers of his novel, we accept and believe in the special Proustian meaning of Time Recaptured so long as we are under the novel's spell. We do so because Proust is a great novelist who makes us full participants in the Proustian world. But the theory, examined coldly, tells us something about Proust as a person—not about how he actually wrote his novel, or how other novels ought to be written or read.

Its personal meaning for Proust is suggested by the special linkage between his theory and his memories of the idealized Combray of his childhood, and of his mother's kisses, which he wanted exclusively for his very own. The theme seems to be the same as the one Keniston (1965) found to underlie the fantasies of his alienated Harvard students: a Pyrrhic victory in the Oedipal conflict; disillusion with the father and with the father's world of adult affairs; ambivalence toward the intrusive mother; longing for return to the Golden Age when mother's love was possessed exclusively, even for return to the womb—or cork-lined room. If "unconscious memory" can retrieve this Golden Age from the corruptions and ravages of time, no wonder that Proust celebrates it. Though it does not at all explain his mastery as an artist, it provides the grand theme of his novel. And its origins, if we are to believe Keniston, draw together in psychological congruence his two auxiliary themes of homosexuality and of disillusionment—and very likely his pathology of asthma as well.

Of course to establish this interpretation persuasively would require a much more careful exegesis than is appropriate here. My point is not: Such is the truth about Proust. It is rather that the combination of a great psychological novel with a great biography provides succulent food for psychological speculation. Here is rich material for the study of lives.

28

Some Thoughts on the Legitimation of Evil

In early 1966, the Council of the Society for the Psychological Study of Social Issues, in a discussion of then-current social problems, expressed deep concern over the indifference of the American people to the large-scale torturing of prisoners by the South Vietnamese troops under American supervision and over the large-scale use of napalm by the American planes in the bombing of Vietnamese villages. Council members felt that the American people had closed their minds to these unnecessary cruelties, an attitude not unlike the defensive attitudes of the German people to the existence of the Nazi extermination camps and not unlike similar attitudes held by most Americans toward the systematic suppression of the Negro people over the past century.

As Milton Rokeach, then president-elect of the Society, put it in a letter to various psychologists, social scientists, social critics and philosophers:

> Council members felt further that all such phenomena could perhaps be considered as but different forms of behavior manifested under conditions wherein evil is socially legitimized. In a symposium on "The Legitimation of Evil" sponsored by SPSSI at the 1965 Annual Meetings of the American Psychological Association, several speakers pointed to the relevance of Hannah Arendt's ideas on the "banality of evil," discussed in her *Eichmann in Jerusalem* [1965], for an understanding of active participation in or passive condoning of evil acts by large numbers of individuals. Arendt's analysis of Eichmann as a banal rather than monstrous person acting in a context of social legitimacy was considered to have important sociopsychological implications extending far beyond an understanding of Eichmann alone. Similar social processes may well account for Stanley Milgram's [1963] finding, in the context of a socially legitimized laboratory experiment on learning, that over 60 percent of Yale undergraduates and New Haven adults obeyed an experimenter's commands to inflict severe physical pain and suffering on other human beings.

In the letter I have just quoted, essays were invited from a number of possible contributors to a proposed symposium volume on this topic. Perhaps because developments in the Vietnam war and in the domestic urban crisis were out of tune with such a cool, intellectualized approach to critical problems of the time, plans for the volume proved abortive. The planned symposium was the context for the following remarks, which I wrote in the fall of 1967.

I still remember my puzzlement when—early in college—I first heard of the "problem of evil." Having been raised outside of any religious tradition (the offspring of assimilated Methodists), I could not grasp why there was a "problem." Not believing in an all-good and all-powerful God, I had no reason to expect or to demand an all-good world. Of course the real world, that of nature as well as that created by man, was a mixed bag. Some things were good, some bad. And good and bad were at least partly a matter of perspective, which might vary as between carnivores and their prey. There was no cosmic moral scheme to be shaken by the unexplained presence of unwelcome facts. There were no promises that, lacking fulfillment, could breed disillusionment. My first naive misunderstanding of the "problem of evil" has turned out to be my lasting understanding of its only substantial meaning: what to do about evil, how to undo it. I have never been surprised that there are things about man and the world that are bad for people. And that, I have always thought, is at root what evil is about.

All the same, the myth of the Garden, the Tree, and the Apple seems to me to express an important truth. It symbolizes a crucial advance in the still recent prehistory of humanity—the discovery of Ought. Taken together with the emergence of language and self-consciousness, "knowledge of good and evil," as reflected in the myth of Genesis, marked the attainment of full human status. One can readily imagine a nonhuman animal that uses tools, and we now know that there are such. But a conscientious, self-conscious creature, a social creature that formulates its experience and its obligations to self and others, cannot be conceived as other than man—or at any rate as a being with whom man would immediately find close kinship. "Knowledge of good and evil" represents the step from unexamined preference to socially-rooted obligation—obligation to God the Father as the myth had it, but also to fathers, to members of family and tribe, and, with increasing awareness, to self. In this context, Evil was not merely what was bad for man; indeed, it sometimes became altogether detached from this meaning. Rather, it was what, for deep social and cultural reasons, men agreed *ought* not to be or *ought* not to be done. As the myth had it, the fact of human responsibility and the possibility of sin depend on the existence of obligations that go beyond preference.

But a social view of the moral sense calls into question the meaningfulness of the phrase "the legitimation of evil," with which this symposium is concerned. If evil is whatever violates socially transmitted and internalized obligations, and obligations are legitimate to the extent that their acceptance is shared in a social group together with the awareness that it is shared, how can evil be "legitimated"? And if it *is* legitimated, does it remain evil? According to the cultural relativism that prevailed among social scientists just before World War II, the meaning of good and evil is contained exhaustively in the transmitted social norms, and "legitimated evil" is either a contradiction in terms or an awkward and vacuous expression like "melted ice" for water.

The critical posture of cultural relativism, while it encouraged respect for the values of each different culture on its own terms, in effect challenged the *general* validity of all historically received values. And the corrosive impact of modern scientific-technical-urban culture, as it spread willy-nilly throughout the world, tended universally to undercut the foundations of traditional values. The ethos of the warrior Sioux, admirable as it may have been as one realization of human potentiality, had clearly become obsolete. Were many of our own values obsolescent? Even in the refined and universalized versions shaped by the great ethical religions, traditional ethics and morals still showed their roots in the tribe. What most modern men would regard as great evil had obviously been perpetrated in the name of tribal values. If today the negative, critical message of cultural relativism seems an inadequate guide and its positive, appreciative message (each culture valid in its own terms) strikes us as sentimental or wrong-headed, we should not forget the deceit, the repression, the carnage enacted throughout history in the name of culture-bound absolutes. The critical and tolerant perspective of cultural relativism remains relevant so long as we have still to outgrow the world of ethnocentric tribes and nations. The necessary transition from this tribal-nationalistic world promises at best to be much more difficult and painful than we had previously thought.

In the language of the old myth, the insights of cultural relativism (for those who share them) involve a second portentous bite into the fruit of the Tree of Knowledge, one that has conjured us far, far from the Garden of Eden. In our new sophistication, we have not only lost the primal innocence of Like and Want; we have also lost the assurance of ethnocentric Ought. As solidary traditional society has given way to individualism, we have to face a plurality of Oughts, personal and cultural. Sophisticated man has to choose and cannot merely receive the version of good and evil that he is to live by. In the absence of genuine community in the new urban society, his moral position often seems painfully exposed.

For middle-aged liberals the encounter with Nazi Germany and involvement in World War II shook the complacency of prior relativism. As an argument against cultural relativism, the fact of Nazi evil had all of the pragmatic cogency and illogic of Dr. Johnson's refutation of solipsism: kicking a rock. For liberals who encountered it, Nazism was unquestionably and close to absolutely evil, with no ifs, ands, or buts—there was nothing relative about it. Liberals found that they could *not* grant the Nazi Weltanschauung validity equal to their own; they discovered that they, in fact, held to value commitments that they were unwilling to regard as valid only "within *this* culture." The existence of Nazism could not undermine the relativist perspective logically; rather, it opened the eyes of those who had proclaimed relativism to the fact that they did not *really* mean it after all; faced with such a disturbing challenge to their own values, they discovered that they could not accept its full consequences.

But just as Dr. Johnson's kick in favor of naive realism hardly resolved the metaphysical question, neither did the moral kick by the Nazis provide a satisfactory basis for ethical standards, free from reliance upon ethnocentric tradition or its other guise, theological authority. The liberals, on their part, continue to grope awkwardly toward a humanistic ethic with rankling doubts about the weight to be given to tradition and about the actual content of emerging ethical codes. The postliberal young—"hippies," New Left radicals and others who have recently cut loose from the Protestant ethic—seem to be seeking, in different directions, to simplify the moral issues.

For some, the experience of Ought has suffered extreme attrition. The "flower children," while they last, seem to be engaged in a touching pretense that the primal innocence of Paradise can actually be regained, where Want and Like are supreme, Ought is restricted to the minimums of "live and let live," and positive value is assigned to ambiguous Love and to intense experience of all kinds. This intended innocence seems, unavoidably, to involve a degree of pretense. For so long as cultural continuity is not entirely broken, gains in moral knowledge and sophistication are basically as irreversible as those in science and technology. If one intentionally turns back to a simpler moral world, it is likely to be at the cost of maintaining denial of the moral complexities with which our still-continuous cultural tradition confronts us, as well as of the practical exigencies of the political world.

Others—the activists of the New Left—also engage in simplifications that are hard for a person reared in the liberal tradition to stomach. The angry young people who have gained the limelight on some of the best American campuses have a vivid sense of Evil and a refreshing sense of principled Ought that admirably governs their political lives. But finding the credentials of traditional liberal values wanting, they are likely to follow their strong moral intuitions into a new absolutism for which the existentialist fiat of commitment seemingly gives them charter. In the name of an intuitive humanism, they tend to cut loose from the modulated discriminations of the humanist tradition. The pragmatic compromises of action in the real political world get written off indiscriminately as hypocrisy and evil. When the American president, identified with an unsavory contemporary version of old-time military power politics, is reviled as no different from a Hitler or a Stalin, and at the same time the more violent romanticism of Black Power is swallowed with scarcely a blink, there is, at best, evidence of moral confusion on the part of potential leaders in moral reform.

These hit-and-run comments, which may seem to stray rather widely from the topic of our symposium, are a necessary preamble to my contribution for two reasons. In order to talk cogently about the "legitimation of evil," I have to locate the terms of the problem in the framework of meanings that they have acquired in the social-moral controversy of recent times. And in order to put my own necessarily personal contribution in perspective, I need to make clear its foundation in a rather old-fashioned liberal outlook—one, to be sure, that exposure to recent history has purged of the old naive *faith* in Progress, but which nevertheless regards the *hope* for progress and the *determination* to attain it as precious human possessions, not to be discarded casually.

My kind of liberalism insists that in the moral realm progress and retrogression are meaningful and can be identified though without complete consensus. It further insists that if we can keep a rather clear view of progress and retrogression—a matter of shades of gray, not of black and white—we will find ourselves with a full and urgent agenda for social and political action that excludes quietism as irrelevant and equally excludes the more apocalyptic forms of activism, however understandable and honorable they may be. Illiberal activism may be a healthy moral exercise for the young as they resist coming to terms prematurely with a flagrantly imperfect society, but it is an inadequate stance for political adults in a world that badly needs the committed contributions of people who can bring *both* fervently held principles *and* pragmatic cogency and skill to bear on a host of complex and difficult but immensely challenging problems. The new powers that man has attained, and the unprecedented levels of organized complexity in human society and culture, make the stakes very high.

In the call for the symposium, three conspicuous cases of legitimized evil were evoked, in which ordinary people have actively or passively gone along with antihuman actions: genocide in the Nazi extermination camps, the barbarities of torture and napalm in the Vietnam war, and the systematic suppression of the Negro people in the United States over the past century. These major historical tragedies were put in the context of Arendt's ideas about the "banality of evil" and of Milgram's provocative—and ethically troublesome—experiment. Contemplation of the readiness with which supposedly civilized citizens have condoned or actively ignored such barbarities sets our problem. For liberals, it has badly shaken our earlier faith, as it turned out ill-grounded, in the goodness of human nature. Pessimistic conceptions of human nature and potentiality, always the stock-in-trade of conservatives, now receive a ready hearing, and echoes of the old theological version of Fallen Man compete with claims, arising from some of the same sources, that God is dead. The symposium is obviously supposed to respond constructively to this predicament of moral consciousness and action: to think it through as honestly as possible in the light of emerging psychological knowledge, not to be immobilized in a state of moral shock.

The instances that the editors call to mind are ones that morally sensitive people are likely to greet with extreme revulsion. Since it is my guess, as an unreconstructed liberal, that the mood of revulsion is leading younger-generation intellectuals toward romantic nihilistic gestures rather than to considered action to improve the real world, my first concern here is to try to break out of tunnel vision focused exclusively on the chamber of recent horrors that is too likely to dominate our view of the problem, and to place these legitimated evils in broader context. My initial argument will be that insofar as the cases with which we are preoccupied differ from the long history of human wrong-doing, they differ because evil was enacted *in spite of* the prevalence of high ethical standards. Human behavior, on the whole, cannot be said to be blacker than before (though deviations like the Nazis do give us doubt); perhaps we may find some hope in the cause of our dismay—that high aspirations for human behavior prevail.

It is easy enough to turn up instances without end to add to Vietnam and Belsen—examples that we would readily agree present Evil, whose legitimacy at the time was scarcely challenged. A brief look at a selected few may serve to highlight what distinguishes the situations with which Arendt and Milgram are concerned.

One struck me not long ago as an adopted Californian: the historically very recent genocide of California Indians, as reported in Theodora Kroeber's popular book *Ishi* (1961). The wide attention that *Ishi* has received seems to have sprung from romantic individualism, which is fascinated by the story of the "last wild Indian," who had been carrying on his precarious traditional life as a hunter and gatherer on the very doorstep of urban California before he turned up in the first decade of the century, a confused ward of modern civilization. I have seen little notice paid to Mrs. Kroeber's low-keyed account, near the beginning of the book, of the heartless genocide that the California ranchers practiced on the peaceable, unorganized Indians of the Sierra foothills. We read in *Ishi* how the ranchers shot the Indians down for weekend sport—not *like* varmints but *as* varmints, wiping out their encampments man, woman, and child, with the wounded left to die. As a relevant fact about Americans, this hits even closer to home than Milgram's provocative data. These were our honored forebears, not the rugged pioneers from whom a tooth-and-claw relation to the savage environment might be understood, but established farmers of the 1870's and 1880's, when the frontier was already only a memory. Worse, these respectable Californians did not have to cook up a fantastic delusive system, a race mythology Nazi-style, to justify their genocide. This was a weekend shoot, sport that also cleared the land of minor predators against poultry. Legitimation, for those who took part in the crime, apparently came easy. They seem to have acted on the folk saying, "The only good Indian is a dead Indian"—without the component of respect felt by the slayers of Plains Indians toward their warrior enemies. People as mere varmints—this is Evil without the formal dress of ideology.

A more notorious example may be more relevant to American dilemmas in the exercise of world power (though echoes of "people as varmints" transpire from Vietnam): the behavior of the European imperial states under the Kipling morality—so recently that our hero of yesterday, Winston Churchill, participated in the action as a young man. The evils of imperialism and colonialism at its height are too well known to need recapitulation here. High cultures were ridden over rough-shod and destroyed, people were killed and imprisoned, autonomous initiative was suppressed for the one-sided gain of the imperial powers. We are still living with the human problems that this nineteenth-century venture left in its wake.

If colonial imperialism was undoubtedly evil from present perspectives, the effort expended to make it seem legitimate differentiates it from the Californian genocide. Obsolete as the talk of the "white man's burden" has become as a moral justification, it reflected the uneasiness felt by European imperialists at the moral quality of their adventure. It was always shabby as an excuse, and it seems impossibly hypocritical today, but it was seriously offered and meant. It does more credit to its Victorian spokesmen than the callous disregard of the white hunters for the feelings of their Indian quarry, or, for that matter, than the Nazi racist ideology that never pretended to be seeking the good of the "lesser races." Not only did it reflect a higher morality in terms of human values; pragmatically, actions carried out in its name served to mitigate somewhat the crassness of colonial rule and unintentionally to lay the groundwork for the postcolonial era. On balance, the process by which colonial evil was legitimated might in itself be regarded as a net good. From the standpoint of the victims (who should have the strongest vote!), hypocrisy in action may be preferable to naked predation.

Another overlapping type of case to complicate our consideration of how evil has been legitimated may be found in the long, still continuing sequence of religious, nationalistic, ideological, and tribal wars. The evil that was involved is from *our* perspective, as we see the damage to human lives and human values. With few exceptions, the participants had no awareness of evil in their own actions: they saw themselves as fighting for the right—for tribe or homeland, for truth, for salvation. God was always on *their* side. We can speak here of "legitimation of evil" only in an abstract, retrospective way that hardly fits the psychological worlds of the participants. For them, the *other* side, the enemy, represented Evil. Their own side, as good, was immediately legitimate, and did not at all require "legitimation." And even from our sophisticated, retrospective view, the things people said they were fighting for—faith, honor, loyalty, and the rest—

appear as goods. If a modern accounting of human values deplores righteous war, we can still find much that is honorable in the warrior. The problems of ethnocentric conflict remain to be surmounted, but it is not these problems that we have in mind when we talk of the legitimation of evil.

In one not very useful sense, to be sure, legitimation of evil can virtually be taken for granted as the normal state of affairs. People have characteristically behaved rather badly toward one another, especially toward strangers who did not fully qualify as people by the prevailing definitions of kinship and tribe. Ever since human society emerged as a moral order, human cultures have provided justification for what people do—and individuals have elaborated their own justifications and rationalizations for their personal actions. According to any "objective" yardstick of human values applied retrospectively, *most* evil—harm done by man to man—is legitimate. It is unlegitimated evil that is the rarity. Satanism and malevolent crime are historically the exception; sanctioned evil is commonplace. Yet there would be no point to this symposium if this juxtaposition of absolute standards and culturally relative norms supporting the common practice of imperfect societies were an adequate analysis.

Hannah Arendt's ideas and Milgram's experimental paradigm become relevant, rather, to a more limited class of situations: ones in which the participants face the attractive option of condoning what they recognize as evil according to moral standards that they themselves accept (have "internalized"), when social support is provided for this easy course. From a psychological perspective, the "legitimation of evil" supposes a situation of moral conflict, not one of moral naiveté. It requires the initial recognition of evil by those who find comfort in considerations that give it legitimacy. Here is where I would inject a first meliorist note in an argument that has thus far granted much of the pessimists' case about the evil men do. I think the issues raised by Arendt are cogent for us, not a result of any widespread or persistent deterioration in human behavior that exposes a hitherto unknown potential for evil in human nature,[1] but from the fact that there has been a progressive acceptance of high standards of humanistic ethics, such that evil that would previously have been taken for granted is now psychologically problematic and morally shocking.

Consider the cases laid before the symposium, and the one I have added, from this perspective. We are appalled by the methodical, technically competent genocide that the Nazis carried out en masse under the very noses of the German people, because we know the Germans as modern people like ourselves, who differed little from us in moral principles and who had lived as friends and neighbors of their Jewish victims. We condemn genocide as a horror wherever it happens, but morally we view the Nazi case as differ-

1. I would not rule out the possibility, however, that life in a machine-ridden age of rationalized, segmental human relations *may* lead to dehumanized deterioration, and I would quickly grant that the technical powers we have acquired vastly magnify our ability to do evil—but also to do good.

ent, say, from that of the slaughter of the Albigensians of Provence in a late Crusade or from today's murderous tribal warfare between Hausas and Ibos in Nigeria. And the psychological problem is different. Somehow people of good will have been led to shut their eyes to monstrous evil that at some level they must have been aware of *as* evil. The good will and the awareness are as essential to the dilemma as the evil, and make the processes by which evil is condoned important to understand.

The case described in *Ishi* is also at least a near fit. We are horrified when we learn of it because we assume that our grandfathers must have had much the same moral outlook as our own. But perhaps, after all, they did not. We are probably right in thinking that the principles they subscribed to about the proper relations of men to men are much like ours. More doubt comes in as to how we and they *apply* the principles—with what degree of universality or restriction of range.

The extent to which people concede full humanity to other peoples and races is still a very shaky business, an advanced front of moral progress where retrogression also appears to occur more easily than in matters of principle. During the North African campaign, I remember hearing a young infantry captain boast of his unconcern in shooting up Algerian herdsmen in the course of company mortar practice. As he put it, there was a bigger indemnity to pay for killing a donkey than for hitting an "Ay-rab." Similar tales emanate from Vietnam. Callousness toward others often takes the form of denying them full status as people.

Did the California ranchers *re*classify the Indians as *de facto* animals for the sake of legitimation—easing a bad conscience that came from lurking recognition of their humanity? Or did they act on a naively ethnocentric definition of what is human, committing evil that they did not sense, with no moral conflict? The distinction, for which we lack evidence, makes a difference in our present analysis. And are we so much more dependably inclusive in our working definition of humankind than our California forebears? We no longer have wild Indians among us against which to make the test, but the readiness with which we participate in the nastiness of guerilla war raises doubts about us. To the extent that the theme "all men are brothers" is embedded in an ethical culture that we all share, dehumanizing the enemy is a tactic for the legitimation of evil. We have already noted, however, that freedom from the kind of moral conflict with which we are concerned here seems still to be the rule with "righteous wars." Perhaps what is most novel about Vietnam is not the acceptance of unusually cruel but technically efficient means, certainly not the dehumanization, but rather the moral revulsion against the war that is expressed by a substantial minority in the major belligerent power.

The long history of oppression of the American Negro during and after slavery raises similar questions as we try to fit it to the present context. According to Gunnar Myrdal's thesis in his classic study of the race problem, *An American Dilemma* (1944), the fit is exact. Seeing the Negro problem as a *white* problem—anticipating the Kerner Commission's diagnosis of "white racism" (*Report of the National Advisory Commission on Civil Disorders,* 1968)—Myrdal depicted the conflict inherent in the minds of white Americans between the principles of the American creed of fairness and equality, to which all had been exposed, and the gross discrimination against Negroes, in which virtually all were accomplices. On this analysis, the array of beliefs and norms in support of discrimination that let people comfortably ignore the plight of the Negro serves in effect to legitimize an evil that is on people's consciences.

But as Myrdal's critics soon pointed out, the evidence for internalized conflict about Negroes on the part of most white Americans was weak. The traditional Southerner inherited from slavery a conception of Negro inferiority and of white paternal obligation that excluded Negroes from the constitutional privileges of the American creed with no apparent psychological inconsistency. For Northerners the ghetto Negro could all too easily be kept out of sight and mind. And, to an unknown degree, the creed had become a matter of lip service, of school learning, of patriotic symbolism unconnected with daily action in the world of human relations. The logical antithesis between creed and discrimination need not lead to a psychological antithesis in the minds of individual Americans who express prejudice or condone discrimination. Strategies based on the assumption of inner conflict, said the critics, could go astray. I would venture that at the time Myrdal was writing, anti-Negro discrimination was more deeply entrenched, more secure, less conflictual or defensive than he assumed.

A quarter century later, Myrdal's thesis is undoubtedly far more true than when he advanced it, thanks primarily to the insistent initiative that blacks themselves have been able to take to make their grievances painfully visible to the whites. Amid the rising tide of urban violence, in which responsible leadership on both sides increasingly goes unheard, I can hardly classify myself as an optimist about the immediate prospects. But I do think that among the few hopeful ingredients in a generally grim situation—a situation that has become desperately grimmer in the aftermath of the assassination of Martin Luther King since I originally drafted this essay—is the extent to which the *potential* conflict that Myrdal identified in white thinking about the "Negro problem" has been made actual. (Another, of course, is the rising self-respect of Negroes.)

That means, to make the obvious explicit, that on the part both of "backlash" reactionaries and complacent liberals a lurking sense of evil is becoming more salient. The status quo, if it is to be maintained, can rest no longer on naive ethnocentrism or on easy neglect of what was after all not very salient perceptually. More than ever before, those who condone or defend injustice to the Negro today have the problem of placating an uneasy conscience. In their predicament we can fairly speak of the legitimation of evil.

But note what has happened in the course of the argument. Legitimation of evil came into discussion with the case of Nazi genocide. We are properly horrified at the fact of genocide in itself, and we are surprised and shocked that a civilized people could have perpetrated it. The crime so deviates from the expected historical norm that we dwell upon the moral rottenness of any social-psychological process that could lend it legitimacy, neglecting the concomitant fact that the *need* to legitimize reflects an underlying moral conflict, a state of psychological inconsistency and thus of vulnerability that provides a more favorable ground for subsequent moral action than undefensive, "innocent" ethnocentrism. When we arrive at the case of the American Negro plight, it is with difficulty that we attain the same sense of horror: oppression of the Negro comes to us with the unpsychological legitimacy of the status quo, and traditionally rested on a framework of assumptions that hardly required subtle psychological maneuvers in its defense. From one appreciative point of view the carrier of naive prejudice may be a more admirable social object than the morally conflicted person who seeks support for his defections. In the struggle for a world in which all people accord one another respect and care, however, it is surely a step ahead for the moral dilemma to emerge that is indicated by the need for legitimation. As in the case of the "white man's burden," the thing is not just to deplore the hypocrisy, but to capitalize upon the vulnerability of old prejudices that it reflects and to open the paths to action on the side of the good.

Before I can bring this view of the legitimation of evil to bear more fully on the possibilities for social action, I must touch on two other matters that bear on my conclusions. One has to do with the changing situation of moral judgment in which modern man finds himself. The other is to make as explicit as I can my still not very clear thinking about an emerging scale of moral judgment that was implicit in my assumptions about the meaningfulness (but not the necessity) of moral progress and my rejection of the extreme relativist position.

One reason why the problem of the "legitimation of evil" becomes salient for us now as it was not before, it seems to me, is that the scope of ethical decision that is demanded of us has increased enormously in recent history. Given the fading relevance of much of the traditional morals of propriety and sexual conduct, which so readily captures our attention, the statement may seem paradoxical. Is it not one of the hallmarks of our time that much of the conventional morality has been dissociated from the realm of ethical decision with which it was previously identified? Yet a little thought gives the assertion strong support. Insofar as the scientific-technical revolution has enormously multiplied man's understanding of nature and power over it, and is in the process of bringing parallel increases in understanding and power over man himself and his social relations, man arrives at a position of unprecedented potential responsibility (which, of course, he may evade). As man gains increasing command over the causal links of determinism, his area of potentially effective free will expands correspondingly. Matters about which he previously had no choice now call for decision. One can view this new moral situation as frightening or as challenging, depending on one's temperamental pessimism or optimism, but one can hardly deny its breath-taking novelty. The evils are bigger, more efficient and complicated; the goods more enticing, if we can envision them; and the demand for choice in the light of emerging knowledge of relations between means and ends more insistent. Which is to say that the domain of ethics and politics is much greater than ever before, with higher stakes.

Partly this is a matter of scale. Genocide on the scale of the extermination camps, holocaust on the scale of Hiroshima, inflicted pain on the scale of napalm raids were out of the question before the present age. The evil to which we become accomplices gets magnified, perhaps beyond the scale to which we have an appropriate human response. How *can* one feel appropriately about megadeaths? It is a grim irony, too, that the theory of rational decision-making has found its principal early application in the analysis of military systems. Rationality (planful choice) seems indeed to have been preempted for the agents of destruction.

But the important qualitative contrast is rather a matter of scope. The old legal phrase, "an act of God," was invoked to cover all manner of calamities beyond human prediction and control, in an odd echo of the theological Problem of Evil. Fatalism—blaming God—was traditional man's only option as he faced a not very friendly world that he little understood and could do little about. It is still the only viable stance for the oppressed and powerless who have been excluded from the benefits of modernity. For privileged participants in the modern world, what a change there has been!—a change that continues at accelerating pace.

When man first became a self-consciously ethical animal, the problems of living in the physical environment still loomed large in comparison with those of the human environment of fellowman and his products. The trend started in the villages of the neolithic revolution has now brought us to a stage in which the man-made environment engulfs us. Our technologies empower us to shape this environment as we will; even when we make the least adequate use of our new-found opportunities, no one seems ready to call our cities an act of God! Just in the last decade, the fearsome and perplexing implications of population growth have dawned on public consciousness. We do not yet know how to plan for a population that is compatible with a good life—but already, plan or no plan is itself a social, a political decision. Expanded choice is upon us, willy-nilly.

The part of the social and behavioral sciences in this development is already clear. Whether or not they fulfill their promise to match for human problems the understanding and control that the natural sciences have yielded over physical nature, they already have brought these problems into the framework of rational analysis and choice in the light of evidence. They have irradicably changed the context of ethical and political discourse. Man is called upon for choice and decision as never before.

This is an exhilarating but a frightening situation, one that we have far from fully recognized and are not at all used to. Our social institutions and habits are still geared mainly to the older order. Most citizens are hardly aware of the range of genuine choices in which they are already unwitting accomplices. Perhaps most do not want to be. But as awareness of the consequences of the novel human situation begins to percolate through the citizenry, many choices that are necessary will be hard to make and to accept in full responsibility. The broadened range of real ethical choice implies the possibility of an increasing range of internalized ethical dilemmas. People may find new need for the supports and stratagems of evasion that we discuss here under the "legitimation of evil." They may flee from rational choice to the realm of existential purity—or absurdity. They may, as Schorske (1967) suggests, reject Reason as intrinsically befouled with Evil, and, like the Romantics before them, embrace Feeling as the only hope of salvation.

But have we any right to talk of evil, outside of the context of the particular moral norms of particular societies? I need at least to lay my own cards on the table, though I cannot expect to resolve in a page or so the persistent problems of ethical philosophy. I am groping for an *historically* relative approach to emerging ethical standards that escapes relativistic bondage to the norms of *particular* historically given societies (though it honors the claims of the culturally relative perspective) yet avoids insupportable pretensions to the status of a timeless absolute.

It does seem to me that the history of man in society displays a cumulative and convergent development of ethical standards, though not in moral practice. Cutting across cultural variation, common standards of human decency and mutual respect within the in-group recur the world over. The great ethical religions, with their convergent principle of the golden rule, prefigure the ethical basis appropriate for a world society that seems to be coming painfully into being through forces quite other than those of ethical decision. Slavery and servitude, once taken for granted, first fell on the defensive, then were rejected by nearly universal consensus. For all the unevenness of human history, for all the casuistry that is necessary in order to apply common ethical principles to culturally specific situations, a thread of cumulativeness appears in the ethical thinking of those who have had the leisure and cultural sophistication to occupy themselves with these matters, akin to what we find in technological advance. Given an emergent human nature in historically developing human society, it should not be surprising that common principles should also emerge as marking the kinds of human relationships that man finds satisfactory.

Of course, not all is continuity. Different types of societies—agricultural and peaceful or pastoral and warlike—highlight different values and give rise to different ethical principles, different priorities for choice. The present headlong rush toward a shared world society in which warfare becomes intolerably destructive carries its own imperatives. It may well be, indeed, that the preservation of pluralisic values, rather than the attainment of universal ones, will need planful care in the future.

That there is an intrinsic progression from crude and traditional parochialism to principled morality gains credibility from the convergent conclusions of contemporary students of the moral development of the individual, such as Kohlberg (1964). There is no reason why ontogeny should recapitulate phylogeny in these matters, as the obsolete "ontogenetic law" would have it. But if higher insights must build on more primitive ones, there is good reason why, by and large, the sequence with which ethical concepts emerge in human history should approximate the one that appears among modern children growing up in culturally sophisticated surroundings. To the extent that such intrinsic sequences appear, we are dealing with facts about the emerging nature of social man and are no longer caught in the particularities of an arbitrarily selected culture.[2]

At our stage in human history, we—a good many of us, with a good deal of agreement—can recognize evil and know what we are talking about. It is, by and large, with cultural lags and variations and distortions, what has proved to be bad for man in society—charged with the felt imperatives and potential shame or guilt that are built into us through love and discipline in our childhood years of utter dependence, as this unthinking charge becomes modulated and the cognitive content that is associated with it become elaborated in our individual progress toward maturity.

This essay, which has been mostly preamble, will have a short conclusion. There *is* evil; man's powers for both good and evil have vastly increased before he at all knows what to do about them; man is capable of condoning evil that he recognizes by relying on such legitimizing supports as he can find—but when he does so, he betrays an inner moral conflict, a state of inconsistency, that can be turned to better ends.

The line of thinking that I have been pursuing finds no special magic in the concept of "legitimation of evil," no hitherto unseen alternative to the old prescriptions for ethical advocacy: work to make the conceptions of man that prevail increasingly universal, less parochial; work to disseminate increasingly humane standards; and work to bring social practice more into line with the best standards of which we are aware. Nothing psychological about this! In the sphere of social life, where we must reckon with the fact that people will not fully agree with one another about these matters, the methods to which we must turn are those of politics.

Social-psychological insight nevertheless yields a few suggestions about relevant considerations in this age-old political-moral process to which men

2. A provocative attempt to draw together a variety of convergent formulations about individual development that are relevant here, and to make explicit the logic of cumulativeness or intrinsic sequence, may be found in Loevinger (1966). She suggests as tag names for her proposed sequential stages: Presocial symbiotic, Impulse-ridden, Opportunistic, Comformist, Conscientious, Autonomous, and Integrated.

of good will should be recruited. One has to do with the inconsistency between precept and action that underlies the search for legitimation. Currently stylish social-psychological theory makes much of a presumed strain toward consistency among a person's beliefs and feelings, or between his attitudes and his behavior. But it would be naive to count very much on such a tendency (as some recent theorists seem to have) to bring people's behavior into line with their moral principles. The whole history of human frailty scores against such a result; the problem of this symposium attests to the human ability to live with moral inconsistency; and a recent intensive look at the psychological consistency theories (Abelson, Aronson, McGuire, Newcomb, and Tannenbaum, 1968) raises searching questions about the circumstances under which strains toward consistency are likely to produce changes in attitudes or in behavior, and those under which they are not. Indeed, the interesting recent studies of children's moral development—a highly productive line of investigation—seem to underscore the relatively loose connections that hold between moral knowledge, moral judgment, guilt, confession and restitution, and moral behavior. The unitary Freudian superego now stands forth as an outright myth.

Perhaps the most that can be said at present about the moral inconsistencies underlying the legitimation of evil is that they present a potential for constructive action. If moral inconsistency is to be resolved in the direction of more ethical behavior, a plausible strategy would make the latent inconsistency as salient as possible—rub people's noses in it—while at the same time seeking to shift the legitimizing social supports, where this can be done, in favor of the outcome that is desired. But this is only a fancy way of rephrasing a standard approach of social advocacy.

A second consideration has to do with the failure of moral consensus that is implicated in much contemporary privatism, hedonism, and escape from confrontation of moral issues: a failure of consensus that dims the perception of evil and may make it the easier to legitimize. The rapidity of social change, the erosion of traditional religious sanctions, the growth of impersonal metropolitan life, and the ill-managed operation of the economic system together have gone far to break up the traditional community, as we are all aware. To a distressing extent society is fragmented into individuals, interests, and ethnic groups that are in poor communication and share little sense of common purpose. This trite diagnosis of the social critics becomes relevant when we realize that one cannot create moral consensus out of whole cloth or simply by preaching. To regain a new consensus to replace what we have lost, we have first to reestablish the reality and the sense of community. Social and political efforts to bring the socially deprived into the community, to eradicate the ghetto and the ghetto mentality, and—in the international sphere—to promote friendly contact among nations toward common ends are not only directed toward goals that are good in their own right; they work toward establishing the conditions in which a more satisfying and a more effective moral consensus can emerge.

As I suggested at the outset, sophistication in ethical thinking accompanied by deepening revulsion to social evil can foster alienation and privatism: individual soul-saving rather than constructive action. By my appraisal, the threats and opportunities in the unprecedented contemporary world demand all the resources of rationality and constructiveness—*and* of love—that we can muster. Revulsion against evil, in the spirit of the early Christians, could indeed usher in a dark age in which evil prevails in the world though souls are saved. Rather than worrying about the legitimacy that people sometimes accord to evil, the urgent task for us is rather to mobilize constructive action for the good.

References

Abelson, R. T., E. Aronson, W. J. McGuire, T. M. Newcomb, and P. H. Tannenbaum (eds.), 1968. *Theories of cognitive consistency.* Chicago: Rand McNally.

Adorno, T. W., Else Frenkel-Brunswik, D. J. Levinson, and R. N. Sanford, 1950. *The authoritarian personality.* New York: Harper.

Ainsworth, Mary D. Salter, and Barbara A. Wittig. In press. Attachment and exploratory behavior of one-year-olds in a strange situation. In B. M. Foss (ed.), *Determinants of infant behavior,* Vol. 4. London: Methuen; New York: Wiley.

Albert, Ethel M., and C. K. M. Kluckhohn. 1960. *A selected bibliography on values, ethics, and esthetics in the behavioral sciences and philosophy, 1920–1958.* New York: Free Press

Allport, F. H. 1924. *Social psychology.* Boston: Houghton Mifflin.

1933. *Institutional behavior.* Chapel Hill: University of North Carolina Press.

Allport, G. W. 1935. Attitudes. In C. Murchinson (ed.), *A handbook of social psychology.* Worcester, Mass.: Clark University Press. Pp. 798–844.

1937. *Personality: A psychological interpretation.* New York: Holt.

1943. The ego in contemporary psychology. *Psychological Review, 50,* 451–478.

1950. *The nature of personality.* Cambridge, Mass.: Addison-Wesley.

1954. *The nature of prejudice.* Cambridge, Mass.: Addison-Wesley.

1955. *Becoming.* New Haven, Conn.: Yale University Press.

1960. Personality: Normal and abnormal. In *Personality and social encounter.* Boston: Beacon. Pp. 155–168.

1961. *Pattern and growth in personality.* New York: Holt.

Allport, G. W., and P. E. Vernon. 1933. *Studies in expressive movement.* New York: Macmillan.

Allport, G. W., P. E. Vernon, and G. Lindzey. 1951. *A study of values: A scale for measuring the dominant interests in personality.* (rev. ed.). Boston: Houghton Mifflin.

Almond, G. A., and S. Verba. 1963. *The civic culture. Political attitudes and democracy in five nations.* Princeton, N. J.: Princeton University Press.

American Psychological Association, Ad Hoc Planning Group on the Role of the APA in Mental Health Programs and Research. Mental Health and the American Psychological Association. 1959. *American Psychologist, 14,* 820–825.

American Psychological Association. 1959. *Ethical standards of psychologists.* Washington, D. C.: APA.

Angyal, A. 1941. *Foundations for a science of personality.* New York: Commonwealth Fund.

Arendt, Hannah. 1965. *Eichmann in Jerusalem: A report on the banality of evil* (rev. ed.). New York: Viking.

Aronson, E., and J. M. Carlsmith. 1962. Performance expectancy as a determinant of actual performance. *Journal of Abnormal and Social Psychology, 65,* 178–182.

Asch, S. E. 1946. Forming impressions of personality. *Journal of Abnormal and Social Psychology, 41,* 258–290.

1952. *Social psychology.* Englewood Cliffs, N. J.: Prentice-Hall.

Atkinson, J. W. 1964. *An introduction to motivation.* Princeton, N. J.: Van Nostrand.

Atkinson, J. W., and N. T. Feather. 1966. *A theory of achievement motivation.* New York: Wiley.

Baldwin, J. M. 1913. *Social and ethical interpretation in mental development.* New York: Macmillan.

Barron, F. 1954. *Personal soundness in university graduate students.* Berkeley: University of California Press.

1963. *Creativity and psychological health.* Princeton N. J.: Van Nostrand.

Barry, H., III, Margaret K. Bacon and I. L. Child. 1957. A cross-cultural survey of some sex differences in socialization. *Journal of Abnormal and Social Psychology, 55,* 327–332.

Baumrind, Diana. 1966. Effects of authoritative parental control on behavior. *Child Development, 37,* 887–907.

1967. Child care practices anteceding three patterns of preschool behavior. *Genetic Psychological Monographs, 75,* 43–88.

Baumrind, Diana, and A. E. Black. 1967. Socialization practices associated with dimensions of competence in preschool boy and girls. *Child Development, 38,* 291–327.

Bayley, Nancy. 1940. Mental growth in young children. *Yearbook of the National Society for the Study of Education, 39* Part II, 11–47.

1966. *The two year old: Is this a critical age for intellectual development?* Durham, N. C.: The Durham Education Improvement Program.

Beals, R. L., and N. D. Humphrey. 1957. *No frontier to learning: The Mexican student in the United States.* Minneapolis: University of Minnesota Press.

Becker, G. M., and C. G. McClintock. 1967. Value: Behavioral decision theory. *Annual Review of Psychology, 18,* 239–286.

Bee, Helen L. 1967. Parent-child interaction and distractibility in 9-year-old children. *Merrill-Palmer Quarterly, 13,* 175–190.

Bell, D. (ed.). 1963. *The radical right* (rev. ed.). Garden City, N. Y.: Doubleday.

Benedict, Ruth. 1934. *Patterns of culture.* Boston: Houghton Mifflin.

Bennett, J. W., H. Passin, and R. K. McKnight. 1958. *In search of identity: The Japanese overseas scholar in America and Japan.* Minneapolis: University of Minnesota Press.

Berelson, B. 1963. Communication, communications research, and family planning. *In Emerging techniques in population research.* New York: Milbank Memorial Fund. Pp. 159–171.

Berelson, B., P. F. Lazarsfeld, and W. N. McFee. 1954. *Voting: A study of opinion formation in a presidential campaign.* Chicago: University of Chicago Press.

Bernstein, B. 1964. Aspects of language and learning in the genesis of the social process. In D. Hymes (ed.), *Language in culture and society: A reader in linguistics and anthropology.* New York: Harper. Pp. 251–263.

Bettelheim, B. 1943. Individual and mass behavior in extreme situations. *Journal of Abnormal and Social Psychology, 38,* 417–452.

Biderman, A. D. 1963. *March to calumny. The story of American POW's in the Korean War.* New York: Macmillan.

Blake, Judith. 1961. *Family structure in Jamaica.* New York: Free Press.

Blake, Judith. 1965. Demographic science and the redirection of population policy. In Mindel C. Sheps and Jeanne Clare Ridley (eds.), *Public health and population change.* Pittsburg: The University of Pittsburg Press. Pp. 41–69.

Block, J. 1961. *The Q-sort method in personality assessment and psychiatric research.* Springfield, Ill.: Charles C. Thomas.

Block, Jeanne H. 1968. Rebellion re-examined: The role of identification and alienation. Presented to conference on Adaptation to Change, Dorado Beach, Puerto Rico, June 22–27 (unpublished manuscript).

Block, Jeanne H., Norma Haan, and M. B. Smith. 1968. Activism and apathy in contemporary adolescents. In J. F. Adams (ed.), *Understanding adolescence: Current developments in adolescent psychology.* Boston: Allyn & Bacon. Pp. 198–231.

Bogue, D. J., and V. S. Heiskanen. 1963. *How to improve written communication for birth control.* Chicago: University of Chicago Family Study Center; New York: National Committee on Maternal Health, Inc.

Bower, T. G. R. 1966. The visual world of infants. *Scientific American, 215,* 80–92.

Bramel, D. 1962. A dissonance theory approach to defensive projection. *Journal of Abnormal and Social Psychology, 64,* 121–129.

Brehm, J. W., and A. R. Cohen. 1962. *Explorations in cognitive dissonance.* New York: Wiley.

Brim, O. G., Jr. 1959. *Education for child rearing.* New York: Russell Sage Foundation.

Bronowski, J. 1956. *Science and human values.* New York: Messner.

Brown, J. F. 1936. *Psychology and the social order.* New York: McGraw-Hill.

Bruner, J. S., Jacqueline J. Goodnow, and G. A. Austin. 1956 *A study of thinking.* New York: Wiley.

Bruner, J. S., and L. Postman. 1948. An approach to social perception. In W. Dennis (ed.), *Current trends in social psychology.* Pittsburg: University of Pittsburg Press. Pp. 71–118.

Buss, A. H. 1961. *The psychology of aggression.* New York: Wiley.

Camelot and psychological tests. 1966. (Special issue) *American psychologist, 21,* 401–477.

Campbell, A., P. E. Converse, W. E. Miller, and D. E. Stokes. 1960. *The American voter.* New York: Wiley.

Campbell, D. T. 1963. Social attitudes and other acquired behavorial dispositions. In S. Koch (ed.), *Psychology: A study of science.* Vol. 6. *Investigations of man as socius: Their place in psychology and the social sciences.* New York: McGraw-Hill. Pp. 94–172.

Cannell, C. F., and R. L. Kahn. 1953. The collection of data by interviewing. In

L. Festinger and D. Katz (eds.), *Research methods in the behavorial sciences.* New York: Dryden. Pp. 327–380.
Carlson, E. R. 1956. Attitude change through modification of attitude structure. *Journal of Abnormal and Social Psychology, 52,* 256–261.
Carroll, J. B. 1951. The interdisciplinary summer seminar on linguistics and psychology. Social Science Research Control *Items, 5,* 40–42.
Carter, L. J. 1966. Social sciences. Where do they fit in the politics of science? *Science, 154,* 488–491.
Cartwright, D. 1949. Some principles of mass persuasion: Selected findings of research on the sale of United States War Bonds. *Human Relations, 2,* 253–267.
Chein, I. 1944. The awareness of self and the structure of the ego. *Psychological Review, 51,* 304–314.
1962. The image of man. *Journal of Social Issues, 18,* (4), 1–35.
Chilman, Catherine S. 1966. *Growing up poor. An over-view and analysis of child-rearing and family life patterns associated with poverty.* Washington, D. C.: Division of Research, Welfare Administration, U. S. Department of Health, Education, and Welfare.
Christie, R. 1956a. Eysenck's treatment of the personality of communists. *Psychological Bulletin, 53,* 411–430.
1956b. Some abuses of psychology. *Psychological Bulletin, 53,* 439–451.
Christie, R., Joan Havel, and B. Seidenberg. 1958. Is the F scale reversible? *Journal of Abnormal and Social Psychology, 56,* 143–159.
Christie, R., and Marie Jahoda (eds.). 1954. *Studies in the scope and method of "The Authoritarian Personality."* New York: Free Press.
Clark, K. B. 1965. *Dark ghetto.* New York: Harper.
Clausen, J. A. 1956. *Sociology and the field of mental health.* New York: Russell Sage Foundation.
Cohen, A. R. 1964. *Attitude change and social influence.* New York: Basic Books.
Coleman, J. S., E. Q. Campbell, Carol J. Hobson, J. McPartland, A. M. Mood, F. D. Weinfeld, and R. L. York. 1966. *Equality of educational opportunity.* Washington, D. C.: U. S. Office of Education (Superintendent of Documents Catalog No. FS5.238. 38001).
Colson, Elizabeth. 1967. Competence and incompetence in the context of independence. *Current Anthropology, 8,* 92–111.
Combs, A. W. 1949. A phenomenological approach to adjustment. *Journal of Abnormal and Social Psychology, 44,* 29–35.
Committee on Educational Interchange Policy. 1960. *African students in the United States: A guide for sponsors of student exchange programs with Africa.* New York: Institute of International Education.
Cooley, C. H. 1902. *Human nature and the social order.* New York: Scribner.
Coopersmith, S. 1967. *The antecedents of self-esteem.* San Francisco: W. H. Freeman.
Couch, A. S. 1962. The psychological determinants of inter-personal behavior. In S. Coopersmith (ed.), *Personality research,* Vol. 2: *Proceedings of XIV International Congress of Applied Psychology.* Copenhagen: Munksgaard. Pp. 111–127.
Couch, A. S., and K. Keniston. 1960. Yeasayers and naysayers: Agreeing response

set as a personality variable. *Journal of Abnormal and Social Psychology, 60,* 151–174.

Crandall, Virginia C., W. Katkovsky, and V. J. Crandall. 1965. Children's beliefs in their own control of reinforcements in intellectual-academic achievement situations. *Child Development, 36,* 91–109.

Curle, A. 1962. Some aspects of educational planning in underdeveloped areas. *Harvard Educational Review, 32,* 292–300.

Davis, J. M., R. G. Hanson, and D. R. Burnov. 1961. *Survey of the African Student.* New York: Institute of International Education.

Deutsch, M., R. Krauss, and Norah Rosenau. 1962. Dissonance or defensiveness? *Journal of Personality, 30,* 16–28.

Devereux, G. 1956. Normal and abnormal: The key problem in psychiatric anthropology. In J. B. Casagrande and T. Gladwin (eds.), *Some uses of anthropology: Theoretical and applied.* Anthropological Society of Washington. Pp. 23–48.

Dewey, J. 1922. *Human nature and conduct.* New York: Holt.

Doob, L. The behavior of attitudes. *Psychological Review,* 1947, *54,* 135–156.

Du Bois, Cora. 1944. *The people of Alor.* Minneapolis: University of Minnesota Press.

1956. *Foreign students and higher education in the United States.* Washington, D. C.: American Council on Education.

Edwards, W. 1954. The theory of decision making. *Psychological Bulletin, 51,* 380–417.

Eisenstadt, S. N. 1964. Education and political development. In D. C. Piper and T. Cole (eds.), *Post-primary education and political and economic development.* Durham, N. C.: Duke University Press. Pp. 27–47.

Erikson, E. H. 1956. The problem of ego identity. *Journal of the American Psychoanalytic Association, 4,* 55–121.

1958. *Young man Luther: A study in psychoanalysis and history.* Austin Riggs Monograph No. 4. New York: Norton.

1959. Identity and the life cycle. *Psychological Issues, 1* (1).

Eysenck, H. J. 1954. *The psychology of politics.* London: Routledge & Kegan Paul.

1956. The psychology of politics and the personality similarities between fascists and communists. *Psychological Bulletin, 53,* 431–438.

Ezekiel, R. S. 1968. The personal future and Peace Corps competence. *Journal of Personality and Social Psychology, 8* (2), *Monograph Supplement,* Part 2.

Festinger, L. 1950. Informal social communication. *Psychological Review, 57,* 271–282.

1954. A theory of social comparison processes. *Human Relations, 7,* 117–140.

1957. *A theory of cognitive dissonance.* Evanston, Ill.: Row, Peterson.

1964. *Conflict, decision, and dissonance.* Stanford, Calif.: Stanford University Press.

Festinger, L., H. W. Riecken, Jr., and S. Schachter. 1956. *When prophecy fails.* Minneapolis: University of Minnesota Press.

Fiske, D. W., and S. R. Maddi. 1961. *Functions of varied experience.* Homewood, Ill.: Dorsey.

Flacks, R. 1967. The liberated generation: An exploration of the roots of student protest. *Journal of Social Issues, 23* (3), 52–75.

Flavell, J. H. 1963. *The developmental psychology of Jean Piaget.* Princeton, N. J.: Van Nostrand.

Foote, N. N., and L. S. Cottrell, Jr. 1955. *Identity and interpersonal competence: A new direction in family research.* Chicago: University of Chicago Press.

Frank, J. D. 1961. *Persuasion and healing, A comparative study of psychotherapy.* Baltimore: Johns Hopkins University Press.

Freedman, R., P. K. Whelpton, and A. A. Campbell. 1959. *Family planning, sterility, and population growth.* New York: McGraw-Hill.

French, J. R. P., Jr., and R. Kahn. 1962. A programmatic approach to studying the industrial environment and mental health. *Journal of Social Issues, 18,* (3), 1–47.

French, J. R. P., Jr., and J. J. Sherwood. 1965. Self-actualization and self-identity theory. Paper No. 107, Institute for Research in the Behavorial, Economic, and Management Sciences, Purdue University (mimeo).

Freud, Anna. 1946. *The ego and the mechanisms of defense.* New York: International Universities Press.

Freud, S. 1933. *New introductory lectures on psychoanalysis.* New York: Norton.

1957. On narcissism: an introduction. In J. Strachey (ed.), *Standard edition of the complete psychological works of Sigmund Freud.* Vol. XIV. London: Hogarth Press. Pp. 73–102.

Frieden, Betty. 1963. *The feminine mystique.* New York: Norton.

Fromm, E. 1941. *Escape from freedom.* New York: Farrar, Straus.

1947. *Man for himself.* New York: Rinehart.

Gardner, J. W. 1951–1952. The foreign student in America. *Foreign Affairs, 30,* 637–650.

Gill, M. 1959. The present state of psychoanalytic theory. *Journal of Abnormal and Social Psychology, 58,* 1–8.

Ginsburg, S. W. 1955. The mental health movement: Its theoretical assumptions. In Ruth Kotinsky and Helen Witmer (eds.), *Community programs for mental health.* Cambridge, Mass.: Harvard University Press. Pg. 1–29.

Gladwin, T. 1967. Social competence and clinical practice. *Psychiatry, 30,* 30–43.

Goffman, E. 1959. *The presentation of self in everyday life.* Garden City, N. Y.: Doubleday Anchor Books.

Goldstein, K. 1948. *Human nature in the light of psychopathology.* Cambridge, Mass.: Harvard University Press.

Goslin, D. A. 1963. *The search for ability: Standardized testing in social perspective.* New York: Russell Sage Foundation.

1967. *Teachers and testing.* New York: Russell Sage Foundation.

Gross, N., W. S. Mason, and A. W. McEachern. 1958. *Explorations in role analysis.* New York: Wiley.

Gurin, G., J. Veroff, and Sheila Feld. 1960. *Americans view their mental health: A nationwide opinion survey.* New York: Basic Books.

Haan, Norma. 1963. A proposed model of ego functioning: Coping and defense mechanisms in relationship to IQ change. *Psychological Monographs, 77* (8, Whole No. 571).

Haan, Norma, M. B. Smith, and Jeanne H. Block. 1968. Moral reasoning of young adults: Political-social behavior, family background, and personality correlates. *Journal of Personality and Social Psychology, 10,* 183–201.

Hall, C. S., and G. Lindzey. 1957. *Theories of personality.* New York: Wiley.

Hallowell, A. I. 1949. Psychological leads for ethnological field workers. In D. G. Haring (ed.), *Personal character and cultural milieu.* Syracuse, N. Y.: Syracuse University Press. Pp. 290–348.

1953a. Culture, personality, and society. In A. L. Kroeber et al., *Anthropology today.* Chicago: University of Chicago Press. Pp. 597–620.

1953b The self and its behavorial environment. In G. Roheim (ed.), *Psychoanalysis and the social sciences,* Vol. 4. New York: International Universities Press.

Hallowitz, E., and F. Riessman. 1967. The role of the indigenous nonprofessional in a community mental health neighborhood service center program. *American Journal of Orthopsychiatry, 37,* 766–778.

Harding, J. S., B. Kutner, H. Proshansky, and I. Chein. 1954. Prejudice and ethnic relations. In G. Lindzey (ed.), *Handbook of social psychology,* Vol. 2. Cambridge, Mass.: Addison-Wesley. Pp. 1021–1061.

Haring, D. G. (ed.). 1949. *Personal character and cultural milieu.* Syracuse, N. Y.: Syracuse University Press.

Hartmann, H. 1958. *Ego psychology and the problem of adaptation.* New York: International Universities Press.

Haythorn, W., A. Couch, D. Haefner, P. Langham, and L. F. Carter. 1956. The behavior of authoritarian and equalitarian personalities in groups. *Human Relations, 9,* 57–74.

Hebb, D. O., and W. R. Thompson. 1954. The social significance of animal studies. In G. Lindzey (ed.), *Handbook of social psychology,* Vol. 1. Cambridge, Mass.: Addison-Wesley. Pp. 532–561.

Heider, F. 1946. Attitudes and cognitive organization. *Journal of Psychology, 21,* 107–112.

1958. *The psychology of international relations.* New York: Wiley.

Heist, P. 1965. Intellect and commitment: The faces of discontent. In O. W. Knorr and W. J. Minter (eds.), *Order and freedom on the campus: The rights and responsibilities of faculty and students.* Boulder, Colo.: Western Interuniversity Commission for Higher Education. Pp. 61–69.

Held, R., and A. Hein. 1963. Movement-produced stimulation in the development of visually guided behavior. *Journal of Comparative and Physiological Psychology, 56,* 872–876.

Helson, H. *Adaptation-level theory: An experimental and systematic approach to behavior.* New York: Harper, 1964.

Herndon, J. 1968. *The way it spozed to be.* New York: Simon & Schuster.

Herskovits, M. J. 1962. *The human factor in changing Africa.* New York: Knopf.

Hess, R. D., and Virginia C. Shipman. 1965. Early experience and the socialization of cognitive modes in children. *Child Development, 36,* 869–886.

Hill, K. T., and S. B. Sarason. 1966. The relation of test anxiety and defensiveness to test and school performance over the elementary-school years: A further longitudinal study. *Child Development Monographs, 31,* (2, Whole No. 104).

Hill, R., J. M. Stycos, and K. W. Back. 1959. *The family and population control: A Puerto Rican experiment in social change.* Chapel Hill: University of North Carolina Press.

Hobbs, N. 1966. Helping disturbed children: Psychological and ecological strategies. *American Psychologist, 21,* 1105–1115.

Hoffman, Lois W., and F. Wyatt. 1960. Social change and motivations for having larger families: Some theoretical considerations. *Merrill-Palmer Quarterly, 6,* 235–244.

Hoffman, M., and Lois W. Hoffman. (eds.). 1964. *Review of child development research,* Vol. 1. New York: Russell Sage Foundation.

1966. *Review of child development research,* Vol. 2. New York: Russell Sage Foundation.

Hoijer, H. 1953. The relation of language to culture. In A. L. Kroeber et al., *Anthropology today.* Chicago: University of Chicago Press. Pp. 554–573.

Horney, Karen. 1937. *The neurotic personality of our time.* New York: Norton.

Hovland, C. I. 1959. Reconciling conflicting results derived from experimental and survey studies of attitude change. *American Psychologist, 14,* 8–17.

Hovland, C. I., I. L. Janis, and H. H. Kelley. 1953. *Communication and persuasion: Psychological studies of opinion change.* New Haven, Conn.: Yale University Press.

Hovland, C. I., A. A. Lumsdaine, and F. D. Sheffield. 1949. *Experiments on mass communication. Studies in social psychology in World War II,* Vol. 3. Princeton, N. J.: Princeton University Press.

Hunt, J. McV. 1961. *Intelligence and experience.* New York: Ronald.

1963. Motivation inherent in information processing and action. In O. J. Harvey (ed.), *Motivation and social interaction: Cognitive determinants.* New York: Ronald Press. Pp. 35–94.

1965. Intrinsic motivation and its role in psychological development. In D. Levine (ed.), *Nebraska Symposium on Motivation 1965.* Lincoln: University of Nebraska Press. Pp. 189–282.

Hyman, H. H. 1942. The psychology of status. *Archives of Psychology,* No. 269.

1959. *Political socialization: A study in the psychology of political behavior.* New York: Free Press.

Hyman, H. H., and P. B. Sheatsley. 1947. Some reasons why information campaigns fail. *Public Opinion Quarterly, 11* (3), 412–423.

1954. "The authoritarian personality"—A methodological critique. In R Christie and Marie Jahoda (eds.), *Studies in the scope and method of "The authoritarian personality."* New York: Free Press. Pp. 50–122.

Inkeles, A. 1966. Social structure and the socialization of competence. *Harvard Educational Review, 36,* 265–283.

Institute of International Education. 1953. *Education for one world: Annual census of foreign students in institutions of higher education in the United States, 1952–1953.* New York: Institute of International Education.

1954. *Education for one world: Annual census of foreign students in institutions of higher education in the United States, 1953–1954.* New York: Institute of International Education.

1962. *Open doors, 1962.* New York: Institute of International Education.

Jahoda, Marie. 1950. Toward a social psychology of mental health. In M. J. E. Senn (ed.), *Symposium on the healthy personality.* New York: Josiah Macy, Jr. Foundation. Pp. 211–230.

1958. *Current concepts of positive mental health.* New York: Basic Books.

James, W. 1890. *Principles of psychology,* Vol. 1. New York: Holt.

Janis, I. L. 1959. Motivational factors in the resolution of decisional conflicts.

In M. R. Jones (ed.), *Nebraska Symposium on Motivation 1959.* Lincoln: University of Nebraska Press. Pp. 198–231.

Janis, I. L., and M. B. Smith. 1965. Effects of education and persuasion on national and international images. In H. C. Kelman (ed.), *International behavior: A social psychological analysis.* New York: Holt. Pp. 190–235.

Joint Commission on Mental Illness and Health. *Action for mental health: Final report of the Joint Commission.* New York: Basic Books.

Kagan, J., and H. A. Moss. 1962. *Birth to maturity: A study in psychological development.* New York: Wiley.

Kardiner, A. 1939. *The individual and his society.* New York: Columbia University Press.

1945. *Psychological frontiers of society.* New York: Columbia University Press.

Katz, D. 1960. The functional approach to the study of attitudes. *Public Opinion Quarterly, 24,* 163–204.

Katz, D., D. Cartwright, S. Eldersveld, and A. McC. Lee. 1954. *Public opinion and propaganda.* New York: Holt.

Katz, D., C. McClintock, and I. Sarnoff. 1957. The measurement of ego defense as related to attitude change. *Journal of Personality, 25,* 465–474.

Katz. D., I. Sarnoff, and C. McClintock. 1956. Ego-defense and attitude change. *Human Relations, 9,* 27–45.

Katz, D., and R. L. Schanck. 1938. *Social psychology.* New York: Wiley.

Katz, D., and E. Stotland. 1959. A preliminary statement to a theory of attitude structure and change. In S. Koch (ed.), *Psychology: A study of a science,* Vol. 3: *Formulations of the person and the social context.* New York: McGraw-Hill. Pp. 423–475.

Katz, E. 1963. The diffusion of new ideas and practices. In W. Schramm (ed.), *The science of communication. New directions and new findings in communication research.* New York: Basic Books. Pp. 77–93.

Katz, E., and P. F. Lazarsfeld. 1955. *Personal influence: The part played by people in the flow of mass communications.* New York: Free Press.

Katz, I. 1967. The socialization of academic motivation in minority group children. In D. Levine (ed.), *Nebraska Symposium on Motivation 1967.* Lincoln: University of Nebraska Press. Pp. 133–191.

Katz. I., and L. Benjamin. 1960. Effects of white authoritarianism in biracial work groups. *Journal of Abnormal and Social Psychology, 61,* 448–560.

Kavanau, J. L. 1967. Behavior of captive white-footed mice. *Science, 155,* 1623–1639.

Kellam, S. G., and S. K. Schiff. 1967. Adaptation and mental illness in the first-grade classrooms of an urban community. *Psychiatric Research Report, 21,* 79–91.

Kelman, H. C. 1961. Processes of opinion change. *Public Opinion Quarterly. 25,* 57–78.

1967. Human use of human subjects: The problem of deception in social psychological experiments. *Psychological Bulletin, 67,* 1–11.

Keniston, K. 1965. *The uncommitted: Alienated youth in American society.* New York: Harcourt, Brace.

Kennan, G. F. 1968. Rebels without a program. *New York Times Magazine,* January 21, 22–23, 60–62, 69–71.

Key, V. O., Jr. (with the assistance of A. Heard). 1949. *Southern politics in state and nation.* New York: Knopf.

1963. *Public opinion and American democracy.* New York: Knopf.

Key, V. O., Jr. (with the assistance of M. C. Cummings, Jr.). 1966. *The responsible electorate. Rationality in presidential voting, 1936–1960.* Cambridge, Mass: Harvard University Press.

Kiell, N. 1951. Attitudes of foreign students. *Journal of higher education, 22,* 188–194, 225.

Kirscht, J. P., and R. C. Dillehay. 1967. *Dimensions of authoritarianism: A review of research and theory.* Lexington: University of Kentucky Press.

Klapper, J. T. 1960. *The effects of mass communication.* New York: Free Press.

Klein, D. C. 1960. Some concepts concerning the mental health of the individual. *Journal of Consulting Psychology, 24,* 288–293.

Klineberg, O. 1950. *Tensions affecting international understanding.* New York: Social Science Research Council, Bulletin 62.

Kluckhohn, C. K. M. 1951. Values and value orientations in the theory of action. In T. Parsons and E. A. Shils (ed.), *Toward a general theory of action.* Cambridge, Mass.: Harvard University Press. Pp. 388–433.

1954. Culture and behavior. In G. Lindzey (ed.), *Handbook of social psychology.* Cambridge, Mass.: Addison-Wesley. Pp. 921-976.

Kluckhohn, C. K. M., H. A. Murray, and D. Schneider (eds.). 1952. *Personality in nature, society, and culture* (rev. ed.). New York: Knopf.

Kluckhohn, Florence R., and F. L. Strodtbeck. 1961. *Variations in value orientations.* Evanston, Ill.: Row, Peterson.

Kohl, H. 1967. *36 children.* New York: New American Library.

Kohlberg, L. 1963. The development of children's orientations toward a moral order: I. Sequence in the development of moral thought. *Vita Humana, 6,* 11–33.

1964. Development of moral character and moral ideology. In M. Hoffman and Lois W. Hoffman (eds.), *Review of child development research,* Vol. 1. New York: Russell Sage Foundation. Pp. 383–431.

Köhler, W. 1938. *The place of value in a world of facts.* New York: Liveright.

Kozol, J. 1967. *Death at an early age: The destruction of the hearts and minds of Negro children in the Boston public schools.* Boston: Houghton Mifflin.

Kroeber, A. L., and C. K. M. Kluckhohn. 1952. *Culture: A critical review of concepts and definitions.* Cambridge, Mass.: Peabody Museum Papers, *47,* (1).

Kroeber, Theodora. 1961. *Ishi.* Berkeley: University of California Press.

Ladimer, I., and R. W. Newman (eds.). 1963. *Clinical investigation in medicine: legal, ethical, and moral aspects: An anthology and bibliography.* Boston: Boston University, Law-Medicine Institute.

Lambert, R. D., and M. Bressler. 1954. Indian students and the United States: Cross-cultural images. *The Annals, 295,* 62–72.

1956. *Indian students on an American campus.* Minneapolis: University of Minnesota Press.

Lasswell, H. D. 1930. *Psychopathology and politics.* Chicago: University of Chicago Press.

1946. Describing the content of communications. In B. L. Smith, H. D.

Lasswell, and R. D. Casey, *Propaganda, communication, and public opinion.* Princeton, N. J.: Princeton University Press.

Lazarsfeld, P. F., B. Berelson, and Hazel Gaudet. 1944. *The people's choice.* New York: Duell, Sloan, & Pierce.

Lecky, P. 1945. *Self-consistency: A theory of personality.* New York: Island Press.

Lefcourt, H. M. 1966. Internal versus external control of reinforcement. *Psychological Bulletin, 65,* 206–220.

Lenneberg, E. H. 1967. *Biological foundations of language.* New York: Wiley.

Levine, L. S., and R. E. Kantor. 1962. Psychological effectiveness and imposed social position: A descriptive framework. *Personnel and Guidance Journal, 40,* 418–425.

Levinson, D. J., and P. E. Huffman. 1955. Traditional family ideology and its relations to personality. *Journal of Personality, 23,* 251–273.

Levy, M. 1952. *The structure of society.* Princeton, N. J.: Princeton University Press.

Lewin, K. 1935. *A dynamic theory of personality.* New York: McGraw-Hill.

1936. *Principles of topological psychology.* New York: McGraw-Hill.

(Gertrud W. Lewin, ed.). 1948. *Resolving social conflicts.* New York: Harper.

(D. O. Cartwright, ed.). 1951. *Field theory in social science: Selected theoretical papers.* New York: Harper.

Lewin, K., Tamara Dembo, L. Festinger, and Pauline S. Sears. 1944. Level of aspiration. In J. McV. Hunt (ed.), *Personality and the behavior disorders,* Vol. 1. New York: Ronald Press. Pp. 333–378.

Lewis, O. 1959. *Five families: Mexican case studies in the culture of poverty.* New York: Basic Books.

Lewis, W. A. 1961. Education and economic development. *Social and economic studies, 10,* 113–127.

Lifton, R. J. 1961. *Thought reform and the psychology of totalism: A study of "brainwashing" in China.* New York: Norton.

Linton, R. 1936. *The study of man.* New York: Appleton.

1945. *The cultural background of personality.* New York: Appleton.

Lippitt, R., Jeanne Watson, and B. Westley. 1958. *The dynamics of planned change.* New York: Harcourt, Brace.

Lippmann, W. 1922. *Public opinion.* New York: Macmillan.

Lipset, S. M., (ed.). 1966. Special Issue on Student Politics, *Comparative Education Review, 10,* No. 2.

Lipset, S. M., and S. S. Wolin (eds.). 1965. *The Berkeley student revolt: Facts and interpretations.* Garden City, N. Y.: Doubleday.

Loevinger, Jane. 1966. The meaning and measurement of ego development. *American Psychologist, 21,* 195–206.

Lowe, C. M. 1959. Value orientations—an ethical dilemma. *American Psychologist, 14,* 687–693.

Lynd, R. 1939. *Knowledge for what?* Princeton, N. J.: Princeton University Press.

Maccoby, Eleanor E., Edith M. Dowley, J. W. Hagen, and R. Degerman. 1965. Activity level and intellectual functioning in normal preschool children. *Child Development, 36,* 761–770.

Maccoby, N. 1963. The new "scientific" rhetoric. In W. Schramm (ed.), *The science of communication. New directions and new findings in communication research.* New York: Basic Books. Pp. 41–53.

Macgregor, G. 1946. *Warriors without weapons.* Chicago: Chicago University Press.

1962. *American Fulbright scholars: The experiences of American scholars in countries of the Near East and South Asia.* Ithaca: Society for applied Anthropology Monograph No. 5.

MacLeod, R. B. 1947. The phenomenological approach to social psychology. *Psychological Review, 54,* 193–210.

Marlowe, D., and D. Crowne. 1964. *The approval motive.* New York: Wiley.

Marvick, D. 1965. African university students: A presumptive elite. In J. S. Coleman (ed.), *Education and political development.* Princeton, N. J.: Princeton University Press. Pp. 463–497.

Maslow, A. H. 1950. Self-actualizing people: A study of psychological health. *Personality Symposia,* No. 1.

1954. *Motivation and personality.* New York: Harper.

McClelland, D. C. 1951. *Personality.* New York: Sloane.

1961. *The achieving society.* Princeton, N. J.: Van Nostrand.

1965. Toward a theory of motive acquisition. *American Psychologist, 20,* 321–333.

McClelland, D. C., J. W. Atkinson, R. A. Clark, and E. L. Lowell. 1953. *The achievement motive.* New York: Appleton.

McDougall, W. 1908. *Introduction to social psychology.* London: Methuen.

McGuire, W. J. 1966. Attitudes and opinions. *Annual Review of Psychology, 17,* 475–514.

1967. Some impending reorientations in social psychology: Some thoughts provoked by Kenneth Ring. *Journal of Experimental Social Psychology, 3,* 124–139.

Mead, G. H. 1934. *Mind, self, and society.* Chicago: University of Chicago Press.

Mead, Margaret. 1928. *Coming of age in Samoa.* New York: Morrow.

1946. Research on primitive children. In L. Carmichael (ed.), *Manual of child psychology.* New York: Wiley. Pp. 667–706.

1952. Some relationships between social anthropology and psychiatry. In F. Alexander and Helen Ross (eds.), *Dynamic psychiatry.* Chicago: University of Chicago Press. Pp. 401–448.

1953. National character. In A. L. Kroeber et al. *Anthropology today.* Chicago: University of Chicago Press. Pp. 642–667.

Merton, R. K. 1957. *Social theory and social structure* (rev. ed.). New York: Free Press.

Merton, R. K., and P. F. Lazarsfeld (eds.). 1950. *Continuities in social research: Studies in the scope and method of "The American Soldier."* New York: Free Press.

Milgram, S. 1963. Behavioral study of obedience. *Journal of Abnormal and Social Psychology. 67,* 371–378.

Miller, D. R. 1963. The study of social relationships: situation, identity, and social interaction. In S. Koch (ed.), *Psychology: A study of a science.* Vol. 5. New York: McGraw-Hill. Pp. 639–737.

Miller, D. R., and G. E. Swanson. 1958. *The changing American parent.* New York: Wiley.

1960. *Inner conflict and defense.* New York: Holt.

Miller, J. G. 1955. Toward a general theory for the behavorial sciences. *American Psychologist, 10,* 513–531.

Mischel, W. 1965. Predicting the success of Peace Corps volunteers in Nigeria. *Journal of Personality and Social Psychology, 1,* 510–517.

1966. Theory and research on the antecedents of self-imposed delay of reward. In B. Maher (ed.), *Progress in experimental personality research,* Vol. 3. New York: Academic Press. Pp. 85–132.

Morris, C. W. 1956. *Varieties of human value.* Chicago: University of Chicago Press.

Morris, R. T. 1960. *The two-way mirror: National status in foreign sudent's adjustment.* Minneapolis: University of Minnesota Press.

Mowrer, O. H. 1950. *Learning theory and personality dynamics.* New York: Ronald Press.

Munroe, Ruth L. 1955. *Schools of psychoanalytic thought.* New York: Dryden.

Murdock, G. P. 1949. *Social structure.* New York: Macmillan.

Murdock, G. P., C. S. Ford, A. E. Hudson, R. Kennedy, L. W. Simmons, and J. W. M. Whiting. *Outline of cultural materials* (3rd rev. ed.). New Haven Conn.: Human Relations Area Files, Inc.

Murphy, G. 1947. *Personality: A biosocial approach to origins and structure.* New York: Harper.

1958. *Human potentialities.* New York: Basic Books.

Murphy, G., Lois B. Murphy, and T. M. Newcomb. 1937. *Experimental social psychology* (rev. ed.). New York: Harper.

Murphy, Lois, and collaborators. 1962. *The widening world of childhood: Paths toward mastery.* New York: Basic Books.

Murray, H. A. 1938. *Explorations in personality.* New York: Oxford University Press.

1951. Toward a classification of interactions. In T. Parsons and E. A. Shils (eds.), *Toward a general theory of action.* Cambridge, Mass.: Harvard University Press. Pp. 434–464.

Myrdal, G. (with the assistance of R. Sterner and A. Rose). 1944. *An American dilemma. The Negro problem and modern democracy,* Vols. 1 and 2. New York: Harper.

National Assembly on Mental Health Education. 1960. *Mental health education: A critique.* Philadelphia: Pennsylvania Mental Health, Inc.

Newcomb, T. M. 1943. *Personality and social change: Attitude formation in a student community.* New York: Dryden.

1950. *Social psychology.* New York: Dryden.

1961. *The acquaintance process.* New York: Holt.

Nisbet, R. A. 1966. *The sociological tradition.* New York: Basic Books.

1968. Crisis in the university? *The Public Interest,* No. 10, 55–64.

Orne, M. T. 1962. On the social psychology of the psychological experiment: with particular reference to demand characteristics and their implications. *American Psychologist, 17,* 776–783.

Osgood, C. E., G. J. Suci, and P. H. Tannenbaum. 1957. *The measurement of meaning.* Urbana: University of Illinois Press.

Osgood, C. E., and P. H. Tannenbaum. 1955. The principle of congruity in the prediction of attitude change. *Psychological Review, 62,* 42–55.

Parsons, T. 1951. *The social system.* New York: Free Press.

Parsons, T., and E. A. Shils (eds.). 1951. *Toward a general theory of action.* Cambridge, Mass.: Harvard University Press.

Passin, H. 1965. Patterns of polity-directed education development: Japan. In J. S. Coleman (ed.), *Education and political development.* Princeton, N. J.: Princeton University Press. Pp. 272–312.

Passin, H., and J. W. Bennett. 1954. The American-educated Japanese. *The Annals, 295,* 83–107.

Peak, Helen. 1955. Attitude and motivation. In M. R. Jones (ed.), *Nebraska Symposium on Motivation, 1955.* Lincoln: University of Nebraska Press. Pp. 149–188.

Peters, R. S. 1960. Private wants and public tradition. *Listener,* July 14, 46–47.

Peterson, R. E. 1966. *The scope of organized student protest in 1964–65.* Princeton, N. J.: Educational Testing Service.

1968. The student left in American higher education. *Daedalus* (Winter), 293–317.

Piaget, J. 1932. *The moral judgment of the child.* New York: Harcourt, Brace.

1952. *The origins of intelligence in children.* New York: International Universities Press.

Rae-Grant, Q. A. F., T. Gladwin, and E. M. Bower. 1966. Mental health, social competence, and the war on poverty. *American Journal of Orthopsychiatry, 36,* 652–664.

Rainwater L. 1960. *And the poor get children.* Chicago: Quadrangle Books.

Report of the National Advisory Committee on Civil Disorders. 1968. New York: Bantam Books.

Riesman, D., with R. Denney and N. Glazer. 1950. *The lonely crowd.* New Haven: Yale University Press.

Reissman, F., and Jean Goldfarb. 1964. Role playing and the poor. In F. Riessman, J. Cohen, and A. Pearl (eds.), *Mental health of the poor.* New York: Free Press. Pp. 336–347.

Ring, K. 1967. Experimental social psychology: Some sober questions about some frivolous values. *Journal of Experimental Social Psychology, 3,* 113–123.

Rogers, C. R. 1947. Some observations on the organization of personality. *American Psychologist, 2,* 358–368.

1961. *On becoming a person.* Boston: Houghton Mifflin.

Rokeach, M. 1960. *The open and closed mind: Investigations into the nature of belief systems and personality systems.* New York: Basic Books.

Rosen, B. C., and R. D'Andrade. 1959. The psycho-social origins of achievement motivation. *Sociometry, 22,* 185–218.

Rosenberg, M. 1965. *Society and the adolescent self-image.* Princeton, N. J.: Princeton University Press.

Rosenberg, M. J. 1956. Cognitive structure and attitudinal affect. *Journal of Abnormal and Social Psychology, 53,* 367–372.

Rosenberg, M. J., C. I. Hovland, W. J. McGuire, R. P. Abelson, and J. W. Brehm. 1960. *Attitude organization and change: An analysis of consistency among attitude components. Yale studies in attitude and communication,* Vol. 3. New Haven, Conn.: Yale University Press.

Rotter, J. B. 1954. *Social learning and clinical psychology.* Englewood Cliffs, N. J.: Prentice-Hall.

1966. Generalized expectancies for internal versus external control of reinforcement. *Psychological Monographs, 80,* (1, Whole No. 609).

Ruebhausen, O. M., and O. G. Brim, Jr. 1965. Privacy and behavorial research. *Columbia Law Review, 65,* 1184–1211.

Ruebush, B. K. 1963. Anxiety. *Yearbook. National Society for the Study of Education, 62* (1), 460–516.

Sampson, E. E. (ed.). 1967. Student activism. *Journal of Social Issues, 23,* (3). Entire issue.

Sanford, F. H. 1950. The use of a projective technique in attitude surveying. *Public Opinion Quarterly, 14,* 697–709.

Sanford, N. (ed.). 1962. *The American college.* New York: Wiley.

Sapir, E. 1934. The emergence of the concept of personality in a study of cultures, *Journal of Social Psychology, 5,* 408–415.

Sarason, I. G. 1960. Empirical findings and theoretical problems in the use of anxiety scales. *Psychological Bulletin, 57,* 403–415.

Sarason, S. B., K. S. Davidson, F. F. Lighthall, R. R. Waite, and B. K. Ruebush. 1960. *Anxiety in elementary school children.* New York: Wiley.

Sarbin, T. R. 1954. Role theory. In G. Lindzey (ed.), *Handbook of social psychology,* Vol. 1. Cambridge, Mass.: Addison-Wesley. Pp. 223–258.

Sargent, S. S., and Marian W. Smith (eds.), *Culture and personality: Proceedings of an interdisciplinary conference held under the auspices of the Viking Fund, November 7 and 8, 1947.* New York: Viking Fund.

Sarnoff, I., and D. Katz. 1954. The motivational bases of attitude change. *Journal of Abnormal and Social Psychology, 49,* 115–124.

Schein, E. H. with I. Schneier and C. H. Barker. 1961. *Coercive persuasion: A socio-psychological analysis of "brainwashing" of American civilian prisoners by the Chinese Communists.* New York: Norton.

Schiff, S. K., and S. G. Kellam. 1967. A community-wide mental health program of prevention and early treatment in first grade. *Psychiatric Research Report. 21,* 92–102.

Schorske, C. E. 1967. Diderot's bombs. Phi Beta Kappa Address, University of California, Berkeley, May (unpublished manuscript).

Schwitzgebel, R. R. 1964. Delinquents with tape recorders. In F. Riesman, J. Cohen, and A. Pearl (eds.), *Mental health of the poor.* New York: Free Press. Pp. 582–588.

Scott, F. D. 1954. The Swedish students' image of the United States. *The Annals, 295,* 136–145.

1956. *The American experience of Swedish students.* Minneapolis: University of Minnesota Press.

Scott, W. A. 1957. Attitude change through reward of verbal behavior. *Journal of Abnormal and Social Psychology, 55,* 72–75.

1958a. Research definitions of mental health and mental illness. *Psychological Bulletin, 55,* 29–45.

1958b. Social psychological correlates of mental illness and mental health. *Psychological Bulletin, 55,* 67–87.

Seeman, M. 1959. On the meaning of alienation. *American Sociological Review, 24,* 782–791.

Selltiz, Claire, June R. Christ, Joan Havel, and S. W. Cook. 1963. *Attitudes and social relations of foreign students in the United States.* Minneapolis: University of Minnesota Press.

Sewell, W. H., and O. Davidsen. 1961. *Scandinavian students on an American campus.* Minneapolis: University of Minnesota Press.

Sewell, W. H., R. T. Morris, and O. M. Davidsen. 1954. Scandinavian students' images in the United States: A study in cross-cultural education. *The Annals, 295,* 126–135.

Sherif, Carolyn W., M. Sherif, and R. E. Nebergall. 1965. *Attitude and attitude change: The social judgment-involvement approach.* Philadelphia: Saunders.

Sherif, M. 1936. *The psychology of social norms.* New York: Harper.

Sherif, M., and H. Cantril. 1947. *The psychology of ego-involvements.* New York: Wiley.

Sherif, M., and C. I. Hovland. 1961. *Social judgment: Assimilation and contrast effects in communication and attitude change. Yale studies in attitude and communication,* Vol. 4. New Haven, Conn.: Yale University Press.

Shoben, E. J., Jr. 1957. Toward a concept of the normal personality. *American Psychologist, 12,* 183–189.

Skinner, B. F. 1957. *Verbal behavior.* New York: Appleton.

Skolnick, Arlene. 1966. Motivational imagery and behavior over twenty years. *Journal of Consulting Psychology, 30,* 463–478.

Smith, M. B. 1949a. Personal values as determinants of a political attitude. *Journal of Psychology, 28,* 477–486.

1949b. Untitled memorandum. In S. A. Stouffer, A. A. Lumsdaine, Marion Harper Lumsdaine, R. M. Williams, Jr., M. B. Smith, I. L. Janis, Shirley A. Star, and L. S. Cottrell, Jr., *The American Soldier,* Vol. 1: *Adjustment during army life.* Princeton, N. J.: Princeton University Press. Pp. 389–390.

1950a. Optima of mental health: A general frame of reference. *Psychiatry, 13,* 503–510.

1950b. The phenomenological approach in personality theory: Some critical comments. *Journal of Abnormal and Social Psychology, 45,* 516–522.

1954a. Psychology and anthropology. In J. Gillin (ed.), *For a science of social man.* New York: Macmillan. Pp. 32–66.

1954b. A program of research on educational exchange. Institute of International Education *News Bulletin, 29* (May), 2–6.

1958. Opinions, personality, and political behavior. *American Political Science Review, 52* (1), 1–17.

1959. Research strategies toward a conception of positive mental health. *American Psychologist, 14,* 673–681.

1960. Rationality and social process. *Journal of Individual Psychology, 16* (May), 25–35.

1961. "Mental health" reconsidered: A special case of the problem of values in psychology. *American Psychologist, 16,* 299–306.

1964. Peace Corps teachers in Ghana. Final report of evaluation of Peace Corps project in Ghana. University of California, Institute of Human Development, Berkeley (mimeo).

1965a. An analysis of two measures of "authoritarianism" among Peace Corps teachers. *Journal of Personality, 33,* 513–535.

1965b. *Determinants of anti-Semitism: A social-psychological map.* New York: Anti-Defamation League of B'nai B'rith.

1965c. Socialization for competence. Social Science Research Council *Items, 19,* 17–23.

1966. Explorations in competence: A study of Peace Corps teachers in Ghana. *American Psychologist, 21,* 555–566.

1968a. Attitude change. *International Encyclopedia of the Social Sciences,* Vol. 1. New York: Macmillan and Free Press. Pp. 458–467.

1968b. Competence and socialization. In J. A. Clausen (ed.), *Socialization and society.* Boston: Little, Brown. Pp. 271–318.

1968. A map for the analysis of personality and politics. *Journal of Social Issues, 24* (3), 15–28.

1969. Competence and "mental health": Problems in conceptualizing human effectiveness. In S. B. Sells (ed.), *The definition and measurement of mental health: A symposium.* Washington, D. C.: National Center for Health Statistics, USPHS. Pp. 99–114.

Smith, M. B., J. S. Bruner, and R. W. White. 1956. *Opinions and personality.* New York: Wiley.

Smith, M. B., and J. B. Casagrande. 1953. The cross-cultural education projects: Progress report. Social Science Research Council *Items, 7,* 26–32.

Smith, M. B., J. T. Fawcett, R. Ezekiel, and Susan Roth. 1963. A factorial study of morale among Peace Corps teachers in Ghana. *Journal of Social Issues, 19* (3), 10–32.

Smith, M. B., Norma Haan, and Jeanne H. Block (in press). Social-psychological aspects of student activism. In B. Rubenstein and M. Levitt (eds.), *Rebels and the campus revolt.* Englewood Cliffs, N. J.: Prentice-Hall.

Snow, C. P. 1959. *The two cultures and the scientific revolution.* New York: Cambridge University Press.

Snygg, D. and A. W. Combs. 1949. *Individual behavior: A new frame or reference for psychology.* New York: Harper.

Spitz, R. A. 1945. Hospitalism: An inquiry into the genesis of psychiatric conditions of early childhood. *Psychoanalytic Study of the Child. 1,* 53–74.

Spranger, E. 1928. *Types of men* (trans. P. J. W. Pigors). Halle: Niemeyer.

Staats, A. W., and C. K. Staats. Attitudes established by classical conditioning. *Journal of Abnormal and Social Psychology.* 1958, 57, 37–40.

Stein, D. D. 1966. The influence of belief systems on interpersonal preference: A validation study of Rokeach's theory of prejudice. *Psychological Monographs, 80,* (8, Whole No. 616).

Stein, D. D., Jane A. Hardyck, and M. B. Smith. 1965. Race *and* belief: An open and shut case. *Journal of Personality and Social Psychology, 1,* 281–289.

Stember, C. H. 1961. *Education and attitude change.* New York: Institute of Human Relations Press.

Stern, G. G., M. I. Stein, and B. S. Bloom. 1956. *Methods in personality assessment: Human behavior in complex situations.* New York: Free Press.

Stouffer, S. A. 1955. *Communism, conformity, and civil liberties.* Garden City, N. Y.: Doubleday.

1962. *Social research to test ideas: Selected writings.* New York: Free Press.

Stouffer, S. A., A. A. Lumsdaine, Marion Harper Lumsdaine, R. M. Williams, Jr., M. B. Smith, I. L. Janis, Shirley A. Star, and L. S. Cottrell, Jr. 1949. *The American soldier. Studies in social psychology in World War II,* Vol. 1: *Adjustment during army life;* Vol. 2: *Combat and its aftermath.* Princeton, N. J.: Princeton University Press.

Stouffer, S. A., L. Guttman, E. A. Suchman, P. R. Lazarsfeld, Shirley A. Star, and J. A. Clausen. 1950. *Measurement and prediction. Studies in social psychology in World War II,* Vol. 4. Princeton, N. J.: Prinecton University Press.

Sullivan, H. S. 1945. *Conceptions of modern psychiatry.* Washington, D. C.: William Alanson White Foundation.

Sutton, F. X. 1965. Education and the making of modern nations. In J. S. Coleman (ed.), *Education and political development.* Princeton, N. J.: Princeton University Press. Pp. 51–74.

Szasz, T. S. 1960. The myth of mental illness. *American Psychologist, 15,* 113–118.

Testing and public policy. 1965. *American Psychologist* (Special issue), *20,* 857–993.

Thibaut, J. W., and H. H. Kelley. 1959. *The social psychology of groups.* New York: Wiley.

Thomas, W. I., and F. Znaniecki. 1918. *The Polish peasant in Europe and America,* Vol. 1. Boston: Badger.

Thurstone, L. L. 1928. Attitudes can be measured. *American Journal of Sociology, 33,* 529–554.

Titus, H. E., and E. P. Hollander. 1957. The California F Scale in psychological research: 1950–1955. *Psychological Bulletin, 54,* 47–64.

UNESCO. 1961a. *Study abroad, 13, 1962.* Paris: UNESCO.

1961b. *World survey of education, III, Secondary education.* New York: UNESCO.

1963. *The development of higher education in Africa. Report of the conference on the development of higher education in Africa, Tanarive, 3–12 September 1962.* Paris: UNESCO.

Useem, J., and Ruth Hill Useem. 1955. *The Western-educated man in India: A study of his social roles and influence.* New York: Dryden.

Vernon, P. E., and G. W. Allport. 1931. A test for personal values. *Journal of Abnormal and Social Psychology, 26,* 233–248.

Veroff, J. 1963. African students in the United States. *Journal of Social Issues, 19,* (3), 48–60.

1967. Social comparison and the development of achievement motivation. Paper presented at the conference on Development of Achievement-Related Motives and Self-Esteem, Graduate Center, City University of New York, October.

von Mering, O. 1961. *A grammar of human values.* Pittsburgh, Pa.: University of Pittsburgh Press.

Watson, Jeanne, and R. Lippitt. 1955. *Learning across cultures: A study of Germans visiting America.* Ann Arbor: Institute of Social Research, University of Michigan.

Wenar, C. 1964. Competence at one. *Merrill-Palmer Quarterly, 10,* 329–342.

Werner, H. 1948. *Comparative psychology of mental development.* (rev. ed.), Chicago: Follett.

Westoff, C., R. G. Potter, and P. Sagi. 1963. *The third child.* Princeton, N. J.: Princeton University Press.

Westoff, C., R. G. Potter, P. Sagi, and E. Mishler. 1961. *Family growth in metropolitan America.* Princeton, N. J.: Princeton University Press.

White, B. L. and R. Held. Plasticity of sensorimotor development in the human infant. In Judith Rosenblith and W. Allinsmith (eds.), *The causes of behavior: Readings in child development and educational psychology* (2nd ed.). Boston: Allyn & Bacon. Pp. 60–70.

White, L. A. 1949. *The science of culture.* New York: Farrar, Strauss.

White, R. K. 1951. *Value analysis: The nature and use of its methods.* Glen Gardner, N. J.: Libertarian Press.

White, R. W. 1952. *Lives in progress: A study of the natural growth of personality.* New York: Dryden.

1959. Motivation reconsidered: The concept of competence. *Psychological Review, 66,* 297–333.

1960. Competence and the psychosexual stages of development. In M. Jones (ed.), *Nebraska Symposium on Motivation, 1960.* Lincoln: University of Nebraska Press. Pp. 97–141.

1963. Ego and reality in psychoanalytic theory. A proposal for independent ego energies. *Psychological Issues, 3* (3).

Whiting, J. W. M. 1959. Sorcery, sin, and the superego. In M. R. Jones (ed.), *Nebraska Symposium on Motivation 1959.* Lincoln: University of Nebraska Press. Pp. 174–195.

Whiting, J. W. M., and I. Child. 1953. *Child training and personality.* New Haven, Conn.: Yale University Press.

Wiest, W. M. 1965. A quantitative extension of Heider's theory of cognitive balance applied to interpersonal perception and self-esteem. *Psychological Monographs, 79* (14, Whole No. 607).

Williamson, E., and J. Cowan, 1966. *The American student's freedom of expression.* Minneapolis: University of Minnesota Press.

Witkin, H. A., R. B. Dyk, Hanna F. Faterson, D. R. Goodenough, and S. A. Karp. 1962. *Psychological differentiation. Studies of development.* New York: Wiley.

Witkin, H. A., Helen B. Lewis, M. Hertzman, Karen Machover, Pearl B. Meissner, and S. Wapner. 1954. *Personality through perception.* New York: Harper.

Wylie, Ruth C. 1961. *The self concept: A critical survey of pertinent research literature.* Lincoln: University of Nebraska Press.

Yarrow, L. J. (1964). Separation from parents during early childhood. In M. L. Hoffman and Lois Hoffman (eds.), *Review of Child Development Research,* Vol. 1. New York: Russell Sage Foundation. Pp. 89–136.

Young, D. 1941. Memorandum of suggestions for research in the field of social adjustment. *American Journal of Sociology, 46,* 873–886.

Zimbardo, P. G. 1960. Involvement and communication discrepancy as determinants of opinion conformity. *Journal of Abnormal and Social Psychology, 60,* 86–94.

AUTHOR'S BIBLIOGRAPHY, 1938–1969

1938

With C. W. Lee. The incidence of neuroticism in relation to age and sex in high school. *Oregon Educational Journal*, 1938, *12*, 10, 24.

1941

With C. P. Stone. Serial discrimination by rats at the choice points of elevated mazes. *Journal of Comparative Psychology*, 1941, *31*, 79–95.

1942

With E. R. Hilgard. Distributed practice in motor learning. Score changes within and between daily sessions. *Journal of Experimental Psychology*, 1942, *30*, 136–146.

1945

Did war service produce international-mindedness? *Harvard Educational Review*, 1945, *15*, 250–257.

1947

The personal setting of public opinions: A study of attitudes toward Russia. *Public Opinion Quarterly*, 1947, *11*, 507–523.

With J. S. Bruner and R. W. White. A group research project on the dynamics and measurement of opinion. *International Journal of Opinion and Attitude Research*, 1947, *1*, 78–82.

Review of Margaret Halsey, *Color blind. Journal of Abnormal and Social Psychology*, 1947, *42*, 142–144.

1948

Review of T. M. Newcomb and E. L. Hartley (eds.), *Readings in social psychology. Journal of Abnormal and Social Psychology*, 1948, *43*, 240–242.

1949

With R. M. Williams, Jr. General characteristics of ground combat. In S. A. Stouffer, A. A. Lumsdaine, Marion Harper Lumsdaine, R. M. Williams, Jr.,

M. B. Smith, I. L. Janis, Shirley A. Star, and L. S. Cottrell, Jr., *The American soldier*, Vol. 2: *Combat and its aftermath*. Princeton, N. J.: Princeton University Press 1949 Pp. 59–104.

Combat motivations among ground troops. In S. A. Stouffer et al., *op. cit.* Pp. 105–191.

The combat replacement. In S. A. Stouffer et al., *op. cit.* Pp. 242–289.

Attitudes of ground combat troops toward rear echelons and the home front. In S. A. Stouffer et al., *op. cit.* Pp. 290–323.

Personal values as determinants of a political attitude. *Journal of Psychology,* 1949, *28,* 477–486.

Did you major in psychology? *Vassar Alumnae Magazine,* 1949, *35,* 5–8.

With J. S. Bruner. Review of D. Krech and R. S. Crutchfield, *Theory and problems of social psychology. Journal of Abnormal and Social Psychology,* 1949, *44,* 283–288.

1950

The phenomenological approach in personality theory: Some critical remarks. *Journal of Abnormal and Social Psychology,* 1950, *45,* 516–522.

Optima of mental health: A general frame of reference. *Psychiatry,* 1950, *13,* 503–510.

Review of T. G. Andrews (ed.), *Methods of psychology. International Journal of Opinion and Attitude Research,* 1950, *4,* 120–122.

Review of T. W. Adorno, Else Frenkel-Brunswik, D. J. Levinson, and R. N. Sanford, *The authoritarian personality. Journal of Abnormal and Social Psychology,* 1950, *45,* 775–779.

1951

Psychology in a liberal education. *Journal of Higher Education,* 1951, *22,* 181–187.

Review of S. S. Sargent, *Social psychology: An integrative interpretation. Psychological Bulletin,* 1951, *48,* 161–162.

Review of G. C. Homans, *The human group. Psychological Bulletin,* 1951, *48,* 449–451.

Review of W. Gee, *Social science research methods. American Economic Review,* 1951, *41,* 748–750.

Review of K. Lewin (D. Cartwright, ed.), *Field theory in social science: Selected theoretical papers. Psychological Bulletin,* 1951, *48,* 520–521.

1952

Social psychology and group processes. *Annual Review of Psychology,* 1952, *3,* 175–204.

With Joan Eager. A note on the validity of Sanford's authoritarian-equalitarian scale. *Journal of Abnormal and Social Psychology,* 1952, *47,* 265–267.

Review of S. L. Payne, *The art of asking questions. American Statistical Association Journal,* 1952, *47,* 97–98.

Review of I. L. Janis, *Air war and psychological stress: Psychological studies of bombing and civilian defense. Psychological Bulletin,* 1952, *49,* 372–374.

Review of G. A. Miller, *Language and communication. Journal of Abnormal and Social Psychology,* 1952, *47,* 734–735.

1953

Recent studies in social psychology. In *Social science frontiers: Annual proceedings of the Middle States Council for the Social Studies, 1951–52,* 1953, *49,* 26–34.

Conference on nonintellective determinants of achievement. SSRC *Items,* 1953, 7, 13–18.

The SSRC and psychology. *American Psychologist,* 1953, 8, 484–488.

Academic freedom in a climate of insecurity: Some perspectives. *Journal of Social Issues,* 1953, 9 (3), 48–54.

With J. B. Casagrande. The cross-cultural education projects: A progress report. SSRC *Items,* 1953, 7, 26–32.

Special review: Some recent texts in social psychology. S. E. Asch, *Social psychology;* L. W. Doob, *Social psychology: An analysis of human behavior;* R. E. L. Faris, *Social psychology;* E. L. Hartley and Ruth E. Hartley, *Fundamentals of social psychology;* G. E. Swanson, T. M. Newcomb, and E. L. Hartley, *Readings in social psychology* (rev. ed.). *Psychological Bulletin,* 1953, *50,* 150–159.

Review of T. Parsons and E. A. Shils (eds.), *Toward a general theory of action. Journal of Abnormal and Social Psychology,* 1953, *48,* 315–318.

1954

Anthropology and psychology. In J. Gillin (ed.), *For a science of social man: Convergences in anthropology, psychology and sociology.* New York: Macmillan, 1954. Pp. 32–66.

Comment on the "implications of separating opinions from attitudes." *Public Opinion Quarterly,* 1954, *18,* 254–265.

A program of research on student exchange. Institute of International Education *News Bulletin,* 1954, *29* (8), 2–6.

Toward scientific and professional responsibility. *American Psychologist,* 1954, *9,* 513–516.

Review of R. Christie and Marie Johoda (eds.), *Studies in the scope and method of "The authoritarian personality": Continuities in social research. The Annals,* 1954, *294,* 198.

1955

Research in the field of international education. In *Handbook on international study.* New York: Institute of International Education, 1955. Pp. 235–252.

Some features of foreign-student adjustment. *Journal of Higher Education,* 1955, *26,* 231–241.

Evaluation of exchange of persons. *International Social Science Bulletin,* 1955, 7, 387–397.

Research and the foreign student adviser. *NAFSA News Letter* (New York: National Association of Foreign Student Advisers), 1955, *6* (8), 1–2.

The conference on cross-cultural research on personality development. SSRC *Items,* 1955, *9,* 27–31.

Review of G. W. Allport, *The nature of prejudice. Journal of Abnormal and Social Psychology,* 1955, *50,* 158.

Review of S. A. Stouffer, *Communism, conformity and civil liberties: A cross-section of the nation speaks its mind. American Sociological Review,* 1955, *20,* 750–751.

1956

With J. S. Bruner and R. W. White. *Opinions and personality.* New York: Wiley, 1956.

Cross-cultural education and cultural change. *International Social Science Bulletin,* 1956, *8,* 585–597.

The future of international exchange programs. *Teachers College Record,* 1956, *57,* 285–289.

Cross-cultural education as a research area. *Journal of Social Issues,* 1956, *12* (1), 3–8.

A perspective for further research on cross-cultural education. *Journal of Social Issues,* 1956, *12* (1), 56–68.

Editorial. *Journal of Abnormal and Social Psychology,* 1956, *52,* 1–4.

Editorial note: This anniversary number. *Journal of Abnormal and Social Psychology,* 1956, *52,* 289.

With L. Bellak. An experimental exploration of the psychoanalytic process: Exemplification of a method. *Psychoanalytic Quarterly,* 1956, *25,* 385–414.

Review of Kate V. Wofford, *The workshop way with foreign students. Journal of Higher Education,* 1956, *27,* 168–169.

1957

Review of L. Festinger, H. W. Riecken, and S. Schachter, *When prophecy fails. Contemporary Psychology,* 1957, *2,* 89–92.

Review of S. G. Putt (ed.), *Cousins and strangers: Comments on America by Commonwealth Fund Fellows from Britain, 1946–1952,* and Cora Du Bois, *Foreign students and higher education in the United States. Journal of Higher Education,* 1957, *28,* 54–55.

1958

Report on the work of the committee on cross-cultural education. SSRC *Items,* 1958, *12,* 40–42.

Opinions, personality, and political behavior. *American Political Science Review,* 1958, *52,* 1–17.

Review of R. Ross and E. van den Haag, *The fabric of society: An introduction to the social sciences. Scientific American,* 1958, *198* (2), 123–128.

Review of R. Likert and S. P. Hayes, Jr. (eds.), *Some applications of behavioral research. Science,* 1958, *128,* 295.

Review of G. V. Coelho, *Changing images of America: A study of Indian students' perceptions. The Annals,* 1958, *319,* 202–203.

1959

Research strategies toward a conception of positive menal health. *American Psychologist,* 1959, *14,* 673–681. Revised from "Development of the concept of creative mental health." In R. H. Ojemann (ed.), *Recent contributions of biological and psychosocial investigations to preventive psychiatry.* Iowa City: State University of Iowa, 1959. Pp 12–27.

Review of G. Murphy, *Human potentialities. Contemporary Psychology,* 1959, *4,* 161–164.

1960

Rationality and social process. *Journal of Individual Psychology,* 1960, *16,* 25–35.

Review of M. Rokeach, *The open and closed mind. Science,* 1960, *132,* 142–143.

Review of I. de Sola Pool (ed.), *Trends in content analysis. American Journal of Psychology,* 1960, *73,* 657–658.

1961

"Mental health" reconsidered: A special case of the problem of values in psychology. *American Psychologist,* 1961, *16,* 299–306.

Recent developments in the field of social psychology. *The Annals,* 1961, *338,* 137–143.

Editorial. *Journal of Abnormal and Social Psychology,* 1961, *63,* 461–465.

Review of M. Janowitz, *The professional soldier: A social and political portrait. Contemporary Psychology,* 1961, *6,* 77–78.

Review of J. C. Nunnally, Jr., *Popular conceptions of mental health: Their development and change. Contemporary Psychology,* 1961, *6,* 397–399.

Review of A. Campbell, P. E. Converse, W. E. Miller, and D. E. Stokes, *The American voter. American Journal of Psychology,* 1961, *74,* 648–651.

1962

Foreword to G. Macgregor, *American Fulbright scholars: The experiences of American scholars in countries of the Near East and South Asia.* Ithaca, N. Y.: Society for Applied Anthropology, 1962, Monograph No. 5, p. 3.

Review of *Social research to test ideas. Selected writings of Samuel A. Stouffer. Science,* 1962, *136,* 869.

Review of L. W. Doob, *Communication in Africa: A search for boundaries. Contemporary Psychology,* 1962, *7,* 377–378.

1963

Personal values in the study of lives. In R. W. White (ed.), *The study of lives: Essays on personality in honor of Henry A. Murray.* New York: Atherton Press, 1963, Pp. 324–347.

With J. T. Fawcett, R. Ezekiel, and Susan Roth. A factorial study of morale among Peace Corps teachers in Ghana. *Journal of Social Issues,* 1963, *19,* (3), 10–32.

1964

Foreign vs. indigenous education. In D. C. Piper and T. Cole (eds.), *Post-primary education and political and economic development.* Durham, N.C.: Duke University Press, 1964. Pp. 48–74.

Review of D. Bell (ed.), *The radical right. Contemporary Psychology,* 1964, *9,* 147–149.

Review of D. C. McClelland, *The achieving society. History and Theory,* 1964, *3,* 371–381.

1965

Motivation, communications research, and family planning. In Mindel C. Sheps and Jeanne C. Ridley (eds.), *Public health and population change.* Pittsburgh: University of Pittsburgh Press, 1965. Pp. 70–89.

With I. L. Janis. Effects of education and persuasion on national and international images. In H. C. Kelman (ed.), *International behavior: A social-psychological analysis.* New York: Holt, 1965. Pp. 190–235.

Socialization for competence. SSRC *Items,* 1965, *19,* 17–23.

Introduction, Kurt Lewin Memorial Award Address, 1965. *Journal of Social Issues,* 1965, *21,* (3), 1–2.

An analysis of two measures of "authoritarianism" among Peace Corps teachers. *Journal of Personality,* 1965, *33,* 513–535.

With D. D. Stein and Jane A. Hardyck. Race *and* belief: An open and shut case. *Journal of Personality and Social Psychology,* 1965. *1,* 281–289.

Review of S. Koch (ed.), *Psychology: A study of a science,* Vol. 6: *Investigations of man as socius: Their place in psychology and the social sciences. Public Opinion Quarterly,* 1965, *29,* 170–178.

Review of G. Katona, *The mass consumption society. Contemporary Psychology,* 1965, *10,* 344–345.

Review of J. C. Davies, *Human nature in politics: The dynamics of political behavior. American Journal of Psychology,* 1965, *78,* 699–700.

Determinants of anti-Semitism: A social-psychological map. New York: Anti-Defamation League of B'nai B'rith. 14 pp. n.d. (1965).

1966

Explorations in competence: A study of Peace Corps teachers in Ghana. *American Psychologist,* 1966, *21,* 555–566.

With N. Hobbs. The community and the community mental health center. *American Psychologist,* 1966, *21,* 499–509.

With R. C. Dillehay and C. A. Insko. Logical consistency and attitude change. *Journal of Personality and Social Psychology,* 1966, *3,* 646–654.

Three textbooks: A special review. R. Brown, *Social psychology;* T. M. Newcomb, R. H. Turner, and P. E. Converse, *Social psychology: The study of human interaction;* P. F. Secord and C. W. Backman, *Social psychology. Journal of Experimental Social Psychology,* 1966, *2,* 109–118.

An ambiguous case for humanistic psychology. A review of A. H. Maslow, *The psychology of science: A reconnaissance. Science,* 1966, *153,* 284–285.

Report of the Conference on Socialization for Competence. April 29–May 2, 1965, San Juan, Puerto Rico. *Current Anthropology,* 1966, *7,* 517–518.

1967

Conflicting values affecting behavioral research with children. *Children,* 1967, *14,* 53–58.

On rereading Proust. A review of G. D. Painter, *Proust,* Vol. 1: *The early years;* Vol. 2: *The later years. Contemporary Psychology.* 1967, *12,* 337–340.

Foreword to J. P. Kirscht and R. C. Dillehay, *Dimensions of authoritarianism: A review of research and theory.* Lexington: University of Kentucky Press, 1967. Pp. v–ix.

1968

Attitude change. In *International Encyclopedia of the Social Sciences,* Vol. 1. New York: Macmillan and Free Press, 1968. Pp. 458–467.

Samuel A. Stouffer. In *International Encyclopedia of the Social Sciences,* Vol. 15. New York: Macmillan and Free Press, 1968. Pp. 277–280.

Competence and socialization. In J. A. Clausen (ed.), *Socialization and society.* Boston: Little, Brown, 1968. Pp. 271–320.

Personality in politics: A conceptual map, with application to the problem of political rationality. In O. Garceau (ed.), *Political research and political theory: Essays in honor of V. O. Key, Jr.* Cambridge, Mass.: Harvard University Press, 1968. Pp. 77–101.

The self and cognitive consistency. In R. P. Abelson, E. Aronson, W. J. McGuire, T. M. Newcomb, M. J. Rosenberg, and P. H. Tannenbaum (eds.), *Theories of cognitive consistency.* Chicago: Rand-McNally, 1968. Pp. 366–372.

With Jeanne H. Block and Norma Haan. Activism and apathy in contemporary adolescents. In J. F. Adams (ed.), *Understanding adolescence: Current developments in adolescent psychology.* Boston: Allyn & Bacon, 1968. Pp. 198–231.

The revolution in mental-health care: A "Bold new approach"? *Trans—action,* 1968, *5* (5), 19–23.

A map for the analysis of personality and politics. *Journal of Social Issues,* 1968, *24* (3), 15–28.

Conference report: International conference on social-psychological research in developing countries. *Journal of Personality and Social Psychology,* 1968, *8,* 95–98.

International collaboration in social psychology: Some reflections on the Ibadan Conference. *Journal of Social Issues,* 1968, *24* (2), 261–266.

With Norma Haan and Jeanne H. Block. The moral reasoning of young adults: Political-social behavior, family background and personality correlates. *Journal of Personality and Social Psychology,* 1968, *10,* 183–201.

A social psychologist in the corridors of power. A review of H. Cantril, *The human dimension: Experiences in policy research. Contemporary Psychology,* 1968, *13,* 136–138.

1969

Competence and "mental health": Problems in conceptualizing human effectiveness. In S. B. Sells (ed.), *The definition and measurement of mental health: A symposium.* Washington, D. C.: National Center for Health Statistics, USPHS, 1969. Pg. 99–114.

The schools and prejudice: findings. In C. Y. Glock and Ellen Siegelman (eds.), *Prejudice U.S.A.* New York: Praeger, 1969. Pp. 112–135.

With Norma Haan and Jeanne Block. Social-psychological aspects of student activism. In B. Rubenstein and M. Levitt (eds.), *Rebels and the campus revolt.* Publication pending.

Name Index

Subject Index